# AN ENORMOUS CRIME

D1407743

# AN ENORMOUS
# CRIME

## THE DEFINITIVE ACCOUNT OF AMERICAN POWs ABANDONED IN SOUTHEAST ASIA

Former U.S. Rep. Bill Hendon (R-NC)
and Elizabeth A. Stewart

THOMAS DUNNE BOOKS
ST. MARTIN'S GRIFFIN ☙ NEW YORK

THOMAS DUNNE BOOKS.
An imprint of St. Martin's Press.

AN ENORMOUS CRIME. Copyright © 2007 by William M. Hendon and Elizabeth A. Stewart. All rights reserved. Printed in the United States of America. For information, address St. Martin's Press, 175 Fifth Avenue, New York, N.Y. 10010.

www.thomasdunnebooks.com
www.stmartins.com

Design by Kelly S. Too
Maps by Xande Anderer, Citizen X Design, and Bill Hendon

"Abraham, Martin and John." Words and Music by Richard Holler. Copyright © 1968 (Renewed). Regent Music Corporation (BMI) International. Copyright Secured. All Rights reserved. Used by permission.

Library of Congress Cataloging-in-Publication Data

Hendon, Bill (William Martin), 1944–
    An enormous crime : the definitive account of American POWs abandoned in Southeast Asia / Bill Hendon and Elizabeth A. Stewart.—1st St. Martin's Griffin ed.
        p.  cm.
    Includes bibliographical references and index.
    ISBN-13: 978-0-312-38538-5
    ISBN-10: 0-312-38538-2
    1. Vietnam War, 1961–1975—Prisoners and prisons, North Vietnamese.  2. Vietnam War, 1961–1975—Prisoners and prisons, Laotian.  3. Prisoners of war—United States—History—20th century.  4. United States—Politics and government—20th century. I. Title.

    DS559.4 .H46 2007
    959.704'37—dc22

                                                                2007014865

First St. Martin's Griffin Edition: October 2008

10  9  8  7  6  5  4  3  2  1

# MR. HENDON'S PERSONAL DEDICATIONS

I dedicate this book and the good I pray will come from its publication:

To my remarkable parents: my dad, "Big Bill" (1914–1973), friend to everyone he met, World War II veteran, successful businessman, civic leader, accomplished outdoorsman, dedicated husband, wonderful father and mentor to his two boys—in a phrase, the best guy you would ever want to know, who died way, way too young—and my dear late mother, "Meme," who went from world's best stay-at-home mom during my childhood and adolescence, to close friend and confidante in the years following Big Bill's death, to self-appointed reality checker and gentle critic after I got elected to Congress and, as she put it, "began to think quite highly" of myself, and finally to unwavering supporter of my oftentimes controversial efforts on behalf of the Indochina POWs after I left Congress. As long as they lived, Big Bill and Meme were always there for me. *Always*. For all they did for me, and meant to me, and mean to me still, I dedicate this book first and foremost to them. In the same breath I dedicate it also to my former wife and my two daughters, who contributed mightily to this effort, and to my brother and the other members of my immediate family as well.

To the wonderful people of Western North Carolina, who extended to me the greatest honor of my life when they hired me back in the early 1980s to represent them and watch out for their interests in the United States House of Representatives.

To two very special men I came to know and admire early on in my congressional career: Sen. Strom Thurmond (R-SC), (1902–2003), who campaigned hard for me during my successful 1980 campaign (and equally hard for me in later campaigns as well), and Lt. Gen. Gene Tighe Jr., USAF (1921–1994), director of the Defense Intelligence Agency when I first arrived in Washington. Each man, I soon found, was devoted to the cause of the Indochina POWs, and each took me under his powerful wings and provided valuable direction to my efforts and much-needed personal assurances that the decisions I was making and the actions I was taking on behalf of the POWs were correct and proper. I will never be able to convey how much these two men meant to me. Nor will I ever be able to adequately describe how proud I was to walk, if for only a brief time, in the long shadow each cast.

To my buddies "the bomb throwers"—the two dozen or so "damn the torpedoes" backbench Republicans and our gutsy, like-minded comrade-in-arms across the aisle, Rep. Frank McCloskey (D-IN), (1939–2003)—who waged all-out war for the POWs in the House during the early and mid-1980s.

To my colleague, chairman, and dear friend Rep. G. V. "Sonny" Montgomery (D-MS), (1920–2006), Southern gentleman, patriot, statesman, honorable not just in title but in everything he did. Sonny headed a House investigation into the POW issue during 1975–1976 and served on a presidential commission that had conducted a similar investigation in 1977. Both had ruled that no POWs remained alive. But then had come the boat people in the late 1970s and with them a floodtide of intelligence saying otherwise—and then, in early 1981, our demands from the backbench that a new national effort be undertaken to get the POWs home. A lesser man would have circled the wagons and used his power to thwart our efforts and protect himself from possible embarrassment; Sonny, however, responded by pledging his full support and urging us on. I greatly admired him for that—and for later making good on his pledge—and for countless other reasons as well, and am honored to dedicate this book and the good that can come from it to him. He was, as everyone who knew him will tell you, a very special guy.

To my fellow intelligence investigators at the Senate Select Committee on POW/MIA Affairs: John McCreary, JD, Col. Bill LeGro, John Holstein, Ph.D., and Col. Nick Nicklas; to Deputy Staff Director Dino Carluccio and to the Select Committee's vice chairman, my former House colleague and longtime friend Sen. Bob Smith (R-NH). Honorable men all; outgunned from 1991 to 1993; but never outclassed.

—BILL HENDON
Washington, DC

## MS. STEWART'S PERSONAL DEDICATIONS

I dedicate this book to my parents, Pete and Marnie Stewart. To Mom, who has always been unwavering in her support of this effort, who raised six children with great courage, wonderful humor and grace, and continues to be a pillar of strength to her family each and every day. To Dad, Col. Peter J. Stewart, USAF— MIA March 15, 1966—a decorated combat veteran of World War II and Vietnam and a devoted father and husband, for having the courage of his convictions, and whose place on the Wall gives me both sorrow and strength. We miss you more than can be put into words. My love for you both is never ending.

—ELIZABETH A. STEWART
Winter Haven, Florida

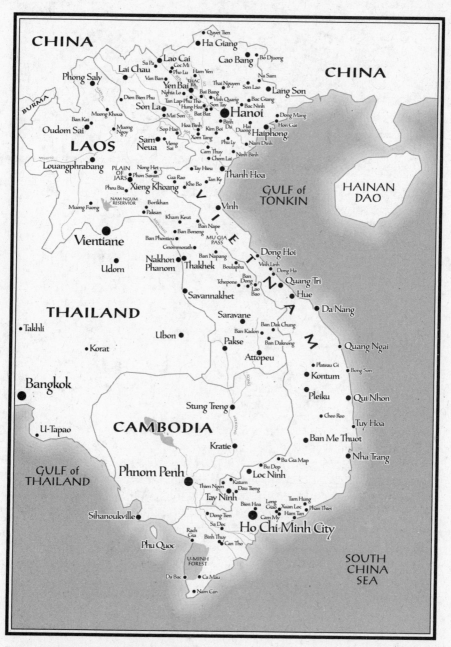

Postwar IndoChina (HENDON/ANDERER)

# · CONTENTS ·

Preface                                                                    xv

## PART I

Introduction                                                                3

CHAPTER 1
The POW Hostage Plan and Its Implementation                                11

CHAPTER 2
Hanoi Bound                                                                 19

CHAPTER 3
American POWs Captured by the Pathet Lao                                    26

CHAPTER 4
American POWs in North Vietnam                                              28

CHAPTER 5
1972: The War Draws to a Close                                             46

## PART II

CHAPTER 6
January 1973: Peace at a Very High Price                                   63

CHAPTER 7
February 1973: A Historic Journey to Hanoi                                 76

CHAPTER 8
February–March 1973: The "Most Tortured" Issue, "The Toughest Sale"        82

CHAPTER 9
Mid- to Late March 1973: The Returnee Debriefs Tell of Hundreds
of American POWs Held Back                                                 92

CHAPTER 10
Spring 1973: "A 'Cancer' on the Presidency"                               98

CHAPTER 11
Spring, Summer, and Fall 1973: The Collapse of the JEC Talks • The
Collapse of the Paris Peace Accords                                    108

CHAPTER 12
1974: The End of the Line for Richard Nixon                            117

CHAPTER 13
January–April 1975: The End of the Line for South Vietnam             120

## PART III

CHAPTER 14
May–December 1975: "Cuba Suggested to Us to Keep
Them Back" • Congress Investigates the Fate of the POWs and MIAs      127

CHAPTER 15
1976: Montgomery Continues His Investigation • American POWs
Seen in Captivity in Both North and South Vietnam                      140

CHAPTER 16
1977: A New President Addresses the Matter of the Unlisted,
Unreturned POWs                                                        156

CHAPTER 17
1978: The Sightings of the Unlisted, Unreturned POWs
Continue • The Refugee Exodus Begins                                   175

CHAPTER 18
1979: A Prison System in Chaos • Convincing Evidence Finally
Reaches Washington                                                     188

CHAPTER 19
1980: Rescue Plans                                                     206

## PART IV

CHAPTER 20
1981: "Gasoline"                                                       215

CHAPTER 21
1982: "The Principle of Reciprocity"                                   224

CHAPTER 22
1983: A Dramatic Change of Course                                      232

CHAPTER 23
1984: Tragedy at Arlington • A Missed Opportunity in the Oval Office   248

CHAPTER 24
1985: "Progress" in the Search for Remains • Freshmen,
Stonewalled on POWs, Turn to Perot • McFarlane Drops His Guard         266

CHAPTER 25
1986: Trench Warfare                                                287

CHAPTER 26
1987: Perot to Hanoi • A Bombshell from General
Vessey • No Evidence?                                               323

CHAPTER 27
1988: "Just Two Bar of Silvers for Each Man"                        347

CHAPTER 28
1989: ". . . The Statute of Limitations Has Been Reached"           367

CHAPTER 29
1990: Sabotaging the Helms/Grassley Investigations • The Bush
Final Report on POWs • Thach's Historic Visit to Washington         378

PART V

CHAPTER 30
1991: One Last Chance to Save the Unlisted, Unreturned POWs         399

CHAPTER 31
1992: The Fragging                                                  408

CHAPTER 32
1993–1995: "The Vietnamese Know How to Count"                       465

CHAPTER 33
1995–2005: "War Legacies"                                           480

Epilogue: A Proposal for President Bush                             483

A Message from the Authors                                          487

Notes                                                              489

Acknowledgments                                                    565

Index                                                             567

As far as Vietnam is concerned, I think that if this document is sustained, and it looks unfortunately to be sustainable, we have the right to ask the present Vietnamese government to place those responsible in war crimes trials.

—ZBIGNIEW BRZEZINSKI, *MacNeil/Lehrer NewsHour,* April 13, 1993, commenting on a previously top secret document found in the files of Soviet military intelligence in Moscow in early 1993 indicating that the North Vietnamese held back some seven hundred American POWs at Operation Homecoming in 1973

If that document is authentic, and it is hard to imagine who would have forged it, for what purpose, then I think an enormous crime has been committed.

—HENRY A. KISSINGER, on the same program

Hanoi, Nov. 19 [2006]

[President George W.] Bush paid a short visit Saturday to the Joint POW/MIA Accounting Command, which is working to account for soldiers missing from several conflicts, including 1,800 from the Vietnam War, which ended more than 30 years ago.

Officials briefed Bush on their efforts as they showed him photos and recovered artifacts, including an old helmet and rusted rifles, and plaster replicas of human bones. Bush listened to the 15-minute briefing, then left without speaking publicly.

Aides say Bush wants to focus not on Vietnam's past but on its future.

—"Bush Fails to Persuade South Korea on Sanctions"
*The Washington Post,* November 19, 2006, p. A24

On Monday, December 8, 1941, the day after Japan's surprise attack on Pearl Harbor, U.S. Navy rescue parties combing the harbor for survivors began hearing tapping coming from deep within the hull of the shattered battleship USS *West Virginia,* which lay smoldering on the bottom near the center of battleship row. According to eyewitnesses, the tapping continued throughout the day and into the night. "I was on guard duty that Monday night," Richard "Dick" Fiske, a Marine Corps bugler on *West Virginia* recalled in 1995. "I could clearly hear tapping coming from inside our ship. It was devastating. We knew they were in there but we couldn't do anything because we were under total blackout in anticipation of another Japanese attack."

Fiske remembered how spirits soared on Tuesday morning when divers with hard hats and air lines arrived to attempt a rescue of the sailors trapped inside his boat and their counterparts who were heard tapping from inside USS *Oklahoma,* which lay nearby. After the divers and a team of welders with cutting torches rescued thirty-two sailors from within *Oklahoma,* operations were begun on board *West Virginia.* "They made five dives on *West Virginia* that afternoon," Fiske recalled, "but they couldn't get to the trapped men because of the extensive damage in the forward part of the ship." Fiske said the divers came back Wednesday and tried again "but still couldn't get through to the trapped sailors. Finally, after fourteen dives, they had to give up."

The tapping continued from deep within *West Virginia* for fourteen more days, until Christmas Eve, Fiske said. "That was the last day I heard them tapping, Christmas Eve. I still dream about it, the noise, the tap, tap, tap. I'll never forget it as long as I live."

*West Virginia* lay on the bottom of Pearl for several months before being moved into dry dock for repairs. "It wasn't until June 1942," Fiske said, "when we opened the forward pump room, that we knew for sure who they were. We found them by the forward generator—Olds, Endicott, and Costin—all firemen first class who took care of the boilers. It looked like they had been tapping with a dog wrench," a special wrench used to ensure tight seals around bulkhead doors. "We also found a calendar. The last entry was on December twenty-third. I'm sure, though, that they tapped until the twenty-fourth, because I remember very clearly, it was on Christmas Eve when the tapping finally stopped."[1]

•  •  •

THE VIETNAM WAR, OR THE AMERICAN WAR, AS THE NORTH VIETNAMESE CALL IT, OFFICIALLY lasted from early August 1964 to late January 1973. More than 58,000 Americans were killed in action or died from wounds or in accidents. More than 315,000 were wounded and survived. Hundreds were captured, imprisoned, and released at war's end during Operation Homecoming. Hundreds more were similarly captured and imprisoned but were held back by the Communists at Homecoming to ensure payment of billions of dollars in postwar reconstruction aid promised them by Richard Nixon and Henry Kissinger. Watergate intervened, the aid was not paid, and these prisoners have never been released.

This is the story of the American prisoners in both groups, those released at Homecoming and those held back. It is told not by the American POWs released at Homecoming, but first by the peoples of Vietnam and Laos who saw or were told about American POWs in captivity and later reported to U.S. officials what they had seen or heard. Scores of these now-declassified reports—each, if you will, a tap on the bulkhead from deep within the wreckage of postwar Indochina—are presented in the chapters ahead. Collectively, they paint a very clear picture of hundreds—*hundreds*—of American POWs held after the war by the Vietnamese and Lao governments.

And, second, the story is told by some of these still-unreleased POWs themselves, a number of whom, following established U.S. escape and evasion (E & E) practices, laid secret codes and/or messages out on the ground that were later picked up by either unmanned reconnaissance drones or U.S. spy satellites passing overhead. The first of these now-declassified coded messages was imaged by an unmanned reconnaissance drone flying over northern Laos in the spring of 1973, just weeks after America's combat role ended with the signing of the Paris Peace Accords; the last was acquired on June 5, 1992, when a U.S. spy satellite passing over a prison in northern Vietnam imaged the name of a still-missing USAF flight officer and his secret escape and evasion code in a field near the prison, and a secret four-digit authenticator matching the identity of another still-missing USAF flight officer along with a valid escape and evasion code in an adjacent portion of the same field. The 1973 message from northern Laos and the 1992 messages from the two missing fliers in northern Vietnam—along with a number of similar, explosive coded messages sent by other captive Americans between the years 1973 and 1992—are also presented in detail in the chapters ahead. Again, each a tap on the bulkhead, each a plea for deliverance, each a clear and unmistakable message from a U.S. serviceman in dire straits saying, "I'm still alive. Get me the hell out of here!"

But not one of these POWs has *ever* been released. Why not, you ask? And not one has *ever* been rescued. Again, why not? And though perhaps a dozen or so are reported to have escaped from various prisons during the postwar years and fled into the countryside, not one has *ever* made it to freedom. Again, why not? And, *hundreds* of POWs? Perhaps the Communists kept a few, but *hundreds*? And even if the Vietnamese and Lao governments did hold back a large number of POWs in 1973, why would they continue to hold them until today? And what of this absurd charge that a thirty-year, bipartisan cover-up spanning *seven* presidential administrations has kept the truth about these prisoners secret?

Does anyone really believe such a cover-up could succeed in Washington, DC, where it is well known that one cannot keep something secret for thirty minutes, much less thirty years?

Read on and you will find the answers to these and many other questions about some very brave—and very abandoned—American servicemen.

Their story begins in earnest in, of all places, Cuba, in the spring of 1961.

# PART I

# INTRODUCTION

. . .

After months of training at secret bases in Guatemala, twelve hundred Cuban freedom fighters departed in ships from Puerto Cabezas, Nicaragua, in mid-April 1961 bound for the Bay of Pigs on the southern coast of Cuba. Their primary mission: Land, establish a beachhead, and hold it long enough to allow a provisional government to be put ashore—a government that would then receive recognition and overt aid from the United States and from anticommunist nations throughout Latin America, and whose forces, if all went as planned, would quickly drive Fidel Castro from power. The U.S. government had trained and equipped the brigade, planned, approved, and financed the invasion, and assured the freedom fighters that U.S. air strikes would destroy the handful of planes comprising Castro's air force on the ground before the invasion was launched. Secure in this assurance that the skies above the beachhead would be theirs, the men of Brigade 2506 went ashore at 2:30 A.M. on Monday, April 17, with high hopes that the overthrow of Fidel Castro was at hand.

These hopes were dashed when the promised preinvasion bombing raids were first cut back and then canceled altogether on orders from Washington. With Castro's air force still intact, the invaders were doomed. By Tuesday, the trapped rebels were pleading by radio for U.S. air cover, telling of government tanks sending merciless crossfire into their ranks and of MiGs diving again and again to strafe men armed only with rifles, machine guns, and bazookas. No assistance was dispatched, however, and the rebels were overwhelmed.

At 5:30 Wednesday afternoon, all organized resistance ceased when the final rebel position at Playa Girón fell. Within hours, the Cuban government announced that its troops had "destroyed in less than seventy-two hours the Army which was organized during many months by the imperialist government of the United States. All the mercenaries," Havana radio declared, ". . . are either dead or prisoners awaiting action by revolutionary tribunals."

The surviving prisoners were taken to Havana that Friday and paraded before the nation's television cameras. Premier Castro then took to the airwaves and delivered a four-and-a-half-hour report to the nation on the invasion. Clearly elated by the rout at Bahía de Cochinos, the victorious Castro charged that President Kennedy was personally to blame for the invasion and ridiculed the American president as an "international bully" who should be likened to Adolf Hitler. Noting that the American government was already calling for clemency for the prisoners, Castro mocked the U.S. gesture, declaring, "They should have asked clemency for the children who were killed by their bombs." All prisoners captured during the invasion, the Cuban leader declared, were considered counter-revolutionaries who "must be shot."

Operation Pluto, the U.S.-backed invasion of Cuba, had ended in total disaster.

*Mid-May 1961*
## WASHINGTON, DC

John Kennedy knew that Brigade 2506 was no band of cutthroats. Many of the freedom fighters, in fact, were not unlike the president himself—charismatic, brave, patriotic, from wealthy Catholic families. Among them were Cuba's finest, grandsons of the old Spanish aristocracy and scions of assorted fortunes. As one observer noted, in capturing them it was as if Castro had captured "the entire Havana Yacht Club." But now here they were—herded around on television like cattle, charged with treason and facing possible execution—and, in the minds of many, all because the American president, acting as mediator between quarreling advisors rather than as a forceful commander in chief, had personally ordered the rebels' air cover withdrawn in the critical early hours of the invasion. The fact that all this weighed heavily on the young president may explain why he moved so quickly when he heard of Castro's offer.

The Cuban premier had been addressing a farmers' rally in Havana on May 17 when he told his audience that a good way to increase agricultural output might be for Cuba to trade the approximately twelve hundred prisoners captured during the invasion to the United States in return for five hundred bulldozers or farm tractors. Within hours of being advised of Castro's remarks, Kennedy was on the phone to Eleanor Roosevelt, asking the former first lady to chair a committee to raise funds to purchase five hundred tractors for Cuba if Castro would free the twelve hundred imprisoned rebels. Mrs. Roosevelt agreed to serve, as did Walter P. Reuther, president of the United Automobile Workers Union, and Dr. Milton S. Eisenhower, president of Johns Hopkins University and brother of the former president. On May 19, only two days after Castro made his offer, committee members wired the Cuban leader to advise him of the formation of the Tractors for Freedom Committee and of their intention to undertake a nationwide drive in the United States to raise the funds necessary to purchase the tractors. "We do this," they told Castro, "as proof that free men will not desert those who risked all for what they thought was right." The three signers concluded by inviting the Cuban leader to immediately send representatives to the United States to work out details for the proposed swap.

Within hours of receiving the committee's offer, Castro paroled ten of the Bay of Pigs prisoners and dispatched them to Washington with his demand: five hundred Caterpillar Tractor Company Super D-8 bulldozers, two hundred equipped with disks for plowing and three hundred with bulldozer blades. Castro estimated that the five hundred bulldozers would cost approximately $28 million. He further informed the committee that the swap was neither an exchange nor a ransom; rather, he said, the bulldozers were to be considered as "indemnification" for war damage caused during the invasion.

Although the committee would have preferred giving Castro only light farm tractors, and found the matter of "indemnity" to be a flagrant effort to direct world attention to America's losing role in the invasion, members chose not to quibble over specifications or semantics. Instead, following their session with the paroled prisoner-representatives, the committee announced it was prepared to meet Castro's demands. Walter Reuther, committee cochair, told a news conference that the committee had given a "firm commitment" to the prisoner delegation that the specified equipment would be sent to Cuba. He also said a similar pledge had been sent to Castro. The committee estimated the cost to be as high as $20 million depending on whether or not the Cuban president continued to insist on the top-of-the-line Super D-8 Caterpillars.

As the Cuban prisoner-negotiators departed for Cuba with the deal, President Kennedy issued a direct personal appeal to all Americans to contribute toward the purchase of the tractors. Calling the prisoners "our brothers," the president expressed confidence that "every American would want to help." He stated that all contributions to the Tractors for Freedom Committee would be tax deductible, and he let it be known that he, as a private citizen, would likely make a contribution to the tractor fund himself. He further declared that the State Department would move quickly to issue previously outlawed export licenses for the tractor shipments and stated emphatically that the Logan Act, a law prohibiting private individuals from negotiating with foreign governments, would not be invoked against the Tractors for Freedom Committee.

The American people responded to the president's appeal by sending thousands upon thousands of contributions to the Tractor Committee's "Post Office Box Freedom" near UAW headquarters in Detroit. Volunteers in cities all across the country moved quickly to form local subsidiary committees to raise funds for the effort. Similar committees also sprang up in a dozen countries throughout Central and South America. In Rio de Janeiro, the president of the Roman Catholic Youth Association opened a drive to buy five tractors to be sent to Cuba in exchange for the prisoners, while in nearby São Paulo, students dressed in prison garb paraded through the streets collecting funds.

The reaction was markedly different, however, on Capitol Hill, where, according to *Time* magazine, a "large part of hell broke loose" over the president's remarks on the tractor swap. Members of both houses of Congress, already angry over Castro's repeated insistence that the tractors be considered reparations for damages caused during the invasion, took to the floor threatening to strip the Tractor Committee of its tax-exempt status and make committee members subject to all provisions of the Logan Act. Still others demanded the State Department halt its issuance of export licenses for the tractors. The attacks were broad-based and bipartisan, with the most serious concern being voiced over the precedent the payments would set. Eloquently addressing the matter of precedent, Democratic Senator Thomas Dodd of Connecticut warned, "Our national concern for the plight of the Cubans . . . should have been evidenced by effective help on the beachhead to enable their just revolution to succeed. By paying Castro's price for a thousand good men, we give him the means to strengthen his enslavement of 6,000,000 others. The American people will, for the first time to my knowledge, be making use of ransom and tribute as an instrument of policy.

If we start to pay tribute now for 1,000 of the one billion communist hostages, where will it stop?"

Former Vice President Richard Nixon, speaking at the Oklahoma State Republican Convention in Oklahoma City, declared the Kennedy plan "morally wrong" and urged his former rival to withdraw his support of the transaction. Nixon declared that America had "decided 100 years ago that human lives are not something to be considered as material or to be bartered on the slave block." To continue with the trade, the former vice president said, "would encourage every tinhorn dictator around the world to try to take advantage of America."

As the political controversy mushroomed, opponents of the plan seized upon the possibility that Castro might use the bulldozers for purposes other than those envisioned by the committee. They began asking, Why such big bulldozers? Did Castro plan to build military installations and missile sites, instead of using them to help his people grow more food? Critics and editorial writers began to liken the proposal to the infamous 1944 offer by Nazi Adolf Eichmann to trade Hungarian Jews for winterized military trucks, one hundred Jews for every truck.

On June 19, unable to defuse the explosive question of possible military use of the bulldozers, the embarrassed committee withdrew its pledge to supply the five hundred Super D-8s. In a telegram to Castro, the members bluntly informed the Cuban premier, "We are prepared to ship [five hundred] agricultural tractors and no other type." The committee then gave the Cuban leader seventy-two hours to accept their offer. Castro replied that he would be willing to forgo the bulldozers and accept the smaller tractors, but because his government considered the U.S. contribution to be indemnity for war damages, the total value of the tractors must approximate the value of the bulldozers, i.e., $28 million. Committee members rejected Castro's proposal out of hand, and when the seventy-two-hour deadline passed at noon on Friday, June 23, announced that the committee was ceasing all operations and returning all contributions received.

For the second time in as many months, John Kennedy had retreated in his high-stakes dealings with Fidel Castro.


*Spring 1962*
## A SECOND CHANCE

Fidel Castro put the Bay of Pigs prisoners on trial for treason in the spring of 1962. The mass trial, held in early May in the courtyard of Havana's Principe Prison, lasted only four days and resulted in guilty verdicts for all 1,179 defendants. Their punishment: thirty years' imprisonment or payment of fines ranging from $25,000 to $500,000 each, the higher amount for each of the three invasion leaders. Casting an eye toward Washington, the military tribunal ruled that payment of the fine would release the individual prisoner from having to serve his thirty-year sentence. Total fines levied: $62 million.

Within hours of the reading of the verdicts in Havana, John Kennedy jumped at this unexpected second chance to free the Bay of Pigs captives. This time he turned to his brother Robert, the attorney general, to raise the money and get the prisoners home.

Using a Cuban refugee organization as a front, Robert Kennedy immediately dispatched the organization's "counsel," famed New York attorney James Donovan, to Havana to negotiate a deal with Castro. Following several months of talks, Donovan, who had negotiated the release of U-2 pilot Francis Gary Powers from the Soviets, struck a deal with the Cuban leader: $53 million payable in medicines, powdered milk, and baby food in return for all the prisoners.

Before the deal could be consummated, the Cuban missile crisis intervened and contact between the two sides was suspended. But when the missile crisis subsided in November, Castro sent word that he was still interested and contact was reestablished. With that, Robert Kennedy and a group of trusted advisors went to work raising the money, with the goal of getting the prisoners home by Christmas. Operating out of offices in the Justice Department, the group made hundreds of calls to executives of pharmaceutical, medical, surgical supply, and food products companies seeking donations for the prisoner deal. On dozens of occasions, Robert Kennedy met personally at the Justice Department with company executives to seek their assistance. At one such meeting, the attorney general reportedly told pharmaceutical executives "my brother made a mistake" at the Bay of Pigs and implied that the prisoner exchange would help rectify that. He followed his remarks with a strong appeal for donations of medicines. Similar appeals for assistance were made to executives of the nation's airline, railroad, and steamship companies. Sometimes the persuasion was less than gentle. The *Minneapolis Tribune* reported that a spokesman for one large corporation facing a government lawsuit said his company received a call from the Department of Justice directing it to supply specific items, plus a specific amount of cash. "We knew we were being blackjacked," the spokesman said, "but there was nothing we could do about it."

Though some of his tactics may have been open to question, the results of Robert Kennedy's efforts were nothing short of astounding. As described in *U.S. News & World Report* at the time:

> The first shipment of the Castro ransom, 32,000 pounds of medicines, was flown from New York to Miami during the night of December 17. . . . After that first shipment, the floodgates were down. By air, truck, and railroad, hundreds of thousands of pounds of baby food, canned goods, medicine [and] medical supplies poured into Florida from every corner of the U.S. . . . Eight domestic airlines began flying 600,000 pounds of supplies to Florida; 19 railroads soon had 80 boxcars on this special run; eight trucking firms were moving 420,000 pounds of supplies from distant points, and 15 shipping companies had put up a ship and the money to move its cargo to Havana. . . . It was a logistical operation almost without parallel except in wartime.

Castro released the prisoners just in time for Christmas. The first four planeloads of freedom fighters arrived to a tumultuous welcome at Homestead Air Force Base outside Miami on the evening of December 23, and by late Christmas

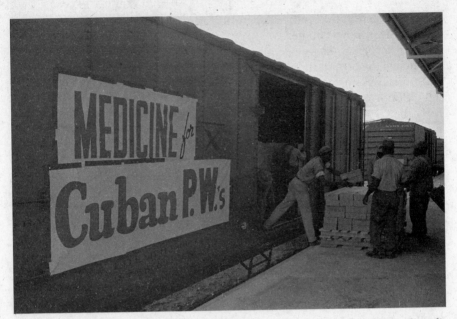

Fort Lauderdale, Florida, December 20, 1962. Longshoremen unload food and medicines bound for Cuba in the Bay of Pigs prisoner exchange. The freighter *African Pilot* will take the cargo to Cuba. (AP/WIDE WORLD PHOTOS)

Eve all surviving prisoners from Brigade 2506 were back in America. Two days after Christmas, the president and Jacqueline Kennedy met privately with the leadership of the brigade at the winter White House in Palm Beach. Then, on December 28, the Kennedys joined the entire brigade and forty thousand wildly cheering Cuban exiles at a welcome home rally at Miami's Orange Bowl. Thunderous cheers rocked the stadium as first the president and then his wife praised the men for their bravery and commitment to freedom. The crowd repeatedly interrupted the president with shouts of "Viva Kennedy" and *"Libertad por Cuba,"* especially when he pledged to see the rebels return to liberate their homeland. Mrs. Kennedy's remarks, delivered in Spanish, evoked equal enthusiasm, with the crowd shouting "Viva Jackie, viva Jackie" and "Jack-k-leen, Jack-k-leen, Jack-k-leen."

After personally greeting many of the freed prisoners who were in formation near the podium, the president and first lady got into their open-topped limousine to depart. As they rode slowly along the sidelines, standing in the back of the open car and shaking the outstretched hands of the exiles, few doubted that John Kennedy had fulfilled his responsibility to those he sent to the Bay of Pigs. The ransomed men of Brigade 2506 were finally home.

Within a week of the Orange Bowl rally, Communist leaders from throughout the world gathered in Havana for ceremonies marking the fourth anniversary of Fidel Castro's rise to power. Following a two-hour parade of military might before a reviewing stand containing some four hundred notables in the Communist world, Castro delivered the keynote address. The Cuban premier, clearly angered by Kennedy's remarks at the Orange Bowl the previous week,

Miami, Florida, December 29, 1962. Jacqueline Kennedy speaks in Spanish at a ceremony honoring former Cuban invasion prisoners released a week ago. She tells the Cubans assembled in the Orange Bowl stadium that she hopes her son, John Jr., will be half as brave as the men of Brigade 2506. President Kennedy stands by her.
(AP/WIDE WORLD PHOTOS)

derided Kennedy as a "vulgar pirate chief" and openly mocked his decision to pay what Castro insisted was "indemnification" to Cuba for damages the United States caused during the Bay of Pigs invasion. "For the first time in history," Castro boasted, "imperialism has paid war indemnification. They call it ransom. We don't care what they call it. They had to agree to pay indemnification."[1]

The delegation from North Vietnam listened attentively.

CHAPTER 1

# THE POW HOSTAGE PLAN AND
# ITS IMPLEMENTATION

. . .

The war may last five, ten, twenty or more years. Hanoi, Haiphong and other
cities and enterprises may be destroyed . . . [but] once victory is won, our people
will rebuild their country and make it even more prosperous and beautiful.
                                                              —HO CHI MINH

John Kennedy was assassinated in Dallas, Texas, on November 22, 1963, some
eleven months after the Bay of Pigs prisoners were released. He was succeeded in
office by his vice president, Lyndon Baines Johnson, the former U.S. Senator
from Texas.

In early 1964, Johnson, while continuing the gradual buildup of U.S. forces
in South Vietnam that Kennedy and he had begun soon after taking office in
1961, approved a covert plan to conduct hit-and-run attacks against coastal targets in North Vietnam. The plan, known as Op Plan 34-A, was a joint South
Vietnamese/U.S. effort designed to interdict supplies, munitions, and Communist troops before they could reach South Vietnam. It called for South Vietnamese PT boats to put South Vietnamese commandos ashore at night to blow
bridges and attack other transportation-related targets; attack North Vietnamese
bases suspected of housing personnel and/or equipment bound for the southern
battlefields and other targets of opportunity—all under the watchful eye of U.S.
destroyers conducting nighttime "intelligence-gathering operations" just outside North Vietnamese territorial waters in the Gulf of Tonkin.[1]

The North Vietnamese were hit and hit and hit again throughout the spring
and summer of 1964, but did not launch any major military response. Then, after South Vietnamese PT boats shelled two North Vietnamese islands in the Gulf
in late July, the North Vietnamese struck back. In the early morning hours of August 2, three of their torpedo boats attacked the USS *Maddox*, one of the U.S. destroyers that had been shadowing the South Vietnamese commando raids. At the
time of the attack, the *Maddox* was conducting its nighttime intelligence-
gathering operations just off the North Vietnamese coast in international waters.

The *Maddox* and U.S. Navy aircraft quickly repelled the North Vietnamese
attack, setting fire to one of the boats and sending the others fleeing, but did
not carry the fight to the nearby port where the boats were believed based.[2]
When news of the attack on the *Maddox*—and the Johnson administration's

less-than-overwhelming response—reached America, a war fever erupted. John-son responded by declaring that any further attacks would be met with over-whelming force and by ordering all U.S. forces operating in the Tonkin Gulf to full battle stations. It was in this charged atmosphere that on August 4, crew-men aboard the *Maddox* and its sister ship the USS *Turner Joy* reported possible but unconfirmed attacks against their vessels during storm-tossed nighttime operations in the Gulf.

Without waiting for confirmation that this second round of attacks had, in fact, occurred, Johnson ordered immediate retaliatory strikes against North Vietnamese coastal targets and ports and submitted what amounted to a decla-ration of war to Congress. The resolution Johnson submitted, which became known as the Gulf of Tonkin Resolution, authorized him, as president, to take "all necessary measures to repel any armed attacks against the forces of the United States and to prevent further aggression" and to provide all needed mil-itary assistance requested by America's allies in the region. Though some sus-pected at the time that the reported attacks on August 4 had not actually occurred and were simply being used by the president and his advisors as a pre-text for widening the war, the Senate approved the Gulf of Tonkin Resolution on August 7, 1964, by a vote of 88 to 2.[3]

Knowing what it all meant—a massive buildup of American troop strength and all-out warfare in the South and perhaps years of ruinous U.S. air attacks against the North—the North Vietnamese began planning for a long and poten-tially very destructive war and, at war's end, a long and difficult period of re-construction. U.S. intelligence officials would soon learn that part of the North Vietnamese plan for the war and its aftermath—a key part, in fact—was based on an important lesson they had learned some eighteen months before from Fidel Castro.

## THE HOSTAGE PLAN

Intelligence collected by the U.S. Central Intelligence Agency during the Viet-nam War indicates that in 1964, the year the United States first bombed North Vietnam, the North Vietnamese Communist Party Central Committee ordered that all North Vietnamese military personnel and civilians be trained to capture American military personnel alive so that they could be used "as hostages to compel the U.S., in the event of a cease-fire, to pay war reparations for the de-struction inflicted upon NVN by the United States."[4]

The CIA reported that North Vietnamese authorities began holding training sessions throughout the country to teach the civilian population the procedures they were to follow in capturing and handling downed fliers.[5] CIA sources fur-ther reported that the main teaching document used in these sessions was a pamphlet titled "Policy on Treatment of American Prisoners," which the North Vietnamese government made available to all civilians. Most of the instruc-tional period at the training sessions, these sources reported, was devoted to the section of the pamphlet that dealt with how Americans were to be captured and searched, how their wounds were to be treated, how they were to be protected from harm and then delivered as quickly as possible to the authorities, etc.[6]

Soldiers of the North Vietnamese army—the Peoples Army of Vietnam (the PAVN) reportedly received similar instruction during basic training or in officer candidate school. The CIA reported that during one session at the Son Tay Officers School west of Hanoi in 1966, the instructor stated that the North Vietnamese government considered U.S. POWs to be of "first-level importance because they will be used as a means of obtaining payment for bomb damages from the U.S. when the war ends." For that reason, the instructor said, Americans must be captured alive whenever possible, protected, and given good treatment.

The instructor went on to explain that downed American airmen were to be captured by

surrounding them and closing in. To shoot to kill was strictly forbidden under any circumstance. If a crew member was armed and resisted capture, he was to be surrounded and volunteers to rush him were to be requested. The volunteers were to charge the man and overpower him. He was not to be killed even if he killed North Vietnamese personnel while resisting capture. . . .

. . . Once capture had been made, the very first act was to search the prisoner for weapons or drugs with which he might kill himself. The prisoner must not be allowed to commit suicide. The second step in the capture was to treat any wounds. Next, the prisoner was to be quickly moved to higher echelons. . . . No one was to be permitted to beat or otherwise mistreat the prisoner. If someone did, he was [to be] criticized. Prisoners were to be given as much food and water as they wanted. . . . All of the prisoner's belongings and equipment were to be confiscated and sent to higher echelons with him. Nothing was to be taken for personal use. If someone did so, he was to be criticized.[7]

To get the POWs back at the end of the war, the instructor told the officer candidates, the United States would have to "exchange equipment for them and build up the country."[8]

In a move that underscored the importance the North Vietnamese placed on the matter of postwar reconstruction, the government in Hanoi created in 1966 the Committee of Inquiry and charged it with keeping a day-to-day tally of the damage caused by American bombs. Those appointed to the committee included top officials from the ministries of Health, Foreign Affairs, and Security, as well as high-ranking PAVN officers, the chief of the PAVN Liaison to the International Control Commission, and the president of the People's Supreme Court. Beginning in 1966, the committee compiled precise information, day by day, factory by factory, village by village, relating to the "material and human damage caused by U.S. bombing."[9]

## HANOI'S PLAN TO CAPTURE AMERICANS ALIVE IN THE SOUTH

Given Hanoi's plan to capture as many Americans alive as possible in the North and use them as hostages to secure postwar reconstruction aid, it came as no surprise to U.S. intelligence officials when they learned of a similar North Vietnamese plan to capture American troops fighting in South Vietnam and use them for the same purpose. The information on the North Vietnamese plan came from PAVN soldiers who had infiltrated down the Ho Chi Minh Trail and had been captured in battle or had turned themselves in to the allies and were later interviewed by U.S. interrogators.

The PAVN told U.S. interrogators that they had been trained in both basic training and officer candidate school to capture *surrendering* Americans alive during combat in the South rather than kill them. The PAVN told of similar training sessions being conducted along the Ho Chi Minh Trail during the long trek to the southern battlefields and of reminders being issued to the troops just before battle.[10]

Wherever the sessions were held, the intelligence indicates the message was the same: Kill as many Americans as possible during battle, but under no circumstances should surrendering Americans be killed; rather, they should be taken alive and quickly removed from the battlefield. PAVN soldiers who violated this policy and executed those Americans who were attempting to surrender or who had already been captured were disciplined.[11]

To assist in capturing Americans during ground combat operations, PAVN soldiers were taught to memorize English-language phrases such as "hands up," "hands down," "surrender, not die," "after me," "go to hospital," "go to safe area," etc.[12] In almost every case, these were the only English words in a PAVN soldier's vocabulary.

The PAVN were also issued 2½" × 3½" "capture cards" prior to battle, which were to be used when direct contact with the prospective American prisoner occurred. Printed on one side were the following English phrases in phonetic Vietnamese and their meanings in English:

Key words to be used while capturing and dealing with American POWs

| (phonetic Vietnamese) | (meaning in English) |
|---|---|
| xo-ren-do o dai | surrender or die |
| gan dao | gun down |
| hen ap | hands up |
| ton rao | turn around |
| not mu | do not move |
| go quich | go quickly |
| xai-lon | silence |
| hoe do men | where are your men |
| con dem | call them |

The reverse side contained a printed message the PAVN were to show the American soldier who was being captured. The message, deliberately misstating the military affiliation of the bearer because the North Vietnamese government refused to acknowledge the presence of PAVN troops in South Vietnam, read in English:

The National Front for Liberation and the Liberation Armed Forces of South Vietnam humanely treat their enemy soldiers who have surrendered [to] them. You are now captured, we do not kill you. Just follow our command!

We will have your arms tied up and take you to a safe place. Stand up and follow us right now! Only then can your life be assured and you be soon untied. Should you hesitate or refuse to go, you would probably get killed as a result of the air raids and artillery from the American side. We should fight as the U.S. troops come; then your life is hardly safe.

Printed at the bottom of the card in Vietnamese was: "Show this to American soldiers when you capture them."[13]

PAVN policy dictated that American prisoners who had not suffered wounds were to be taken directly to the capturing unit's headquarters for interrogation. As stated on the "capture card," these prisoners were to be moved away from the battlefield as quickly as possible for fear they and their captors would be caught in the artillery barrages and air strikes the allies routinely rained down on withdrawing Communist forces.

Wartime intelligence collected from PAVN sources shows that this fear was indeed justified. One PAVN told U.S. interrogators that nine American prisoners who were being escorted away from their point of capture in Kontum Province in the Central Highlands had been caught in one such artillery barrage. The source said that five of the Americans and one guard had been killed, and that all had been buried in a mass grave next to the trail.[14]

Another PAVN told of seeing two badly injured American servicemen being carried on stretchers by PAVN soldiers in Quang Tin Province on South Vietnam's northern coast. He said the litter bearers told him the Americans had been captured uninjured in fighting the previous day but had been wounded when a U.S. armed reconnaissance plane attacked the group as they were moving away toward a liberated area.[15]

Yet another PAVN told how fellow troops had captured twenty-six U.S. soldiers during a battle in Quang Tri Province, the northernmost province in South Vietnam. He reported that the prisoners were being moved from the battlefield under guard when they and their guards were attacked by allied aircraft. He reported that ten American prisoners were killed in the attack and four others wounded, one seriously. He also said that three of the PAVN guards were killed and two others wounded. The source added that a PAVN doctor came to the site of the attack and treated the wounded prisoners and that the Americans and their guards then resumed their journey to a base camp in a secure area.[16]

According to a number of the PAVN sources, official policy dictated that all wounded Americans be taken to the nearest field hospital for treatment. Those who were wounded so severely that they could not walk were to be carried.[17]

Though the intelligence indicates general PAVN compliance with the stated PAVN policy of capturing rather than killing Americans who were attempting to surrender and caring for rather than killing those who had been wounded, revenge killings did occur on a number of occasions. Among these were the killings that occurred during the Battle of the Ia Drang Valley in 1965 when

PAVN troops sought out the American wounded and executed as many of them as possible, and the killings of American pilots and aircrewmen that reportedly occurred along remote sections of the Ho Chi Minh Trail in Laos.[18]

## THE QUALITY OF THE INTELLIGENCE · THE QUALITY OF THE PAVN AS INTELLIGENCE SOURCES

U.S. interrogators found early on that the information provided by the PAVN concerning the American prisoners they had reportedly seen was often highly specific as to date and circumstance. The interrogators concluded that the PAVN were aided in their recall by two factors. First, the soldiers relied on recent specific frames of reference in their highly regimented lives to help them remember the exact date of their sighting—the date they completed basic training, the date they started marching south, the date they crossed the border into Laos, the date they crossed a certain river during infiltration, the date they arrived at a certain rest station along the Ho Chi Minh Trail, the date they arrived in South Vietnam, etc. Second, U.S. interrogators ascribed their highly specific descriptions of the circumstances surrounding the sighting of the American or Americans and the often detailed descriptions of the prisoners to the fact that most PAVN had never before seen an American and when they did the event created an indelible impression upon them.[19]

Given the novelty of seeing an American and the apparent impact that such sighting had on the PAVN, U.S. interrogators were not surprised to find that the education and intelligence level of the individual PAVN sources seemed to have little bearing on the quality of intelligence each provided. Barely literate PAVN

Two PAVN soldiers captured in South Vietnam in 1967.
(U.S. ARMY)

were often able to recall the physical characteristics of individual American POWs they had seen in detail sufficient to allow interrogators to combine the descriptions and the reported date of the sighting with known U.S. battle losses and determine the identity of the Americans with reasonable certainty. On the other end of the education spectrum, captured PAVN doctors were, as one might expect, able to recall clearly the specific surgical procedures they performed on wounded American servicemen in the South and in several cases were able to provide interrogators with their former patients' names. Captured PAVN nurses and medics were likewise able to remember the specific medications and first aid procedures they administered to dozens of wounded Americans on the battle-fields and at aid stations and at field hospitals in the South.

Given where they had come from, what they had seen along the way, and their uncanny ability to recall date and detail, the PAVN were fertile ground indeed for U.S. intelligence officials hungry for information about missing Americans. Their value to the intelligence community was enhanced by the fact that, apparently believing that what they said about American POWs would not adversely affect their country's war effort, the PAVN were generally willing to share this information openly and without apparent intent to deceive.[20]

U.S. military interrogators operating at or under the auspices of one of Saigon's two main interrogation centers, the Combined U.S./South Vietnamese Military Interrogation Center (CMIC) or the National Interrogation Center (NIC), conducted most of the PAVN interrogations. As a matter of routine, at the end of each interview the interrogator assigned each case an evaluation of F-6 on the standard intelligence community evaluation scale. This meant "credibility of source unknown/credibility of information cannot be judged."[21] The F was routinely assigned for the obvious reason that each captured or surrendered PAVN had, by virtue of his past service, never before provided intelligence to the U.S. government and thus had not established himself as a reliable source over time. The 6 was routinely assigned because the information provided by the source had almost always originated behind enemy lines and thus did not lend itself to on-site verification.

In addition to the standard letter/number evaluation, the interrogator would often add comments concerning the demeanor and perceived truthfulness of the source. An example of one interrogator's comments and the relationship of these comments to the letter/number evaluation assigned to the PAVN source is noted below:

## COMMENTS OF THE COLLECTOR

5. (u) Source was cooperative during the interrogation and answered all questions willingly. He appeared to be of average intelligence and correctly responded to control questions with acceptable consistency. The interrogator felt that source was not withholding information and related facts to the best of his ability. Source appeared to be truthful during the interrogation.

6. Evaluation: Source F Information 6[22]

Individual administrative evaluations aside, in the final analysis U.S. intelligence officials considered the PAVN to be rock-solid sources of intelligence on

U.S. POWs. The deputy director of the CIA would later state that captured PAVN provided "very valuable information on the Communist prison system, techniques, and policy of exploiting prisoners, locations of prisons, and, less frequently, actual identification of prisoners.[23] Sedgwick D. Tourison Jr., a U.S. Army warrant officer who interrogated many PAVN for the CMIC during the war, would later pay these soldiers the intelligence community's highest possible compliment. Tourison, who received special commendation for his outstanding service at CMIC from the head of the center, Maj. Gen. Joseph A. McChristian, USA, and went on to work for the Defense Intelligence Agency in Washington, wrote of the PAVN, "There were a lot of observations we could make about those soldiers from north of the seventeenth parallel. We found that most simply told the truth when asked questions."[24]

## VIETCONG POLICY RELATING TO THE CAPTURE AND TREATMENT OF AMERICAN SERVICEMEN

Intelligence collected during the war from captured Vietcong and from Hoi Chanhs—Communist Southerners who turned themselves in to the South Vietnamese government under the Chieu Hoi (open arms) program—indicates the Vietcong generally followed PAVN guidelines when dealing with American prisoners.

The VC, like their northern cousins, operated under the principle that "once captured, the prisoners served a more 'useful' purpose [if] they were kept alive."[25] Just like the PAVN, the VC were instructed to capture Americans alive whenever possible.[26] The VC considered American servicemen to be "excellent hostages" who would be traded at war's end either for reconstruction aid or for Vietcong prisoners held by the South Vietnamese.[27] One VC source told U.S. interrogators that "for one returned officer pilot, the U.S. had to compensate NVN with a factory." He also reported hearing that the rate of exchange for prisoners would be "one U.S. soldier . . . for 10 VC soldiers."[28]

Vietcong sources reported that torturing American prisoners or harming them in any way was strictly prohibited, and that any VC who did so was to be subjected to "severe punishment."[29] The exact form of punishment appeared to vary from unit to unit. One VC source reported that his unit was instructed that anyone who shot an American who had ceased resistance and come forward with his hands up would himself be shot.[30] In other units the penalties for killing an American who could have been captured ranged from demotion in rank to severe reprimand.[31]

Combat atrocities and revenge killings did occur, and the captured VC and the Hoi Chanhs occasionally reported the details of these events.[32] Despite the atrocities, MACV, the U.S. Military Assistance Command in Vietnam, stated in its 1970 *Command History* that "the VC continue a policy of leniency towards captured Americans. . . . Some atrocities . . . have occurred, but they stand out because they have been so few."[33]

Like the PAVN, VC soldiers were ordered to "learn . . . by heart" several English phrases that would aid them in capturing Americans. These phrases included *"hen-xap"* (hands up), *"hon-t"* (halt), *"gan-dao-n"* (throw your weapon down), *"xit-dao-n"* (sit down), *"get-ap"* (get up), and *"gau"* (go).[34]

The VC were under orders to take all Americans who were captured unhurt to higher headquarters for interrogation. If the escort force was subjected to an air strike en route to the headquarters area, members were to give first priority to the safety of their prisoner.[35]

VC policy dictated that those Americans who had been wounded and left for dead on the battlefield or wounded during capture were to be given first aid and then removed to the nearest aid station or field hospital for additional treatment. According to MACV, the administration of this medical care to wounded GIs was "the most often adhered to [tenet] of VC policy regarding American prisoners."[36] One captured VC reported that in instances where VC cadre and U.S. POWs required medical treatment at the same time, the American prisoners were given attention first, unless the VC were more seriously wounded.[37]

"Instances where the VC have killed wounded Americans in lieu of taking them prisoner," MACV declared in its 1970 *Command History*, "are extremely rare."[38]

CHAPTER 2

# HANOI BOUND

· · ·

A mountain of intelligence collected from PAVN and VC sources during the war indicates that hundreds upon hundreds of American servicemen—soldiers, marines, and airmen—were captured in South Vietnam and sent to North Vietnam for long-term imprisonment.

The intelligence reports telling of the transfer of American POWs from the battle areas in the South to the prisons of North Vietnam indicate that the prisoners were moved by foot, truck, van, jeep, train, fixed-wing aircraft, helicopter, motorized sampan, riverboat, and/or Chinese freighter. They were carried on stretchers or in hammocks if they were unable to walk, or were forcibly strapped to stretchers or hammocks and carried if they refused to walk.

The intelligence indicates that several of the early captures were moved to North Vietnam by helicopter or fixed-wing aircraft from airfields in Cambodia and Laos. The intelligence further indicates that in 1966 these transfers by air slowed as the PAVN and the VC began sending captured Americans to the North overland, either via the Ho Chi Minh Trail through South Vietnam, Cambodia, and Laos or directly across the DMZ into North Vietnam. The intelligence indicates these land routes continued in use until the war ended for America in 1973.

## THE MOVE NORTH

The wartime Ho Chi Minh Trail that carried the Americans north from the southern battlefields bore little resemblance to the narrow, single trail that had carried the first shipment of arms to the Vietminh in 1959. By 1966, the North Vietnamese had developed the Trail into a series of north-south roads, trails, and waterways joined to a labyrinth of east-west feeder roads. Along the major corridors, they had constructed large base camps called *binh trams* (literally, binh [soldier] tram [stopping point][1]) and had manned them with anywhere from about four hundred to more than one thousand personnel. These personnel oversaw the movement of southbound supplies and provided food, shelter, medical care, postal services, etc., for (1) southbound PAVN; (2) PAVN who had been wounded or had become ill in the South and were returning to North Vietnam for treatment or convalescence; (3) Vietcong officials traveling to North Vietnam for various reasons; (4) the children or orphans of Vietcong who were traveling to North Vietnam for study; and (5) American, South Vietnamese (soldiers of the Army of the Republic of Vietnam [ARVN]), South Korean (soldiers of the Army of the Republic of Korea [ROK]), and other free world POWs who had been captured in South Vietnam, Cambodia, and southern Laos and were being taken up the Trail to North Vietnam for long-term confinement.

Between the large *binh trams* on the major corridors and also along the smaller east-west feeder roads, the North Vietnamese had also constructed a series of small rest and resupply stations called commo-liaison stations. These stations were located approximately one day's march apart and were manned by armed "commo-liaison agents" who provided security and served as escorts and guides.[2]

The sightings of American prisoners being moved to North Vietnam for long-term confinement began in earnest in early 1966. According to PAVN and VC who saw the American prisoners and then were later themselves captured and interrogated by U.S. intelligence personnel, and according to other wartime intelligence sources, here is some of what took place in the South and along the infiltration routes during 1966, the first full year of reporting:

- A PAVN soldier reported that he observed fifteen U.S. and twenty-five ARVN POWs in Moi Pass in Binh Dinh Province, located on SVN's central coast, in late February 1966. The prisoners were walking north in single file accompanied by five armed guards. The Americans were wearing brownish-green uniforms, combat helmets, and boots. The source was told they were being taken to Hanoi.[3]
- A Communist soldier reported that his unit captured four members of the U.S. "1st Airborne" during a battle in Pleiku Province, SVN, in the Central Highlands on March 30, 1966. The prisoners were led away toward Cambodia. The source was told they would probably be flown to NVN by helicopter. The source reported that "it was common knowledge that NVN used helicopters between NVN and Cambodia."[4]
- A PAVN soldier reported that he was infiltrating with his unit along the Ho Chi Minh Trail in Cambodia west of Pleiku in the spring of 1966 when he

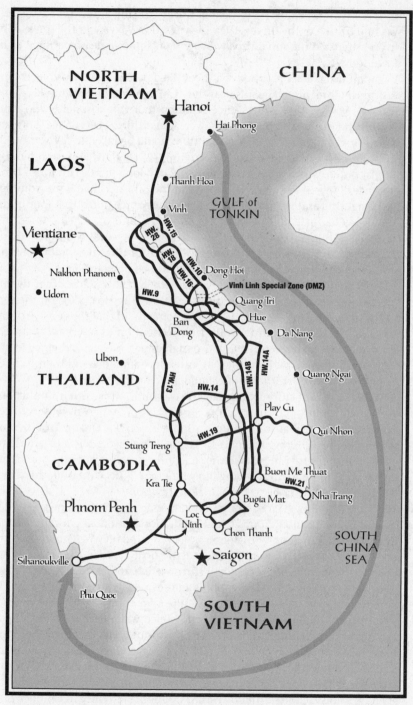

The Ho Chi Minh Trail according to the North Vietnamese and Vietcong.
(HENDON/ANDERER)

observed two three-quarter-ton panel trucks crossing a river on a barge. He
was told by one of the drivers that a few U.S. POWs were in the trucks. The
drivers later said the Americans were being taken to a nearby airfield to be
flown to NVN.[5]

- A Communist soldier reported that he walked past two U.S. prisoners being
escorted by three armed guards near the Laotian border in Kontum Province,
SVN, on May 1, 1966. The source reported that the prisoners, who wore
dark green fatigues and black shoes, were about thirty years of age. Both appeared tired and sad. The guards said they would be taken to NVN.[6]

- A Communist soldier reported that on June 12, 1966 his unit captured five
U.S. and ten Korean soldiers during a day-long battle in Binh Dinh
Province, SVN, on the central coast. All of the prisoners had been wounded
in the fighting and left on the battlefield. The source noted that four of the
Americans had patches on their sleeves with a bird on it. The Americans
were taken to infantry headquarters where their wounds were treated and
they were fed. They were kept by source's unit for three days and then sent
to NVN in the company of an interpreter and eight guards.[7]

- A PAVN soldier reported that he was told by a fellow soldier that twenty
Americans had been captured during a battle at Tuy Hoa, SVN, on the central coast, during June or July 1966. The soldier said that four or five of the
Americans had been slightly wounded. He went on to say that the Americans would be taken to Gia Lai (VC designation for Pleiku Province in the
Central Highlands) by foot, then by truck to Cambodia and then to NVN
by air. "We have our airfields in Cambodia," the soldier said.[8]

- A PAVN medical doctor reported that he was infiltrating with his unit along
the Ho Chi Minh Trail in Laos on June 27, 1966, when he observed ten
American prisoners at infiltration station #10 west of Quang Tri Province,
the northernmost province in SVN. The POWs all wore black pajamas and
were bound together in pairs with parachute cord. A guard said the Americans would be escorted to Quang Binh Province, NVN, and from there they
would be taken by truck to their final destination.[9]

- The same PAVN medical doctor reported that approximately one week later,
he and his infiltration group shared infiltration station #35, located farther
down the Trail in Laos, with a group of twelve U.S. POWs. Guards told the
doctor that the POWs were pilots, but the doctor noted that most of the
prisoners wore olive drab fatigues. Three were barefoot and lamed by foot
injuries; the others wore leather boots and seemed to be in good health. The
men were tied in pairs by nylon parachute cord at one wrist. They were fed
rice, canned tuna, unripe mangoes, and boiled water because it was important to keep them in good health. The doctor believed they had been held
in a POW camp for some time before they began their trek north. A guard
said the Americans would be escorted to Quang Binh Province, NVN, and
from there they would be taken by truck to their final destination.[10]

- A PAVN soldier reported that he was in Quang Tri Province in October 1966
when he heard other PAVN talking about six American POWs who were
being held in Cam Lo district in the province. Four were said to be
wounded. The soldiers said that the POWs were to be sent north of Vinh

Linh, in the Vinh Linh Special Zone (DMZ), to recover from their wounds, and that after they had recovered they would be sent on to Hanoi.[11]

- A PAVN soldier reported that he had seen a captured U.S. pilot at commo-liaison station #7 along the Ho Chi Minh Trail in Kontum Province, SVN, in October 1966. The source was told that the pilot had been held at the station for four or five days. He was further told that on his first night at the station the American had caught his guards sleeping and had taken one of their AK submachine guns and escaped into the jungle. A group of ten or twelve PAVN had been sent out to recapture him. The group had specific orders to find and recapture the American and not to shoot him or harm him in any way during the recapture process. When the PAVN caught up with the pilot, he began shooting and four PAVN were killed. The survivors waited for the pilot to expend all the ammunition in the single clip he had and they then recaptured him and returned him to the station. The source was told that following his interrogation the American was taken to Cambodia. From there he was to be sent to Hanoi.[12]

- A PAVN soldier reported that an American sergeant was captured by Communist forces during an attack on a U.S. artillery base in Binh Dinh Province on the central coast in October 1966. The prisoner stayed at regimental headquarters for six days before he was sent to division and then transferred to NVN.[13]

- A Vietcong soldier reported that he observed in mid-November 1966 four U.S. pilots who had been shot down and captured in the vicinity of the Vinh Linh Special Zone (DMZ). The Americans, uninjured and still dressed in their flight uniforms, were kept in caves out of view of the local populace for fear they might be harmed. After three days, they were taken to Hanoi in a military truck.[14]

- A classified CIA source reported that he observed three U.S. pilots walking under guard north of the DMZ in Quang Binh Province, NVN, in December 1966. Policemen escorting the pilots said they had been captured several days earlier in the Vinh Linh Special Zone. The pilots all wore one-piece dark gray flying suits that were splattered with mud. They had badly swollen feet and one walked with a cane. All appeared sad. After an evening meal, the prisoners and their guards continued their journey north at night to avoid detection by allied aircraft.[15]

- A PAVN soldier reported that while infiltrating with his platoon into Binh Dinh Province, on SVN's central coast, during December 1966, he passed within one meter of a U.S. POW who was being escorted by Communist soldiers. The source reported that the American wore green fatigues and black boots. One of the escorts said the prisoner was being taken to NVN.[16]

- A classified CIA source reported that eight American prisoners were detained by the VC in a village just inside Cambodia on December 22, 1966. The source reported the village was located about four hundred meters from the border with Tay Ninh Province, SVN. The source reported that the prisoners were tied up and were awaiting transfer to NVN.[17]

- A Vietcong soldier reported that his regiment captured four U.S. First Air Cavalry Division soldiers on December 27, 1966, during a battle in Binh

Dinh Province. The Americans were sent to division headquarters, then to Military Region 5 headquarters, and finally to NVN where they would be detained for possible exchange after the armistice.[18]

- A Communist soldier reported that he saw one U.S. and approximately twenty ARVN POWs southwest of Tuy Hoa City on SVN's central coast in late December 1966. The American wore a green military uniform with two ribbons over the left pocket and was accompanied by two guards. The source was told that American prisoners were taken by truck to Dar Lac Province on the SVN/Cambodia border and put aboard a plane and flown to NVN.[19]

As combat heated up in the South, so too did the intelligence telling of American soldiers, marines, and airmen being captured alive and moved to North Vietnam for long-term imprisonment. In July 1968, after reviewing only forty-five intelligence reports received during late 1967 and the first half of 1968, CIA officials in Saigon published a classified memorandum titled "Northward Movement of U.S. Civilian and Military Personnel Captured in South Vietnam." The memorandum read in part:

This review of 45 reports, most of which were received during late 1967 and the first half of 1968, suggests that the North Vietnamese Government, during the period May 1967 to July 1968, moved from fifty to several hundred American personnel captured in South Vietnam northward along established lines of infiltration and transport through Cambodia, Laos and across the DMZ. . . . The same roads, footpaths, guides, vehicles and systematically numbered way stations were utilized—southward for the infiltration of NVA troops and supplies, northward for transfer of American prisoners and NVA wounded to NVN. . . . No definite route across the DMZ could be determined from the reports received; the evidence is substantial enough, however, to conclude that some of the Americans captured in First Corps of RVN were being moved into NVN across the DMZ. Nine reports and two NVN radio broadcasts mentioned a total of about 150 American POWs [moving across the DMZ]. . . . The North Vietnamese Government, however, did not acknowledge or allow public reference to or photography of any American prisoner in North Vietnam who had been captured in South Vietnam or Laos. In view of these facts, the population of American prisoners in NVN could be considerably larger than the number of American pilots considered captured or MIA over NVN alone.[20]

Later in the war, in August 1970, personnel at the USAF's 6499th Special Activities Group, after reviewing more than eleven hundred intelligence reports about American POWs their group had acquired from captured PAVN and Hoi Chanhs since January 1, 1968, said this in a classified twenty-eight-page synopsis of that intelligence dated August 31, 1970:

There appears to be a definite trend toward the moving of all PWs to North Vietnam, whenever feasible. This movement, primarily from South Vietnam

to North Vietnam, has been reported across the DMZ and north on the infiltration trails in Laos. . . .

. . . North Vietnamese policy toward the treatment of U.S. PWs seems to be
centered around one idea, namely the bargaining potential of the U.S. PWs
during future negotiations with the United States. Accordingly, indications
are that PWs generally have not been mistreated upon capture. Except for a
few instances, treatment of downed pilots upon shootdown seems to be
within the humane guidelines of the stated North Vietnamese policy. There
are indications that treatment during confinement is much more harsh. . . .

. . . The intention of this study has not been to pinpoint camp locations
nor to identify those personnel whose status should be changed from MIA to
PW or from MIA to KIA. [Rather], [t]he main thrust . . . has been towards . . .
showing that North Vietnamese PWs who were first hand sources to the incidents involving U.S. aircrew members provide highly useful and voluminous information for the analysis of the plight of the many hundreds of U.S.
PWs believed interned in North Vietnam. . . . [21]

The intelligence reporting would continue throughout the war. An analysis
of just the 1966 reports presented above and approximately 150 additional similar reports received from 1967 to 1973, subtracting for possible duplicate sightings of the same American or groups of Americans, shows that well over one
thousand American POWs were sent to North Vietnam during the war for long-
term imprisonment. [These approximately 150 selected reports covering the period from 1967 until the end of the war can be found at www.enormouscrime
.com, Chapter 2, "Selected Declassified Wartime Intelligence Reports Telling of
the Movement of American POWs From the Southern Battlefields to North Vietnam for Long-Term Imprisonment, 1967–1973".]

## SOME AMERICAN POWs REMAIN IN CAMPS IN THE SOUTH

Intelligence received during the war indicated that in addition to the large number of American POWs sent north for long-term imprisonment, the VC were allowed to keep a small number of American prisoners under their own control in
the South on a semipermanent basis.[22] The intelligence indicated that these
prisoners were held in primitive camps in the U-Minh Forest in the far southern
portion of the country,[23] in Loc Ninh and Tay Ninh provinces north and northwest of Saigon,[24] in camps just across the border in Cambodia,[25] and at a prison
known as T-15 in the northern province of Quang Ngai. T-15 reportedly held
about a dozen U.S. servicemen, including a doctor.[26]

Subsequent intelligence received during the war indicated that the American
POWs held by the VC in some of these camps, but not all, were later moved to
North Vietnam.

# CHAPTER 3

# AMERICAN POWs CAPTURED
# BY THE PATHET LAO

. . .

Intelligence collected during the war indicates that Pathet Lao policy relating to the capture, treatment, and disposition of U.S. POWs was virtually identical to that employed by the PAVN and the Vietcong.

Like the Vietnamese, Pathet Lao soldiers were under strict orders to capture Americans alive and treat them well. According to one intelligence source, these orders were personally signed by Prince Souphanouvong, the Pathet Lao leader, and distributed to PL units throughout the country.[1]

As was also the case with the PAVN and VC, approved procedures for capturing American pilots and servicemen were "required reading" for all PL officials and soldiers.[2] PL troops were reminded of these procedures prior to entering combat and were threatened with punishment if they disobeyed.[3] One intelligence source reported that because "the higher cadre had given the order that the prisoners be kept alive . . . the lower ranking personnel did not dare try and ignore this order."[4] Another source told how one group of PL physically carried an American pilot for more than ten miles to deliver him alive to PAVN forces after he refused their order to walk.[5]

Wartime intelligence collected in Laos indicates that American prisoners were generally well treated by the PL after capture. A 1971 CIA review of this intelligence led agency officials in Vientiane to declare that "American POWs are reported to be well treated—they have been given medical attention, their rations apparently are on par with those of a PL officer, and there have been no reports of torture or inhumane treatment." These intelligence officials also concluded that in regard to the critical matter of the final disposition of Americans captured in Laos, they "fall into two categories—those who are captured in the Lao panhandle and those who are captured in northern Laos. It appears that those who are captured in the panhandle are escorted through the infiltration system directly to North Vietnam while those who are captured in northern Laos are escorted to prisons in Houa Phan/Sam Neua Province where they are detained on a semi-permanent basis or transferred to North Vietnam."[6]

## THE PRISONERS IN SAM NEUA

The fact that the PL held American POWs in cave prisons in and around their mountain redoubt in Sam Neua Province, some two hundred miles northeast of the Lao capital of Vientiane, was a matter of little dispute among U.S. intelligence officials during the war. Intelligence sources told of American pilots being held in the area from the spring of 1965 until the spring of 1972. The accounts were highly specific in nature, beginning with the eyewitness account from a PL defector describing the imprisonment of U.S. Air Force pilots David L. Hrdlicka and Charles Shelton in 1965 and ending with a highly detailed eyewitness account of eight American pilots being held in a cave prison in 1972—a report so specific that the source, a PL telephone repairman, was even able to give U.S. interrogators the telephone number at the prison where he said the Americans were being held.[7]

Sandwiched between the 1965 and 1972 accounts were a number of similar reports telling of Americans held in the Sam Neua caves.[8] These and other intelligence reports led the CIA in February 1969 to publish a classified list of more than a half dozen *confirmed* PL prisons in Sam Neua that held or had held American POWs.[9]

Several wartime intelligence reports from Sam Neua suggested that American POWs held there were periodically transferred to North Vietnam. A CIA source reported that one of these transfers occurred in late 1968:

> . . . In late December 1968, 27 Americans held prisoner by the Pathet Lao /PL/, and three other prisoners believed to be either Thai or Lao, were assembled in Ban Hang Long /VH 132629/ in Houa Phan [Sam Neua] Province before being sent to North Vietnam. The 27 Americans represented all Americans the PL held captive in Laos. The reason given for sending them to North Vietnam was that they were to be used in prisoner exchanges between the North Vietnamese and the South Vietnamese governments.
>
> . . . Before the American prisoners were released to North Vietnamese Army /NVA/ personnel, an agreement was reached between the North Vietnamese government and the Neo Lao Hak Sat [PL] Central Committee whereby all Americans captured in Laos would be sent to North Vietnam where they would be used in prisoner exchanges with the South Vietnamese government. For several weeks before the American prisoners were turned over to the North Vietnamese, teams of NVA and PL propagandists circulated throughout northeast Laos explaining the importance of releasing all American prisoners to the NVA to assist the North Vietnamese government in its negotiations with the South Vietnamese and American governments.[10]

Following the apparent emptying of the Sam Neua prisons in late 1968, additional human intelligence from the area told of other American pilots—perhaps new shootdowns or pilots moved from other locations—being held there in 1969.[11] The presence of Americans was confirmed on October 11, 1969, when a manned U.S. reconnaissance aircraft photographed twenty or more American prisoners and an undetermined number of their guards at the Ban Nakay Teu Cave Prison complex in Sam Neua. Several of the American POWs were seen in the photography standing around the entrances to the cave prison itself, which was located at the base of a sheer karst formation, while others were seen along with guards on the camp volleyball court located just northeast of the cave. An enlargement of the portion of the photograph of the American

POWs on the volleyball court showed one blond-haired American POW relieving himself at courtside at the moment the reconnaissance aircraft roared by.[12]

Later, a CIA source, unaware of the existence of the then-highly classified reconnaissance photographs of the Americans at Ban Nakay Teu, reported that
twenty American pilots were being held in the Ban Nakay area during the time
period the reconnaissance photographs were taken.[13] Intelligence officials believed that the twenty American pilots cited in the CIA report were almost certainly the same Americans photographed near the cave entrance and on the
volleyball court on October 11, 1969.

The continued presence of Americans in Sam Neua late in the war was indicated by additional human intelligence from the area and by the public statement of a high PL official who declared in April 1972 that his government was
holding many American POWs in the caves of northern Laos.[14]

None of the American POWs released at Operation Homecoming in 1973 reported they had been detained in the Ban Nakay Teu Cave Prison complex or in
any of the other half dozen *confirmed* PL prisons in Sam Neua Province that held
American POWs.[15]

CHAPTER 4

# AMERICAN POWs IN NORTH VIETNAM

. . .

The air war over North Vietnam was in reality two separate wars, one fought
during the Johnson administration and the other during the administration of
Richard Nixon. The sustained bombing of the North under President Johnson
began in early March 1965, some seven months after the Gulf of Tonkin incident and lasted until March 31, 1968. This three-year effort, punctuated by periodic halts in the attacks designed to induce North Vietnamese concessions,
went by the code name Operation Rolling Thunder. The North Vietnamese call
the Rolling Thunder campaign either "the U.S. War of Destruction" or "the First
U.S. War of Destruction."

Richard Nixon won the 1968 election but did not resume the bombing of the
North until the spring of 1972 when Hanoi's forces invaded South Vietnam. The
bombing was intensified in December of 1972 when the Paris peace talks broke
down and Nixon ordered B-52s sent against targets in the Hanoi-Haiphong area.
All bombing of the North ended with the cessation of the B-52 raids in late De-
cember. The first bombing campaign of 1972 was officially code-named Opera-
tion Linebacker. The second campaign in December was code-named Operation
Linebacker II but became better known as the "Christmas bombing." The North
Vietnamese refer to the Linebacker raids of 1972 collectively as "the Second U.S.
War of Destruction."

Wartime intelligence reports indicated that hundreds of American pilots and aircrewmen were captured alive after being shot down over North Vietnam during the course of the war. The intelligence indicated that when battlefield conditions permitted, these prisoners were taken immediately to Hanoi, "where," as one intelligence source said, "all U.S. pilots had to go."[1] Intelligence sources reported that pilots and aircrewmen captured in the North were moved to Hanoi by jeep, car, truck, fixed-wing aircraft, and helicopter.[2]

A number of intelligence sources reported that wartime conditions sometimes precluded the immediate transfer of prisoners to Hanoi. These sources reported that when this occurred, the Vietnamese housed the Americans in transit camps or regional prisons near their point of shootdown until they could be moved safely to the Vietnamese capital.[3] These camps and prisons included the Cam Thuy (Cam Chu) prison in Thanh Hoa Province,[4] the Tran Phu prison in downtown Haiphong,[5] and the Bac Giang prison northeast of Bac Giang City.[6] The intelligence suggested that prisoners were collected at these facilities for varying periods of time before being taken to Hanoi in groups.

## THE IMPRISONMENT AND EXPLOITATION OF AMERICAN POWs IN NORTH VIETNAM

The U.S. intelligence community amassed volumes of intelligence during the course of the war relative to the imprisonment and exploitation of American POWs in North Vietnam. This intelligence related not just to the pilots and aircrewmen captured in the North but also to the Americans captured in South Vietnam, Cambodia, and Laos who had been moved to North Vietnam for long-term confinement.

A great deal of the human intelligence about Americans held in the North was acquired in South Vietnam from captured or surrendered PAVN soldiers who had seen the Americans prior to leaving the North to begin infiltration (see Chapter 1). Other human intelligence sources included clandestine CIA sources (spies), foreign diplomats and military personnel, friendly foreign intelligence services, businessmen and others who visited North Vietnam, members of the foreign press, foreign news accounts, information provided wittingly and unwittingly by the North Vietnamese themselves in their broadcasts, publications, and propaganda activities, American prisoners who were periodically granted early release by the North Vietnamese, and other sources.

Tactical reconnaissance photography was acquired by both drone and manned aircraft and used to assist U.S. personnel in their analysis of the information provided by the human sources.

## THE AMERICANS AT HANOI'S HOA LO PRISON AND AT THE HOA LO CENTER

A number of intelligence sources reported during the war that they had learned U.S. POWs were being held in an old French prison on Hoa Lo Street in downtown Hanoi. One source reported in 1966 that the prison was located "directly across the street from the Cuban embassy."[7] Another reported the prison was "down the street from the embassy of the United Arab Republic."[8] Yet another described the prison in 1967 as being "west of the Hanoi People's Court" and provided a map sketch of the area.[9] Prewar and wartime maps of Hanoi and wartime reconnaissance photography[10] showed the prison to be exactly where the sources described. (See map page 31, point 1.) Other sources reported they had personally observed American prisoners in and around Hoa Lo prison. In 1968, a classified CIA source reported he had observed an American prisoner sweeping the sidewalk under guard at the entrance to the prison.[11] Another source, a PAVN soldier, reported that he had gone to Hoa Lo in 1970 to visit his cousin who was being held there, and while he was inside the prison he personally observed several American prisoners. His cousin told him they were pilots and that there were seventy to eighty of them in the prison at the time.[12] Still another Vietnamese source reported that he had been held prisoner in Hoa Lo during that same period and that in spite of the fact that Vietnamese prisoners were strictly isolated from the Americans, he had been able to count approximately one hundred U.S. prisoners in the American section during one meal period.[13] One source reported that he had been told that U.S. pilots were being held at Hoa Lo and that if they resisted their interrogators' efforts, they were beaten.[14] Another reported that "nearly everyone in Hanoi knew it [Hoa Lo] was a detention center for American POWs."[15]

Based on the early intelligence and testimony received from a handful of POWs who had been granted early release, U.S. officials assigned Hoa Lo DIA reference number N-43, meaning "North Vietnamese prison number 43." Officials would employ a similar numbering procedure at other facilities in the North as intelligence about American POWs became available.

In addition to the reporting on the old French prison on Hoa Lo Street, U.S. officials learned from a CIA source of "extreme sensitivity" about another detention facility for U.S. POWs located in Hanoi that also went by the name "Hoa Lo," this the Hoa Lo Detention/Interrogation Center, located some four blocks south of Hoa Lo prison N-43. The CIA source reported that this facility, which he referred to as the "Hoa Lo Center," was housed in an old French Security Service compound on the south side of Nguyen Thuong Hien Street at map coordinates WJ 88132408. (See map page 31, point 2.) The source's sketch of the area matched published maps in every detail.

The source reported that the Hoa Lo Center had been used as a prison for North Vietnamese civil prisoners after the French withdrew but had been converted to its present use in late 1963 or 1964. He said the center handled only American officer pilots or aircrew members shot down over North Vietnam. He reported that some of the prisoners who had been shot down in the provinces around Hanoi had been brought directly from their point of capture to the center. He said the center did not handle captives brought from South Vietnam.

The source reported that he visited the facility on three occasions. He said that during one visit in October 1969, he observed approximately fifty American prisoners being held there. Most were thin, pale, weak, and dejected.

CIA officials in the field were quick to point out that "the Hoa Lo Center should not be confused with the Hoa Lo Prison located at WJ 883248." Distribution of their report on the Center, which they labeled "particularly sensitive,"

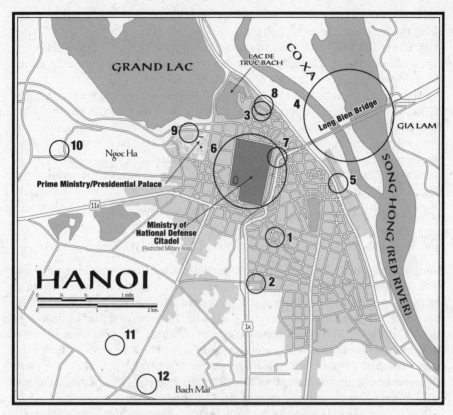

Selected locations where U.S. POWs were reported detained during the War, Hanoi, DRV. (HENDON/ANDERER)

was restricted to a very limited number of very high U.S. government officials.[16] Perhaps for that reason, the facility was not assigned an official DIA name and "N" number.

## THE HUMAN SHIELDS

In the summer of 1966, at about the same time the early intelligence on Hoa Lo N-43 was being received, U.S. officials received the first in what would become a steady stream of wartime intelligence reports telling of U.S. POWs being used by the Vietnamese as human shields to protect critical military and civilian targets in the North from attack by American bombers. Among the first reports indicating the Vietnamese used American POWs for this purpose was one from Cuba in July 1966, just weeks after Ho Chi Minh had threatened to put American POWs on trial for war crimes. The CIA reported that month from Havana that a high Vietcong official visiting Cuba had stated that rather than be placed before firing squads, American fliers would be "moved to a concentration camp in the vicinity of U.S. bombing targets in North Vietnam."[17] Another CIA source reported sometime later that the Vietnamese had, in fact, established POW camps in 1966 "near NVA military bases in the hopes that the Americans will not bomb the bases for fear of hitting their own people."[18]

By the fall of 1967, as one source later said, it had become "common knowledge in Hanoi that . . . U.S. POWs had been placed in strategic areas, presumably to discourage U.S. bombing of important installations."[19]

Intelligence reports telling of American POWs being deployed as human shields at specific targets soon began pouring in, and they continued unabated until late 1972. Highly specific as to location and rich in detail, these reports told of Americans being deployed or imprisoned at key government buildings and ministries, airfields, bridges, manufacturing and munitions plants, communications facilities, waterworks, and electric power plants throughout the North—all for the obvious or stated purpose of thwarting U.S. bombing attacks on those facilities.

## Human Shields at the Hanoi Electric Power Plant • DOD Target JCS-81[20]

A number of sources told U.S. officials during the war that American prisoners were being used as human shields to prevent U.S. attacks on Hanoi's thermal electric power plant. The power plant, Vietnam's largest at the time, was located in a residential area just east of Truc Bach Lake in northwest Hanoi. (See map page 31, point 3.) The Vietnamese called the plant the Yen Phu Electric Power Plant for a nearby hamlet; U.S. intelligence officials referred to the facility as the Hanoi Thermal Power Plant, JCS-81 or simply Hanoi TPP, JCS-81.[21] The plant was periodically photographed for targeting purposes and thus its location was well-known to pilots and members of the U.S. intelligence community.[22]

A PAVN soldier told U.S. interrogators that he observed first five and then six Americans when he walked past the facility on two occasions during mid-April 1966. He was told by a friend's father who worked at the plant that twenty U.S. POWs were housed within the complex and that they were kept there to prevent an attack by U.S. aircraft.[23]

The CIA reported that sightings of American POWs inside the power plant complex occurred during December 1966 and February 1967.[24]

Another PAVN soldier reported that twenty American prisoners were detained during 1967 in numbered "houses" on the power plant grounds along Pham Hong Thai Street. He said a second group of twenty Americans were being detained across the street in a former Chinese school adjacent to the power plant director's office. Prisoners from both locations, the source said, were assigned to work details inside the power plant complex. The soldier provided a sketch of the facility and surrounding structures, which exactly matched photography of the facility.[25]

A PAVN soldier who had worked as a truck driver's assistant in Hanoi told U.S. interrogators that he saw approximately twenty American POWs being held at the power plant during June, July, and August 1967. He said he observed the POWs during his weekly food deliveries to the facility. He estimated there were twenty Americans being held at the plant, all Caucasians and all dressed in white pajama-type clothing with blue stripes. The soldier said he heard that the

POWs were put in a bunker during air strikes. He provided a sketch of the power plant and the surrounding structures.[26]

Another PAVN soldier reported that he saw eight U.S. POWs on the grounds of the power plant on July 20, 1967. He said the prisoners were performing various chores such as carrying charcoal and preparing a fence for repainting. He said he was told that approximately thirty to forty U.S. POWs were being permanently detained in the power plant. He said the North Vietnamese government detained the POWs in this location to save the plant from destruction by bombs. "If the U.S. pilots bombed the plant," he explained, "they would be killing thirty to forty of their fellow countrymen."[27]

Another PAVN soldier reported seeing fifty to sixty American POWs at the Hanoi power plant during July 1967. He said the men were held there to deter American air attacks. He further said that the Americans, some of whom he saw painting the interior of a building in the complex, appeared undernourished.[28]

A PAVN soldier reported seeing two different groups of U.S. POWs in October 1967 in the area of the Hanoi electric power plant. He said the the prisoners, who were wearing light and dark blue striped pajamas and black rubber sandals, were pushing, pulling, or walking alongside carts loaded with bricks.[29]

Yet another PAVN soldier reported that he, too, observed American POWs being held in the vicinity of the power plant during October 1967. He told U.S. interrogators that he observed between thirty and forty American prisoners at the old Chinese school on Yen Phu Street. The soldier said that when he saw the Americans, some were engaged in a volleyball game, some were playing basketball, and others were sitting around by themselves or in groups talking or singing to the accompaniment of a guitar. He said the POWs were all dressed in black pajamas and rubber sandals but some of the men playing ball had removed their shirts. He also mentioned that the men playing ball were shouting to one another and in general appeared to be happy. The soldier provided a sketch of the Chinese school complex.[30]

A classified intelligence source told U.S. interrogators that he visited the Hanoi power station in January 1968 and saw U.S. prisoners at forced labor in the immediate vicinity of the station. He said he also saw placards written in Vietnamese indicating that U.S. pilots were in the power station.[31]

Another classified CIA source reported that he visited the Yen Phu power plant in early July 1968 and saw six U.S. POWs in the office building of the plant. He said the prisoners were handcuffed and were seated on two benches in a corridor. All were Caucasian and appeared to be from thirty to forty years of age. They wore black pajamas and rubber sandals. The source said he asked why the POWs were being held at the plant and was told they were held there to keep the plant from being bombed. He was told that Hanoi was "filled with spies" and that the North Vietnamese government thought these spies would report that the prisoners were being detained at the plant and that on the basis of that information the plant would be spared from a bombing attack.[32] During this same time period, a third classified CIA source reported the presence of two U.S. POWs at the Chinese school across the street.[33]

Based on the intelligence indicating that American POWs were being detained at the Hanoi thermal power plant, U.S. officials designated the facility TPP N-59, meaning Thermal Power Plant, North Vietnamese prison #59.

## Human Shields at the Long Bien Bridge in Hanoi • DOD Target JCS-12

A number of intelligence sources told U.S. officials that American POWs were being used as shields at another important target located just down the Red River from the Yen Phu power plant in Hanoi. This target was the 5,532-foot-long steel and concrete rail/highway bridge spanning the river between Hanoi and Gia Lam. (See map page 31, point 4.) The bridge, which the Vietnamese called the Long Bien Bridge for the tiny hamlet at its western terminus, funneled all rail traffic from China and the port of Haiphong into Hanoi and on to points south. It was considered among the most important military targets in North Vietnam.

The Americans called the imposing bridge by the name the French had given it, the Paul Doumer Bridge, for the colonial governor-general who had overseen its construction at the turn of the century. Targeting officials in the Pentagon referred to it as the Red River Highway and Railroad Bridge (JCS-12).

The CIA received word at the end of July 1967 that as of mid-July 1967 "approximately 100 American prisoners were engaged every day in painting the Red River Bridge in Hanoi."[34] Responding to the report, CIA officials consulted their sources familiar with the area and analyzed photographs of the bridge. They discovered what they believed could be a detention facility for the described Americans. The facility, a former French jail, was located on Co Xa Island in the middle of the river at a point almost directly under where the bridge crossed the island. A human intelligence source reported the presence of a guard inside the facility during July, thus indicating that the jail was an active facility.[35] File photographs of the bridge showed the jail in detail, complete with flagpole and a sign over the front door.[36]

Knowing that the Pentagon was planning to bomb the bridge for the first time in the near future, CIA Director Richard Helms sent the information on the jail and the pictures to Secretary of Defense Robert McNamara on August 10, 1967. Helms told McNamara, "Since the joint chiefs have recently added this bridge, Hanoi Highway/RR Bridge (Paul Doumer Bridge) to the Rolling Thunder strike target list, you might wish to instruct them that any strikes on this bridge should avoid this island which may house American prisoners."[37]

At midmorning the next day in Southeast Asia—just hours after the dispatch of the Helms memorandum in Washington and almost certainly before McNamara received and read it—U.S. officials launched their long-planned, first-of-the-war attack on the bridge. The attack, undertaken on the afternoon of August 11 (local time) by USAF pilots flying strike aircraft from bases in Thailand, resulted in the destruction of one of the overwater bridge spans located east of the island and the partial destruction of one of the spans crossing the island.[38]

The Vietnamese immediately began repairing the damaged spans and were able to reopen the bridge by early October. The United States responded by attacking the bridge in force on October 25, this time knocking down the second span away from the island on the Gia Lam side. "I estimate," a CIA analyst wrote, "that the span knocked out is not more than 125 yards from the building on the island tentatively identified as a prison camp."[39]

The Vietnamese repaired the October damage and reopened the bridge within a month. The Americans then delivered a staggering one-two punch by attacking the bridge on December 14 and 18 with a combined total of almost one hundred 3,000-pound bombs. Poststrike photography showed five consecutive spans in the water and bomb craters bracketing the island jail.[40] As a result of the December raids, the Defense Intelligence Agency (DIA) distributed an advisory declaring that the jail on Co Xa Island was now "incapable of functioning as a detention facility" and was therefore "inactivated" as a potential site for the detention of American POWs.[41]

It has never been determined if any Americans were detained in the jail on Co Xa Island before, during, or after the 1967 raids.

The possibility of the presence of American POWs in the Co Xa jail notwithstanding, a number of other sources reported during the war that the Vietnamese deployed large numbers of Americans on, under, and around the bridge after the late 1967 bombing attacks.

A classified CIA source reported that about one hundred American POWs were taken to the bridge daily from Hoa Lo Prison during March 1968 to do repair work on the damaged structure. The source stated that a large American flag was to be raised at the onset of any U.S. fighter bomber attack in order to deter bombing of the bridge. When CIA officials asked the U.S. Joint Prisoner Recovery Center (JPRC) to comment on this report, JPRC personnel replied that it "reinforces other reports of U.S. personnel being used by the North Vietnamese both to repair and protect key rail and highway bridges and electrical power stations." According to CIA officials, a similar request for comment from the U.S. Seventh Air Force brought this reply: "There is one report that in 1967 the North Vietnamese put U.S. POWs to work scraping rust off the Long Bien Bridge, reportedly giving them radios with which to contact and warn off any U.S. planes. A sign indicating the U.S. POWs were working on the bridge was reportedly also there. There were no indications, however, that a U.S. flag was ever used."[42]

Another source, a PAVN soldier, also reported American prisoners at the bridge during March 1968. The soldier told U.S. interrogators that he personally observed forty U.S. prisoners who were helping the Vietnamese repair bomb damage on the Gia Lam end of the bridge. He reported that four middle spans of the bridge had collapsed due to U.S. bombing and were being repaired by a North Vietnamese engineering unit. He said he saw the North Vietnamese unit working at disassembling the collapsed spans while the U.S. prisoners transported gravel for use on the bridge foundations. The soldier said about ten PAVN soldiers were transporting gravel along with the Americans, and it seemed to him as though these soldiers guarded the prisoners at the same time they themselves worked. He said the Americans were bearded and thin and wore light yellow uniforms.[43]

Yet another PAVN soldier reported that he and five friends observed approximately one hundred U.S. POWs who were "nonchalantly gathered" on the bridge on an unrecalled day during May or June 1968. He said the prisoners were engaged in no noticeable work, were not bound in any way, and appeared simply to be passing the time in idle conversation while occasionally tossing stones into the river below. The soldier said that all the Americans seemed healthy and well fed. He added that morale appeared to be good, as many of the men were laughing and talking. The group was guarded by a number of armed public security agents. The soldier reported that all the prisoners wore dark blue pajamas and olive Chinese Communist canvas shoes. He said each prisoner had a triangular-shaped name tag pinned to the left breast pocket of his pajama shirt. The tag contained the name, rank, and nationality of the prisoner plus additional information the soldier could not recall. He remembered the names of two of the prisoners and provided them and their physical description to U.S. interrogators.[44]

Another PAVN soldier reported that he observed approximately one hundred U.S. POWs working under guard on the Long Bien Bridge in late 1968. He said the POWs were working in two groups of fifty each at opposite ends of the bridge. He told U.S. interrogators that he approached to within five meters of the group working on the Hanoi side and watched them for approximately ten minutes as they went about repairing metalwork. He said the Americans, all of whom were Caucasian, appeared healthy. They were dressed in American fatigues or white pajamas with blue vertical stripes. The soldier reported the group was guarded by approximately fifteen PAVN guards armed with AK-47s. One of the guards said the POWs were American pilots shot down over North Vietnam who had volunteered to help repair the bridge.[45]

A classified CIA source reported that he was crossing the Long Bien Bridge in a train in February 1969 when he saw ten Caucasian Americans scraping paint and rust from the bridge's ninth span. The source said the Americans were dressed in black shorts and shirts and were under the escort of several armed security guards.[46] A different CIA source reported that approximately ten American prisoners were seen sweeping the bridge in September 1969. This source also reported the prisoners were dressed in black shorts and shirts.[47] Yet a third classified CIA source reported seeing about twenty-five U.S. POWs at the Hanoi end of the bridge in February 1970. These prisoners were reportedly dressed in navy blue trousers and blue or white shirts. The source said that all were Caucasian and all appeared healthy and at ease. The source noted that some of the prisoners carried notebooks and made occasional notations. The group was under the escort of ten armed public security personnel.[48]

U.S. investigators received a solid lead in 1972 about the location of the prison where some of the Long Bien Bridge prisoners may have been held. The information came from a classified CIA source who said he picked up the lead while on the bridge in early November 1967. The CIA described the source's account:

In early November 1967 while traveling through Hanoi . . . [source] observed 10 men, some of whom were standing and others sitting on the western end of the Paul Doumer Bridge at [map coordinates] WJ 89132658. Two policemen guarded the men and a third policeman told [source] that the men were U.S. prisoners of war (POW's) repairing the bridge. From [a point at map coordinates] WJ 88982652 [source] observed the POW's for almost 30 minutes and did not see them do any work. He remarked that it appeared more like "taking in fresh air." Another member of his group asked their North Vietnamese guide while at [map coordinates] WJ 88852646, also at the western end of the bridge, where the U.S. POW camp was located. The guide answered by pointing to the southeast.[49]

Given the topography of the city southeast of the bridge and the fact that several sources had reported the presence of Americans in a prison located some five hundred yards southeast of the bridge's western terminus, it appeared that the guide was referring to the prison that one Vietnamese source had called the "Black Ferry Camp," apparently after the ferry located close by.[50] (See map page 31, point 5.) The "Black Ferry" source had told of seeing an unknown number of American POWs in the camp in June 1967, and three other sources had reported seeing forty U.S. POWs at what was believed to be the same camp in 1969.[51] Based on this intelligence, the facility south/southeast of the bridge had been assigned DIA reference number N-89 (North Vietnamese prison #89).[52]

## Human Shields at North Vietnam's Pentagon, the Ministry of Defense Citadel in Hanoi • DOD Target JCS-57

The heavily fortified Ministry of Defense Citadel—North Vietnam's Pentagon—is located three blocks south of the Hanoi thermal power plant and five blocks west of the Long Bien Bridge. (See map page 31, point 6.) The Citadel's 150-year-old walls, over ten feet high and six to eight feet thick in some places, stretch for two miles around the compound, forming a small hidden city within the Vietnamese capital.

During the French colonial period, the compound had served as the French military's northern headquarters. It housed the Air Ministry, infantry and artillery headquarters commands, senior officers' residences, and a number of barracks for colonial infantry and artillery regiments and a contingent of "native riflemen." A military prison occupied the northeast corner of the compound. A half mile to the southwest a soccer field and bleachers occupied the southwest corner. A military hospital and dozens of large barracks and administrative structures filled the southern end of the compound.[53]

In 1945,[54] after turning their backs on their allies, the French, and capturing as many of them as possible, the Japanese had interned over four thousand French and other allied prisoners in the barracks and the hospital inside the compound.[55] The French had reclaimed the facility when they returned to the North after the war but had been forced to turn it over to the Vietminh following the Vietminh victory at Dien Bien Phu in 1954.

After 1954, the Vietnamese had put the Citadel to the same uses as the French. They had headquartered their Ministry of Defense in the northwest corner of the compound and placed the numerous supporting commands in houses and office buildings all along the tree-lined streets that crisscrossed the heavily guarded "hidden city." A number of senior military officers had taken up residence in homes inside the compound, and PAVN troops had occupied the old French barracks. The military hospital at the southern end of the compound continued to function as before, and also as before, the Citadel compound continued to be among the most secure military areas in all of North Vietnam.

U.S. intelligence officials got their first hint that the Vietnamese might be holding American prisoners inside the Citadel from, of all places, a news account that appeared around the time the North Vietnamese were threatening war crimes trials for the American POWs. The account, dispatched from Hanoi by the Agence France-Press in <u>mid-July 1966</u>, read in part: "The people are under the impression that at present the location of the imprisoned American pilots in Hanoi is not fixed in one spot. Sometimes they are held in the central detention camp [Hao Lo, the 'Hanoi Hilton'] and other times they are held in the barracks within the fort. According to the regulations of Hanoi, these captured pilots are not considered as 'prisoners of war,' but 'war criminals.' "[56]

U.S. intelligence officials analyzed the AFP report and declared that "the 'fort' is believed to refer to the Citadelle, now occupied by the Ministry of National Defense."[57] (It has long been suspected, though never proved, that North Vietnamese officials provided the "speculation" about the Citadel to AFP in hopes publication of the information would dissuade the United States from bombing the compound.)

In the spring and summer of 1967, the North Vietnamese undertook a more obvious public effort to protect the Citadel from U.S. attack. They did this by converting a government film studio compound located at 17 Ly Nam De Street—directly across the street from the northern end of the Citadel's east wall—into a prison for American POWs and then inviting selected members of the foreign press into the facility to interview and photograph the Americans held there. (See map page 31, point 7; map page 39, point 1.)

The North Vietnamese began their PR effort by allowing the East German agency DEFA to film portions of a documentary on American POWs at the new camp. When U.S. intelligence officials later analyzed the documentary, titled *Pilots in Pajamas*—plus still pictures taken during the filming at the camp, some of which were published in the October 20, 1967, edition of *Life* magazine—they were able to match the images with human intelligence and closely approximate the prison's location. When reconnaissance photos confirmed the prison compound was indeed the old film studio at 17 Ly Nam De Street, U.S. officials officially designated it Hanoi PW detention installation Citadel, N-62.[58] U.S. officials would later discover that the American prisoners detained there called the prison the "Plantation," after the stately but run-down French villa located just inside the compound's main gate.

Three American prisoners were granted early release from the Plantation in February 1968. One of them, Air Force Capt. Jon D. Black, told U.S. officials that American POWs were not only being held at the Plantation on the east side of Ly Nam De but also across Ly Nam De Street inside the MND Citadel compound.

U.S. officials, mindful of the existence of the old French military prison in the northeast corner of the Citadel compound, surmised that the Americans Black referred to were being held there. When reconnaissance photography confirmed that the prison was an active facility, U.S. officials assigned it the designation Hanoi PW camp, MND, N-67, the letters MND standing for Ministry of

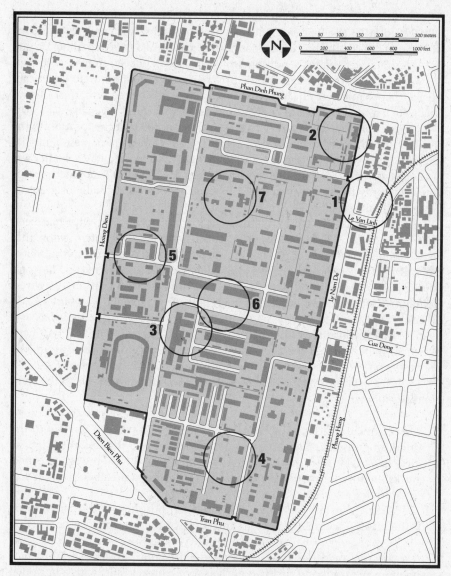

Reported wartime human shield deployments in the vicinity of the Ministry of National Defense Citadel, Hanoi, DRV. (HENDON/ANDERER)

National Defense.[59] U.S. officials would later learn that the Americans held at this camp called the facility "Alcatraz." (See map page 39, point 2.)

U.S. officials quickly discovered that Captain Black was not the only person that February who knew about American POWs being held inside the Citadel compound.

A captured PAVN soldier convalescing during February 1968 at a hospital in South Vietnam told U.S. interrogators that a year earlier—in 1967—he had delivered food to a prison for U.S. POWs located fifty meters northeast of the soccer stadium that occupies the southwest corner of the Citadel compound. (See map page 39, point 3.) The soldier said he had personally observed "many" Americans while he was inside the prison compound and that he had talked to some. He said the Americans were quite friendly and told him they had been studying the Vietnamese language. The soldier said the prisoners, most of whom were Caucasian, were all pilots and were all dressed in green or cream colored uniforms. He said they were fed three meals a day consisting of meat, fish, and vegetables.

U.S. interrogators who interviewed the soldier noted that the location of the described prison had not been kept secret by the North Vietnamese and that several other PAVN soldiers at the hospital where the captured PAVN soldier was interrogated reported that they too had seen the facility. The interrogators noted that only the source who had delivered the food had actually been inside the prison compound.[60]

Later in February, a North Vietnamese medical technician who had been captured in South Vietnam during the Tet offensive told U.S. interrogators that he had seen a large number of American prisoners being detained in the southern end of the Citadel during late 1967. The technician referred to the compound as the "Tran Phu Military Compound," for the street that runs east-west along most of the Citadel's southern boundary. (See map page 39, point 4.)

The technician said that he had gone to the prison on three occasions as a member of a medical team that periodically provided treatment for the Americans held there. He said the team included two doctors, one other intern [the source was an intern at the time], four corpsmen, and the team's driver.

U.S. interrogators described the technician's account of his visits to the compound as follows:

> After being admitted to the camp the group would proceed directly to the American house. . . . The group would divide into two sections at the house, one section taking care of the exterior parts of the body and the other section checks the interior part of the body. Source was not a member of either section, just an observer.
>
> . . . There were approximately 400 American prisoners in the camp. None of the prisoners were seriously ill and most of them seemed to be in good health. . . . The personal appearance of the prisoners was neat. They were all clean shaven and dressed in clean green shirts and trousers. The shirt buttoned up the front and had two pockets, one on each side, with a buttoned down flap. The trousers buttoned up the front and had two pockets; belts were not utilized. Some of the prisoners wore their shirts tucked inside of their trousers and others were left out. The prisoners wore undershirts and undershorts of assorted colors. All prisoners wore a type of tire tread sandals (Ho Chi Minh sandals) and some of them wore socks.
>
> Source was not at the camp when the prisoners were fed but had heard that they were fed three meals a day consisting of rice, fish sauce, vegetables and small portions of meat.[61]

Subsequent interrogations of the source yielded the following additional information:

- Source drew a detailed sketch of the prison compound and the route he and his group followed when going there. He indicated that just as their vehicle pulled up to the prison gate from the west, they passed a soccer field located ten meters south of the road.[62] The sketch very closely matched official maps of the area.
- Source pointed out the location of the camp on a map, indicating it was in the southern part of the Citadel compound at map coordinates WJ 880255. This location is approximately three hundred meters southeast of the soccer field.[63]
- Source said the buildings in the compound, including the "American house" where the prisoners were quartered and the administration building where some were examined, had previously served as barracks.[64]
- Though source personally estimated there were 400 American POWs in the camp, he was told by personnel in the administrative section of the camp that the compound actually housed between 350 and 375 American prisoners.[65]
- Source was able to determine from conversations with the administrative staff and from viewing the prisoners' medical records that most of the prisoners were Air Force officers. Only occasionally, he said, did he see records indicating that a prisoner was a U.S. Naval officer.[66]

The reports from the Citadel continued. In May 1968, a PAVN soldier told U.S. interrogators that he had personally observed approximately thirty U.S. POWs being detained in a troop barracks in a section of the Citadel just north of the soccer field. (See map page 39, point 5.) The soldier said he had seen the Americans in late 1966. He said the senior captain in charge of interrogating the Americans had told him they were pilots captured in North Vietnam who were undergoing interrogation in the compound. The captain had also said the Americans would later be returned to their prison in Hanoi City. The soldier reported that the Vietnamese had taken various measures to ensure that none of the pilots he had seen committed suicide during interrogation.[67]

Sometime prior to 1970, another source also reported the presence of American POWs inside the Citadel compound, which the source called the "Ly Nam De PW camp." This source described the prison camp as being situated "in the heart of a large MND military camp and military cadre housing facility . . . off of Ly Nam De Street." U.S. interrogators wrote that the location the source described was "in actuality, . . . the Ministry of National Defense or the Citadel."[68] (See map page 39, point 6.) Finally, a North Vietnamese defector told CIA interrogators late in 1970 that prior to his defection in September 1969, the North Vietnamese held U.S. POWs "in the Ly Nam De area." When the defector drew a sketch of where the Americans were reportedly being held, U.S. officials immediately recognized it as being inside the northern half of the Citadel compound.[69] (See map page 39, point 7.)

The wartime intelligence, then, showed there was little cause for debate within the U.S. intelligence community as to whether or not American POWs were being detained in and around the Ministry of National Defense Citadel in downtown Hanoi. Agence France-Press had first suggested that American POWs were being held "in the barracks within the fort," and then human intelligence sources and photographic intelligence had reported Americans being held in (1) the old film studio across the street from the Citadel compound (the "Plantation"); (2) the old French prison in the northeast corner of the Citadel compound ("Alcatraz"); (3) an interrogation facility just northeast of the soccer field inside the Citadel compound; (4) barracks southeast of the soccer field inside the Citadel compound; (5) barracks north of the soccer field inside the Citadel compound; (6) "the heart" of the Citadel compound; and (7) the northern half of the Citadel compound. (See map page 39, points 1–7.)

The Ministry of Defense Citadel—the very headquarters of the North Vietnamese war effort—was never bombed.

## Human Shields at Other Military Targets in Hanoi

In addition to those prisoners reportedly used as human shields at Hanoi's thermal power plant, at the Long Bien Bridge, and at the Ministry of Defense Citadel, U.S. POWs were reportedly deployed as shields at at least a half dozen other military targets in Hanoi.

A PAVN soldier told U.S. interrogators that he saw six U.S. POWs in May 1967 working on the grounds of the main Hanoi waterworks, which is located just east of Truc Bach Lake and just north of the Hanoi thermal power plant.[70] (See map page 31, point 8.)

Another PAVN soldier told U.S. interrogators that he observed twenty-five American POWs in a small prison compound located at the northeast corner of the Hanoi Zoological Garden on September 2, 1967. He said he was allowed to view the Americans for a period of approximately thirty minutes. He reported that there were five buildings in the compound and that a guard told him the facility was designated the "4th NVA PW camp."[71] The soldier drew a sketch of the area, which matched published maps in almost every detail, and U.S. reconnaissance photography confirmed the existence of the facility at the exact location the soldier had reported.[72] Studying the photography, U.S. officials saw that the camp was located approximately 100 yards from the Prime Ministry and some 250 yards from the Presidential Palace. (See map page 31, point 9.)

An examination of reconnaissance photography taken of the prison facility during its construction showed that at the same time the Vietnamese were building the prison they were also constructing a large bomb shelter immediately south of the Prime Ministry.[73] It was widely reported at the time that President Ho Chi Minh and Prime Minister Pham Van Dong not only maintained offices in the Prime Ministry and Presidential Palace buildings but also lived in separate small houses on the palace grounds.[74]

A PAVN soldier told U.S. interrogators he observed several U.S. POWs in October 1967 who were being held in a walled facility directly adjacent to the Ngoc Ha waterworks in the western part of the city.[75] (See map page 31, point 10.) U.S. reconnaissance photography confirmed the existence of the walled facility at the exact location the soldier had reported. The facility, which had five guard towers along its perimeter walls, contained a number of barracks-type buildings, administrative buildings, a mess hall, and a parade ground. Weapons positions were apparent both on the roof and immediately in front of one of the large administrative-type buildings. Additional weapons positions and ten anti-aircraft artillery pieces, all believed to be 57mm, were located just outside the prison compound. Based on the intelligence and the reconnaissance photography, U.S. officials designated the Ngoc Ha facility the Hanoi Army Barracks West and Possible PW Camp, N-63.[76]

Another PAVN soldier reported that he observed as many as twenty American POWs working on the grounds of the Trung Qui Mo munitions factory in southwest Hanoi during July 1967. (See map page 31, point 11.) He said the factory was protected by antiaircraft guns mounted on the roofs of buildings in and around the factory grounds, and that he had been told that the prisoners were deployed at the factory to "preclude air strikes by U.S. aircraft."[77]

Finally, a classified CIA source reported that American POWs were being held during April 1971 in an enclosure at a radio communications station located just north of Bach Mai Airfield on the southern outskirts of the city. He drew a sketch of the facility and later traced his journey to the facility on a map that had on it only the Bach Mai Airfield and two major nearby road intersections. CIA officials found that both his sketch and his map track were accurate when compared to reconnaissance photography of the area and declared that the facilities sketched and described by the source "conform closely to those at Hanoi Radio Communications Station, Bach Mai." This station, officials knew, was located just north of the airfield at a point just to the east of the village of Cu Loc.[78] (See map page 31, point 12.)

## Human Shields at Other Military Targets in North Vietnam

Intelligence reports indicate that the North Vietnamese did not restrict their deployment of American prisoners to military targets in the city of Hanoi.

One source reported that he observed American POWs in 1967 who were being used to protect a thermal power facility in Ha Dong, just southwest of Hanoi, from American bombing.[79] (See map page 45, point 1.)

A PAVN soldier reported seeing U.S. POWs on a number of occasions at a prison located ten meters from the Nam Dinh thermal power plant (JCS Target 82.15)[80] in downtown Nam Dinh, a major city located some forty-five miles downriver from Hanoi. (See map page 45, point 2.) The soldier, who said he lived near the prison, told U.S. interrogators that he observed the Americans on a number of different occasions. He said he was told by a friend who worked as a cook at the prison that approximately one hundred American POWs—all pilots—were held there. The soldier reported the prisoners did no work and were allowed to leave the compound in groups of five and walk around the city with an unarmed guard.[81]

A source reported that twice during 1966 he had personally observed U.S. POWs scraping rust off of the Song Thuong Bridge (JCS Target 18.23)[82] in the city of Bac Giang located some thirty miles northeast of Hanoi (See map page 45, point 3.) He said he learned from citizens that the POWs were there to protect the bridge from U.S. bombing.[83]

A PAVN soldier reported that he saw three hundred American prisoners inside a prison in an area inside the sprawling Thai Nguyen steel complex (JCS Target 76)[84] north of Hanoi. (See map page 45, point 4.) The soldier said he saw the Americans in <u>April 1966</u> while he was on a food collection detail at the prison. He described the prison as being located in the Luu Xa area and within the steel mill complex (Luu Xa is a village immediately adjacent to the steel mill complex).[85] He said the prisoners were dressed in two-piece striped uniforms with white, blue, or yellow stripes. He said he was unaware of the rationale behind the color differences. The soldier said that all the prisoners appeared to be in good health. He said he observed no maltreatment of the POWs and noted that no prisoner work details were in progress during his hour-long visit to the facility.[86]

[A classified CIA source later reported that three hundred U.S. POWs were moved out of Thai Nguyen prison and taken in February or March 1968 to a prison near Tuyen Quang City, west of Thai Nguyen.[87] Meanwhile, another source, this one a PAVN soldier, reported that he personally observed approximately two hundred U.S. POWs some ninety days later who were reportedly being taken *to* Thai Nguyen. The soldier said that he saw the Americans arrive at Bo Ha Village east of Thai Nguyen in eight six-wheeled trucks, and when the trucks stopped at a government-run comfort station and the Americans got out, he was able to observe them closely for approximately five minutes. He reported they were dressed in variously colored striped pajamas and appeared to be strong and healthy. He said a large, orderly crowd assembled to watch the POWs, and members of the crowd said the Americans "were being taken to visit the Thai Nguyen steel plant."][88]

Another PAVN soldier reported that he saw a large number of American POWs almost daily during <u>October, November, and December 1968</u> at a prison camp located one kilometer northeast of the Phuc Yen MiG base (JCS Target 6)[89] just north of Hanoi. (See map page 45, point 5.) The soldier said that MiG-17, MiG-21, and MiG-23 aircraft were based at Phuc Yen and that there were fifty or more antiaircraft positions of various caliber around the prison camp and airfield. The soldier's description of the camp location placed it northeast of the MiG revetments leading to the east end of the runway.[90]

The soldier said he was inside the prison camp on two occasions and had the opportunity to see many of the American POWs held there. He also saw a number of South Vietnamese, Korean, and Filipino prisoners who were quartered separately from the Americans. He said the Americans were "non-flyers who had been captured at Khe Sanh and other locations in SVN." He also said a camp guard told him one thousand five hundred American prisoners were held at the camp. [A later analysis of declassified U.S. intelligence holdings, screened for duplicate sightings, indicates that perhaps nine hundred Americans had been reported moved to North Vietnam from the South by late 1968.[91] (See Chapter 2.) The discrepancy between that number and the unreasonably high number of American POWs cited by the guard might be explained by one or more of the following: (1) The guard may have actually said that the total number of allied prisoners held at the facility—American, South Vietnamese, Korean, and Filipino—was one thousand five hundred; (2) the guard could have been mistaken, boasting, or lying; (3) the soldier could have been mistaken, boasting, or lying, or an agent sent by Hanoi to deceive U.S. intelligence officials; (4) both

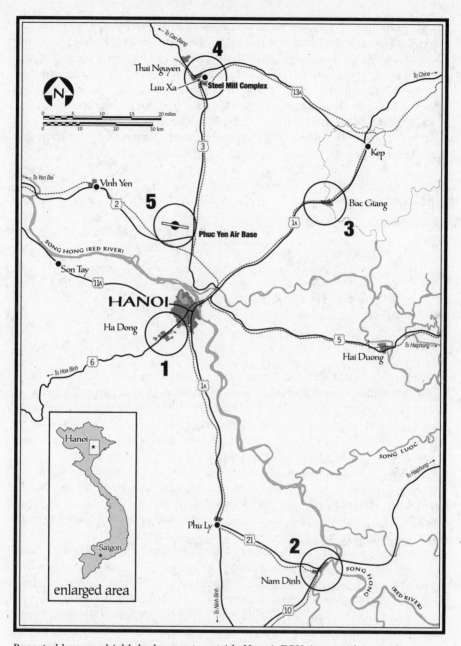

Reported human shield deployments outside Hanoi, DRV. (HENDON/ANDERER)

could have been mistaken, boasting, or lying; (5) the American interviewer could have misunderstood what the soldier told him; or (6) any combination of the above possibilities could have occurred. Whatever the explanation, the unreasonably high number of Americans cited in the report remains unexplained.]

The obviously inaccurate number of American prisoners cited in the report notwithstanding, the soldier went on to say that the ARVN held at Phuc Yen "were used to carry rice" and that the Americans were used to "repair bridges because the North Vietnamese thought that American pilots would see that American PW's were there and would not bomb the bridges."[92] Perhaps. But given that the POWs' reported place of confinement was a mere one thousand meters from the MiG revetments at the east end of the Phuc Yen runway, it seems clear it wasn't just bridges the Americans at Phuc Yen were protecting.

The Phuc Yen MiG base is the present-day Noi Bai International Airport serving Hanoi.

CHAPTER 5

1972

# THE WAR DRAWS TO A CLOSE

. . .

In the spring of 1972, Richard Nixon ordered the first sustained bombing of the North Vietnamese heartland since President Johnson had suspended Rolling Thunder strikes against the North on March 31, 1968. The spring 1972 bombing campaign, code-named Operation Linebacker, was launched on May 8 in response to the massive three-pronged North Vietnamese invasion of the South that had taken place several weeks earlier.

The Linebacker campaign, accompanied by the first ever mining of the key North Vietnamese port of Haiphong, was massive in scope and devastated many areas of the North that had escaped even the furious attacks of Johnson's Rolling Thunder. The North Vietnamese reacted to the bombing with what *The Washington Post* called "new depths of bitterness."[1] By June they had consigned "Nic~xon" to a place above even "Gion~xon," "Mac~Na~ma~ra," and "Oet~mo~len" on their list of most-hated Americans.[2]

Rejecting outright the concept of unintentional but unavoidable "collateral damage," the Vietnamese accused Nixon in press conference after press conference that spring and summer of deliberately targeting churches, schools, hospitals, leprosaria, dikes, sluices, dams, and other civilian structures and demanded at every opportunity and through every possible forum that the bombing be stopped. The North Vietnamese conducted repeated press tours of bomb-damaged civilian areas, decrying the damage and loss of innocent life. They raised the specter of Communist bloc retaliation by bringing Russian sailors before the press to tell how they had been bombed and their fellow sailors killed and wounded while aboard ship in North Vietnamese waters. Later they trotted out an East German boat captain with a similar story. And then a Communist Chinese boat captain. When this had no impact, they invited foreign intellectuals to Hanoi, as they had during the Rolling Thunder raids, to convene war crimes trials in hopes of forcing Nixon to end the bombing.[3]

When these efforts had no apparent impact, the North Vietnamese began parading American POWs before the media to condemn the bombing and to call for its immediate end. The CIA's Foreign Broadcast Information Service (FBIS; pronounced "FIBIS")—the agency organ tasked with reporting developments in the foreign press—reported in late June that media outlets in Hanoi and East Germany had broadcast statements by U.S. POWs who called for an end to the Linebacker raids because of the danger the bombing posed to them and their fellow POWs. "The bombing raids greatly endanger our lives," a captive U.S. pilot had said in an interview broadcast on East German television on June 20.[4] FBIS further reported that media outlets in Hanoi, Havana, East Berlin, and Tokyo broadcast similar appeals by American POWs in late June and early July. In each case, the American prisoner or prisoners said essentially that "the bombing endangers our lives; stop the bombing."[5] Nixon and his advisors remained unmoved, dismissing the comments as either antiwar rhetoric offered by the group of prisoners in Hanoi who were known to oppose the war, or as statements made under duress. The bombing continued.

The North Vietnamese made another attempt to halt the bombing by hosting the famous American movie actress and antiwar activist Jane Fonda for two weeks in mid-July. Accompanied by North Vietnamese representatives and members of the domestic and foreign press, Fonda toured a number of bomb-damaged areas around Hanoi, including the Bach Mai hospital, which had been struck by U.S. bombs in late June while U.S. aircraft were attacking military targets nearby.[6] She also met with and lectured a small group of American POWs at the "Zoo" POW camp at Cu Loc, just west of the Bach Mai Airfield, and made repeated radio appeals to U.S. pilots based throughout Southeast Asia encouraging them not to fly their assigned bombing missions. In a move that proved especially controversial, Fonda held a news conference and posed for pictures while seated in the gunner's seat of an antiaircraft gun in a gun emplacement outside Hanoi.[7] These pictures inflamed passions throughout the U.S. military and may have been the cause of the reported subsequent U.S. air attacks on military sites Fonda had visited during her two week stay in the North.[8]

*Summer–Fall 1972*
## THE NORTH VIETNAMESE DECIDE TO SETTLE • LE DUC THO AND HENRY KISSINGER AGREE ON A PEACE TREATY

The United States and North Vietnam, along with the South Vietnamese and the Vietcong, had held public peace talks off and on since just after the Tet Offensive in 1968. In February 1970, as the public talks ground on with little hope of real progress, Nixon's National Security Advisor Henry Kissinger and a small team of advisors had entered into secret negotiations with the North Vietnamese in Paris. On the American team with Kissinger were his chief deputy Winston Lord, and aides John Negroponte, Peter Rodman, and George Aldrich. (Later Army General Alexander Haig and Assistant Secretary of State William Sullivan would join the team.) Facing them across the table were the DRV's

[Democratic Republic of Vietnam, i.e., North Vietnam] two chief negotiators, Le Duc Tho and Xuan Thuy, Nguyen Co Thach, (pronounced Win Co Tock); Phan Hien (pronounced Fon HEE un), Lu Van Loi, and several other North Vietnamese. The South Vietnamese and Vietcong were not parties to the secret talks.

According to the official North Vietnamese record of the secret Paris negotiations, *Le Duc Tho–Kissinger Negotiations in Paris,* Le Duc Tho and Xuan Thuy concluded in late July 1972 that from the North Vietnamese perspective the best time to settle the war through diplomacy would be in the heat of the upcoming 1972 U.S. presidential campaign. Toward that end, Tho and Thuy set out to "gradually direct . . . [Kissinger] towards our position of settlement" from early August until the Republican party convention in late August and then settle "around October."[9]

The North Vietnamese record states that Tho and Thuy used first the August and then the September negotiating sessions just as they had planned, gradually moving Kissinger closer and closer to a settlement. Then, on October 8, Tho presented Kissinger with North Vietnam's draft peace plan. The North Vietnamese plan called for (1) an immediate in-place cease-fire, the effect of which was to allow the North Vietnamese to keep approximately two hundred thousand PAVN soldiers in the South;[10] (2) the creation of a new Council of National Reconciliation and Concord, designed to promote implementation of the signed agreements, maintain the cease-fire, decide the procedures and modalities for general elections in the South, and organize and conduct these elections; (3) the withdrawal of all U.S. troops from the South; and (4) a massive program of postwar reconstruction of the North to be funded by the United States. In return for all that, the North Vietnamese pledged to cease offensive military operations in the South and return within sixty days all American POWS they and the Vietcong held and render an accounting of Americans listed as missing in action and those who had been killed in action or had died from wounds, disease, etc.

Kissinger, by his own admission, embraced the North Vietnamese offer immediately.[11] Then, according to Kissinger biographers Marvin and Bernard Kalb, following three days of clarifying negotiations, he agreed to the North Vietnamese position on all major points with only minor changes. The Kalbs wrote that at least two of Kissinger's top aides—Alexander Haig and John Negroponte—considered this a major error. "The smartest thing we could have done was fly back to Washington, get a good night's sleep, clear the fog out of our minds, check out the draft carefully, with ourselves and with the South Vietnamese, and then return to Paris for another hard look at the agreement with the North Vietnamese," the Kalbs quoted one official as saying. "But no, Henry would have none of that. He wanted the deal, and he wanted it then." Another official was quoted as saying "The North Vietnamese calculation was that the U.S. was so eager that once they gave us a treaty, we would jump at it. And they were right."[12]

Critiquing Kissinger's decision to settle so quickly, the Kalbs themselves later declared that had "Kissinger . . . been negotiating with the Russians or the Chinese, he no doubt would have been extremely meticulous about every syllable; but with the North Vietnamese, after more than three years of painful negotiations, and with only four weeks remaining before the presidential election, he seemed more concerned about nailing down the deal than about making sure that every detail was correct—an attitude that played right into Le Duc Tho's hands."[13]

Kissinger sealed his acceptance of the North Vietnamese plan in a 2:00 A.M. toast to Le Duc Tho on October 12, 1972, declaring that he and his staff would "come to Hanoi . . . to pay our respects to the heroic people of North Vietnam and to begin a new era in our relationship."[14] In what would become an oft-quoted reflection, he later called his acceptance of the agreement "my most thrilling moment in public service."[15]

Kissinger and members of his team quickly flew back to Washington to brief President Nixon. Then Kissinger, leaving Haig in command in Washington, re-turned to Paris with Negroponte to clear up some loose ends and continued on to Saigon to present the fait accompli to South Vietnamese President Nguyen Van Thieu.[16] Incredibly, Kissinger believed he would have little trouble selling Thieu on the accords, this in spite of the fact that two hundred thousand heav-ily armed PAVN would be allowed by the treaty to remain in the South and that by creating the new Council of National Reconciliation and Concord, "Wash-ington and *Hanoi*" had agreed in principle, as *Newsweek* would report, "on a blueprint for a new South Vietnamese Government."[17] "All of us [on the plane en route to Saigon] except John Negroponte thought that Thieu would be over-joyed by the agreement," Kissinger later wrote.[18] Negroponte, according to Pulitzer Prize–winning author Seymour Hersh, "expected the South Vietnamese President to defend himself 'like a trapped tiger.'"[19]

As it turned out, Negroponte proved the more accurate predictor of Oriental behavior. And no wonder. Two hundred thousand PAVN troops remaining in the South *permanently*? A new South Vietnamese government designed in part by *Hanoi*?

## *Saigon*
## "TO BE OR NOT TO BE"

Though the Americans had striven mightily to keep the South Vietnamese in the dark on what had transpired in Paris, Thieu had already learned of the treaty's provisions by the time Kissinger and his team arrived at Saigon's Tan Son Nhut airport on Wednesday evening, October 18. The South Vietnamese president had received a copy of the agreement only hours before from his armed forces, who had found the copy late in the previous afternoon in a Viet-cong commissar's bunker in Quang Tin Province, south of Da Nang. The events surrounding the embarrassing find were later described by Nguyen Tien Hung and Jerrold L. Schecter in their landmark book *The Palace File:* "The documents were flown from the field by helicopter and light plane to Danang. By midnight they were on President Thieu's desk," Hung and Schecter wrote. Thieu "read them as soon as they arrived—and realized that Communist cadres in an iso-lated province of Central Vietnam knew more about the details of the Paris Talks than he did."[20]

Having carefully read the documents, Thieu realized it was a surrender contain-ing virtually everything Hanoi could have dreamed of—a coalition government in the South, at least ten PAVN divisions supported by armor, heavy artillery and surface-to-air missiles stationed in the countryside, resupply through the DMZ, and, of enormous consequence, no Americans around to keep the Communists at bay with their B-52s and tactical aircraft.

According to Hung and Schecter, Thieu, now knowing Kissinger was coming "with a proposal that made fatal concessions to Hanoi, . . . in anger and sadness," called in his top advisors "to discuss the American betrayal and how to prepare for Kissinger's visit."[21] Kissinger, expecting smooth sailing with Thieu, had planned to spend two days in Saigon and then fulfill his secret pledge to Le Duc Tho to fly directly to Hanoi to initial the final agreement.

On Thursday morning, the 19th, Kissinger and members of his team arrived at the Presidential Palace for their first meeting with Thieu, his National Security Council, and other South Vietnamese officials. Kissinger, himself the principal briefer during this three-and-one-half-hour meeting, explained his position and assured the group that one major portion of the agreement "met every proposal we had put forward" and that another was "far better than the terms we had offered publicly or privately."[22] With the Vietnamese listening courteously, the briefing continued in an "orderly and unabrasive" manner and ended amicably.[23] At a second brief meeting late in the afternoon, Kissinger reportedly told Thieu that the agreement represented "a collapse of the North Vietnamese position" and that Le Duc Tho had cried when making this "concession . . . for the sake of peace." "To make the assertion that the Communists cried set us on our guard," Thieu aide Hoang Duc Nha later said. "Communists don't cry. Either Kissinger was naïve or he thought we were stupid."[24]

At the third round of talks the next morning, Thieu began to press Kissinger for answers. As Kissinger began his reply, Rudyard Kipling's famous warning about hustling the East again rose like a specter over the American delegation. According to Kissinger biographers Marvin and Bernard Kalb, when Thieu asked why he had not been given advance word of the agreement, Kissinger—despite the fact that the North Vietnamese, the Vietcong, the Russians, and the Red Chinese all had copies—claimed the agreement "was too sensitive . . . to be entrusted to the regular diplomatic couriers or to be cabled through normal diplomatic channels." When Thieu told Kissinger that "there is no doubt about" the fact that the Vietnamese-language version of the treaty called for a coalition government with the Vietcong, Kissinger insisted that the matter was only a "misunderstanding" that could easily be cleared up with the North Vietnamese. And when Thieu told Kissinger that the occupation of South Vietnamese territory by North Vietnamese troops was illegal in that it had been achieved at gunpoint and that he therefore refused categorically to yield sovereignty over any portion of South Vietnam, Kissinger answered that the United States had decided two years earlier, in the fall of 1970, to drop its insistence that the North Vietnamese withdraw their forces and that there was no reason to fear the presence of the PAVN in the South because, given that the treaty prohibited further infiltration, those PAVN already in the South would, over time, simply "wither away."[25]

Predictably, things went downhill quickly after Kissinger's remarkable performance on the 20th. At a working group meeting the next day, Nha—acting on behalf of Thieu, who had boycotted the meeting—presented Kissinger with a preliminary list of twenty-six proposed changes to the agreement. When Kissinger indicated the United States would not or could not resolve a number of the important points, an angry Nha told Kissinger, "We have fought this war for fifteen years—to accept this? It would be like surrendering to the Communists. We cannot sign this agreement."[26]

Kissinger met with Thieu twice on Sunday, the 22nd. At the first meeting, held in the morning before a quick side trip Kissinger had planned to Phnom Penh, Thieu told Kissinger, "We don't think this agreement is acceptable to us and we don't think we can sign it in its present form."[27] The South Vietnamese leader went on to explain that he well understood that the problem for America was how to end its involvement in the war, but for him it was a matter of life or death for his country. Kissinger would later write that Thieu made this statement "with some dignity."[28] Thieu would later recall that he had said, "For me, it is a question of life and death! To be or not to be!"[29] Kissinger pressed on, offering his standard rebuttal to each of Thieu's objections. The meeting ended with a pledge from Thieu that he would consult further with his cabinet and advisors during the day and would give Kissinger his final decision on the accords after the White House Advisor returned from Phnom Penh that evening. Strangely, Kissinger left the meeting, in his words, "encouraged" and quickly sent a cable to Washington declaring, "I think we finally made a breakthrough."[30]

Kissinger made the short, 130-mile flight to Phnom Penh just after noon to personally brief Cambodian leader Lon Nol on the proposed accords. Kissinger later wrote that he received Lon Nol's unqualified agreement and returned to Saigon for his meeting with Thieu "excited at the prospect of success."[31]

But again, Kipling intervened. An angry Thieu greeted Kissinger by declaring, "I do not appreciate the fact that your people are going around town telling everybody that I have signed. I have not signed anything. I do not object to peace, but I have not gotten any satisfactory answers from you and I am not going to sign."[32]

Kissinger became enraged and accused Thieu of being "the obstacle to peace." "If you do not sign, we're going to go on our own," Kissinger declared.[33] Kissinger, by his own admission, then attempted to explain away Thieu's objection to the presence of the PAVN troops by declaring that "we have not recognized the right of North Vietnam to be in the South."[34] The debate quickly became personal. Addressing Thieu's interpreter, Kissinger asked, "Why does your President play the role of a martyr? He does not have the stuff of a martyr."[35] Strong words, indeed, in the face-conscious Orient. Thieu struck back with equally strong words, angrily demanding of Kissinger, "Why are you rushing to get the Nobel prize?"[36] Kissinger and Thieu continued to trade insults until U.S. Ambassador Ellsworth Bunker intervened and asked Thieu if his decision not to sign was final. "Yes, that is my final position," Thieu responded. "I will not sign and I would like you to convey my position to Mr. Nixon. Please go back to Washington and tell President Nixon I need answers."[37]

Kissinger cabled Nixon after the disastrous meeting that Thieu's demands "verge on insanity."[38] The following morning Kissinger paid one last, brief call on Thieu. The South Vietnamese president gave the White House envoy a letter for Nixon stating that he, Thieu, wanted to sign a peace treaty but only under the right terms and at the right time. The two leaders shook hands and Kissinger and his party left for Tan Son Nhut.[39] Kissinger and his team then departed not for Hanoi, as they had originally planned, but for Washington to lick their wounds and regroup.

Thieu addressed the nation by radio and television the day after Kissinger departed and declared that the South Vietnamese government would not sign the Paris accords unless all North Vietnamese troops were withdrawn from the South. "If they [the North Vietnamese] want U.S. troops to withdraw," Thieu said, "they must also withdraw their troops back to the North." Thieu told his people that the peace agreement was a product of the North Vietnamese and warned that "the communists could only hope to win if our ally betrays us and sells us out." Addressing the possibility that Kissinger and Nixon might do just that, Thieu warned that "in any peace solution the final decision should be ours. Nobody can sign a cease-fire agreement or a peace settlement without the signature of the Government of the Republic of Vietnam."[40]

Hung and Schecter would later quote Thieu as saying Kissinger "had come not as a comrade in arms, but to advocate the North Vietnamese cause"; that he "gave me the impression that he was a representative of Hanoi, not America"; that he "was not on my side but on the side of Le Duc Tho and advocated his position."[41]

## *Washington, DC*
## "WE BELIEVE THAT PEACE IS AT HAND"

Kissinger arrived back in Washington on Monday, October 23, knowing he would soon have to return to Paris and try to get Tho and the North Vietnamese to go along with at least some of the changes proposed by Saigon.

Three days after his return to Washington—and after the North Vietnamese had released the terms of the draft agreement to the press in Hanoi—Kissinger held a press conference in Washington to explain the proposed treaty to the American public. Declaring, "We believe that peace is at hand," Kissinger told the assembled White House press corps that the final agreement would be signed after one last negotiating session with the North Vietnamese, which he predicted would last "no more than three or four days." He went on to suggest that all remaining questions could be resolved (in talks scheduled to begin on November 20) "within a matter of weeks or less."[42]

Nixon won reelection on November 7 in a landslide. Kissinger, believing that the election results would force Thieu into submission, immediately dispatched Haig to Saigon with a demand that Thieu and the South Vietnamese now *support the treaty without change*. Haig presented Thieu with a letter from Nixon—which had been written, as was customary, by Kissinger—that forecast "grave consequences" for Thieu and the people of South Vietnam if he continued to oppose the accords.[43]

Rather than submit to the Nixon/Kissinger demand, Thieu and his National Security Council forcefully renewed their earlier demand that all North Vietnamese troops be withdrawn from the South, even spelling out how the withdrawal should take place and what weapons the North Vietnamese should take with them.[44] Haig returned to Washington empty-handed and by now increasingly concerned that the vaunted agreement might actually be, as many in the media were suggesting, a total sellout of the South. [Keyes Beech, the famed *Chicago Daily News* correspondent in South Vietnam, later said of the period, "When the terms of the Paris Agreement were made public, even the antiwar correspondents, the young ones, said, 'Well, this is a sellout.' And of course it was."][45]

Thieu and his advisors ratcheted up the pressure on November 18 by presenting Bunker with a list of sixty-nine modifications to the agreement and publicizing the list.[46] In the face of this latest development, Nixon, now clearly concerned about charges he was betraying the South, changed course and informed Thieu by letter that, though he held out little hope that the North Vietnamese would agree to withdraw their troops from the South, he had personally instructed Kissinger to seek "to the maximum extent possible" to incorporate Thieu's proposed changes in the agreement.[47]

Kissinger departed for Paris on the 19th under the most difficult circumstances imaginable. First had come Thieu's public demand for the sixty-nine changes. Next, shortly before Kissinger's departure, the Soviet Union's ambassador to the United States, Anatoly Dobrynin, had warned him the North Vietnamese were angry.[48] Then, on the very day of his departure, *The Washington Sunday Star* had published a front-page article in which Kissinger openly bragged about his negotiating prowess and appeared to claim credit for many of Nixon's major foreign policy successes.[49] The article, which shocked and titillated official Washington and the entire international diplomatic community, had embarrassed Kissinger and placed him on the defensive with his boss, his peers and, most important, his image-conscious interlocutors the North Vietnamese. To make matters worse, only hours before his first meeting with Le Duc Tho was to have begun in Paris on the morning of the 20th, the South Vietnamese Senate handed him a stinging public rebuke by voting overwhelmingly to reject the draft treaty until such time as all North Vietnamese troops were withdrawn from the South.[50]

Kissinger, then, in spite of Nixon's landslide victory at the polls only two weeks before, entered the critical negotiations in Paris from a position of profound weakness. Tho, the hardened revolutionary and master reader of men and political landscapes, was ready.

*November 20–25, 1972*
## THE PARIS NEGOTIATIONS

Kissinger attempted to finesse his troubles by leading off the first round of talks with gifts for Le Duc Tho and Xuan Thuy and a renewal of his earlier invitation to Tho that he come teach at Harvard. Kissinger then presented what he himself later called a "stirring speech."[51] The speech contained a series of lighthearted attempts at self-effacing humor, with Kissinger taking note at one point of the unflattering article in the *Sunday Star* and remarking at another time that he had contributed to the unity of the two zones of Vietnam because "both North and South Vietnam hate me now."[52]

Tho, cold, aloof, and unmoved, responded by assailing Kissinger in a prepared five-page speech. Dashing any hope Kissinger might have had for an early
settlement, Tho told Kissinger, "You swallowed your words," and then warned
ominously that "if modifications [to the October 8 text] are . . . requested, continued war is unavoidable."[53] Kissinger, under direct orders from Nixon, pressed
on and presented Thieu's sixty-nine proposed changes. Tho replied by telling
Kissinger, "If these are your last, unchangeable proposals, settlement is impossible." Kissinger declared that these were his last proposals but that they did not
constitute an "ultimatum." With that, the two sides agreed to recess until the
following morning.[54]

Tho moved quickly on the second day of talks to take maximum advantage of
the weakened Kissinger. He began by "most energetically" rejecting Kissinger's
proposal that PAVN forces be withdrawn from the South and declaring "unacceptable"[55] the proposed changes to the Council of National Reconciliation—the
entity that by now not only the South Vietnamese but also the Associated Press,
United Press International, *Newsweek,* Pham Van Dong, and almost everyone
else had publicly labeled a "coalition government." Tho then stunned Kissinger
by making new and significant demands of his own. Telling Kissinger that because the United States had not signed the October 8 agreement at the agreed
time and that therefore "we cannot accept any longer what happened in October," Tho demanded additions to the draft text that would guarantee the release
of all political prisoners held by the Thieu regime (some thirty-eight thousand
Vietcong) and the withdrawal not just of all American troops from the South
but all U.S. civilians doing army-related work there as well.[56] Kissinger would
later write that he considered Tho's new demands "more worrying" even than
his rejection of Thieu's sixty-nine demands. It was, Kissinger wrote, "the stuff of
which deadlocks are made."[57]

Following an unproductive session on November 22, Kissinger opened talks
on the 23rd by dropping what he called "Saigon's less important nitpicks" and
concentrating primarily on the matters of the coalition government, the presence of the two hundred thousand PAVN troops in the South, and the sanctity
of the DMZ.[58] Kissinger attempted to extract concessions from the North Vietnamese on all three of these issues, but Tho steadfastly refused, telling Kissinger,
"We have made our utmost effort." When Kissinger pressed Tho further on
points relating to the proposed coalition government, the official North Vietnamese record states the meeting grew "very tense."

> Le Duc Tho pounded on the table:
> —. . . We'll make no concessions on these points!
> Kissinger said:
> —I'll have to ask the President to give his views!
> Le Duc Tho told him:
> —It's up to you. If there is a settlement, peace will be restored. If there is no
> settlement, the war will continue.

With that, the North Vietnamese record states, "the discussions ended in a
heavy atmosphere."[59]

Having gotten nowhere using gifts, flattery, humor, guile, reason, anger, veiled threat, or any of his other negotiating tactics, Kissinger resorted to actual threat when the talks resumed the next morning, the 24th. The threat came in the form of a message from Nixon, which Kissinger read aloud to Tho as the session began. In the message, Nixon chastised Tho for pounding on the table the day before and informed Kissinger that "unless the other side shows its willingness to take into account our reasonable concerns, I direct you to discontinue the talks and we shall have to resume military activities until the other side is willing to negotiate on honorable terms."[60] Tho was unmoved and declared, "We cannot sign an agreement in which there is a clause to the effect the NVN forces shall be withdrawn from SVN." When Kissinger proposed that the North Vietnamese at least reposition one hundred thousand of their troops to the northern provinces of SVN, Tho refused, adding pointedly that threats like the one just received from Nixon were "futile."[61] When the meeting ended in stalemate, Kissinger cabled Nixon that "there was no possibility that we could come near anything that would satisfy all of Thieu's requirements."[62]

The following morning, Kissinger, frustrated and angry over the fact that he now had a worse deal than when he had arrived, recessed the talks and headed back to the United States to report to Nixon. "We were caught in a vise," Kissinger later wrote, "Thieu on one side . . . Hanoi on the other."[63]

## NIXON DECIDES TO SETTLE

Kissinger returned to the United States and met with the president late in the evening of November 25th. The meeting, which lasted approximately one hour, took place at the Waldorf-Astoria hotel in New York, where Nixon was staying at the time. Though no public record of what the two men said is known to exist, Nixon wrote in his diary following the meeting, "we now have no option but to settle."[64] Kissinger, who for some unexplained reason made no mention of the meeting in his memoirs, later wrote in apparent reference to what had transpired only that "we decided to bring matters to a head."[65] Whatever was actually said that night at the Waldorf, it is clear that the two most powerful men in the U.S. government had finally decided that no matter the cost, they would bring America's participation in the war to an end once and for all.

Why, that night, after ten long years of fighting and, for Nixon and Kissinger, almost four years of negotiating, the decision to settle? Some believe that Nixon came to this historic decision after learning firsthand of the depth of Tho's intransigence. Others cite Nixon's increasing concern over Watergate—concern Nixon had expressed to his chief of staff H. R. Haldeman just prior to leaving for New York earlier that day. "The main thing involved here is to protect the Presidency," Nixon had declared during a strategy session with Haldeman on how best to contain the burgeoning scandal.[66] When one adds to these two possible reasons Nixon's well-known desire to wrap up the war during his first term, his oft-professed fear that members of the new Congress would cut off all funding for the war when they convened just after New Year, and the high level of expectation raised by the Kissinger declaration that "peace is at hand"—an expectation that Nixon feared if left unfulfilled would cost the administration dearly both at home and abroad—a clear rationale for settlement emerges. But regardless of *why* the decision to settle was made, it is clear from the known record that by the end of the evening of November 25, 1972, Nixon had decided to end America's involvement in the war no matter the cost. Having made the decision, he and Kissinger immediately set in motion a four-step plan for carrying it out.

Kissinger began the process the next morning, by inviting Thieu's personal representative to the Paris talks, Nguyen Phu Duc, to come immediately to Washington to meet with him and Nixon. The plan was, in Kissinger's words, for Nixon to "brutalize" Duc and let him know in no uncertain terms that a final, irrevocable decision had been made to settle with the North Vietnamese with or without Saigon's approval. The delivery of this message, step one in the plan, took place in the Oval Office on the 29th. Nixon later wrote that he told Duc that "it was not a question of lacking sympathy for Saigon's predicament; but we had to face the reality of the situation."[67] Step two involved informing the North Vietnamese that Kissinger would return to the Paris talks in early December with the intention of making what Kissinger called "a maximum effort." On November 27, the North Vietnamese were notified that Kissinger planned to return to Paris.[68]

Step three involved the president, in the following order, (1) informing the Joint Chiefs that the treaty was about to be signed; (2) ordering them to pledge their unqualified support for the treaty *sight unseen;* (3) having Kissinger then brief them on the treaty's contents; and finally (4) directing them to draw up contingency plans for a massive bombing and mining campaign against the North Vietnamese heartland in the event the concluding talks with Tho collapsed or an agreement was reached and subsequently violated by the North Vietnamese.

Nixon and Kissinger summoned the Joint Chiefs to the Oval Office for a meeting on November 30 to brief them as planned. In his memoirs, Kissinger twice notes that the meeting occurred but omits any mention of his own participation.[69] The official record of the meeting, originally classified "Top Secret Sensitive <u>Exclusively Eyes Only</u>" and declassified in 1992, shows that Kissinger played a pivotal and deeply troubling role.

According to the official record, taken down by Haig, those present that day along with the president, Kissinger, and Haig were Defense Secretary Melvin Laird, his deputy Kenneth Rush, Chairman of the Joint Chiefs Adm. Thomas Moorer, USN, Adm. Elmo Zumwalt, USN, Gen. Creighton Abrams, USA, Gen. Robert E. Cushman Jr., USMC, and Gen. Horace M. Wade, USAF. Haig's official record shows that Nixon began by telling the group that the new Congress would cut off all funding for the war when it convened in January and that this fact made it imperative that the agreement negotiated by Kissinger be signed. Stating unequivocally that "as of January 3, 1973, when the Congress reconvenes, continuation of the war is no longer a viable proposition," Nixon told the Chiefs, "It is important that America's military express pride in the accomplishment of the proposed agreement." He added, "If all of the sacrifices are not to be in vain, the military cannot criticize it."

Having sufficiently warned the Chiefs, the president then called on Kissinger, who stated he would "touch upon the agreement's main provisions, the changes made in Paris last week, and what is in store for the coming week."

Kissinger proceeded to review the treaty chapter by chapter. When he came to the chapter containing the provision creating the new governing body for the South, Kissinger told the Chiefs the new entity was "meaningless, . . . merely a figleaf, . . . eyewash." The provision for the new body was so bad for the Communists, Kissinger said, that "it is difficult to see how Madame Binh [the PRG— Provisional Revolutionary Government of South Vietnam—(Vietcong) representative to the Paris talks] could accept it after ten years of bloody struggle. All she has obtained is membership in a committee that has no power." When Kissinger had completed his presentation, Nixon declared again that the Chiefs as U.S. spokesmen "must accept it and be proud of the agreement."

Kissinger continued, and when he got to the treaty provision that allowed the approximately two hundred thousand PAVN currently in South Vietnam to remain there permanently, he told the Chiefs that "the fact is that the agreement does not legalize the presence of North Vietnamese troops in the South." He went on to declare that "contrary to some misunderstandings there is no legal basis for them being there." Then, perhaps for emphasis, he reiterated, "Hanoi cannot keep its army in the South." The official record shows that no objections to these statements were raised by anyone in attendance.

Nixon, his national security advisor having performed as planned, then moved to end the proceeding by directing Admiral Moorer to review plans for the resumption of mining operations in North Vietnamese harbors and the use of B-52s over Hanoi in the event that either the concluding talks set for December 4 in Paris broke down or that an agreement was signed and the North Vietnamese subsequently violated it. He told Moorer to be prepared for either contingency.[70]

Next came the fourth and what Nixon and Kissinger hoped would be the final step: Kissinger's return to Paris, his presentation of the administration's "maximum effort," and Tho's speedy acceptance. Kissinger was confident he would pull it off with ease, telling Nixon just before his departure for Paris that there was a seventy–thirty chance the North Vietnamese would agree to a final settlement after only two days of talks.[71]

## December 4–13
## THE PARIS NEGOTIATIONS

Two sessions of talks between Kissinger and Tho were scheduled in Paris on Monday, December 4, a "private" session in the morning followed by an "official" session in the afternoon.

The official North Vietnam record shows that in the very first moments of the morning session, Tho attacked Kissinger with a vengeance and quickly derailed any hope for an early settlement. Catching the unsuspecting Kissinger completely off guard, Tho defiantly declared:

Reviewing the last six days of meeting [the November 20–25 talks], we have realized that you did not respond to any of our demands. . . . You even came here with threats. . . .

In the past ten years of war, we have known all the atrocities of war. Particularly under the Nixon administration, the atrocity has been pushed to the

extreme. We also understand that without a settlement the war will be merciless. You may bring your B-52s to raze Hanoi and Haiphong. You say that your
President is determined; we know that he is determined to invade and devas-
tate our country. We have not misunderstood him. We have undergone tens
of millions of tons of bombs and shells equaling 500–600 atomic bombs, but
we are not afraid. We are determined to oppose you. We will not submit; we
cannot accept being slaves. That is why your threats and your breach of
promises prove that you are not really serious in negotiation.[72]

Kissinger, obviously taken aback by the unexpected attack—and perhaps also
by Tho's knowledge of the administration's plan to deploy B-52s against Hanoi
if need be—quickly retreated. He first offered only what he later called "a
stripped-down version of the minimum changes for which we would settle,"
and then sought a recess to consider what had transpired and formulate the
American negotiating strategy for the afternoon session.

When the parties returned to the table, Tho denounced Kissinger again, rejected all of Kissinger's proposed changes, added several major changes of his
own, and withdrew nine of the twelve changes he had accepted in the November round of talks.[73] It thus became clear that the North Vietnamese had no intention of settling, not in two days or two hundred. Nixon later described in his
diary what had occurred: "Henry went back to Paris firmly convinced that he
would quickly . . . reach agreement with the North Vietnamese. . . . The North
Vietnamese surprised him by slapping him in the face with a wet fish."[74]

As it turned out, the events of December 4 forced Kissinger into a defensive
posture from which he could not recover. The talks dragged out for a week, with
Tho toying with Kissinger, granting him concessions one day and retracting
them the next, agreeing on a point during one session and renegotiating the
same point during the next. "I had come to Paris on December 4 with instructions from Nixon to settle," Kissinger later wrote, but "each day we seemed farther away from an agreement. . . . There was no intractable substantive issue
separating the two sides, but rather an apparent North Vietnamese determination *not to allow the agreement to be completed*."[75] Negroponte later called Tho's
performance "contemptuous of the United States."[76]

On December 12, the North Vietnamese finally made their intentions clear.
Tho, with critical questions still on the table and the two sides, in the words of
the Vietnamese, still "far apart" on a number of matters, informed Kissinger that
he was suspending the talks and returning to Hanoi for consultations.[77] The
talks broke off the following day with a frustrated and disappointed Kissinger
accusing Tho of bad faith, charging that he had allowed "just enough progress
each day to prevent a breakup but never enough to bring about a settlement."[78]
Kissinger departed immediately for Washington to consult with Nixon. Tho left
two days later for Hanoi via Moscow and Beijing.[79]

Step four in the Nixon/Kissinger plan to end the war quickly had ended in
total failure.

## OPERATION LINEBACKER II • THE B-52s POUND HANOI, HAIPHONG, AND THE NORTH VIETNAMESE HEARTLAND

Following consultations with Kissinger and Haig in the Oval Office on the morning of December 14, Nixon ordered the Joint Chiefs to launch the massive bombing campaign against the North Vietnamese heartland that he had discussed with them in the Oval Office on November 30. The campaign, code-named Operation Linebacker II, would be the first ever no-holds-barred B-52 assault on targets in and around Hanoi.

Though the Chiefs had been warned by the CIA in mid-October that the North Vietnamese were reportedly deploying American POWs as human shields at the Hanoi thermal power plant and other strategic targets in the Hanoi area during the summer and fall—and that five or six American POWs had reportedly been killed in Linebacker raids in early September—officials charged with Linebacker II target selection of necessity targeted the power plant and other lucrative military targets. (The source of the mid-October CIA report was a member of the International Control Commission [ICC], a body made up of representatives from Canada, India, and Poland who investigated violations of the Geneva accords and served as semiofficial "referees" between the warring sides).[80]

When finalized, the Linebacker II strike plan called for a series of massive co-ordinated air assaults by B-52s and assorted tactical aircraft against railroad yards, airfields, power plants, radio communications facilities, bridges, and storage facilities throughout Hanoi and its environs; in areas west, north, and northeast of the capital; and in and around the port city of Haiphong.[81] The bombing was set to begin on the evening of December 18, Hanoi time.

Operation Linebacker II began, from the Vietnamese perspective, when a pilotless American spy plane skimmed over Haiphong on the morning of December 18 at 10:52 A.M. local time. Another, coming from the mountains of Laos, flew over Hanoi at about the same time. "Judging that a raid . . . was impending," a PAVN officer later wrote, ". . . the AA Defense and Air Force Command . . . warned the AA batteries."[82]

One hour later on the Pacific island of Guam, the first wave of B-52s took off from Andersen AFB and began their eight-hour flight to North Vietnam. Their route would take them north of the Philippines and over the South China Sea to South Vietnam, then on to Cambodia, where they would turn north and follow the route of the Mekong to northern Laos. There they would form up with other B-52s from the U.S. base at U-Tapao, Thailand, creating a stream of bombers in the first wave alone that would stretch for seventy miles. The formations would enter North Vietnamese airspace northwest of Sam Neua Province, Laos, and attack the North Vietnamese heartland from the west and northwest. A second and then a third wave would follow. One hundred and twenty-nine B-52s would strike the North on this first night of raids alone.[83]

At 4:00 P.M. that afternoon, Hanoi time, Le Duc Tho arrived at Hanoi's Gia Lam airport from Paris after stops in Moscow and Beijing. According to the North Vietnamese, "As soon as Le Duc Tho had left Gia Lam airport and reached his home at Nguyen Canh Chan Street, at the centre of Hanoi, strategic B-52 bombers poured a great roar of bombs onto Hanoi, Haiphong, and several other cities."[84]

Col. Larry Guarino, USAF, who by December 18 had spent some 2,744 days in captivity in the North as a prisoner of war, was ecstatic at the sounds that enveloped Hoa Lo prison that evening. "The antiaircraft fire and the SAM launches were deafening!" he later wrote. "Then came the bombs, and by the long volley of explosives, we knew immediately the birds were B-52's! . . . The sky lit up and we all jumped up onto the pad to look out. . . . God, we were excited! . . . laughing, crying, yelling, 'Hit the bastards, Dick! Give 'em hell! . . . Way to go Dick,' we screamed, 'kick the shit out of them!' "[85]

The United States bombed the North unmercifully every night until Christmas, when Nixon declared a one-day truce. When the North Vietnamese did not accept his offer to resume negotiations, Nixon resumed the bombing on the 26th with a vengeance, quadrupling the number of B-52 sorties flown on the 24th. Kissinger, reflecting on the period, would later say, "The North Vietnamese [had] committed a cardinal error in dealing with Nixon: They cornered him. Nixon was never more dangerous than when he seemed to have run out of options. He was determined not to have his second term tormented like the first by our national trauma—especially when a settlement had seemed so near."[86]

The North Vietnamese passed the word to Kissinger's staff in Paris on the 28th that they were willing to resume negotiations in Paris in early January. The next day Nixon ordered an end to the bombing. At 7:00 A.M. Hanoi time on December 30, B-52 operations against the North Vietnamese heartland ceased.[87]

# PART II

# CHAPTER 6

JANUARY 1973

PEACE AT A VERY HIGH PRICE

. . .

There is one unbreakable rule of international diplomacy. You can't get something in a negotiation unless you have something to give.
                        —RICHARD NIXON, address to the nation, March 29, 1973

We insisted that . . . it was a voluntary act, not an "obligation" to indemnify
Hanoi. It may have been hairsplitting but to us it involved a point of honor.
                        —HENRY KISSINGER, about the Nixon administration's commitment
                                            to help rebuild North Vietnam after the war

The North Vietnamese had been battered severely by the B-52s. At year's end,
with their stocks of SAMs almost totally depleted and much of their war-making
machinery a smoking ruin, they were undeniably at the mercy of the huge
bombers of the U.S. Air Force.[1]

Battered, too, was the man who had dispatched the B-52s. Nixon had been
vilified in the world's press for ordering the bombing, and doubly condemned
when word emerged that the Bach Mai hospital in suburban Hanoi had been hit
yet again by U.S. bombs and that this time twenty-eight persons, including two
doctors, had been killed.[2] The pressure on Nixon to settle once and for all was
enormous.

Adding to the pressures generated by the bombing and the unfortunate collateral damage at Bach Mai were ominous new developments in the Watergate
investigation, which by late December had reached into the West Wing and was
threatening Nixon's closest advisors, H. R. Haldeman and John Ehrlichman.
Howard Hunt was facing jail and Charles Colson was expressing concern that
either Haldeman or Ehrlichman or both might have been more deeply involved
than had been indicated.[3]

It was under the twin dark clouds of the fallout from the December bombing
and an increasingly threatening Watergate investigation that Nixon met with
Kissinger at Camp David on January 6 to finalize strategy for the talks slated to
begin on the 8th in Paris. Nixon wrote in his diary, and later in his memoirs that
he "put it to Henry quite directly that even if we could go back to the October 8
agreement that we should take it. As far as our situation here is concerned," he
told Kissinger, "the war-weariness has reached the point that [renewed bomb-
ing] is just too much for us to carry on. . . ." Nixon wrote that "Henry, of course,

is going to continue to play the hard line, indicating that I might resort to resumption of bombing in the Hanoi area, even though I have told him that as far
as our internal planning is concerned we cannot consider this to be a viable option. . . . As I told him goodbye at the door of Birch Lodge," Nixon recalled, "I
said, 'Well, one way or another, this is it!' "[4]

*January 1973*
## PARIS

Le Duc Tho returned to the Paris talks in early January a very angry man; angry
not just that Nixon had unleashed the B-52s on the Vietnamese capital, but that
he had done so only three and a half hours after Tho had returned from Paris on
the 18th and that during the raids on the 21st, one bomb had impacted a mere
four hundred yards from Tho's home near the citadel in northwest Hanoi.[5]
Taken in concert, these events had clearly led Tho to suspect that the
Americans—Nixon, Kissinger, or whoever—had deliberately tried to embarrass
him, or worse.

The North Vietnamese record of the first session of the January talks shows
just how indignant Tho was. "You resumed the bombing of North Vietnam just
at the moment I reached home. You greeted my arrival in Hanoi in a very courteous manner!" Tho declared. ". . . You thought that by doing so, you could submit us. You were mistaken." When Tho continued to severely criticize the
United States for the bombing, Kissinger himself grew angry, telling Tho, "I
have heard many adjectives in your comments, I propose that you should not
use them!" According to the Vietnamese, the atmosphere was "tense" and remained so throughout the session.[6]

Once they had blown off steam at the morning session on the 8th, both sides
agreed on an agenda during the afternoon session and then, yielding to the realities each faced, moved quickly to settle. William Sullivan, the assistant secretary of state who had joined the Kissinger team in October and was present at
this round of talks, later summed up those realities: "We were on the verge of
some degree of anarchy . . . in the United States because of our continuation in
Vietnam. So our time was relatively limited and they knew it. . . . Now, on the
other hand, they also were aware, after they shot off their last SAM-2s, that they
were naked as jaybirds as far as defending themselves was concerned, and they
were not totally certain that Nixon wouldn't pull the madman routine. . . .
They had fired the last one [of their SAMs] at the B-52's. . . . We could have really clobbered them."[7]

On January 9, after only two days of talks, the two sides agreed on a final
treaty that was, according to Kissinger team member George Aldrich, "not all
that different from the [October] draft."[8] A relieved Kissinger reported to Nixon
that night that "we settled all the outstanding questions in the text of the agreement, made progress on the method of signing the agreement, and made a constructive beginning on the associated understandings."[9]

One of those "associated understandings" yet to be settled was the matter of
the payment of war damages to North Vietnam, a nonnegotiable North Vietnamese demand that Le Duc Tho had long described as "one of the most

important . . . in the agreement."[10] Another of the "associated understandings" was the matter of the return of the American POWs held by Hanoi. Equally non-negotiable from the American point of view, the return of the POWs was, according to Kissinger, not just one of the most important issues facing the United States, but *the* most important. "There was no single other objective as important to us as the POWs," Kissinger would later say. "POWs/MIAs were the absolute, irreducible demand."[11]

The two sides began discussions on these two critically important and closely linked matters at the negotiating session on January 11. Unknown to anyone at the time, the discussions would continue, at different venues and with different negotiators, into the twenty-first century.

## NORTH VIETNAM'S DEMANDS FOR WAR DAMAGES

It was a well-known fact even during the early days of the war that the North Vietnamese planned to demand war damages in return for the American POWs they held. Wartime intelligence reports had shown convincingly that the North Vietnamese had undertaken a program to capture American servicemen alive both in the North and in the South and use them as hostages to ensure that North Vietnam would be compensated for damages inflicted by American bombers. It was also well-known that Hanoi had formed the Committee of Inquiry in 1966 to keep a day-to-day tally of the bomb damage—street by street, village by village, factory by factory—and that the final bill would be presented to the Americans for payment at war's end (see Chapter 1).

Knowing North Vietnam's intention to use the POWs they held as hostages, Johnson administration officials had entertained a plan in late 1966 to pay ransom for the American POWs the North Vietnamese held at that time. The plan, put forth by the State Department and patterned after the effort by President Kennedy and his brother Robert that had freed the Bay of Pigs prisoners four years earlier, had called for a cease-fire to be followed by the payment of medical supplies, foodstuffs, pesticides, and other nonmilitary supplies and materials to North Vietnam in return for the POWs. When the head of the State Department's POW Committee, Ambassador-at-Large Averell Harriman, had asked the Joint Chiefs to evaluate the plan and comment on it, the Chiefs had rejected the proposal, citing among other reasons their belief that the payment of ransom would be taken as a sign of weakness, could offer propaganda opportunities to the North Vietnamese, would set a bad precedent, and would give aid and comfort to the enemy.[12]

When the Paris talks had convened following the bloody Tet Offensive in 1968, the North Vietnamese had publicly set forth in ominous, unmistakable terms their intention to use the American POWs they held as hostages to ensure the payment of reparations at war's end. State Department official Philip Habib, a member of the U.S. delegation to the talks at the time, later recalled how clear North Vietnam's intentions had been:

I was a member of our negotiating team in Paris. . . . In one of the first lists of negotiating points put forward by the North Vietnamese, the Communist side bracketed the release of prisoners with what they described as "U.S. responsibility for war damage in Vietnam" in a single numbered point. Although humanitarian issues such as POW/MIA's have been subjects of disagreement in the settlement of other past conflicts, I know of no instance in which an adversary so openly treated this humanitarian problem in this way. . . . We thus recognized from an early date what we were up against.[13]

In May 1968, at about the same time the Paris talks had convened, the Office of the Secretary of Defense had commissioned the RAND Corporation to conduct a study to examine "various military-political aspects of war termination in Vietnam." The study, titled "Prisoners of War in Indochina," had been published in classified form in late 1968 and again with minor changes when the Nixon administration had come to power in January 1969. The 1969 version had confirmed what the North Vietnamese had said at the Paris talks and had offered the Nixon negotiators the following insights on what they might encounter when trying to secure release of the American POWs held by Hanoi:

- We may fairly assume that in the future, as in the past, North Vietnam's major considerations in dealing with prisoner releases will be material and political rather than moral or humane.
- Since [U.S. prisoners] constitute one of the Communists' greatest bargaining assets, we may assume that the price for the release of American PWs will be commensurately high and could take the form of political, military and/or monetary demands. . . .
- It is not to be assumed that humanitarian reasons, a desire to abide by the Geneva PW Convention, or even commitment to an agreement reached during negotiations will induce the DRV to hand over all prisoners during the negotiations for a cease-fire, or promptly after a settlement has been reached. To rely on such a likelihood would be to ignore the Viet Minh's past tendency to use PWs in their custody as a means of gaining political objectives.
- A quid pro quo that the DRV is likely to demand—and one that the United States may want to consider accepting, is the payment of "reparations" to North Vietnam in exchange for U.S. prisoners.
- Should the United States agree to pay reparations, it might be able to obtain from the DRV a complete list of U.S. prisoners, particularly if payments were in any way tied to numbers of prisoners. Release of prisoners probably would take place in installments as reparation payments were made. If reparations were paid in a lump sum, Hanoi might simultaneously release all American prisoners.
- The United States could avoid giving the appearance of paying reparations or ransom money if it could reach its agreement with the DRV in private, and if all funds paid out to Hanoi were then publicly labeled part of the U.S. contribution to a postwar recovery program of the kind proposed by President Johnson in his regional development plan at Johns Hopkins University, in April 1965.

- No matter what terms are agreed upon, it would be unduly optimistic to believe that the DRV and the VC will release all U.S. prisoners immediately after conclusion of an agreement in the expectation that the United States will meet its military, political, or monetary commitments. More likely, they will insist on awaiting concrete evidence of U.S. concessions before releasing the majority of the American prisoners, and will retain some of them until all U.S. commitments have been fulfilled.

By the time the Nixon administration took power in January 1969, then, there was no doubt in anyone's mind—Vietnamese or American—what the North Vietnamese wanted and how they planned to get it.

## WHAT AND HOW MUCH? THE LONG AND TORTURED DEBATE OVER THE FORM AND AMOUNT OF WAR DAMAGES TO BE PAID TO THE NORTH VIETNAMESE

U.S. and North Vietnamese records show that the debate over the exact form of payment and the exact amount the United States would be required to pay at war's end toward the reconstruction of North Vietnam had been long and tortured.

The North Vietnamese record shows that Kissinger, clearly aware of North Vietnam's long-standing demand for war damages, had offered to help rebuild the postwar North at his very first secret meeting with Tho, which had taken place in Paris on February 21, 1970.[14] Tho, after considering the offer, had informed Kissinger that the U.S. payment had to be in the form of reparations and not aid. Kissinger had refused, stating that the money would be "economic aid, . . . a voluntary act of good will."[15] Later, in July 1971, Tho had again insisted that the payment be in the form of reparations rather than aid, and Kissinger had again refused, declaring the concept of reparations to be, according to the North Vietnamese record of the meeting, "unacceptable and unnegotiable."[16] North Vietnamese records indicate that in August 1971, Kissinger had conveyed to the North Vietnamese an oral commitment from Nixon regarding postwar aid for North Vietnam, stating, "One month after the agreement on principle, the President will request the Congress to allow and to finance a 5-year programme of aid to the Indochinese countries . . . amounting to about 7.5 billion dollars, out of which no less than 2 billions will be reserved for the DRVN."[17] Kissinger later wrote that he made clear to the North Vietnamese that this $2 billion commitment was neither to be a written part of the peace agreement nor would it be considered reparations.[18]

Nixon's $2 billion offer put forth by Kissinger in August 1971 had served to satisfy the North Vietnamese until the bombing of North Vietnam had recommenced in the spring of 1972. In late summer 1972, as the Linebacker raids had continued to devastate the North, Tho had more than doubled his demand for damages to $4.5 billion. As an inducement, he had offered to stop using the word "reparations" and to substitute in its place "the responsibility of the US to contribute to the reconstruction of Vietnam and to heal the wounds of war."[19] Kissinger, without agreeing to any increase over and above the previously offered

$2 billion, had countered that the United States was ready to enter into an agreement to rebuild Indochina, but only verbally.[20] In response, the North Vietnamese had demanded again that they receive $4.5 billion and that the U.S. commitment be made a written part of the accords. Kissinger had agreed during the final hours of negotiations in early October to convey the U.S. commitment in written form but had insisted that the specific sums involved would not appear in the treaty but rather would be pledged in a separate letter from Nixon.[21] According to the Vietnamese, Kissinger had concluded the October 1972 talks by agreeing that the U.S. payment would be in "an amount of about three billion U.S. dollars."[22]

But then, of course, the B-52s had flown north in the Linebacker II raids and new calculations had to be made. The North Vietnamese, it turns out, had begun these calculations on the very first night of the bombing, when they had ordered their Commission of Inquiry—the group charged with calculating war damage in the North that now operated under the name DRVN Commission for Investigation of the US Imperialists' War Crimes in Viet Nam—into the streets, clipboards in hand. The group's Chairman, Col. Ha Van Lau, who had served as a member of the North's delegation to the public Paris Peace Talks from 1968 to 1970 and would later become Vietnam's postwar ambassador to the United Nations,[23] and members of the commission had worked tirelessly throughout late December. The commission had published its preliminary report, titled "The Late December 1972 U.S. Blitz on North Viet Nam," just before Kissinger had departed for the Paris talks in early January. The commission report stated that Linebacker II ordnance had "rained down on 5 cities, 17 provinces and Vinh Linh area, including over 300 villages, 14 townships, 11 towns, destroying large numbers of cultural, educational, medical, economic and social establishments, water conservancy and public utility works such as schools, hospitals, pagodas, temples, churches, State farms, agricultural cooperatives, factories of consumer goods, markets, workers' living quarters, residential quarters, dikes, dams . . . [etc.]." The report presented a street-by-street analysis of damage inflicted on hard-hit sections of Hanoi, Haiphong, and four nearby provinces, citing the damage by specific street address, describing casualties by name and circumstance, and even counting and listing the number and size of all bomb craters in selected specific areas. Nothing was too insignificant to be reported; even damage to the flower beds and trees in the Haiphong town square was included in the tally.

Kissinger had viewed the Department of Defense poststrike bomb damage assessment photography of military targets prior to his departure for Paris and knew well what the bombers had wrought.[24] What he did not yet know was how much it was going to cost him over and above what he had pledged to the North Vietnamese in October.

## NORTH VIETNAM'S FINAL BILL

Tho presented North Vietnam's revised demand to Kissinger on January 11. He demanded $5 billion in reconstruction funds, a $2 billion increase over Kissinger's October commitment. Tho also demanded that Kissinger travel to

Hanoi within ten days of the signing of the accords to meet with Premier Pham Van Dong and confirm to him that payment would be forthcoming as promised. Kissinger agreed to make the trip but would only take Tho's demand for $5 billion under advisement until the next scheduled negotiating session set for January 13.[25]

Tho repeated his demand for $5 billion in reconstruction funds when the two sides reconvened on the 13th. Kissinger responded that after the signing of the agreement Nixon would send a letter to Pham Van Dong that would specify the principles that would govern U.S. participation in the postwar rehabilitation of North Vietnam and contain a firm declaration of the amount the United States would pay. Kissinger then presented Tho with a proposed draft of the letter that stated that the U.S. participation would be in the amount of $3 billion over a five-year period, subject to the approval of Congress. Tho immediately rejected both the amount of the payment and the provision on congressional approval, demanding instead $4.5 billion and a declaration in the letter that the money would be paid by the United States "without any political conditions." After a lengthy discussion, Kissinger and Tho agreed that their deputies would review both the wording of the letter and the final amount of aid and that both matters would be settled before the initialing of the agreement, which was now scheduled to take place on January 23.[26]

Kissinger departed for Washington on the afternoon of the 13th for final consultations with Nixon. He planned to return to Paris in time to conclude the discussions on postwar reconstruction and to learn for the first time how many POWs the North Vietnamese held and how and where the prisoners would be released—a matter the North Vietnamese had steadfastly refused to discuss until the U.S. contribution to postwar reconstruction was addressed to Hanoi's satisfaction. He and Tho would then initial the accords on the 23rd. A formal signing ceremony would follow on the 27th, with Secretary of State William P. Rogers signing for the United States and North Vietnamese Foreign Minister Nguyen Duy Trinh signing for the DRV.

Haig and Negroponte flew to Indochina during the mid-January break to brief allied leaders on the postwar aid issue. In Vientiane, Haig informed Prime Minister Souvanna Phouma that "we are convinced the Politburo [has] made the decision to settle and that they are greatly interested in rebuilding their homeland and want our assistance." He further told Souvanna Phouma that Nixon "is not naïve regarding Hanoi's intentions. He knows they do not want to abandon their struggle but only its character, [but] that they are weak and that they must change the character of the struggle to political insurgency. . . . We intend to help Hanoi just enough to provide an incentive for them to handle themselves in a proper way."[27] In Phnom Penh, Haig told Cambodian President Lon Nol that the North Vietnamese "are in trouble and want to shift the character of the war and keep their main forces at home." He added that the United States would grant postwar economic aid to the North Vietnamese and that it would be "not enough that they could make trouble but enough to make them behave."[28]

Kissinger, for his part, would later write, "I believed then . . . that the agreement could have worked. We hoped that with the program of assistance . . . we might possibly even turn Hanoi's attention (and manpower) to tasks of construction [rather than war]. Hanoi was indeed instructing its cadres in the South to prepare for a long period of *political* competition. We would use our new relationships with Moscow and Peking to foster restraint."[29]

Kissinger returned to Paris as planned and met with Tho on the morning of January 23. He began by asking Tho about the U.S. POWs, but Tho replied only in generalities, saying that the U.S. pilots captured in North Vietnam would be handed over to the United States in Hanoi; those prisoners captured in the South would likewise be returned in Hanoi, and those captured in Laos would be returned only after North Vietnam exchanged views with "its friends in Laos." Still refusing to provide Kissinger a list of the POWs Hanoi planned to release, Tho, according to the North Vietnamese record, "reiterated the question of the US contribution to the healing of the wounds of war."[30]

According to the North Vietnamese record, Kissinger, in reply, "handed to the Vietnamese delegation a draft of the US Note regarding the reconstruction of North Vietnam and promised that on January 30, 1973 the official note would reach us. . . . It was finally agreed to be 3 billion 250 million dollars . . . [and] soft loans would be 1.5 billion dollars. The grant aid would be confirmed by an official letter and [the] other assistance by a note."[31]

Tho, knowing that the United States did not expect repayment of the "soft loans," officially accepted the American offer of $4.75 billion and agreed to provide the U.S. side with a list of POWs to be released. The list, he informed Kissinger, would be handed over in two installments, the first at the official signing ceremony on January 27, the second when the official Nixon letter was received. Kissinger assured Tho that the Nixon letter would be delivered on January 30. With that assurance, all negotiations ended and Tho and Kissinger initialed the final agreement at 12:45 P.M. Incredibly, as Kissinger initialed the final document, Tho knew precisely what the North Vietnamese were getting for the prisoners—money to rebuild their country, and lots of it—but Kissinger had absolutely no idea how many American POWs the North Vietnamese would release in return.

Kissinger returned quickly to Washington to brief Nixon, Congress, and the nation on the accords. He would later say that he kept the amount of aid secret from everyone except Nixon "so that the Vietnamese couldn't trumpet it around as reparations."[32] Following the congressional briefings, he met with the leadership of the National League of Families of American Prisoners and Missing in Southeast Asia, a group of family members who had banded together during the war to demand better treatment for their missing loved ones, to brief them on the treaty's specifics relating to POWs and MIAs. "We have absolute assurance that all American prisoners of war held anywhere in Indochina will be released," Kissinger told the group during a meeting in the Roosevelt Room at the White House. "We will get a list tomorrow and we will check this list against our own. Then we'll know how many they claim and where we stand. . . . We . . . do not believe they will hide any POWs."[33]

## HOW MANY? THE LONG AND TORTURED DEBATE OVER THE NUMBER OF AMERICANS HELD PRISONER BY THE COMMUNISTS

Hanoi had kept the number of American POWs it held a closely guarded state secret throughout the war. Though the U.S. negotiators in Paris during the Johnson years—Averell Harriman, Cyrus Vance, Philip Habib, and the others—and Kissinger and members of his team throughout the Nixon years had all repeatedly pressed the North Vietnamese for an official, complete list of prisoners, no such list had ever been provided.

Admittedly, the North Vietnamese had provided two lists to opponents of the war in 1970, but the United States had officially rejected both as being inaccurate and incomplete. The first list, turned over to antiwar activist Cora Weiss in June of 1970, had contained the names of 335 POWs.[34] Though Weiss had insisted at the time that the list contained the names of every American held captive by the North Vietnamese, the CIA had rejected it, declaring that "intelligence reporting establishes beyond reasonable doubt that there are U.S. PWs in North Vietnam whom the North Vietnamese have not admitted [holding] and do not intend to admit holding."[35]

The other list, turned over to representatives of Senators Edward M. Kennedy (D-MA) and J. William Fulbright (D-AK) just before Christmas 1970, had contained the names of 368 Americans reportedly held in captivity in the North.[36] Though Secretary of Defense Melvin Laird had deemed this list to be "an authentic North Vietnam Government statement of the status of the 368 men listed," he had declared:

I do not accept it as a complete list of all the prisoners held in North Vietnam. . . .

The list is not an accounting for the approximately 1,625 men lost in Southeast Asia. Nor is it an adequate accounting for those men lost only in North Vietnam. There is no mention of the men lost in South Vietnam, Laos, or Cambodia. It lists only a small percentage of the men lost in North Vietnam. . . . We have ample reason to believe that the North Vietnamese hold more men than [those] listed.[37]

In mentioning the figure of 1,625 men, Laird was referring to Americans listed in late 1970–early 1971 as either known prisoners of war or as missing in action. Pentagon officials had long held that "a significant number" of the MIAs were, in fact, being held prisoner.[38]

In the absence of a full accounting by the North Vietnamese and Pathet Lao, the United States had been left with the very difficult task of trying to estimate the number of POWs the Communists actually held. When the peace talks had begun to bear fruit in the fall of 1972, the Joint Chiefs had directed that a task force be formed at CINCPAC to determine as closely as possible who by name among those listed by the United States as POW and/or MIA might realistically be expected to return alive when the accords were signed and prisoners released. The task force was composed of approximately fifteen to twenty mostly field-grade officers and headed by Brig. Gen. Eugene F. Tighe Jr., USAF (pronounced "tie"), the director for intelligence for the U.S. Pacific Command. Tighe would later say that the task force had carefully analyzed the wartime intelligence acquired from human sources, photographs, and interviews of POWs that had appeared in the North Vietnamese and foreign press; mail from the few prisoners who had been granted mail privileges to see if their letters contained, as some did, coded messages relating to the prison population; evidence relative to each serviceman's loss incident, including testimony from wingmen, fellow soldiers, or other eyewitnesses; U.S. radio traffic relating to loss incidents; intercepts of Communist radio traffic, etc.

Following an intensive, month-long investigation, Tighe and his staff had determined it was reasonable to believe that between nine hundred and one thousand two hundred specific individual American servicemen were candidates for release when peace came. (The task force report has never been declassified. Tighe told investigators on the Senate Select Committee on POW/MIA Affairs in 1992 that he remembered the figure to be between nine hundred and one thousand men.[39] The chairman of the Joint Chiefs during 1972–73, Adm. Thomas Moorer, USN, told committee investigators that he remembered the number cited in the CINCPAC task force report to be one thousand two hundred men.[40] The discrepancy might be explained by the fact that Tighe also told investigators that he had expected the number on the "evidential list" to swell when the fate of some four hundred Americans involved in "off the scope losses"—those men who had simply disappeared over enemy territory without a trace—was finally determined.)[41]

Whatever the precise number of American POWs believed by U.S. authorities to have been alive at war's end, Kissinger and his team would later say they were well briefed on the matter of the POWs and MIAs during the closing days of the Paris negotiations. Kissinger would tell Senate investigators that he and his team had at their disposal "all the current information [on POWs and MIAs] that CIA and the Defense Department had available" and that the information had been "fully studied."[42] Team member Winston Lord, who later described himself as "the most central figure [on the team] below Kissinger,"[43] later told Senate investigators that Kissinger himself "was in charge" of the POW issue and called "inconceivable" the suggestion that Kissinger or members of his team might not have been fully briefed on the prisoner issue during the period of the Paris negotiations. Lord told investigators:

> I want to make very clear that any information in the government on prisoners of war or . . . missing in action . . . obviously Kissinger and the President would fully be aware of this. . . . it's inconceivable [to say that the two men were not privy to all available intelligence on POWs and MIAs]. Let's just take the President. . . . Of course he was going to demand, . . . as would Kissinger and all his top aides, to know what the hell was going on. I mean roughly how many people. Every time somebody was shot down, were they prisoner, were they killed?
>
> So it would be inconceivable that they didn't have the full information available to them. . . . They certainly did.[44]

Lord further recalled that at the time the accords were signed, he himself had had "a sense that we were talking about— . . . whatever the figures were—a few thousand or something."[45]

## *January 27, 1973*
## THE PARIS ACCORDS ARE SIGNED • THE NORTH VIETNAMESE TURN OVER THE FIRST LIST OF POWs

On January 27, Lord, representing the Kissinger team, watched as Secretary of State William P. Rogers signed his name sixty-two times to the Paris Peace Accords.[46] It was only then, with the United States bound by Article 21 to "contribute to healing the wounds of war and to postwar reconstruction of the Democratic Republic of Vietnam and throughout Indochina," that the North Vietnamese presented the American side with the first of its two lists containing the names of American and other allied prisoners the DRV planned to release. As required by Article 8 (a) of the accords, all of the prisoners were to be released within sixty days. Article 8 (b) required the North Vietnamese to later account for those who remained missing in action.[47]

The January 27 list was in reality three separate sets of lists. The first set contained two lists, both prepared by the Ministry of National Defence Democratic Republic of Vietnam (the North Vietnamese). The first list was titled "U.S [*sic*] Pilots Captured in the Democratic Republic of Viet Nam." This list contained the names of 491 pilots and aircrewmen, some of whom were marked "dead" or "released." When those marked "dead" or "released" were deducted from the total, the names of 456 pilots and aircrewmen remained. On the second list, the name of one civilian American pilot appeared along with the names of three prisoners of other nationalities. Thus, the total number of American pilots and aircrewmen to be released who had been captured in North Vietnam was <u>457</u>.[48]

There were three lists in the second set, all prepared by the Provisional Revolutionary Government of the Republic of South Viet Nam (the PRG, i.e., the Vietcong). The first, "List of U.S [*sic*] Military Personnel Captured in South Viet Nam," contained the names of ninety-three prisoners who would be released. The other two lists in this set were of those U.S. servicemen who had died or been killed in captivity (thirty-four men) and those whom the PRG had periodically released during the war (twenty-four men). Thus the total number of U.S. servicemen to be released who had been captured in South Vietnam was <u>93</u>.[49] (One more name would later be added, bringing the total to 94).

The third and final set of lists, also prepared by the PRG, related to U.S. civilians and foreign nationals captured in South Vietnam. The first list in this set, "List of Civilian Personnel of the United States and Other Foreign Countries Captured in South Viet Nam," contained the names of twenty-seven Americans, two West Germans, two Filipinos, and one Canadian who would be released. This list was accompanied by two others, one listing the names of seven U.S. civilians captured in the South who had died in captivity and the other listing five Americans captured in the South who had earlier been released. Two additional lists contained the names of foreign civilians captured in the South who had died in captivity and foreign military personnel and civilians captured in the South who had earlier been released. The total number of U.S. civilians to be released who had been captured in South Vietnam was 27.[50]

A quick recapitulation of the January 27 lists showed that the total number of Americans to be returned by the North Vietnamese at Operation Homecoming was

| | |
|---|---|
| U.S. pilots and aircrewmen captured in North Vietnam | 457 |
| U.S. military personnel captured in South Vietnam | 93 |
| U.S. civilians captured in South Vietnam | 27 |
| Total number of Americans to be returned | 577 |

Flash messages containing the names of those on the lists went out from Paris that evening to the Pentagon and other government addressees.[51]

## February 1, 1973
## THE NIXON LETTER IS DELIVERED · THE NORTH VIETNAMESE TURN OVER THE SECOND LIST OF POWs

On February 1 (rather than on January 30 as previously agreed to), the United States delivered the Nixon letter to a North Vietnamese representative in Paris and received in return the second and final list of American POWs to be released at Operation Homecoming. The letter, titled "Message from the President of the United States to the Prime Minister of the Democratic Republic of Vietnam February 1, 1973," pledged that, as required by Article 21 of the treaty, the United States would contribute approximately $4.75 billion in reconstruction funds and food and commodity assistance to North Vietnam over a five-year period, payment to be made "without any political conditions." A separate note stated that the contribution would be made subject to U.S. "constitutional provisions," meaning the payments required by the treaty and committed by Nixon in the letter would have to be appropriated by the U.S. Congress.[52] At Kissinger's insistence, the letter and its contents would be kept secret from the public and from the U.S. Congress for the remainder of his and Nixon's government service.

The February 1 list contained the names of only nine Americans and one foreign national, a Canadian missionary, all of whom had been captured by North Vietnamese forces operating in Laos.[53] It was understood that the North Vietnamese would hand these prisoners over to U.S. authorities in Hanoi rather than in Laos.

## "STUNNED," "SHOCKED," "INCONCEIVABLE," "MY GOD, LOOK AT THE DISPARITY"

Members of the Kissinger team and the Tighe task force reviewed the lists and knew instantly that the situation was ominous. "We were stunned by the lists we got," Kissinger team member Peter Rodman would later tell Senate investigators. "We got lists that we knew were inadequate or at least very puzzling on both Vietnam and Laos."[54] Tighe, at his office at CINCPAC when he got his copy of the Vietnamese lists, was "shocked" by what he read. "When we got the initial list of those that were going to be returned the disappointment was dramatic," Tighe later told Senate investigators. "My reaction was that there was something radically wrong with the lists versus our information and that they should have contained many more names. That was my personal judgment and that was a collective judgment of all those that had worked compiling the list."[55] Tighe described how he had compared the North Vietnamese lists with the one he and his task force members had developed and immediately took them both to the CINCPAC, Adm. Noel Gayler, USN, and told Gayler, "My God, look at the disparity." Tighe recalls that Gayler sent the comparison to the Joint Chiefs in the form of a report. "I don't remember the numbers," Tighe told Senate investigators, "but . . . it just sits in my memory that we got back about half of the ones we anticipated to get back. . . . In my mind's eye, it was about half."[56]

Nixon, for his part, was so concerned over the paucity of names on the February 1 list—the list the United States had received in return for his written pledge of $4.75 billion in reconstruction funds—that he ordered his deputy national security advisor, Brig. Gen. Brent Scowcroft, USAF, to immediately send a strong note of protest in his name to the North Vietnamese delegation in Paris. In the note, Nixon questioned the accuracy of the February 1 list and warned the North Vietnamese that unless a more complete accounting was rendered, Kissinger's upcoming trip to Hanoi to discuss the implementation of America's postwar reconstruction program might not end in success. Declaring the February 1 list of prisoners in Laos "unsatisfactory," Nixon told the North Vietnamese that "it is inconceivable that only ten . . . men would be held prisoner [there]." He further stated that:

> The United States side has on innumerable occasions made clear its extreme concern with the prisoner issue. There can be no doubt therefore that the implementation of any American undertaking is related to the satisfactory resolution of this problem. It should also be pointed out that failure to provide a complete list of prisoners in Laos or a satisfactory explanation of the low number thus far presented would seriously impair the mission of Dr. Kissinger to Hanoi.[57]

The concern that Nixon, Kissinger, Scowcroft, and their entire team felt on the night of February 1 was no doubt heightened the following day when the CIA sent Kissinger fresh intelligence relating to the North Vietnamese prisoner lists. In a February 2 report, the agency advised Kissinger that a Vietcong cadre had recently reported that "the list of U.S. POW'S given to the United States was not a complete one and that the communists in fact held 'over a thousand' prisoners."[58] Additional concern arose several days later when word was received that Communist gunners had shot down a USAF EC-47Q electronic surveillance aircraft near Binh Tram #44 on the Ho Chi Minh Trail in southern Laos on February 5. According to at least three separate intercepted Communist radio transmissions received in the hours following the shootdown, four U.S. aircrewmen had been captured alive and were being held prisoner. In one intercept, the Communists stated that "the people involved in the south Laotian campaign have shot down one aircraft and captured the pilot/pilots." In an associated transmission, the sending unit stated, "Group is holding four pilots captive and the group is requesting orders concerning what to do with them." In yet a third associated radio transmission, a Communist unit declared, "Group has four pirates. They are going from 44 to 93. They are having difficulties moving along the road."[59] Given the PAVN numbering system for the binh trams, BT 93 would have logically been located north of BT 44 in an area of the Truong Son Mountains southwest of the A Shau Valley.[60]

It was in this environment that Kissinger and three members of his team—Sullivan, Lord, and Rodman—and a small number of other administration officials departed Washington on the morning of February 7 for Hanoi.[61]

Three days of critical talks with Pham Van Dong, Le Duc Tho, and the other top leaders of the Democratic Republic of Vietnam lay ahead. The fate of all of the American POWs, listed and unlisted, and the future of South Vietnam hung in the balance.

# CHAPTER 7

# FEBRUARY 1973

# A HISTORIC JOURNEY TO HANOI

. . .

Hanoians had been doing a lot of celebrating in the days leading up to Kissinger's arrival in their city on February 10. Their cause for celebration was not just the end of the bombing and the coming of peace but also the specific peace agreement reached in Paris, which they and their leaders had considered a stunning victory for the DRV.

The North Vietnamese leadership had been so thrilled with the outcome in Paris they had ordered the entire peace agreement read over Hanoi radio word-for-word, including the protocols, only hours after Tho and Kissinger had put their initials to it on January 23. The transcript of the broadcast, which had taken place over a two-day period punctuated by long periodic interruptions of patriotic music, covered thirty typewritten pages.[1] Then, on the 26th, *Nhan Dan,* the official Communist party daily in Hanoi, had run a lengthy story about the accords under a huge banner headline that proclaimed in red ink, "A Great Victory for Our People."[2] With nationwide rallies and celebrations set to begin when the accords were formally signed on the 27th, the Communist Party Central Committee had issued approved slogans for use at the celebrations. These included "Hurrah for the Paris agreement on ending the war and restoring peace in Vietnam," "Hurrah for the great victory of the heroic people of North Vietnam," "Hurrah for the great victory of the heroic people of South Vietnam."[3]

Slogans at the ready, the North Vietnamese had gathered at celebrations throughout the country on January 28, the first full day of peace. Radio Hanoi had described the mood in the capital:

Hanoi . . . today throbs with joy over the great victory of the nation. . . . All the streets in the capital city, from the main shopping centers . . . to the smallest alleys, are flooded in a sea of flags which calls back to the mind of every Vietnamese the stirring days in August 1945 when the century-old colonial rule was overthrown.

This afternoon more than twenty thousand people . . . gathered at the [B]a Dinh square [where Ho Chi Minh had declared independence on September 2, 1945] to celebrate the great victory of the resistance.[4]

The Hanoi Domestic News Service had reported that at one celebration in Quang Ninh Province, the coastal area northeast of Haiphong where America's first pilot prisoner, Lt. (j.g.) Everett Alvarez Jr., USN, had been shot down following the Gulf of Tonkin incident eight and one half years before, "more than 8,000 youths, workers, and self-defense agents took to the streets to . . . greet' our people's great victory."[5]

"We have won," the Army daily *Quan Doi Nhan Dan* had declared in a lengthy editorial on the 28th, "Vietnam Has Won a Great Victory."[6] The following day the party daily *Nhan Dan* had offered an editorial of its own, "The Historic Victory and the New Situation in the South." This lengthy editorial had outlined what the party envisioned would occur in the South in the months ahead:

With the success in signing the Paris agreement on Vietnam, our South Vietnam's revolution has entered a new phase. . . . Through the negotiations, the national council for reconciliation and national concord will be set up at various levels. Our southern compatriots will decide their political future by themselves through the genuinely free and democratic elections. The unification of our country will be gradually achieved through peaceful means.

. . . The Paris agreement is an important legal and political basis and an effective weapon for the southern compatriots and combatants in the struggle from now [on].[7]

Then had come Tet and the beginning of spring, which this year the Vietnam News Agency had officially declared the "Spring of Victory." "Hanoi is adorning itself more gloriously . . . than ever, for the first Tet (Lunar New Year festival) in peace after years of war," VNA had reported. "Joy and pride can be seen on everybody's face, the joy of a regained peace and the pride of big victory in a protracted and bitter struggle."[8]

On February 3, the first day of Tet, Tho and Nguyen Duy Trinh, who, respectively, had initialed and signed the peace agreement at Paris, had returned to Hanoi to heroes' welcomes. VNA had reported that

Today, the first day of the lunar new year, the Hanoi population [gave] a rousing and most enthusiastic welcome to Le Duc Tho . . . and Nguyen Duy Trinh . . .

At the Gia Lam airport bedecked with flags . . . , thousands of representatives of various strata of the Hanoi population, bouquets in hands, waited for the arrival of the two distinguished diplomats.

At 13:00 hrs, the plane touched down. Le Duc Tho and Nguyen Duy Trinh alighted, cheerfully waving to the welcomers. They were greeted at the gangway by Premier Pham Van Dong and Vice-Premier Le Thanh Nghi who gave them a warm handshake and a tight hug amid the burst of fire crackers and stormy ovation of the crowds.[9]

From the airport ceremony, Dong, Tho, Trinh, and other officials had been driven to the Presidential Palace for a welcome home ceremony attended by President Ton Duc Thang—the elderly, little-known successor to Ho Chi Minh (Ho had died in early September 1969), other officials of the North Vietnamese government, members of the diplomatic corps, and members of the press. VNA had reported that Dong told those assembled, "We are very happy and enthusiastic to greet the great victory of our people in our protracted and hard and certainly victorious struggle. This is a victory on all the military, political and diplomatic fronts." VNA had further reported that "President Ton Duc Thanh and other party and state leaders, diplomatic envoys and other representatives proposed toasts to greet the great victory of the Vietnamese people."[10]

It was into this environment that Kissinger and his team landed at Phuc Yen on the morning of February 10.

*February 10–13*
## THE KISSINGER/PHAM VAN DONG MEETINGS IN HANOI

Though the CIA had warned Kissinger prior to his departure that it was possible the Vietnamese "will play your visit . . . as proof of Hanoi's 'victory,'" and that Kissinger and his team might be made to look like "barbarian chiefs coming to pay tribute,"[11] there was no evidence of any of that when Kissinger's plane touched down. Instead, Kissinger was welcomed planeside by a warm and gracious Tho, who Kissinger later said "greeted me almost affectionately."[12] Nguyen Co Thach, Tho's key deputy at Paris, likewise greeted his counterpart William Sullivan more as an old friend than a vanquished foe. Lord, Rodman, and the others were greeted similarly. Amid the wreckage of the Phuc Yen MiG base that morning, all seemed to have been forgiven.

Following a trip into the city, Kissinger and his team met for three and one half hours with Prime Minister Pham Van Dong, Tho, and other top North Vietnamese leaders. In his initial cable to Nixon describing what had transpired, Kissinger wrote: "The North Vietnamese today were obviously most eager to normalize relations. They made fulsome protestations of their peaceful intentions and of their having made a basic decision to take a peaceful course. They assured us that they would bring about a ceasefire in Laos within the next two or three days."[13]

In a second cable, Kissinger reported that Dong had wanted to talk about reconstruction aid during that first meeting, but that he (Kissinger) had "refused" until the matters of cease-fires and the North Vietnamese withdrawals from both Laos and Cambodia were addressed.[14] Kissinger later wrote in his memoirs that Dong had declared that he and his government wanted to establish a new long-term relationship with the United States and would implement the Paris agreement scrupulously, but had warned also that if a new relationship did not develop between the two countries on a solid basis of mutual interest, the Paris agreement would be "only a temporary stabilization of the situation, only a respite." Kissinger considered this comment by Dong to be "an ominous hint of renewed warfare."[15]

Kissinger then raised the matter of the prisoners, presenting Dong with a number of narrative accounts of the loss incidents of men who were known to have been captured alive but had not shown up on the list of those prisoners to be released. Kissinger later wrote in his memoirs that the U.S. side "knew of at least eighty instances in which an American serviceman had been captured alive and had subsequently disappeared," and that "none of these men were on the list of POWs handed over after the Agreement." Where were they, Kissinger asked Dong, calling special attention to nineteen cases where pictures of the captured Americans had appeared in the media. According to Kissinger, Dong replied noncommittally that "the lists handed over to us were complete" and made no attempt to explain the discrepancies. Kissinger further quoted Dong as telling him that "experience had shown that owing to the nature of the terrain in Indochina it would take a long time, perhaps a year, to come up with additional information. . . ."[16]

According to William Sullivan, the North Vietnamese "took all the files [on the POWs] and told us they'd be back in touch." They accepted the files, Sullivan later said, in an atmosphere of "maximum cooperation."[17]

On the second day of meetings, Dong again raised the issue of reconstruction aid. Kissinger, however, again put the prime minister off and chose first to discuss technical issues relating to implementation of the agreement, violations allegedly committed by the North Vietnamese, and the matter of a cease-fire in Laos. Kissinger reported to Nixon that the atmosphere was "very cordial" and the general mood "constructive."[18]

Finally, on the 12th, the third day of his meetings with Dong, Kissinger could no longer avoid a discussion of reconstruction aid, a discussion he had told Nixon hours before would "no doubt prove difficult."[19] The source of Kissinger's concern clearly was his fear that Dong would seek to up the ante over and above the $4.75 billion Nixon had already agreed to in his February 1 letter—and the fact that if he (Kissinger) did not agree to the new figure, Dong would delay or cancel the release of the first American POWs, *which was scheduled for later in the morning just across the river at Hanoi's Gia Lam Field.*[20]

In an effort to head off any move by Dong to squeeze more money out of the treaty, Kissinger poor-mouthed, opening the morning's discussion with what he called "a long pitch on our Congressional problems" and then spending an entire hour explaining in detail the difficult legal and constitutional requirements of congressional authorization and appropriations.[21] "I pointed out how our actual aid levels in recent years always fell short of our request," he later reported to Nixon. "I stressed that it was hard enough to get money for our friends, let alone for those with whom we have just been at war." But in the end, Kissinger told Nixon, "I reaffirmed your intention to seek aid as part of an Indochina effort, because it reflected our traditional policy, was part of our undertaking with the DRV, and was in our own self-interest."[22]

To Kissinger's obvious relief, the remainder of the discussion "went smoothly . . . and we avoided many of the shoals that I expected. They accepted our basic approach of shifting all discussion into a joint US-DRV economic commission; they did not try to raise the target figures we had agreed upon; we agreed that we would not mention any total sums; and they concurred in other procedures which should make congressional approval easier."[23]

Across the Red River at Gia Lam, meanwhile, the POWs were nervously waiting. They had left Hoa Lo prison earlier in the morning, but when they had arrived at the sprawling airfield they had found there had been a "delay," and their buses had been directed to a holding area about a mile from the terminal. "We unloaded the buses [at the holding area]," Navy Capt. Howard Rutledge recalled. "Our guard told us that there would be a delay as both sides hammered out the final details of the turnover." Rutledge later wrote:

> We stood around nervously. At first there were feeble attempts at joking about our predicament. Then we lapsed into silence. About noon the Vietnamese brought us something to drink and some stale sandwiches. We ate them, hoping this was our last meal in Vietnam. No one wanted any trouble. There was too much to lose. . . .
> We could see the international control teams scurrying around. There was nothing to do but wait.[24]

Navy Capt. Jeremiah Denton would later write that at the first sight of the airport a long, loud cheer had arisen from the prisoners on his bus. "But [there were] no Americans planes. There had been a delay, and I prayed there hadn't been a last-minute hitch."[25] Everett Alvarez, longest held among the fliers shot down over the North, later recalled the delay lasted more than two hours.[26]

Denton later wrote that "Shortly after noon we heard a low, deep droning, and in moments a beautiful sight appeared in the clear sky: the high tail and swept wings of an American C141. Another cheer, then back on the buses; a short drive to the release point; a long table; some foreign guys in uniforms."[27]

VNA would further describe the scene at the release point:

> The "dean" of the group, and also of all the other American flyers still in North Vietnam detention camps, was Everett Alvarez, Jr, Lt JG, Calif., who was shot down in a navy bomber over the coal-mining Province of Quang Ninh on August 5, 1964, the very first day of the U.S. air war against North Vietnam.
> Next to him in the list was astronaut-pilot Robert Harper Schumaker [sic], Lt Cdr, Navy, whose detention has lasted 7 full years by yesterday.
> . . . When the first white four-engine C-141 was taxing [sic] down toward the apron in front of the control tower, the first returned American stepped into the enclosed area nearby, over which a green parachute was hung to provide a temporary shelter for the members of the ICCS and the military

delegations of the DRV and the U.S., who sat facing one another across two adjoining tables and chatted with ease.

Man after man, the returned Americans, clad in beige blouses and dark green trousers, stepped in at the call of their names.[28]

Denton, who would rise to the rank of rear admiral and later be elected United States senator from Alabama; Alvarez, who would become deputy director of the Peace Corps and later deputy administrator of the Veterans Administration; Shumaker, who would also make rear admiral; Lt. Col. Herschel "Scotty" Morgan, USAF, who would later run for Congress from western North Carolina; and others boarded the first C-141 and departed for Clark Field in the Philippines just as the second C-141 landed.

The handover procedure was then repeated. Lt. Col. Robinson Risner, USAF, who would later make brigadier general; Cmdr. James B. Stockdale, USN, who would become rear admiral and later a candidate for vice president of the United States; Rutledge, who would later make two runs for the U.S. Congress from Oklahoma; and others boarded the second C-141 and departed.

Then the remaining POWs, including Maj. Samuel R. Johnson, USAF, who would later be elected to the U.S. Congress from Texas; and Capt. Charles G. Boyd, USAF, who would become the only returnee to attain the rank of four-star general, formed up and boarded the final C-141. Capt. James Mulligan, USN, the senior POW, later wrote in his prison memoir that "We lurched into the air" and when the pilot announced "Gentlemen, we're airborne" over the aircraft loudspeaker system, "the plane echoed with the cheers and yells of liberation. We were on our feet, pounding each other on the back, hugging the nurses, grasping each other's hands," Mulligan wrote. Mulligan said that pandemonium reigned as those aboard greeted one another and shouted, " 'We made it! We made it! We made it!' Over and over! And over and over! 'We made it!' "[29]

With this first group of America's ransomed POWs safely out of Hanoi and on their way home, Henry Kissinger took some well-earned time off and went for a tour of the Hanoi Art Museum.[30]

Later in the afternoon, Kissinger met again with Dong to iron out details of a joint communiqué to be issued simultaneously from each country's capital after Kissinger's departure. He and Dong then spent what Kissinger reported to Nixon was "a relaxed hour's conversation, mostly on the course of the war and the negotiating history."[31]

Dong hosted a going away dinner for Kissinger and his delegation that evening. Kissinger would report to Nixon that the atmosphere was "very easy and cordial."[32] When Dong rose to speak, he praised his American visitor, expressing "delight"[33] that Kissinger had come and offered what Kissinger reported was "a very warm toast reaffirming his country's strong desire for better relations."[34]

In an effort to hurry those relations along, Kissinger invited Le Duc Tho to visit the United States as his guest, possibly as early as June.[35]

Goodwill was in abundance as Kissinger's historic visit came to an end.

# CHAPTER 8

FEBRUARY–MARCH 1973

THE "MOST TORTURED" ISSUE,

"THE TOUGHEST SALE"

. . .

It isn't hard to understand why the hottest topic of the day in Washington is that of U.S. aid to Hanoi.
—MAX LERNER, "Will Aid Alter Hanoi Leaders' Lifestyle?" (1973)

Henry Kissinger left Hanoi the next morning having accomplished a great deal. First, he had satisfied the wary and untrusting Pham Van Dong that América would honor its commitment to help rebuild the North—and in doing so had ensured that the first group of American prisoners were, in fact, released (albeit belatedly) and that the other listed POWs would soon follow. Second, he had received reassurances that those Americans known to have been prisoners who were not on the lists—as well as those Americans missing in action—would be accounted for. And third, he and Pham Van Dong had undertaken what both sides considered concrete steps toward normalized relations.

The joint communiqué was released as planned by the two sides in their respective capitals the next day. The communiqué declared that "concrete steps" had been examined that could lead to normalization of relations between the two former enemies and told of the creation of a U.S.-DRV Joint Economic Commission to develop plans for the postwar reconstruction of the North.[1] *Pacific Stars and Stripes*, the authorized newspaper of the U.S. Pacific Command, would carry the story on the front page of its February 16 edition under the headline "U.S., Hanoi Tell Plan to Rebuild Vietnam." The story read in part:

> Washington (UPI)—The United States and North Vietnam will create a joint economic commission to oversee rebuilding of the war-torn country with U.S. dollars, the two sides announced Wednesday.
>
> A communiqué issued by the White House and Hanoi on four days of talks by President Nixon's envoy, Henry A. Kissinger, and North Vietnamese leaders in Hanoi, listed no specific figures for U.S. post war aid.
>
> But the language displayed a new cordiality between the two nations.

For most of the returnees who read it—either at Clark or on one of the C-141s that began taking them on to stateside hospitals that Friday—the *Stars and Stripes* article was troubling, to say the least. After all the torture, pain, and deprivation that came with years of captivity—and the billions of dollars spent and the thousands of aircraft lost and the hundreds of their fellow pilots and aircrewmen killed and missing trying to *destroy* North Vietnam—Uncle Sam was going to *rebuild it with U.S. dollars*? No way in hell, they said, almost to a man.

And they weren't the only Americans who felt that way.

## THE "MOST TORTURED" ISSUE, "THE TOUGHEST SALE"

The news that Kissinger and Pham Van Dong were no longer just talking about postwar aid to North Vietnam but had actually set up a commission to administer it set off a firestorm on Capitol Hill. Rep. H. R. Gross (R-IA), a perennial critic of foreign aid, labeled the commission "the conduit for a handout" and noted that "we probably won't have anything to say about setting up the conduit, but we'll have a whole lot to say about what goes into it. I'm opposed to paying them anything."[2] Assistant Senate Democratic leader Robert C. Byrd (D-WV) said he would never vote to provide aid to North Vietnam. Sen. Hubert H. Humphrey (D-MN) said he could not vote to provide funds to rebuild the port of Haiphong when much of Washington's ghetto had not been rebuilt since it was ravaged by riots in 1968.[3] Other comments from the Hill were generally reflective of those made several days earlier by the powerful chairman of the House Ways and Means Committee, Rep. Wilbur D. Mills (D-AK), who had said that aid to North Vietnam would be "an awful bitter pill for Congress to digest. I just don't like to give a bunch of fellows I can't describe as anything other than murderers and hoodlums money out of the federal treasury."[4]

Surveying the congressional landscape, *The Washington Post* opined editorially that of all the post-Vietnam issues facing America, "reconstruction aid to Indochina may become the most tortured."[5] Nixon had conducted a survey of his own and also knew that passage of his aid proposal would be difficult. "We have the toughest sale we ever had," he told Haldeman and Scowcroft in an Oval Office meeting the day after the joint communiqué was released. He added that the depth of congressional resistance required that he himself rather than Kissinger had to "sell the aid program" in order to ensure its passage.[6]

Declassified White House records indicate that Nixon began his fight for aid on February 15 by seeking the support and assistance of the Joint Chiefs during a luncheon with the Chiefs and Secretary of Defense Elliot Richardson at the Pentagon. Seeking the Chiefs' help in dealing first with the returning POWs, and then with the Congress, Nixon told the Chiefs he feared that "if too many stories come out about the bad treatment accorded our POWs, [this] could jeopardize the chances of getting aid . . . through the Congress." He then expressed his additional concern that if the returning POWs rejected the idea of aid to the North, "that would kill it in Congress." JCS Chairman Adm. Thomas Moorer promised Nixon, "We will take care of this problem." Nixon then asked the Chiefs to personally contact selected senators and members of Congress and "convince them of the necessity of aiding North Vietnam on a national interest basis, not through any idea of reparation or humanitarism [*sic*]. Aid to North Vietnam," the president said, "should be pushed as an investment in peace." He ended his appeal by stating his additional concern that "the doves will oppose [reconstruction aid] because they think it would come out of welfare."[7]

Nixon met with his cabinet the following morning at the White House and, following a lengthy discussion on foreign trade, he briefed those present on his aid proposal for North Vietnam. Repeating what he had said to his advisors and to the Joint Chiefs and Richardson the day before, Nixon acknowledged that "North Vietnam aid will be tough to sell" and reiterated that "[it] is not being done on a humanitarian basis but for pure national interest." He offered justification for the program by explaining that reconstruction aid to the North Vietnamese "will draw them toward their own problems, have them turn inward, and will give us some measure of influence over their behavior." Official notes of the meeting show that the discussion then led to Nixon revealing his contingency plan for the aid in the event Congress ultimately refused to appropriate the funds:

[Secretary of State William P.] ROGERS: Tell Congress to wait until they know what we want and why. We have spent so much. Why let it all go down the drain now?

THE PRESIDENT: I would like every member of the Cabinet to take the Rogers line. Don't ask them [congressmen and senators] to support it now, but just to keep quiet. Wait and see. . . .

ROGERS: Particularly say shut up until the prisoners are home. Aid was in the agreement.

THE PRESIDENT: An excellent point. Also, the Johnson Administration began this. If everyone will wait until the prisoners get back, this will give us time to turn some people around.

[Budget Director Roy L.] ASH: People want to know where the money is to come from.

THE PRESIDENT: Hold it close for now, but I will say that aid will not come at the expense of domestic programs; it will have to come from the national security budget.[8]

## NORTH VIETNAM CONVENES SPECIAL SESSION OF NATIONAL ASSEMBLY TO RATIFY PARIS ACCORDS, U.S. PLAN TO REBUILD NORTH

Back in Hanoi, meanwhile, reconstruction aid was also a matter of high-level discussion. On February 20, more than four hundred Communist party leaders from all over the North gathered at a special session of the National Assembly to, according to VNA, "acknowledge and hail the great victories of our compatriots and combatants," officially ratify the Paris accords, and chart a postwar course for their country.[9]

Addressing the assembly's opening session, Prime Minister Pham Van Dong declared, "We must . . . build a new economic system and make preparations for . . . large scale and rapid development. . . . Our capital's armed forces and people pledge to make every effort in labor, production, and work to heal the wounds of war rapidly, build socialism in the north, and carry out properly President Ho's teachings: 'After the day of victory our people will rebuild our country into a bigger and more beautiful one.'" Dong told the assembly that toward that end the Paris agreement "says that the obligations [*sic*] of the United States is to contribute to healing the wounds of war and to postwar reconstruction of the Democratic Republic of Vietnam and throughout Indochina." He further declared that the agreement created conditions for the establishment of "a new, equal, and mutually beneficial relationship" between the DRV and the United States.[10]

In reply to Dong's address, Truong Chinh, chairman of the National Assembly Standing Committee, declared:

The National Assembly hopes that the Hanoi compatriots, who proved creative and valiant in combat, will be more creative and valiant in labor and peace. With the impetus of their past victories, let our compatriots . . . overcome rapidly the aftermath of the war, restore and develop properly our country's economy and culture, and build a bigger and more beautiful capital city, as taught by Uncle Ho, so as to secure a happy and joyful life for the capital's people. . . .

At the same time, let them strive to support the struggle of our southern compatriots in general and of Hue and Saigon sister-cities in particular for implementation of the Paris agreement on Vietnam in order to advance toward peaceful reunifying the fatherland [as reported].[11]

After two days of speeches, presentations, and discussions involving representatives of "the political parties, religions, mass organizations, ethnic minorities, the armed forces, and the localities," the assembly voted unanimously to approve the Paris agreement.[12] In his closing address, Ho's successor, President Ton Duc Thang, told the delegates that "Peace has been restored in our beloved country" and that "our people's brilliant development period has begun." He added:

Our country's future is really bright. Our people have acquired many new favorable conditions. . . . We must hold aloft the banner of peace and national concord, implement all provisions of the Paris agreement strictly and scrupulously and demand that the parties signatory to the agreement also respect and scrupulously implement it.

We must strenuously emulate in rebuilding our war-ravaged country.[13]

Radio Hanoi reported that as the assembly concluded its work in historic Ba Dinh Hall that afternoon, "Everyone looked at . . . Uncle Ho's statue . . . and had the impression that he was still alive, sharing the people's and nation's joy on the days of great victory."[14]

The Paris accords having been ratified by the National Assembly, Pham Van Dong wrote Nixon on February 23 to confirm his government's understanding of and agreement with Nixon's February 1 letter outlining the principles that would govern the U.S. contribution to the postwar reconstruction of North Vietnam. Dong confirmed Nixon's letter point by point, suggested a date for the first meeting of the Joint Economic Commission, and named the DRV representatives to the commission. A careful reading of the text showed that Dong had taken note

of the 10 percent devaluation of the U.S. dollar announced since the Nixon letter had been dispatched, and had made his acceptance of the U.S. contribution
based on the dollar's higher value on February 1, not the current value.[15]

With Dong's letter of acceptance, the matter of reconstruction aid had, from
the North Vietnamese perspective, evolved from a matter of secret negotiation
to a treaty obligation that had been (1) confirmed by Nixon in both official secret correspondence and official public statements; (2) confirmed by Kissinger
in Paris and Hanoi; (3) announced by both governments in a joint communiqué
following Kissinger's departure from Hanoi; and (4) ratified by North Vietnam's
National Assembly. And now, from the North's perspective, at least, all that was
left was for the Joint Economic Commission to meet and decide which specific
projects would be funded and for the money to be paid.

## NIXON, KISSINGER, ROGERS, DEFENSE OFFICIALS PUSH FOR CONGRESSIONAL APPROVAL OF RECONSTRUCTION AID TO NORTH VIETNAM

U.S. Secretary of State William Rogers went to Capitol Hill on February 21 to testify in support of the administration's aid proposal. According to AP, Rogers, testifying before the Senate Foreign Relations Committee, "refused to rule out
reconstruction aid to North Vietnam by presidential order if Congress fails to
appropriate the funds" and "three times called for 'restraint' by members of
Congress in making adverse comments on the aid issue, at least until American
troops are out of Vietnam and all American prisoners are released."[16]

Perhaps thanks to Rogers's testimony, the administration began to pick up a
slow trickle of public support for its aid proposal in the Senate and seemed to be
making headway even in the more conservative and strident House of Representatives. Press reports showed Senators J. William Fulbright (D-AR), the powerful chairman of the Foreign Relations Committee, Edward M. Kennedy
(D-MA), and Ted Stevens (R-AK) being sympathetic to aid and Senate GOP
leader Hugh Scott (R-PA) predicting that "after everyone has made his pitch,"
aid would likely pass.[17] [Hill insiders believed passage was, in fact, likely, and
that when Nixon and the House Democratic leadership got down to the really
serious horse trading, a compromise aid package might well emerge. After all,
Nixon would enter the negotiations with a 68 percent approval rating in public
opinion polls, compared to an embarrassing 26 percent rating for Congress.][18]
On the House side, Otto Passman (D-LA), the respected and feared chairman of
the House Appropriations Subcommittee that would handle any request for aid
to Hanoi, let it be known that while he much preferred forty-year, no interest
loans to North Vietnam in place of direct grants, he would not rule out approving such grants if the administration insisted.[19] Other congressmen, however,
were less charitable. Ohio's powerful Democrat Wayne L. Hayes told *Time* magazine, "They'll be ice skating in hell the day I vote any assistance for that bunch
of murderers in Hanoi." *Time,* however, suggested that Hayes and other House
Democrats might be using their refusal to vote for aid only "as a club to force
Nixon to yield in his running battle with Congress over his impounding of
funds already appropriated [for other programs]."[20]

Kissinger held a news conference at the White House on the 22nd to report on his trip to Hanoi and to join in the push for postwar aid. AP, reporting Kissinger's remarks under the headline "Kissinger: Hanoi Aid is Investment in World Peace," quoted Kissinger as saying that the administration was "asking for support for the idea of such a program, not on economic grounds and not even on humanitarian grounds primarily, but on the ground of attempting to build peace in Indochina and therefore to contribute to peace in the world." AP further quoted him as saying he had not discussed precise figures with the North Vietnamese and had gone to great lengths to explain to them that "the fate of whatever recommendations we made depends on a decision by Congress." AP went on to say Kissinger "left the impression that the White House was counting on Congress to vote the necessary funds."[21]

In an interview with NBC News correspondent Barbara Walters broadcast several days later, Kissinger called for support of the aid plan and noted that "the sums that are in question will not make a decisive difference [in overall U.S. spending]." He added that he believed the North Vietnamese were considering a "peaceful revolution . . . for the first time in their history and in their lives."[22]

Nixon publicly joined the aid offensive in early March, telling a news conference the same thing he had confided to his cabinet two weeks before, that reconstruction aid for North Vietnam would be drawn from the national security budget rather than from funds for domestic purposes. "As far as any assistance program is concerned," Nixon said, "it will be covered by the existing levels for the budget which we have for national security purposes. It will not come out of the domestic side of the budget." He added that providing aid to Hanoi would serve "the interests of peace."[23] The day following his news conference, Nixon was joined in his public call for aid by both Defense Secretary Elliot Richardson and Deputy Defense Secretary William P. Clements. According to United Press International, Richardson, addressing a Pentagon news conference, endorsed reconstruction aid to North Vietnam as "a very important insurance policy" for maintaining peace in Southeast Asia. In remarks prepared for the annual Veterans of Foreign Wars conference in Washington, Clements said, "I believe a reasonable program for future economic assistance to the countries of Southeast Asia—including North Vietnam—is an investment in peace. . . . such an economic aid program would provide, in my view, a form of insurance that Hanoi will live up to the agreement it signed in Paris."[24]

*March 15, 1973*
## THE U.S.-DRV JOINT ECONOMIC COMMISSION CONVENES IN PARIS • THE DRV PRESENTS ITS FIVE-YEAR PLAN

The U.S.-DRV Joint Economic Commission met for the first time in Paris on March 15. In what the U.S. side would report was a "friendly" atmosphere, the North Vietnamese led off the proceedings by presenting an "exhaustive . . . catalogue of destroyed facilities and arrested development" and the broad outline of a plan for reconstructing the damage. Finance Minister Dang Viet Chau, head of the DRV delegation, declared that there were three main elements to the plan: reconstruction of destroyed facilities, general socioeconomic development, and the most urgent needs of the population. He proposed that the JEC reach a final agreement on the amount of aid in each element within thirty days.

According to the declassified U.S. delegation's reports of the proceedings, Maurice Williams, deputy director of the U.S. Agency for International Development (USAID) and head of the U.S. delegation, responded by "sound[ing] an optimistic note that in the right framework . . . a major program of reconstruction would be possible." Williams "held out prospects of a major advance of the DRV economy and encouraged the DRV to seek its objectives by peaceful and economic competition." He "accepted the general agenda suggested by Chau but [noted] that it was an ambitious one and that it might not prove possible to meet his time-table." Williams also "emphasized the historic turning-point the US and DRV had reached: after long hostility the DRV had undertaken in the Agreement to embark on the path of peace, leash the dogs of war, return its soldiers to the barracks, forge guns into plows, and place the pursuit of economic reconstruction to the fore. Scrupulous observance of signed agreements would make possible a major U.S. contribution to reconstruction throughout Indochina. He expressed confidence that, with the energies and determination of the DRV population devoted to peace and reconstruction, there was no reason why the DRV could not attain high levels of industrial and agricultural achievement."[25]

At the commission's second session held four days later, Williams confirmed to Chau that the U.S. reconstruction program would, as President Nixon's letter had outlined, extend over a period of five years. Williams also told Chau that "normalization of US-DRV economic relations would be an essential part of the reconstruction program, in order to transfer resources and technology effectively." He noted that "in practice [the] reconstruction program could not be separated from other economic relationships such as transportation, banking, trade, communications and thus the two matters must be considered together."[26]

Williams subsequently reported that the atmosphere at the first two meetings was "correct and businesslike" and that there was "an absence of invective and exaggerated rhetoric." He advised his superiors that "at this stage, they [the North Vietnamese] seem to be making a remarkable effort to be agreeable. The DRV presentations are succinct, relevant and intensely serious." He also reported that "mistrust of US intentions impels the DRV to emphasize a speedy conclusion of JEC deliberations."[27]

At the third meeting, on March 22, Williams stressed the need for periodic reporting to ensure that the aid was being used for its intended purpose and undertook a detailed discussion on establishing priorities for aid deliveries. Preliminary discussions were held concerning the anticipated proposal by the Vietnamese of the specific projects to be funded by the United States. Chau proposed to discuss those projects at the next meeting, which was scheduled for the following day. After this third meeting ended Williams, referring to the mistrust he had mentioned previously, reported to Washington that "[we] believe our delegation has convinced DRV that we are serious in our efforts to develop a program upon which we can agree."[28]

Chau presented the DRV five-year plan to the American side at the fourth meeting the following morning. (It should be noted that by doing so, the North

Vietnamese were signaling their desire to abide by the terms of the Paris accords for at least those five years, knowing as they did that any serious violations on their part would result in immediate suspension of aid by the United States.) The proposed plan called for the United States to contribute in five areas: (I) industry, (II) agriculture and fishing, (III) transport and telecommunications, (IV) maintenance of production and stabilization of living conditions, and (V) cash. Williams submitted the Vietnamese proposal to Washington by classified cable later that day:

### DRV-PROPOSED FIVE-YEAR SHOPPING LIST

I. ON INDUSTRY

1. An iron and steel complex, annual output: 1.5 million tons of steel (including: ore extraction and enrichment, production of coke, cast iron, steel; steel rolling . . . )
2. Truck, truck-crane, tractor, bulldozer and excavator plants. Annual output:
    a. Trucks (loading capacity: up to 10 tons) and truck-cranes: 15,000 units,
    b. Tractors, bulldozers, excavators: 6,000 units.
3. A shipyard for the building of sea-faring transports of 10,000 ton-burden. Total annual output: 100,000 tons.
4. A diesel railway engine plant. Annual output: 100 units.
5. A factory of diesel motors up to 2,500 hp for ships and railway engines. Total annual output: 300,000 hp.
6. A factory of high tension electrical equipments. Annual output: 3,000 tons.
7. A thermo-power station of 1,200 MW.
8. An oil refining and petrochemistry complex, refining 4 million tons of crude oil per year.
9. A nitrogenous fertilizer plant. Output: 1,000 tons $NH_3$ per day.
10. Two cement factories. Annual output per unit: 1.2 million tons.
11. A sheet glass factory. Annual output: 10 million square meters.
12. Two textile complexes. Annual output per unit: 100 million meters. (including: spinning, weaving, dyeing and printing . . . )
13. A silk and rayon weaving factory. Annual output: 20 million meters.
14. Five chipboard plants (including also the production of glue).
15. Four plants producing prefabricated houses. Annual output per unit: 1,000 apartments.
16. A plant producing refrigerators and air conditioners. Annual output: 50,000 units.
17. A sanitary porcelain wares plant. Annual output: 5,000 tons.
18. A brassware plant. Annual output: 2,000 tons.
19. A synthetic paints plant. Annual output: 10,000 tons.
20. A mashed bananas and lyophilized bananas factory. Annual output: 3,000 tons.
21. A wristwatch and alarm clock factory. Annual output: 500,000 units.

22. A leatherette plant. Annual output: 2 million square meters.
23. A metal wrapping paper plant. Annual output: 1,000 tons.
24. A wool spinning and woolen carpet-making factory. Annual output: 5,000 tons.
25. Five food processing [plants] for livestock. Output per unit: 10 tons per day.
26. Five drills capable of drilling at least 5,000 meters deep, along with shafts, tubes and other equipments, tools and materials required.

Regarding the above-mentioned plants and factories, the US party will supply:

1. Projects, complete equipments, spare parts, such building materials and building machines which are not available in Viet-Nam.
2. Licenses, technical documents and all the required know-how.

II. ON AGRICULTURE AND FISHING INDUSTRY
   1. For machine and tractor stations:
       a. 2,000 crawler tractors of 100 hp type.
       b. 5,000 crawler tractors of 75 hp type.
       c. 10 plants for major repairs and restoration of tractors.
   2. For irrigation work:
       a. Equipment for ten construction teams in irrigation works.
       b. Twenty suction-dredgers (250 cubic meters per hour per unit).
   3. For leveling bomb craters in rice fields:
       a. 500 bulldozers of 100 hp upwards type.
   4. Complete equipments for:
       a. Three agricultural colleges.
       b. Six agricultural research institutes (on food plants, industrial plants, animal husbandry, agricultural mechanization, soil research, etc.)
   5. Fertilizers and food for livestock:
       a. Two million tons of nitrogenous and kali fertilizers.
       b. Twenty million US dollars worth of food for livestock.
   6. Fish trawlers, total power: 200,000 hp.

III. TRANSPORT AND TELECOMMUNICATIONS
   1. Sea transport:
       a. A seaport with a shipment capacity of five million tons per year.
       b. A floating port with a shipment capacity of two million tons per year.
       c. An over 10,000 ton floating dock.
       d. A 300-ton floating crane.
       e. Ten port cranes of up to 15-ton lifting capacity.
       f. Equipments for 10 port construction teams.
       g. Four suction-dredgers, each with the capacity of 2,500 cubic meters per hour.

      h. Ten suction-dredgers, each with the capacity of 500 meters per hour.

      i. Cargo ships and tankers with a total capacity of 400,000 tons.

2. Railways:

      a. 50 diesel railway engines.

      b. 1,000 freight cars.

      c. 100 specialized freight cars.

      d. Equipments for ten railways construction teams.

      e. Equipments for five tunnel construction teams.

      f. 500 truck-cranes up to 15-ton cranes.

      g. 70,000 tons of rails.

      h. 1,500 meters of big bridges.

3. Roads:

      a. 1,000 trucks (loading capacity: up to 25 tons per unit).

      b. 70,000 tons of girders for bridges.

      c. Equipments for 30 road-building teams.

4. Telecommunications:

      a. Networks of automatic telephones including automatic telephone exchanges totaling 40,000 subscribers, telephone apparatuses and wires . . .

      b. Networks of wave carriers of up to 40 channels, totaling 1,500 km.

      c. Ten networks of microwave carriers.

## IV. MAINTENANCE OF PRODUCTION AND STABILIZATION OF LIVING CONDITIONS

1. Living conditions:

      a. Foodstuff: five million tons of rice, wheat flour, maize, soya bean, etc.

      b. Clothing:

          (1) 250,000 tons of cotton.

          (2) 50,000 tons of cotton and rayon yarn.

          (3) 50,000 tons of synthetic yarn.

          (4) 200 million meters of cloth.

          (5) 5,000 tons of combed wool.

          (6) 5,000 tons of raw wool.

          (7) 5 million feet of leather.

2. Housing:

      a. 2 million square meters of prefabricated houses and warehouses.

      b. 50,000 tons of corrugated galvanized sheet steel.

      c. 3 million cubic meters of logs.

      d. 1,500,000 tons of building and shaped steel.

3. Paper:

      a. 50,000 tons.

4. Pharmaceutical materials:

      a. 2 million US dollars worth.

5. Materials for production:
   a. 800,000 tons of thick steel plate and steel for machine use.
   b. 40,000 tons of copper.
   c. 40,000 tons of aluminum.
   d. 6 million tons of crude oil.
   e. 50,000 tons of synthetic rubber.
   f. 15 million US dollars worth of industrial chemicals.

V. CASH
   A cash amount equivalent to 25% of the total amount will be set aside
   for the purchase of equipments, goods, etc. . . . from other countries.[29]

Williams noted in his classified report that Chau had said "the DRV would
probably need some technicians from the US to assist with project implementation and perhaps it would be necessary to send some North Vietnamese to the
US for technical training."[30]

A quick look at just one small item on the North Vietnamese list illustrated
the breadth and depth—and, in this case, the "length"—of the problem the
United States now faced: the amount of "cloth," alone, demanded by the North
Vietnamese—200 million meters (124,274 miles)—was enough to circle Earth at
the equator *five times*. Viewed through the eyes of many Americans—including
a number of members of the House and Senate—delivery of this one item alone
would be tantamount to rewarding the Communists with a gift of over two
miles of "cloth" for every American killed during the war. And then, of course,
there were all of the other items on the North Vietnamese list.

A very bitter pill. A very tough sale, indeed.

CHAPTER 9

MID- TO LATE MARCH 1973

THE RETURNEE DEBRIEFS TELL OF HUNDREDS

OF AMERICAN POWs HELD BACK

. . .

Intelligence about unlisted, unreturned POWs was received in Washington
throughout mid- to late March. Some of that intelligence came from Southeast
Asia, but by far the most came from the debriefs of the American POWs already
released. By the time the last groups of listed POWs were being readied for release from Hanoi on March 27, 28, and 29, there should not have been any
question in any U.S. official's mind that the Communists—primarily the North

Vietnamese, but the Pathet Lao as well—were holding back significant numbers of American prisoners.

## THE MID- AND LATE MARCH INTELLIGENCE AND OTHER INFORMATION FROM SOUTHEAST ASIA ABOUT UNLISTED POWs

A classified report sent exclusively to Henry Kissinger from CIA Director James Schlesinger on March 20 revealed that a Vietcong lieutenant colonel who served on the military intelligence staff of VC Military Region 4 in South Vietnam had "said on 12 March 1973 that the figure of 585 U.S. POW's, which was released officially to the U.S. Government in its negotiations over the POW's, had been developed only as a 'bargaining figure' by the VC for negotiating purposes with the United States" and that in reality, "since the 1954 involvement of the United States in Vietnam, many additional POW's have been captured, and the prisoners not yet listed by the communists will be a subject of direct, secret negotiations between Hanoi and the United States." According to the CIA report, the VC lieutenant colonel said that "Hanoi will use these POW's as a 'bargaining tool' to obtain additional 'concessions' from the United States."[1]

On March 22, the White House received a classified cable from U.S. ambassador to Laos G. McMurtrie "Mac" Godley stating that "we believe the LPF [Lao Patriotic Front, the Pathet Lao] holds, throughout Laos, more prisoners than found on the DRV list."[2] On the 23rd, Godley sent another classified cable advising officials in Washington that a Swedish television crew had just reported to embassy personnel that a Pathet Lao official had informed them during a just-completed visit to Sam Neua Province that the PL currently held "[some U.S. POWs]."[3]

Press reports from Vientiane, meanwhile, suggested that the number of Americans held by the Pathet Lao might approximate one hundred. A UPI report published in *Pacific Stars and Stripes* on the 25th quoted U.S. sources in the Lao capital as saying they believed that perhaps as many as one hundred American prisoners "still may be alive" in Laos and noted concern among U.S. officials in Laos that the Pathet Lao planned to "hold them back as pawns in the continuing struggle in Indochina."[4] CBS News anchorman Walter Cronkite reported on the 26th from Vientiane that up to two hundred U.S. pilots had survived their shootdowns in Laos and that one hundred of them might still be alive in captivity.[5]

Valuable information for sure. But, it turned out, only a tiny fraction of what Washington already knew about the unlisted, unreturned POWs.

## WHAT THE RETURNEES HAD TOLD ABOUT UNLISTED AMERICAN PRISONERS

The matter of unlisted POWs had been among the first items raised by U.S. officials when they had debriefed the returnees during February and March. The returnees had been queried about unlisted prisoners on the planes leaving Hanoi, then at Clark Field during their stays there—stays that generally lasted three to five days—and finally during the more extensive debriefs that were conducted in stateside hospitals, etc., in the days following their return to the United States.

Once, twice, a third time, and perhaps again over a period of several weeks, the returnees had been grilled: "What do you know about other Americans not on the lists?"

An analysis of the returnees' responses had shown that:

- A number of returnees had reported that their wingman or fellow crew member had certainly or almost certainly been *killed during shootdown or had died from injuries sustained during ejection or at the hand of an unruly mob after landing.*
- A few of the returnees had reported that their wingman or fellow crew member had certainly or almost certainly *survived his loss incident* but had not for whatever reason shown up alive in the known prison system.
- Many returnees had told of one particular Air Force officer who had been *beaten to death* by guards following a failed escape attempt in Hanoi in 1969.
- A number of returnees had told of a small number of named prisoners who had *died in captivity from illness.*
- Many of the returnees had reported seeing, interacting with, or knowing about several named prisoners who were in very bad physical and/or mental condition and were *last known to be alive in Hanoi prisons or hospitals,* but whose names had not shown up on the lists of those prisoners to be returned. Some of the returnees had felt these men had *died in captivity;* others had stated they believed they *might still be alive.*
- One returnee, Capt. Douglas B. Peterson, USAF, who would later become the first postwar U.S. ambassador to Vietnam, had told of a perfectly healthy American prisoner who was *inexplicably segregated* from his fellow POWs at a Hanoi prison one evening and *never seen again.*[6]

Though the returnees' statements relative to these individual, named Americans had been helpful in solving isolated, specific cases, this information had done little to answer the larger question of the fates of the hundreds of men Brig. Gen. Tighe and his CINCPAC task force had expected to be released. The answers to that larger question, it turned out, were to be found in the written personal histories the returnees had created during their debriefing sessions.

## THE RETURNEES' PERSONAL HISTORIES

The personal histories the returnees had reconstructed with the assistance of their debriefers had described each man's experiences from the time just prior to his loss incident all the way up to his release and repatriation. For the returnees captured late in the war, the period covered in the personal history was comparatively short and the task of recounting all events and experiences relatively simple; for those captured during the Rolling Thunder campaign or in the South during the mid- to late 1960s, time in captivity was measured in years rather than months and the task more difficult.

Regardless of a returnee's period of confinement, each had recounted and documented to the best of his ability everything he had experienced—the events involving his loss incident, capture, field interrogation, movement to initial place of confinement, initial confinement, initial interrogation and torture if any, movement to subsequent place/places of confinement, subsequent interrogation and torture, medical treatment if any, communication and resistance methods employed, morale, diet, health, escape attempts, and any other matters of interest to the returnee or his debriefer.[7]

One of the first things Homecoming officials had done with the returnees' personal histories was carefully examine all information relating to the prisons in North Vietnam where the returnees said they had been held and the approximate dates the returnees reported they had been held in each. Officials first condensed this information into the following table:[8]

| NAME | LOCATION | DATES OF USE |
|---|---|---|
| *Alcatraz | North Central Hanoi | 25 Oct 67–9 Dec 69 |
| | | 1 Jul 70–17 Aug 70 |
| *Briarpatch | 33 miles WNW of Hanoi | 13 Sep 65–20 Sep 65 |
| | | 1 Dec 65–2 Feb 67 |
| | | 5 Feb 71–9 Jul 71 |
| **Camp Faith | 9 miles W of Hanoi | 14 Jul 70–24 Nov 70 |
| **Camp Hope (Son Tay) | 22 miles WNW of Hanoi | 23 May 68–14 Jul 70 |
| **Dirty Bird | Northern Hanoi | 29 Jun 67–25 Oct 67 |
| **Dogpatch | 105 miles NNE of Hanoi | 14 May 72–31 Jan 73 |
| ***Farnsworth | 18 miles SW of Hanoi | 29 Aug 68–25 Nov 70 |
| *Hanoi Hilton (Hoa Lo Prison) | Central Hanoi | 11 Aug 64–28 Mar 73 |
| *Mountain Camp (Mountain Retreat) | 40 miles NW of Hanoi | 12 Dec 71–28 Jan 73 |
| *Plantation | Northeast Hanoi | 6 Jun 67–30 Jul 70 |
| | | 25 Nov 70–16 Mar 73 |
| ***Rockpile | 32 miles S of Hanoi | 21 Jun 71–14 Feb 73 |
| *Skidrow | 6 miles SW of Hanoi | 7 Jul 68–19 Aug 71 |
| | | 9 Sep 71–4 Nov 71 |
| | | 16 Dec 71–1 Jan 72 |
| *Zoo | SW suburb of Hanoi | 20 Sep 65–26 Dec 70 |
| | | 8 Feb 71–10 Mar 71 |
| | | 14 Jun 71–10 Jul 71 |
| | | 24 Sep 71–29 Mar 73 |

*Camps used for detention of PWs captured both in North Vietnam and outside North Vietnam.

**Camps used exclusively for detention of PWs captured in North Vietnam.

***Camps used exclusively for detention of U.S. PWs captured outside Vietnam and subsequently moved to North Vietnam.

Then officials compared the information in the table to the wartime intelligence. It was these comparisons that proved beyond any doubt that the North Vietnamese were holding back hundreds of American POWs.

## THE COMPARISONS PROVE DEVASTATING

In retrospect, it is hard to imagine which of the revelations gleaned from the comparisons proved most stunning.

Surely at the top of the list was the fact that no returnee—not one—reported he had been detained at, on, under, or in the immediate vicinity of the Long Bien Bridge in Hanoi, even though a variety of independent wartime intelligence sources had reported American prisoners were being used to shield the bridge from U.S. attack (see Chapter 4).

And consider this: No returnee—not one—had reported being detained at any of the following other locations where wartime intelligence sources had also reported American POWs being deployed as human shields:

- the main Hanoi waterworks near the Hanoi thermal power plant
- the POW camp behind the Presidential Palace in northwest Hanoi
- the POW camp adjacent to the Ngoc Ha waterworks in the western part of Hanoi
- the Trung Qui Mo munitions factory in southwest Hanoi
- the detention compound at the Hanoi radio communications station just north of Bach Mai airfield
- the Ha Dong thermal power facility reportedly located just southwest of Hanoi
- the POW camp reported adjacent to the Nam Dinh thermal power plant in downtown Nam Dinh City, forty-five miles downriver from Hanoi
- the Song Thuong Bridge in Bac Giang City, thirty miles northeast of Hanoi
- the POW camp reported at Luu Xa, within the Thai Nguyen steel complex forty miles north of Hanoi
- the POW camp reported just north of the Phuc Yen MiG base north of the capital

Where were all these American POWs?

And where were the several hundred American POWs reported in the wartime intelligence to have been held within the walls of the MND Citadel compound in northwest Hanoi? Where were *they*? Ten returnees had reported they had been held at "Alcatraz," the small jail located directly behind 4 Ly Nam De Street in the Citadel compound's extreme northeast corner, but what of the several hundred other American POWs reported in the wartime intelligence as being held at other locations throughout the sprawling and heavily guarded "hidden city"? (See Chapter 4.) Where were these American POWs?

And what about all of the POWs reported in the wartime intelligence to have been detained as human shields at the Hanoi Thermal Power Plant ("Dirty Bird")? Where were they? Approximately thirty returnees had reported they had been held at the power plant for varying periods of time from late June until late October 1967, but the wartime intelligence had shown American POWs being held there not only during this period but also long before and long after.[9] So where were the other American prisoners, those reported by intelligence sources to have been held at the power plant in mid-April 1966, December 1966, and

February 1967—*long before* the returnees reported being held there—and in January 1968, July 1968 and during the Linebacker bombing campaign in 1972, *long after*? Were only the wartime intelligence sources who saw or told of U.S. POWs at the power plant from June to October of 1967 telling the truth?

The more one compared the information in the returnees' personal histories to the wartime intelligence, the more discrepancies one found. Though virtually all of the returnees had reported being detained at some point at Hanoi's Hoa Lo Prison ("Hanoi Hilton"), not one reported having been processed through or detained at the Hoa Lo Center, the reported interrogation and detention center for aircrewmen shot down over the North, which the wartime intelligence had indicated was located four blocks south of Hoa Lo Prison (see Chapter 4). Where were the American prisoners reported at this facility?

Though none of the returnees shot down in the North reported having been moved to Hanoi by helicopter or fixed-wing aircraft after capture, the wartime intelligence had indicated this had occurred on a number of occasions (see Chapter 4). Where were these men?

Though none of the returnees reported having been held in several specific temporary holding facility/transit camps in the North prior to transfer to Hanoi, several wartime intelligence sources had reported the presence of American POWs in these facilities (see Chapter 4). Where were these POWs?

Then there was the devastating news from the returnees who had been captured in South Vietnam and moved to North Vietnam for long-term confinement. (See Chapter 2 and www.enormouscrime.com, Chapter 2.) They had described their trip up the Ho Chi Minh Trail in detail that mirrored the wartime intelligence almost word-for-word—the *binh trams* and commo-liaison stations, the special food and medical care afforded the northbound American prisoners, the injured or sick Americans being carried on litters by their captors, the captured ARVN and the South Vietnamese children and other civilians moving north up the Trail along with the Americans, the PAVN moving south down the Trail, movement by train once inside North Vietnam, etc.[10] The catch was that only ninety-three (plus the one added later) American military personnel and twenty-seven civilians captured in the South were on the list to be released from Hanoi, but the wartime intelligence showed that more than one thousand American military personnel—and a small number of civilians—had been captured in South Vietnam and other southern battle areas and moved to North Vietnam for long-term detention. Where were the rest of the military prisoners from the South?

Additional analysis of information provided by the southern returnees released in Hanoi had shown that none had reported having been moved to North Vietnam by helicopter, fixed-wing aircraft, or Chinese freighter, as various wartime intelligence reports had indicated. Where were the men in these reports?

And what about the American POWs reported in the wartime intelligence to have been moved from time to time from PL prisons in Sam Neua Province, Laos, to Hanoi for long-term detention? (See Chapter 3.) None of the returnees had told of being held by the PL in Sam Neua and later being moved to Hanoi. Where were these American prisoners?

Where, indeed, were *all* these American prisoners?

The obvious answer was that if any of the wartime intelligence on POWs was to be believed—and much of it had been confirmed in both general and specific terms by the returnees—then the North Vietnamese had held them back—several hundred who had been captured in the North and hundreds more who had been captured on the battlefields of the South and later moved to North Vietnam for long-term confinement. The twin facts that these prisoners were not being returned by the North Vietnamese at Operation Homecoming—and that the U.S. government knew at the time they were not being returned—would for more than thirty years remain among the most closely guarded secrets of the Vietnam War.

By late March, then, information in U.S. policy makers' hands made it clear to all but the "purposely blind," that the North Vietnamese were holding hundreds of American POWs who were not going to be released at Operation Homecoming. It was surely equally clear, from the long history of the Paris negotiations and the five-year reconstruction plan the North Vietnamese had recently presented to the American side at the Joint Economic Commission talks in Paris, that it was going to cost Uncle Sam dearly—perhaps almost $5 billion—to get them back.

And then, of course, there was the matter of the POWs the United States believed the Pathet Lao were holding.

It would have been an extremely difficult proposition even in the best of times.

For Richard Nixon, late March 1973 was not the best of times.

CHAPTER 10

SPRING 1973

"A 'CANCER' ON THE PRESIDENCY"

. . .

Watergate came crashing down on Richard Nixon just as the final group of listed POWs was being readied for release in late March.

Nixon would later recall the precise moment it happened: It was just after 10:00 A.M. on Wednesday, March 21, when White House counsel John Dean informed him during a meeting in the Oval Office, "We have a cancer—within—close to the presidency."[1]

Dean went on to explain his statement by relating the following points he had established in a review of the scandal that Nixon had asked him to prepare.

- Acting under pressure from Nixon's trusted White House aide Charles Colson, an official at the Committee to Re-elect the President (CRP) had personally ordered the late May and mid-June 1972 break-ins at Democratic National Committee (DNC) Headquarters in Washington's Watergate complex. (It was the second break-in in June that had resulted in the arrests of the Watergate burglars.)

- Several members of the White House staff in addition to Colson had known of the break-ins in advance.
- Some members of the White House staff had received and utilized transcripts of intercepted messages picked up by a bug the GOP burglars had placed in a DNC office telephone during the first Watergate break-in.
- Following the arrests of Watergate burglars Howard Hunt, a former CIA agent who had worked in the White House up until sixty days before the first Watergate break-in, and James McCord, another former CIA man who was employed as security coordinator by the Committee to Re-elect the President at the time of the break-ins, members of the White House staff had offered clemency to both. Dean characterized these actions as "bad, . . . the very sort of thing that the Senate is going to be looking most for." (Sen. Sam J. Ervin's Senate Select Committee on Presidential Campaign Activities, the Ervin Committee, was investigating the break-ins.)
- In addition to offering clemency, some members of the White House staff had paid hush money to Hunt and McCord in an effort to buy their silence and prevent White House involvement in the burglaries from surfacing prior to the 1972 election. Dean told the president the money had been paid from a $350,000 White House "cash fund" after White House Chief of Staff H. R. Haldeman and Domestic Affairs Advisor John Ehrlichman had determined there was "no price too high to pay" to prevent disclosure prior to the election.
- Hunt, who along with McCord and the other Watergate burglars was to be sentenced two days later, was now demanding more money and threatening to "bring John Ehrlichman . . . to his knees and put him in jail" unless the funds were paid immediately. Dean informed the president that Hunt was referring to Ehrlichman's authorization of the 1971 burglary of Daniel Ellsberg's psychiatrist's office in Los Angeles, which Hunt had participated in, "and apparently some other things." Dean told Nixon that Hunt was demanding $122,000 and that the deadline for payment was "close of business yesterday."[2]

Nixon later recalled that he asked Dean how much money would be needed and that Dean estimated the payments for all the defendants would require a million dollars over the next two years. Nixon said he told Dean finding such a large amount of money would not be easy, but that he (Nixon) knew where we could get it. Then, calling Howard Hunt a "time bomb," Nixon asked Dean, "don't you have to handle Hunt's financial situation damn soon?" and then answered his own question, saying "You've got to keep the cap on the bottle that much in order to have any options—either that or you let it all blow right now." "At the moment," Nixon told Dean, "don't you agree that you'd better get the Hunt thing?" adding, "you've got no choice with Hunt but the 120 or whatever it is. Right? Would you agree that that's a buy-time thing, you better damn well get that done, but fast?"

"I think he ought to be given some signal . . . ," Dean replied.[3]

Tape recordings of the meeting subsequently revealed that Nixon told Dean twelve times that the money had to be paid to Hunt.[4] Nixon went on to write in his memoirs that after his meeting with Dean he "called Rose Woods [Nixon's personal secretary] and asked her if we had any unused campaign funds. She told me that we did—she would have to see how much. It turned out to be $100,000. . . ."[5]

The following day, hush money from an unstated source was paid to Hunt "via John Mitchell," Nixon's close friend and former attorney general who served as head of the Committee to Re-elect the President.[6]

*Friday, March 23*
## THE WATERGATE BURGLARS ARE SENTENCED

On Friday, two days after Nixon's damning insistence that hush money be paid to Howard Hunt, Hunt and the other Watergate burglars were brought before U.S. District Judge John J. Sirica in Washington for sentencing. In addition to Hunt, those scheduled to-be sentenced were McCord, G. Gordon Liddy, whom the press called the "mastermind" of the operation, and four anti-Castro CIA operatives from Miami known collectively to court watchers as "the Cubans." All seven defendants had been arrested during or shortly after the second Watergate break-in on June 17, 1972, and had subsequently been charged with conspiracy, burglary, wiretapping, and eavesdropping. Hunt and the Cubans had pleaded guilty to avoid trial; McCord and Liddy had fought the charges but had been found guilty in Sirica's court in late January 1973. Despite a number of offers of leniency in return for their testimony, all seven men had steadfastly refused to cooperate with prosecutors since their guilty pleas and/or convictions.

The sentencing hearing had barely gotten under way when Sirica announced that he had received a letter from McCord stating that he had decided to cooperate with Sirica and government prosecutors in an effort to minimize his punishment. Sirica then read McCord's letter aloud in open court.

McCord wrote that unnamed others had been involved in the burglary plot, that political pressure had been applied on him and the other defendants to plead guilty and remain silent, and that certain defense witnesses had perjured themselves during his and Liddy's trial. McCord concluded the letter by requesting a meeting with Sirica to further discuss the matters he had raised.[7]

After reading the letter aloud, Sirica announced that he had accepted McCord's offer and would meet with him the following week. Sirica also declared that he would feel free to disclose whatever McCord told him to both the Watergate grand jury and the Ervin Committee. He then postponed sentencing McCord until after the meeting.[8]

Liddy was then called forward to be sentenced. Sirica asked the former FBI agent if he wished to speak. "I have nothing to say, your honor," Liddy replied. Sirica offered Liddy a second opportunity to make a statement and again Liddy refused. Sirica sentenced Liddy to six years, eight months to twenty years in prison and fined him $40,000.[9] The unexpectedly harsh sentence elicited audible expressions of shock from courtroom spectators. Sirica declared that the sentence was designed as a deterrent to others, not for rehabilitation, and ordered Liddy back to jail pending his transfer to the federal penitentiary at Danbury, Connecticut.[10]

Sirica then turned his attention to Hunt and the Cubans. He began by conditionally imposing extremely harsh sentences—thirty-five years in prison and a $40,000 fine for Hunt and forty years in prison and a $50,000 fine for each of the Cubans—and then declared that he would defer final sentencing for three or more months in hopes that each of the defendants would decide to cooperate.[11] He ordered the five back to jail to consider his proposal.

As Liddy, Hunt, and the Cubans were being returned to jail, McCord left the courthouse in the company of his attorney and headed to a meeting with Samuel Dash, chief counsel to the Senate Watergate panel.

The unraveling of Watergate had begun.

## McCORD FINGERS DEAN • NIXON NOW EXPOSED

McCord met with Dash for three hours that Friday afternoon and again for three more on Saturday. On Sunday the 25th, Dash, in what Nixon would later call "a blatantly prejudicial move,"[12] called a news conference and announced that McCord had supplied him with additional names of persons involved in the Watergate cover-up and had begun offering "a full and honest account" of the conspiracy. Dash offered no specifics as to who the additional persons might be. He did say, however, that the Watergate committee might grant McCord immunity from further prosecution and added that he, Dash, planned to contact attorneys for the remaining six convicted men that day to ask them also to aid the committee's inquiry.[13]

Given the charged political atmosphere in Washington at the time, it is no wonder that the names McCord divulged to Dash were quickly leaked to the press. Nixon later wrote that he was at his villa in Key Biscayne, Florida, that Sunday when "we learned that the next morning's *Los Angeles Times* was going to report that McCord had 'told Senate investigators' that [CRP official Jeb Stuart] Magruder and Dean had had prior knowledge of the Watergate break-in."[14] Nixon, for good reason, was mortified. He had repeatedly insisted to Dean *only four days earlier* that hush money be paid to Hunt, and now Dean, having been fingered by McCord, would almost certainly be called to testify before the Watergate committee. If the committee granted Dean immunity, would he testify that the president of the United States had personally directed—in fact, insisted—that hush money be paid to one of the Watergate burglars? Nixon would later write that the *Times* article represented "a major new stage in my perception of the seriousness of the Watergate issue."[15]

The *Los Angeles Times* story appeared as scheduled the following day.[16] Haldeman joined Nixon at his villa for a strategy session that would end up lasting six hours. "The immediate question," Haldeman later wrote, "was Dean."[17]

At Nixon's direction, Haldeman phoned Dean to sound him out. Nixon later described the crucial Haldeman-Dean conversation: "[Haldeman told me that] Dean had said, 'The more I look at it, the more I am convinced that if we try to fight it we're going to lose eventually, and the longer we take to lose, the worse we are going to look.' Dean told Haldeman that we should revive the idea of going before a grand jury to talk about everything, without invoking executive privilege."[18]

The news about Dean was devastating. Dean had to be contained, but how? Nixon and Haldeman continued discussing the matter for several more hours but could not reach a decision. They returned to Washington late that night to continue their discussions.

*March 27, Washington*
## A MATTER OF SCHEDULING?

Nixon and Haldeman were greeted upon their return to work the following morning by an article in *The Washington Post* trumpeting the fact that now even the Republican members of the Senate Watergate Committee were calling for Dean to appear before the committee in public session. The *Post* also reported that the committee had voted to allow live television coverage of the hearings.[19]

Nixon met with Haldeman and Ehrlichman and press secretary Ronald Zeigler in the Oval Office shortly after 11:00 A.M. to discuss ways to head off any appearance by Dean before the committee. Nixon later wrote that he and the group "considered an idea that Dean [himself] had [long before] suggested of appointing a special presidential commission with extraordinary powers that would be structured somewhat like the Warren Commission that had investigated President Kennedy's assassination."[20] Under this scenario, Haldeman wrote in his diary at the time, Nixon would create what Haldeman called a "superpanel" [sic] and would give it power to "remove Federal employees, levy fines, and [im]pose criminal sanctions, etc." Everyone involved in the Watergate scandal, Haldeman went on to explain, would agree to waive trial by jury and "tell everything" to the panel in secret sessions. As envisioned by Haldeman, panel members would then deliberate each case and render their decisions. "Proceedings in secret, decisions final," Haldeman wrote in his diary, adding that the advantages of having such a panel were twofold: "One, nothing will be done until after the '74 elections, and two the P [president] maintains the ultimate stroke with the power to pardon at a later point. . . ."[21]

Nixon, already planning to address the nation following the scheduled release of the last group of POWs by Hanoi later in the week, told those assembled that before making any announcement of a "Watergate Commission," he wanted "to get Vietnam out of the way." A partial transcript of a tape recording of the meeting shows this exchange between Nixon and Ehrlichman, the latter apparently making reference to the *Post* articles:

EHRLICHMAN: This story and, uh, this one, uh, this, this Watergate thing is
    potentially very debilitating around, but we have to devote a large part of
    our time to keeping people busy in, uh . . .
PRESIDENT: I know. . . .
PRESIDENT: . . . I don't believe that I should go out on national television like
    tonight or tomorrow and go out on the Watergate Commission and then
    come on the next day on national television on Vietnam. . . . My view
    would be to get Vietnam out of the way, and maybe get this right if you
    could. I think that gives you time."[22]

The plan, then, appears to have been that the president would address the nation on Vietnam as planned on Thursday the 29th and, as he put it, "get Vietnam out of the way." Then there would be time to deal with Watergate. But what did the president mean when he said "get Vietnam out of the way"? Was he simply proposing a schedule; prioritizing the tasks that lay before him, saying, "Let's do Vietnam first, then Watergate"? Or did he have, as critics would later charge, something more sinister in mind?

## GETTING VIETNAM OUT OF THE WAY

The last of the listed American POWs—sixty-seven in number—were released by the North Vietnamese as scheduled on Thursday, March 29. The men departed from Hanoi's Gia Lam field in two USAF C-141s, the final plane lifting off at approximately 4:00 P.M. local time (4:00 A.M. Thursday Washington time).[23]

At 9:00 P.M. that evening, the president, as planned, addressed the nation from the Oval Office. Noting that when he had taken office over four years before, "five hundred and fifty thousand Americans were in Vietnam . . . [and] hundreds were held as prisoners of war in North Vietnam." Nixon declared that "the day we have all worked and prayed for has finally come. For the first time in 12 years, no American military forces are in Vietnam. All of our American POW's are now on their way home." He added, "There are still some problem areas, [including] . . . an accounting for all missing in action in Indochina."[24]

Critics would later charge that Nixon's declaration to the nation that "all of our American POWs are now on their way home," coming as it did on the heels of his earlier statement to Ehrlichman that he wanted to "get Vietnam out of the way," suggested he had deliberately and knowingly written off the unlisted, unreturned POWs so he could concentrate on saving his threatened presidency. In the early 1990s, Nixon would respond to this explosive charge by saying that his comment to Ehrlichman had been taken out of context.[25] Kissinger, weighing in on Nixon's behalf, would declare at the same time that all he and the president knew about unreleased POWs was that the provisions of the Paris accords relative to the MIAs had not, as Nixon had stated in his address, been complied with.[26]

Nixon's deeds in the days just after his March 29 speech would lend credence to the critics' charge and belie his and Kissinger's later explanation.

## POWs REPORTED ALIVE IN SOUTHEAST ASIA

On April 9, less than two weeks after the president had informed the nation that the war was over and that all the POWs were on their way home, newspapers came alive with reports of American servicemen still held captive in Southeast Asia.

*Pacific Stars and Stripes* ran an AP story that morning reporting that ARVN soldiers recently released from North Vietnamese prisons had returned home and said that American prisoners of war were still being held in Communist camps in remote areas of North Vietnam. The *Stars and Stripes* report, filed from

Saigon, said the ARVNs had recently seen the Americans in prison camps in the Chinese border provinces of Cao Bang and Lang Son and in Thai Nguyen Province north of Hanoi. AP added that "there is a widely held belief among U.S. officials in Indochina that additional American POWs may be held in Communist jungle and mountain camps."[27]

Much closer to home that day, *The New York Times* and the *Chicago Tribune* reported that a Chicago woman, Mrs. Phyllis Allard, was saying that she was certain her son and perhaps as many as twenty-five other U.S. servicemen she had seen with him in a prison camp in Cambodia in 1972 were still being held prisoner by the Communists. Allard's son, Spec. 4 Richard M. Allard, USA, who had been carried as missing in action since the crash of his helicopter near the South Vietnamese–Cambodian border in 1967, had not been among the POWs released at Operation Homecoming.[28]

The *Times* account of the Allard story read in part:

Chicago, April 8 (AP)—A chicago [*sic*] woman says she is certain that American soldiers are being held as prisoners in Cambodia because she saw her son while he was a prisoner in a Cambodian prison camp.

Specialist 4 Richard M. Allard is listed as missing in action by the Army. The Pentagon, asked for comment, said that it was unaware of his being held in Cambodia.

Mrs. Allard . . . told the story of a visit to Indochina in January 1972. . . . She said she and her three other children had previously identified Specialist Allard from film clips released by the Viet Cong. . . .

"They walked me . . . into a room. I was there alone.

"Then an official and a man in uniform with a rifle helped my son into the room. They let go of him and I saw that he had difficulty walking. He was very weak. I went over to him to help hold him up and I touched him. . . ."

Mrs. Allard said she told her casualty assistance officer, Capt. Robert Morris, of her trip when she returned.

"They questioned me, then I didn't hear for two months, three months," she said.

Mrs. Allard said the big question in her mind now was, "Since I saw him, why does our Government continue to say there are no such places where our men are? When I went through the hallways of the prison camp, I saw about 25 men, all tied up."

Arthur C. Egan, Jr., a reporter for The New Hampshire Sunday News, which published a story about Mrs. Allard today, said he talked to a high ranking officer at Fort Sheridan, Ill., about the case.

Mr. Egan said that the military official asked that his name be withheld and said that the only reason the Pentagon would not fully confirm the story was "then that would be admitting the Communists are still holding American P.O.W.'s."[29]

*The Washington Evening Star* featured an expanded version of the Allard story later that afternoon. The front-page article was accompanied by a large picture of the youthful, attractive Mrs. Allard clutching her passport and travel documents and gazing at photos of her son laid out before her. "I saw my son. I touched him. I talked to him and I saw at least 25 other men there," she declared in the lengthy article. The *Star* reported that a Pentagon spokesman, when asked by the Associated Press whether it was possible Allard "is or has been a prisoner in Cambodia," he replied, "We're not speculating on the possible. We're left with only one thing. We just don't know."[30]

### April 11, 12:04–12:29 P.M.: *The Oval Office*
### "IT IS BETTER . . . TO BE CERTAIN . . . THAN IT IS TO BE UNCERTAIN"

At noon on April 11, two days after the press articles about living POWs, Dr. Roger Shields, the Pentagon official in charge of POW recovery operations, came to the White House to meet privately with Nixon and Deputy National Security Advisor Brent Scowcroft in the Oval Office. Scowcroft wrote at the time that Shields had been summoned so that the president could "thank [him] for his work on the POW/MIA issue and discuss the results of Operation Homecoming."[31] Transcripts of tape recordings of the meeting obtained from the National Archives in 1997 reveal, however, that Nixon had far more to say to Shields than just a simple "thank-you."

After the participants posed for pictures, Nixon told the thirty-three-year-old Shields that he thought it would "be useful to get a little firsthand report from you."[32] After additional introductory remarks by the president, Shields began to describe what had taken place when he had gone to Hanoi to help pick up the first group of POWs released on February 12.

"Now, Mr. President, I wish you could have been in Hanoi when that first . . . bus came around the corner," the assistant to an assistant secretary of defense told the president. ". . . To see those men, ah, I could have flown back to Clark without the use of the airplane. It was the greatest point of my life."

Nixon responded, "But what, but what, how did, tell me about it."[33] Shields continued with an emotion-packed discourse. When he had finished, Nixon got to the point of the meeting.

"You, ah, incidentally, you, you are working on the MIA?" the president asked. When Shields responded that he was, Nixon said, "[T]he, ah, the main thing there, of course, is to just [unintelligible] be known that these bastards probably aren't going to come out with anything. Ah, we have got to make an enormous effort in the public relations sense as well as what we do, ah, as I'm sure you know . . . I mean letters to the MIA [families]."[34]

Continuing, Nixon said:

I can think of those families that have waited so long, always hoping, and, of course, always wondering, you know . . . well, maybe, maybe somebody's alive. . . . I think the main thing is certainty . . . and I am in a . . . mood on that to say, look, it's over now, it's over, we can't find them. . . . They've got to figure we are doing everything we can to be sure that we have found everybody. But on the other hand, we must not destroy the certainty that they have. It is better to be certain, the man is gone, than it is to be uncertain. . . .

Follow up, follow up okay? . . . That's all. You go all that way to get all of that
behind us [unintelligible] you know what I mean."[35]

Shields held a press conference at the Pentagon the day after his Oval Office
meeting with Nixon and Scowcroft. When asked about the possibility that some
POWs might still be alive, Shields declared, "We have no indication at this time
that there are any Americans alive in Indochina."[36] The resulting headline and
lead paragraph on page A10 in the next morning's *Washington Post* could well
have been written by the president himself: "All U.S. POWs Free, Pentagon
Maintains," the headline read. Below it, the article began, "The Pentagon said
yesterday it has no evidence there are any more U.S. prisoners of war still alive
in Indochina."

Similar stories with similar headlines appeared in newspapers around the
country and at military bases around the world. " 'No More POWs in Indochina,' " the *San Francisco Examiner* declared. "US Thinks POW Account Now
Closed," the *Boston Evening Globe* reported. *Pacific Stars and Stripes* informed its
readers, "POW Unit Boss: No Living GI's Left in Indochina."

For the second time in as many weeks, Richard Nixon had sentenced the unlisted, unreturned POWs to life in Asian prisons without parole. This time, in a
move laced with irony, he had enlisted the services of a man named Shields to
help him do the deed.

## "THERE WAS NO CHOICE BUT TO FOLLOW HIS DIRECTIVE"

To the obvious dismay of U.S. officials, the problem of the unlisted, unreturned
POWs reared its ugly head again in late spring when a PAVN defector told U.S.
newsmen in Saigon that he had personally seen "six prisoners whom he believed
were Americans who had not yet been released." In a move that would become
standard procedure in dealing with similar accounts of unreturned POWs in the
future, American officials implored the press to play down defectors' statements
about living POWs. A U.S. embassy telegram to the secretary of state and National
Security Council (NSC) officials in the White House explained what occurred:

> NVA rallier/defector Nguyen Thanh Son was surfaced by GVN to press June 8
> in Saigon. In follow on interview with AP, UPI and NBC American corre-
> spondents, questions elicited information that he had seen six prisoners
> whom he believed were Americans who had not yet been released. American
> officer present at interview requested news services to play down details; AP
> mention was consistent with embargo request, while UPI and NBC after talk
> with embassy press officer omitted item entirely from their stories. . . . [37]

The impact U.S. officials had had on the UPI and NBC correspondents present
at the interview was explained clearly in the embassy telegram. The impact on
the AP correspondent soon became evident when the AP account appeared in
*The New York Times* under the headline "Told to Attack Peace Units, Alleged Defector Reports." The article began with the statement "A man identified as a
North Vietnamese junior officer who said he had defected to South Vietnam said

today that he had been ordered to attack international peacekeeping planes and convoys investigating alleged Communist violations," and then, omitting any mention of the fact that the defector, Nguyen Tan Son, had said he had personally observed six prisoners whom he believed were Americans who had not yet been released, quoted Son as saying he believed the North Vietnamese were still holding some American prisoners. "They want to keep United States prisoners because there are many problems to be settled with the United States Government," the article quoted Son as saying. "They want to keep prisoners in case the United States Government launches war again. They will have some prisoners."[38]

For *New York Times* readers, the AP account was, admittedly, a story about American prisoners, but hardly the eyewitness account reported by the defector.

Had it all been just everyday Saigon embassy spin control, just another edition of the infamous wartime "five o'clock follies"? Or, as critics would later charge, had word been passed down the official chain of command—from the president to the Pentagon and State Department and then to the U.S. embassy in Saigon—that there were to be no living, unreturned POWs and that everyone should act accordingly? Nixon's assistant secretary of defense for legislative affairs during 1972 and 1973, John O. "Jack" Marsh, the highly respected former conservative Democratic congressman from Virginia who would later serve as a key White House advisor to President Gerald R. Ford and as secretary of the army for eight years under Ronald Reagan, would later offer this insight:

> Watergate hit the White House just as the POWs were repatriated. I believe . . . President Nixon fully intended to negotiate for remaining POWs plus bodies, check of crash sites and accounting for all MIAs. It seems obvious that his attention had to shift, if not for his own good, at least for what he must have felt was the image in the world of the U.S.
>
> What really happened?
>
> He was commander-in-chief. If he asked that the position of the DoD and State Department be "we have no reason to believe there are more POWs in Indochina," there was no choice but to follow his directive. Right?[39]

On June 15, the president, speaking at the unveiling of the cornerstone of the Everett McKinley Dirksen Congressional Leadership Research Center in Pekin, Illinois, declared "for the first time in 8 years, all our prisoners of war are home here in America."[40]

SPRING, SUMMER, AND FALL 1973
THE COLLAPSE OF THE JEC TALKS • THE
COLLAPSE OF THE PARIS PEACE ACCORDS

. . .

Despite all the torture and mistreatment we received as prisoners of war, I
would not now personally oppose reconstruction aid to North Vietnam, as I
understand it is envisioned by the President. . . .

If they can get that from the United States, in terms of the three-four-five
billion dollars President Nixon is talking about—a fraction of the budget we
were putting out for the war year by year—I think we would have accomplished a great thing in preserving peace.

—CAPT. JEREMIAH A. DENTON JR., USN, "Capt. Denton's Own Story,
An Ex-POW Remembers"

The Nixon administration remained under siege throughout the spring. Haldeman and Ehrlichman had been forced to resign in late April, and FBI agents had
been dispatched to the West Wing to guard their offices and files. By June, investigators were closing in on many fronts. Nixon later recalled that by this
time formal inquiries were being conducted by the Ervin Committee and four
other congressional committees; the FBI; the General Accounting Office; grand
juries in Los Angeles, New York, Florida and, Texas; and the Miami, Florida, district attorney's office. In addition, more than a dozen civil suits had been filed
against the Watergate burglars and conspirators, other current and former
White House and CRP officials, and the CRP itself. At the offices of *The Washington Post*, meanwhile, a crack team of investigative reporters and editors
churned out one damaging story after another.

Deprived of the counsel of his two most trusted advisors and overwhelmed
by the forces arrayed against him, Nixon turned the day-to-day operations of
the White House over to Haig, whom he had chosen to replace Haldeman as
chief of staff, and foreign policy and national security decision making over to
Kissinger. Kissinger later recalled that the transfer of power to him was so complete that he became, in his own words, "endowed with quasi-presidential authority" in matters of foreign policy and national security affairs.[1] "I . . . found
myself in a truly extraordinary position," Kissinger later said of the time. "I . . .
had become a Presidential surrogate."[2]

From late spring on, there was no question in anyone's mind who was running American foreign policy. It was, by turn of fate—and by his own
admission—Henry Kissinger.

## BREAKING THE BAD NEWS TO THE NORTH VIETNAMESE

Throughout the spring, the North Vietnamese had continued to anticipate the reconstruction aid pledged to them in the Paris accords and in the still-secret Nixon letter. They considered the aid a solemn obligation of the United States, and though they were well aware that stories of torture told by the returnees had soured any chance that Congress might approve such aid, they were counting on Nixon to grant the aid by executive order, something Secretary of State William Rogers had earlier publicly refused to rule out.[3] By June, however, they began to see that Nixon might not survive in office, and they grew restive and began pressing hard for the money that had been promised them. It fell to Kissinger, the surrogate president, to convey the bad news that there would be no aid—under any circumstances, from any account, or through any channel.

Kissinger's task was daunting for a number of reasons, not the least of which was that failure to pay the aid would constitute a material violation of the Paris accords, something Kissinger sought to avoid if at all possible. To avoid such an outright violation, Kissinger, according to his closest aide at the Paris talks, Winston Lord, decided that the United States would not confront the North Vietnamese with a flat out "no" on aid but would instead, in Lord's words, "play them along" at the JEC talks with no intention of ever reaching a final decision. Lord told Senate investigators in 1992 that the thinking was, "[S]crew these guys; they're not going to get any money out of us; we'll just play them along with this endless commission and talk and vagueness. . . . The game was to play it out in a vague way that would take forever."[4]

As a first step in the "game," Kissinger had temporarily suspended the aid talks earlier in the spring, citing alleged North Vietnamese "violations" of the accords. However, when warned by Le Duc Tho in May that North Vietnamese patience was growing thin, Kissinger had flown to Paris for an extended series of meetings with Tho. In a joint communiqué issued at the conclusion of these talks on June 13, Kissinger had publicly pledged that the U.S. delegation would return to the JEC talks within four days and would complete work on the first phase of the aid program for North Vietnam by July 2.[5]

The official declassified U.S. record shows that when the JEC talks reconvened in secret session in Paris on June 18—the first such session since the North Vietnamese had presented their five-year plan to the U.S. side back on March 23—the chief North Vietnamese delegate, Finance Minister Chau, "continually stressed urgency and sought to speed up review for completion of all major substantive issues" within one week. The chief of the U.S. delegation, Maurice J. Williams, however, demurred, informing Chau that before the United States was to fulfill its obligation to contribute postwar aid to the DRV, the DRV must first prevail on its ally the Khmer Rouge to agree to an immediate cease-fire in Cambodia.[6]

Clearly disappointed by Williams's demand but intent on resolving the aid issue quickly, Chau responded the following day by scaling back North Vietnam's request for aid in a number of categories that were considered sensitive by the

U.S. side, placing more emphasis on housing and other civilian needs and less on heavy industrial projects.[7] Unmoved by the conciliatory gesture, Williams again demurred, reiterating that the North Vietnamese would have to secure a cease-fire in Cambodia before any final aid program could be approved. The matters of aid and a Cambodian cease-fire were, he told Chau, "inseparable."[8]

At the next meeting of the JEC on June 22, Chau again urged the U.S. side to "complete its operations with all possible speed."[9] On the 29th, with the July 2 deadline rapidly approaching and no aid plan in sight, Chau again expressed concern over the pace of the talks and again stressed the urgency of the U.S. side developing a concrete aid proposal.[10] A classified report written at the time by members of the U.S. delegation noted that this emphasis on urgency was one of the "cardinal principles" advanced by the DRV. Another was the "allegation that US assistance to DRV is a special moral obligation distinguishing it from conventional aid programs."[11]

The North Vietnamese grew testy when the July 2 deadline came and went without any movement from the U.S. side. On July 5, three days after the deadline, Chau resorted to polemics, accusing Williams and the United States of not respecting the agreed-upon agenda and of lacking "serious intent." He further declared that his government "would insist that agreements be reached rapidly and duly recorded in formal, signed documents."[12]

When a week passed and still there was no agreement, Chau demanded that a definite date be set for beginning implementation of the first year's portion of the five-year aid plan he had presented back in March. Williams telegrammed Washington that "Chau has not attempted to disguise his rancor and deep suspicions" over the delays and reported that Chau had lent "special emphasis" to the matter of setting a definite date, "terming it the *sine qua non* of successful negotiations."[13] Several days later, Williams further reported that Chau's deputy had informed members of the U.S. team "that stipulating an effective date was for the DRVN the acid test of U.S. credibility." Unmoved, Williams responded to the North Vietnamese statement by stressing to Chau the need for congressional approval of any aid program and of the fact that "our efforts will not bear fruit in terms of reconstruction assistance from the U.S., unless the DRV contributes more actively to a settlement in Laos and Cambodia."[14]

By mid-July, the talks were at a critical point. At the technical level, where day-to-day meetings had continued in the shadow of the back-and-forth policy debate between Williams and Chau, experts had finally come to agreement on the specific items that would be included in any first-year aid plan the U.S. side might approve.[15] The U.S. side estimated the cost of this first-year program to be in the range of $600 million to $1 billion.[16] Clearly sensing that a resolution might be near, Chau advised Williams on the 19th that he wished to conclude and sign an agreement "this week." Williams, however, again rebuffed Chau, telling him that "no further progress would be possible in moving forward a reconstruction proposal without tangible progress on a settlement in Laos" and warning him that before any agreement could be implemented there would have to be "(a) Congressional appropriation of funds, (b) conclusion of a Bilateral Country Agreement, (c) conclusion of a Program Agreement, (d) agreement on appropriate JEC mechanism for implementation including the possible stationing of American officials in Hanoi—all of these and several other steps preceding the opening by the United States of letters of commitment which would permit the purchase and shipment of goods, from the United States to North Vietnam."[17]

The imposition of these additional conditions proved too much for the Vietnamese. On July 23, Chau called for a recess in the talks and announced he was returning to Hanoi for consultations. He issued a statement prior to his departure accusing the United States of having "deliberately raised all kinds of obstructions to drag on the talks and thereby prevent the signing of the documents on the agreed questions."[18] Radio Hanoi quickly joined in the fray, demanding that the United States "scrupulously implement Article 21 of the Paris agreement" and warning that "the United States must bear responsibility for the delay in the work of the joint economic commission."[19]

The North Vietnamese walkout was apparently just what Kissinger had hoped for. U.S. officials responded by putting the word out that the United States was in no hurry to grant any aid to North Vietnam—and then insulted the North Vietnamese by announcing that Williams would soon be heading to Upper Volta to discuss a U.S. aid program for the "severe drought" affecting that country.[20]

With that, the deliberations of the Joint Economic Commission ended. The commission would never meet again. Kissinger and his team had won the "game"—there would be no treaty violation, neither would there be any aid. A win-win for the U.S. side. Total victory.

But at what cost?

*September 1973*
## ENTER COMRADE FIDEL

Though Kissinger would declare in the third volume of his memoirs published in 1999 that "all evidence at the time and even more since in the various accounts of the North Vietnamese commanders leaves no doubt that Hanoi was preparing for a military showdown from the day the peace accords were signed,"[21] many Indochina experts familiar with the proceedings of the Joint Economic Commission have long believed it was the demise of the commission in late July that led directly to the demise of South Vietnam. And why not? Kissinger had stated in an earlier volume of his memoirs (1982) that Pham Van Dong told him during their discussions on postwar aid in Hanoi in February 1973 that the North Vietnamese wanted to establish a new, long-term relationship with the United States and would implement the Paris agreement scrupulously, but warned him that if a new relationship did not develop between the two countries on a solid basis of mutual interest, the Paris agreement would be "only a temporary stabilization of the situation, only a respite." Kissinger considered Dong's statement to be "an ominous hint of renewed warfare."[22]

An expert familiar with the proceedings of the JEC, D. Gareth Porter, Ph.D., author of *A Peace Denied: The United States, Vietnam and the Paris Agreement,* editor of the two-volume collection of Vietnam-era documents *Vietnam: The Definitive Documentation of Human Decisions,* and a consultant to a congressional committee that investigated the matter of the POWs and MIAs in the mid-1970s, wrote in 1977:

> There was every reason to believe that Hanoi was interested in seeing the military provisions of the agreement fully implemented. Secretary of State William Rogers testified before a Congressional committee on June 5, 1973: "We find that the North Vietnamese are conducting themselves as if they want the Paris Agreement to be carried out, and . . . in a way that suggests that they have come to the conclusion that continuation of military activities does not make sense." Rogers added that he thought Hanoi was "looking forward to programs of rehabilitation, reconstruction."
> . . . Kissinger's refusal to keep his end of the bargain took away the last incentive which Hanoi had to maintain a defensive military posture in the South, and led ultimately to the drive that brought Saigon's collapse."[23]

A series of events that occurred in the weeks immediately following the North Vietnamese walkout at the JEC talks suggests that Dr. Porter—not Dr. Kissinger—had it figured right.

The first of these events occurred in early September, when Cuban Premier Fidel Castro traveled to the Summit Conference of Nonaligned Countries in Algiers and called on all in attendance to join with Cuba in providing money and manpower to help rebuild Vietnam.[24] Following the summit, Castro flew to Hanoi where, speaking at a welcoming banquet given in his honor, he told Vietnamese leaders about the plea he had put forth on their behalf in Algiers, declared that he had been pleased by the response, and formally announced that Cuba would henceforth assist in the reconstruction of Vietnam and, that as part of that effort, would send "labour brigades" to Vietnam to "take part in rebuilding hospitals, agricultural and stockbreeding centres and communication lines and other activities."[25]

Why, now, this move by the Cubans and the nonaligned nations to rebuild Vietnam? Had the North Vietnamese really and truly given up all hope of receiving the reconstruction aid promised them by the Americans at Paris? And if so, what did all this mean for the future of the accords, the cease-fire, the South, the region?

Two days after his arrival in Hanoi, Castro, in the company of Premier Pham Van Dong and other Vietnamese leaders, flew to Dong Hoi in war-ravaged Quang Binh Province located just north of the DMZ. After a side trip to the still-devastated village of Vinh Linh, where near-constant Allied bombing and shelling had forced villagers to live around-the-clock for years in underground tunnels, Castro informed Communist party officials and military leaders of his efforts at the Algiers summit and outlined how his country would, as part of a larger program to rebuild war-damaged facilities and restore the cities of Vietnam, build a new hospital in Dong Hoi.[26] Then, leaving Pham Van Dong behind, the following day the Cuban leader and members of his delegation and a team of lower-ranking North Vietnamese officials set out overland to the DMZ and entered South Vietnam to rally PAVN and Vietcong troops stationed there.

Communist press accounts filed at the time indicate that the Cuban leader first traveled to the city of Dong Ha—which had been under joint PAVN/VC control for many months—and while there conducted a walking tour of portions of the city, talked informally with some of the citizenry, and "watched the intense and animated actions of the workers of the liberation communications branch, who were rapidly repairing the bridge . . . which had fallen into the riverbed.[27]

Castro proceeded west along Route 9 to meet with soldiers at a cluster of firebases near Cam Lo and to attend a ceremony in his honor at nearby "historic Hill 241," where the Communists had reportedly scored a major victory during the Easter Invasion. Liberation Radio reported that at the first firebase, Castro, "standing on the roof [of] a ferroconcrete bunker surrounded by sandbags piled meters wide at Tong Lam firebase, a strong point on the McNamara electronic defense line, . . . met many heroes who had come here from various different regions to welcome the Cuban guests." Castro then moved to another firebase nearby, where "various armed units of the province [had] assembled . . . with guns in hands" to welcome him. Liberation Radio later described how, "listening to stories about battles against the Americans, while standing right on top of a U.S. bunker, Prime Minister Fidel was constantly smiling with immense satisfaction. He said: each victory of Vietnam is also a victory for the Cuban people."[28]

Castro then attended the public rally, where citizens from throughout the province greeted him with flags, applause, and shouts of "Vietnam—Cuba! Long live Fidel!"[29] Introduced by a Communist official who praised him for being the first leader of a friendly country to visit the liberated areas of South Vietnam—an act the official described as "an event of extremely great significance that will vigorously encourage the South Vietnamese people to advance in the new stage"—Castro responded with lengthy praise for the Communists' victories over the French, the Americans, and the "puppet" forces of the Republic of Vietnam, and then told those in attendance that, in view of these "initial victories . . . the complete liberation of South Vietnam and peaceful reunification of your country are just a matter of time." In closing, he quoted Ho Chi Minh's famous statement that "after the U.S. aggressors are defeated, we will rebuild Vietnam 10 times more beautiful" and assured his audience that the Cuban people were "constantly and closely" with them in their effort to rebuild their country.[30]

Liberation Radio reported that following his speech, "Prime Minister Fidel—clad in a military uniform of the same color as those worn by the South Vietnamese Liberation Armed Forces combatants and wearing the Dien Bien Phu Victory Badge—left the rostrum and rejoined the liberation soldiers. The prime minister took from the hands of one of our combatants the traditional [battle] flag of his unit with its sparkling medals and held it high, very high, as if he was advancing along with our combatants."[31]

Liberation Radio went on to report that the soldiers then presented Castro and members of his delegation with "war trophies . . . some M-79's . . . some M-16s—U.S. fast-firing automatic rifles, . . . an old gun of the guerrillas in Hai Thong village, a heroic unit which had scored a great achievement in annihilating U.S. air cavalrymen . . . [and] a traditional unit flag which had been carried through many violent battles." Not to be outdone, officials of the Provisional

Revolutionary Government (the PRG, the Communist government that, in name at least, ruled the Communist-controlled areas of the South), presented Castro and his delegation with "an M-48 tank, a large, modern U.S. tank, which the southern armed forces and people had captured during their battle to liberate Quang Tri."[32]

Liberation Radio reported that shortly after his speech, Castro and members of his delegation "left the liberated areas for home." Concluding its coverage of the Cuban leader's historic visit—and underscoring the impact the visit had on the southern Communists—the announcer closed with these words: "The image, words and gestures of Prime Minister Fidel Castro, the first top leader of the party and government of a socialist country in the Western Hemisphere to set foot in the southern liberated land, have brought strong encouragement to the South Vietnamese people and further hardened their conviction in final victory. In this land of the heroic south, the voice of Fidel, the voice of the world peoples who support Vietnam in its anti-U.S. national salvation struggle, will forever resound."[33]

Why, now, had Castro, blood brother to the North Vietnamese, long their most trusted and respected comrade-in-arms, their most revered friend—and now a leader in the effort to rebuild their country—traveled into South Vietnam to rally the Communist troops stationed there? Rally them for *what*?

For those who might have asked that question at the time, a plausible answer would not be long in coming.

## THE NORTH VIETNAMESE MOVE TO TAKE THE SOUTH BY FORCE

Fidel Castro had been gone only several weeks when, in early October, members of the Central Committee of the North Vietnamese Communist party met in Hanoi and officially decided to take the South by force.

Or, as British historian and Vo Nguyen Giap biographer Peter Macdonald later put it, decided to give "priority to a military offensive [in the South] instead of emphasizing political warfare."[34]

Or, as PAVN General Van Tien Dung (pronounced "Zung"), who would later direct the assault on the South and the capture of Saigon, said in his postwar account of the period, *Our Great Spring Victory,* "They [the members of the Central Committee] . . . pointed out clearly: 'The revolutionary road for the South is the road of revolutionary violence. Whatever the situation, we must seize the opportune moment [in Vietnamese, this is *thoi co,* a fundamental concept in military strategy], maintain a course of strategic [military] offensive, and give active guidance to advance the revolution in the South. The problems of gaining people, gaining administrative control, and developing the real strength of the revolution are the urgent and basic demands in the new phase.' "[35] [Though not well known in the West, Dung had served at Giap's right hand since the earliest days of the revolution. One of Giap's key commanders at Dien Bien Phu in 1954, Dung had headed the Vietminh delegation to truce negotiations convened at Trung Gia, north of Hanoi, after Dien Bien Phu, and had then led victorious Vietminh troops across the Paul Doumer Bridge to take control of

Hanoi. Later in 1954, Dung had been appointed PAVN chief of staff, a position he would hold until 1974, when he would replace Giap as PAVN commander in Chief.][36]

Peter Macdonald later wrote that once the decision had been made, "the stage was set for the final act—the liberation of the South."[37] Richard Nixon, in *No More Vietnams,* later wrote that immediately following the decision, "Hanoi's leaders sent orders to its military commanders to start going on the offensive. It was the beginning of the third Vietnam War."[38]

Hanoi's order to fight was announced by the Vietnam News Agency (VNA) in Hanoi on October 15. The brief order directed "all officers and men of the main forces army, the regional army, the militia, and all guerrilla, home-guard and security forces across South Vietnam to . . . fight back at the Saigon administration . . . [at] any place and with appropriate forms and force."[39]

When Communist forces in the South received the order, they quickly began moving from a generally defensive posture to the offense, and the "third Vietnam War," as Nixon called it, was under way.

## A REMARKABLE CASE OF POOR TIMING

On October 16, the day after VNA broadcast Hanoi's directive to Communist forces based in the South that they should begin offensive military operations, the Nobel Committee of the Norwegian Parliament, in what would go down as surely one of the greatest examples of poor timing ever recorded, bestowed the Nobel Peace Prize jointly upon Kissinger, who had recently been promoted to the post of U.S. secretary of state, and Le Duc Tho. Kissinger issued a formal statement saying that "nothing that has happened to me in public life has moved me more than this award."[40] Tho, however, his eyes now on another prize, declined the award. "When the Paris agreement on Vietnam is respected, guns are silenced, and peace is really restored in South Vietnam, I will consider the acceptance of this prize," he said in his letter rejecting the award.[41]

## A DRAMATIC, LAST-MINUTE AMERICAN EFFORT TO SAVE THE SOUTH AND THE UNLISTED, UNRETURNED POWs AS WELL

Indications are that in the days shortly after he received word that he had won the Nobel, Kissinger—surely having been informed of the North Vietnamese directive to the southern troops, and surely knowing that, thanks to his own performance at Paris, approximately two hundred thousand heavily armed PAVN troops remained in the South legally and that because of their presence there any full-scale conflict would inevitably lead to a Communist victory, and perhaps feeling also some degree of guilt or unease for planning to head off to Oslo to accept the Nobel Peace Prize under these circumstances—reportedly dispatched his military assistant, Maj. Robert "Bud" McFarlane, USMC, to meet with the Vietnamese, make amends, and put in place a process that he hoped would save the South and the unlisted, unreturned POWs as well.

According to what McFarlane would later tell two U.S. congressmen (Hendon and Rep. John LeBoutillier [R-NY]), he had been sent to meet with North Vietnamese officials sometime during the latter half of 1973 to offer them an initial sum of $100 million in medical aid if North Vietnam would return the American POWs they held. McFarlane explained to the North Vietnamese that the money would come from USAID funds and that the U.S. side intended that if they cooperated, the $100 million would be only the first tranche of postwar aid the U.S. government would provide. McFarlane said that he had told the North Vietnamese the funds were to be used to purchase medicine and medical supplies for the people of Vinh, the heavily bombed city located just north of Dong Hoi in the North Vietnamese panhandle. According to McFarlane, the Vietnamese had replied that they would report the offer to higher authorities and that he should return the following day for an official reply. McFarlane said that he had returned the next day as instructed but had been told by the Vietnamese, "[T]hanks, but we think we'll wait for the entire $4.75 billion." [McFarlane had a long career at the NSC. He joined the NSC staff in July 1973 as military assistant to Kissinger. When Kissinger took on the additional title of secretary of state and moved to the State Department in September 1973, McFarlane stayed at the NSC as a foreign policy specialist. He worked there under Kissinger's deputy, Brent Scowcroft, until both resigned following President Gerald Ford's defeat in the 1976 elections. In early 1982, McFarlane returned to the NSC as deputy to President Ronald Reagan's second national security advisor, Judge William Clark. McFarlane succeeded Clark as national security advisor in October 1983 and served in that capacity until December 1985, when he resigned.[42] McFarlane made the above statements about his trip and the offer of medical aid while meeting with then U.S. Reps. Hendon and LeBoutillier in his West Wing office in early 1982. When questioned by U.S. Senate investigators a decade later about his statements, McFarlane denied under oath that he had made the statements described above or had discussed the matter of the trip or the offer with the two congressmen either during the meeting in his West Wing office or at any other time. He further denied that he had ever made such a trip and stated that to his knowledge no such trip had taken place. He also denied that he had ever made any such offer to the North Vietnamese and stated that to his knowledge no such offer had ever been proffered.[43] A year later, however, in 1993, Lt. Col. Oliver North, USMC (Ret.), who had served under McFarlane at the NSC from 1983 to 1985, stated that "ten years before I worked for him at the National Security Council in the Reagan Administration, Robert C. "Bud" McFarlane, then an assistant to Dr. Henry Kissinger, was dispatched to offer Hanoi $100 million in medical and humanitarian aid in return for any prisoners remaining after 577 American POWs were repatriated in Operation Homecoming."[44] Thus, in addition to McFarlane himself, North is the third former U.S. official known to have described the Kissinger/McFarlane offer, the other two being Hendon and LeBoutillier.]

Their decision to take the South by force irrevocable, the North Vietnamese intensified their attacks throughout southern Indochina during late fall, and by December the outlook for South Vietnam had grown increasingly bleak. Shortly before Christmas, Kissinger, in Paris for what would turn out to be his final meeting ever with Le Duc Tho, told reporters that America wanted nothing more to do with Vietnam. Kissinger biographers Marvin and Bernard Kalb wrote that Kissinger "was determined that the United States would never again become enmeshed in Vietnam. 'We are not going to make ourselves the principal party . . . to that whole mess,'" they later quoted him as telling a small group of reporters on December 20. "'We spent four years trying to get out. We are not going to get back in.'"[45]

On that tragic note, one of the most remarkable years in the history of American foreign policy came to an inauspicious end.

Next would come one of the most remarkable years in American political history.

Working late at the presidential retreat at Camp David on the night of December 23, Richard Nixon wrote across the top of a page of notes: "Last Christmas here?"[46]

CHAPTER 12

1974

THE END OF THE LINE FOR RICHARD NIXON

. . .

One day I had the opportunity to ask Kissinger what he thought of our intelligence. Not speaking of Vietnam, but generally. He was getting this big flow of intelligence from CIA world-wide at the time. What did he think of the value of it? And he thought for a moment and then he said, "Well, when it supports my policy it's very useful." And I think this is the heart of the problem. It is that American policy is not formulated in response to what the intelligence shows. We first formulate the policy, and then we try to find the intelligence to support it.
        —THOMAS POLGAR, CIA chief of station, Saigon, 1972–1975, *Tears Before Rain*

In spite of the administration's firm policy that all the POWs were home, many relatives of those men who had not returned at Operation Homecoming continued to believe their loved ones remained in captivity in Indochina. Responding to the concerns of these families—concerns that had increased markedly when the first anniversary of the Paris accords came and went and still there was no news from Hanoi or Washington—Kissinger agreed to meet with members of the Executive Board of the National League of POW/MIA families in early February 1974 to respond to questions.

The meeting took place in the Roosevelt Room of the White House on February 9. Declaring that he would be "perfectly honest," Kissinger told those present that "it is my own genuine belief that there are no more POWs held in North Vietnam. . . . I myself can't believe that they hold anyone. They would have no reason to, and our returning prisoners also believe that all of whom they knew were returned. . . . I don't believe they hold any more prisoners." Following a lengthy exchange, one of the family members told Kissinger, "[Y]ou have been very pessimistic. You don't give us much hope." "It is better to tell you the truth," Kissinger replied.[1]

Just across the hall in the Oval Office, meanwhile, Richard Nixon was under relentless attack from Special Prosecutor Leon Jaworski, the Watergate grand jury, Judge John Sirica, members of the House Judiciary Committee—who by now were actively pursuing impeachment—and, of course, the team at *The Washington Post.* "The biggest danger I saw . . . ahead," Nixon later wrote of the period, "was that both the Special Prosecutor and the House Judiciary Committee would begin requesting more and more tapes. . . . For me the continuing nightmare of the tapes was the possibility that, given enough time and enough tapes, they might find what they were looking for. . . . The ones I had already reviewed were bad enough; now what might be on the others haunted us all." Nixon called the tapes "an enemy within."[2]

On March 1, the Watergate grand jury indicted Mitchell, Haldeman, Ehrlichman, Colson, and three other former White House or CRP officials for their roles in the cover-up.[3] As a consequence of these indictments, Sirica, acting at Jaworski's request, soon issued a subpoena for the tapes of sixty-four presidential conversations. When Nixon refused to turn them over, Jaworski appealed to the Supreme Court to force the president's compliance.[4] While the high court considered the case, the House Judiciary Committee scheduled televised hearings to consider formal articles of impeachment against the president. On the very day the hearings were to begin, July 24, the Supreme Court ruled that Nixon must comply with the Sirica subpoena and surrender the tapes "forthwith." The vote was eight to zero.[5] (Associate Justice William H. Rehnquist did not participate in the decision, having recused himself due to his previous association with former Attorney General John Mitchell at the Justice Department.)

Several hours after the Supreme Court ruling, Judiciary Committee Chairman Peter Rodino (D-NJ) convened his committee and began formal hearings on the proposed articles of impeachment.[6] As millions watched on television, committee members debated the president's fate for two days and then, on the 27th, voted to approve a first article of impeachment. This article charged Nixon with making false statements to investigators, withholding relevant evidence, approving or counseling perjury, interfering with the Justice Department's investigation, approving the payment of hush money to Watergate defendants, passing on information about the investigation to his aides who were suspects, making false statements to the American people about White House involvement in Watergate, and causing defendants to believe they might receive clemency in return for their silence. The article, officially Article I but known as "the obstruction article," passed by a vote of twenty-seven to eleven. All twenty-one Democrats on the committee voted in favor of the article, as did six of the committee's seventeen Republicans.[7]

On the 29th, the committee voted on a second article, this one charging Nixon with abuse of power. The charges ranged from Nixon's alleged use of the FBI and IRS to harass his political opponents through unlawful wiretaps and discriminatory tax audits to his reportedly maintaining a secret investigative unit within the office of the president for the purpose of engaging in covert, illegal activities to illegally interfering in the work of the FBI, the Justice Department's Criminal Division and its Office of the Watergate Special Prosecutor, and the Central Intelligence Agency. The vote on Article II, the "abuse of power" article, was twenty-eight to ten: twenty-one Democrats and seven Republicans in favor, ten Republicans against.[8]

On July 30, the Committee approved Article III, which charged Nixon with defying the committee's subpoenas for tapes and documents. The vote on the "subpoena article" was along party lines, twenty-one to seventeen. Following this vote, committee members voted down two additional proposed articles, Article IV, the "Cambodia article," which accused the president of concealing the secret bombing of Cambodia, and Article V, the "personal finances article," which accused Nixon of tax fraud and unconstitutional receipt of emoluments from the federal government for his private homes. Both failed on identical twenty-six–twelve votes.

Its work done, the committee adjourned shortly after 11:00 P.M. on the 30th to begin writing its final report. When completed, the report was to be sent to the full House for debate and votes on each approved article of impeachment.[9]

Nixon, himself a former congressman and knowledgeable in the ways of the House, counted noses. When his count showed he would surely be impeached, he informed Haig he would resign.[10]

Nixon announced his resignation in a nationally televised address on the evening of August 8. He submitted his formal letter of resignation the next morning, to take effect at noon that day.[11] Following a farewell address to friends, supporters, and staff in the East Room of the White House that morning, he walked with his family to the South Lawn and departed by helicopter for Andrews Air Force Base and a flight home to California.[12] Within a month's time he would be pardoned by his successor, Gerald R. Ford, and would never stand trial for any crime allegedly committed while president.[13]

Though Richard Nixon was able to avoid criminal prosecution for his actions in the Watergate scandal, others caught up in Watergate and associated criminal activities did not fare so well. Watergate mastermind G. Gordon Liddy, unrepentant to the end, would spend approximately four and one half years in prison. His accomplice, Howard Hunt, would serve thirty-three months.[14] The Cubans would all serve lesser sentences: Virgilio Gonzales and Eugenio Martinez would each serve fifteen months, Frank Sturgis thirteen, and Bernard Barker twelve.[15] James McCord, who had written the bombshell letter to Sirica that promised cooperation and signaled the unraveling of the cover-up, would serve just sixty-eight days.[16]

John Mitchell would be convicted of conspiracy, perjury, and obstruction of justice and would serve nineteen months in federal prison. Haldeman would be convicted of conspiracy and obstruction of justice and would serve eighteen months. Ehrlichman would be convicted of conspiracy to obstruct justice and perjury in the Watergate affair and conspiracy in the Ellsberg case. He would also serve eighteen months. Colson, who had pleaded guilty to obstruction of justice for his role in the Ellsberg affair, would spend seven months in prison.

Magruder, charged with perjury and obstruction of justice, would also serve seven months. Dean, who had provided a treasure trove of information to prosecutors, would serve only four.[17]

Barring a miracle, the unlisted, unreturned American POWs—victims of Watergate just as surely as all the president's men—would serve life.

CHAPTER 13

JANUARY–APRIL 1975

THE END OF THE LINE FOR SOUTH VIETNAM

. . .

> By his failure to act decisively and ruthlessly to clean his campaign and White House of loyalists who had blundered and, yes, committed crimes, he became ensnared in a cover-up that would destroy his presidency. . . . And when he went down, Southeast Asia and everything 58,000 Americans had bled and died for went down with him.
>     And that is upon the conscience of us all.
>                         —PATRICK J. BUCHANAN, "Completing the Watergate Picture"

> Nixon's ruin led to a cascade of catastrophic events—the crude and humiliating abandonment of Vietnam and the Vietnamese, the rise of a monster named Pol Pot, and millions—millions—killed in his genocide. . . . What a terrible time. Is it terrible when an American president lies and surrounds himself with dirty tricksters? Yes, it is. How about the butchering of children in the South China Sea. Is that worse? Yes. Infinitely, unforgettably and forever.
>                         —PEGGY NOONAN, "The Legend of Deep Throat,
>                                         Was Mark Felt Really a Hero?"

Just as 1973 will always be remembered by historians as the year America finally withdrew from Vietnam, and 1974 as the year the Nixon presidency came to an end, 1975 will be forever marked as the year South Vietnam fell to the Communists.

In Indochina, the Gregorian New Year began with the North Vietnamese Politburo in the midst of an historic conference in Hanoi. The conference, which had begun on December 20, had been convened so that the members could debate plans for the final push to capture the South.

As the conference wound toward conclusion in early January, the members adopted their final operational plan to take the South, which they entitled the "1975–1976 two-year strategic plan." Politburo member Gen. Van Tien Dung, who would be chosen by his colleagues to implement the plan and lead the attack on the South, later wrote that the plan called for widespread offensives during 1975 and complete liberation of the South in 1976.[1]

At the conclusion of the Politburo conference on January 8, Le Duan (pronounced "Zu-anh"), first secretary of Vietnamese Workers party and leader of the Politburo, told his fellow members that implementation of the plan must begin at once. "The Americans have withdrawn, we have our troops in the South, and the spirit of the masses is rising," Duan said. "This is what marks an opportune moment. We must seize it firmly."[2]

Members of the Politburo chose as their first target what the Vietnamese refer to as the Tay Nguyen, the Central Highlands. They chose Dung to lead the campaign and ordered him to depart for the South as soon as possible. Before Dung's departure, the leadership met again and determined the first target in the Central Highlands campaign would be Ban Me Thuot, a major town located approximately two hundred miles northeast of Saigon. (See map page 122, point 1.)

Dung left for the South on February 5. He traveled from Hanoi to Dong Hoi by plane, and then by car to the DMZ, where he boarded a motorboat and traveled west up the Ben Hai River to the Headquarters of the PAVN 559th Force, the command created in May 1959 to construct the Ho Chi Minh Trail. After receiving assurances from various commanders that all rice, ammunition, gasoline, and transport vehicles needed for a successful campaign would be available to him, Dung went on by car to the A Shau Valley, where he celebrated Chinese New Year. The following day he departed for Front Command Headquarters located in the jungle west of Ban Me Thuot.[3]

## *March 10, 1975*
## THE CENTRAL HIGHLANDS CAMPAIGN BEGINS

Following several weeks of preparation and a series of diversionary attacks in the Pleiku/Kontum area, Dung's forces opened fire on Ban Me Thuot at 2:00 A.M. on March 10. By midmorning the following day, after just thirty-two hours of fighting, the city was in Communist hands.[4]

Sensing an "opportune moment," Dung cabled Giap and sought permission to quickly move his victorious forces to the northeast to capture or encircle Phu Bon (Cheo Reo) and then back to the northwest to "surround and wipe out" Pleiku. (See map page 122, points 2 and 3.) "Enemy morale in the Tay Nguyen is collapsing," Dung told Giap, ". . . they are weakened and isolated. . . . Our forces [on the other hand] are still strong and in good spirits, guaranteed with logistics, and the weather is still to our advantage. . . . We propose you discuss this in the military committee and report to the Political Bureau, and afterwards send us your guidance."[5]

The Politburo approved Dung's request and advised him by telegram the following afternoon that he should "rapidly wipe out the remaining enemy units in Bon Me Thuot" and then move quickly toward Phu Bon (Cheo Reo ) and Pleiku.[6] On March 15, however, before Dung's forces could reach either city, a critical order by South Vietnamese President Thieu that all ARVN forces in the Pleiku/Kontum area abandon their positions and move eastward to the coast changed everything.

Thieu gave the order to his commanders on the morning of March 15 to begin the pullout from the Central Highlands.[7] According to the ARVN chief of staff at

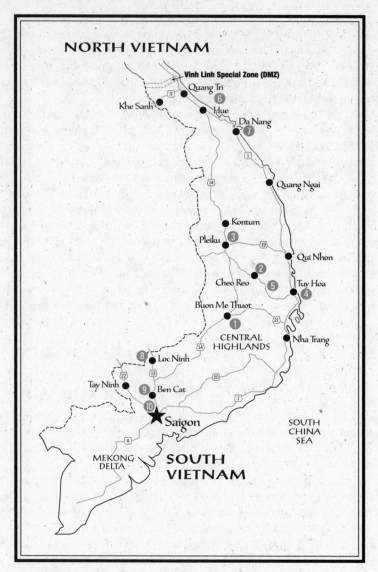

The fall of the South, March–April 1975. (HENDON/ANDERER)

the time, Gen. Cao Van Vien, Thieu's plan was that the ARVN units would move to the coast, defend the coastal cities as best they could, and then fall back as necessary to defend Saigon, its surrounding provinces, and the Mekong Delta. Vien later wrote that the Saigon area and the delta were "our untouchable heartland, their reducible national stronghold."[8] Sensing an "opportune moment," Dung cabled Giap on the morning of the 11th and sought permission to quickly move his victorious troops to the northeast to capture or encircle Phu Bon. When the pull-out order was passed to the ARVN troops, pandemonium broke out; orders were issued, countermanded, then issued again. Finally, on the evening of the 16th, the first convoys were able to pull out, bound for Tuy Hoa on the coast. (See map page 122, point 4.) Tragically, however, their route of escape took them to Phu Bon (Cheo Reo) and directly into the path of PAVN units moving to assault the town. On the 17th, Dung's forces cut the road between Phu Bon (Cheo Reo) and the coast, causing a massive traffic jam, and then began a series of merciless attacks on the trapped two thousand-vehicle ARVN convoy. (See map page 122, point 5.) The resulting carnage was without precedent in the war. According to one authoritative source, only seven hundred of seven thousand ARVN rangers, only twenty thousand of the other sixty thousand ARVN soldiers, and only one hundred thousand of the estimated four hundred thousand civilians in this doomed "Convoy of Tears" ever reached the coast alive.[9]

It was, Dung later wrote in his memoirs, the "turning point in the war."[10]

## *March 20*
## THE CAMPAIGN TO TAKE SAIGON BEGINS

Members of the Politburo in Hanoi had closely monitored the events in the Central Highlands. At a meeting on March 20 they concluded that *thoi co,* the "opportune moment," had arrived and that the attack on Saigon planned for the fall of 1975 should begin at once. They also determined that their fellow Politburo member Le Duc Tho should leave for the South immediately to help plan and oversee the attack. Five days later, when reports from the South indicated a further deterioration of ARVN fortunes, members met again and formally resolved "to liberate Saigon before the rainy season [summer]."[11]

In the South, meanwhile, the northern provinces were descending into chaos. Hue was abandoned on March 25, and on the 28th the PAVN bombardment of Da Nang began. (See map page 122, points 6 and 7.) The following day the ARVN began evacuating the city by boat. By March 30, Da Nang and all of the former ARVN I Corps were in North Vietnamese hands.[12]

Tho arrived at Dung's Front Command Headquarters near the Cambodian border west of Loc Ninh on the afternoon of April 7.[13] (See map page 122, point 8.) The following morning, he met with the combined leadership of Communist forces in the South and laid out the Politburo's plan to take Saigon. Dung later wrote that Tho informed those present that three members of the party's Central Political Bureau, he (Tho), Pham Hung, and Dung, had been appointed to lead the assault on the South Vietnamese capital.[14]

At dawn on April 26, Dung departed for his forward command post located northwest of Ben Cat. (See map page 122, point 9.) Tho and Hung joined him there on the 28th.[15] At 5:00 A.M. on the 30th, Communist forces attacked Saigon "from all directions."[16] By noon, the city was theirs. (See map page 122, point 10.)

Dung, Tho, and Hung came down from their forward command post near Ben Cat on May 1 to examine their prize, now already renamed Ho Chi Minh City. Driving past Tan Son Nhut Air Base, they entered the city and proceeded to the headquarters of ARVN General Staff, where they found the computers still running.[17]

Within hours, Le Duan, Gen. Vo Nguyen Giap, and a host of other dignitaries began streaming in by plane from Hanoi to congratulate the victors and inspect the spoils. Then came the formal victory celebration, held at the former Presidential Palace, now renamed Independence Palace and adorned with a huge picture of Ho Chi Minh. Ho's successor, Ton Duc Thang, flew down from Hanoi to participate. Surrounded by Dung, Tho, Hung, and a number of other dignitaries, Ton addressed those in attendance from a balcony overlooking the palace grounds. One author described the celebration that day as "the largest gathering of personalities and legendary figures of the Vietnamese Revolution ever."[18]

Le Duc Tho addressed his fellow leaders at a banquet later in the day. "It is impossible to fully describe the barbarous crimes committed by the U.S. imperialists and their henchmen against our nation," he told those assembled, "and likewise it is also impossible to resolve in just 1 or 2 days the grave consequences caused by the U.S. war of aggression in our country. Therefore, our people's task of rebuilding the country is enormous and arduous. We must quickly stabilize the people's lives, maintain public order and security, resolutely punish stubborn counterrevolutionary elements, truly heal the war wounds, build a self-sustaining economy and a democratic and progressive national culture, so as to bring prosperity and happiness to all the people."[19] Speaking the following day to a group of "people's representatives," Tho added, "[N]o imperialist will ever dare set foot again in Vietnam, a country which has, in its 4,000 year history, fought twice against the most powerful enemy aggressors of the world and completely defeated them all."[20]

When the speeches were done and the celebrating ended, the North Vietnamese moved quickly to address two of the most pressing tasks Tho had outlined. First, they began rounding up and imprisoning members of the South Vietnamese military as well as South Vietnamese government officials, diplomats, policemen and other civil servants, teachers, and other supporters of the Thieu regime who remained in the country. Their goal: break the Southerners in both body and spirit so they would never again have any desire to fight. Next, clearly no longer in fear of American retaliation, they moved forcefully to ransom the unlisted, unreturned American POWs "Cuban style" for the reconstruction aid promised them by Nixon and Kissinger.

These two state-sponsored efforts—each born of vengeance, each coldly calculated—would go on for years. One would succeed. The other would fail, but not for lack of effort.

The "fourth Vietnam War" was under way.

# PART III

# CHAPTER 14

MAY–DECEMBER 1975

"CUBA SUGGESTED TO US TO KEEP
THEM BACK" • CONGRESS INVESTIGATES
THE FATE OF THE POWs AND MIAs

. . .

> Two weeks after the North Vietnamese army had taken over Saigon, there came to my house five colonels of whom there was Colonel Le Phuong. All these colonels were of the General Van Tien Dung's staff. During the conversation, Le Phuong confidentially whispered to me . . . "we still keep about 800 American pilots alive of whom the majority are of notorious families. We will exchange these pilots with conditions. . . ."
>
> [I told Le Phuong,] "I believe we have released all the American pilots one year ago in [the] exchange of war prisoners after [the] Paris agreement." The Colonel explained, "we are not so stupid to do that. Cuba suggested to us to keep them back for future negotiations, just as Cuba itself had done previously."
>
> —Statement of DIA Source 13590

During the Republic of Vietnam's final hours, millions of South Vietnamese were forced to make a painful decision: flee their homeland, their ancestors, and their families, or stay in Vietnam and face the consequences of defeat at the hands of an enemy hardened by thirty years of civil war.

Tens of thousands of high-ranking ARVN officers, high officials of the South Vietnamese government, and those civilians and military personnel closely associated with the American government chose to leave. Thousands of them were able to escape on last-minute American evacuation flights out of the beleaguered capital. Some commandeered helicopters and flew to U.S. ships operating off the coast, while others piloted Republic of Vietnam Air Force (RVNAF) planes and helicopters to neighboring countries.[1] Many thousands took to boats with their families and comrades and headed for the open sea. Though some were undoubtedly lost at sea, most made it safely to U.S. Navy ships or merchant ships waiting offshore and then on to nearby countries.[2] Tragically, hundreds of thousands who wanted to flee were not able to do so.

In the days following the collapse of the South, Communist officials announced over the radio that all members of the RVN armed forces, all elected officials, all officials and employees of the RVN government, and all policemen, teachers, and others associated with the former regime were required to attend a brief "reeducation course," and that upon completion of the course all would be released and allowed to return to their homes and families.[3] These radio announcements notwithstanding, the truth about what *really* happened—the truth about the North Vietnamese program to, as Le Duc Tho had put it, "resolutely punish stubborn counterrevolutionary elements"—would not reach the West until the late 1970s when refugees fled Vietnam by the tens of thousands and told what had happened when the unsuspecting Southerners arrived for class.

Two of those refugees, one a former college instructor from Saigon, the other a former ARVN major named Thai Phi Long, later offered accounts of the period that proved representative of thousands of others that would be collected and analyzed by the U.S. government in the postwar years.

This, the former college instructor later told U.S. officials, is how the long nightmare for the Southerners began:

Shortly after April 30, 1975 or beginning early May, the communist armed forces and the local committee militias gained control of almost all of the areas of South Vietnam. During the first few days, there were no apparent atrocities or killings from the regime, but the people were still in anguish waiting for new things to happen. All movements inside the country from cities to cities were checked and limited. No more gasoline for trucks and cars. The only way to get it was to buy illegally from secret sources supplied by the VC army truck drivers.

In early May 1975, the VC local administration committees, usually in charge of small areas in Saigon, with the help from one soldier in uniform carrying a rifle and one or two secret policemen with pistols K54, in small groups of about 5 or 7 persons went to every house in the designated areas for a population census, a people registration. The new registration gave the communists detailed personal data of all persons living in each house, so anybody without their names in the records would be caught by the police which were soon established in every area.

In mid-May, soldiers and non-commissioned officers of the former regime were called to present themselves at certain local centers or schools for studying the new government's policy of clemency. After 3 days at the centers, all of them, in hundreds of thousands, returned to their homes. Radios and newspapers, the communist organs, proclaimed the reeducation policy as the best policy of clemency for anyone involved with the former regime. People outside thought that there would be no harm to go to reeducation centers or camps, because they had seen soldiers and NCO coming back home after 3 days there. The terrible mistake was that people didn't understand the difference between NCO and higher officers and leading officials of the old regime. Soldiers and NCO were not the main targets of the VC.

The return of the soldiers and NCO made a loud propaganda for the clemency policy. Then a few days later, on May 20, higher officers from captain ranks up to colonel and general officer as well as government officials, ministers and senators and members of the house of representatives were called up for enrollment in their future reeducation studies. Some were told to bring a 10 day ration with them; others were told to bring a 30 day ration. People knew that the soldiers and NCO who had already been released had been told to bring a three day ration with them, so the 10 day rations or the 30 day rations for higher officers at the centers were thought logical and sensible.

The enrollment took place in about 30 big schools in Saigon, the schools with high walls or safe railings around. Once inside, it was difficult to get out, except through the gate or sentinel, consisting of an armed platoon.

I presented myself for political indoctrination at one of the centers, a parochial school in Saigon, because, besides being a college instructor, I had also served 4 years as a lieutenant in the armed forces of the Republic of Vietnam. When I reported to the school, I saw thousands of professional people, doctors, engineers, teachers, etc. who also happened to have served as military officers, active or reserves.

After 3 days at the school, all of us, about 5,000 men, were suddenly awakened at 1 am and led into the Russian Molotova trucks carrying exactly 50 persons in each truck, with complete cover above. The convoy of hundreds of trucks left at 2 am on deserted streets and headed to Tay Ninh province, 100 km northwest of Saigon.

At 8 AM, the convoy went through the city of Tay Ninh and reached Trang Lon, a former US 11th Cavalry division fortified stronghold, about 8 km from the provincial city. Outside this camp we saw hundreds of empty Molotova trucks bringing other "captured" into the camp. Trang Lon, with the diameter of 4 km and a perimeter of barbed wire and mine field thick, was an excellent prison camp. We were now "captured prisoners."

. . . The term "Reeducation Camp" was completely unfamiliar to South Vietnamese officials and laymen from 1954 to 1975. Had we understood how the reeducation camps have been, we wouldn't have gone into the prison camps prepared very carefully and cunningly by the Vietnamese Communist (VC) regime.[4]

Former ARVN Maj. Thai Phi Long told a similar story:

I and millions of officers and men of the Armed Forces of the Republic of Vietnam and government officials who were unable to escape in time and leave Vietnam at the last minute were stunned by the sudden developments and historic events of 30 April 1975. The cruel troop convoys of the North Vietnamese communists pouring into Saigon created apprehension for everyone.

However, during the initial days of their takeover of South Vietnam, the communists didn't touch anyone. They didn't make arrests, didn't kill and didn't take any revenge. And they didn't shrink from throwing out many communiques to appeal over the radios or through propaganda and information units sent to all streets and alleys in wards and quarters to make loudspeaker announcements. The communists also disseminated their 8- and 10-point policies of humanitarian clemency for all elements of the "puppet army and puppet administration." Those who previously had worked for "the Americans and puppets," if they presented themselves to the closest

Military Training Committee in order to go for re-education for a limited period of time, would be issued a certificate that they would return to the normal life of a citizen on completion of the re-education.

Then, the communists began to apply this re-education plan in a truly sophisticated and scientific manner. The period of study was stipulated as follows:

—three days for enlisted men
—seven days for noncommissioned officers
—ten days for company-grade officers
—one month for field- and general-grade officers and similar time periods for officials of the Government of the Republic of Vietnam, depending on the former rank and position of each person.

The communists implemented this re-education program in a truly serious and open manner, dispelling in part our initial worries and suspicions. The enlisted men were sent for re-education first. After exactly three days, they were issued certificates to return to their homes to live normal lives with their wives and children. Then the noncommissioned officers went for re-education for seven days, and they, too, received certificates and were free to go home. The officers of all grades had to wait until June 15, 1975, before they were called to go for re-education.

I can never forget June 15, 1975, the day when all field- and general-grade officers said good-by to their wives and children to be away from their families temporarily for one month to go for re-education. Each carried a small handbag containing a few sets of clothing, some essential items and a little dry food, which everyone thought would be enough to last for 30 days, after which they would return home. We reported in person at collection points in Saigon to go to the re-education camps. We told each other that 30 days would not be long for us. Everyone said: Going to study to get a certificate and then return home is truly funny. Everyone wanted to fulfill that "re-education" obligation.

Many convoys of Molotova trucks completely enclosed by canvas transported us from the different collection points in Saigon (which since then is being called Ho Chi Minh City) to many former camps of the Armed Forces of the Republic of Vietnam in places such as Bien Hoa, Long Khanh, Hoc Mon, Tay Ninh, Cat Lai, etc., which were used for the re-education. Each truck carried 30 persons plus two communist escorts tightly clasping AK-47 rifles, who sat in the rear of the truck to guard us and be ready to open fire on anyone trying to escape.

The trucks left Saigon at 2100 hours and arrived at their destinations at 0500 hours the next morning, a distance of from 10 to 60 or 70 kilometers, for which they had to drive constantly without stop, using up a full eight hours. The communists did this to disorient us, but they were clumsy. Besides, how could they maintain secrecy with us, who were from South Vietnam and were overly familiar with the geography in South Vietnam, especially those of us in the military who had traveled all over and know nearly all of South Vietnam.

The days in the re-education camp passed by very quickly. First 10, then

20, and then 30 days went by. This was the "milepost" that we felt we had to reach to receive a paper certifying that we had attended re-education in order to return to our families. But, we were not allowed to go home after that 30-day "milepost." We also felt that we had not "received" any re-education at all. Each day we only performed the tasks of maintaining camp sanitation, and we collectively cooked our own meals. In the evenings we learned songs and then went to bed.

. . . One day, after the 30 days, the camp commander had us "go to class" and talked to us about the reform and re-education policy of the Vietnamese communist Party and State. We asked him, "The 30 days are up. Why can't we go home?" He solemnly replied, "The communique of the Military Management Committee told you fellows to bring along enough personal items and money for one month. It didn't say that the re-education period was one month." Without a bit of shame, the camp commander continued, "Now, the State will issue you additional clothing, blankets, mosquito nets and essential items for long-term re-education. . . . You fellows served as lackeys for the French and then the American imperialists to oppose and sabotage the Revolution during the past 30 years. Your minds have been crammed with reactionary thinking. Your crimes are immense. Neither the heavens nor the earth can forgive them. They are crimes which could not be erased by death by firing squad many times over. But, the Party, State and Revolution will not shoot you to death. They leniently spare you from death and allow you to undergo re-education. By rights, you fellows should take re-education for 30 years, the length of time that you opposed and sabotaged the Revolution. But the Party and State are lenient toward you and are letting you undergo re-education for a limited period of time. Those who advance early will be allowed to go home first. Those who have not advanced yet will have to stay for further re-education. Anyone who obstinately continues to oppose and be reactionary will be severely punished. So, you are the ones who will determine for yourselves whether you go home early or late. The Party and State have a lenient and humane policy, opening the way for you fellows to pardon your enemies and cooperate with those who join with you. Do you fellows understand?"

When the camp commander stopped talking, all of us were stunned and worried; our faces had turned a grayish purple in color, our hearts were filled with a piercing pain as though a knife had been driven into our chest. . . . And we slowly left the assembly hall and went back to our individual tents. No one raised his head to look at the others any longer. A dark curtain fell to cover our lives and the awful things that might happen to us. We could only sit back and wait, and accept everything that would come to us. We agreed and told each other, "This is the first 'debt' that we must pay to the Vietnamese communists, and it also is the first 'gift' that the communists are giving us."

The communists had laid their trap and had easily caught the whole pack of us in it to subsequently apply their punishment and revenge measures through the Party and State's so-called "humane and lenient" policy. We knew that we were naive and stupid to let the communists deceive us into going for re-education. Later, we regularly comforted each other by saying,

"We are the stupidest of the stupid people in the world for turning ourselves in to be imprisoned by the communists."[5]

It had been another stunning victory for the North Vietnamese. Without firing more than a few shots, they had rounded up hundreds of thousands of South Vietnamese and locked them securely behind "barbed wire and mine field thick" in former U.S. and ARVN military bases all over the South.[6]

With their grip on the South now firm and order assured, the North Vietnamese got on with their next priority, securing the funds needed to rebuild their country.

## THE NORTH VIETNAMESE EFFORT TO RANSOM THE UNLISTED, UNRETURNED POWs "CUBAN STYLE" FOR THE BILLIONS OF DOLLARS OF RECONSTRUCTION AID PROMISED THEM AT PARIS

A review of the historical record leaves little doubt that in early June, just weeks after they had captured the South, the North Vietnamese launched a carefully planned effort to ransom the unlisted, unreturned POWs "Cuban style" for the reconstruction aid the United States had promised at Paris in 1973.

The record indicates that Pham Van Dong himself kicked off the effort in a speech to the DRV Fifth National Assembly in Hanoi on June 3. "We demand that the U.S. Government truly respect Articles 1 and 4 of the Paris agreement on Vietnam regarding the basic national rights—the independence, sovereignty, unity, and territorial integrity—of Vietnam and that it strictly implement the spirit of Article 21, regarding its obligation to contribute to healing the wounds of the criminal war of aggression waged by the United States in both parts of Vietnam," Dong declared. "On that basis, and in accordance with the principles of equality and mutual benefit, the Government of the Democratic Republic of Vietnam will normalize relations with the U.S.—in accordance with the spirit of Article 22 of the Paris agreement on Vietnam—and will settle other remaining problems with the United States."[7]

Lest anyone not understand what Dong had meant by "other remaining problems," Vice Premier Nguyen Duy Trinh, who had signed the Paris accords on behalf of the DRV, addressed the delegates the following day:

The United States . . . has refused to live up to its commitment in the [Paris] agreement. We persistently demand that the U.S. Government fulfill its obligations as provided for by the Paris agreement. . . . On this occasion, the Government of the Democratic Republic of Vietnam declares that all the basic principles of the Paris agreement on Vietnam must be strictly observed. The United States must fully respect the national rights of the Vietnamese people, end for good its interference in the internal affairs of South Vietnam, and fulfill its obligation of contributing to healing the wounds of war and to post-war reconstruction in both North and South Vietnam.

. . . The end of the war, the restoration of peace throughout Vietnam's territory and the fulfillment by the U.S. of its obligation as mentioned above

will create conditions for the establishment of new, equal and mutually beneficial relations between the Democratic Republic of Vietnam and the United
States in the spirit of Article 22 of the Paris agreement on Vietnam. All the sequels of war concerning Vietnam and the U.S., such as the United States'
contribution to healing the wounds of war in both zones of Vietnam, the
search for Americans missing in action, as well as the exhumation and repatriation of the remains of Americans killed in the war, are pending problems
that need to be settled soon. The DRV Government is ready to discuss with
the U.S. Government on how to solve these problems.[8]

The leaders having set the agenda, the party organs immediately went to
work spreading the news that the DRV was ready to fulfill its obligations under
the Paris accords to search for Americans missing in action and exhume and
repatriate the remains of Americans killed in action if the United States would
provide the reconstruction aid it had pledged. On June 10, Radio Hanoi repeated
Trinh's linkage of the matters of aid, the MIAs, and the repatriation of remains.[9]
The following day, *Nhan Dan* addressed the issue again:

With regard to . . . Article 21, . . . we resolutely point out that since the U.S.
Government was . . . the destroyer of the Vietnamese nation, it must contribute to healing the wounds of war and to postwar reconstruction in both
parts of Vietnam. This is an unshirkable [sic] responsibility and obligation.
This is also a debt owed to the Vietnamese people which the United States
cannot dodge.
    The war has now ended completely and real peace has been restored
throughout Vietnam. This situation has created conditions for resolving the
problems of the consequences of war between Vietnam and the United
States, such as the U.S. contribution to healing the wounds of war in both
parts of Vietnam, the search for American MIAs and the exhumation and
repatriation of the remains of Americans who died in Vietnam.
    These problems still exist today and no progress had been made in resolv-
ing them because of the U.S. attitude which lacks seriousness and goodwill.
The DRV Government showed its seriousness and goodwill when it stated
that it is ready to hold discussions with the U.S. Government to resolve
them. It is obvious that everything now depends on the U.S. attitude.[10]

After monitoring the broadcast in Bangkok, UPI dispatched the following
story:

North Vietnam said today there can be no search for the 2,500 missing and
dead Americans in Indochina unless the United States provides postwar aid
to North and South Vietnam. It said Hanoi was ready to discuss the issue
with the United States.
    The statement was contained in a commentary in the North Vietnamese
Communist Party newspaper Nhan Dhan [sic] broadcast by Radio Hanoi and
monitored here. U.S. officials here said it was the first time they have known
the North Vietnamese to link the two subjects in such a direct manner.[11]

When word reached Washington that the North Vietnamese were prepared to address the matter of the MIAs if the United States would fulfill its promise to provide reconstruction aid, the administration's response was succinct and—given that less than six weeks had passed since PAVN tanks had rolled into Saigon—highly predictable. The Paris accords, White House spokesman Ron Nessen declared, had "no more practical meaning," and the decision by the North Vietnamese to link progress on the MIA issue to the receipt of reconstruction aid was "cruel." Bottom line: "No sale."[12]

Nessen's statements, though surely in line with the thinking of most Americans at the time, provoked a shrill response from Hanoi. Assailing what they called the unilateral "scrapping" of the Paris agreement by the White House as "a betrayal and violation of international law," the North Vietnamese accused the United States in a commentary broadcast over Radio Hanoi on June 16 of shirking its responsibility under Article 21 "to make war reparations for actions in the criminal U.S. war of aggression in both parts of Vietnam." Then, responding to Nessen's charge that North Vietnam's linking the search for the MIAs to receipt of postwar aid was "cruel," the commentator declared that "the White House wants to wash off its responsibilities under the Paris agreement and for the relatives of the American servicemen killed and missing as well. This," he said, "is indeed a cruelty."

The commentator went on to state that "the DRV side has on several [recent] occasions said that the problem of searching for U.S. servicemen missing in action is not difficult to resolve . . . [and that] the DRV side stands ready to hold discussions and consultations with the U.S. side to carry out this work." Continuing, he declared:

The reason why this problem [MIAs] remains outstanding is due to the U.S. attitude which lacks seriousness and good will. While adamantly pressing for a search for Americans missing in action, the United States has sought to evade its responsibility for implementation of several articles of the Paris agreement. It has persistently refused to implement Article 21 concerning (war reparations) and contributions to the reconstruction of Vietnam and throughout Indochina. . . .

The war has now ended completely, and genuine peace has been restored throughout Vietnam. This situation has created favorable conditions for resolving the sequels of war concerning Vietnam and the United States. The decisive factor is whether or not the U.S. administration is ready and has goodwill.

Our people's stand and attitude are very clear. As the 3 June statement by Premier Pham Van Dong has clearly said, the United States must truly respect Articles 1 and 4 of the Paris agreement on Vietnam regarding the basic national rights—the independence, sovereignty, unity, and territorial integrity—of Vietnam, and it must strictly implement the spirit of Article 21 regarding the U.S. obligation to make war reparations for its action in the war of aggression in both parts of Vietnam. On that basis, and in accordance with the principles of equality and mutual benefit, the DRV Government will normalize relations with the United States—in accordance with the spirit of Article 22 of the Paris agreement on Vietnam—and will settle other remaining problems with the United States.

Therefore, the U.S. administration's erroneous statements which distort or deny the Paris agreement or the shirking of its responsibility for the implementation of this agreement only hinder the normalization of relations between the United States and Vietnam. Furthermore, they also deadlock the settlement of outstanding problems between the two countries.[13]

On June 21, Pham Van Dong dispatched a letter to twenty-seven members of the U.S. Congress in which he repeated his country's willingness to begin the search for the MIAs if the United States would provide the reconstruction aid it had promised.[14] A press account of the letter that appeared later in the *Bangkok Post* left no doubt what was afoot:

### HANOI LINKS MIA SEARCH TO US AID

North Vietnamese Premier Pham Van Dong says his government is ready to pursue the fate of Americans listed as "missing in action" (MIA) in Vietnam but has linked the search for MIAs to US aid in the reconstruction of Vietnam.

Dong, in a letter to . . .[15]

## U.S. HOUSE CREATES SELECT COMMITTEE TO INVESTIGATE FATE OF POWs/MIAs

Responding to the Pham Van Dong correspondence—and to the pleas for help that were pouring into congressional offices from POW/MIA family members distraught over the administration's rejection of Dong's offer to search for their loved ones—members of the U.S. House of Representatives voted on September 11 to create a new select committee to conduct "a thorough study and investigation of the POW/MIA problems resulting from the war in Indochina."[16] Officially designated the House Select Committee on Missing Persons in Southeast Asia, the committee quickly became known as the Montgomery Committee after its popular and highly respected chairman, the conservative Democrat from Mississippi, G. V. "Sonny" Montgomery.

Before Montgomery could hold his first hearing, Kissinger, speaking to members of the Southern Governors' Conference in Orlando, admitted that he knew well what the North Vietnamese were up to, and, in doing so, highlighted the enormity of the task Montgomery and his committee faced. "I negotiated with the North Vietnamese for four years," Kissinger told the assembled governors, "and they have used the anguish of Americans for blackmail for all this period. First they used the prisoners; now they are using the missing in action. . . . I feel that they will [continue to] use the missing in action for their political purposes, [but] we do not believe that American foreign policy should be shaped by the holding of hostages—and, even less, by the remains of Americans who died in action."[17]

Hostages? Blackmail? Montgomery and his colleagues surely now knew their task would not be an easy one. What they did not know, however, was the lengths Kissinger and other top administration officials would go to ensure that their effort to account for those missing in action and the unlisted, unreturned POWs would fail.

## MONTGOMERY GOES TO WORK

Montgomery began his investigation with a series of introductory fact-finding hearings in September and October. He then decided to take members to Paris in early December to meet with the North Vietnamese, and, if all went well, to travel to Hanoi and Vientiane later in December for additional meetings.

To prepare for the overseas meetings, Montgomery and his entire committee attended a working breakfast with Kissinger at the State Department on November 14. Near the top of everyone's list of questions for the secretary was the matter of whether or not the North Vietnamese might really be holding American prisoners, either as ransom as Kissinger had implied in Orlando back in September, or for any other reason. Also near the top of everyone's list was the matter of the secret letter from Nixon to Pham Van Dong—a letter that no one on the committee had yet seen. Did it exist? If so, what did it say?

According to the official committee reports of the November 14 meeting, Kissinger said that "he did not believe the Vietnamese held any [living prisoners of war], since there was no purpose for them to do so."[18]

Committee member Rep. Henry Gonzalez (D-TX), who like the other members had heard the rumors of the Nixon letter, asked Kissinger if there were "any side memorandums, any codicils, any letters or missals or writings or verbal understandings that have not been disclosed?" Kissinger answered with a categorical no. On the matter of postwar aid, Kissinger told the members, "I gag at direct aid. . . . We'll discuss economics, trade, but not Article 21. . . . They want normalization more than we do. They have to come to us."[19]

As planned, Montgomery and several members of the committee flew to Paris in early December to meet with the North Vietnamese. At a meeting held on December 6, the chief North Vietnamese delegate, Vo Van Sung, the DRV's ambassador to France, began by pressing his visitors for the postwar reconstruction aid promised at Paris. He then told them that while all living POWs had been returned in 1973, agencies of his government were "carrying out the research of missing U.S. personnel," and "we hope we can find some."[20] Afterward, Sung told reporters that North Vietnam wanted relations "not only normal but friendly" with the United States, but he "added the condition that Washington must observe the 1973 Paris treaty terms calling for the United States to pay for rebuilding war-torn North Vietnam."[21]

Committee members returned to Washington buoyed by Sung's statement but convinced they would get nowhere with the Vietnamese leaders in Hanoi unless they had something tangible to offer. In hopes of securing some sort of inducement, Montgomery and two of the three Republicans on his committee, Paul N. "Pete" McCloskey Jr. (R-CA) and Benjamin A. Gilman (R-NY), met with President Ford at the White House four days before their scheduled departure for Hanoi. Official committee notes of the meeting show that Ford assured his three old friends that he was interested in doing whatever he could to help solve the POW/MIA dilemma and encouraged them to make it clear to the Vietnamese that, while more information was required about Americans still unaccounted for, he was willing to "move forward on the basis of reciprocity." Ford told the congressmen that to get the ball rolling, they "should ask the Vietnamese for their shopping list," their "list of quid pro quos."[22]

Unlike his secretary of state, the president, it appeared, might actually be willing to deal.

## December 21–23
## HANOI

Chairman Montgomery wasted no time in Hanoi asking the Vietnamese what they wanted in return for cooperation on the MIAs. Speaking at the opening session of talks on December 21, Montgomery first thanked the chief North Vietnamese representative, Deputy Foreign Minister Phan Hien, (Fon HEE un), who had been a member of the North Vietnamese delegation to the Paris peace talks, and the other North Vietnamese officials present for the DRV's "continuing research on American personnel missing in Viet Nam." Montgomery then told them: "The President has explicitly stated that he is prepared to reciprocate gestures of good will. In furtherance of this, he asked us to request from you a listing in writing of the gestures by the United States you consider of importance."[23]

Before Hien could reply, the three other members of the committee who had made the trip chimed in with suggestions on how the United States might respond to North Vietnamese progress on the MIA issue. McCloskey declared that tangible progress might convince the Congress to end the trade embargo against the DRV; Gilman suggested that the United States might assist the DRV in oil exploration and that this might hasten normalized relations; Richard Ottinger (D-NY) suggested that the United States could help with trade assistance, with technical help with mine deactivation, and by allowing international organizations to give humanitarian assistance.[24]

D. Gareth Porter, a staff consultant to the committee and note taker at the session, described Hien's response:

> Phan Hien's response to these suggestions . . . indicated that Hanoi was determined to pursue a different approach. Hien immediately launched in[to] a detailed discussion of the Nixon letter to Pham Van Dong and the Joint Economic Committee negotiations. He quoted from the Nixon letter and listed the points on which the U.S. and DRV delegations to the JEC had agreed before the U.S. suspended the talks. Despite protestations by the Committee members that the Congress could not reinstate the Paris Agreement, Hien concluded, "We are prepared to carry [out Article 8(b) relative to MIAs] fully if you carry out fully Article 21." It would be "impossible to carry out one and not the other," he said.[25]

Montgomery and his colleagues were stunned and embarrassed. Hien had read aloud from the Nixon letter—the very existence of which Kissinger had denied to the members, face-to-face, prior to their departure from the United

States. Hien had also cited what he said was an agreement between the U.S. and North Vietnamese delegates at the JEC talks, an agreement the committee likewise had not been advised of.

Montgomery attempted to regain the initiative by asking Hien for a copy of the Nixon letter, but Hien, adding insult to injury, refused to allow the Americans even to see the document, much less have a copy of it. Hien did, however, give Montgomery what the chairman had asked for in his opening remarks, "a listing in writing of the gestures by the United States you consider of importance." The "listing" Hien handed over was the first-year postwar reconstruction program the American and North Vietnamese JEC representatives had approved just prior to the collapse of the JEC talks at Paris in late July 1973 (see Chapter 11). Titled "First Year Program For Reconstruction and Healing the Wounds of War," it included diesel railroad locomotives, freight cars, rail line, dock facilities, refrigerator ships, assorted barges, fishing and shipping vessels, cement plants, food-processing plants, prefabricated housing plants, plumbing fixtures plants, sheet glass plants, chipboard plants, textile and knitwear plants, a leatherette plant, tractor repair plants, a fertilizer plant, livestock food-processing plants, steel mills, a high-tension electrical equipment plant, a thermal power plant complete with substations and transmission line, more than three thousand bulldozers, scrapers, and excavators, seventeen thousand tractors, and hundreds of millions of dollars' worth of other items.[26]

"We want to know in substance what you are going to do," Hien declared after handing over the list. Then he "strongly hinted as well that the Vietnamese would make substantial information available on MIAs only when agreement had been reached with the U.S. on helping to 'heal the wounds of war' in Vietnam. Asked for details about the DRV agency on the search for MIA's, Hien replied, 'Frankly, we can't give you figures, but when agreements have been reached on both big problems, we won't keep anything secret.' "[27]

Humiliated and angered by his lack of knowledge of the Nixon letter and the JEC list—and surely recoiling from the contents of both—the conservative Montgomery told the Vietnamese, as he would later recall, "just as plain as I am talking to you, that they are not going to get reconstruction aid from the United States and that we weren't going to bargain or pay blackmail."[28]

The following day Montgomery and his members accepted the remains of three American pilots at a repatriation ceremony and then paid a courtesy call on Prime Minister Pham Van Dong. According to official committee records of the meeting, the American side stressed to Dong "the importance of resolving the MIA issue as a means of bringing the two countries together." Those same records show that Dong in return "stressed the importance of reciprocal gestures" and "urged the Select Committee to use its influence to induce the U.S. Government to help heal the wounds of war."[29]

"Codel [Congressional Delegation] Montgomery" departed the next morning for Vientiane and talks with officials of the new Pathet Lao government, the government of the Lao People's Democratic Republic (LPDR). The Communist Pathet Lao, the congressmen knew, had gained total control of the country only weeks before, when, after forcing King Savang Vatthana to abdicate his throne on December 2, they had seized the few key government agencies and installations that remained under royal control and announced the formation of a new government.[30] The congressmen knew, too—or, given their mission, *should* have known—that, in one of their first official acts, the PL had unveiled the new government's foreign policy, one aspect of which was a demand that the United States fulfill its obligation under the 1973 Lao Peace Accords to contribute to the healing of the country's war wounds.[31]

Committee records show that the members held only one meeting in Vientiane, this with the hard-line chief of cabinet of the Foreign Ministry, Soubanh Srithirath (pronounced SUE bon). The members asked Soubanh for information on five fliers who were last known to have been alive in Lao hands and thirteen who had reportedly been killed in a crash near Pakse late in the war. Soubanh replied that no Americans remained alive in his country, that information on those who had died would be provided to the U.S. side when it became available, and that the United States should pay the LPDR reconstruction aid as required by the 1973 Lao Accords.[32]

Following their brief and unproductive stop in Vientiane, the members flew on to Bangkok. The following day, Christmas Eve, they headed back to the United States to lick their wounds, make another attempt to secure a copy of the Nixon letter, and hear from an array of expert witnesses as to whether or not American POWs might still be alive in Indochina.[33]

## A ROUGH CHRISTMAS FOR FOUR OTHER AMERICANS

Unknown to the four congressmen, at around the same time they departed Bangkok and headed home, four other Americans—these servicemen—were being sighted in Vietnam and Laos in the most desperate of circumstances.

According to what one eyewitness would later tell U.S. officials, two Americans, both emaciated and wearing tattered military uniforms, were seen surrendering to Communist authorities just outside the former Tan Son Nhut Air Base in Ho Chi Minh City around Christmastime. The Americans were said to have been hiding out in someone's house near the base but had been forced to turn themselves in when their protectors could no longer feed them. The Americans had reportedly surrendered in the market crowd to protect the identity of the people who had harbored them. They apparently had been in hiding since the fall of Saigon some eight months before.[34]

A young Laotian man would later report to U.S. authorities that around Christmastime he and his mother had observed two American prisoners—both said to be pilots—who were being jeered and hectored at a Pathet Lao political rally near the Pathet Lao capital at Sam Neua. According to what the young man later told U.S. authorities, the two pilots were standing together on a stage with the recently deposed king and queen of Laos as the crowd denounced the king and queen for being puppets of the U.S. government and the pilots for the destruction and killing they had caused.[35]

# 1976

## MONTGOMERY CONTINUES HIS INVESTIGATION • AMERICAN POWs SEEN IN CAPTIVITY IN BOTH NORTH AND SOUTH VIETNAM

. . .

> Sometime between April and July 1976, . . . source overheard a camp cadre . . . tell other cadre that in Vinh Phu [Province], . . . NVN, the [Hanoi Government] was holding 180 US POW's who were not released in 1973. The objective in holding them after 1973 . . . was to follow the "Cuban" style of holding American's after a conflict in order to obtain an advantage in future dealings with the U.S.
>
> JCRC Report, M85-004, Hearsay of 180 US POWs Held in North Vietnam

Chairman Montgomery and his colleagues returned to Washington following their embarrassing encounter with Phan Hien and went right to work trying to secure a copy of the Nixon letter. Montgomery first sought information about the letter from former President Nixon himself, and when this bore no fruit, officially requested a copy from the National Security Council. Deputy National Security Advisor Brent Scowcroft declined the request, citing executive privilege.[1]

Undeterred, Montgomery and the members met again with Kissinger at the State Department in March and asked him for a copy of the letter. Kissinger this time acknowledged the letter's existence but refused to allow the members to see it.[2] He assured them, however, that "we never said [in the letter] we were going to provide this money."[3]

Two weeks later, Kissinger sent an official note to the North Vietnamese stating in diplomatic language that the Paris Peace Accords were dead and that any promises of aid made by the United States at Paris would not be honored.[4] Livid, the Vietnamese responded with a note accusing the United States of shirking its obligation to contribute to the healing of the wounds of war[5] in Vietnam and, several days later, by reading key portions of the Nixon letter over Radio Hanoi. Following the reading of portions of the letter, the announcer declared that "the United States has swallowed its promise and dodged its responsibilities . . ." and is clearly "trying to evade its blood debt toward the Vietnamese people."[6]

Though the North Vietnamese had now placed the essence of the Nixon letter squarely in the public domain, a copy was never made available to Montgomery and his committee. The historic letter would not be released in written form until it was declassified by Carter administration officials in June 1977, long after the select committee had completed its work, filed its final report, and passed from the scene.[7]

## THE DEVASTATING TESTIMONY OF THE EXPERT WITNESSES

Concurrent with his and the other members' efforts to obtain a copy of the Nixon letter, Montgomery had continued holding hearings and receiving testimony from expert witnesses in an attempt to determine whether or not American POWs might still be alive in captivity. As it turned out, the testimony of four of these expert witnesses—three former POWs and one of America's most highly respected wartime commanders—proved especially damaging to the cause of the unlisted, unreturned POWs.

The first of the four expert witnesses to testify had been returnee Lt. Cmdr. George Coker, USN. Coker, an A-6 bombardier-navigator who had been shot down over North Vietnam in the summer of 1966 and had spent six and a half years in captivity—some of it under extremely harsh conditions—had distinguished himself as a tough resister and was highly respected by the other returnees. Coker also enjoyed the little-known distinction of being one of the few returnees who had been deployed as a human shield at two different locations—first at "Dirty Bird," the Hanoi Thermal Power Plant (target JCS 81) where he and a cell mate engineered a successful escape but were recaptured the following day, and later at "Alcatraz" in the northeast corner of the MND Citadel compound (target JCS 57).

Coker, presenting his testimony in written form, had begun by establishing his bona fides:

> I have talked to people in the Navy and the Air Force, and to a great extent the Army, the DOD representatives and to the State Department. I know their attitudes. . . . I think I can speak as a consensus of opinion. It's purely unofficial, but I can guarantee that I do speak for a consensus.
>
> How did I get some of these credentials, especially speaking for POW's? . . . Well, I can give you this little bit of factual type of data: There is nothing that took place in the POW system that I am not aware of. I am not the only person who can say that; but there are not too many who can.[8]

Having made clear that he was speaking (1) for administration officials handling the POW issue, (2) for the returnees, and (3) as an expert on the prisons where American POWs had been held during the war, Coker had then declared the following:

> - Most of the MIA's were dead the second that they were called MIA. . . . More than likely . . . most of them were killed outright, right then . . . but they're carried as MIA. They are KIA, even though in our minds we get them confused. There is no way these people are going to appear—there's no way that they can come home as a POW because they're dead.
> - There are no POWs [in Laos]. The guys, if they made it to the ground alive . . . probably died there in that area, if not immediately, within a couple of days to 1 or 2 weeks. Laos killed him; it just gobbled him up.

- The only reason they [the North Vietnamese] keep you is because you are worth something to them. . . . If you cease to be good to them as a political hostage, they're going to get rid of you, because they're not going to spend money to feed you, to clothe you, to shelter you, and to guard you. If you're not good for something to them, they're going to get rid of you. So for this reason . . . I have come to the conclusion that I don't think there are going to be more people over there alive. There's no reason for them to be alive.
- I know the vast, huge majority of POW's support me in this attitude, all live POW's came home.[9]

The second blow had been struck in mid-February when the committee heard from Adm. John S. McCain Jr., USN (Ret.), the legendary and highly respected commander in chief of U.S. forces in the Pacific from 1968 to 1972 and the father of returnee Cmdr. John S. McCain III, USN.[10]

Testifying in open session on February 18, Adm. McCain had stunned observers when he had declared in his introductory remarks that "I don't have to tell you that Johnny, along with many other POW's have some very strong opinions on the subject that you're about to embark on. It's a very fine thing this committee has taken on its shoulders, the responsibility of clearing the books as far as the missing in action are concerned. There comes a time when this must be done."[11]

*Clearing the books?*

Though McCain's statement about how the returnees felt about the likelihood that POWs might remain alive in captivity in Southeast Asia had tracked with what Coker had said, Montgomery had gone on to press the legendary admiral for his own personal opinion on the matter. McCain had answered Montgomery by stating that he did not think there was any question but that some Americans remained alive in Indochina, but that the number was "small . . . very small . . . very, very few . . . maybe 20 or 30" and that any who were alive were "working for [the] Communists."[12]

Rear Adm. William P. Lawrence, USN, a highly respected naval aviator imprisoned by the North Vietnamese for more than five and a half years prior to his release in March 1973, had administered the third blow while testifying before the committee in early March. When asked by Chairman Montgomery if he believed there were any American servicemen still held captive in North Vietnam, Lawrence had replied:

Well, of course, this is an opinion based on my best educated analysis of the situation. I feel that the North Vietnamese released all of the American prisoners, because the list of names that we had coincided with the list of people who were released, died in captivity, et cetera.

I perceive that they had a very strong incentive to release all of the Americans in order to facilitate the peace agreement. They knew that in order to achieve a peace agreement and to obtain the agreement of the Americans to withdraw from Vietnam, that they had to release the POW's. So it is my opinion that they did release all the Americans in Vietnam. I see no indications from the actions of the North Vietnamese that they still have any

Americans still alive in North Vietnam.[13] [Lawrence would later tell author Al Santoli that the North Vietnamese kept him and the other POWs who were returned at Operation Homecoming alive because "they knew we had hostage value.[14] Lawrence, who had been in one of the final selection groups for the Mercury space program before his June 28, 1967, shoot-down, had served as John McCain's immediate superior during McCain's detention at Hoa Lo. McCain would later describe Lawrence as "my dear friend and revered commanding officer in Hanoi . . . universally respected . . . a remarkable commander [with whom] I shared . . . every question or concern I had."][15]

Finally, in late March, a third returnee had appeared before the committee to address the question of live prisoners. Former CIA contract pilot Ernest C. Brace, had been one of the nine "Laos prisoners" released by the North Vietnamese during Operation Homecoming. A former marine and a decorated Korean War pilot, Brace had been captured in May 1965 in northern Laos by PAVN troops. Following capture, he had been force-marched to an area of North Vietnam near Dien Bien Phu and imprisoned there under the most hellish of conditions for over three years. In October 1968, he had been transferred to Hanoi and, after a brief stop at Hoa Lo (the "Hanoi Hilton"), had been taken to the "Plantation" and placed in a cell in the solitary confinement lockup. Shortly thereafter, John McCain III, who by chance occupied an adjoining cell, had contacted him and instructed him to place the tin cup in his room up to the wall and use it to transmit his voice through the wall. Brace had done so, and, as he would later state, soon he and McCain were talking to one another "almost as easily as we were speaking on the phone." Brace would later write that he and McCain talked for hours every day for an entire year, discussing music, movies, news, sports, etc., and telling one another "things we would never say to anyone else." Though their daily discussions had ended in December 1969 when they had been caught communicating and had been moved to Hoa Lo and placed in widely separated cells, the two would remain the closest of friends.[16]

Brace testified that he and the other eight "Laos prisoners" released from Hanoi during Operation Homecoming had all fallen into the hands of North Vietnamese troops operating in Laos and that none had ever been held by the Pathet Lao. In spite of this fact, Chairman Montgomery asked Brace if the Pathet Lao might still be holding American POWs and, if so, why. The following exchange occurred:

MR. BRACE: I see no reason for the Laotians to be holding any Americans in Laos. There is no propaganda value. We were not workers. We haven't worked in the fields. We are pretty soft compared to their standards.

I see no reason for the Pathet Lao to hold American prisoners. There is nothing to be rebuilt in Laos that I can see, unless you want to rebuild the city of Vientiane, which was never really wrecked. But I think as far as Americans being alive in Laos, I would say that it is a possibility, but it is very unlikely.

THE CHAIRMAN: A possibility, but very unlikely?

MR. BRACE: Very unlikely. I see no political reason for it, I see no practical reason for it from the Laotian standpoint whatsoever.[17]

Concluding, Brace expanded his comments to North Vietnam, telling Montgomery, "My own personal feeling is that it is done, it is over, there is nobody captured prior to 1973 that is going to come out of North Vietnam at this time alive."[18]

## SOUTHERN VIETNAM

Around the time Adm. McCain and the three former POWs were presenting their expert testimony in Washington, American servicemen were being seen in captivity at numerous locations in both southern and northern Vietnam. Those prisoners' plight would not become known until many months (or even years) later when the persons who had observed or heard about them were able to escape from Vietnam and tell U.S. officials what they had seen or heard.

In April, three Americans dressed in torn and dirty military uniforms were reportedly seen being taken into custody by Communist officials in a forced labor area located some ten miles west of the former U.S. air base at Bien Hoa. (See map page 145, point 1.) The Americans were reportedly hiding out in an underground bunker near the former Phu Loi military camp when a bulldozer being used in a land-clearing operation hit the bunker and opened it, exposing the three men inside. According to a South Vietnamese man who reportedly was present at the time and saw the three Americans emerge from their damaged hideout, one of them could not stand on his own and had to be supported by the others. The witness reportedly said that all three were Caucasian and that all had long hair and long beards, leading him to surmise they had either long ago escaped from prison or had been hiding out since the fall of Saigon a year before.[19]

On May 12, a South Vietnamese truck driver pressed into service by the Communists had a chance encounter with American POWs while delivering a load of wheat and other foodstuffs to a storage shed located on the grounds of the former U.S. Army base at Long Binh, northeast of Ho Chi Minh City. (See map page 145, point 2.) According to what the truck driver later told U.S. intelligence officials, he had been directed by PAVN soldiers to pull his truck into the shed on a remote section of the base and, soon after he had done so, to his surprise some ten American prisoners and a like number of PAVN guards armed with AK-47 rifles came walking into the shed. The truck driver said that as he watched, two of the Americans got up into the bed of his covered truck and began dragging sacks of wheat and other foodstuffs to the back, where the other Americans took them and placed them on their shoulders and carried them away. He further said that at one point he climbed up into the truck to help the two Americans who were dragging the sacks, and that one of the Americans told him that the group of American prisoners numbered twenty-two men. The truck driver described the Americans as all being skinny and having very closely cut hair. Some were wearing gray trousers, others gray shorts, and some were wearing gray T-shirts while others were bare chested.[20]

At approximately 11:00 A.M. on an unrecalled morning in May, an ARVN prisoner confined to one of the reeducation camps in the Ham Tan reeducation camp system located east of Ho Chi Minh City near the coastal city of Ham Tan was out of his camp on a work detail when he observed two Caucasian prisoners in VC custody. The ARVN would later tell U.S. officials that the sighting had taken place at a rice distribution point on the southeast slope of Mt. May Tao, a

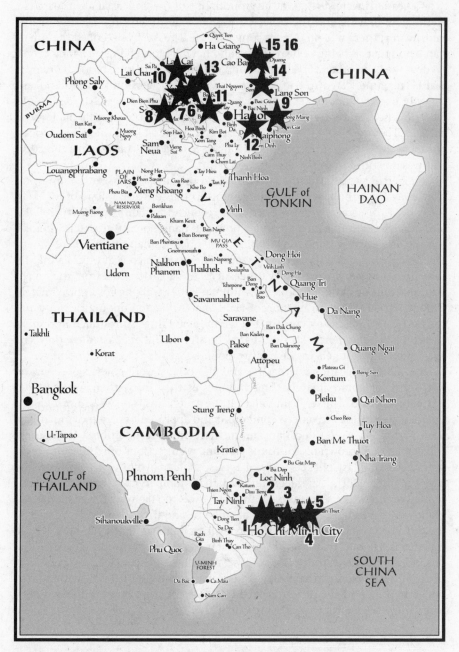

Selected 1976 sightings of U.S. POWs in Vietnam. (HENDON/ANDERER)

2,310-foot-high outcropping located some twenty-five kilometers northwest of Ham Tan. (See map page 145, point 3.)

The ARVN prisoner said that he and other members of his work detail observed the two Caucasians off and on for approximately one hour, and that during a period when he and three of his work party were resting near where the two Caucasians were sitting on the ground, one of the Caucasians whispered in Vietnamese that he and the other Caucasian were Americans. Because guards were nearby, there was no further conversation. The ARVN described the American who spoke as being of heavy build and having blond hair and a long beard. He described the other as being of slim build and having long blond hair and a beard. This American also had restricted use of the fingers on his left hand, apparently due to a poorly set broken wrist. Both Americans were dressed in old ARVN trousers and tattered black shirts and were wearing sandals made from old tires. The ARVN told U.S. officials that after about an hour the two American prisoners left with their escort, pulling a cart loaded with rations in a direction that was downhill from the distribution point.[21]

Some eight weeks after the two American prisoners were seen hauling supplies away from the rice distribution point on the southeast slope of Mt. May Tao, an ARVN sergeant imprisoned at a reeducation camp just north of the mountain was out of his camp on a wood- and bamboo-cutting detail when he and the other ARVN inmates with him came upon a small prison where Americans were being held. The sergeant would later explain to U.S. officials that he and approximately thirty to forty other ARVN inmates departed from their reeducation camp on foot early one morning and after walking for approximately five or six hours in the direction of Ham Tan they came upon a prison camp consisting of three newly constructed bamboo buildings surrounded by a crisscross type bamboo fence. He said that as he and the others passed by, they saw four American prisoners inside the compound. (See map page 145, point 4.)

The ARVN sergeant said that he and the others were able to observe the Americans for approximately three minutes as they made their way past the prison compound. The sergeant said that the Americans were walking around in a garden area inside the fenced compound and appeared to be removing insects from plants. All were Caucasian and all were wearing traditional Vietnamese conical hats and brown peasant-type clothing with sections of white cloth sewn over the two breast pockets and a larger section of white cloth sewn on the backs of their shirts. The sergeant said that numbers and letters had been printed on the white sections of cloth, but he was too far away to them. The sergeant went on to tell U.S. officials that when he and the other ARVNs passed by the prison several days later on the way back to their camp, they did not see the Americans. He said that a few months later, however, his group passed by the prison again and this time they saw two Americans inside. (See map page 145, point 5.) He explained that these Americans were tilling the soil with garden hoes when he and the others arrived but dropped their hoes and stared back when they realized they were being watched.[22]

## THE MASS TRANSFER OF REEDUCATION CAMP INMATES TO NORTHERN VIETNAM FOR LONG-TERM IMPRISONMENT

In addition to not yet knowing of the isolated sightings of small groups of American prisoners that were taking place in southern Vietnam during the spring and summer of 1976, U.S. intelligence officials did not know either that the victorious North Vietnamese, after having spent the better part of a year investigating, interrogating, indoctrinating, terrorizing, and brutalizing those held in reeducation camps in the South, had begun to transfer tens of thousands of hard-core senior military officers, intelligence operatives, former high officials of the South Vietnamese government, and others who had not "done well" during their first year in reeducation to camps and prisons in the North for long-term reeducation. (Tens of thousands of lower-ranking Southerners remained captive in the southern camps, some for many years.)

The story of the transfer of the Southerners to the North and their subsequent confinement there would be told by thousands who survived the ordeal and later fled Vietnam. One of those Southerners, former ARVN Maj. Thai Phi Long, who so eloquently described the roundup and imprisonment of the Southerners following the fall of Saigon (see Chapter 14), also offered details of the transfer of the Southerners to the North. Major Long's account, received by U.S. officials in 1981, would prove representative of the eyewitness accounts of thousands of his comrades:

On the night of 10 April 1976, the communists took us by truck convoy from our reeducation camp near Saigon to the New Port docks in Saigon. When we arrived at the docks around midnight, we saw many other prisoners who had been transported there from other camps. The communists assembled us, took roll call, divided us into groups of 300 persons each and took the groups one after another down to ships—the type of landing ships used by the army—and locked us up down in the very bottom of the ship. Many escort troops armed with AK-47 rifles stood guard over us on the deck of the ship. We asked one another whether or not they might be taking us for imprisonment on Phu Quoc [Island] or Con Son [Island].

After traveling on the ship for four days and nights, they put us ashore. As we set foot on the mainland we couldn't figure out where we were, in part because it was nighttime and in part because we were overly tired and hungry and thirsty after being locked in the ship's hold for four days, sleeping sitting up and in stinking filth [because we had to go to] the bathroom in place. Suddenly, a voice echoed over a megaphone being held by a cadre standing on the deck and pointing it at us, saying, "I welcome all of you to the Socialist Northern Region of Vietnam. Here you will have favorable conditions for studying well and making progress." We all were stunned to hear this. The guide cadre said that we were at the port of Vinh.

We lined up in a single file in groups of 65 persons and, surrounded and closely guarded by many military escort troops and public security personnel in yellow uniforms, we followed the surveillance cadres. Each group of 65 was moved up onto a railroad car parked 500 meters away. We couldn't get all 65 persons onto the car, which normally was used to haul livestock. They shoved us until we all were aboard and stepping on each other, because there was not enough room. Then they closed and locked the door. In the entire railroad car, there were no openings for looking outside other than a few small cracks in the sides of the car.

The next day, as the train was moving past a point, it slowed down. We heard many voices outside jeering and denouncing us, and [the sound of] bricks and stones being thrown against the railroad car. We vied with one another to get a peek through the cracks and learned that this was Hanoi and that the people of Hanoi had been invited to come out "to line up and welcome" us. The train traveled for another day, and then we disembarked at the Yen Bai Railway Station. Two of my friends Lieutenant Colonel Nguyen Xuan Minh and Major Hoang Duc Nguyen, died as a result of [the trip]. The communists put their stiff bodies in a Red Cross vehicle and took them away. Many people were standing and waiting to see us at the Yen Bai Station. They looked at us with accusing glances. One person was surprised and said, "My God! Look how big these puppet soldiers are. They are so big and so tall!!!" An extremist said with an angry voice, "They should be big. They squeezed and exploited the people and lived high with many benefits. Why wouldn't they be big and tall!" After stopping for about half an hour at Yen Bai, we were put on another Molotova truck convoy to be transported to many different locations in the jungles.

A camp was set up for every 200 officers. These camps were scattered in the mountainous jungle region of Hoang Lien Son, Lao Cai, Son La and Nghia Lo Provinces near the border of China. The communists forced us to do labor right from the first day that we set foot there. The guards told us "you must labor energetically in order to turn stones into rice so that you can eat. No one can sit idle, living at the expense of others." Now, we began to taste the communists' "prisons" in the North and the persecution measures that they in turn applied to punish us and to take revenge against us. They placed the blame on the American imperialist aggressors in Vietnam for creating a war to destroy the country, for crippling the national economy, and for causing hunger and hardship for the people.[23]

Other Southerners later reported they had been moved by boat from the Mekong Delta to Vinh and then on by train to Yen Bai.[24] Still others would report they had been taken in boats from ports in the South to the northern ports of Haiphong[25] and Hon Gai[26] and transferred to railroad cars, trucks, or buses for the trip to Yen Bai. In the end, no matter who the Southerner was, or what was his port of embarkation in the South or port of debarkation in the North, the story was almost always the same: trucks at night to the southern ports; packed, foul-smelling ships to the northern ports; packed, foul-smelling railroad cars, trucks, or buses to Yen Bai (and, quite often, the sight of their dead countrymen being unloaded from the packed railroad cars there);[27] and then movement overland from Yen Bai to reeducation camps throughout the North.

By the summer of 1976, thousands upon thousands of Southerners had been transferred out of the southern camps to new places of confinement in the

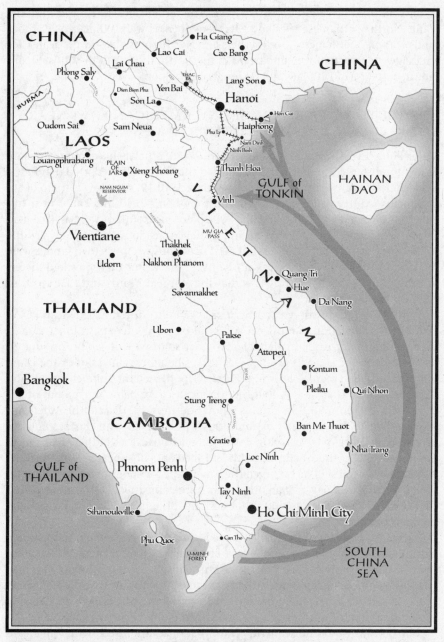

The mass transfer of South Vietnamese prisoners to North Vietnam, 1976–1977.
(HENDON/ANDERER)

North. Unknown to the Communists—or perhaps they just didn't care—as a result of the transfers, *America's postwar eyes and ears were now in place deep inside the "Socialist Northern Region of Vietnam."* Soon, great numbers of additional "friendly" eyes and ears—those of the Southerners' families who would begin coming north for periodic visits—*would join the intelligence network*. All the while, North Vietnamese eyes and ears were open as well. When tens of thousands of these Vietnamese—Southerners and Northerners alike—would later flee and tell what they had seen and heard in the North, the fate of the unlisted, unreturned American POWs would no longer be in doubt.

## THE SOUTHERNERS BEGIN SEEING AMERICAN POWs NEAR THE REEDUCATION CAMPS OF NORTH VIETNAM

Major Long, the ARVN who had described to U.S. officials his capture and subsequent transfer to long-term reeducation in the North, also reported that in the weeks following his arrival in the North in late April 1976, he saw a group of approximately thirty American POWs who were being held in a camp near his, which was located across the Red River at a point just south of Yen Bai. (See map page 145, point 6.) He said that he and his fellow reeducation inmates saw the Americans on approximately ten different occasions when the two groups were working in the same area. Long said he never got closer than hundred meters from the Americans but clearly saw that they all had beards and that seven or eight of them were black.[28]

Soon, other newly arrived Southerners began encountering American POWs near their reeducation camps. An ARVN airborne lieutenant colonel arrived from the South at a camp in Nghia Lo Province southwest of Yen Bai on June 30 just in time to see sixty to seventy U.S. POWs being marched out of the camp under guard. (See map page 145, point 7.) The lieutenant colonel would later tell U.S. officials that he was told the Americans were being moved out of the camp to make room for him and his fellow Southerners. He said the Americans were dressed in red pajama-type uniforms with vertical white stripes and appeared weak. Some were carrying PAVN-issue field packs and others had rolled-up sleeping mats. Almost all were white skinned and all appeared fairly old. The lieutenant colonel said he observed the Americans for about five or ten minutes until PAVN guards began marching them three abreast out of the camp in a northeasterly direction. He said the Americans disappeared into the forest and he never saw them again.[29]

Later in the summer, in August, a reeducation camp inmate on a bamboo-cutting detail near his camp in Son La Province, southwest of Nghia Lo, came upon six Caucasians in prison clothes who were also cutting bamboo. (See map page 145, point 8.) The inmate would later tell U.S. officials that the Caucasian prisoners, all of whom were thin and weak, appeared to be forty years of age or older. They were guarded by at least one armed public security guard.[30]

U.S. officials would subsequently learn that in addition seeing the Americans described above—all of whom were clearly prisoners—the newly arrived Southerners encountered a single American in the Yen Bai area who was in a different status. This American, seen by hundreds and perhaps thousands of Southerners, was approximately thirty years old and was said by camp cadre to have remained in Vietnam voluntarily after the signing of the Paris accords in 1973. He was often seen driving a truck, repairing PAVN motor vehicles, and maintaining the generators that provided power for the reeducation camps in the region.

The guards said the American's Vietnamese name was "Nam." A number of Southerners would later correctly identify "Nam" as former U.S. Marine Corps Pvt. Robert Garwood.[31]

## NORTHERNERS ALSO SEE AMERICAN POWs

U.S. intelligence officials would later find that the newly arrived Southerners weren't the only ones encountering American prisoners in the North in 1976. Many Northerners would later flee and report that they, too, had seen American POWs being detained in the northern part of Vietnam that year.

A North Vietnamese man saw several American pilots in early 1976 inside a large prison located about a twenty-minute walk off of Route 183 near Hon Gai. (See map page 145, point 9.) The man later told U.S. officials that a friend who was with him at the time pointed out the prison and told him that American pilots captured during 1972 were being held there. It was then that he observed the American prisoners, who were dressed in baggy striped uniforms and appeared skinny. Some had red faces, apparently from exposure to the sun.[32]

A Northerner employed as a motor grader operator on a road project at Coc Mi, near Pho Lu in the far northwest had almost daily encounters that summer with a group of Caucasian prisoners who were assigned to break rocks on his road project. (See map page 145, point 10.) The motor grader operator later told U.S. officials that he assumed the Caucasians were American prisoners of war because of their appearance; because they were always guarded and because they wore striped uniforms with "POW" written on the back in Vietnamese. He drew a map of the area where the sightings occurred and said he believed the Americans had been kept at a prison camp located just up the road from where he had seen them.[33]

In August, a PAVN captain reportedly saw a truck carrying an undetermined number of American prisoners who were being held at a prison camp in a mountainous area at Ba Vi village, about twelve kilometers from Son Tay.[34] (See map page 145, point 11.)

In October, a North Vietnamese doctor traveling by bus from Hanoi to Haiphong reportedly saw fifteen to twenty American POWs in a truck near Hai Duong. (See map page 145, point 12.) The American prisoners were chained together in pairs and wore striped POW uniforms. All appeared sick or injured. The doctor had reportedly seen many American POWs before and was thus certain that the prisoners in the truck were Americans.[35]

In November, two civilian criminals on a work detail northeast of Thac Ba Lake, the large man-made hydroelectric reservoir just north of Yen Bai, reportedly saw approximately thirty Caucasian prisoners in the back a Molotova truck that passed by their worksite. (See map page 145, point 13.) The two criminals reportedly were able to see that the prisoners' hands were bound in front of them and that armed guards also occupied the truck. The two criminals reportedly said the truck was headed in the direction of Hanoi, and as it passed by, the overseer of their work detail pointed to it and declared, "That is the truck that is carrying American prisoners."[36]

At about 8:00 A.M. on an unrecalled day in 1976, armed PAVN security guards were seen being posted along both sides of the main street of Na Sam, a small town located near the Chinese border at a point just northwest of Lang Son. After viewing the scene for approximately fifteen minutes, a resident saw six or seven trucks rumble through town along the deserted main street. The resident later told U.S. officials that each truck had its cargo compartment covered with metal sheets to prevent observation of the contents, but that a PAVN security guard said the trucks contained U.S. POWs who were being transported to nearby Dong Khe County in Cao Bang Province.[37] (See map page 145, points 14 and 15.)

Late in 1976, an electrician wiring a cave that served as the underground portion of a prison complex near Dong Khe City in Cao Bang Province saw eight U.S. pilots incarcerated there. The electrician later told U.S. officials that the prison was located at the village of Bo Djuong, which he said was approximately five kilometers off the main highway between Na Sam and Cao Bang. (See map page 145, point 16.) He described the aboveground portion of the prison as a high-security facility with writing on the walls that indicated that as many as 180 U.S. pilots had been held there during the war. He said that this main, aboveground portion of the prison backed up against steep mountains, and in one of those mountains, at a point less than one hundred meters to the rear (southeast) of the prison proper, was a large cave that the Vietnamese were using as an underground detention facility. The electrician estimated that this cave could hold several hundred prisoners. He told U.S. officials that he observed the eight American prisoners from a distance of two to three meters while he was wiring this cave for electricity. The prisoners were wearing red striped prison uniforms and were talking among themselves when he observed them. He also said cadre told him the men were former U.S. pilots.[38]

## WASHINGTON

Back in Washington, Chairman Montgomery and members of his committee had no way of knowing about the American POWs being sighted throughout Vietnam during 1976. That information would become known only many months—and in some cases many years—later when the sources who had seen the Americans or heard about them would escape from Vietnam and tell what they had seen or heard. Declassified CIA records indicate, however, that agency officials were in possession of intelligence that indicated a probability that American POWs were alive in Vietnam in 1976 and that this intelligence was withheld from the committee.

Here is what the record shows: In February 1976, Montgomery wrote to the director of central intelligence, George H. W. Bush, and requested that someone from the agency come and testify before the committee as to "whether any Americans are still being held as prisoners of war, as 'war criminals,' or in any other category as a result of U.S. involvement in Southeast Asia."[39]

In response to Montgomery's request, Director Bush dispatched his deputy director, Lt. Gen. Vernon A. "Dick" Walters, USA, to testify. Walters appeared before the committee on March 17 to, in his words, "represent the Director as spokesman for the intelligence community on the subject of intelligence efforts to determine the status of the men still carried as prisoner of war—PW—and missing in action—MIA—in Southeast Asia." In written and oral statements to the committee, Walters declared:

- There has been no substantive reporting, confirmed or confirmable, of Americans still being held captive in North Vietnam.
- Since the fall of Saigon in April 1975, no substantive reports have been received concerning U.S. personnel unaccounted for in North Vietnam.
- A review of the intelligence community's holdings shows that we have no confirmed information that additional American PW's are still being held in captivity in Southeast Asia or elsewhere as a result of the Indochina war.[40]

When asked point-blank by Montgomery whether any intelligence relating to living POWs "is being held back from this committee," Walters replied, "Absolutely none, Mr. Chairman. It would be inhuman to do such a thing to the families and I am sure that we would stretch every desire to protect sources and methods if we had any information we could give those families. We do not have any additional information."[41]

Walters's testimony went over well on the Hill, where both he and Bush were highly respected by members of both parties.

In mid-April, however, alarm bells sounded when the committee learned from a confidential source that Soviet Ambassador Anatoly Dobrynin and one other member of the Soviet delegation in Washington had reportedly been heard to say after the war that the North Vietnamese were still holding some ninety-three American POWs. Believing the CIA was already in possession of this information, committee members demanded that the agency explain why they had not been briefed on Dobrynin's statement and forcefully renewed their request that all intelligence the agency held that indicated POWs might still be alive be turned over to the committee for review.[42]

Responding to the committee members' concerns, a CIA official acknowledged in a draft internal memorandum prepared in August for Director Bush that the agency was, in fact, in possession of intelligence that "can be interpreted as indicating a probability that there are still American PWs alive in North Vietnam." The official cited several examples, the most significant of which were the fact that the American POWs used as human shields at Hanoi's Long Bien Bridge (Paul Doumer Bridge) had not been returned at Operation Homecoming and that the agency was in receipt of several postwar intelligence reports that quoted various North Vietnamese and Vietcong officials as stating the DRV was still holding American POWs. "Not all of these reports," the official wrote, quoting North Vietnamese and Vietcong officials, "have been brought to the attention of the Select Committee." The memorandum raised the question as to whether the CIA's position that "there is no . . . reliable information" that American POWs are still held in North Vietnam should be reevaluated since doing so "at this point in time presents a delicate problem."[43]

Senate investigators would later discover that the intelligence cited in the CIA August draft reevaluation was not the only intelligence the agency held in the summer of 1976 suggesting that American POWs were still being held prisoner by the North Vietnamese. Also in the agency's possession was potentially explosive photographic intelligence acquired from spy satellites that suggested the presence of American POWs inside a maximum security prison at Dong Mang, just north of the northern port of Hon Gai. This satellite photography, which had been taken during 1975 but had been examined for evidence of American POWs only in mid-1976, showed what both CIA and DIA photo interpreters believed could be a series of pilot distress signals laid out in Morse code in roof tiles on the roof of one of the walled, high-security lockups inside the prison compound.[44] The signal was believed by the experts to be the universal U.S. pilot distress signal—the letter *K*—which had been given to all U.S. pilots and aircrewmen during the war with instructions that they display it by whatever means available if they were shot down.[45]

According to CIA records declassified in the early 1990s, the existence of the satellite photography was a closely guarded secret in the summer of 1976, known only to Director Bush, RADM James B. Stockdale, who was stationed at the Pentagon at the time and had been consulted because of his experiences as a POW, and a very few others.[46]

The absence of any mention of the satellite photography and the suspected pilot distress codes in the official record of the Montgomery Committee proceedings strongly suggests that this critical intelligence was not made available to the committee. The similar absence of the information about the human shields who did not return from the Long Bien Bridge in Hanoi (and many other military targets as well) indicates that this critical information too was withheld from the committee. Likewise, there is no mention in the committee's published record about the postwar intelligence reports quoting Communist officials from both the North and South saying Hanoi was still holding American POWs. Nor does the record show that Walters ever returned to the Hill to amend his testimony that no intelligence was being withheld from the committee.[47]

A comparison of information in the committee's public record with wartime intelligence that remained classified until the early 1990s indicates that the CIA was not the only U.S. intelligence agency withholding critical intelligence on live POWs from Montgomery and his members. DIA officials, for their part, provided the committee with declassified maps and annotated reconnaissance photos of the famous Ban Nakay Teu cave prison complex in Sam Neua Province Laos, including one photo of the area just outside the cave entrance labeled "Recreation Area with Net."[48] Nowhere in the committee record is there any indication DIA also provided the highly classified October 11, 1969, reconnaissance photos showing some twenty American POWs playing volleyball on that exact same recreation area—none of whom returned at Operation Homecoming (see Chapter 3).

## MONTGOMERY COMMITTEE WRAPS UP ITS INVESTIGATION, DECLARES ALL POWs/MIAs DEAD

Stymied on all sides—first by the North Vietnamese and their unyielding demand for reconstruction aid, then by Nixon, Kissinger, and Scowcroft on the matter of the Nixon letter, and finally by CIA and DIA on the intelligence—

Montgomery and the members of his committee wrapped up their investigation and, in mid-December, issued their final report.

In their findings relative to the contentious matter of reconstruction aid, committee members declared the obvious by stating that "the Socialist Republic of Vietnam [the name of the newly unified country] has called for selective implementation of the Paris Peace Agreement, specifically Article 21 dealing with American reconstruction aid to Vietnam, in exchange for POW/MIA information under Article 8B," but added bluntly that "the Congress and the Administration will not agree to any conditions even faintly resembling blackmail in order to gain an accounting."

Regarding the Nixon letter, the members declared only that "the Department of State failed to inform the select committee fully, prior to its visit to Hanoi, of the details of the correspondence between the Governments of the United States and Vietnam."

On the explosive question of living POWs, the members—almost certainly having been deprived of critical intelligence by their own government, and almost certainly having been influenced by the testimony of the expert witnesses, and having no way of knowing what was actually going on in Indochina at the time—declared their belief that "no Americans are still being held alive as prisoners in Indochina, or elsewhere, as a result of the war in Indochina." They added that this belief reflected the position of the national intelligence community that "there is no reliable evidence that any unaccounted for POW's/MIA's are still being held in Indochina."

With that, the committee returned to the treasury nearly half of the $350,000 allocated for its investigation and, on the last day of the congressional term, ceased to exist.

Hundreds of new reports of Americans held in captivity and years of rancorous national debate over the POW/MIA issue lay ahead.

George H. W. Bush would be in the last months of his presidency in 1992 when another U.S. spy satellite would pick up two fresh pilot distress codes in a field some four hundred feet northwest of the same Dong Mang prison shown in the 1975 satellite photography. The codes shown in this imagery, acquired on June 5, 1992, would include two classified USAF escape and evasion codes, the secret four-digit authenticator of a missing U.S. Air Force captain, and the last name of a missing U.S. Air Force major.

Neither of these fliers, nor any of the hundreds of the other unlisted, unreturned American POWs described in the other postwar intelligence, have yet been released.

# CHAPTER 16

1977

# A NEW PRESIDENT ADDRESSES THE MATTER OF
# THE UNLISTED, UNRETURNED POWs

. . .

Has anybody here seen my old
  friend Abraham?
Can you tell me where he's gone?
He freed a lot of people,
But it seems the good they die
  young.
You know, I just looked around and
  he's gone.

Anybody here seen my old friend
  John?
Can you tell me where he's gone?
He freed a lot of people,
But it seems the good they die
  young.
I just looked around and he's gone.

Anybody here seen my old friend
  Martin?
Can you tell me where he's gone?
He freed a lot of people,
But it seems the good they die
  young.
I just looked around and he's gone.

Didn't you love the things that they
  stood for?
Didn't they try to find some good
  for you and me?
And we'll be free
Some day soon, and it's a-gonna be
  one day . . .

Anybody here seen my old friend
  Bobby?
Can you tell me where he's gone?
I thought I saw him walkin' up over
  the hill,
With Abraham, Martin and John.

—"Abraham, Martin and John,"
Words and music by Richard Holler

More than thirty-five of the American POWs declared dead by the Montgomery Committee were seen in early 1977 on a work detail just outside Lai Chau Province Town, near the Chinese border in far northwest Vietnam. (See map page 158, point 1.)

The Americans were seen by a group of ARVN soldiers who were themselves on a work party near their reeducation camp. One of them later told U.S. officials that the American prisoners, whom he estimated numbered between thirty-five and sixty, were all dressed in black collarless prison uniforms and appeared haggard and emaciated. Some, he said, wore wooden sandals and some had on *non las,* the Vietnamese conical hats. He added the Americans were all carrying food and water containers and field tools and were speaking among themselves in English as he and the other ARVN inmates passed nearby.[1]

Due east of Lai Chau near the Red River town of Pho Lu, meantime, another eighteen "dead" American prisoners were reportedly being seen regularly at one of the subcamps in the Phong Quang (Coc Mi) Prison complex, located just up the road from where the motor grader operator had repeatedly seen the American POWs working on the road gang the previous summer (see Chapter 15). (See map page 158, point 2.) These Americans, a majority of whom were said to be U.S. Special Forces and the others pilots, were reportedly being seen by a former ARVN Marine Corps second lieutenant imprisoned at Phong Quang (Coc Mi) who had been tasked to deliver food and water to the Americans' camp. They were reportedly held two to a cell in an underground lockup located some three kilometers southwest of the main Phong Quang (Coc Mi) prison.[2]

In the South during early 1977, other Southerners were encountering other "dead" Americans all along a roughly hundred-kilometer-long stretch of the Cambodian border northwest of Saigon. In January, a former South Vietnamese naval officer undergoing reeducation near Katum, a small village located near the border in northern Tay Ninh Province, saw two Caucasian prisoners and their guards while he and fellow South Vietnamese inmates were on a logging detail near their camp. (See map page 158, point 3.)

The former naval officer later told U.S. officials that he and his fellow inmates believed the two Caucasians were Americans based on their appearance and manner. Both men, he said, were tall, fair skinned, and very thin. One had long blond hair, the other long brown hair. Both were dressed in long-sleeved yellow uniforms with broad brown vertical stripes and rectangular patches over the left breast. Both were carrying bundles of wood that hung Vietnamese-style from the ends of carrying poles. They were guarded by four guards carrying rifles.

The former naval officer said the two Americans and their guards passed by approximately twenty meters from where he and the others were working and that when the Americans saw the South Vietnamese work party they smiled and one raised his fingers in a V sign. The former naval officer said that he and several others returned the V until one of the guards forced the American to put down his hand. The former naval officer added that no words were spoken, and that the two Americans and the guards continued on their way and soon passed out of sight.[3]

Just after Tet, three Americans were reportedly taken into custody after Communist authorities discovered them hiding in the cellar of a house near Suoi Cut, northeast of legendary Nui Ba Den (Black Virgin Mountain). (See map page 158, point 4.) According to what a South Vietnamese woman later told U.S. officials, she and her mother were at the house waiting to see the owner, an herbal medicine doctor, when several security policemen from the Tay Ninh police station arrived and informed the doctor that a complaint had been filed against him and that they had come to search the premises. The woman said that she and her mother went outside and waited while the security police conducted their search. She said that during the course of the search they heard the security police screaming at the owner that they had discovered a trapdoor in the floor and three Americans hiding below it in a cellar. The security police then began beating the owner and, as the woman and her mother watched, dragged him from his house and took him away. The woman told U.S. officials that neither

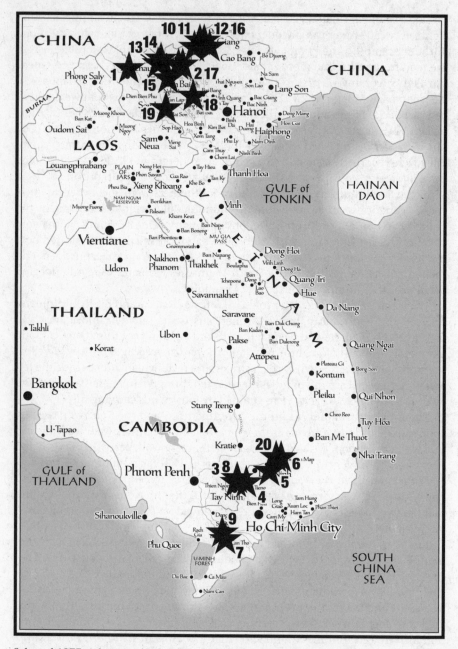

Selected 1977 sightings of U.S. POWs in Vietnam. (HENDON/ANDERER)

she nor her mother saw the three Americans and assumed the security police had planned to wait until after dark to bring them out. She added that she later learned from her mother that the herbal doctor's house and all his belongings had been confiscated.[4]

Several weeks after the reported discovery of the three Americans near Suoi Cut, two American prisoners were reportedly seen in an old French detention facility at Ba Ra Mountain, just south of Phuoc Binh (Song Be). (See map page 158, point 5.) According to an ARVN soldier who was reportedly held in reeducation in the area and reportedly saw the two Americans while out of his camp on woodcutting detail, he and other members of the detail were shown the two American prisoners by a Communist cadre during a rest period. The ARVN reportedly said that one of the Americans was black with the rank of private or PFC and the other one, who was Caucasian, was a sergeant or perhaps an officer. The ARVN reportedly said that both Americans were very thin and tired looking and that he felt very sorry for them. The cadre, speaking to the assembled ARVNs, reportedly told them that if they had captured prisoners like the two Americans they would not have been put in reeducation. The cadre then reportedly explained that U.S. leaders had signed an agreement in Paris to provide reconstruction aid to Vietnam when the POWs were returned, but that even after some of the POWs were returned there was no aid, so they continued to hold these POWs.[5]

A few weeks after the reported sighting of the two American POWs at Ba Ra Mountain, several tall Caucasians were reportedly seen on a tree-cutting detail in an area near the Cambodian border west of Bu Gia Map. (See map page 158, point 6.) According to the ARVN reeducation camp inmate who reportedly saw them, the Caucasians were tall, very thin, had full beards, and were dressed in brown and white striped uniforms.[6]

Word that all these Americans were still being held prisoner would not reach U.S. officials in Washington for years.

*Early 1977*
## WASHINGTON

Back in Washington in early 1977, the new U.S. president, Jimmy Carter, had announced during the opening days of his administration his intention to normalize relations with the SRV. Knowing the charged emotions associated with the MIA issue, however, and knowing that many of the nation's veterans as well as many among the POW/MIA families were unhappy with the Montgomery Committee's findings, Carter pledged that there had to be a satisfactory accounting of the MIAs before normalization could take place and that he would appoint a presidential commission to achieve such an accounting before any steps to normalize were undertaken.

In mid-February, Carter appointed his five-member Presidential Commission on Americans Missing and Unaccounted for in Southeast Asia. He named retired United Auto Workers president Leonard Woodcock as chairman and directed the commission to depart immediately for Southeast Asia to seek information about the missing and, if all went well, to informally explore ways to begin a new postwar relationship with the SRV. (Though the ink was barely dry on Congressman Sonny Montgomery's findings that no prisoners remained alive in Indochina, Montgomery was appointed to a seat on the commission. Also appointed were former Senator Mike Mansfield [D-MT], former Ambassador

Charles W. Yost, and Mrs. Marian Wright Edelman, director of the Children's Defense Fund.)[7]

The North Vietnamese, undoubtedly believing that Carter and Woodcock were seeking live POWs and might therefore be willing to address their demand for postwar reconstruction aid, hailed the appointment of the new commission. In a diplomatic note delivered to the United States in late February, the Vietnamese welcomed the commission's proposed visit to Hanoi and, as they would do often in the days and weeks ahead, took one more opportunity to restate their now-familiar position on the relationship between MIAs and postwar reconstruction aid: "In order to contribute to making the Vietnamese-U.S. meeting fruitful, the Vietnamese side is prepared to examine and solve with goodwill the question of Americans missing in action and other matters of interest to the United States. The U.S. side should adopt the same attitude regarding the U.S. contribution to the healing of the wounds of war and to postwar reconstruction in Viet Nam and other matters of interest to Viet Nam."[8]

"Prepared to examine and solve with goodwill the question of Americans missing in action." Not a bad start.

And had Carter and Woodcock had any interest whatsoever in recovering live prisoners, it might have developed into something big. But the record shows that they did not, and it did not.

## "THE WHOLE POINT . . . WAS TO DECLARE . . . THE MIAs . . . DEAD"

That Carter and members of his administration and Woodcock and members of his commission had no interest whatsoever in recovering live prisoners—and, in fact, actually set out from the beginning to declare all the MIAs dead—is a matter of little debate.

- Author Nayan Chanda, in his widely acclaimed history of the period, *Brother Enemy,* quotes a Carter State Department official as saying privately that "the whole point of the Woodcock trip was to declare that the MIAs are all dead."[9]
- Cyrus Vance, Carter's secretary of state, wrote to Carter at the time that the members of the Woodcock Commission, "understanding just how difficult, emotional and politically sensitive this issue [the MIAs] is, . . . are determined to do everything possible to assist the Administration in putting the problem behind us so that movement toward normalization can proceed."[10]
- Richard Holbrooke, an assistant secretary of state whose portfolio included Vietnam, and whose deputy, James Rosenthal, would serve as Woodcock's chief of staff, later said that the commission's "only real mission [was] to bring back remains and stress to [the Vietnamese] the importance of a full accounting [of the dead]."[11]
- Zbigniew Brzezinski, Carter's national security advisor, later stated that during the period of the Woodcock Commission the matter of the MIAs was raised only by "extreme right wingers" and "wasn't really a central issue."

"The prevailing view," Brzezinski later said, was that "we were dealing with KIA's and not MIA's," and thus the main mission of the Woodcock Commission was to see "whether we . . . [could], in the wake of the war, normalize relations."[12]

Given the feelings of these Carter administration officials at the time, it is not surprising that they did not respond aggressively when, in early and mid-March, they received two separate intelligence reports from the CIA, both quoting SRV officials as saying Hanoi was still holding American POWs, both making reference to the upcoming talks with Woodcock. The first report was dispatched from CIA headquarters on March 8.

## THE CIA INTELLIGENCE OF MARCH 8

Career diplomat James Rosenthal had served with distinction in Vietnam during the war. Seriously wounded when Vietcong terrorists attacked the U.S. embassy in Saigon in 1967, now, ten years later, Rosenthal was country director at the Vietnam, Laos, and Cambodia desk at the State Department. As trusted right hand to Assistant Secretary of State Richard Holbrooke, he had been chosen to accompany the Woodcock Commission to Vietnam as chief of the commission's staff. It was in early March, as Rosenthal was busy making arrangements for the commission's trip, that he was listed as a recipient of the first of two classified, closely held messages from the CIA that quoted Vietnamese officials as saying the Hanoi government was currently holding American POWs.

In this first message, received by Rosenthal just days before the delegation was scheduled to depart for Hanoi, William W. Wells, the agency's veteran deputy director of operations, advised Rosenthal that four days earlier, a CIA contact in West Germany had learned from a Vietnamese embassy employee in Bonn that the SRV was holding American prisoners of war as a "trump card" that they planned to use in the upcoming negotiations with the United States. According to the embassy employee, the POWs would not be released until the promised U.S. postwar financial aid was forthcoming. The CIA reported that the embassy employee had boasted that the Vietnamese, "as victor in the Vietnam war, would take advantage of this situation in negotiating with the U.S. for aid in economic reconstruction."[13]

It was as if a mole in General Motors headquarters had tipped Woodcock off to the company's negotiating strategy just prior to critical contract talks back in Detroit.

*Mid-March*
**HANOI**

Woodcock and his team, including Roger Shields, who had joined the delegation as Department of Defense staff representative, departed for the Far East on a USAF jet on March 13. After a stop in Hawaii and an overnight stay in the Philippines, the delegation switched to a smaller plane and departed Clark Field for Hanoi on the morning of the 16th. They arrived at Hanoi's Gia Lam Airport that afternoon at 2:45 P.M. Hanoi time.

A UPI reporter accompanying the delegation described the scene at Gia Lam:

Vice Foreign Minister Phan Hien stepped out [from a crowd] of some 50 officials and soldiers . . . and shook the hands of the five-member Commission sent by President Carter to find out what happened to 2,550 Americans missing from the Indochina War.

State Department officials accompanying the Commission expressed surprise. "Phan Hien is here," one diplomat said. "This is more than we expected."

Hien joined the welcome moments after two lower ranking foreign ministry officials met the Commission at planeside in an airport almost bare of planes and humanity.

There were no bands, no flags, no banners, no flowers and no speeches. "But there was Hien," the U.S. diplomat said.

"And that means this has been a very pleasing, very warm welcome," he said.

. . . Even though the American bombing of Hanoi halted only three years ago, the politeness of the welcome possibly reflected the Vietnamese desire for moving toward normal diplomatic relations with Washington, which could bring them the western aid they need and want.[14]

Following the airport welcome, Woodcock, Hien, and the others left for the Government Guest House for a welcoming session hosted by Foreign Minister Nguyen Duy Trinh. In opening remarks, Woodcock told Trinh, Hien, and the other Vietnamese present that the commission had come to help resolve the MIA issue and that President Carter hoped their visit would establish a basis for a new relationship between the two countries. Trinh thanked Woodcock for his remarks and then repeated for his visitor the SRV's position on MIAs. Vietnam, he said, "has done its utmost to implement Article 8B by research into the missing question. . . . Within the limits of our ability we have done our best. . . . We believe the United States should also show its good will by . . . carrying out Article 21 and in line with the Nixon letter of February 1, 1973." Trinh added, "[T]hat's the article on economic aid."[15]

Formal talks got under way the next morning, the 17th. Hien, heading the Vietnamese delegation, immediately began hammering the American side for the reparations he had helped win at Paris. "Vietnam," Hien said, "is willing to forget the past and look to the future, but the problems of the past, left over from the past, have to be solved. There are two major questions left over, (1) the question of the missing; and (2) . . . the U.S. response to the postwar reconstruction of Vietnam." He cited the Nixon letter as one basis for Vietnamese claims.

When Woodcock responded that the United States no longer had any responsibility for the Nixon letter, Hien countered by citing the U.S. responsibility under Article 21 of the Paris accords and questioned how, if Article 21 was not enforced, could Article 8B be enforced? Hien insisted that one side cannot be expected to implement the treaty while the other refuses to carry out its own responsibilities. "We have done our utmost on 8B and will continue these efforts," he declared, "but when we ask our people to help [in the search for missing Americans], we'll be asked about the obligation of the U.S. to heal the wounds of war, and what will we say? Vietnamese families have lost members and homes from U.S. bombs. If we told our people to help [with] the missing question without the United States doing its job," Hien went on, "I would lose my job with the Foreign Ministry." Rejecting any thought of normalizing relations before first receiving reconstruction aid, Hien told the commission, "Better to tighten the belt than to lose self respect."

The Americans questioned Hien about the possibility that some U.S. POWs might still be alive in Vietnam. In a remarkable ploy, Hien answered by reading aloud the findings of the Montgomery Committee and declared his complete agreement with Montgomery's conclusion that all American prisoners had either been released or were dead. He then dropped a tantalizing hint that would be heard by U.S. negotiators again and again in the future. "All Americans who remained in Vietnam and had 'registered' have been allowed to leave," he declared. When questioned by commission member Marian Wright Edelman about those who might not have "registered," Hien replied he had no way of knowing about them, because, he said, "they had not registered." When Edelman inquired further if it was likely that all Americans had heard of the "registration requirement," Hien said that no Americans were kept in prisons and "you can draw your own conclusions from what I have said."[16]

As the first full day of talks drew to a close, it was clear to the American side that, just as the CIA had reported from Bonn, the Vietnamese planned to use the prisoner issue for all it was worth. But were the Vietnamese really holding living American POWs, as the embassy employee in Bonn had reportedly said, or was Phan Hien simply bluffing about the "unregistered Americans" in an attempt to leverage American aid?

In only a matter of hours, the CIA would dispatch new intelligence addressed to Rosenthal that would indicate Hien was not bluffing. Not in the least.

## THE CIA INTELLIGENCE OF MARCH 16

At the very moment Hien was laying his case for aid before the American delegation in Hanoi, officials at CIA headquarters in Langley, Virginia, were in the process of sending Rosenthal yet another secret dispatch about U.S. POWs being held in Vietnam. Given that Rosenthal, as chief of staff of the commission, was facing Hien across the negotiating table in Hanoi at the time, the contents and the timing of the CIA report were truly electrifying.

The CIA report, dated March 16, 1977, stated that in January, Ambassador Hardi, Indonesia's ambassador to Hanoi had reported to Indonesian officials that Phan Hien himself and other North Vietnamese officials with whom Hardi was in contact had told Hardi that "there were American prisoners of war (POW's) still remaining in Vietnam and that these POW's posed a problem to the opening of diplomatic relations between the SRV and the United States."

Phan Hien, the CIA report continued, had told Hardi that these POWs included some who did not want to return to the United States.[17]

Given the obvious importance of this CIA report, it is unthinkable that Rosenthal, as chief of staff to Woodcock, would have kept its contents from his chairman. What, then, did Woodcock do with the explosive information? The commission's official trip report, submitted to President Carter after the commission returned to Washington, makes no reference to the intelligence or to Woodcock acting on it. The report does state that Woodcock held two private sessions with Hien during his visit but does not reveal what was discussed at those two meetings. No declassified notes of the two meetings are known to exist. Woodcock, in a telephone interview with coauthor Hendon in 1987, refused to discuss what occurred during the two meetings and said that he did not recall ever seeing the March 16 CIA intelligence report or being told of its contents. Phan Hien has twice refused to meet with the authors to discuss either his reported statement to Indonesian Ambassador Hardi or what occurred during his private meetings with Woodcock in Hanoi.[18]

What is known is that during an official meeting between the two delegations on the 18th, Hien presented Woodcock with a five-page aide-mémoire stating the official SRV position on MIAs and postwar aid. In the document, Hien, on behalf of his government, (1) quoted again what the Montgomery Committee's final report had stated, that no American servicemen remained alive in North Vietnam after the war; (2) declared that all Americans who had remained in the country after the fall of Saigon and had registered themselves with the Foreign Service of Vietnam had been allowed to leave; (3) promised that the SRV was actively seeking "information about the Americans still considered missing"; and (4) stated that the SRV "will welcome the U.S. contribution to the postwar reconstruction of Viet Nam." Attached to the document was a drastically scaled back version of the aid list Hien had given to the Montgomery Committee back in December. This new version contained only cereals (rice and wheat); cotton yarn and synthetic fiber; tractors; bulldozers; fertilizer; trucks; cement; steel to be used for the construction of houses, schools, and hospitals; and pharmaceutical raw materials and medicines. The aide-mémoire noted that the SRV was eager to hold talks with the United States on additional aid and trade-related matters and was prepared to normalize relations with the United States.[19] Concluding his remarks, Hien informed his guests that as a "special gesture" of goodwill, the Vietnamese would turn over the bodies of twelve deceased American pilots to members of the commission just prior to their departure, which was scheduled for the next morning, the 19th. (Vietnamese officials had made a similar macabre gesture four months earlier when they had presented Montgomery and members of his committee with the remains of three American pilots.)

Woodcock and the members of his delegation hosted a farewell dinner for the Vietnamese that evening. The following morning, they returned to Gia Lam and, after receiving the remains of the twelve pilots and conducting a brief repatriation ceremony at planeside, said their good-byes and departed for Vientiane for a quick meeting with the Pathet Lao.

The commission's official trip report shows that during their brief stop in

Vientiane, Woodcock and members of his delegation were treated to a familiar refrain:

> The Lao made clear to the Commission that they connected the MIA problem with that of U.S. assistance to "heal the wounds of war" and rebuild their country. They expressed the belief that the two problems should be resolved together, since both resulted from the war. They noted that if one speaks of humanitarian concern for the MIA's, one must also think of the damage Laos suffered at U.S. hands during the war. They said that the Lao people could be expected to search for MIA information only when they see that the U.S. Government is interested in healing this damage and helping reconstruct the country. In more general terms, they indicated that the MIA problem can be resolved when there is a new relationship between the two countries and when U.S. policy has changed from hostility to friendship.[20]

This very clear message from the Pathet Lao in hand, Woodcock and his delegation hurriedly returned to the airport, flew back to Clark Field, reboarded the larger USAF jet that had brought them from the United States, and departed for Washington to report their findings to the president.

## *Washington*
## WOODCOCK REPORTS HIS FINDINGS

Chairman Woodcock and his team went to the White House within hours of their arrival back in Washington to personally report their findings. Meeting with President Carter in the Cabinet Room, Woodcock presented his hastily prepared report, which contained nine primary conclusions. Among them were these: (1) there was no evidence to indicate that any American POWs remained alive anywhere in Indochina; (2) the Vietnamese had given assurances that they would look for "MIA information and remains"; (3) the Vietnamese did not link their providing of information on MIAs and remains to the receipt of aid; and (4) the Lao called attention to the difficulty of MIA search efforts in view of the difficult terrain in their country but undertook to provide information and remains as they were found.[21] Carter praised the commission for its "completely successful mission" and told Woodcock, "I'm very proud of what you've done."[22]

Carter, Woodcock, and Mansfield then went to the White House Briefing Room to meet with reporters. The president led off by labeling the commission's trip "superb" and declaring that "every hope that we had for the mission has been realized." He went on to declare that the Vietnamese "have not tied together economic allocations of American funds with the MIA question" and that "they've also suggested that we reinitiate diplomatic discussions in Paris without delay." Carter said he would accept the Vietnamese offer "immediately" and closed by again praising the commission for having "performed their assignment in an absolutely superlative way."[23] (Two days later, Carter would write to Woodcock that "You have contributed substantially to the healing of our own war wounds. . . . Your compassionate yet firm negotiating abilities elicited the maximum possible response from the Vietnamese and

Laotians. I hope that knowledge of this will always be a source of satisfaction to you.")[24]

Carter was asked at a news conference the following week if his statements regarding the Woodcock Commission's trip had meant that he had changed his previously stated position that there had to be a satisfactory accounting of the missing before relations with Vietnam could be normalized. He responded that in his opinion the Vietnamese had done "about all they can do" on the matter of the MIAs. "I don't have any way to prove that they have accounted for all those about whom they have information," he said. "But I think, so far as I can discern, they have acted in good faith."[25]

Chairman Woodcock went to the Hill on April 1 to present his findings to members of the Senate Foreign Relations Committee. In prepared remarks, Woodcock first told the senators that there was "no evidence that any American prisoners from the Indochina conflict were still alive." Then, addressing the question of aid, he explained:

> Throughout the commission's meeting with the Vietnamese, they expressed their strong interest in receiving aid from the U.S. This was expressed as an American "responsibility" and "obligation. . . ." They mentioned three ways of looking at what they claimed was our responsibility to contribute to their postwar reconstruction: legal, humanitarian and on the basis of reciprocity. They said they were ready to be flexible in discussing how aid might be provided, though they continued to cite Article 21 of the Paris Accord as an element of their position. In addition, they referred to our providing aid as a matter of conscience or moral obligation. . . . They did not specifically link aid to an MIA accounting, although they noted the "inter-relation" of various issues including these two.[26]

When asked by Senator Robert Griffin (R-MI) how the commission had come to its finding that no American POWs remained alive, Woodcock replied, "We were told that by the Vietnamese. We were [also] told that in Vientiane by the Lao government representatives. Obviously we have no proof, because proof could only be if we had physical control and we were allowed to go and search. They say no Americans are held alive against their will. I add to that just good common sense, and the passage of time. Why would they be holding Americans against their will?"[27]

## Early May
## PARIS

With the unlisted, unreturned POWs now declared dead by President Carter's own commission—the second official declaration of death for the men in fewer than four months and, counting Nixon's, the third to date—Richard Holbrooke, James Rosenthal, and several other State Department officials flew to Paris in early May to meet with Phan Hien and begin the process of normalizing relations.[28]

As the talks got under way on the 2nd, neither Holbrooke nor Rosenthal confronted Hien with the recent CIA intelligence that quoted Hien himself as saying the SRV was holding American POWs. Holbrooke did not confront Hien with this critical intelligence because, as he would swear under oath to Senate investigators in 1992, he had never been informed of its existence. "Nobody at the Pentagon, the CIA, the State Department or anyone else gave us anything resembling information or evidence that people were still alive," Holbrooke declared. "Nobody told us there was a possibility [anyone was alive]. Had we heard that there was a possibility, it would have reshaped the mission, obviously. If some staff member had come in there and said to us, listen, we think there might be people still alive, and we think we ought to make an all-out effort, that would have been the first mission, for the most obvious of reasons. You go for the live people first."[29]

Rather than confront Hien on the matter of living prisoners, Holbrooke informed him that the United States would no longer block Vietnam's entry into the United Nations and that the two sides should move rapidly toward normalization without any preconditions. To Holbrooke's amazement, the Vietnamese diplomat responded by pushing a copy of the Nixon letter across the table and saying, "You want relations with us? Give us this money you owe us."

"I said, 'you can't be serious,'" Holbrooke later told Senate investigators, "[but] the Vietnamese said, 'Why? The President of the United States promised this to us.' It was then," Holbrooke continued, "that I realized that it was more than a negotiating ploy, that they really believed it. . . . I want to stress this. The Vietnamese took [the Nixon letter] very seriously. The Vietnamese . . . believed the Kissinger-Nixon letter to have standing. . . . Our position [however] was simple: . . . That letter has no standing, . . . it is an outrageous document . . . which should never have been sent."[30]

When Hien steadfastly refused to accept his position on the Nixon letter, Holbrooke attempted to break the logjam by proposing that the United States and Vietnam immediately and unconditionally normalize relations—with no reconstruction aid being paid—and that he and Hien call a press conference at once to make the joint announcement. Hien refused, arguing again that normalization of relations between the two countries was contingent upon the payment of the reconstruction aid promised by the United States in the Paris accords and the Nixon letter. When no accord could be reached, both sides agreed to adjourn the talks with the pledge to meet again in two weeks.[31]

Speaking to reporters after the talks broke off, Hien made no official mention of Holbrooke's "unconditional" offer to normalize relations. Instead, according to a later *New York Times* account, he "maintained that 'a contribution to healing the wounds of war and to reconstruct the country' was an American obligation that must be 'linked' to establishment of relations"; declared such aid had been pledged in a letter from President Richard M. Nixon at the time of the 1973 Paris cease-fire agreement in the amount of $3.25 billion, plus another billion or billion and a half in 'concessional aid,' and indicated that Hanoi still demanded that amount."[32] (The *Washington Post* would later report that Hien also told reporters that in addition to the $4.25–4.75 billion promised by Nixon, his country was also demanding payment from the United States of an additional $150 million for assets of the former South Vietnamese government held under American control.[33] This raised the total Vietnamese demand to almost $5 billion.)

Word of Hien's public demands reached Washington within minutes of his press conference and immediately set off a firestorm in the American capital. Secretary of State Cyrus Vance, appearing at a hastily called press conference at the State Department, acknowledged that the Vietnamese were demanding specific sums of economic assistance as a precondition to normalization but stated emphatically that U.S. negotiators "have made clear to the Vietnamese that we will not pay any reparations."[34] Later in the day, members of the U.S. House, perhaps unmoved by Vance's assurances, voted after only ten minutes of debate to prohibit the Carter administration from using any funds "for the purpose of negotiating reparations, aid or any other form of payment to the Socialist Republic of Vietnam."[35]

Holbrooke later told Senate investigators that when word of the House vote reached him in Paris, he telephoned Hien and told him that by making public his demand for reconstruction aid "you have severely compromised your government's limited chances of achieving the objective they seek." When Hien asked why this was the case, Holbrooke replied, "You don't understand the United States. . . . The American public is not in a mood to give you money and, as I have told you repeatedly, the Nixon letter has no standing. I am very sorry you have done this because it will impede any chance we have for progress."[36]

*May, Hanoi*
## "WE STAND FOR AN OVER-ALL, PACKAGE DEAL SOLUTION"

Hanoi's reaction to Vance's public statements, the congressional vote on aid, and Holbrooke's rebuke of Phan Hien was swift and predictable. Quoting the Communist party daily *Nhan Dan,* Hanoi radio declared on May 11 that "the United States continues with its erroneous policy . . . and has in recent days advanced slanderous arguments against our government's correct stand, deliberately trying to dodge its obligation and responsibility to healing the wounds of war and rebuilding Vietnam." Citing the "irrefutable U.S. responsibility" for war damages in Vietnam, the radio commentator repeated the Vietnamese government's willingness to resolve matters left over from the war. "Specifically," the commentator said, "these matters include the seeking of information on missing Americans, the U.S. contribution to healing the wounds of war and to postwar reconstruction in Vietnam and the normalization of relations between the two countries . . . [which] are interrelated because they are the contents of three of the provisions of the Paris agreement on Vietnam."[37]

On May 14, the PAVN daily *Quan Doi Nhan Dan* accused Washington of "conducting a strenuous campaign to distort our government's correct stand and to create an illusion about the so-called U.S. good will to rapidly normalize relations between the two countries while it tries to shirk its pledged responsibility to contribute to healing the wounds of war in Vietnam." The paper further charged that "Mr. Carter wants to show that he is more reasonable than Nixon concerning the normalization of relations with Vietnam, but he is following in Nixon's footsteps by evading the fulfillment of the U.S. obligation to

Vietnam. . . . A new chapter in the history of Vietnam-U.S. relations can be opened only when the United States clearly shows genuine responsibility in solving problems left over by the past."[38]

The Vietnamese turned up the heat three days later in a commentary broadcast over Hanoi radio:

President Carter and his [word indistinct] had many times spoken of the so-called U.S. fine intention to open a new era in the Vietnam-U.S. relations and of their readiness to look forward to the future. But how can they look forward to a future and open a new era in the Vietnam-U.S. relations while a number of problems of the past remain unsettled, including the U.S. obligation to contribute to healing the wounds of war and postwar reconstruction in Vietnam?

The new era in the Vietnam-U.S. relations can be opened only when the United States gives up its hostile policy toward Vietnam and seriously fulfills its obligations toward Vietnam.

The prospects for the new era in the relations between the two countries depend on the U.S. fulfillment of its commitments.[39]

Anti-U.S. rhetoric reached a fever pitch on May 23 when *Nhan Dan* published a scathing article accusing the United States of wanting to implement only articles of the Paris accords beneficial to it. The daily charged that the U.S. refusal to contribute to postwar reconstruction in Vietnam was "a preposterous action in the life of the present community of civilized nations . . . [which] tramples upon the most elementary provisions of international law." Continuing, *Nhan Dan* declared:

The United States cannot elude its obligations as provided for in 21 of the Paris agreement. Instead, it must fulfill them with all its conscience and responsibility. Nobody else than the U.S. Presidential commission had acknowledged during its visit here that if the Paris agreement on Vietnam is considered invalid, so is 21 as well as 8B of the agreement; and if 8B remains valid, so does 21.

The stand of the government of the Socialist Republic of Vietnam is so just and clear. We stand for an over-all, package deal solution to the three questions which are closely interrelated. They are: (1) the seeking of information on Americans reported as missing in action in Vietnam and the solution of remains of Americans who died in the Vietnam war (Article 8B of the Paris agreement); (2) the U.S. contribution to healing the wounds of war and to post-war reconstruction in Vietnam (Article 21); and (3) the normalization of the relations between Vietnam and the United States (Article 22).

In the implementation of Article 8B, the Vietnamese government has done all it possibly can and its good will is undeniable.

On the contrary, we hold that to implement Article 21 of the Paris agreement is an undeniable obligation of the United States in terms of the jurisdiction of the Paris agreement, of international laws as well as of human morality and conscience.

We are prepared to create all favorable conditions for the United States to contribute to post-war reconstruction of Vietnam.

The Vietnamese people are ready to look forward to the future. However, the future can by no means be completely divorced from the past which has left a number of outstanding questions which will stand in the way of the normalization of relations between the two countries if they are not solved adequately. The sole obstacle to be overcome is the stubbornness and short-sightedness of those in the U.S. ruling circles who are urging the solution of a question of concern to the U.S.—the MIA—while trying to elude the solution of a question of concern to the Vietnamese side—the application of Article 21 of the Paris agreement on Vietnam.

The United States must not elude its obligations but strictly fulfill them. Only in this way can the present negotiations between Vietnam and the United States be fruitful to both sides.[40]

Reading the invective coming out of Hanoi, and mindful of the demands Phan Hien had made to Holbrooke in Paris, Carter administration officials now knew for sure that unless they agreed to address in some way the matter of post-war reconstruction aid, progress toward reconciliation with Vietnam and, as the Vietnamese had repeatedly said, progress in the effort to account for the "un-registered" American servicemen, was impossible. They also knew that with Holbrooke poised to return to Paris for further talks with Phan Hien, a final decision on what to do about Vietnam had to come very soon.

So what was it going to be? The three-part "over-all, package deal solution" the Vietnamese had proposed, where the United States would contribute to postwar reconstruction as required by the Paris accords, the Vietnamese would fully account for the MIAs and return the remains of the dead as required by the Paris accords, and the two countries would normalize relations—essentially, where the United States would trade reconstruction aid for the MIAs—or no solution at all?

Anybody here seen my old friend John? Anybody here seen my old friend Bobby? Can you tell me where they've gone?

## GETTING OUT

Carter and his men opted not to provide the reconstruction aid the Vietnamese were demanding, and, in late May, moved swiftly to extricate themselves from the mess they were in.

The NSC began the extrication process on May 25 by recommending that Carter tone down any expectation that the upcoming Paris talks might produce results on the MIA issue. In making the recommendation, an NSC official said it was necessitated by "the inability of two bitter enemies swiftly to place the past behind them, as the President had hoped." The official cited both the recent "vitriolic" Vietnamese attacks on the United States and the strong congressional sentiment against aid to Vietnam as contributing to his recommendation. He went on to say that though the president "had raised public expectations that the Vietnamese were going to be more forthcoming on MIA information . . . , the hardened mood makes it unlikely that we will be obtaining more information on MIAs . . . [and] we may be in a deep freeze for at least many months."[41]

The second step in the process occurred the following day when Defense Secretary Harold Brown dispatched a memorandum to Carter recommending that the administration begin the process of officially declaring dead all Vietnam-era servicemen currently listed as POW or MIA. Brown, who had served as secretary of the air force during President Johnson's Rolling Thunder campaign, offered the following as part of the rationale for his recommendation:

> It is true the Southeast Asian governments probably have more information about our missing men than they have given to us. There is no reason to believe, however, that continuing to carry servicemen as missing in action puts pressure on Hanoi to provide information on our missing men. In fact, the opposite is probably true; it puts pressure on us to make concessions to Hanoi.
>
> Given the overwhelming probability that none of the MIAs ever will be found alive, I believe the time has come to allow the Secretaries of the Army, Navy and Air Force to exercise their responsibilities for status reviews as mandated by law even though we have not received a full accounting.[42]

The third step in the extrication process took place in Paris in early June when Holbrooke and Hien met again as scheduled. This step was well planned and took little time: When Hien reintroduced the SRV's "three point package solution" of MIAs, reconstruction aid and normalization of relations, and repeated for two days Vietnam's demand for approximately $5 billion in aid, Holbrooke simply broke off the talks and returned to Washington.[43]

Carter himself took the final step out of the quagmire ten days later by agreeing with Brown and ordering that the process of officially declaring all remaining Vietnam era POWs and MIAs legally dead should begin.[44] A DOD spokesman would later tell the press that the decision to declare the men dead had been made "primarily due to the lapse of time since the end of the war."[45]

By mid-June, the crisis had passed. With amazing swiftness—in fact, within the space of just three weeks, from May 25 until June 16—the president himself, National Security Advisor Zbigniew Brzezinski, Secretary of Defense Harold Brown, Secretary of State Cyrus Vance, Assistant Secretary of State Richard Holbrooke, Country Director James Rosenthal, and the others had successfully freed themselves from the grip of a tenacious enemy.

Back in Vietnam, other Americans were not so lucky.

*Summer and Fall*
## VIETNAM

Sometime in June, at about the same time their commander in chief was having them declared dead in Washington, three weak, emaciated Americans wearing old military uniforms were seen under guard at the front gate of a reeducation camp the Communists had constructed on the grounds of the old Binh Thuy Air Base, near Can Tho in Vietnam's Mekong Delta. (See map page 158, point 7.)

The three were seen by a South Vietnamese man who had come to visit a relative held at the camp. The man later told U.S. officials that the three Americans were wearing old fatigue uniforms and were barefoot and had their hands bound behind their backs. All three appeared very dirty and all had long, unkempt hair and beards. He said a crowd had gathered around the Americans and there was much commotion and he heard someone in the crowd say they had been caught that very day hiding out in a tunnel complex beneath the air base. Someone in the crowd said the three had been hiding in the tunnel for the past two years and that several years' supply of food and a generator had been discovered in the tunnel.[46]

In July, the American prisoner who had flashed the V sign to the ARVN work party near the Cambodian border and the other American seen with him back in January were both reportedly sighted again near the Katum reeducation camps.[47] (See map page 158, point 8.)

Later that summer, an American who had reportedly just escaped from a prison near the Mekong River town of Sa Dec (pronounced "SAY deck"), some twenty-five kilometers north of the Binh Thuy Air Base, was seen on the run in the business district in downtown Sa Dec. (See map page 158, point 9.) According to what one of many reported onlookers would later tell U.S. officials, he (the onlooker, a South Vietnamese man) was waiting for a bus at the Sa Dec bus station on an unrecalled day during September when the American, who was completely nude, came running across the street and into an ice cream plant located in front of the bus station. The onlooker described the American as having no hair and being "skin and bones." He said the man stood about six feet tall and appeared to be between thirty-five and forty years old and that given his appearance he was sure the man had had no food or medicine for a long time.

The onlooker told U.S. officials that he and at least fifty other Vietnamese bystanders followed the American into the ice cream factory to see what was going on. He said that a girl named [redacted] and other female employees of the ice cream factory screamed at the sight of the naked man. He said the manager then closed the plant door, told the female employees to be quiet, gave the American a Cambodian shirtlike piece of clothing to put on and some food, and then helped him climb over the fence in the rear of the plant and flee. The onlooker said that after approximately fifteen minutes had elapsed, a Communist policeman arrived and dispersed the crowd.

The onlooker went on to say that he heard someone say that the American had just escaped from a prison in the area and that the police were looking for him. The onlooker concluded by telling U.S. officials that he did not know what happened to the American after he fled from the ice cream factory.[48]

Far to the north, meanwhile, in the mountainous border reaches of northern Vietnam, an ethnic Chinese political prisoner imprisoned at the maximum security Quyet Tien (pronounced "Wet Tin") political prison complex continued seeing approximately fifty American POWs who had been held at the prison with him since late 1973–early 1974. (See map page 158, point 10.) This prisoner would later tell U.S. officials that cadre at this infamous political prison complex, which the Asian inmates variously called "Gate to Heaven Prison," "Gate to God Prison," and "Vietnam Siberia," told him and other Asian inmates the Americans were pilots and aircrewmen. He said the cadre also said the Americans had apologized and had offered to "rebuild every bridges, roads and buildings they have destroy[ed] if we would set them free, yet we still cannot release them." The prisoner also told U.S. officials that the Americans had reportedly told some of the Taiwanese commandos who were being held at Quyet Tien that if they ever got out of the prison and the country to "please report to the U.S. Government about them." Two commandos would later confirm the presence of American POWs in Quyet Tien.[49] (See map page 158, points 11 and 12.)

Not far from Quyet Tien, two American prisoners in a group of eighty reportedly being moved by rail during the summer of 1977 were said to have been killed in a train wreck near Chapa (Sa Pa).[50] (See map page 158, point 13.) Just up the road from Sa Pa meanwhile, approximately a dozen American prisoners were seen under guard at the Lao Cai Medical Dispensary. (See map page 158, point 14.) A Northerner who observed them, a carpenter who was visiting a friend at the dispensary, later told U.S. officials that the Americans were being treated on the second floor of the facility. He said that when he saw them they were wearing green pajama-type clothing with vertical white stripes. All had beards and some were freshly bandaged, including some who had bandages around their heads. The Americans reportedly remained at the dispensary for more than a week.[51] U.S. officials surmised that the bandaged American prisoners seen undergoing treatment at the Lao Cai Medical Dispensary were among the survivors of the reported train wreck at nearby Sa Pa.

Some thirty miles southeast of Sa Pa, meantime, a former field-grade ARVN counterintelligence officer who was being marched with fellow prisoners from one reeducation camp to another saw three American POWs loading fertilizer onto a three-quarter-ton Russian truck at a cooperative near the village of Van Ban. (See map page 158, point 15.) The ARVN officer later told U.S. officials the Americans were wearing purple striped prison uniforms and Ho Chi Minh sandals. He said that all three appeared to be about thirty years old, had blond hair and beards, and were very skinny but not sickly. He said they were guarded by three Vietnamese soldiers, two armed with AK-47s and the other with a pistol.[52]

In the fall, American POWs were seen again at the Quyet Tien political prison near the Chinese border. (See map page 158, point 16.) This time, the Americans—six or seven in number—were seen by a female circus performer who was part of a troupe that had come to the prison to perform for the cadre. The woman later told U.S. officials that all of the American prisoners she saw during her visit to Quyet Tien were Caucasian. She said that some were dressed in light blue hospital-type pajamas, while others had on striped pajamas. She further said that the camp commander told members of the troupe that the prisoners were American pilots and that they were being held at Quyet Tien because it was a "special camp."[53]

American POWs were seen yet again in the vicinity of the Phong Quang (Coc Mi) Prison complex near Pho Lu during late fall. (See map page 158, point 17.) These Americans, approximately ten in number, were seen by the same carpenter who had earlier seen the Americans being treated at the Lai Cao Medical Dispensary. The carpenter told U.S. officials that his second sighting of the ten or so American prisoners occurred as he drove by their work site on the way to pick up some lumber. He said that these Americans, dressed in striped uniforms with writing on them and wearing PAVN-issue canvas shoes, were loading rocks onto the back of a truck at the time he passed by. He also provided U.S. officials with a hand-drawn sketch of the area where the sighting took place.[54]

During this same general time frame, a group of ARVN officers on a work detail in the jungle near their reeducation camp somewhere in the North reportedly happened upon a group American POWs who were also on a work detail. One of the ARVNs would later state that the Americans were all white and skinny. He would go on to state that one of the ARVNs approached the Americans and wrote with his finger in the dirt, "POW?" and one of the Americans responded in a similar fashion by writing, "U.S. POW."[55]

In Hanoi, meanwhile, a Vietnamese official from Saigon who had been summoned by the minister of water conservancy to discuss future water projects was reportedly told by the minister that the SRV was holding U.S. POWs to obtain $3.2 billion in aid and that some of the money would be used to support water projects.[56]

In November, an ARVN commando who had been imprisoned in the North since the early 1970s was transferred to one of the subcamps of the Tan Lap–Phu Tho prison complex southeast of Yen Bai and tasked to clean the individual cells of the prisoners being held there. (See map page 158, point 18.) The commando later told U.S. officials that when he began his work he found that the prison was composed of sixty individual, isolated rooms that had been built in such a way as to prevent communication and that forty-nine of these rooms each contained one American POW. He said that the Americans were forced by the guards to vacate their rooms and stand outside while he performed his work, and that they were not allowed to communicate with him or one another in any way. He said that the guards referred to the Americans only by rank and room number, i.e., "the Captain in room 5, the Major in room 40." The commando told U.S. officials that he saw the American prisoners daily from November 1977 until he was freed by Communist authorities in August 1978.[57]

In December, an opium smuggler observed a group of approximately twenty Caucasian prisoners whom he believed to be Americans who had just returned from a work detail and were entering the main gate of a prison located just north of Son La Province town. (See map page 158, point 19.) The smuggler later told U.S. officials that the Americans had apparently just gotten down off a nearby truck, which he said still had shovels and other labor tools in the back, and were walking double file into the prison under guard when he observed them. He provided U.S. officials with a hand-drawn sketch of the facility.[58]

Back in the South near the Cambodian border, meanwhile, an ARVN major on a work detail west of Bu Gia Map encountered a light-skinned American prisoner with a thick beard in the jungle one morning around Christmas. (See map page 158, point 20.) The ARVN major later told U.S. officials that when he first saw the emaciated prisoner he was startled and wondered if he was seeing "a Russian or a ghost." He explained that as he approached to within approximately three meters of the man, the man said to him in a weak voice, "Morning," and that he then realized the prisoner was an American. He said he asked the American what he was doing there and that he replied that his name was "Captain Patrick" and that he and two other Americans were being held nearby.

The ARVN major said that he told Patrick "this is Christmastime 1977" and that he was an ARVN major "in the same situation as him." The major told U.S. officials that upon hearing that, Patrick asked him that if he ever got out of jail to "try to tell about his story to anybody who can help."[59]

Unknown to Captain Patrick and the other unlisted, unreturned POWs who were being seen throughout the SRV during 1977, it would now be only a few more months before both Northerners and Southerners alike began fleeing the country by the thousands and telling their stories.

CHAPTER 17

1978

# THE SIGHTINGS OF THE UNLISTED, UNRETURNED POWs CONTINUE • THE REFUGEE EXODUS BEGINS

. . .

American prisoners of war were seen in captivity throughout unified Vietnam during 1978. They were observed in and around prisons and work camps from Haiphong, Phu Ly, Phu Tho, Ham Yen, Nghia Lo, and other locations in the North to near Katum, Thien Ngon, Loc Ninh, Phan Thiet, Bu Dop, Bu Gia Map, and other points in the South. The sightings began in January and continued unabated through December. On a number of occasions, the American prisoners reportedly communicated directly with the person or persons who saw them, asking for a cigarette, begging for food, or pleading for deliverance.

Also during 1978, famine, social unrest, persecution, and the threat of renewed warfare led tens of thousands of Vietnamese—many of whom had seen or heard about American POWs being held in captivity after 1973—to flee their homeland for a better life. As a result, some five years after Operation Homecoming, reports that hundreds of the unlisted, unreturned POWs were still alive and held captive finally began making their way to U.S. officials in Washington.

For the unlisted, unreturned POWs, 1978 would be a seminal year.

## THE SIGHTINGS OF THE UNLISTED, UNRETURNED POWs CONTINUE

Just prior to Tet, a North Vietnamese inmate being held at Tran Phu Prison in the northern port city of Haiphong encountered four American pilots while doing janitorial work near the Americans' cell. (See map page 177, point 1.) The inmate later told U.S. officials that the pilots, all of whom were Caucasian, were wearing dark blue-gray clothes. He also recalled that one of the men's trousers were so short that they reached only to the middle of his calf. The inmate said that all four Americans were very thin and had beards. (He explained that the Americans were not allowed to have razors or other metal implements in their cell and that the only time they could shave was during their monthly bath.) The inmate further said that on one occasion one of the American pilots, who had a heavier build than the others and a very long beard, smiled at him and made a sign with his hands and whispered, "cigarette, cigarette."

"The reason I know they were American pilots is because the communist security people told me that," the inmate told U.S. officials. "They also let me know that each American pilot was worth two-three factories, so they had to keep them for trade."[1]

Just after Tet, in February, a middle-aged man was joyriding one evening with his brother on a Honda motorbike on a narrow, winding mountain road just west of Phu Ly, a city located some fifty kilometers south of Hanoi, when the two came upon three PAVN soldiers leading two Caucasian prisoners along the road. (See map page 177, point 2.)

The man later told U.S. officials that his brother was operating the motorbike at the time and when he (the brother) saw the three soldiers and their two prisoners in the headlamp, he slowed immediately and then began easing the bike past the five men on the narrow road. The man said the three guards and two Caucasian prisoners were moving in the same direction as the motorbike and that he and his brother passed alongside them at a very low speed at a distance of one meter. As they passed, they could see that the Caucasians were wearing gray prison uniforms with the letters "BSR" printed on the backs. Both of the prisoners appeared thin and weak. One appeared to be in his fifties, the other younger. The older man had a short growth of gray hair that appeared to have been shaved sometime in the recent past; the younger prisoner's head was shaved bald. Both had stubble but no beards, and both had their wrists bound behind their backs. The man told U.S. officials that his brother, who lived in a nearby village and knew the area well, later surmised that the two Caucasians were being taken to a prison camp known as Trai Ba Sao (Camp Ba Sao), which was located just up the road.[2]

North of Yen Bai near the village of Ham Yen, meanwhile, two Swedish workers employed at a Swedish aid project reportedly happened upon a small group of American prisoners who were working under guard on a road gang. (See map page 177, point 3.) (The Swedish aid project, a large paper mill located at the village of Bai Bang, had a satellite forestry compound at Ham Yen, very near to where the sighting reportedly took place.)[3] A Norwegian engineer working at the paper mill at the time would later leave Vietnam and report that the two Swedes told him that when the American prisoners saw them, one of the Americans shouted, "Tell the world about us," before guards threatened the two Swedes with weapons and ordered them out of the area.[4]

In late June, a schoolteacher living in Saigon traveled to the North by train to visit her husband who was undergoing reeducation at the Tan Lap–Phu Tho prison complex southeast of Yen Bai. While walking along a rural road toward the prison complex with a group of other wives, the women came upon fifteen to twenty Caucasian prisoners working under armed guard in a field adjacent to

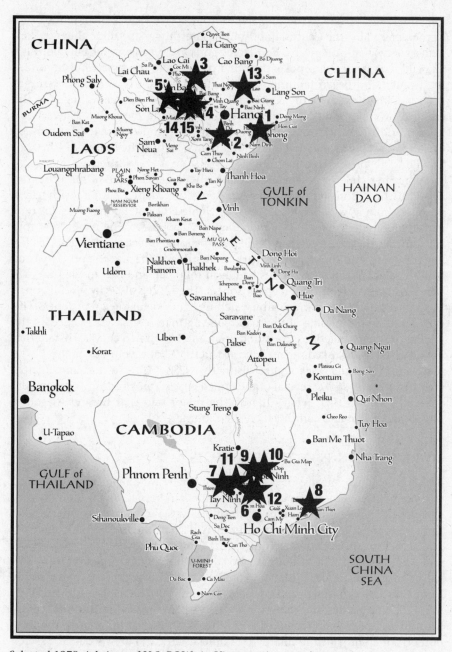

Selected 1978 sightings of U.S. POWs in Vietnam. (HENDON/ANDERER)

the road. (See this map, point 4.) The schoolteacher later told U.S. officials the Caucasians were chopping and hoeing the ground with long-handled implements as guards armed with AK-47s stood nearby. She said the Caucasians were wearing blue prison uniforms, some of which were faded almost white from long use and exposure to the sun. She went on to say that as she and the other women passed by, the Caucasian prisoner nearest the road said to them in Vietnamese, "I-we-are Americans. You ladies go back to Saigon and tell about it!" She said that as the man spoke, the other prisoners in the group looked toward the women and began fanning their open-collared shirts as if they were hot from working. Just after the American spoke, one of the guards yelled at the group of wives, "Don't look over here, hurry up and move on!" The schoolteacher and the others moved along quickly. She added that they continued walking for approximately four more hours before they reached the Tan Lap–Phu Tho visitor reception center.[5]

Soon after the wives' encounter with the American POWs near the Tan Lap–Phu Tho prison complex in late June, an ARVN major returning with fellow prisoners from a work detail southeast of Nghia Lo came upon a Russian truck parked alongside the road. (See map page 177, point 5.). The major later told U.S. officials that the truck was headed in the same direction as he and his fellow prisoners, and though it was dark at the time, as he and the others passed by they saw that the side curtains had been rolled up and that inside the truck were approximately thirty foreign prisoners. The ARVNs also saw several armed Vietnamese guards standing nearby watching over several foreign prisoners who were standing by the side of the road relieving themselves. The major said the foreign prisoners all looked sickly and weak and had drawn cheeks. He said that as he walked by, he asked the men in the truck, "What is your nationality?" and that someone in the truck replied distinctly, "USA." He said that immediately after the prisoner spoke, several of the armed guards came running over and demanded, "What's that, what's that?" The major said that he and the other ARVNs kept silent and continued on their journey.[6]

## MORE SIGHTINGS IN THE SOUTH

Back in the South, meanwhile, American prisoners were reportedly being seen at several different locations along the Cambodian border northwest of Saigon, near an ARVN reeducation camp north of the coastal city of Phan Thiet, and at a prison at an unknown location somewhere deep in the southern highlands.

The first of the reported sightings near the Cambodian border occurred in mid-April when a medical student who was part of a mobile medical team providing treatment to ARVN inmates confined to a reeducation camp east of Tay Ninh City saw two American prisoners at the camp. The medical student later told U.S. officials that the camp was located some thirty kilometers east of Tay Ninh in an isolated, unpopulated area of dense forest. He pinpointed the location on a map provided to him by U.S. officials and also drew a detailed sketch of the facility.[7] (See map page 177, point 6.)

The medical student said that the inmate population at the camp totaled about five hundred men, most former members of the South Vietnamese Air Force. He went on to say that he observed the two American prisoners at two different times during his team's visit to the camp. He said the first observation occurred when he was conducting examinations of the South Vietnamese inmates in the prison dispensary and noticed the two walking across the prison yard approximately seventy-five to one hundred meters away. He said that the second sighting occurred when the Americans were brought into the dispensary and, as he stood nearby, were examined by doctors on his team.

The medical student described one of the Americans as being Caucasian, thin, about twenty-eight years old, six feet tall to six-three, with hazel eyes, light brown hair, and hair on his chest. He said the other was also Caucasian, about thirty-one years old, about six feet tall, with brown eyes and white hair and had a scar the length of a finger directly on his right kneecap. He told U.S. officials that while the American prisoners were being examined, he heard one of them say in English to the doctor who was examining him, "Help me gain freedom!" The medical student said that this doctor's name was Dr. [portion of name redacted] Hong. According to DIA records, at this point in the interview process the medical student "offered lengthy criticisms of the U.S. Government because it was not taking action to help return these American prisoners from VN."[8]

Also near the Cambodian border in Tay Ninh Province, at about 3:00 P.M. on an afternoon in late June, a former ARVN corporal who was in the business of selling roofing thatch to PAVN installations was sitting parked in his old De Soto truck just outside the former U.S/South Vietnamese base at Thien Ngon when he saw a GMC truck approaching from within the base. The former corporal later told U.S. officials that as the GMC pulled onto the highway and started north in the direction of the Cambodian border, he observed from a distance of about three meters approximately twenty to twenty-two gaunt Caucasian prisoners wearing leg irons and two armed escorts sitting in the back. (See map page 177, point 7.) He said the Caucasians were wearing black pajamas and/or olive drab clothing and all had long hair and beards.[9]

In October, two Vietnamese men walking along a rural road near Tam Hung Village, north of the coastal city of Phan Thiet, had a face-to-face encounter with a group of seven undernourished Caucasian prisoners and the four armed cadre accompanying them. (See map page 177, point 8.) The two Vietnamese later told U.S. officials that they observed the prisoners and their guards from a distance of three meters as the two groups walked past one another in opposite directions along the road. They said the prisoners and their guards were heading in the direction of the nearby Ca Tot prison and appeared to be returning from a work detail. The two Vietnamese described the Caucasians as being between the ages of twenty-five and thirty-five and having fairly long hair. Some, they said, had facial hair and others had long beards. The two Vietnamese said that as the Caucasians passed, several of them asked for food by motioning to their stomachs and by making other gestures.[10]

Also in October, an employee of the Loc Ninh national rubber plantation and his driver were arrested by Communist authorities and temporarily detained in the jungle near Loc Ninh, a city located near the Cambodian border northwest of Saigon. The employee, a Northerner by birth who had lived in the South since 1954, later told U.S. officials that while being held in one of four tents in a jungle clearing, he and his driver observed three Caucasian prisoners, whom they presumed to be Americans, who were being detained some four meters away in an adjoining tent. (See map page 177, point 9.) He told U.S. officials that when one of the Caucasians saw that he and his driver had seen him, the

Caucasian attempted to communicate with them by sticking his leg out of his tent and shaping letters in the dirt with his toe. He said that as he and his driver watched, the Caucasian drew a *W* followed by an *I* and had just completed the third letter, which he said might have been an *R*, when he suddenly pulled his leg back into the tent and closed the flap. The employee told U.S. officials that one of the guards then rushed to the tent where he and his driver were being held and demanded to know what they had seen. He said they told the guard they had seen nothing. The employee told U.S. officials that he and his driver were released later in the day after a local Communist official he knew intervened on their behalf.[11]

During November, the wife of an ARVN general reportedly saw a group of American prisoners working near a road near Bu Dop, just northeast of Loc Ninh. (See map page 177, point 10.) According to what one refugee would later tell U.S. officials, the wife had been en route to see her husband, who was being held in reeducation in the area, when she came upon the Americans. She reportedly heard one of the prisoners make a deliberate attempt to communicate with her and from his voice recognized that he was an American. The prisoner reportedly exclaimed, "There are thirty Americans kept here. We all need food. If you bring food for us, the American Government will reward you!"[12] Another refugee would tell U.S. officials roughly the same story, and further describe the thirty Americans as being malnourished and very thin, having long hair and long beards, and wearing tattered clothing. This refugee would also say that as he had understood it, the general's wife had been headed to nearby Bu Gia Map rather than to Bu Dop, and that she had been going there to visit her nephew, not her husband.[13]

Back at the Katum reeducation camp near the Cambodian border in neighboring Tay Ninh Province, two Caucasian American prisoners—perhaps the same two sighted near the camp in January and then again in July 1977 (see Chapter 16)—were reportedly seen during the time the camp was being evacuated in late 1978. (Escalating border tensions during late 1978 led the Vietnamese to evacuate prisons and reeducation camps located near the Cambodian Frontier.) (See map page 177, point 11.) According to what one ARVN who learned of the sighting later told U.S. officials, an ARVN inmate and four other individuals were reportedly assisting in the evacuation and had just exited the camp kitchen with a load of utensils when they observed the two Americans. The ARVN inmate reportedly said that each American was blindfolded and had his hands tied behind his back from wrist to elbow. The inmate also reportedly said that as he and the others watched, the two Americans were placed in the back of a Russian Molotova truck and driven away in the opposite direction from which the Vietnamese prisoners were being taken.[14]

Just south of the Katum camp, meantime, a number of Caucasian American prisoners were reportedly seen in the custody of PAVN soldiers in the Phu Khuong District of Tay Ninh Province. According to the Vietnamese Muslims (Cham) who reportedly saw the Americans, they (the Cham) were gathering wood on the lower slopes of a medium-sized mountain in an area near the border with Binh Duong Province when they observed the Americans being escorted down the mountain. (See map page 177, point 12.) The Cham were unable to pinpoint the exact location where the sighting took place but reportedly said that the PAVN operated a sugar mill and a rock quarry in the immediate area.[15]

Finally, in the South during 1978, a South Vietnamese schoolteacher imprisoned somewhere in the mountains was reportedly on a wood-gathering detail near his prison when he and a fellow inmate became lost and, after walking for some time in the jungle, stumbled upon a small prison camp that contained several American prisoners mixed in with Vietnamese inmates. The teacher reportedly later said that he had been able to talk briefly with one of the Americans, and this man, whom he described as tall and bearded, had implored him to "tell the U.S. government we are still alive and being held prisoner." The teacher reportedly said that when he and his fellow inmate heard this, they became frightened and ran away. After his release from prison, the teacher would send the information about the American prisoners and the tall, bearded American's plea for deliverance to the U.S. government by a trusted family friend.[16]

## STILL MORE SIGHTINGS IN THE NORTH

In December, a North Vietnamese bus driver saw a number of American POWs in a prison located inside a military camp near the village of Son La (Son Lao), near Bac Son, northeast of Hanoi. (See map page 177, point 13.) The bus driver later told U.S. officials that he had gone to the camp to deliver a shipment of personal merchandise to the prison camp commander. He said that after unloading the merchandise, the camp commander had invited him to remain for dinner and after dinner had taken him on a tour of the facility. The bus driver said that it was during this tour that he observed the American POWs.

The bus driver told U.S. officials the Americans were "wearing clothes that were faded brown in color" and eyed him coldly, not knowing what he was up to. He said they were fed part rice and part sorghum, "the kind previously used to feed hogs," and were in "a sorry state, very thin and pale." He said that the warden told him, "Our party and our state are not stupid. We have spent a large amount of money to feed and guard those men. We want to use them to bargain and set a price for their release with the U.S. imperialists. The reason we need to keep those flying bandits and headmen . . . is because these bandits have killed many of our comrades. Our people, our party and our state will make the claims, which our children can enjoy."[17]

At about the same time the bus driver saw the American "flying bandits and headmen" at the camp northeast of Hanoi, the ARVN major who had come upon the disabled truck carrying American prisoners near Nghia Lo earlier in the summer (see page 178) had a chance encounter with a single American prisoner at a medical detention facility inside the Tan Lap–Phu Tho K-1 Prison southeast of Yen Bai. (See map page 177, point 14.) The major would later tell U.S. officials that he had been transferred to Tan Lap–Phu Tho in December and that soon after arriving had become sick and had been taken to the special medical detention facility to await treatment. He said that while waiting, he encountered and conversed with a lone American prisoner who appeared to be awaiting treatment for a leg infection. The major said the American told him his name was "Jackson," and that there had been fifteen other Americans previously held at Tan Lap–Phu Tho K-1 with him but that the others had recently been moved out of the camp. The major described Jackson as being about five foot seven, skinny, with long hair, a long beard, and sunken cheeks, and having an infected wound on his right leg. He said Jackson wore a red and white striped prison uniform and scratched himself constantly during their time together.

The major told U.S. officials that when the guards finally heard him and Jackson talking, they intervened and took Jackson away. The major added that he soon heard the sound of a car starting outside and surmised Jackson was being taken out of the camp. He said he never saw Jackson again.[18] A PAVN defector would later report to CIA that two unidentified prisoners had told him that around 1978–1979 they had seen a group of U.S. POWs being transferred out of the main, K-1 prison compound at the Tan Lap–Phu Tho prison complex. (See map page 177, point 15.) These Americans were rumored to have been taken to a location fifteen kilometers to the east.[19] The main rail line to Hanoi lies approximately fifteen–sixteen kilometers east of Tan Lap–Phu Tho K-1.[20]

## THE REFUGEE EXODUS BEGINS

Concurrent with the sightings of the American prisoners that were taking place throughout Vietnam during 1978, events were occurring in the region that would cause thousands of refugees, some of whom had seen or heard about American prisoners in captivity after the war, to flee Vietnam and seek asylum in other countries. These refugees would be followed in the years ahead by tens of thousands and then hundreds of thousands more, many hundreds of whom had also seen or heard about American servicemen held captive long after Operation Homecoming. By the mid-1980s, a task force of U.S. intelligence experts headed by a former director of the Defense Intelligence Agency would declare that the intelligence about POWs these refugees provided constituted "possibly the finest human intelligence data base in the U.S. post World War II experience."[21]

But for now, in 1978, the saga of the "boat people" and the "land refugees"— and the intelligence they brought with them—was just beginning.

## THE PERSECUTION OF THE ETHNIC CHINESE

The refugee exodus that began in 1978 had its origin in southern Vietnam in the months following the fall of Saigon. It was then that Communist authorities had attempted to increase food production by setting up "new economic zones" throughout the countryside and ordering tens of thousands of Southerners to leave their homes in the cities and move to these zones to work the land. Many Southerners had complied, but most of the South's estimated one million ethnic Chinese, who traditionally had been among Vietnam's most successful and privileged minorities, had refused.

The ethnic Chinese, known as Hoa or the Hoa people (pronounced "Wah"), had long been regarded as Vietnamese citizens in all respects except that they were not subject to the military draft. Given the fact that by Vietnamese standards, at least, these businessmen, shop owners, and traders had led a somewhat privileged existence, especially in the capitalist South, it should have surprised no one when they had refused to give up their way of life and become farmers as the victorious Communists had dictated.[22]

Though the Hoa people's refusal to give up their businesses and move to the collective farms had angered the conquering Communists, the authorities had initially made no effort to force the Hoa to comply. During 1976 and 1977, however, as agricultural output fell far below even minimal projections, the Communists had begun to publicly blame the Hoa for the shortage of food and had again called on them to move to the new economic zones. When few Hoa had complied, many hungry rank-and-file Vietnamese had begun to express hostility toward their once-respected and well-liked countrymen.

By early 1978, hunger was rampant in the South and the hostility and political unrest it bred were rapidly spreading. Seeing what was occurring, Communist authorities began to fear that their Socialist experiment in the South might actually fail and knew that if this occurred the "glory of the revolution" would be forever tarnished. And so, to overcome the food shortages and ensure the success of socialism in the South, Communist officials in the early spring declared the situation with the Hoa an "urgent problem" and moved to forcefully eject them from the cities and relocate them to the collective farms in the countryside.

Vowing to abolish once and for all the "trade and business practices of [these] bourgeoisie and switch them to [food] production," Vietnamese authorities in March sent thousands of armed cadre first into Cholon, Ho Chi Minh City's Chinese quarter, and then into other southern cities to "meet bourgeois tradesmen to persuade them to give up trade and take up production." "These bourgeoisie tradesmen," Ho Chi Minh radio declared the day the first assaults began, are "carrying out black market activities, hoarding goods and cash, monopolizing the economy and market, raising the prices of goods, disrupting the state's purchasing activities, undermining the market, engaging in dishonest business activities and flooding the market with fake goods, thus making the laboring people's livelihood increasingly difficult."[24] Press reports later quoted eyewitnesses as saying that many people were killed during the "meetings" in Ho Chi Minh City's Cholon district alone.[25]

In the North, meanwhile, a similar but less violent crackdown was launched against the Hoa living there. These Northern Hoa, having lived under a collectivist system since 1954, were far less profit oriented than their southern cousins; many, in fact, had long held jobs with the central, provincial, and local governments, or had worked in hospitals, schools, research facilities, and other quasi-governmental organizations. It was reported that prior to the events of 1978, almost a quarter of all ethnic Chinese living in Hanoi were employed by the central government.[26]

In early spring, however, in spite of their long service to and close association with governments at the national, provincial, and local levels and with various quasi-governmental institutions, the northern Hoa came under heavy—though essentially nonviolent—attack. With few exceptions, every ethnic Chinese citizen employed at every level in every agency of the central government was dismissed. Similarly, those Hoa employed in provincial or local government agencies, hospitals, schools, research facilities, and the like were terminated as well. Then, just as they had done in the South, Communist authorities accused the northern Hoa of selling goods on the black market and decreed that anyone who had cash "above the permitted limit" and could not give a satisfactory explanation of his or her sources of income would have the money confiscated. And as it turned out, of course, only the Hoa among the many Northerners who bought and sold goods on the thriving black market would be found to have cash "above the permitted limit."[27]

## FIRST COME THE HOA, THEN THE SOUTHERN VIETNAMESE

Faced in the South with confiscation of their businesses and forced relocation to state-run farms, and in the North with the loss of their jobs, their shops, and in many cases their life's savings, tens of thousands of Hoa began pulling up stakes in the spring of 1978, saying their good-byes and fleeing to nearby countries to begin new lives. Vietnamese officials, eager to rid the country of these once-respected but now-despised citizens, set up offices at points along the Chinese border and in coastal towns to help facilitate their departure.[28] (This was in marked contrast to the government's policy toward ethnic Vietnamese, who were subject to arrest and imprisonment if caught trying to escape.)

By the end of June, it was estimated that some 150,000 Hoa had crossed by land directly into southern China. Untold thousands more had boarded small boats and ridden the southwest monsoon toward the Philippines or up the coast to China, Macau, Hong Kong, Taiwan, South Korea, or Japan.[29] Thousands more, meanwhile, had been evacuated on ships and aircraft dispatched by the governments of China, Taiwan, and Hong Kong.[30]

Meanwhile, the Communist Chinese, enraged by Vietnam's assault on their kinfolk, began striking back by launching hit-and-run raids at points all along the countries' 750-mile-long border. Concurrently, the Khmer Rouge—undoubtedly at the direction of their patrons the Communist Chinese—began carrying out similar raids against Vietnamese citizens, villages, and military installations all along the Cambodian-Vietnamese frontier. By summer, the fighting along both borders had intensified to the point that the threat of an all-out, two-front war was very real.

It was at this point, during the summer of 1978, that thousands of South Vietnamese—disgusted with the food shortages, harsh conditions, and repression that characterized life in the postwar South, sensing that another bloody war was about to break out along the Cambodian border, and seeing the ease with which the Hoa were departing—began boarding rickety boats themselves and heading to the Philippines or up the coast to Macau, Hong Kong, and points beyond.[31] Other Southerners, meanwhile, chose an even more risky route, striking out overland through the killing fields of Cambodia for Thailand.

In the fall, the monsoon winds began their yearly shift toward the south and were soon carrying many more thousands of Hoa and South Vietnamese alike—now collectively the "boat people"—toward southern Thailand, Malaysia, Singapore, Brunei, Indonesia, and Australia. Almost overnight, the number of boat people making landfall in the countries closest to Vietnam became staggering.

By early November, forty thousand Vietnamese refugees—two-thirds of them ethnic Chinese—had reportedly come ashore in Malaysia alone. And this would prove only the beginning; within a year, the population of a single, tiny previously uninhabited island off the Malaysian coast would go from zero to forty thousand persons.[32]

Brian Eads, writing in Singapore's *New Straits Times* in December 1978, offered this rationale for the Southerners' decision to flee:

> Life in socialist Vietnam is harsh, and promises to become harsher still. The quickening pace of "socialist transformation" and collectivization is thwarting entrepreneurs. A sequence of droughts and floods means severe shortages and food rationing. The young face the prospect of compulsory military service, and possible death or mutilation on the Cambodian border. The skilled and educated of the former Saigon regime are finding rehabilitation a deadeningly slow process.
>
> What's [in store] for most is a life of ill-rewarded pioneer farming in the "new economic zones." Mistakenly or not, South Vietnamese in increasing numbers are preferring the uncertainties of the South China Sea.
>
> . . . The people leaving are the bitter, indigestible leftovers of the former regime's American-financed affluence. . . . While the risks—storms, pirates, hunger and thirst—are considerable, the prize—resettlement in a western country and the chance of prosperity—is sufficiently tempting.[33]

"Bitter, indigestible leftovers" to some, but bearers and providers of "possibly the finest human intelligence data base in the U.S. post World War II experience" to others.

## THE REPORTS OF IMPRISONED AMERICANS BEGIN MAKING THEIR WAY TO THE U.S. GOVERNMENT

No sooner had the early land refugees and boat people settled into their camps than word began to spread that some had seen or heard about American servicemen being detained by the Communists long after the war had ended. Slowly at first, and then, because of the increasingly explosive nature of the information, at a quickened pace, the refugees' reports began making their way to DIA's Special Office for POWs/MIAs at Arlington Hall, just south of the Pentagon in Washington. Declassified DOD and CIA documents indicate that these reports moved through any one of four separate "intelligence pipelines."

The first "pipeline" carried reports acquired from refugees <u>by CIA agents</u> operating in the countries where the refugee camps were located. These reports were sent from CIA stations in the Far East to officials at Agency Headquarters in Langley, who then forwarded them on to the Special Office for analysis.

The second "pipeline" carried reports acquired from refugees <u>by camp relief workers, members of the staffs of the various camps, camp resettlement officials, etc.</u>, and forwarded to the Joint Casualty Resolution Center (JCRC) at the U.S. embassy in Bangkok. JCRC was the primary U.S. government field agency

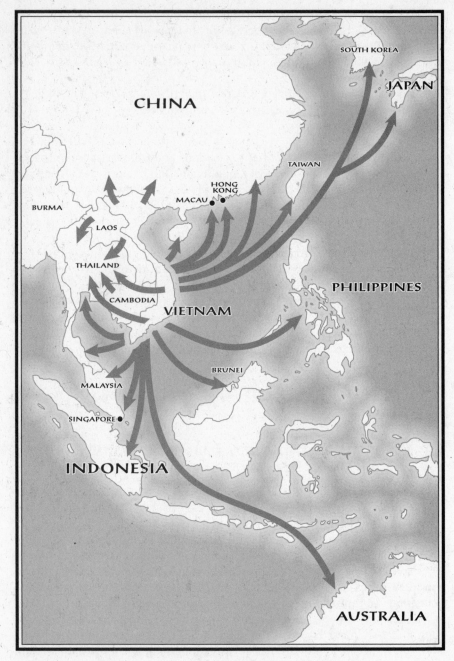

Countries of first asylum for Indochinese refugees. (HENDON/ANDERER)

responsible at the time for investigating the fate of the some two thousand five
hundred Americans still missing or unaccounted for. JCRC officials, upon receiving these reports, would task interviewers to travel to the camps, interview
the refugees who had reported the information about missing Americans, write

up detailed reports of the interviews, and forward those reports to the Special Office for analysis.[34]

The third and fourth "pipelines" involved reports acquired directly from refugees by the National League of Families and another POW/MIA family organization, the National Forget-Me-Nots. These "pipelines" developed when officials at the League and the Forget-Me-Nots began hearing rumors about the early refugee reports about live POWs and, in an effort to acquire as much information about their loved ones as possible, placed advertisements in Vietnamese-language magazines calling on refugees with information about POWs and MIAs to send that information *directly to their organizations*. The ads, soon read by untold thousands of refugees in the camps—and by thousands more who had been permanently resettled to countries throughout the world—yielded large numbers of additional reports about captive Americans. League and Forget-Me-Not officials forwarded these reports on to officials at the Special Office, who then tasked either JCRC, if the refugee source was still in a camp in the Far East, or, if the refugee had already been resettled to another country, the Defense Attaché Office (DAO) at the U.S. embassy in the country where the refugee now resided, to contact the source, conduct an in-depth interview, and report the results of that interview back to the Special Office for analysis. The resulting reports thus traveled through either the "advertisement to League/Forget-Me-Nots to Special Office to JCRC and back to Special Office 'pipeline'" (if the refugee source was still in his or her camp in the Far East) or the "advertisement to League/Forget-Me-Nots to Special Office to DAO and back to Special Office 'pipeline'" (if the refugee source had already been resettled to another country).[35]

By the end of 1978, the first of what would become hundreds of reports telling of American servicemen still held captive in Indochina after the war were at long last beginning to make their way through the various intelligence "pipelines" that ran from the camps in the first-asylum countries in the Far East and from second-asylum countries throughout the world where the refugees were being permanently resettled to the Defense Intelligence Agency's Special Office for POWs/MIAs in suburban Washington. It would now be only a matter of months before senior DIA officials would analyze these and other reports and conclude that American prisoners of war were, in fact, still alive in Communist prisons in Indochina.

## THE VIETNAMESE INVASION OF CAMBODIA

The simmering border tensions between Vietnam and the Chinese-backed Khmer Rouge exploded on Christmas Day when Vietnamese forces launched a lightning invasion of Cambodia. Streaming down out of the Central Highlands behind heavy armor and under the cover of attack aircraft and helicopters, the seasoned PAVN quickly routed the outnumbered and outgunned Khmer Rouge. Within less than two weeks, the PAVN would take the capital of Phnom Penh and begin pushing what was left of the Khmer Rouge west and north toward the Thai border.

Humiliated by the collapse of the Khmer Rouge troops they had equipped and trained—and still smarting from Vietnam's terror campaign against their kinfolk the Hoa—China's leaders would retaliate in early 1979 with a full-scale invasion of northern Vietnam.

The North Vietnamese, long having planned for just such an eventuality, would be ready.

CHAPTER 18

1979

A PRISON SYSTEM IN CHAOS • CONVINCING
EVIDENCE FINALLY REACHES WASHINGTON

. . .

As part of their overall planning for their Christmas Day 1978 invasion of Cambodia, the Vietnamese high command had determined early on that it was likely the Chinese would launch a retaliatory invasion across the border of northern Vietnam soon after PAVN troops had entered Cambodia. In anticipation of just such a move, the Vietnamese in the fall of 1978 had begun beefing up their defenses at key points along the Chinese border, removing for security reasons all Hoa still living in the border areas, and evacuating border area prisons and reeducation camps they felt might be threatened by an invading force. The defensive buildup, the removal of the ethnic Chinese, and the evacuations of the prisons and reeducation camps all continued into the early weeks of 1979.

It was during the evacuations of the northernmost prisons and reeducation camps in early 1979 that two of the most dramatic postwar sightings of American prisoners ever reported to U.S. authorities occurred. The first involved American prisoners reportedly seen by an ARVN officer at the Dogpatch Camp (Loung Lang PW Camp N-124) at Bo Djuong near the Chinese border in Cao Bang Province.[1] (See Chapter 15.) The other involved American pilots seen by a North Vietnamese political prisoner and his fellow inmates when they were evacuated from one of the maximum security subcamps of the Phong Quang (Coc Mi) Prison complex near Pho Lu in Lao Cai Province and transferred to a prison in Kim Boi District, Hoa Binh (Ha Son Binh) Province southwest of Hanoi where Americans were being detained.

The sighting at Dogpatch reportedly occurred when an ARVN officer being evacuated from the aboveground section of the camp saw American prisoners being evacuated from the nearby underground portion of the camp. (See map page 190, point 1.) The ARVN officer reportedly told a close relative, who later brought the story out of Vietnam and shared it with U.S. officials, that he saw two different groups of American prisoners at the camp that day. According to the relative, the officer said he saw the first group as they were getting up onto a

GMC truck. He said these Americans were wearing olive drab, inmate-type uniforms and appeared gaunt and emaciated. He also said that some were missing limbs and others had bandages on their heads, and that many among the group [perhaps thinking they were going home] were yelling and laughing as they climbed aboard the truck.

According to the relative, the ARVN officer, despite having been warned by camp guards not to look around, continued to watch as another group of similarly dressed American prisoners—these unable to see—were led by camp personnel out of the same underground portion of the camp located adjacent to the main camp and loaded onto a second truck.

According to the relative, the ARVN officer said that though he had been held at the camp for more than three years, this was the first time he realized Americans were being held in the underground portion of the facility.[2]

The sighting of American pilots at the jungle camp near Hanoi would prove equally dramatic. This sighting occurred when a group of forty-two North Vietnamese inmates were evacuated from the Phong Quang (Coc Mi) Prison complex near Pho Lu in Lao Cai Province and taken by truck to a prison located adjacent to a PAVN military camp in the jungles of Kim Boi District in Hoa Binh (Ha Son Binh) Province, southwest of Hanoi.[3] (See map page 190, point 2.) According to what one of the North Vietnamese inmates later told U.S. officials, when he and the other North Vietnamese prisoners disembarked and entered the new prison, they found that fifty to sixty foreign prisoners were being held in one section of the facility.

The inmate, who was serving a life sentence for blowing up a North Vietnamese military train, told U.S. officials that camp cadre told him and the other newly arrived Vietnamese inmates that the foreign prisoners were American pilots. The inmate said he saw the Americans often over a period of weeks when they were taken out of the American section for interrogation. He described them as being big and tall and "bushy with beard, mustache and whiskers." He said all were white, very thin and pale, and wore striped prison uniforms and leg chains.

The inmate told U.S. authorities that during February, "three persons and I . . . [were ordered into the American section of the prison] to bury an American prisoner of war who died of malaria. He died but his friends didn't bury him. They kept him there for two or three days, and they read and sang things which I heard but didn't understand. This person was very tall. And his frame was such that, if fat, he would be very large. He had a scar on his face and wore a bracelet on his wrist on which were some letters that I didn't understand."[4]

The inmate went on to say that there was no coffin for the dead American, so he and the three Asian inmates assisting him wrapped the body in two empty fertilizer bags—"one to wrap the head part and one used to wrap [the] two-legged part"—and carried it to a nearby cemetery and buried it. He said there were approximately twenty other graves in the cemetery, but he could not discern whether they were Vietnamese or American.

The inmate further said that in July he and the some other Vietnamese inmates were able to escape. He said that, traveling alone, he made his way south to Xuan Loc and then later fled overland across Cambodia to Thailand. In addition

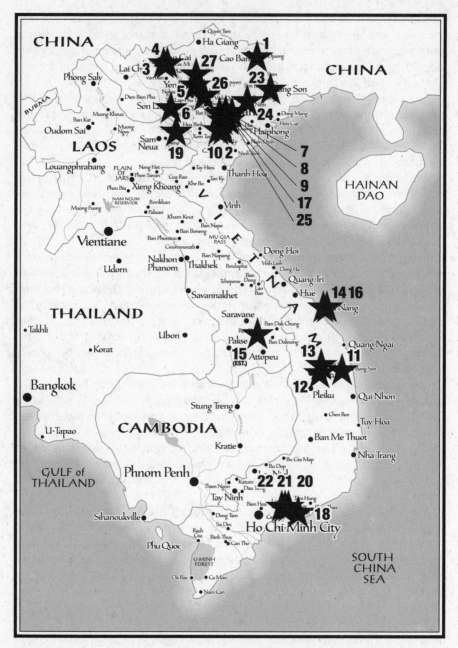

Selected 1979 sightings of U.S. POWs in Vietnam and Laos. (HENDON/ANDERER)

to providing the details of his encounters with the Americans at Kim Boi, he provided U.S. officials with a detailed drawing of the Kim Boi Prison, the cemetery where he and the others buried the dead American pilot, and the nearby North Vietnamese military camp.[5]

It would turn out that the handicapped and blind American prisoners reportedly seen at Dogpatch and the fifty to sixty American pilots seen at the Kim Boi prison southwest of Hanoi were only some of the many American prisoners reportedly seen during the chaotic period that preceded the Chinese invasion.

- Two different groups of American POWs were reportedly evacuated from the immediate area around the province capital of Lao Cai, located at the Chinese border where the Red River enters Vietnam.[6] (See map page 190, points 3 and 4.) Some of the Americans in both of these groups were reportedly taken to Yen Bai and imprisoned there.[7] (See map page 190, point 5.)
- Approximately fifty tall Caucasian prisoners believed to be American POWs were seen bathing just outside a large cave near Mai Son, in Son La Province. (See map page 190, point 6.) The man who saw the Americans later told U.S. officials that one of the guards told him the prisoners were being temporarily housed in the cave and that "in the near future our government will return them to their country."[8]
- In Hanoi, a group of some thirty-five American prisoners was reportedly seen shortly after they arrived at Hoa Lo Prison (Hanoi Hilton) in early January. (See map page 190, point 7.) The Americans were reportedly observed on the first floor of the prison by a group of Vietnamese prisoners who were being held at Hoa Lo at the time. Within several days of the Americans' arrival, the Vietnamese prisoners were reportedly transferred out of Hoa Lo to a prison south of Hanoi. There, they reportedly told a number of Vietnamese inmates at the new facility about the thirty-five Americans they had seen at Hoa Lo. One of those Vietnamese inmates later fled Vietnam and told U.S. officials what he had been told.[9]
- Two other sources would also report the presence of American POWs at Hoa Lo during this period.[10] (See map page 190, points 8 and 9.)
- In early February, an American POW said to be a field grade officer reportedly escaped from a prison camp in a mountainous area of Hoa Binh (Ha Son Binh) Province, the same province where the North Vietnamese political prisoner had seen the fifty to sixty American pilots and helped bury the one who had died. (See map page 190, point 10.) A North Vietnamese man who fled Vietnam and told U.S. officials about this reported escape said that as a result of the escape, the entire foothills area of the province had reportedly been placed under tight security control and citizens had been prohibited from carrying any foodstuffs or water with them when they left their houses.[11]

*Mid-February–Mid-March*
## THE CHINESE INVADE . . . AND THEN QUICKLY WITHDRAW

On February 17, two hundred thousand to three hundred thousand Chinese People's Liberation Army (PLA) troops supported by aircraft and artillery stormed across the border into northern Vietnam.[12] Employing human wave attacks and a scorched earth policy, the PLA quickly captured four northern provincial capitals.[13] Then, in early March, in the face of determined Vietnamese counterattacks and threats of Soviet retaliation along the Sino-Soviet frontier, the Chinese began withdrawing back across the border.[14] By mid-March, the withdrawal was complete and the fighting replaced by isolated artillery duels and what the Vietnamese call "mouth fighting." The artillery duels and name-calling would go on for months.

## THE RELOCATION OF THE DISPLACED AMERICAN POWs

Intelligence received later from a number of independent sources indicates that after the brief but bloody war with the Chinese, the Vietnamese did not send the American prisoners they had evacuated from the border area prisons back to those prisons for continued detention, but instead transferred them—and perhaps other American prisoners as well—to detention facilities located in areas considered totally and permanently safe from any future Chinese attack.

- In March, PAVN personnel attending an official briefing at the old U.S. air base at Bien Hoa near Ho Chi Minh City were informed that some of the American POWs held in the North would be moved to South Vietnam "for their safety because of the Chinese aggression in the north."[15]
- In May, a list of those American prisoners who were to be moved to the South was reportedly circulated in Ministry of Interior offices in Ho Chi Minh City.[16]
- In June, a former South Vietnamese police captain working with his fellow reeducation camp inmates on a logging detail northeast of their camp near Pleibong in the Central Highlands observed a column of approximately fifty American prisoners and their guards moving along a trail during a heavy rainstorm. The police captain later told U.S. officials that as he and the other members of his crew watched, the group stopped for a rest within yards of where he and his fellow inmates were working. (See map page 190, point 11.) The police captain said the Americans were all wearing gray pajama-type uniforms and ponchos or pieces of plastic to protect them from the rain. He said he heard one of the guards accompanying the Americans tell one of his guards that the Americans had recently arrived at Bong Son (Hoai Nhon) by train from North Vietnam. He said the guard further said that the POWs were being marched to a former U.S. military camp near Kontum, where they would be imprisoned.[17] (See map page 190, point 12.) Other sources later reported that the Americans had been taken to the former military base at Plateau Gi, located some forty-two kilometers northeast of Kontum, and imprisoned there.[18] (See map page 190, point 13.)
- On an unknown date during the period of the Chinese invasion, more than two hundred American POWs reportedly left an unknown location in North Vietnam in trucks spaced between two and three hours apart and traveled south to Da Nang. (See map page 190, point 14.) A former South Vietnamese public servant later told U.S. officials that he had learned from Communist soldiers, businessmen, travelers, and others whom he had encountered on the streets, in restaurants, and in the markets that these American prisoners were dressed in tattered clothing and appeared sickly and undernourished. He said that after resupply in Da Nang the prisoners

were reportedly taken west into Laos and imprisoned there. (See map page 190, point 15.) He said he also heard that sometime prior to 1981 the Americans were moved from Laos to Tay Ninh Province, near the Cambodian border northwest of Ho Chi Minh City.[19]

• At around midnight on August 12, 1979, a military train carrying American and ARVN prisoners reportedly arrived at the central Da Nang railroad station after a nonstop trip from Hanoi. (See map page 190, points 16 and 17.) A Vietnamese refugee later told U.S. officials that he had learned of the prisoners from a friend of his, a member of the Ho Chi Minh Youth League who worked for the railroad support company in Da Nang, who said he had boarded the train during its stop and provided water to the prisoners. According to the refugee, the railroad support company employee told him the following morning that the train was composed of twelve cars and had locomotives at both the front and rear. The employee reportedly described the cars as unmarked, gray-colored "military cars" made of steel plate and having small apertures, which he took for gun ports. He reportedly said that after boarding the train he found that each car held approximately thirty prisoners, all of whom were chained to the roof, along with approximately ten guards. The employee reportedly further said that while he was doling out water, several of the Vietnamese prisoners told him that they and the other Vietnamese prisoners on board were former high-ranking South Vietnamese officers. According to the employee, all of the prisoners—South Vietnamese and American alike—were clean shaven and wearing new military uniforms, a fact that led him to believe they were being prepared for a prisoner exchange.[20] He reportedly added that the South Vietnamese prisoners did not appear to be as healthy as the Americans. He also reportedly said that security around the rail station was unusually tight for several days before and after the military train's arrival on the night of August 12, and that when the train departed at approximately 12:30 A.M., public security forces were stationed all along the tracks leading south from the central station.[21] Though the employee reportedly told U.S. officials that he had not heard where the train was going, subsequent reporting would indicate the American prisoners were taken to the Ham Tan area near the coast east of Ho Chi Minh City and imprisoned there.[22] (See map page 190, point 18.)

• At about 5:00 P.M. on a September afternoon in 1979, six Soviet trucks loaded with American POWs and Vietnamese guards were seen pulling into a Pathet Lao seminar camp located some six kilometers south of Sop Hao in Sam Neua Province (postwar name Houaphan Province), Laos. The camp, located in a valley near the small village of Ban Nameo (Ban Na Keo), was one of a half dozen or so small camps lying along the Vietnamese-Lao border in the area where the Song Ma (Horse River) flows out of the "Gorilla's Eye" into Vietnam. (See map page 190, point 19.) A Royal Lao inmate who witnessed the arrival later told U.S. officials that the Americans—mostly Caucasian and a few blacks—were placed in the southwest end of the same building where he and sixty-four other Lao prisoners were being held. The

inmate, a former lieutenant colonel in the Royal Lao Army, said the new arrivals all wore long dark blue pants and matching short-sleeve shirts. He
also said that he later learned there were 111 American prisoners in the
group and that all were pilots who had been captured in Vietnam during
the war. He said he also learned the Americans had been brought to Sop
Hao from a location near the China-Vietnam border because of Chinese
military activity in the border area. The Royal Lao lieutenant colonel explained that the 111 Americans were periodically transferred from his
camp at Sop Hao to other camps close by. He said that after several months
the Americans would be returned to Sop Hao and after a stay of several
months they would again be transferred to a different nearby camp. He
said the Americans were fed canned fish and fresh chicken, pork, beef, and
potatoes that were brought from Vietnam especially for them, and added
that the Lao inmates had to catch their own fish and ate only curries made
from locally grown vegetables.[23]

• In late 1979, most probably in either October or early November, a resident
of Long Khanh Province (postwar name Dong Nai Province) east of Ho Chi
Minh City reportedly was awakened late one night by noise he associated
with the uncommon action of a train stopping near his home. When the
man arose to see what was happening, he reportedly saw that a train had
stopped to let passengers disembark. The man reportedly later stated that
as he watched, approximately seventy old, thin, and bearded American
prisoners got off the train under armed guard and proceeded on foot in a
westerly direction and disappeared into the forest. (See map page 190,
point 20.) The train, believed to be from North Vietnam, reportedly then
continued on its way toward Ho Chi Minh City. The man reportedly said
he later heard the Americans were taken to a POW camp nearby.[24] (See map
page 190, point 21.)

• Sometime during 1979, eighty American POWs were reportedly seen being
brought into a prison camp at Xuan Loc in Long Khanh Province (Dong
Nai Province). (See map page 190, point 22.) These Americans were said to
have been moved to the area from Lang Son near the Chinese border to escape the Chinese invasion.[25] (See map page 190, point 23.)

## OTHER AMERICAN POWs REMAIN CAPTIVE IN THE NORTH

Intelligence reports would later indicate that not all the American POWs held in
the North during the period of the Chinese invasion were moved to Southern
Vietnam or to Laos for safekeeping.

A Northerner employed during 1979 as a driver for the Central Film Documentary Studio in Hanoi would later flee to Hong Kong and tell U.S. officials
that sometime around midyear he had been tasked to assist in the filming of
two U.S. POWs at a government installation located an hour and a half's drive
by truck northeast of Hanoi at a point just north of Bac Ninh City. (See map
page 190, point 24.)

The employee told U.S. officials that although he had normally been assigned as a driver for the film studio, he had been ordered by the leader of the studio filming team, a Mr. Phung, to assist in a one-time film project due to a shortage of personnel. The employee said that on the day of the filming he and other members of the ten-member film crew left Hanoi by truck, crossed a pontoon bridge over the Red River and, after proceeding through the countryside for some ninety minutes, arrived at their destination. After entering the compound, which he said was surrounded by a 2.5-meter-high masonry wall, he and the other team members dismounted and entered a masonry-type building to begin their work. He described the building as being composed of six equal-sized rooms and a community-type latrine at one end. He said he was assigned the job of holding an electric cord for one of the cameramen, and that while other team members were setting up lights and arranging furniture, he and the cameraman began filming the individual rooms. He said that each room was equipped with a wooden, German-style bed with mattress, one pillow and one white sheet, a small wooden nightstand, and a small wooden table with a Formica top on which rested a thermos bottle for water and two drinking glasses. He also said that each room was lighted by a small reading lamp that rested on the bedside table and a light located in the middle of the ceiling.

The employee said that the two American POWs the team had come to film were in two of the individual rooms that he and the cameraman filmed. He described one of the Americans as a Caucasian with no apparent injuries or wounds, of medium build, approximately five-eleven, with short blond hair and wearing white sleeping pajamas with one-inch vertical stripes and rubber sandals. The employee stated the other American was similar in appearance to the first, but he was unable to describe this prisoner in detail because he did not see him clearly.[26]

In November, several months after the filming of the two American prisoners north of Bac Ninh, approximately ten American POWs were reportedly interviewed and filmed by members of an eight-man Vietnamese government team at a PAVN film studio located at the Nga Tu So intersection, where National Route 6 and Route 606 (the "Hanoi Beltway") come together in Hanoi's southwestern suburbs.[27] (See map page 190, point 25.) These American POWs were reportedly observed by a driver employed by the state-operated films distribution firm who had brought the government team to the guarded compound to interview and film the Americans. The driver would later flee Vietnam and tell CIA officials what he had seen and heard at the film studio that day.

The driver told CIA officials that he personally observed the American prisoners as he waited outside the building while the filming took place. He said that all the Americans were Caucasians in their twenties with crew cuts and that all were dressed in white pajamalike uniforms with vertical blue or pink stripes. He explained that following the filming, which he said took approximately one and a half hours, team members told him that at first the Americans had covered their faces with their hands and had refused to be filmed, but they had eventually been persuaded to cooperate. He said the team members also said that during the filming the Americans had been asked about the circumstances of their capture, how they had been treated by their captors, and the identities of their parents and close relatives. He said the team members mentioned that special attention had been paid to relatives who owned or worked for big industrial enterprises in the United States, and that prisoners who had relatives in this category had been isolated and interviewed separately. He also said that the team members told him that at one point the Americans had been asked what they wanted, and they had replied they wanted to be allowed to send and receive mail freely.[28]

On a Thursday morning in mid- or late November, word began to circulate around the Swedish paper mill complex at Bai Bang, northwest of Hanoi, that two American servicemen had escaped from a nearby prison camp and entered the walled, secure Swedish administrative compound seeking asylum. (See map page 190, point 26.) Word had it that the Americans had disguised themselves as Vietnamese peasants by dressing in peasant clothes and traditional Vietnamese conical hats.

A West German engineer who was installing machinery at the mill would later state that after hearing the rumor about the two Americans that morning, he and a French engineer on assignment at the mill both personally observed the two American escapees at about 3:00 P.M. that afternoon inside the Swedish administrative compound. The West German said that he and the Frenchman observed the two Americans as they were escorted by three Swedish camp guards up a flight of stairs that led from the main office to the main drive that ran through the camp and then helped into a Toyota pickup that was parked on the drive. He said a Swedish woman who was manager of food services at the •compound and who was with him and the Frenchman at the time pointed to the two Americans and said, "Those are the two Americans who came into the camp last night."[29] The West German said that both of the Americans were thin and appeared to have been living under difficult conditions for a long time. Both appeared to be thirty–thirty-five years old; one was blond, the other had darker hair. He said that both Americans were wearing fresh new clothes, which he said he later learned had been provided by the Swedes from the compound's Sports Shop. He said that as he, the Frenchman, and the female Swedish food service manager watched, the Toyota truck carrying the two Americans and their Swedish escorts moved down the main drive, turned onto the road leading to the camp medical clinic, and disappeared from sight.

The West German said that the following day he learned that Swedish authorities, fearing a diplomatic incident, had denied the Americans' request for asylum and had returned them to Vietnamese control. He said that when he heard this he became enraged and confronted one of the chief Swedish engineers in the section of the mill where he worked. "Why did you give the American soldiers back to the Vietnamese?" he said he had demanded of the Swede. "I cannot understand why you did this!" According to the West German, the Swede raised his hands chest high and replied, "I cannot discuss this with you! It is not my business to discuss this with you! We should not discuss this! I am sorry!"[30]

Subsequent reporting would quote a Swedish employee who was based at the paper mill's satellite forestry compound at Ham Yen during November 1979 as saying the two American escapees had entered and asked for asylum at the forestry compound at Ham Yen (see map page 190, point 27)—rather than at the administrative compound at Bai Bang—and that they had *then* been taken to "Little Sweden," the administrative compound where the West German engineer said he, the French engineer, and the Swedish manager of food services saw them.[31] The Ham Yen–based Swede would also reportedly say that he had actually talked with the two Americans, whom he identified as Walter Schmidt and Todd Melton.[32]

Though it would be many months and even years before word of the sighting of Schmidt and Melton and the other 1979 sightings reached Washington, reports that were already in the pipeline and arrived at DIA during November— the very month the American POWs were reportedly being filmed at the studio in the southwest Hanoi suburbs and Schmidt and Melton were reportedly being handed back to the Vietnamese at Bai Bang—proved sufficient to convince top U.S. intelligence officials that American POWs were, in fact, still alive in captivity in Indochina.

## *Late 1979*
## U.S. OFFICIALS BECOME CONVINCED POWs ARE ALIVE IN SOUTHEAST ASIA

Lt. Gen. Gene Tighe, USAF, who as director for intelligence for the U.S. Pacific Command during the last months of the war had headed the CINCPAC task force responsible for determining the number of American POWs that might reasonably be expected to be returned at Operation Homecoming, had been named director of DIA in June 1977.

Given his wartime experiences with the POW/MIA issue, Tighe had taken a special, personal interest in the early refugee reporting that had trickled into Washington during 1977 and 1978 and had repeatedly pressed the analysts at the Special Office to pursue every report and to keep him advised of their progress. To his dismay, Tighe had soon discovered a disturbing trend in the analysis coming out of the Special Office. The analysts and managers were routinely ruling that those refugees who reported seeing deserters; American civilians trapped at the fall of Saigon (all of whom had later been released or accounted for); American missionaries, humanitarian aid workers, trekkers, etc., or American POWs held in captivity *during* the war were all being declared truthful witnesses and their stories believed. But those refugees who had testified they had seen American POWs in captivity *after* the war were all being declared either unscrupulous charlatans looking for a quick buck or a green card, none of whom could be believed, or agents sent by the North Vietnamese as part of an elaborate conspiracy to deceive the United States into believing there were living prisoners so that the United States would change its policy and pay to help rebuild North Vietnam in hopes of getting them back. Tighe would later say that these early attempts to discredit the refugees who had seen Americans in captivity after the war were outrageous and had left

Lt. Gen. Eugene F. Tighe Jr., USAF, Director,
Defense Intelligence Agency
September 1977–September 1981.
(OFFICIAL USAF PHOTO)

him very disappointed and frustrated.[33] He would later declare publicly that
the analysts had exhibited a "mindset to debunk" the intelligence on live
POWs.[34]

In July 1979, Tighe—and the unlisted, unreturned POWs—had gotten a big
break when Rear Adm. Jerry O. Tuttle, USN, had been appointed DIA's vice
deputy director for intelligence, a post with direct line authority over the Special
Office. Tuttle, who had flown more than two hundred missions over the North
in carrier-based A-4s,[35] had been appalled at the negative attitudes he found at
the Special Office. He would later explain that the personnel in the office had
exhibited "a mindset that the POW/MIA issue was officially over in 1973 when
our people were repatriated"[36] and that as a consequence the office "made a
morgue look like a three-ring circus."[37]

To remedy the situation, Tuttle first ordered the office moved from Arlington
Hall Station just south of the Pentagon to a complex on the Pentagon's first
floor where he could personally ride herd on the operation.[38] He then began
monitoring the nation's fledgling POW effort on a day-to-day basis, pushing the
analysts to schedule follow-up interviews, insisting that they arrange polygraph
examinations where indicated, requiring them to use the latest satellite imagery
to aid them in their analyses and, perhaps most important, demanding that
they turn out objective, unbiased reports. "I was a mean SOB down there,"[39]
Tuttle later said when discussing the steps he had taken to clean up the mess he
had found at the Special Office.[40]

To deal with the flood tide of refugees now coming ashore in Southeast Asia,
a new program of aggressively screening all new refugee camp arrivals for
POW/MIA-related information was instituted. All the while, Tuttle himself provided Tighe with a daily, blow-by-blow report of what was going on in the nation's POW/MIA recovery effort.[41]

By the end of October 1979, DIA's postwar tally of refugee reports relating to

Americans held captive after Operation Homecoming, by date the report was received at DIA, looked like this:[42]

|      | JAN | FEB | MAR | APR | MAY | JUN | JUL | AUG | SEP | OCT | NOV | DEC | Total |
|------|-----|-----|-----|-----|-----|-----|-----|-----|-----|-----|-----|-----|-------|
| 1975 | 0   | 0   | 0   | 0   | 0   | 0   | 0   | 3   | 0   | 2   | 3   | 2   | 10    |
| 1976 | 0   | 0   | 0   | 1   | 0   | 0   | 0   | 0   | 5   | 0   | 3   | 5   | 14    |
| 1977 | 6   | 3   | 1   | 0   | 0   | 3   | 3   | 2   | 2   | 1   | 1   | 5   | 27    |
| 1978 | 2   | 0   | 4   | 6   | 5   | 8   | 14  | 5   | 7   | 8   | 9   | 9   | 77    |
| 1979 | 34  | 10  | 26  | 59  | 23  | 43  | 49  | 74  | 13  | 30  | ... | ... | 361   |

In November, fifty-eight new reports would be received. Among them would be three which, when viewed in context with the other reporting and with a radio intercept acquired during November, would convince Tighe, Tuttle, and other senior DIA officials that American POWs were still alive in captivity. The first of the three November reports would come from an ethnic Chinese mortician who had fled Hanoi to Hong Kong, the second from a former ARVN colonel who had fled by boat from the South to Malaysia and had recently resettled in France, and the third from a prized North Vietnamese defector who, after having been transferred from Hanoi to the South, had escaped by boat to Malaysia and had later been granted asylum in France.

## REPORT 1: THE ETHNIC CHINESE MORTICIAN

In early November, the American embassy in Hong Kong learned that an ethnic Chinese Vietnamese refugee residing in a refugee camp in Hong Kong possessed information about the disposition of U.S. remains in North Vietnam. During initial interviews in Hong Kong, it became apparent that the refugee could not only provide apparently reliable information concerning deceased Americans but also had firsthand knowledge of three American stay-behinds and hearsay knowledge of other Americans.

Tuttle, reading the report of the refugee's interviews that had been dispatched to DIA, sensed the value of the information and arranged that the man be flown to Washington at once for further interviews.[43] When the nervous refugee—fearful of SRV retaliation and unable to utter a word of English—failed a polygraph administered prior to his departure from Hong Kong, the analysts and officials at the U.S. mission recommended the trip be canceled.[44] Tuttle, however, believing that the refugee possessed potentially valuable information, ordered that preparations for the trip continue. When the still-nervous refugee arrived at Dulles Airport outside Washington in mid-November, Tuttle and his wife were there in person to greet him and put him at ease.[45]

During some sixty hours of interviews that took place over a two-week period, the refugee told U.S. officials that from 1956 until 1979 he had been employed in the Directorate of Cemeteries for Hanoi City. He said that during that period he had personally prepared the skeletal remains of some four hundred deceased U.S. servicemen, remains that had not yet been returned by the Vietnamese. He also reported that between 1974 and January 1979, he had personally observed three unidentified Americans in Hanoi who he was told were U.S.

military pilots who had cooperated with the Vietnamese by providing information on weapons systems and, at war's end, had requested asylum. He also reported that he had obtained information about a small group of former U.S. military personnel said to be working at an airfield northwest of Hanoi who had also cooperated with their captors and had also requested asylum.

At the conclusion of the interviews, the "mortician," as the refugee was now called, passed a polygraph concerning his preparation of the four hundred remains and his sighting of the three former pilots who had requested asylum.

Analyzing the information gleaned from the interviews, Tuttle quickly determined that the key elements of what the mortician had told him and the analysts about his long career working with French and American remains, the inner workings of the North Vietnamese remains program, and the personalities involved in that program mirrored information already in U.S. intelligence files. Given all this, and the fact that he had passed the second polygraph, Tuttle and the analysts chose to discount the results of the initial polygraph and declared that the mortician was a credible witness and that based on his testimony, "It appears likely that the Socialist Republic of Vietnam is withholding a substantial number of remains . . . [and] possibly that at least three unidentified Americans are still in Vietnam."[46]

Though the mortician had spoken only of remains and stay-behinds, his testimony had provided an unexpected and significant boost to Tighe's and Tuttle's efforts to find living POWs. Many now believed that because the Vietnamese were lying about not withholding remains, and lying about not harboring stay-behinds, there was a good chance they were lying also when they said they weren't holding live POWs.

## REPORT 2: THE FORMER ARVN COLONEL

In late October, a former ARVN colonel living in France had written to the National League of Families volunteering to provide information on live POWs being detained in Vietnam.[47] League officials had forwarded the letter to Admiral Tuttle, who, upon reading it, had ordered officials at the U.S. Defense Attaché Office at the U.S. embassy in Paris to contact the refugee and interview him as soon as possible.

On November 7, DAO officials interviewed the refugee at his temporary residence in a refugee center in southern France. The refugee identified himself as a former ARVN colonel and explained that he had traveled to the Loc Ninh area north of Saigon with a trusted former associate in late October and again in early November 1978 to scout out an overland escape route to Thailand. The colonel explained that his associate, who had served as one of his NCOs during the war, was a truck driver who hauled exotic woods like teak and ebony from collection points in the jungle to a sawmill in Saigon, and that he (the truck driver) had agreed to allow him to go along on trips to areas near the Cambodian and Lao borders in an effort to assist him in finding an escape route out of the country. The colonel said that during both trips he and his associate had observed a group of twenty-five to thirty American prisoners working under guard at a logging camp located approximately 7.5 kilometers southeast of Loc Ninh.[48]

The colonel explained that during the first trip, on October 26, 1978, he traveled to the logging camp with the truck driver and his eight-man crew of Oriental men—seven laborers and their supervisor. He said that when the truck arrived the camp at about 3:15 P.M., he saw (and was later able to count) twenty-five American POWs, working in three teams, carrying logs from the jungle and stacking them at the loading site for eventual pickup by the crew that had just arrived. He said the Americans were closely guarded by two officers armed with pistols and five PAVN soldiers carrying AK-47s. The supervisor of the truck driver's work crew told him the prisoners were Americans and that speaking to them or trying to communicate with them in any other way was prohibited.

The colonel said that most of the Americans were wearing black and white striped uniforms but that two had on all-black uniforms with a white panel bearing some unidentified characters on the back of the shirt. He said the prisoners were all skinny and unshaven and had long, unkempt hair and seemed tired and moved slowly and listlessly. He went on to say that when the Americans had finished hauling and stacking all of the logs, they were escorted under guard to their compound, which was located within sight of the log pile at a point some 150 meters away. Only then, the colonel said, were members of the truck's crew allowed to approach the log pile and begin the task of loading the logs onto the truck. The colonel said the crew completed their work at approximately 7:00 P.M. and the truck departed for Saigon immediately thereafter.

The colonel told DAO officials that a week later, on November 2, he and the truck driver returned to the camp alone in hopes they might be able somehow to communicate with the Americans. He said that during this trip they observed what they believed was the same group of American POWs they had seen the previous week, but this group numbered twenty-eight rather than twenty-five. The colonel said that twenty-five of the twenty-eight Americans were working in a garden plot located in a section of the camp, while two were preparing a meal over an open fire and another carried water. He said that neither he nor the truck driver had been able to get close enough to the Americans to communicate with them; however, they had learned from children of members of the security force that the prisoners were indeed Americans.

At the conclusion of the interview, the colonel drew a detailed sketch of the camp and the surrounding area, showing the town of Loc Ninh, the rubber plantations that lay between Loc Ninh and the camp, the road leading to the camp, the small steel bridge the truck had crossed just prior to pulling into the camp, the point where the driver had parked the truck, the nearby log pile where the Americans had stacked the logs, the five-building detention compound where the Americans had been taken after they had completed hauling and stacking the logs, the garden plot where he and the truck driver had seen the Americans working during their second visit to the camp, and the small buildings that housed the security force, the children of whom had confirmed to him and the truck driver during their second visit that the prisoners held at the camp were Americans.[49] He also provided DAO officials with the names of the truck driver and the supervisor and their addresses in Vietnam and suggested that U.S. officials contact the truck driver specifically and ask him to return to the camp as quickly as possible and to report back if the Americans were still there so that the United States could rescue them. He further suggested that U.S. officials could easily confirm the presence of the camp by comparing his map and verbal description of the camp's location to recent satellite photography of the area.[50]

DAO officials would note in a report of the interview session dispatched to Washington two days later that the colonel had "seemed very confident and sure in describing what he saw and the physical details of the area in which he saw it."[51]

Tuttle read the DAO report of the colonel's two sightings and immediately went into overdrive. He first directed that recent imagery of the Loc Ninh area be ordered up and analyzed for evidence of a camp similar to the one the colonel had described.[52] He then ordered the analysts to work with the CIA to develop a CIOP (clandestine intelligence operational proposal) outlining the best way for U.S. officials to contact the truck driver and communicate with him over an extended period.[53] Finally, he directed that an interview team be assembled and dispatched to France at the earliest possible time to conduct a series of follow-up interviews with the ARVN colonel.

The interview team was preparing to depart for France when word came down that a DIA photo interpreter studying satellite imagery of the Loc Ninh area taken in mid-April 1979—some seven months earlier—had discovered a camp matching the colonel's description at the exact spot the colonel had described. In a memorandum chronicling the discovery, a DIA official reported that "PI analysis indicates that the source's description of the area checks out with photography taken about seven months ago" and that the "facility is located at coordinates [redacted] and is approximately one kilometer to the Southeast of [the village of] Shrok Xa Neo.[54] The official further stated that "for purposes of identity, the facility is being referred to as Shrok Xa Neo possible PW detention facility" and indicated that its discovery would be one of the topics covered in a classified congressional briefing planned for November 29.[55]

Then came the report of the prized defector, a former PAVN officer assigned during and after the war to the North Vietnamese equivalent of the Defense Intelligence Agency.

## REPORT 3: THE PRIZED DEFECTOR

In mid-October, the French newspaper *Le Matin* had published an article that quoted a North Vietnamese defector who had been granted asylum in France as saying that a number of Americans—stay-behinds and POWs alike—were still alive in Vietnam.

After a series of unsuccessful attempts to locate the defector, U.S. officials finally found him in November and scheduled a series of in-depth interviews. The interviews were conducted by a DIA debriefing team in Paris from November 22 to 26.

During twenty-one hours of formal debriefings and approximately nine hours of casual conversations over dinner, the defector, named Le Dinh, told team members that in 1971, while a senior lieutenant in the North Vietnamese

Army, he had been assigned as an intelligence analyst in Department C-14 in the North Vietnamese Ministry of Defense. According to Le Dinh, C-14 was a research and analysis office in the "Political General Department" (aka the "General Staff Political Directorate" or simply the "General Political Directorate") of the Ministry of National Defense. The department, he told the already-knowing interviewers, performed a role roughly equivalent to that of the U.S. Defense Intelligence Agency.

Le Dinh said his office exercised administrative control and coordination over several sections, including those responsible for the administration and exploitation of U.S. POWs, and that in his capacity as an analyst, he had access to policy documents and other information concerning American POWs in Vietnam between 1970 and early 1975, when he was reassigned to a new position. He explained that both during the war and after Operation Homecoming, he had had direct responsibilities for planning and coordinating interrogation efforts against U.S. POWs, had had access to dossiers maintained on the POWs, had personally visited some of the detention facilities that held Americans, had seen documents referring to U.S. POWs and their places of detention, and had heard his superiors and other personnel talk about American POWs and the detention camps.

Speaking to the crucial issue of American POWs held by the North Vietnamese after Operation Homecoming, Le Dinh told his interviewers that on several occasions he had heard general-grade officers state that the SRV continued to hold approximately seven hundred U.S. POWs that could be used to force the U.S. to pay reparations. He also reported he had heard a rumor in his department that shortly after the People's Republic of China had seized the Paracel Islands in 1974, the entire population of a camp containing U.S. POWs and about sixty guards located somewhere near the northern border with China had disappeared without a trace.

Addressing the matter of stay-behinds, Le Dinh reported that he had personally observed a group of thirty-three "progressive" Americans in Hanoi on four or five occasions in the latter half of 1974 and offered physical descriptions of three.

In their interim and final reports of their interviews with Le Dinh, team members wrote that

- Le Dinh was very cooperative and is willing to participate in follow-up interviews.
- Le Dinh proved intelligent, self-confident, eloquent, politically aware, and fervently idealistic.
- Le Dinh's account of his position in the Ministry of Defense appears to be authentic.
- In his capacity as an analyst, Le Dinh had access to policy documents and hearsay information concerning US PWs in Vietnam between 1970 and early 1975.
- The details which he presented to the debriefing team leaves [sic] little doubt that he possesses some authentic information about US PWs.

- Le Dinh demonstrated that he had access to information about the North Vietnamese agency responsible for U.S. PW matters.
- Le Dinh demonstrated accurate knowledge about U.S. PWs and PW detention facilities known prior to 1973.
- Le Dinh cited stories he had heard which accurately reflect life in the PW camps.
- Further evidence of Le Dinh's access to the PW camp system was demonstrated by his ability to identify from photographs the names and positions of several North Vietnamese personalities associated with U.S. PWs. Enough is known of some of these personnel to believe that Le Dinh's identifications are accurate.
- Much of the information which Le Dinh furnished regarding the personalities in the General Headquarters is confirmed as accurate.
- His information about organization, missions, and personalities within elements of the Vietnam Ministry of Defense, including the identities of individuals known to have been associated with matters related to U.S. PWs, demonstrates his access to PW/MIA information within this ministry.[56]

Tighe would later say that, given Le Dinh's bona fides and the fact that his statement about the SRV holding seven hundred POWs tracked closely with the difference between the number of expected returnees he and his task force had developed for CINCPAC in the waning days of the war and the actual number of POWs released at Operation Homecoming, he knew at once that Le Dinh was a credible source who possessed accurate information. Tighe would later add that he had been particularly impressed by a statement Le Dinh had made in the *Le Matin* article—but apparently had not repeated to the DIA debriefers—concerning one simple fact that Le Dinh believed constituted proof that the North Vietnamese were still holding American POWs after the war: The offices and sections within the North Vietnamese government concerned with the administration and exploitation of American POWs had not been closed down after Homecoming but, in fact, had continued to function throughout the 1970s.[57]

## THE RADIO INTERCEPT TELLING OF THE TRANSFER OF AMERICAN AND THAI POWs WITHIN LAOS ON NOVEMBER 15, 1979

On December 3, officials at the National Security Agency advised Pentagon officials that a recent intercept of a Pathet Lao radio transmission had revealed the presence of three American POWs in Laos on November 15, only 18 days before. The text of the intercept showed that the Americans and four hundred Thai prisoners had been moved that day from Vieng Sai in Sam Neua Province in the north to Vientiane and then on to Attopeu (pronounced "At-tuh-poo") Province in the south to work in the mines.[58] (See map page 205.)

The radio intercept sent shock waves through the DIA. Tighe would later say that when it was received—coming as it had on the heels of the reports of the mortician, the ARVN colonel, and the prized defector Le Dinh—there was no

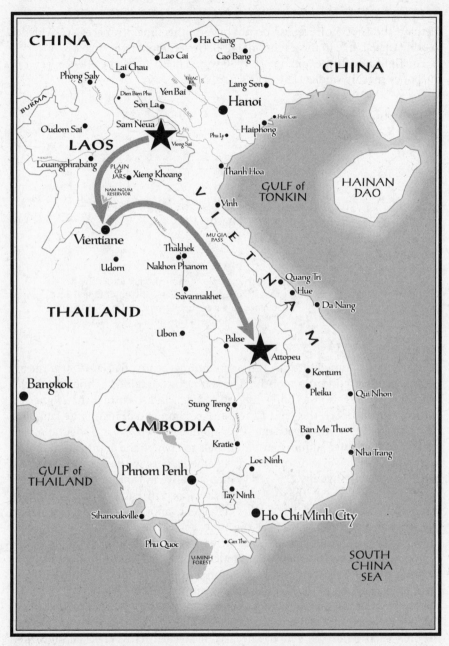

The November 15, 1979, transfer of U.S. POWs from Vieng Sai to Attopeu.
(HENDON/ANDERER)

longer any doubt that American POWs were still alive.[59] On the 12th, a visibly excited Air Force colonel who worked for Tuttle announced at a meeting that it was
the opinion of his office that U.S. POWs "are in fact still alive in SEA."[60] Tuttle, in
an update sent to Tighe on December 18, was only slightly less enthusiastic,

declaring, "We are convinced more than ever that Americans are being held in Vietnam and Laos, however, we do not have, at this time, the necessary evidence to bring that charge to the attention of U.S. Government policymakers."[61]

For Tighe and Tuttle, job one in 1980 would be to get that evidence, get it to the policy makers, and get the POWs home.

CHAPTER 19

1980

RESCUE PLANS

. . .

I strongly hope you still have the pities on them who are under the danger.
—Lao refugee to JCRC officials in Thailand after informing them he
had repeatedly seen American POWs on work details in
northern Laos during 1979 and early 1980

Refugee reports poured into the Pentagon during the first half of 1980 at the average rate of forty-five per month.[1] Though none contained actionable intelligence, i.e., intelligence so compelling, so specific, and so current that Tighe and Tuttle could approach the Joint Chiefs and recommend a mission be launched to rescue the POWs involved, the sheer number of reports and their apparent credibility led Carter administration officials to change the administration's official policy on POWs. The old policy statement that "we have no credible evidence to indicate that any U.S. servicemen are alive in captivity and being held against their will in Southeast Asia" was scrapped in late summer and a new statement adopted. This new policy statement, approved by U.S. officials in charge of the POW/MIA issue at the time, including the State Department's John Negroponte, read, "There is an increasing number of reports that Americans may be held against their will in Indochina. The U.S. Government has thus far been unable to substantiate this information and priority effort will continue to be assigned to investigating these reports."[2]

All the while, Tighe and Tuttle, intent on determining exactly where American prisoners were being held and, if possible, rescuing them, continued insisting that each report be vetted, checked, rechecked, cross-checked, and then checked again. Their efforts paid off in the fall when, according to Tighe, they found two targets—one in Vietnam and another in Laos—and began developing plans to rescue American POWs believed held at both.

# THE AMERICAN POWs AT CAMP K-55,
# TAY NINH PROVINCE, VIETNAM

In mid-October 1980, a former ARVN major who had reached Singapore by boat reported to U.S. officials that just before his recent departure from Vietnam he had seen twenty-one American POWs at a POW camp known as K-55 in Tay Ninh Province northwest of Ho Chi Minh City. He described the camp as being located just outside the village of Dau Tieng (pronounced dow tee-ING), also known as Tri Tam, near Nui Ba Den, the famed Black Virgin Mountain. On the day the major reported his information to U.S. officials—October 18, 1980—just sixty-three days had elapsed since he had seen the American prisoners inside the camp.

The major's account was dispatched to Washington on October 31. Tuttle read it and, struck by both the convincing nature and timeliness of the initial reporting, ordered up a background check of the source, a pattern analysis of other sightings in the Dau Tieng area, a search of satellite imagery of the Dau Tieng area already on file, and priority acquisition of new imagery. He also directed that a second, in-depth interview of the major be scheduled in the United States.

The major was flown to the United States and interviewed and polygraphed in California during late November and early December. During the November interviews, he told DIA analysts that after the fall of the South, he and some members of his battalion had escaped capture and had fled into a jungle area north of Saigon. There, he said, operating from abandoned U.S. firebases, he and his men had for a period of several years conducted hit-and-run attacks against PAVN truck convoys operating on National Routes 13 and 14. He explained that he had been replaced as commander of the resistance battalion in mid-1978 and sent to Ho Chi Minh City to acquire classified documents from Ministry of National Defense offices. The effort, however, became compromised and he was arrested and sentenced to seventeen years in prison.

The major told U.S. officials that immediately following his trial he had been taken by truck to prison camp K-55 near the Cambodian border in Tay Ninh Province. He described the prison as being located in an open area just northwest of Dau Tieng village. He recalled two distinct landmarks that were easily visible from the camp: the smokestacks of the Dau Tieng rubber-processing plant to the east and the imposing Nui Ba Den to the west.

The major said that shortly after entering the camp he had seen a group of American prisoners who were being held in a separate section of the camp. He saw these Americans daily from as close as twenty meters over a period of seven months. He counted the American prisoners on several occasions and was certain there were twenty-one in the group. The Americans wore an assortment of plain peasant garb. Most had beards and, though one walked with a severe limp, all appeared in reasonably good health. Occasionally, the American prisoners were permitted to play football or soccer in a large field at the edge of the camp. The major was told by camp cadre that the Americans were mostly aircrewmen who had been captured in Laos and North Vietnam. According to the cadre, they had been transferred to K-55 from North Vietnam after the Chinese invasion.

The major told DIA analysts that he was transferred out of the K-55 camp in April 1979 and moved to another prison facility near Katum. He said that the twenty-one American POWs were still at K-55 the day he was transferred. He told interviewers that after several months at the new camp, he was able to escape and make his way back to Ho Chi Minh City, where he hid out until he could make arrangements to flee the country by boat. He said that twelve days before his scheduled departure, he returned to K-55 disguised as a cattle herder to see if the American POWs were still there. He said he got close enough to the camp to visually confirm the presence of at least five to seven American prisoners inside the compound. He then quickly departed the area and returned to Ho Chi Minh City, convinced that the entire group of twenty-one Americans he had last observed in April 1979 were still at the camp that day, August 15, 1980.

The major said he departed Ho Chi Minh City for his boat rendezvous on August 27. The following day he and a number of other Vietnamese passengers set sail from Rach Gia, near Vietnam's southern tip, bound for Malaysia. After six days and nights at sea, he and his fellow passengers were rescued by a passing ship and taken to Singapore. He informed refugee officials in Singapore on September 5 that he wished to meet with an appropriate Department of Defense official to report what he had seen at Dau Tieng. Several weeks passed until, on October 18, a U.S. DOD officer contacted him and took down his information about the twenty-one Americans.[3]

During the November interviews, the major drew a highly detailed sketch of Camp K-55 and its environs.[4] Satellite imagery confirmed the existence of a camp at Dau Tieng that almost exactly matched the major's verbal descriptions and hand-drawn sketch of the camp.[5] At this point, the existence of K-55 was considered confirmed.

Throughout the interviews, the major repeatedly expressed an urgent desire that the United States quickly launch a rescue operation to free the American prisoners at Dau Tieng. He pointed out forcefully that the camp was lightly defended and located in an open area near the Cambodian border and so a small heliborne force could easily rescue the prisoners. He volunteered to accompany the rescue party to help ensure the success of the mission.

Following two days of interviews, the major was administered a polygraph examination by a DOD certified polygraph examiner. The following are the relevant questions asked by the examiner and the answers given:

Did you observe 21 American prisoners of war near Dau Tieng?
ANSWER: Yes.
Did you observe 21 American prisoners of war this August?
ANSWER: Yes.
During the period from September 78 to about April 79, is it correct that you
   were imprisoned near Dau Tieng?
ANSWER: Yes.

It was the opinion of the examiner that the major had been truthful in all his responses. On December 4, the polygraph charts were independently reviewed by the deputy chief of the USAF polygraph program, who concurred with the opinion of the original examiner.[6]

In his official report of the interviews and polygraph examination, the DIA

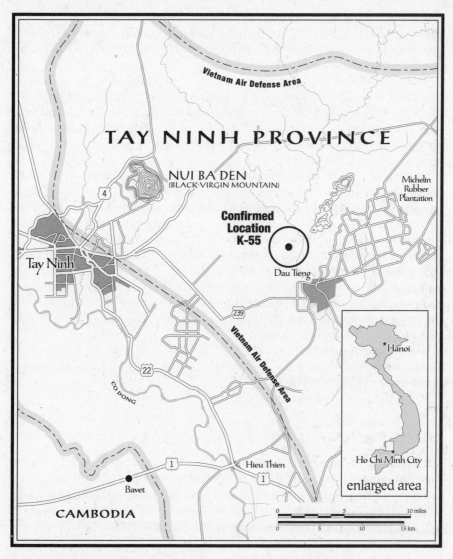

Confirmed location of Camp K-55 (XT 452 515) NW Dau Tieng, SRV.
(HENDON/ANDERER)

analyst in charge of the case described the major as "a highly self confident individual who expressed himself with poise and apparent sincerity." The analyst
further stated that the major was "eager to supply information beyond what is
requested regarding his past, about anti-government activities in the SRV, and
about current events in the SRV, as well as about the topic of U.S. PW/MIA in the
SRV." The major's stated motivations were cited as "anger at the SRV government for having violated the terms of the Paris peace agreement, a desire to
demonstrate his gratitude to the U.S. for its selfless and prolonged support of
the Republic of Vietnam, a desire to help his former American comrades in arms

who are still being held as prisoners of war and a humanitarian concern for the families of the U.S. POWs." The analyst added that the major was a member of a wealthy, upper-class family and had not requested any special considerations, promises, or remuneration from the DIA.[7]

Tighe would later say that when he read the interim report of the sightings at Dau Tieng and viewed the imagery, he began preliminary planning for the dispatch of a helicopter assault force to rescue any Americans who might still be at K-55. He went on to say, however, that lingering concern in the Pentagon over the failed attempt to rescue the hostages in Iran earlier in the year had forced him to cancel the mission.[8]

In early December, as Tighe and Tuttle pondered what if anything could be done about the twenty-one Americans the major had seen at Dau Tieng, Thai intelligence intercepted another Pathet Lao radio transmission telling of the movement of American POWs inside Laos. This intercept, the text of which was dispatched to DIA on December 2, involved the pending transfer of twenty American and sixteen Lao POWs from the northern province of Oudom Sai to the capital of Vientiane.[9] Though the information in the intercept was considered further proof that American POWs were alive in Laos, the fact that the Lao had not discussed when the transfer would occur or the exact location where the Americans would be taken left Tighe, Tuttle, and their planners with little to go on from an operational standpoint.

Twenty-one American POWs at Dau Tieng, Vietnam—but just out of reach! Twenty American POWs, these just across the border from Thailand in Laos—but when, and exactly where?

Then Tighe and Tuttle got their break.

## THE AMERICAN PRISONERS AT GNOMMORATH, LAOS

Ten days after the receipt of the SIGINT (signals intelligence) about the twenty American prisoners being moved from Oudom Sai Province to Vientiane, Tuttle informed Tighe there was promising new evidence that American POWs were being held in a jungle camp southeast of Gnommorath (pronounced nom-or-ROT), in central Laos. Unlike the camp at Dau Tieng, Vietnam, this camp was a mere forty-two miles from the Thai border and only fifty-two miles from the former U.S. air base at Nakhon Phanom.

Tuttle explained that CIA had just advised DIA that thirty U.S. POWs were being held at a prison camp in the Gnommorath area in mid-November, and that the information about the Americans had come from one of the agency's most reliable and highly placed human intelligence sources operating inside Laos.

Tuttle informed Tighe that when the CIA report had been received, he had moved quickly to review old satellite imagery of the Gnommorath area and to acquire new imagery on a priority basis. The old imagery had revealed the presence of a highly secure prison camp located southeast of Gnommorath in an isolated area just off of Route 12, the main road leading across central Laos from the Mekong to the Mu Gia Pass.[10] Tuttle told Tighe that the area would be the focus of the new imagery, which he said would probably be received sometime within the next ten days.[11]

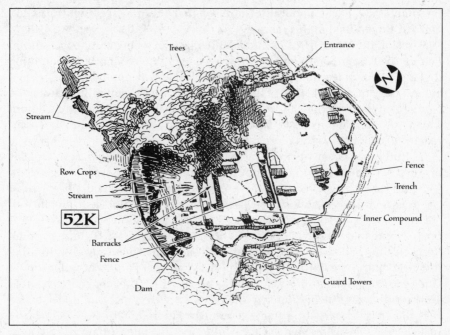

Detention camp southeast of Gnommorath, Laos, December 1980.
(DIA, WITH HENDON ANNOTATIONS)

The new imagery was nothing short of stunning. The prison camp, immediately dubbed "Fort Apache" for its stockade-like appearance, consisted of an outer compound surrounded by a six- to eight-foot-high stockade-type fence and a second, inner compound located near the center of the camp that was separated from the outer compound by a trench and another stockade-type fence. This inner compound contained a number of buildings, most noticeably two long structures thought to be barracks for the prisoners.[12]

Located just outside the inner compound fence were two guard towers and an automatic weapons position. The thatched-roof guard towers, both with platforms approximately twelve feet above the ground, appeared to be positioned for observing activities in the inner compound. Also in the outer compound was an area of cultivated row crops located adjacent to the inner compound fence. In the row crops, photo interpreters clearly saw the number 52 followed by the letter K dug into the ground. Each character was approximately nine feet high and six feet wide. The characters were placed so that they could not be seen from either of the two guard towers.[13]

Aware of the 1975 imagery of the prison in North Vietnam that photo interpreters had believed showed the K laid out in Morse code on the roof of one of the prison lockups, Tighe, Tuttle, and everyone else with knowledge of escape and evasion codes knew instantly that the K in this new imagery could mean only one thing: At least one American aircrewman was trying to signal that he was still alive and being held at the facility. Given that the K was preceded by the number 52, Tighe and Tuttle surmised that the message might read "52 downed airmen held in this camp."[14]

Based on the prior HUMINT (human intelligence) telling of Americans being held in the Gnommorath area and the December satellite imagery confirming the presence of at least one U.S. aircrewman inside Fort Apache, Tuttle ordered around-the-clock surveillance of the facility. Then, on December 30, he called in representatives from the CIA to brief them on all the recent intelligence from Laos and to formally request that their agency send a team overland to Gnommorath to conduct ground reconnaissance.

To Tuttle's amazement, the CIA representatives were openly hostile to his briefing and the proposition that any living American POWs were being held in Laos. First labeling the recent radio intercept about the planned movement of the twenty American and sixteen Lao POWs from the northern province of Oudom Sai to the capital of Vientiane "a fraud," the CIA representatives went on to declare that it in spite of the HUMINT, SIGINT, and IMINT (imagery intelligence) Tuttle had just outlined, it was "unlikely" that American POWs were being held anywhere in Laos and especially at the Fort Apache prison at Gnommorath. That facility may hold prisoners, the CIA representatives told Tuttle, but it was "highly unlikely the prisoners were American." They added that the risks entailed in sending a team to Gnommorath were "extremely high."[15] The CIA representatives told Tuttle that in spite of their reservations, they would report his request to their superiors.

With friends like these, Tuttle later said, who needed enemies?

## FRESH SIGINT TELLING OF AMERICAN POWs ALIVE IN LAOS

On New Year's Eve, the day after Tuttle's negative encounter with the CIA representatives, an intercept of another PL radio transmission arrived at the Pentagon, this one telling of American POWs in Attopeu Province, Laos on December 27, only four days before.

The new intercept, acquired by a Thai intelligence detachment monitoring Pathet Lao communications on the morning of December 27, Indochina time, stated in part: ". . . Refer to the Politbureau [sic], Ministry of Defense, that because U.S. and Thai POWs have been identified by [Thais], Politbureau [sic] orders they be removed from Attopeu Province. Aircraft will pick up POWs at the airfield on 28 Dec at 12:30 Hours.[16] Thai intelligence reported the message was signed by Gen. Kamtai Sipundon [sic] [pronounced Kam Tie], supreme commander of the Lao People's Liberation Army.[17]

Hearts raced for an instant as officials thought of rushing a rescue team from Thailand to the little-used Attopeu airfield to snatch the Americans right off the tarmac or pierced steel planking or whatever it was there, but then sank when everyone realized it was too late—the time the POWs were to have been at the airfield for removal had passed by seventy-two hours.

Seventy-two hours!

(Senate intelligence investigators would find in 1992 that Thai military/intelligence personnel monitored the movement of a large aircraft into and out of the Attopeu airfield during the period specified in the above cable.[18])

# PART IV

# CHAPTER 20

# 1981

## "GASOLINE"

. . .

The near miss at the Attopeu airport in late December caused such a stir that the anti-POW crowd at Langley had no choice but to go along with Tuttle's request that a ground reconnaissance team be dispatched to Gnommorath. On January 17, 1981, Tighe formerly requested that CIA plan and undertake an attempt to confirm the existence of American prisoners at Gnommorath, and CIA agreed.[1] The approved plan called for an all-Asian, CIA-trained and -equipped team to travel overland to Gnommorath, conduct visual reconnaissance of the area, take photographs of the entire camp with emphasis on the inner compound, and return to Thailand. If the photos offered conclusive proof that Americans were being held in the camp, a U.S. Delta Force team from the Joint Special Operations Command (JSOC, pronounced JAY-sock) at Fort Bragg, North Carolina, would be launched from a secret base in Thailand to liberate the Americans.

In late January, after a momentary scare over a report that the Americans had been removed from Gnommorath, CIA officials in Thailand and JSOC officials at Fort Bragg began preparing for the joint operation. Tuttle, working with the Joint Chiefs, coordinated the overall effort from the Pentagon.

*Fort Bragg, North Carolina*
### DELTA FORCE/JOINT SPECIAL OPERATIONS COMMAND · OPERATION POCKET CHANGE

Preparations for the Delta Force assault and rescue phase of the operation began under tight security at Fort Bragg in early February. The effort, code-named Operation Pocket Change, was JSOC's first rescue mission since the joint command had been formed in the wake of the debacle at "Desert 1" in Iran.

Lt. Col. Lewis H. "Bucky" Burruss, USA, who had been deputy on-ground commander at "Desert 1," was chosen to lead the Pocket Change assault force. Burruss would later recall that the intelligence showing Americans at Gnommorath had been "very good" and that morale during the planning phase of the operation was "sky-high." "It was a kick-ass time at Delta during Pocket Change," he later said. "Not only did we have good intel, we had good morale too, because we knew that this time, unlike 'Desert One,' we had a commander in chief who would back us up if the going got tough." (Ronald Reagan had just taken office as the nation's fortieth president.)

Burruss also recalled that Delta planners argued from the beginning that one of their recon teams, rather than a CIA team made up of indigenous personnel, should handle the on-ground reconnaissance at Gnommorath. Burruss said that Delta's plan called for the deployment of a recon team made up of men from the First Ranger Battalion backed up by a "hatchet force" heavy reaction unit secreted at Nakhon Phanom, Thailand. The hatchet force, Burruss later said, would have been sent in to extract the Delta recon team if its members had gotten into serious trouble. Burruss later recalled that when planners at JSOC received final word that Asians employed by the CIA—and not a Delta team—would handle the on-ground reconnaissance, the brass at JSOC had protested vigorously. But in the end, he said, they had been forced to stand down on the reconnaissance portion of the mission and concentrate exclusively on planning and training for a successful rescue. "Assuming all had gone well with the CIA recon team and POWs had been confirmed in the camp," Burruss later said with confidence, "we would have launched our assault from either NKP or a nearby isolation site, and I promise you, we would have gotten those POWs out."[2]

Lt. Col. Herschel S. "Scotty" Morgan, USAF, who had been shot down over North Vietnam in 1965 and had spent almost eight years in captivity in various prisons in the North, served as the director of logistics at JSOC during Pocket Change. Like Burruss, Morgan remembers the enthusiasm that swept through the unit when word came down that President Reagan had personally okayed plans for the mission. "My job at JSOC was to plan for, provide, and pre-position all the equipment needed for a successful extraction," Morgan later said, "and with President Reagan personally behind the mission the way he was, it was a planner's dream. We could get everything we needed, from the most sophisticated radar jamming technology all the way down to the new squad automatic weapons and special ammunition for the assault force." Morgan later recalled that Pocket Change was going to be a "surgical strike, a quick in and out, and believe me, we had the troops, the firepower, and the political backing to pull it off."

According to Morgan, JSOC sent its planners to northern Thailand to check out several of the old U.S. air bases and to make a quick study of the Thai road network. "We carefully checked the roads up in the northeast," he later said, "to make sure we could sneak our heavy equipment in by truck and avoid the attention airborne delivery would create." Other planners, meanwhile, began targeting Vietnamese radar sites in the mountains east of Gnommorath and calculating the size and reaction times of various hostile forces in the area. These planners quickly became convinced that the assault force would have sufficient time to empty the camp and return safely to Thailand, given their ability to neutralize all enemy radars in the area and the fact that it would take Pathet Lao MiG 21s based at Vientiane forty-three minutes to arrive over Fort Apache once they got word of the assault.[3] Morgan later recalled that while all this was going on, plans were being drawn up for an exact, full-scale replica of Fort Apache to be built on Tinian Island in the Pacific for training purposes. "All in all," Morgan later said, "the whole operation was very well planned, and though nobody wanted to start another big war over there, from the White House on down it was clear that we were going to do whatever it took to get our prisoners out of that camp."[4]

*Thailand*
# THE CIA GROUND RECONNAISSANCE MISSION
# TO FORT APACHE

After a series of delays involving the planning of the ground reconnaissance mission and the hiring, outfitting, and training of indigenous personnel in Thailand, the CIA's thirteen-man, all-Asian reconnaissance team crossed the Mekong in late March and headed overland to Fort Apache.

While the team was en route through central Laos during April, friendly intelligence agents monitoring Pathet Lao radio traffic in the Fort Apache area intercepted a low-power voice transmission—believed to be from a walkie-talkie—in which a guard assigned to the Fort Apache camp was heard complaining to another party about the poor working conditions at the camp. As agents listened, the guard first decried the lack of female companionship afforded him and his fellow guards and then went on to complain about the poor quality of the food, declaring "even the Americans in the long building receive better food than we do."[5]

Unaware of what awaited them at Fort Apache, the CIA reconnaissance team continued on its overland trek.

The team reached the area of the camp in early May. After reconnoitering the area, team members hurriedly established a base camp in a cave located within sight of the camp. Several hours later, the two leaders of the team left the cave, approached to within several hundred meters of the Fort Apache compound, and began photographing the camp and its occupants. In the crucial inner compound, site of the two long, windowless buildings, they observed and photographed several guards, several Asian prisoners, and one tall, dark-haired prisoner whom they believed could have been Caucasian. They also observed what appeared to be prepared food and water being taken into one of the long buildings and waste buckets being removed. After observing and photographing the facility for approximately two hours, the team leaders returned to the cave, joined back up with their comrades, and headed back to Thailand.[6]


## "WE DIDN'T WANT TO PUT GASOLINE ON THE ISSUE"

The reconnaissance team returned safely to Thailand in early May. Team leaders quickly contacted their CIA handlers to turn in their film and report their observations. In-depth debriefings followed.

After hearing the statements of both team leaders that they had observed one possible Caucasian prisoner in the inner compound and had also observed prepared food and water being taken into one of the long buildings and waste buckets being removed, CIA officials in Thailand determined that a second reconnaissance team—this one to include at least one American—should be dispatched to Gnommorath at once for a second look. On May 19, these officials cabled their superiors at CIA headquarters in Langley seeking approval of their plan to dispatch another team to Fort Apache. Included in the request was the specific statement that "both [men] claimed to have seen a tall dark haired person who could—repeat—could have been Caucasian."[7]

In a move that would later fuel charges of conspiracy and cover-up, the information on the sightings of the possible Caucasian prisoner was initially held back from the Pentagon. When later asked by Senate investigators why this had occurred, William G. Graver, a veteran CIA officer who at the time was in his fifth year as chief of the agency's East Asia Division at CIA headquarters, said the information was withheld because CIA officials "did not want to put gasoline on the issue."[8]

*Gasoline?*

On the morning of 21 May, two days after CIA headquarters personnel had received—and withheld—the crucial information about the sighting of the possible Caucasian prisoner, a banner headline reading "Mercenaries Sent to Laos Seeking MIAs" appeared at the top the front page of *The Washington Post.* First reporting that "[t]he United States financed and helped train a secret force of mercenaries who went into Laos earlier this month to determine if Americans were imprisoned in a jungle camp there, as covert overflights by satellites and spy planes had suggested," the article then declared the secret force "returned a few days ago without any evidence that Americans were in the camp, chilling the hopes that the earlier photographic intelligence had raised in the minds of some Pentagon officials." Continuing, the article told how members of the team had been issued cameras to take pictures of the camp's inhabitants, but how upon their return "photo interpreters [had] scrutinized all the photography . . . and concluded that there were no Americans in the jungle camp."

Any chance that a second team would return to Gnommorath—and that Lieutenant Colonel Burruss and his men might rescue any Americans held there—evaporated the instant the *Post* hit the streets. At a meeting held at the Pentagon at 7:30 on the morning the article appeared, the brass were angry. "The Chairman wants to know who leaked this," one general declared. "Find the SOB," demanded another.

By the time the meeting ended at 8:30, it was official: Operation Pocket Change, was history.[9]

## MORE PUBLICITY ABOUT THE POWs AND A NEW EFFORT TO FREE THEM

On Memorial Day weekend, just ten days after the *Post*'s revelations about the mission to Fort Apache, *Post* readers and millions of other Americans from coast to coast found the cover of their Sunday *Parade* magazine adorned with a collage of a wartime picture showing a dazed, injured American pilot standing in his flight suit amid a crowd of angry onlookers in North Vietnam. Emblazoned across the cover was a banner declaring, "OUR MEN STILL HELD BY VIETNAM, They're Alive and We Want Them Back." Inside, readers found a feature-length article that began with the equally unambiguous declaration, "Dozens of American prisoners of war are still being held in Vietnam and Laos and the U.S. is determined to get them back." An accompanying article quoted Green Beret Lt. Col. Nick Rowe, who had escaped from a Vietcong POW camp during the war, as saying that prior to his escape, he had found it difficult to accept the fact that the

(© *PARADE* MAGAZINE. REPRINTED WITH PERMISSION)

price required by his Communist captors for his freedom might be too high for the U.S. government to pay. "I only hope," Rowe declared in the article, "that the price for the ultimate freedom [of those still held today] is not too high for our country to pay."[10]

The combination of the *Post* revelations about Gnommorath and the *Parade* article about American servicemen held captive by the Vietnamese elevated the matter of the POWs to topic number one at Memorial Day ceremonies held throughout the country that weekend. On this seventh Memorial Day after the fall of Saigon, countless Vietnam veterans came to feel that their worst fears about their missing comrades were now being realized—and that perhaps the last shots of America's most unpopular foreign war had not yet been fired.

Spurred by the *Post* and *Parade* articles and by Memorial Day speeches exhorting them not to forget the POWs in Indochina, thousands of Americans wrote to the president and to their senators and congressmen demanding that the government take whatever diplomatic or military steps were called for to get the men home. A number of Vietnam veterans volunteered to return to active duty with the proviso that they would be sent back to Southeast Asia to help rescue their abandoned comrades.[11]

President Reagan responded to the national outpouring of concern by holding a ceremony in the Rose Garden on June 12 to publicly pledge to the nation that his administration would do all it could to find living prisoners and gain their release. Some two weeks later, congressional leaders convened a public hearing to examine the plight of the POWs and called General Tighe as their star witness. Tighe, frustrated by his failure to rescue POWs from Dau Tieng and the Attopeu airport in 1980 and from Gnommorath only weeks before, stunned those in attendance by testifying in open, public session that he was "absolutely certain" that American POWs were still being held captive in Southeast Asia. He also called for a renewed effort by the Congress and the administration to get the prisoners home.[12]

Bill Hendon, a freshman congressman at the time, was a member of the House POW/MIA Task Force and present at the committee hearing when Tighe testified. Also present was Hendon's freshman colleague and close friend, John LeBoutillier (R-NY), who served on the POW/MIA task force and on the task force's parent committee, the Committee on Foreign Affairs. Both congressmen had followed the Gnommorath mission day by day throughout the winter and spring, and, like others, had been deeply disappointed when the mission had been compromised.

Now, with Tighe's testimony, they had reason for renewed hope. "[Hendon] and I were just totally blown away by Tighe's testimony in public session that the men were still alive," LeBoutillier later said. "*We* knew, of course, that they were [alive], but this was the director of defense intelligence, testifying to the fact before the U.S. Congress in open session. I'll never forget it—'*absolutely certain.*'" LeBoutillier went on to say that he and Hendon were sure Tighe's statement "would be big news the next day, not just on the Hill, but all across town and, via the media, all across America."

To the congressmen's surprise, however, Tighe's statement did not appear the following day in the *Post* or any of America's other major newspapers. Nor, to their knowledge, the next day. Nor the next, or the next, or the next. Nor was there any buzz about what the general had said in the halls or on the floor of the House. Perplexed, the two congressmen contacted senior members of the task force and the Foreign Affairs Committee to see what they had planned in response to Tighe's testimony. The two congressmen's message to the senior members was a simple one: "Tighe told our committee last week he was certain U.S. POWs are alive. Nothing happened. No press, no follow-up strategy sessions by the task force or the full committee, nothing in Armed Services, nothing in Veterans Affairs, nothing on the Senate side and, as far as we can determine, nothing downtown. What the hell is going on?"

To a man, the senior congressmen replied that other than holding additional hearings and issuing additional press releases, there was really nothing more in the short term that Congress could or would do. "The administration runs the Delta Force teams and the foreign aid programs," one said, "and it's going to take one or the other to get these men home. It's the administration's job, not ours. It's their ball game to win or lose." Another added that because of the failed Gnommorath raid there was little chance a similar mission would be approved anytime soon. "They will never attempt another rescue," this member said, "it's just too risky politically. They were lucky to get through the Gnommorath thing without it being labeled another fiasco like 'Desert 1' and they know it. And anyway, Tighe is set to retire in a matter of weeks and Tuttle has been reassigned, so don't look for much action on this issue in the months ahead."

Amazed and disappointed, the two congressmen called Tighe and invited him back to the Hill for a private meeting. Maybe the general—soon to retire after an illustrious thirty-nine-year career—would have some last-minute advice on how to go about getting the prisoners home.

Meeting with Tighe over lunch in Hendon's Capitol Hill office, the two congressmen told their guest of their frustration over the lack of media response to his historic testimony and explained in detail what they had heard from their more senior colleagues. Tighe responded that he too had been surprised by the lack of response to his statement and expressed agreement with the assessment that the publicity over the Gnommorath mission had severely reduced the chances that POWs would be rescued anytime soon. Tighe then said that he had been giving the matter serious thought since the congressmen's invitation and had concluded that the best approach from here on out would be diplomacy—a bold, new, groundbreaking diplomatic initiative to free the men. He had concluded that Laos, which he characterized as "the soft underbelly of communist Indochina," was the place to begin.

In a little over an hour the three men settled on a plan. Tighe would have his senior analysts draw up plans for a secret, official diplomatic mission to Laos as if he, Tighe, were the traveler. The plans would include a flight itinerary, a schedule of proposed appointments with U.S. and friendly foreign officials in the region, proposed appointments with Pathet Lao and North Vietnamese officials, biographies of top Pathet Lao and Vietnamese government officials, negotiating strategies, various quids that might be offered for the prisoners, and the like. Tighe would then give the plans to the congressmen, who would depart as soon as possible to begin negotiations with the Lao for the release of the POWs. "Your main task is to find out what the Lao want for the prisoners and then use your contacts in the White House to try to get it for them," Tighe said. He added that "for now, Vietnam can wait. If you are successful with the Lao, the Vietnamese will follow."

Knowing that Tighe would soon retire from active duty, the congressmen urged him to accompany them to Laos. He declined, saying with a chuckle that "if the Communists got hold of me and strung me up and put a needle in my arm, I am afraid they might learn far more than they could ever imagine. So I had better not go. You two will be fine alone."

On his way out the door, Tighe thanked the congressmen for the lunch and added, "I'm convinced this is now the only way we can get them out of that hellhole alive. I'll have the briefing book to you in forty-eight hours."[13]

Tighe had the briefing book delivered by courier within forty-eight hours as promised. Armed with their playbook, the congressmen began making arrangements to travel secretly to Laos during the upcoming Labor Day recess.[14]

## A FINAL INTELLIGENCE UPDATE BEFORE DEPARTURE

As the Labor Day recess approached, Hendon contacted Tighe again for any last-minute advice or late-breaking developments. After first underscoring the importance of the recommendation in the briefing book that a courtesy call be paid to the Vietnamese in Bangkok at some point during the trip, Tighe indicated additional good intelligence had continued arriving at DIA since their meeting in Hendon's office, and suggested the congressmen arrange to be briefed on that intelligence prior to their departure. There was no question, Tighe told Hendon, that American prisoners were being held in large numbers in both Vietnam and Laos. "But we can count them when we get them home, can't we," Tighe said. "Godspeed and good hunting."

Hendon and LeBoutillier contacted a friend at the Special Office in late August and learned that, as Tighe had said, DIA had received several good intelligence reports about live POWs that Hendon and LeBoutillier and other members of the POW/MIA Task Force had not yet been briefed on. One of these reports, Hendon and LeBoutillier learned, came from an ARVN officer who escaped from a reeducation camp in Vietnam in November 1980 and later fled to Thailand and told U.S. officials there that, prior to his escape, he periodically observed approximately thirty American prisoners imprisoned near his camp and was told by camp guards that all were American aircrewmen captured in North Vietnam. The ARVN said he witnessed the deaths of several of the Americans and, convinced as he was the others would die off in time, volunteered to return to Vietnam to get current information so the men could be rescued. U.S. officials in Thailand declined his offer.[15] A second seemingly credible sighting from Vietnam came from another former ARVN officer who recently reported that he observed a group of about ten American POWs being brought into his prison in North Vietnam under guard in January 1981, just seven months before. The prison in question, Hendon and LeBoutillier learned, was believed located just south of Hanoi.[16]

Regarding sightings of Americans being held in Laos, Hendon and LeBouillier learned that a Lao refugee currently residing in the United States had recently told U.S. officials he saw American POWs the preceding year in a Pathet Lao camp in northen Laos. The refugee, who passed a polygraph, explained that he and two coworkers were delivering a truckload of supplies to the PL camp when they saw several manacled, emaciated Caucasian prisoners being escorted to a camp bath point under guard. The refugee told U.S. officials he asked a PL soldier at the camp who the prisoners were and the soldier replied they were Americans and that fifty of them were being held in the camp.[17] Then came what the two congressmen considered under the circumstances to be the most exciting and promising of the recent intelligence reports. This report, dispatched to DIA from the U.S. embassy in Vientiane only days before, stated that a European official working in Laos saw a group of Caucasian prisoners performing forced labor under guard on a road gang in the northern part of the country earlier in the summer. The report said the European, who embassy personnel believed was a United Nations refugee official . . . was riding in a helicopter with a high-ranking Lao Communist official when he looked below and observed the group of Caucasians working the road. According to the report, the U.N. official asked the Communist official who the Caucasians were and the Communist official replied they were Americans and Australians "left over from the war."[18]

## IMPLEMENTING THE PLAN

Arriving in Laos by motorized sampan from Thailand over the Labor Day holiday, the two congressmen had barely cleared the customs shack on the north bank of the Mekong when they were informed that they were scheduled to meet the following day with the deputy vice minister of foreign affairs, Soubanh Srithirath. Soubanh had long been active in Lao-U.S. affairs and had been heavily involved in the LPDR's dealings with the Montgomery Committee in 1976 and the Woodcock Commission in 1977. He was known to be a tough negotiator who was unyielding in his demand that the LPDR must receive postwar reconstruction aid from the United States before any search for the MIAs could be undertaken.[19]

At their meeting the following day, the congressmen informed Soubanh that they had come to help improve relations with the Lao and asked what specific measures the United States could take to bring about that improvement. Soubanh, aloof and cool but speaking without rancor, matter-of-factly characterized America as a hit-and-run driver that had devastated his country and departed without helping the victims. "Our people deserve assistance," he said, "medicines and medical supplies, hospitals, ambulances, schools, irrigation projects and other things. So you should help heal the destruction you caused, that is the best way to improve relations between our two countries."

The congressmen, never mentioning POWs, promised Soubanh they would return to Washington and see what they could do. Following a series of meetings with lower-ranking Lao officials over the next two days, the congressmen, by now convinced that their effort would take many months or perhaps even several years to complete, departed for Bangkok and home.[20]

The congressmen returned to Washington and, as Tighe had suggested, reported their findings to the White House. Having determined during their return flight that a modest $200,000 worth of medical supplies would be a doable task in Washington and an acceptable first step in Vientiane, the congressmen took their proposal first to presidential counselor Edwin Meese III and then to Deputy Secretary of State William Clark, Director of Central Intelligence William J. Casey, and Peter McPherson, the director of the Agency for International Development (AID). The plan was ultimately approved and the first portion of the medicine—the first tranche, in State Department terms—was dispatched from Thailand on December 15.[21]

The congressmen returned to Laos over the Christmas recess to check on the delivery of the medicine and for further meetings with Soubanh. After delivering boxes of medical specialty items to their host, and following initial meetings in Vientiane, they were flown by Lao military aircraft to Savannakhet Province town in the central panhandle to tour a hospital. Upon their return to Vientiane, Lao officials made a formal request that the congressmen provide aid to the hospital at Savannakhet and added cryptically, "We understand the principle of reciprocity." After further meetings, the congressmen departed for Washington on New Year's Day to report on their progress and to attempt to free up additional shipments of medicine, these for the hospital at Savannakhet.

Due to the hostile relations that existed between the two countries at the time, the Lao had not allowed the head of the U.S. mission in Vientiane, chargé d'affaires William W. Thomas Jr., to accompany the two congressmen on their trip to Savannakhet. Shortly after the congressmen departed for the United States, however, Thomas filed a glowing report of their visit, pointing out that "no American had been given such a reception in recent years and that the invitation to visit Savannakhet, while it may have had ulterior motives, was special recognition that Americans had not received since the LPDR took over [in 1975]." Thomas went on to write that, "several long conversations with the Congressmen have given me a good idea of what they hope to accomplish. First, they are primarily interested in obtaining the release of live American MIA'S who they are certain are being held by the LPDR. They believe that Soubanh Srithirath has the key to the release of these prisoners and—I think correctly—that they have established a good relationship with him. They also consider that . . . American medical assistance will serve as an adequate earnest of American good intentions toward the LPDR which will allow them to pursue their search for American MIA'S. To this extent they are interested in further deliveries of medical supplies to Laos and probably would consider it a severe setback if such supplies are not delivered. . . . I consider that the results of the visit were favorable from the point of view of the Lao, the USG, [a]nd the Congressmen themselves. I believe they have established a good working relationship with Soubanh Srithirath, and I welcome further visits."[22]

The "Lao Initiative," as administration officials now called the effort, was gaining momentum.

CHAPTER 21

1982

"THE PRINCIPLE OF RECIPROCITY"

. . .

Thomas's glowing report to the State Department proved both good news and bad for the fledgling Lao initiative. The good news was that the report helped to quickly free up a second tranche of medicine for the Lao. This tranche, three times the size of the first, was dispatched from Thailand in early January. On the other hand, the bad news was that shortly after the dispatch of the second tranche, hard-liners at State and DOD began rushing things and demanding an immediate quid pro quo from the Lao.

Proclaiming, "We've given 'em the medicine now they've got to give us the POWs," these officials made a formal request of the Lao in late January that a DOD team be allowed to come to their country immediately to discuss MIAs.

When the request was quickly denied, the hard-liners cited the denial as reason to cancel the entire initiative.

Concerned that the initiative was in peril, the congressmen returned to Laos in mid-February to check on the arrival of the most recent tranche of medical supplies and, because of the pressure being generated by the hard-liners in Washington, to broach for the first time the matter of the POWs.

Meeting privately with Soubanh and his note taker at the Foreign Ministry, the congressmen had barely said hello when their host apologized for his government's refusal to allow the DOD team into the country to discuss MIAs. "We will be happy to discuss this matter with you, but we will not discuss it with them," Soubanh declared. Then, speaking from notes, he told the congressmen that "in response to your humanitarian gestures, we have decided to change our policy in regard to your MIAs, and we have instructed our village officials to begin searching for living MIAs as soon as possible." Soubanh cautioned his guests to have patience. "There is still much ill will in the provinces that must be overcome," he said, "and you must have patience. But as we told you during your last trip, Congressmen, our government understands the principle of reciprocity on this issue."[1]

"We're getting a lot of heat from the hard-liners in our own government," one of the congressmen told Soubanh.

"So am I," he replied with a wry smile.

The congressmen thanked Soubanh and told him they would return to Washington and do what they could to overcome the hard-line elements and keep the initiative alive.

Entering their embassy car outside the Foreign Ministry, they knew they were in deep trouble. "Reagan," they said out loud at the same instant, then headed back to the embassy residence to pack.

*Winter/Spring*
## GETTING THE WORD TO THE PRESIDENT

The congressmen called the White House upon their return to the United States to request an appointment with the president. Because of the recent shake-up in the national security advisor's office—Deputy Secretary of State William Clark had just moved to the White House to replace Richard Allen as national security advisor—they were told to channel their request through Clark's deputy, Robert C. McFarlane. The congressmen did so and within a matter of days met with McFarlane at his office in the basement of the West Wing to brief him on the initiative and deliver their formal request to see the president.

After bringing McFarlane up to speed on the initiative and discussing in detail the recent breakthrough with the Lao, the congressmen asked that they be given an appointment to see the president. McFarlane, perhaps attempting to correct what he later called the "foreign policy drift that infected the administration" under the now-departed Allen,[2] told them that not only could they not see the president, but that they must also shelve their initiative for the foreseeable future and cease all contact with the Lao. It was, McFarlane declared, time to "back off."[3]

Given that McFarlane was now the number three man in the White House foreign policy apparatus behind the president and Clark, the congressmen had no option but to agree to his directive. First telling McFarlane of their disappointment and then assuring him they would do as he said, they thanked him for the meeting and departed.

Faced with a now-hostile White House and the cutoff of all further medical aid to the Lao, the congressmen advised the Lao that there had been a "slight delay" and that the American side of the initiative was on hold until the summer, when the congressmen believed things would improve. The message conveyed, the congressmen went about their regular duties and began actively preparing for the upcoming congressional elections. Then, in early April, they received word from the Pentagon that DIA had just received another "Tell the world about us!" sighting from Vietnam. This sighting, the congressmen were told, had occurred in Thanh Hoa (pronounced "Tan Wah") Province in the North in the spring of 1980. They immediately recognized that this was the same area where the ARVN captain had seen the thirty American POWs in October 1980 and had volunteered to return to the area to gather intelligence on the Americans so that they could be rescued.[4]

Learning of this new report from Thanh Hoa, the congressmen determined they must try again to meet with the president. They contacted McFarlane's office, but again their request was denied.

The congressmen were still smarting over McFarlane's latest rebuff when they learned in early May that the DIA had just received new intelligence indicating that an estimated three hundred American POWs were being held prisoner in Laos. This information, which had been acquired by U.S. military intelligence personnel in Japan, had reportedly originated with a member of the staff of the Japanese embassy in Vientiane.[5]

For the congressmen, this new report was the last straw. On May 12 they called McFarlane's office and demanded that McFarlane arrange a meeting with the president so they could brief him on the Lao initiative. When McFarlane again refused, the congressmen contacted White House Chief of Staff James Baker and asked that he arrange the appointment for them. Baker refused, saying the president's schedule was full and that he would soon be leaving town, first for a vacation in California and then to the G-7 Economic Summit in Europe. "Sorry," Baker said, "but it will be several months, and even then I can't promise anything."

It was then that LeBoutillier told Baker that if he and Hendon were not allowed to see the president before his departure for California they would stand up during Reagan's next address to Congress and walk out. Baker replied that he would see what he could do. The following day he called back to advise the congressmen that they were on the schedule to meet with the president on the afternoon of the 24th.

## "BIGGER THAN THE RED SEA"

The congressmen met with the president, Baker, and McFarlane in the Oval Office on the afternoon of May 24. They found the president his usual gracious self from the onset. After brief introductory conversation, the president asked rhetorically, "Well, how are we going to resolve this?"

"Respectfully, sir," Hendon replied, "as John and I see it there are really only three options: we either buy 'em, we steal 'em, or we forget 'em."

"Well," Reagan said quietly, "we will never forget them."

"We know that, sir," Hendon replied, "and that's why we are here."

The congressmen began briefing the president of their travels to Laos, the shipments of medicine, and the resulting decision by the LPDR to begin searching for living Americans. They told Reagan that to keep the initiative going they needed another shipment of medicine at once and funds to cover their travel expenses to Laos, expenses they had heretofore been paying out of their own pockets. They concluded by saying they would like to return to Laos over the July 4th recess and that it was essential that a new tranche of medical supplies be delivered prior to their arrival. They ended their presentation by telling the president that they were convinced that if the medical supplies kept flowing, the Lao would, in time, "find" and release living prisoners.

Reagan appeared deeply moved by what he had heard. After a long, thoughtful pause, he said quietly and with more than a hint of emotion, "If we could get these men back, it would be bigger than the Red Sea." He told the congressmen that he would indeed help them with their initiative and directed McFarlane to work with them on the particulars of funding, additional tranches of medicines, and the receipt of other government support where possible. The president asked the congressmen to send McFarlane a proposal for another shipment of medical supplies and to make sure it was received at the White House before his (Reagan's) departure for Europe. He also told the congressmen that the government would reimburse them for all expenses they had incurred to date and would cover all future travel costs.

The congressmen agreed to send the proposal for medicine and a list of their expenses and, after assuring the president they would do their best to make the initiative work, thanked him and departed. They returned immediately to Capitol Hill, dictated one memorandum relating to additional medical supplies and another related to past travel expenses and couriered both to McFarlane that afternoon.[6]

McFarlane called Hendon several days later to follow up on the Oval Office meeting and the information the president had requested. Pertinent portions of Hendon's phone notes of his conversation with McFarlane show that the following was said.

McFarlane reported, "The president brought up your meeting again the next morning. He said that he had thought about it overnight and that he was impressed. . . . He said you and John had done a first-class job . . . had established your bona fides . . . and had acted very discreetly. . . . He made it clear to me in firm terms that he wanted to be helpful on the travel and on the whole project. . . . I have a firm commitment to handle."

He continued, "The president's position would be [that] he is pleased by what you have done. The U.S. government has endorsed what you have done. The U.S. wants to improve relations with the Lao. We want some tangible action, i.e., the physical return of remains or prisoners. . . . He said he thought it was up to the Lao, now, to reciprocate. He would like remains or prisoners with no further movement by U.S. [meaning after the upcoming July tranche had been sent]."

McFarlane asked, "Can you and John go back? The president said he wants me to help with a return visit."

Hendon told McFarlane that the planned July shipment of medical supplies discussed in the Oval Office meeting and in the congressmen's memorandum of May 24 must be shipped immediately or there would be no reason to return to Laos. He asked, "Has the shipment been dispatched?"

"I don't think so," McFarlane replied.

"Please get it going *now*."

"Yes, I'll do that."

"Get it there before July 1, we go July 5. Okay?"

"Okay."[7]

*July, Laos*
## "SOME PEOPLE BELIEVE THE TIGERS ATE ALL YOUR MEN . . ."

In late June, LeBoutillier chose not to continue his participation in the Lao initiative. On July 7, Hendon, traveling alone, arrived at Vientiane's Wattay Field by U.S. government C-12 aircraft from Bangkok. He was taken immediately to the Foreign Ministry for a scheduled meeting with Vice Minister Soubanh.

Soubanh greeted Hendon warmly and introduced him to Dr. Ponemek Daraloy, the LPDR's vice minister of public health, who, Soubanh said, would be Hendon's official host during his brief six-hour visit.

Following three-way discussions at the Foreign Ministry, Dr. Ponemek drove Hendon to Vientiane's Mahosot Hospital for a room-by-room, ward-by-ward inspection of the dilapidated and virtually abandoned multistory facility.

The hospital, though of modern design and structurally sound, was in a deplorable state. In the rooms that formerly had housed patients, windows swung useless on their hinges, bed frames and springs lay rusting on dirty concrete floors, mosquitoes swarmed in the corners. In the operating rooms, rectangular holes cut through the outer walls marked the site of long-gone window-type air conditioners; X-ray machines, their control panels hanging open and wires dangling out, stood useless. Buckets of caked, dried blood hung from hooks at the feet of several filthy operating tables.

"The price of your victory," Hendon wanted to say but quickly extinguished the thought.

At the conclusion of the tour, Ponemek gave his guest a list of equipment and supplies he said the Lao would need to enable them to reopen the hospital. Scanning the short two-page French-language list, which included radiology; dental and surgical supplies; air conditioners for the delivery room, the ICU, and the various operating rooms, two heavy-duty washers and two heavy-duty dryers for the laundry; and four small buses for the transport of patients, Hendon told Ponemek, "This is very reasonable. I am sure we can provide this. It may take several months, but we can do it."[8]

The two men then returned to Ponemek's broken-down car to depart. As Ponemek prepared to drive his guest back to the Foreign Ministry, he turned to him and said, "[A]s Mr. Soubanh has told you, we understand the principle of reciprocity in our dealings with you and your government. Some people believe the tigers ate all your men. I am not one who believes that. I have people in all the provinces. I believe some of your men are still alive, and if you will help us, I believe we can find them."

Ponemek drove Hendon back to the Foreign Ministry following their conversation at Mohosat. After good-byes to Ponemek and Soubanh, Hendon was taken to Wattay Field where he boarded the waiting C-12 and departed for Bangkok. Shortly after arriving in Bangkok he boarded a westbound Pan Am flight for New York and home.

## THE ADMINISTRATION CHANGES OFFICIAL POLICY ON LIVING POWs

On July 9, in remarks prepared before Hendon's trip to Vientiane, Secretary of Defense Caspar Weinberger told POW/MIA family members gathered in the Washington area for the thirteenth annual meeting of the National League of Families that the administration had changed official government policy on the POW/MIA issue. "[W]e [now] proceed under the assumption that at least some Americans are still held captive by the Indochinese Communists," he stated, citing "over 400 first-hand sightings" as reason for the change. He told the families that determining the fate of their loved ones was now "a matter of the highest national priority."[9] Soon after Weinberger's speech, his statement on POWs was formally adopted as official U.S. policy and disseminated in written form throughout the government.[10]

## "REHABILITATION OF PEOPLE'S LIVELIHOOD"

Hendon and the NSC's new director of Asian Affairs, Lt. Col. Richard Childress, USA, worked during August to cost out the supplies requested by Ponemek and begin making arrangements for their shipment. According to NSC estimates, the cost of the entire list of supplies and equipment was less than a quarter of a million dollars, excluding freight and the extra charge involved in special ordering the buses for October–November delivery.[11]

While arrangements were being made to purchase and ship the supplies and equipment, a four-member delegation from the National League of Families traveled to Vientiane in mid-September to seek information on missing Americans. Lao officials informed their visitors that no American POWs were being held by the Lao government but acknowledged that some might still be held in remote regions of the country without their knowledge. They then presented the delegation with a short list of development projects that they said would be needed to begin the "rehabilitation of people's livelihood in provinces heavily affected by war in Laos during the years 1964–72."[12]

Retired Green Beret Col. Earl Hopper, whose son was missing in action over North Vietnam, was chairman of the board of the league at the time and a

member of the league delegation. Hopper later said that he had not been surprised when the Lao had presented their list of development projects, because
Lao officials in New York had told league officials prior to the delegation's departure that they desperately wanted reconstruction aid and hoped the league
would pressure the U.S. government to grant it.[13] "They had talked in generalities in New York," Hopper later recalled, "but in Vientiane they told us exactly
what they wanted—schools in these districts, hospitals in these towns, irrigation projects in these provinces, and the like."

Hopper's main interest, of course, was live POWs, and it didn't take long before he became convinced that the Lao were holding them. "During the talks
with the Lao, it became perfectly obvious they were holding our men," Hopper
later said. "And they made it abundantly clear that they had to get the schools,
hospitals, and the like before they would consider releasing them." Hopper
added, "They just basically told us, 'You help us out with our needs and we'll
help you out with yours.' "[14]

Ron Miller, an ABC News correspondent who accompanied the league delegation, later agreed with Hopper's assessment about living POWs. "I had been
covering the POW issue since the fall of Saigon," Miller recalled, "and I had
never seen anything like this. The Lao as much as said, 'Your POWs are stashed
away in the caves. Help us rebuild our country and we'll give 'em back.' They
put on an amazing performance, and I remember thinking as I left Vientiane to
file my story that something really positive was taking place."

Miller also remembered that upon his return to the United States he had
been surprised and pleased to find that State Department officials had responded favorably to a story he had filed from Southeast Asia indicating that
POWs might still be alive. "State's reaction was 180 degrees different from previous POW stories, which they had always tried to disparage," Miller later said.
"This time, they responded by saying that they assumed some POWs were alive,
that they were encouraged the Lao were saying the same thing, and that they
looked forward to cooperating with the Lao government to resolve the matter. It
was amazing. Suddenly, after years of denials from both sides, officials in both
capitals seemed to be saying, 'Hey, we can work this out.' "[15]

## A PROPOSAL FROM THE LAO

Twenty-six Republican congressmen—Hendon and LeBoutillier among them—
were defeated in the November midterm elections.

Ten days after the election, Hendon, with six weeks still to go in his congressional term, returned alone to Vientiane for a series of meetings with the Lao.
His purpose was to advise the Lao that he would be leaving government service
and that it was his strong belief that if the Lao initiative was to succeed, the Lao
must begin working with the U.S. chargé in Vientiane, William W. Thomas,
whom they had heretofore pointedly excluded from all aspects of the Hendon-
LeBoutiller trips. Thomas had steadfastly supported Hendon and LeBoutillier in
their efforts, in spite of both the rude treatment afforded him by the Lao and
the pressure he had received from members of his own embassy staff who were
opposed to any form of rapprochement with the Vientiane government. Given

that opposition within the embassy, Hendon knew that Thomas, rather than one of his staff, had to be the man in charge.

Meeting with Soubanh and other officials at the Foreign Ministry, Hendon told them that Thomas was a friend of the Lao people and of the Lao initiative and that it was critically important that they bring Thomas on board as his replacement. The Lao quickly agreed to do so and, in an effort to get their new relationship with Thomas off to a good start, invited Hendon and Thomas to fly by helicopter to Xieng Khouang Province in the north for a weeklong tour of the war-ravaged Plain of Jars [Plaine des Jarres] (PDJ). Hendon and Thomas accepted the invitation and departed for the PDJ the following day in the company of two officials from the Lao Foreign Ministry. Hendon and Thomas remained there for a week, meeting with province and local officials and being taken on tours of war-damaged towns and villages, on visits to the homes of wartime casualties, and to meet with those wounded in recent encounters with the antipersonnel mines that still littered the landscape.

Upon the group's return to Vientiane, Thomas and his wife hosted a reception-buffet at the official residence on the evening of the 23rd. The event, which was designed to serve as a going-away party for Hendon, was attended by Vice Minister of Foreign Affairs Soulivong Phasitthideth, Dr. Ponemek, and a number of lower-ranking Lao officials.[16] Hendon and Thomas were both surprised at Soulivong's presence, Hendon because he had never met the vice minister and Thomas because Soulivong had never before accepted an invitation to an official U.S. function.[17]

Midway through the event, Soulivong pulled Hendon aside for a private conversation. "We regret very much that you lost the election," he began. Then, with a smile coming to his face, he said, "but I have a proposal that may make the pain go away. I propose that our two countries normalize relations at once and that you come back to Vientiane as America's ambassador. We are prepared to extend full diplomatic relations to your country—immediately and without precondition—and we invite you to return here as your country's first ambassador. What do you say?"

*Early December*
## WASHINGTON

Hendon returned to the United States and reported Soulivong's offer to McFarlane in his White House office in early December. After reviewing with Hendon what had transpired with the Lao and carefully weighing Soulivong's offer, McFarlane chose a middle course. "It's not yet time to normalize," he declared. "There may be a way, however, to keep this thing moving forward. We'll put you in the Pentagon working for Rich [Armitage] as a consultant. You can work with him, get to know him and Paul Wolfowitz over at State. Working out of the Pentagon, you can continue traveling to Laos and we will continue shipping the medicine. In six months we'll reassess, and if there has been measurable progress, we'll consider upgrading [the embassy] and sending you back as ambassador."

"Deal," Hendon said.

What a year it had been:

- "Our government understands the principle of reciprocity on this issue."— Soubanh Srithirath
- "We proceed under the assumption that at least some Americans are still held captive."—Caspar Weinberger
- ". . . 400 first-hand sightings . . ."—Caspar Weinberger
- "If you will help us, I believe we can find them."—Ponemek Daraloy
- "Officials in both capitals seemed to be saying, 'Hey, we can work this out.'"—Ron Miller
- "Bigger than the Red Sea."—Ronald Reagan

Would 1983 see a parting of the waters?

CHAPTER 22

## 1983

# A DRAMATIC CHANGE OF COURSE

. . .

The atmosphere in the basement ballroom of the Hyatt Regency Hotel in Crystal City, Virginia, was ripe with anticipation on the morning of January 28, 1983, as relatives of the POWs and MIAs gathered to hear an address by the president of the United States. The families, some five hundred strong, had convened in special session at the suburban Washington hotel to commemorate the tenth anniversary of the signing of the Paris Peace Accords and, more important, to hear from the one man they were sure could bring their loved ones home.

Entering to "Hail to the Chief" and flanked on the stage by his secretary of defense, his national security advisor, the chairman of the Joint Chiefs of Staff, and a former Vietnam-era POW, Ronald Reagan disappointed no one. "You watched as we disengaged from Vietnam and many of our prisoners of war returned for an emotional homecoming," he told the families. "You've seen task forces and committees hold hearings and issue reports that attempted to foreclose hope. But as the tragic flow of refugees from Indochina began a few years ago, those columns of humanity who had suffered hunger and thirst and disease and piracy brought with them firsthand live sighting reports of American prisoners held captive after 1973. As this information was investigated, respected figures in the intelligence community reached personal conclusions that these reports were credible, even though the circumstances of the sightings prevented confirmation. . . . Today, I want you to know that your vigil is over. Your government is attentive and intelligence assets of the United States are fully focused on this issue. . . . I pledge to you, we will take decisive action on any sighting report that can be confirmed."

When the applause died down, the president then went on to send a message to the Lao. Explaining that "some of [our] approaches must be done quietly," he declared that "progress on the POW/MIA issue will be the principle measure of [Lao] sincerity. I wish to recognize publicly their positive steps to date, and call upon them to continue with us this humanitarian effort to end the years of uncertainty that you have endured."[1]

After delivering additional remarks and praising the families for having kept their vigil, the president ended his speech with an emotional tribute to the missing. As he left the ballroom, family members cheered, embraced, and even wept. "I've been waiting 15 years to hear something like that," the mother of an MIA told *The Washington Post*. "He's given us hope."[2]

Seventy-two hours later, in a truly incredible stroke of bad luck, that hope began to evaporate on the banks of the Mekong River in northeast Thailand.

## THE WAR HERO, CLINT EASTWOOD, WILLIAM SHATNER, AND THE PRESIDENT OF THE UNITED STATES

On January 31, three days after the president's speech, the *Bangkok Post* reported in a front-page story that a retired U.S. Army Green Beret had led a team into Laos several months before in an unsuccessful effort to rescue American POWs. The *Post* identified the leader of the team as forty-three-year-old Lt. Col. James "Bo" Gritz (pronounced "Grieghts"), and said that Gritz was currently in northeast Thailand preparing for another mission. Citing knowledgeable sources, the *Post* said that Gritz and his team were financed in part by American actor Clint Eastwood and suggested that President Reagan himself might have personally authorized the missions or have been otherwise involved. The article pointedly made reference to the fact that Reagan had pledged to relatives of the missing the previous Friday that he would take "decisive action" to free any American POWs proved to be in captivity.

The *Post* article went on to say that that an administration spokesman in Washington had denied any official U.S. government involvement in the Gritz affair and had declared that the former Green Beret's actions were "very unhelpful to our effort to make progress on PoW-MiA . . . matters." The *Post* also quoted U.S. sources in Bangkok as having expressed concern that Gritz's actions might have a negative impact on U.S.-Lao relations. "We're just starting to make some little progress in our relations with Laos," the *Post* quoted one American as saying. "The Laotians are just starting to show us progress in our talks with them. Just one incident like this thing could queer our whole relationship with Vientiane for a long time." The *Post* noted that "the United States has diplomatic relations with Laos, but they have been cool since 1975, and only about six Americans serve in the Embassy in Vientiane."[3]

Given Reagan's widely quoted pledge to the families that POWs would be rescued if their presence could be confirmed, the story of Gritz and his team proved irresistible to the world's press. Agence France-Press, reporting from Bangkok only hours after the *Post* article appeared, declared provocatively, "A commando unit of 16 former United States 'Green Berets' is preparing in Thailand for a raid inside Laos to liberate U.S. prisoners of war, the *Bangkok Post* said today."[4] News organizations, anticipating a sensational story was in the works, rushed reporters to northeast Thailand to find and interview Gritz and his team and—they hoped—some recently liberated POWs as well.

Reporters soon located Gritz and his team, sans POWs, in the sleepy Mekong River town of Nakhon Phanom. Though dismayed to discover that no POWs had been rescued, the reporters nonetheless found a major story in the jaunty, charismatic Gritz and a very talkative member of his team.

On February 22, *The Washington Post* reported in a front-page story filed from Thailand that a member of Gritz's team had said that Eastwood had gone to see Reagan at the president's ranch in California prior to the first Gritz mission and had told the president of Gritz's upcoming raid. According to the *Post,* after being told of the planned raid, Reagan had told Eastwood that if Gritz's team brought one live POW back, he, Reagan, would "start World War III to get the rest."[5] With hordes of nuclear freeze activists working the halls of Congress to stop the president's proposed military buildup, White House officials were justifiably horrified at the *Post's* reference to the president. Their horror was compounded on the 28th when *The Los Angeles Times* revealed that LeBoutillier, apparently believing the cat was already out of the bag, had provided *Times* reporters with details of his earlier trips with Hendon to Laos and the administration's sending medical supplies to the Lao in hopes of gaining the release of living American POWs. "World War III" on the one hand, "ransom" on the other; either or both to be employed to gain release of living POWs still held captive by the Communists ten years after the American withdrawal. Hendon, monitoring it all from his Pentagon office, was certain things could not possibly get any worse.

That same day, February 28, Gritz and two members of his team were arrested by Thai authorities and charged with possession of high-powered radios, which at the time was a serious offense in security-conscious Thailand. When word that the men were in jail reached the United States, media interest in Gritz surged, and as a result he became an instant folk hero to the POW/MIA family members and to many Vietnam vets. The usually staid *Washington Post* stoked the fire, publishing a lengthy profile of Gritz, complete with combat lore and a picture of him being visited at his Nakhon Phanom jail cell by the daughter of a missing air force pilot.[6]

Readers of *The Washington Post* article—and other similar articles that appeared at the time—learned that Bo Gritz had been a true military hero during the Vietnam War. The son of a B-17 pilot killed in action over France during World War II, he had joined the Special Forces in 1957 and had later served four tours of duty in Vietnam. During those tours, he had reportedly led indigenous troops behind enemy lines on more than a hundred missions, and in the process had earned over sixty medals, including a double handful of Silver and Bronze Stars.

According to the *Post,* retired General William C. Westmoreland, commander of U.S. forces in Vietnam from 1964 to 1968, had remembered Gritz in his memoirs as being a "daring young commander." Retired Army Brig. Gen. William Yarborough, who had served as commander of U.S. Special Forces at Fort Bragg during the war, was quoted as saying that Gritz had "a lot of leadership and charisma" and "there was no question about his skills as a soldier. He has been in some of the tightest places a man can be and survive," Yarborough said, "[and] if I were in combat, I'd love to have this guy with me."

The *Post* went on to report that Gritz had held several prestigious assignments after the war, including a tour in the Pentagon where he served as the army's liaison officer to the U.S. House of Representatives. It was during his Pentagon tour in the late '70s, the *Post* said, that Gritz had become privy to the increasing flow of intelligence that told of American POWs still imprisoned in Indochina. The intelligence, coupled with the lack of response from those he would later call the "faint hearts" in the Pentagon and "pot-bellied" bureaucrats elsewhere in Washington, had moved Gritz deeply. He had protested loudly within the ranks, and when his protests had failed to spark interest in the POWs, he had retired from the army in early 1979 to pursue the POW/MIA matter in the private sector.

In 1980, after making several trips to Thailand to establish contact with members of the Lao resistance and gather fresh intelligence on POWs, Gritz had returned to the United States to raise money for a rescue mission. He reportedly received support from defense contractors, veterans' groups, officers of the National League of Families, and several big-name Hollywood movie stars. William Shatner, who later called Gritz "a modern-day Sergeant York," reportedly contributed $10,000; superstar Eastwood, $30,000.

Following a period of training at a site in Florida, Gritz and a small team of Americans had departed for Thailand in the fall of 1982 to make final preparations for a mission into Laos. After renting a house in Nakhon Phanom, Gritz had expanded his team to include a number of Asians and, on the night of November 27, had led his men across the Mekong into Laos. After traveling only several kilometers through the Lao countryside, the team had been ambushed and forced to return to Thailand empty-handed.

Following the mission, Gritz had returned to the United States for a brief stay and then, in January 1983, had returned to Thailand to attempt a second mission. It was then that the *Bangkok Post* had published its story.

*The Washington Post* profile of Gritz sparked even more media interest, and on March 4, Gritz, moments after he was released on bail pending his trial, appeared on ABC's *Good Morning America* by telephone hookup from just outside his jail cell in Nakhon Phanom. In the course of his conversation with host David Hartmann, he revealed that he had acquired intelligence on live POWs in Laos and would release it when he returned to the United States.[7]

Gritz was tried later in the week and found guilty of possessing the radio. He was given a one-year suspended sentence, fined approximately $700, and told to leave the country.

Upon his return to the United States, Gritz was invited to testify before a U.S. House Foreign Affairs subcommittee on his activities in Laos and Thailand. During his testimony on March 22, he was asked to produce the evidence on living POWs he had promised to reveal upon his return. To the great dismay of the POW/MIA families who packed the hearing room, Gritz acknowledged that he had no firm evidence, only, he said, "evidence that might be presented to a convention of clergymen to prove that God exists."[8]

"This is ridiculous," one leader of a Vietnam veterans' organization who was in the audience said when Gritz had finished. "He is exploiting people. This issue should be put to rest."[9]

After the hearing, members of the press, apparently sharing the veteran leader's sentiments, unleashed a torrent of negative media accounts aimed directly at Gritz and his men. With stunning swiftness, Gritz and his "combat tested commandos" who had launched such a "daring raid," became "ragtag drifters," "buccaneers," "dreamers," and "desperadoes" who were on a "quixotic," "amateurish," and "feckless" mission; the whole affair "tragicomic," "bizarre." And on and on it went.[10]

Rep. G. V. "Sonny" Montgomery (D-MS), when asked for his reaction to Gritz's testimony, laid the blame for the whole Gritz affair at the feet of the president, who, Montgomery implied to *Washington Post* columnist Mary McGrory, made serious mistakes when he "gave the poisoned pot another stir when he went before the National League of Families in January, gave the problem of the missing-in-action 'highest national priority' and mentioned the 'live sighting' reports."[11]

Though Montgomery was believed by some to be a less than objective observer—his Montgomery Committee and the Woodcock Commission on which he served had, after all, declared in 1976 and 1977 that no POWs remained alive—his response, coming as it did from one of the House's most respected conservative Democrats, added to the perception that the POW issue was a minefield Ronald Reagan should never have been allowed to approach, much less strike out across.[12]

## THE END OF THE LAO INITIATIVE

During the time of the Gritz controversy, Hendon, whose office was in the 4C-840 East Asia and Pacific Affairs suite, was deep into a study of all postwar POW-related intelligence in the division's files. One day soon after Gritz's ill-fated testimony on the Hill, someone asked, "Have you heard? Gen. Dick Secord's working on Central America now, just down the hall."

"Who is Dick Secord?" Hendon asked.

"Working in Laos, I thought you knew," the reply came. "He ran the secret war in Laos. He's the best in the business when it comes to counterinsurgency ops. He had been working the Saudi AWACS deal for the SECDEF but now he's helping with our operations in Central America."

On occasion Secord and an entourage would rush past the EAPR office suite and word would sweep through the suite that the legendary figure had just passed by in the hall. The type of electricity that accompanies any exciting, high-powered figure was in the air. Something big was going down in the Central American offices just on the other side of the bulkhead, and Secord was a key player.

Though not privy to the classified reporting coming out of Central America, Hendon knew from discussions around the office and from news articles that things were going badly for the administration in its efforts to defeat the pro-Soviet, pro-Cuban forces fighting in Central America. In El Salvador, the

U.S.-backed Salvadoran army was in full retreat. Just to the south of El Salvador, U.S.-supplied and -trained contra rebels were going nowhere in their efforts to overthrow the Marxist-Leninist Sandinista government of Nicaragua. Hendon found that among many in the Pentagon, there was a fear that Soviet- and Cuban-backed forces might actually gain control of the entire area from the Panama Canal to the Rio Grande on the U.S.-Mexican border. Secretary Weinberger, in fact, had said that if things continued to deteriorate in the region, the United States might have to "pull ourselves out of Europe, and out of Japan and Korea, and establish some sort of Fortress America concept" along its southern border.[13]

Weinberger's hyperbole notwithstanding, Hendon knew that huge shipments of arms were indeed pouring into the region from the Soviet Union, East Germany, Libya, and other Eastern Bloc and third world countries—tanks, trucks, helicopters, artillery pieces, antiaircraft guns, mortars, machine guns, AK-47s and other small arms, and untold thousands of tons of ammunition and explosives. He also knew that Soviet and Cuban advisors were in abundance in the region and that Cuban military forces were participating in actual combat operations in both El Salvador and Nicaragua. All this, of course, was cause for concern, but in mid-April, the United States came face-to-face with something far more menacing than these conventional weapons and the Soviet and Cuban advisors. Nicaragua's Defense Minister Humberto Ortega (brother of Sandinista leader Daniel Ortega and, along with Daniel, a member of the nine-man Sandinista National Directorate that ruled the country) declared in an interview published in *The New York Times* and later picked up by *The Washington Post* that the Sandinistas "would consider accepting Soviet missiles if asked." The *Times* reported that a proposal to deploy the missiles—reportedly nuclear-tipped intermediate range ballistic missiles,—had been made by a high official of the Soviet Central Committee named Vadim V. Zagladin. Ortega told the *Times* that when the final decision on the missiles was made it would be treated as a "state secret" and went on to stress that it was the "sovereign right" of Nicaragua to form whatever military alliances it deemed necessary.[14]

The news about the Soviet IRBMs, the huge influx of arms, and the rapidly deteriorating situation in El Salvador put the administration on a war footing. Officials quickly threw together a comprehensive four-point plan outlining how they planned to deal with the crisis and then requested that a joint session of Congress be convened so that the president could present the plan to the Congress and the American people.

On the evening of April 27, some two and a half weeks after the first article about the missiles had appeared, President Reagan addressed the nationally televised joint session. Telling the assembled lawmakers that he had called the joint session to head off a crisis in Central America that "directly affect[s] the security and well being of our own people," the president spoke of the huge influx of arms and war matériel into Nicaragua; the presence of Cuban, Soviet, East German, Libyan, and PLO advisors there; the Soviet threat to station nuclear missiles there—"five minutes from the United States"—and Nicaragua's decision to consider accepting those missiles; the guerrilla war in El Salvador—and the fact that that guerrilla war was being "directed from a headquarters in Managua, the capital of Nicaragua"; the threat to Honduras, Guatemala, and Costa Rica posed by the Nicaraguan government; and a host of lesser matters.

After declaring that "the goal of the professional guerrilla movements in Central America is as simple as it is sinister—to destabilize the entire region from the Panama Canal to Mexico," Reagan went on to say that "we cannot be certain that the Marxist-Leninist bands who believe war is an instrument of politics will be easily discouraged. It is crucial [though] that we not become discouraged before they do. Otherwise the region's freedom will be lost and our security damaged in ways that can hardly be calculated."

Then, after calling on the members to join him "in a program that prevents Communist victory," the president outlined the administration's new four-point plan for the region, calling for increased emphasis on human rights, expanded economic aid, beefed-up security assistance, and a pledge to support dialogue and negotiation over military conflict whenever possible.

The president ended his speech with these grave words: "In summation, I say to you that tonight there can be no question: The national security of all the Americas is at stake in Central America. If we cannot defend ourselves there, we cannot expect to prevail elsewhere. Our credibility would collapse, our alliances would crumble, and the safety of our homeland would be put in jeopardy.[15]

*The New York Times* wrote the following day that the president's taking his case to the joint session was "unusual"; *USA Today* characterized it as "rare"; the *Los Angeles Times* called it "extraordinary."[16] Regardless of the adjective used to describe the event and/or the venue, the message in these stories and in similar stories that appeared that day across the country and the world was the same: Ronald Reagan saw danger—mortal danger—in the gains the Marxist-Leninists were making in Central America, and he was determined to take whatever steps were necessary—unusual, rare, extraordinary, or whatever—to reverse those gains, ease the threat to the United States, and restore stability to the region.

Hendon was sitting in his office one morning reading intelligence reports and awaiting approval for a long-planned trip to Laos[17] when Armitage came to the door with bad news. "We're going to back away from POWs for a while, Billy," Armitage, a giant of a man, said, taking up the entire doorway as he always does. "I'd like for you to move over to the China desk while Jim Riordan's on vacation, and then I need you to help Jerry and Stu with some projects they've got working. Then if there's time before your contract runs out you can get back to your project. And who knows, things may improve and we may extend your contract. But for now, we need your help with these other projects." (Jim Riordan, a Marine Corps lieutenant colonel, handled China affairs for the East Asia and Pacific region. His younger brother had been MIA since November 11, 1966, when the carrier-based Grumman S2E he was aboard had failed to return from a mission over the Gulf of Tonkin. Col. Jerry Venanzi, USAF, who had spent five and a half years as a POW in North Vietnam, served as principal advisor to the secretary of defense for POW-MIA affairs; Commodore Stu Ring, USN, Hendon's immediate boss, headed all EAPR operations. Ring reported directly to Armitage, the deputy assistant secretary of defense for East

Asia and Pacific Affairs. Hendon held all four—Rioridan, Venanzi, Ring, and Armitage—as well as the other officers and civilians assigned to the region, in very high regard.)

Hendon was taken aback by the unexpected development but told his boss that he would, of course, do as he had directed.

After a stint on the China desk and completion of several mundane projects for Venanzi and Ring—including the preparation and printing of the DOD POW/MIA newsletter, no less—Hendon returned to his intelligence project. His plan was first to examine any intelligence reports that had come in during his absence and then to begin anew his detailed study of the division's POW intelligence files.

Hendon was no more than thirty minutes into the stack of new intelligence when he came across two reports that literally took his breath away. The first was a report the Special Office had recently received from CIA stating that one of their sources in Hong Kong had seen a large group of American pilots being held in a prison compound in downtown Hanoi within the last nine months. The sighting, which had been confirmed by CIA polygraph, seemed to Hendon to be especially compelling.

The other report, filed by U.S. officials in Thailand, contained information received during their recent debrief of a Lao medical doctor and a friend who together had defected to Thailand. According to the report, the doctor was identified as [Hendon redaction], daughter of [Hendon redaction], the LPDR's [high LPDR official, Hendon redaction] during the early 1980s.

The report stated that when U.S. officials had asked the newly arrived doctor if she had any knowledge of American POWs being held in Laos, she had replied that she did not. The report went on to say, however, that when interviewers had posed the same question to the female companion in a separate interview, the companion had replied that the doctor had recently told her that (1) before defecting to Thailand she had worked at the Health Ministry for a doctor named Ponemek Daraloy; (2) Dr. Ponemek was in charge of providing health care for the American POWs currently held in Laos; and (3) Dr. Ponemek had pointed out to the doctor the location where he was providing treatment for the American POWs. The companion had told U.S. officials that the doctor had not told her the exact location Dr. Ponemek had pointed out, and had not actually seen the Americans, only the place where Dr. Ponemek showed her he was caring for them.[18]

"That little son-of-a-*bitch*!" Hendon said of his Lao friend as he reached for the phone to seek an appointment with Armitage.

Standing in Armitage's D-Ring office the next morning, Hendon went over the remarkable news from Thailand and asked that he be given one more shot at Ponemek. Telling Armitage he realized the Lao initiative was hanging by a thread, he requested that he nevertheless be allowed to return to Laos at once to meet again with the very man now reported to be providing medical care to some of the American POWs the PL were holding. Given this new information on Ponemek, Hendon said, surely it was worth the minimal cost and risk involved.

Armitage, standing behind his desk, shook his head. "Can't do it," he told Hendon, "this thing is over for now." When Hendon expressed his displeasure, Armitage stiffened and replied, "Look, Congressman, it's over. These men serve at the pleasure of their commander in chief, and when he decides it's time for them to come home, they'll come home."

"I understand, Rich," Hendon told Armitage.

But Hendon did not really understand, and so shortly after his meeting with Armitage he took his notes about the two intelligence reports and perhaps a dozen other recent ones in the EAPR files and went down to the Special Office to see what his old friends from Lao Initiative days were doing to investigate them. He was stunned by the reception he received. His friends, even the senior military officers, hardly knew him. When Hendon asked them about the recent intelligence reports and what was being done to investigate each, their responses were vague and evasive; their demeanor defensive and sometimes even hostile. When Hendon pressed them for answers about their findings in each case, they declared almost defiantly that all eyewitnesses who recently reported seeing live American POWs in captivity after the war had been determined to be lying or confused about what they had seen. None, they said, had actually seen American POWs. When Hendon asked the reasons for those determinations, their replies showed they were debunking the sightings for what Hendon considered to be the most spurious and outrageous of reasons. Hendon left convinced of two things: first, a dramatic change had come over the Special Office and a cover-up was now under way there, and second, given the scope of the cover-up and its wide-ranging implications, this was no rogue operation—direction, support, and cover had to be coming from far up the chain of command.

## THREE LAST ATTEMPTS TO RESTART THE LAO INITIATIVE

In spite of Bo Gritz's rough treatment at the hands of the press following his testimony to Congress, public support for rescuing the POWs had continued to build throughout the spring of 1983. Many Vietnam vets had vowed to emulate Gritz and launch raids of their own if the administration did not soon rescue their compatriots; in fact, several vets incarcerated in American jails had even petitioned the Pentagon to send them on "Dirty Dozen–type" missions to rescue the POWs, if they could earn their freedom in return.[19] Vets and nonvets alike, meanwhile, had formed POW/MIA activist organizations in cities and towns all across America. Countless fund drives had been undertaken, speeches given, vigils held. How ironic, Hendon thought, that as public support for the prisoners had grown, efforts by the U.S. government to get the men home had all but ceased.

Troubled by what Armitage had told him and haunted by the recent sighting in Hanoi and especially by the doctor's friend's revelations about Dr. Ponemek, Hendon in early May went to see Deputy Assistant Secretary of State for Asian and Pacific Affairs Paul Wolfowitz at his State Department office and, later, Childress in his office in the Old Executive Office Building next to the White House to see if he could convince either or both to restart the Lao initiative by approaching Ponemek and negotiating for the prisoners' freedom.

Meeting alone with Wolfowitz, Hendon cited the new intelligence from

Hanoi, reviewed the Lao initiative and his relationship with Dr. Ponemek, and described the recent intelligence indicating that Ponemek himself was caring for the American POWs held in Laos. Hendon suggested to Wolfowitz that he (Wolfowitz) approach the Lao and seek the release of the POWs within the framework of the Lao initiative, i.e., medical supplies, hospitals, schools, infrastructure improvements, etc., in return for the prisoners the Lao held. "President Reagan is in favor of this approach, Paul," Hendon told Wolfowitz. "Call Bud [McFarlane] and ask him. He'll confirm it. Ronald Reagan wants to negotiate the release of these prisoners."

Hendon was ill prepared for Wolfowitz's simple reply. "We can't let him, Congressman," the deputy assistant secretary said in a measured, professorial tone. "The price might be too high."[20]

Hendon later met with Childress in the Old EOB office suite he shared with Marine Corps Lt. Col. Oliver North. Hendon found his old partner in the Lao initiative to be cold, aloof, and purposefully distant. The meeting went worse than the one with Wolfowitz.

In mid-May, as Hendon continued reading report after report of American POWs being held captive, he decided as a last resort to take his case directly to McFarlane. Meeting with McFarlane and Childress in McFarlane's West Wing basement office on May 13, Hendon went over a number of intelligence reports he had brought with him from the Pentagon and then made the same plea to McFarlane that he had made earlier to Wolfowitz and Childress: Approach Ponemek. When McFarlane refused, tempers flared and unpleasant words were exchanged. When the meeting ended, there was no doubt in any of the participants' minds that the Lao initiative or any similar effort to negotiate the release of POWs from Communist prisons in Indochina was over.

His bridge to the White House now burned, Hendon returned to his Pentagon office to get his affairs in order and prepare for his now certain departure. Then, several days later, came the heartbreaking news from around the water cooler: Thousands of U.S. M-16s captured by the North Vietnamese at the fall of Saigon—some still packed in their original crates—were showing up on the battlefields of Central America, killing Salvadoran soldiers, killing U.S.-backed contra rebels and, perhaps, killing the American advisors who were ever more frequently accompanying them into combat. "You sure you still want pay those little bastards for the POWs?" Hendon was asked by one of the lieutenant colonels in his EAPR suite.

For Hendon, the revelation about the M-16s was shattering. First had come the firestorm over Gritz, then the Soviet missile threat, and now this. Hendon sat in his office digesting the news. "There is no way in hell Ronald Reagan can negotiate for the POWs under these circumstances," he said to no one. He felt naïve, foolish, a child in a man's game, embarrassed by his advocacy.

## THE ADMINISTRATION'S NEW PLAN FOR DEALING WITH THE POWs

In late May, as Hendon was wrapping up his work and preparing to depart, word began to circulate around EAPR that the administration was getting completely out of the live POW issue and would concentrate its efforts instead on the less difficult task of repatriating remains. Future progress on the POW/MIA front, word had it, would be measured in terms of crash sites visited and bodies recovered rather than living prisoners returned. The buzz was that administration officials, fearing a backlash from the families, would protect their flanks by offering the two top officials in the Washington office of the National League of Families government jobs. Given what Armitage had said to him and what he had discovered at the Special Office, Hendon believed the office rumors were almost certainly true.

And sure enough, during late May and early June the plan to co-opt the two League officials began to unfold. The first indication came when a letter written on National Security Council stationery signed by Childress went out to the chairman of the board of the National League of Families on May 17, four days after Hendon's contentious White House meeting with McFarlane and Childress. In the letter, which was given wide distribution among the families, Childress informed the league's chairman at the time, George Brooks, a retired school custodian who lived in Newburgh, New York, that League executive director, Ann Mills Griffiths, had been upgraded to "principal member" on the U.S. government's POW/MIA Interagency Group. (As Brooks already knew, the POW/MIA IAG (pronounced in single letters, "I-A-G")—one of hundreds of IAGs formed within the federal government over the years to administer matters that spanned more than one agency's jurisdiction—had, since its creation in 1980, included representatives of the Department of State, the Department of Defense, the Defense Intelligence Agency, the National Security Council, congressional committees with jurisdiction over the POW/MIA issue and, in an observer and largely ceremonial status, Griffiths representing the National League of Families.)[21] Now, Childress was telling Brooks and the families, Griffiths would no longer be relegated to observer status but would be brought to the table as one of the principal members or, as Childress declared, a "full partner in even the most sensitive initiatives."[22] Childress, the NSC representative on the IAG, went on to inform Brooks that he had decided to defer attending the National War College to work with Griffiths and the League to resolve the POW issue once and for all. "If we ever have a chance," Childress told Brooks, "it is with the current team." Childress concluded by telling Brooks to "keep the faith, we are doing our level best to break the speed limits."[23]

The second shoe dropped on the POWs within days of the Childress letter when Griffiths's assistant and longtime confidante, League public affairs director Carol Bates, received a telephone call from Rear Adm. Jerry Paulson, USN, Tuttle's replacement at DIA, informing her that DIA would like her to come to work as a paid, full-time employee at the DIA Special Office for POWs in the Pentagon. Though surprised by Paulson's call—Bates had long had an adversarial relationship with the special office, had no experience in intelligence matters, and would later profess that she had "no idea" why Paulson had offered her the job[24]—she quickly accepted and announced in the League newsletter that she would resign her position with the League and go to work full-time at DIA.[25]

By mid-June, the administration plan was in place. The two top officials employed in the National League of Families Washington office—Executive Director Ann Griffiths and her assistant, Director of Public Affairs Carol Bates—were both now working on the government side of the equation, Griffiths—the only nongovernment member of any interagency group among the hundreds that existed throughout the U.S. government—as principal member of the POW/MIA IAG; Bates in the DIA Special Office for Prisoners of War and Missing Persons in the Pentagon.

To the unsuspecting families, members of Congress, veterans' organizations, and POW activists, the appointment of Griffiths and Bates appeared to be a major breakthrough in the fight to return live prisoners, and for good reason. Griffiths had gained a reputation in Washington as a fierce fighter for the men she was convinced remained captive in Indochina. Living POWs, everyone knew, were her passion—her brother was among the missing—and she had not been reticent in speaking out about the fact that American servicemen remained imprisoned in Indochina.

- In late 1979, during her first year as League executive director, Griffiths, while spearheading the organization's effort to recover living prisoners, had declared in her official newsletter that "the preponderance of evidence clearly indicates that Americans are being held against their will in Southeast Asia."[26]
- In late 1979, the League board of directors had unanimously approved a new policy statement declaring that evidence from Southeast Asia proved POWs were still alive and that the primary focus of all League efforts should be to gain release of those prisoners. This new policy statement, written by Griffiths herself, stated:

  The Board of Directors of the National League of Families of American Prisoners and Missing in Southeast Asia has obtained sufficient evidence to prove that American prisoners are being held in Southeast Asia.
      The primary focus of all League actions and decisions is to secure the release of these Americans and ensure their return to the United States. . . .[27]

- In March 1981, in her capacity as League executive director, Griffiths had demanded that the Reagan administration "initiate [simultaneous] rescue operations as soon as feasible to as many locations as possible" to liberate the POWs being held in Southeast Asia.[28]
- In June 1981, in her capacity as League executive director, Griffiths had testified before Congress that she was "absolutely positive" live POWs were being held against their will in Indochina and had again called for their immediate rescue.[29]
- In 1982, in her capacity as League executive director, Griffiths and her assistant, Bates had launched a nationwide League advertising campaign that featured ads proclaiming, "Americans Are Alive in Southeast Asia" and "American POW/MIAs are Alive in Vietnam."[30]

By 1983, then, the time of her elevation to principal member of the IAG, few could hold a candle to Griffiths when it came to advocacy on behalf of living

POWs. Except, perhaps, Bates, who, as executive director until replaced by Griffiths in the late 1970s and as Griffiths's right hand ever since, had worked doggedly for the live prisoners—advertising their plight, testifying on their behalf, demanding their immediate rescue.

In the eyes of many family members and Vietnam vets, Reagan/Bush officials could not possibly have picked two better people to fight for the live POWs. However, almost immediately after Griffiths and Bates were brought aboard, strange things began to happen on the POW front.

## THE SHIFT TO REMAINS

The first public hint that something was up, and that the administration did, in fact, intend to shift its focus to recovering remains rather than live prisoners, came in late June when Secretary of State George Shultz traveled to Bangkok to attend a conference of foreign ministers sponsored by the Association of Southeast Asian Nations (ASEAN) (pronounced AH-see-anh).

In remarks delivered to the ASEAN foreign ministers and at a joint press appearance following the conference, Shultz, rather than broaching the issue of live prisoners, denounced the Vietnamese for withholding the remains of several hundred deceased American servicemen. Calling Vietnam's actions "cruel and heartless," Shultz informed reporters that "we have intelligence that suggests the remains of quite a sizeable number [of U.S. servicemen] are in hand but have not been turned over to us." For the POWs, the next day's headlines in *The Washington Post* spelled trouble: "Shultz: Hanoi Holds Remains of U.S. MIAs" and "Shultz Accuses Vietnam of Withholding Remains of American Servicemen."[31] Not living POWs, as only months before, but remains.

Earl Hopper, who as League board chairman had led the League delegation to Laos the previous fall, recalls being deeply concerned by Shultz's statements. "Every League member I knew wanted the focus to be on getting the prisoners back first, then finding the MIAs, and then remains, in that order," Hopper later said. He went on to explain that "the families believed we had a team in place that not only agreed with us, but was now in a position to get the men home— that is, Reagan in the Oval Office, Childress at the NSC, Griffiths with her full-time seat on the IAG, and Bates working full-time at DIA. But here comes Shultz, asking for ASEAN's help in getting back *remains*! We were shocked and angry and felt betrayed, and let it be known that we planned to strenuously object at the League's annual meeting in Washington in July."[32]

When administration officials learned of the coming protest at the League's annual convention in Washington in mid-July, they dispatched Childress to confront Hopper and the others.

Speaking to the assembled families on July 15, a now much-changed and far more pugnacious Childress, after alluding to the "potential disaster for us all in Central America," opened fire with all barrels.

Declaring that it "is time for straight talk from us to you," Childress told the families that administration policy called for a "genuine partnership with the National League of Families" but warned that "the last thing we can afford is the slightest indication that you and the government are not in agreement that the ultimate resolution of this issue lies in Hanoi, not Washington." Alluding to the uproar over Shultz's comments about the recovery of remains, Childress told the families, "If you want to point fingers, don't point them here, point them East, toward Hanoi."

Childress moved to undo the president's pledge made to the families at the League meeting back in January that their "vigil is over," a comment that had been taken by all in attendance to mean that the live POWs would soon be coming home. First declaring that the president and his administration had "never promised specific results," Childress explained that the president's pledge made "in January that your long vigil was over" had been misinterpreted and that what the president had really meant was that "your vigil for years was to obtain government attention and priority [and] you have it now."

He then admonished the families to support the president and not listen to "the vocal minority that is inherently opposed to the government." He explained that though the administration was "always open to ideas, constructive criticism and proposals for constructive cooperation, . . . none of us have time for carping, grandstanding or abuse." He concluded his remarks by warning the assembled parents, wives, sons, daughters, brothers, and sisters of the missing that the "frustration that causes such reactions is understandable, but also understand that we tire of unreasonable behavior or demands."[33] Virtually everyone in the room was stunned. Even Carter administration officials had never talked to them like that.

Following Shultz's remarks in Bangkok in June and Childress's lecture to the League convention in July, more and more family members began to believe that there might be some truth to the rumor that the administration for some unexplained reason *really had* abandoned the search for live POWs. For many, that belief became conviction in August, when Griffiths sent out a special edition of the League newsletter that contained ominous news about living prisoners.

In this issue of the newsletter, which would become known in family circles as the "POW Death Warrant," Griffiths, saying she was writing "to inform you of where the [POW/MIA] issue stands," told the families that she could no longer state that POWs remained alive in captivity in Southeast Asia. In this stunning reversal of her long-standing position to the contrary, her testimony to Congress that she was "absolutely positive" that prisoners remained in captivity, and her and Bates's declaration in the League advertisements they had run all over the country declaring "American POW/MIAs are Alive in Vietnam"—Griffiths flatly declared that "confirmation that POWs are still captive has not yet been obtained." In an effort to assure the families that she was in a position to know, she then declared, as she would many times in the years ahead, that "close scrutiny of U.S. government efforts is my job as executive director, representing you in the Interagency POW/MIA Group (IAG)."[34]

Coming as it had from one of their own with access to virtually all of the classified government intelligence reports on POWs, Griffiths's statement about living POWs was believable to many of the families. Coming from Ann, they believed, as awful as the news was, it simply had to be true. Other family members, now totally convinced the fix was in, were enraged. Soon cries that the executive director had sold out to the government coursed through the "telephone trees" that connected the League membership. Within days, several members of the board and a number of rank-and-file League members were demanding Griffiths's resignation. In the raging debate that ensued, venomous charges and countercharges were exchanged. As happens so often in volunteer-type advocacy organizations, close friends became bitter enemies. "It quickly became a civil war," one family member later recalled, "with no middle ground whatsoever. There was no gray, just black or white; you were either with the group who wanted to rescue the live prisoners, or you were with Griffiths, Childress, Armitage, Wolfowitz, Bates, and those who were now saying there weren't any and wanted to spend the entire U.S. effort searching for remains."

*Late Summer and Fall*
## CENTRAL AMERICA

Weinberger and Armitage joined Ollie North for a well-publicized tour of the front lines in Central America in early September.[35] Days later, Undersecretary of Defense Fred C. Ikle, the third-ranking official at the Department of Defense, issued a public call for total military victory in Central America. In remarks prepared for delivery to the Baltimore Council on Foreign Affairs on September 13, Ikle declared, "Let me make this clear to you. We do not seek a military defeat for our friends. We do not seek a military stalemate. We seek victory for the forces of democracy."[36]

The following month, in a move that would have a profound impact on administration initiatives in Central America, President Reagan ordered U.S. forces to storm the tiny Caribbean island of Grenada, where a bloody coup had placed in jeopardy the lives of hundreds of American students studying at a U.S.-run medical school outside the island's capital of St. George's. The U.S. invasion force, composed of Navy Seal teams and more than six thousand U.S. Marines and U.S. Army airborne rangers backed by helicopter gunships, Navy attack aircraft, and USAF AC-130 Spectre gunships, quickly rescued the medical students and then went on to attack and overwhelm leftist Grenadan and Cuban forces stationed on the island. More than six hundred Cubans were captured in the fighting.[37]

On the morning after the invasion, as victorious U.S. forces began mopping-up operations all across the island, the first of the rescued American medical students were evacuated to the United States on USAF C-141 transports. In a scene that touched the hearts of most Americans who witnessed it—Democrats and Republicans, conservatives and liberals, hawks and doves—one of the first of the returning students, Jeff Geller of Woodridge, New York, dropped to his knees and kissed the tarmac. "I have been a dove all my life," Geller exclaimed to newsmen. "I just can't believe how well those Rangers [performed]. Those Rangers deserve a lot of credit. I don't want anyone to say anything bad about the U.S. military." Stephen Hall of Hastings, Florida, said, "[T]he military actions and our subsequent return were extremely impressive and we are very proud to have been with the U.S. servicemen. . . . I am very, very proud to be an

American." Another student exclaimed, "God bless America, God bless Reagan, God bless our military."[38]

The ghosts of Vietnam for a moment exorcised, the Reagan administration went on the offensive in Central America. In early November, Weinberger pointedly refused to rule out a U.S. invasion of Nicaragua and dispatched the saber-rattling Ikle to the region on a "fact-finding tour." During his trip, Ikle called for increased military aid to the region, announced that the ongoing U.S. military exercises in Honduras that had been scheduled to end shortly would be extended indefinitely, and declared that a force of one thousand U.S. combat engineers would be dispatched to Costa Rica, Nicaragua's southern neighbor, to begin joint exercises there. He then joined Weinberger in refusing to rule out an American invasion of Nicaragua.[39] On November 18, a combined U.S. Marine/Honduran Army force stormed the Honduran coast in a mock invasion exercise. "It's probably going to give the Marines more useful training than the Hondurans," a U.S. officer said in remarks obviously directed at the Sandinistas just across the border in Nicaragua.[40] Two days later, a leading Costa Rican newspaper quoted the U.S. ambassador to Costa Rica as saying that the United States could not live with the subversive and activist Marxist-Leninists in Managua and that an invasion by the United States to topple that government was "not impossible." Then, on November 25, The Washington Post reported that several Central American countries were pushing the United States to invade Nicaragua before the Sandinista government became any stronger and before the upcoming presidential campaign kicked off in the United States.[41]

In December, rumor began to spread that USAF crews were flying America's most potent anti-insurgency weapons, the much-feared AC-130 Spectres, down from the U.S. mainland at night, decimating leftist forces with the aid of sophisticated night vision and computerized targeting equipment and then flying back to the United States under the cover of darkness before the plane's presence over the battle zone could be confirmed.[42] In mid-December, Reagan, speaking to a meeting of the Medal of Honor Society in New York, made no specific mention of the Spectres but did, however, send a very clear message to the Sandinistas on the matter of a U.S.-led invasion of their country. "Our military forces are back on their feet and standing tall," the president told America's most decorated heroes, ". . . and now the world knows that, when it comes to our national security, the United States will do whatever it takes to protect the safety and freedom of the American people." Referring to the negative feelings many in the United States had toward the U.S. military after Vietnam and the damage done to the American psyche by the Iran hostage crisis, Reagan declared, "(O)nce again, it's an honor to wear the uniform and serve our country. . . . Our days of weakness are over."[43]

As the year came to a close, few who followed the situation in Central America closely had any doubt about what Ronald Reagan and his advisors had in mind for the Sandinista government of Nicaragua in the months ahead. Reagan personally detested the Sandinista's leader, Daniel Ortega, whom he derisively referred to as "that little Marxist who flies up to New York to the UN to buy his designer glasses," and he clearly believed that Ortega's Marxist-Leninist

Sandinistas and the Soviet missiles they might allow to be based in their country constituted a direct and potentially deadly threat to America's national security. Purely and simply, Reagan and Company believed the Sandinistas—and
the Russians and Cubans based in their country—had to go.

CHAPTER  23

1984

TRAGEDY AT ARLINGTON • A MISSED OPPORTUNITY

IN THE OVAL OFFICE

. . .

The furor within the League over Griffiths's perceived abandonment of the live
prisoners and her increasingly cozy relationship with the administration had
continued to build throughout late 1983. In December, a particularly divisive
session of the League board had almost resulted in Griffiths's dismissal.

By mid-January 1984, the attacks on the League executive director reached
such a level that Armitage was forced to personally intervene to save her. On
January 21, at Childress's request, Armitage warned the League board by letter
that if Griffiths was fired, her replacement, whoever he or she might be, would
not be given a seat on the IAG, and that as a consequence the League "would
then be in the same position as other POW/MIA groups." The threat did the job
and Griffiths was again saved.[1]

Emboldened by their victory, Armitage and Childress took Griffiths—
without her board's knowledge or consent—to Hanoi in mid-February on what
Griffiths later characterized as "the highest level mission to Vietnam since the
end of the war."[2] Board Chairman Earl Hopper was incredulous, telling one equally
astonished family member at the time that Griffiths now appeared to be "taking
instructions from the USG instead of from the Board for whom she works." The
situation, Hopper said, had grown "embarrassing and difficult."[3]

Central America, meanwhile, was ready to explode at any minute. In mid-
January, a commission headed by Henry Kissinger that had been studying U.S.
involvement in the region officially declared that U.S. security was now "threatened directly in the area as a result of Soviet and Cuban intervention."[4] Coinci-
dentally, on the same day Kissinger released his finding, Sandinista antiaircraft
gunners opened fire on a U.S. helicopter flying in the vicinity of the Nicaraguan-
Honduran border and, after the pilot steered his craft to a crash landing just inside Honduran territory, shot and killed the pilot as he stood beside the downed
chopper surveying the damage.[5]

Given the charged atmosphere in the region and the cowardly manner in which the Sandinistas had killed the American pilot, many thought the incident would become the region's real-life Gulf of Tonkin incident and set off the much-rumored U.S. invasion of Nicaragua. This seemed at the time to be entirely possi-ble, given that several thousand American combat troops—all eager to avenge their comrade's death—were conducting maneuvers along Nicaragua's northern border, and thousands more of like mind were stationed at bases and on ships from the U.S. mainland to Panama—all ready, willing, and able to do to Nicaragua exactly what they had done to Grenada.[6]

President Reagan did not order the invasion as many in the administration had hoped he would. Instead, in February he secretly authorized the mining of Nicaragua's ports.[7] Several weeks later, two Panamanian fishing boats struck mines in the harbor at El Bluff, on Nicaragua's east coast. Then, on March 1, a Dutch freighter was damaged by a mine in Corinto harbor, the country's largest, on the Pacific coast.[8] Days later, another freighter, this one owned by a consor-tium of Central American governments, struck a mine while attempting to en-ter the Corinto harbor. On March 13, Daniel Ortega, facing increasingly serious disruptions at his ports, issued an appeal to "all governments of the world" to provide military and technical assistance to help Nicaragua defend itself.[9]

By the ides of March, the air was heavy with war.

It was precisely then, on March 15, that Ann Griffiths set in motion what would turn out to be one of the most shameful chapters in the history of the United States government.

## THE FRAUDLENT SELECTION OF THE UNKNOWN SOLDIER

Just as she had fought hard for the live POWs prior to 1983, Ann Griffiths had toiled to prevent the government from interring the remains of an Unknown Soldier from the Vietnam War at the Tomb of the Unknown Soldier at Arlington National Cemetery. The reason for her crusade was later described in a book on the Unknown written by William M. Hammond of the U.S. Army's Center of Military History:

On 18 June 1973, shortly after the last American troops withdrew from South Vietnam, Congress directed the Secretary of Defense to select the re-mains of an unidentified American serviceman killed in the war for burial in the Tomb of the Unknown Soldier at Arlington. It seemed reasonable that among all the casualties of the war the military services would find an Un-known, but scientists at the U.S. Army's Central Identification Laboratory at Honolulu had managed to name all but a few of the American dead and re-mained confident that they would ultimately identify the rest.

Complicating the process of selection was the fact that the government of Vietnam had failed to render a full accounting of the hundreds of Amer-ican servicemen who were known to have fallen into its hands during the war. Over the years, the families of those servicemen had pressed for some official word of their relatives' fate, and they objected to the declaration of an Unknown for the Vietnam War on the grounds that the act would al-most certainly diminish official efforts to recover the missing—in effect, symbolizing to all concerned that the war was over and the issue was no longer important.[10]

Though accurate, Hammond's comments did not adequately reflect the passion felt by many of the POW/MIA families, who, simply put, viewed any attempt to entomb an Unknown as the ultimate act of betrayal of those left behind. "Everyone knew that the day the government entombed the Unknown Soldier was the day the POW/MIA issue was over," one family member later said. "It was every metaphor you could think of—the last chapter, the closing of the book, the final buzzer, the last out in the ball game, the fat lady singing, or whatever—to us, it was all of those things and more wrapped into one little ceremony."

In 1981, John O. "Jack" Marsh, President Reagan's new secretary of the army, had suggested that the administration comply with the 1973 congressional directive and move quickly to name a Vietnam Unknown. Griffiths, then a rabid advocate for the live POWs and observer member on the IAG, had strongly opposed the action. "The National League of Families is opposed to any ceremony at this time," she wrote Marsh in late 1981, "primarily due to the Central Identification Laboratory's findings that there are no qualified remains in U.S. possession." She further objected to the interment on the grounds that it "would be publicized as the 'end of a sad chapter in American history' and otherwise promoted to 'put the war behind us.'" Griffiths told Marsh that "the weight of the evidence is convincing that Americans are still held captive in Indochina" and that determining their fate "should precede a ceremony which historically has occurred after such problems have been resolved."[11]

When Marsh, ignoring Griffiths advice, had advised Weinberger in June 1982 that the Central Identification Laboratory known as CIL, or CILHI, did, in fact, possess remains that met the legal requirements for the Unknown and that he had concluded that the selection process should begin, Weinberger had sided with Marsh and had recommended to National Security Advisor William Clark that the selection process proceed and that the official interment ceremony be held on Memorial Day, 1983.[12]

With that, Griffiths had gone into overdrive. Writing Weinberger in July 1982, she had told the secretary that the League was opposed to the interment of "any remains now held" because, she said, "substantial identification information already exists on each of the four remains now in U.S. possession." She had gone on to warn Weinberger that "there could be adverse public reaction" if this fact became known and suggested that, in lieu of allowing the selection process to proceed, Weinberger should order the army to issue "a clear statement that qualified remains are not available and may never be due to technical expertise attained [by the CIL]."[13]

Childress, at the time still totally committed to the search for live POWs, had sided with Griffiths against Weinberger and Marsh. Childress had told his boss, National Security Advisor Clark, that there were no good candidates among the four not-yet-identified sets of remains held by the CIL and had advised Clark that he should meet with Weinberger and pointedly warn him of the potential for intense controversy if any of the four unqualified candidates be selected. Among the points Childress had suggested that Clark raise with Weinberger was the fact that "we simply can't have the public believe we created an unknown for interment."[14]

When Clark had conveyed this message to Weinberger, Weinberger had relented. Later describing the events surrounding Weinberger's decision, William Hammond wrote in his history of the Vietnam Unknown, "In 1982, . . . [the] families convinced the administration of President Ronald Reagan to postpone selection of an Unknown on the grounds that the few bodies that remained unnamed might still be identified."[15] Thanks to Griffiths, there would be no Vietnam Unknown, no "closing of the books."

Things changed dramatically, however, on March 15, 1984, when Griffiths, just back from her trip to Hanoi with Armitage and Childress, suddenly reversed her position and, without consulting her board, informed Marsh by letter that the League was now in favor of moving ahead with selection and interment of the Vietnam Unknown.[16]

## THE SELECTION OF LT. MICHAEL BLASSIE

Administration officials moved quickly and with well-oiled precision after receiving the green light from Griffiths on March 15.

On the 16th, Weinberger advised the president by memorandum that the League was now in favor of the selection and interment of the Vietnam Unknown and that "we have one set of remains which cannot be identified and which, although not as complete as we would like, meets the legal requirements for the Vietnam Unknown and therefore is qualified." The interment ceremony, Weinberger told Reagan, would be held some two and a half months later on Memorial Day, May 28, 1984.[17]

Five days after Weinberger notified the president, Maj. Johnie Webb, USA, commander of the CIL, officially certified that the remains of the American serviceman Weinberger had referred to had been "determined to be unidentifiable."[18] In fact, however, the remains certified by Webb as "unidentifiable"—remains known at CIL as "X-26"—were those of Lt. Michael J. Blassie, USAF, and Webb had to have known it when he signed the certification. (Lieutenant Blassie, as Webb and many others knew at the time, had been shot down on May 11, 1972, near An Loc, South Vietnam, while piloting his A-37 on a strike against Communist forces. Some five months after his plane had gone down, ARVN troops had recovered Blassie's partial remains, along with his military ID card, another item of identification, portions of his flight suit, part of an ejection seat, a life raft, and several other items. These remains and some of his personal effects were later transferred to CIL and designated "X-26.") Word circulated that Webb had faked the certification because of intense pressure from Washington.

On April 4, Webb received a call from the Pentagon directing him *to take three items relating to Lieutenant Blassie's identity out of the X-26 file and place them in a file titled "Blassie, Michael J. (1853-0-01)."* He was also directed to send all documents that remained in the X-26 file to Washington and to certify in writing that he had destroyed any duplicate copies. Webb complied with the directives that same day.[19]

Weinberger announced to the nation on April 13 that the Unknown had been selected and that interment would take place on Memorial Day.[20] Understandably, his announcement stunned the League board, which up to that point had been kept in the dark by Griffiths. Responding quickly, the acting chairman of the League, Anne Hart, wrote President Reagan on behalf of the board requesting that he personally intervene and stop the ceremony until there had been a full accounting of all the POWs and MIAs.[21] "We were aghast at what Ann [Griffiths] had done," Hart later said, "and we knew that if the president didn't stop it, the nation would quickly lose interest in the POW issue and those held prisoner would never get out of Indochina alive."[22] Hart's husband, Capt. Thomas T. Hart, USAF, a navigator on an AC-130 Spectre gunship, had been missing since his plane had been shot down in December 1972 during a mission over the Ho Chi Minh Trail in Laos.

Though embarrassing to Griffiths, Hart's letter was not viewed as a serious threat either at the Pentagon or at the NSC. One of Marsh's deputies, displaying a remarkable degree of cynicism, told his boss that inasmuch as the League's opposition was "focusing on its perception the Government's commitment to their cause will be reduced and not on the wisdom of interring the designated remains, it seems that the ceremonies will be relatively untainted."[23] Marsh then told Weinberger by memorandum that he didn't expect the League's opposition to "significantly degrade the positive aspects of the event" and assured Weinberger that "prior to the public announcement, we fully briefed and coordinated the Vietnam Unknown decision with the Executive Director of the National League of Families (NLF)."[24]

Over at the White House, meanwhile, McFarlane advised Reagan to ignore the League board's objection and to inform Hart by letter that the ceremony would go on as planned. He went on to assure the president that "we successfully resisted Congressional and veterans group pressure to inter an unknown prematurely for the past two years in order to assure ourselves that the remains to be interred are unidentifiable. We brought Ann Griffiths, the Executive Director of the League in Washington, into the technical process and she is satisfied in this regard."[25]

The unknowing Reagan, to the relief of everyone involved in the effort, signed the letter to Anne Hart.[26] With this last hurdle crossed, preparations for the ceremonies, which would be the most extensive since the funeral of President John F. Kennedy in 1963, moved into high gear.[27]

## THE CEREMONIES

Salvadoran President-elect José Napoleón Duarte was in Washington to meet with President Reagan and to lobby Congress for more military aid[28] on the same day Reagan ordered that flags in the nation's capital would remain at half-staff over the Memorial Day weekend in honor of the Vietnam Unknown.[29] As protesters massed outside Duarte's northwest Washington hotel carrying signs painted with Vietnam-era peace symbols and messages demanding "NO MORE

VIETNAM WARS!"[30] the nation's capital prepared for the arrival of the remains of the Unknown and a four-day, almost continuous ceremony to honor him.

By the time the casket containing Blassie's remains arrived at Andrews Air Force Base at 2:00 P.M. on Friday, May 25, the Pentagon public affairs machinery had gone out of its way to assure the assembled press corps that the Unknown was, truly, unknown. "The serviceman chosen to be placed in the Tomb of the Unknowns has remained unidentified and will now forever remain so," Pentagon spokesman Maj. Robert Shields told *The Washington Times*. He added that in spite of pressure from various veteran groups to entomb a soldier from the Vietnam War, "we resisted the pressure—not because of political reasons—but because we thought we should try and identify everybody. . . . To say that the efforts made to identify remains have been intensive and exhaustive," Shields declared, "is an understatement."[31]

Shields told *The Washington Post* that there had been pressure for some time from the veterans' groups to bury an Unknown, but, he said, "We were hardheaded. We refused to believe that we couldn't identify him." The *Post* went on to report that "the Armed Services Graves Registration Office Board, along with other military superiors, finally concluded that further search for an identity was futile." The *Post* further reported that the relatives of those missing in action were opposed to the burial out of fear it would end the search for their loved ones. League chairman Earl Hopper was quoted as saying the League board had voted to oppose the interment because "we felt that since the burial of any individual is a terminal act, meaning everything is finished, the same impression would be conveyed to the American public and they would feel the interment was the final act of the Vietnam war."[32]

Had the tough, patriotic Hopper, who had served in World War II, Korea, and Vietnam, known at the time what was really going on, one can only imagine what he would have said and done that day.

The casket containing Blassie's remains was taken immediately from Andrews Air Force Base by hearse to the U.S. Capitol. Plans called for the casket to lie in state in the Capitol Rotunda until noon on Memorial Day, when it would be taken by horse-drawn caisson to Arlington Cemetery for the formal interment ceremony.

Minutes after arrival at the Capitol, the casket, preceded by a procession of dignitaries led by Gen. John Vessey Jr., Chairman of the Joint Chiefs of Staff, was carried into the Rotunda where President Reagan, members of his cabinet, members of Congress, and other dignitaries awaited.[33] The president, standing before the casket that lay on the catafalque that had held Lincoln, Kennedy, and other presidents, delivered the brief eulogy. "We may not know of this man's life," the president said, "but we know of his character. We may not know his name, but we know his courage." The chief naval chaplain prayed, "[N]ow that he is known only to Your grace, he will forever be an influence to all the people of this beloved country."[34] A *New York Times* reporter witnessing the moving ceremony would write that before reaching the Rotunda, the Unknown had "traversed some sensitive national political ground and withstood the most sophisticated attempts of forensic pathologists to identify him."[35]

More than one hundred thousand people filed through the Capitol Rotunda to pay their respects over the weekend. Then, at noon on Memorial Day, pall-bearers carried the casket out of the Capitol and placed it on the caisson for the slow, three-mile trip to Arlington.

A cordon of honor composed of 1,750 men and women representing all branches of the military lined both sides of the route all the way to Arlington. Police estimated they were joined by 250,000 spectators, some of whom lined the route ten-deep.

*The Washington Post* reported that as the procession made its way toward Arlington, "more than 100 rumpled, often bearded war survivors, some pushing friends in wheelchairs, marched out to claim a place in the parade." Several of the vets, the *Post* noted, "carried the black flag of the League of Families of American Prisoners and Missing in Southeast Asia." "POW-MIA," "Don't Let Them Be Forgot" [sic]. The *Post* said when reporting the message on the flags.[36]

The caisson, pulled by six white horses, reached the Vietnam Veterans Memorial at precisely 1:00 P.M. Manning one of the POW/MIA booths at the memorial at the time were Robert and Lynn Standerwick, two of four children of Air Force Col. Robert Standerwick, who had been missing in Laos since 1971. Colonel Standerwick had parachuted safely from his stricken F-4 and radioed that he was wounded and that enemy troops were approaching, but he had not been heard from since. The Standerwicks were among dozens of children of missing men and a like number of Vietnam vets who handed out literature at the memorial to publicize the plight of the POWs.

"It's just another nail in the coffin," Lynn told a *Washington Times* reporter. "Their purpose is to show the war is over and all the men are home."

"That's what the unknown soldier's for," her brother explained. "They're closing the doors."[37]

After pausing for a moment of tribute at the "Wall," the caisson carrying Blassie's remains continued on around the Lincoln Memorial and across Memorial Bridge to Arlington.

At precisely 2:00 P.M., the interment ceremony, attended by the president, Weinberger, the leaders of the nation's military, and some four thousand invited guests, began in the hilltop amphitheater with the playing of the National Anthem. In a special place of honor in the audience, the national commanders of the major American veterans' organizations took the place of the family of the Unknown, a function DOD had deemed "a very great honor." Present were the national commanders of the Veterans of Foreign Wars, AMVETS, the Blinded Veterans Association, the American Legion, the Military Order of the Purple Heart, the Veterans of World War I of the USA, the Marine Corps League, the Paralyzed Veterans of America, the Legion of Valor, the Congressional Medal of Honor Society, the Disabled American Veterans, the American Ex-Prisoners of War, the Vietnam Veterans of America, and the United Vietnam Veterans Organization. Also present were heads of the American Gold Star Mothers and the Gold Star Wives of America.[38] The National League of Families had been issued an invitation, but the board had declined to send an official representative. Though the board had instructed Griffiths that she could not attend, she reportedly nevertheless did, reportedly wearing a black veil to conceal her identity.[39]

The president, saying that "we close no books, we put away no final memories," paid honor to the missing and called on Hanoi to "heal the sorest wound of this conflict, return our sons to America, end the grief of those who are innocent and undeserving of retribution." Then, proving again, as he had at the earlier ceremony in the Capitol Rotunda, that he could not possibly have known what some in attendance knew, he presented the Congressional Medal of Honor to Blassie and said, "About him, we may well wonder as others have: As a child, did he play on some street in a great American city, did he work beside his father on a farm in America's heartland? Did he marry? Did he have children, did he look expectantly to return to a bride? We will never know the answers to those questions about his life."[40] Following the president's remarks, pallbearers carried Blassie's casket to the nearby Tomb of the Unknown. Along the way, the U.S. Army Band played the hymn "Holy, Holy, Holy."

The casket was placed over the open crypt facing the Tomb, which bore the words "HERE RESTS IN HONORED GLORY AN AMERICAN SOLDIER, KNOWN BUT TO GOD."[41] After representatives of the Jewish, Orthodox, Catholic, and Protestant religions read the graveside prayers customary to their faiths, the president placed a wreath at the head of the casket. Following a twenty-one-gun salute, the chaplain of the U.S. Coast Guard gave the blessing. At the conclusion of the blessing, three rifle volleys were fired and "Taps" was sounded. While the band played "America the Beautiful," the pallbearers folded the flag that had covered the casket since its departure from the Central Identification Laboratory in Hawaii and presented it to their commander, who in turn presented it to President Reagan.[42]

Ronald Reagan could not possibly have known it, but from start to finish, the entire undertaking had been a scam, a hoax, a public relations extravaganza designed, just as some of the POW/MIA families had charged, to close the book on the Vietnam War and bring to an end the corrosive national debate about American servicemen still held hostage in Southeast Asia more than a decade after America's withdrawal.[43]

## MOVING ON

With the coming of summer it became clear that administration officials were doing everything they could to put the live prisoner issue in the past.

In early July, *The New York Times* reported that Secretary of State Shultz, speaking in Singapore while en route to the annual meeting of ASEAN ministers being held in Jakarta, "stressed that there was no evidence that any American prisoners of war were alive" in Indochina.[44]

Then, on July 20, the president, speaking on the South Lawn of the White House to members of the League and a group of returned POWs who had gathered to commemorate National POW/MIA Recognition Day, passed up the opportunity to repeat the pledge he had made to the families only eighteen months before that their "vigil is over" and announced instead three new initiatives aimed at *recovering remains*—one involving the recovery of remains from the Korean War. In his speech, the president reported that:

- The administration had pressed the government of North Korea for an accounting and would continue to do so, and that U.S. officials had received information from U.S. soldiers who had fought in Korea about possible grave locations in South Korea, and that any remains found in those graves would be returned to the deceased's next of kin.
- The Vietnamese government had, three days before, turned over "the remains of several more U.S. servicemen" and had agreed to additional technical talks to be held in August.
- The Lao government had, just hours before the ceremony began, agreed in principle to excavate a U.S. crash site. The president termed this development "good news."[45]

Not once in his three-page speech did the president make any reference to living POWs. However, in reporting on the speech, *The New York Times* did, noting that "American officials have said there is no verified evidence that any [POWs] are alive."[46]

Shortly after the president's declaration to the families and the returnees that the administration would henceforth focus its time, effort, and resources on the recovery of remains, a prominent Democrat congressman, House Veterans Affairs Subcommittee Chairman Douglas Applegate (D-OH), went before the House Foreign Affairs Committee's Subcommittee on Asian and Pacific Affairs to declare that he was "fearful" the Reagan administration was covering up evidence of live American POWs. In the wake of Applegate's incendiary charge, the activist families and the activist Vietnam vets approached General Tighe and pleaded with him to come out of retirement and head a commission to investigate the live POW issue. When Childress and Griffiths got wind of the plan, they contacted Tighe and invited him to meet them at a downtown Washington restaurant for lunch. Tighe would later testify that Griffiths told him she and Childress wanted to meet "because of the increasing pressures they were feeling for an investigation of the POW issue."

Tighe said that during the luncheon, which he characterized as "very long and agonizing," Childress and Griffiths both expressed fear that "this whole thing [the matter of living POWs] was going to present President Reagan with another hostage issue that they claim defeated Carter." Tighe said that both "were very concerned about it [a hostage crisis], and they said before he [President Reagan] left his first term there was going to be a major operation that would satisfy me and . . . [that I should] just keep my mouth shut, that this was all being planned, and don't rock the boat." Tighe said he was told, "Stay away from the press. . . . Stay quiet because at the end of the first Reagan tour [term] there was going to be a very major breakthrough in this whole thing and they were going to rescue a lot of people, or words to that effect."

Tighe went on to say:

They referred to the plan to really take action before the first term of President Reagan was over, and [they requested] that I be as quiet as possible during the interim, that there were great things coming.

And that was the purpose of getting me there to the luncheon. It was very unusual. I had not met Childress before. And the message was very, very clear. Please shut up; we've got something big coming and we don't want another hostage thing clouding the reelection chances of the President. . . .

I knew exactly what he was talking about. He was promising me that they had a large POW sighting and they were about to do something about it. I had no doubt about it [what Childress had meant].

When a Senate investigator asked Tighe, "Did Childress ever say that there were live Americans that he was aware of," Tighe replied, "In effect, he said of course we know there are live Americans. This was part of the conversation that led up [to] this whole thing. . . . [i.e.,] we can't stand another hostage thing, and before he leaves his first term the President will surprise you with a large operation."

Tighe would go on to say that because he had believed that there was an impending rescue operation, he had kept his mouth shut about live POWs lest he jeopardize that mission. "I really got snakebit," Tighe said. ". . . I was afraid anything I even said about the issue might open up and reveal something very sensitive. . . . I don't think I spoke nearly as freely to anybody about . . . [live POWs] for quite a while."[47]

Luckily for the unlisted, unreturned POWs, just at the time Tighe—for the most honorable of reasons—stayed quiet about live POWs, another American, no Boy Scout but for honorable reasons as well, was deciding to speak out.

## THE REEMERGENCE OF ROBERT GARWOOD

In 1965, a U.S. Marine Corps private from Indiana named Robert Garwood had been captured in I Corps in South Vietnam by members of a Vietcong unit.[48] At the time of his capture, Garwood had been less than two weeks shy of completing his thirteen-month tour of duty.

Following capture, Garwood had been taken to a primitive jungle camp and imprisoned there with other captured Americans. Following the death of a Special Forces officer he had befriended in the camp, Garwood had become disillusioned with the U.S. effort in South Vietnam. Soon his name began appearing on antiwar leaflets the VC were distributing, and a voice believed to be his was heard on Liberation radio urging U.S. forces to stop fighting. In September 1970, he had been transferred to North Vietnam. He had chosen not to return to the United States when the listed American POWs had been released at Operation Homecoming in 1973.

As previously noted, many of the ARVN prisoners moved to the Yen Bai area in North Vietnam in 1976 for long-term reeducation had throughout the late 1970s seen an American performing chores in and around the ARVN camps, driving and repairing vehicles for the PAVN, repairing camp generators, and the like. It was later determined that this American was Robert Garwood.

In February 1979, during the period of chaos that preceded the Chinese invasion, Garwood, in Hanoi on a resupply mission, had managed to pass a note to a Westerner at a Hanoi hotel. The note said simply, "I am American in Viet

Nam Are you interested?" followed by the signature "Robert Russell Garwood" and Garwood's military service number.[49]

The recipient of the note, a Finnish employee of the World Bank who was based in Washington, DC, had responded affirmatively and had approached Garwood. In the ensuing conversation, Garwood had asked the Finn to contact the U.S. State Department and seek the department's help in getting him out of Vietnam. According to the Finn, Garwood had said he was a prisoner of war and was being held in a POW camp in a mountainous area approximately 150 kilometers from Hanoi. Garwood had further said that he knew of fifteen other Americans staying in his and other camps and indicated that there were probably more American POWs imprisoned in northern Vietnam.

Following his discussion with Garwood, the Finn had contacted the Swedish ambassador in Hanoi with news of his encounter. The ambassador had reported the incident to his government in Stockholm by cable, and the Swedish government had passed the information to the U.S. embassy in Stockholm.[50] On February 14, the U.S. State Department in Washington had announced that Garwood was still alive in Vietnam and had requested that the Vietnamese make immediate arrangements for his departure.[51]

Garwood was released by the Vietnamese on March 21, 1979. He returned to the United States and was charged with desertion—a capital offense—collaboration with the enemy, and several lesser crimes.

Facing a barrage of questions about his knowledge of living POWs, Garwood had, on the advice of his civilian attorney, Dermot Foley of New York, who served as counsel for the National League of Families and whose brother, Maj. Brendan Foley, USAF, had been missing in action in Laos since late 1967, refused to discuss any information he possessed concerning Americans remaining in Vietnam "pending resolution of his pending court proceedings."[52] However, Foley, after telling the press that at his direction Garwood would not publicly discuss the matter of Americans remaining in Vietnam, had offered a hint of what Garwood knew when he told *The New York Times* in late May 1979 that "it's fair to say that Bobby has a belief that there are men still over there."[53]

After a brief period of recuperation, Garwood had been returned to duty by the Marine Corps and, in 1981, been put on trial at Camp Lejeune, North Carolina. During the court-martial proceedings, Garwood's navy psychiatrist had testified that Garwood had reported seeing "a couple of hundred other Americans still in captivity in Vietnam and [had] complained of being unable to make that information public." The psychiatrist, Capt. Benjamin R. Ogburn, USN, had testified that Garwood "knew that there were other Americans still in Vietnam and he felt that should be brought out." In response to Ogburn's revelations, the presiding judge, Col. R. E. Switzer, USMC, had ruled that Garwood's statements about POWs remaining in Vietnam were irrelevant and had ordered those statements stricken from the record and disregarded by the jurors.[54]

The military court had ultimately found Garwood not guilty of desertion but guilty of collaborating with the enemy and of striking a fellow prisoner. Garwood had been ordered dishonorably discharged from the Marine Corps with loss of back pay. His civilian attorney at the time, John Lowe, had immediately filed an appeal and, as Foley had previously done, had advised his client not to say anything more about the remaining American prisoners pending the outcome of the appeal. Following his conviction, Garwood had dropped out of sight.

Hendon had become intrigued with the Garwood case after reading some of the information in Garwood's classified files in the Pentagon in 1983. Upon leaving the Pentagon in June 1983, Hendon had attempted on several occasions to contact the secretive Garwood but had been unable to do so. Finally, in March 1984, Hendon, acting on a tip, had found Garwood working as a mechanic at a service station on Lee Highway in Arlington, Virginia, just a stone's throw from the Pentagon.

Hendon had introduced himself to Garwood and had asked him if he would be willing to talk about the prisoners he had described to his psychiatrist. "The families, but more importantly, the POWs themselves," Hendon had told the former marine, "desperately need your help."

Garwood had replied that he had, in fact, seen a number of American POWs in captivity in North Vietnam long after the war, but that on advice of his lawyers he could not talk about it, publicly or privately, and he hoped Hendon understood. Hendon had assured Garwood that he did understand and left his business card, telling Garwood that if things ever changed, to please call him.

## Late September 1984
## "I WANT TO CLEAR MY CONSCIENCE AND HELP THESE MEN"

Six months passed. Then, in late September 1984, Garwood had contacted Hendon by phone and told him that he could no longer remain silent about the American prisoners he had seen. "I just can't live with this anymore," Garwood had told Hendon, who by now was campaigning for his old congressional seat. "I want to clear my conscience and help these men in any way I can," Garwood had said. "If it costs me my back pay and even my freedom, so be it, but I have to put this behind me and I have to do it now. It's time to lay the bomb out there and take whatever comes as a result."[55]

Hendon, locked in a heated political campaign, did not have time to give this unexpected development the attention it deserved. However, he could not send Garwood to the Pentagon, where the DIA analysts would have had a field day savaging the dishonorably discharged former marine. After thinking for a moment, Hendon suggested that Garwood tell his story to a respected newspaper. "Those sons of bitches didn't want to hear about the POWs during your trial," Hendon told Garwood, "so maybe they should read about them in the paper." Hendon went on to explain that if the newspaper believed Garwood was telling the truth and decided to publish his story, then, first, the POWs would benefit, because their story would be in the public domain for everyone to see, and second, Garwood would benefit by being protected from the piranhas in the Pentagon, because his story would already be known and there would be no way the government could misrepresent what he had said. "I think you should do it," Hendon said.

Garwood agreed, and after further discussion with Hendon decided to tell his story to *The Wall Street Journal,* which, he said, "would be read not only in Washington but also in Hanoi by the people who are still holding the men I saw."

The decision made, Hendon told Garwood that he did not want to hear anything about his story until he read it in the *Journal.* Hendon then hung up and called *Journal* reporter Bill Paul, who Hendon knew had an interest in the Vietnam POWs, and told Paul that Garwood was finally ready to talk. Paul contacted Garwood by phone and then met with him in person to begin what would become a series of conversations followed by a vetting process that Hendon later learned spanned many weeks.

*December 4, Washington*
## A CALIFORNIA CONGRESSMAN CONFRONTS HIS PRESIDENT

Ronald Reagan defeated Walter Mondale in a landslide in the November elections. Hendon, aided by the huge turnout for Reagan, won reelection to his old House seat.

Hendon was in Washington in early December for freshman class orientation when the *Journal* published Paul's story. In the article, which appeared on the front page of the December 4 issue under the headline "Robert Garwood Says Vietnam Didn't Return Some American POWs," Garwood was quoted as saying he had seen American POWs at five different, specific locations in the North after Operation Homecoming and had heard they were being held at other locations in the North as well. Paul wrote that he (Paul) had contacted both General Tighe and Admiral Tuttle and advised them of the locations, and both men had said that several were consistent with information provided by other intelligence sources.

Reading the lengthy article, Hendon immediately recognized from his own work with the classified intelligence that four of the five locations cited by Garwood were locations where other sources had also reported seeing American servicemen in captivity long after Operation Homecoming. Hendon did not recall seeing reports of Americans being held at the fifth location.

As fate would have it, on the afternoon the *Journal* story appeared, members of the Republican freshman class went to the White House for a get-acquainted meeting with President Reagan. The meeting, attended by Hendon and some twenty other members-elect, was held in the Cabinet Room.

When the meeting convened, the president, seated at his traditional place at the cabinet table with the usual phalanx of administration officials seated behind him along the windowed doors, immediately mesmerized his new troops with his patented wit, charm, and self-effacing grace, pausing briefly from time to time to offer his guests one of his favorite Jelly Belly brand jelly beans that sat in a jar on the table. When he concluded his remarks and opened the floor for questions, Robert K. Dornan (R-CA), who had been reelected to the congressional seat he had given up in 1982 in what turned out to be an unsuccessful run for the U.S. Senate, literally exploded out of his seat with a copy of the *Journal* in his hand.

Hendon recalls that Dornan, almost shouting at his fellow Californian, waved the *Journal* in the air, passionately recited several passages, and then told the president that "some in your administration are letting you down, not serving you well, Mr. President, on the POW issue." As best as Hendon can remember, Dornan then went on to say something like somebody had better get serious about these prisoners, they are being tortured and they are being ignored by the bureaucrats in your own administration, and then declared that as a former chairman of the House Task Force on POWs and MIAs, he knew "all about the intelligence" and pleaded with the president to seize the moment and take whatever actions were necessary to get the prisoners home.

The president responded to Dornan's outburst by saying that his administration was deeply committed to the POWs, but that every time officials pursued a lead it turned out to be a dead end.[56] He then turned around in his chair and asked National Security Advisor Robert McFarlane, who was seated behind him, to arrange a briefing for him on the Garwood sightings. Hendon remembers that McFarlane, who appeared quite embarrassed by what had just occurred, responded that he would do so at once.

Hendon collared Dornan in the Roosevelt Room on the way out. Telling his old friend first about how Garwood's sightings matched reports from other sources and then about the problems he had encountered in the Pentagon, Hendon warned Dornan that the fix was in and that whatever briefing the president might receive would surely be rigged. "The lid's on," Hendon said. "They are trying to put this thing in the history books, Bob, and they will never *ever* tell the president or anyone else the truth about how Garwood's sightings match the other intel." After a brief discussion, it was decided that Hendon would find out what he could about the upcoming briefing and see if he and Dornan could attend to keep the proceedings honest.

## THE POW SPECIAL OFFICE

On the 5th, the day after the Garwood article appeared, the *Los Angeles Times* ran a follow-up article that quoted a Pentagon spokesman as saying that the Garwood story contained "a great deal of information, none of which is corroborated with other information we have."[57] Hendon, more angry than surprised, called the Pentagon after hearing of the *Times* article and scheduled an appointment with Special Office personnel the following day. His intention was to ask them to change DOD's official public statement on corroboration and to determine, if possible, the status of the presidential briefing.

On December 6, the day of Hendon's scheduled meeting with Special Office personnel, *The Washington Times* published a front-page story about the Garwood revelations entitled "Garwood: Can a collaborator help bring the MIAs home?" The article identified Garwood as "the Vietnam War's longest held POW returnee," and quoted him as saying he was willing to return to Vietnam at any time "to locate prison camps where he estimates 60 to 75 U.S. soldiers remain in secret captivity." "I would go in a heartbeat," Garwood was quoted as saying. "I could recognize those camps absolutely, and the Vietnamese would not be able to deny what I told them."

The article went on to explain that the thirty-eight-year-old former marine, "the only man tried for treasonous activity during the war—and later exonerated of the most serious charges against him— . . . [had] led a life of complete seclusion in the Virginia suburbs since his court-martial ended in 1981," but had "burst back into view this week when, in a published interview, he reiterated claims that many POWs remain behind in Vietnam, that he has seen them, and that he knows the names of about a dozen." Garwood was quoted as saying he had "made his decision to reveal the detailed information about the POWs when he realized that he was the only living link between the men he believes missing and the long-anxious and desperate families in the U.S." Garwood's new information, the article declared, was "electric to those interested in the fate of about 2,500 men missing-in-action or unreturned from POW camps."

Meeting at the Pentagon later in the day with Col. John Oberst, USAF, the head of the Special Office; Oberst's civilian deputy, Charles Trowbridge; and several analysts, Hendon told Oberst that Dornan had raised the Garwood story at the White House and asked Oberst if there might be a presidential briefing in the works. Oberst responded that he and DIA director, Lt. Gen. James A. Williams, USA, were scheduled to brief the president in the Oval Office the next morning.[58]

Hendon then stated what all in attendance already knew: first, that corroboration has always been considered "the best lie detector," and second, that at least four of Garwood's sightings were corroborated by other intelligence already in DIA files. Hendon then asked Oberst to correct DOD's public statement denying there was any corroborating intelligence and pledge that he and Williams would brief the president fully about all of the corroborating intelligence that existed. When Oberst refused both requests, Hendon, citing the intelligence from memory, asked Oberst to have one of the analysts pull the specific files so that everyone could go over them together to ensure that there was no mistaking the fact that these sightings corroborated Garwood's.[59]

Oberst told Hendon that such an examination of the intelligence files would not be possible because, "you haven't been sworn in yet and you don't have the necessary security clearance. Come back in January after you've been sworn in, and we'll go over it then."

"Well, fine, I will," Hendon replied, "but in the interim I need your assurance that when you and General Williams brief the president tomorrow morning you will inform him that at least four of Garwood's sighting are, in fact, corroborated by other sightings and information in your files."

"What I tell the president is classified and will remain classified," Oberst replied.

Harsh words were exchanged and Hendon departed.

## ONE LAST TRY

Hendon returned to his Capitol Hill hotel from the Pentagon and placed a call to M. B. Oglesby, Reagan's chief of congressional affairs, and invited Oglesby to come by for a brief meeting. When Oglesby arrived at Hendon's room that afternoon, Hendon told his old friend, who had been at the White House meeting on the 4th and had witnessed Dornan's outburst, that he had just come from a meeting at DIA and was convinced that Oberst and Williams planned to deceive the president about the Garwood sightings in the upcoming briefing. Hendon told Oglesby that he and Dornan would like to attend the briefing as observers to keep Williams and Oberst honest.

"They're gonna lie like dogs, B.," Hendon told Oglesby, "but with me and Dornan knowing what we know about the intelligence, we believe that if we're there, just sitting there with our mouths shut, our mere presence will prevent Williams and Oberst from lying to the president. We won't open our mouths unless the president asks us to, you have my word." Saying that the stakes were enormous and that he believed the lives of the prisoners hung in the balance, Hendon implored Oglesby to agree to his and Dornan's proposal. Oglesby refused.

Hendon countered with a proposal that he and Dornan be given five minutes with the president either before or after the DIA briefing. Oglesby again refused.

"Goddamnit, B.," Hendon told Oglesby, "there is a huge cover-up going on over at DIA on this issue—Dornan was Chairman of the POW Task Force, I was a member of the task force, we have studied the intelligence carefully, and I worked at the Pentagon last year and I know firsthand that they are covering this thing up. And now, with Garwood's sightings and his offer to show us exactly where the POWs were held, we have an opportunity to fix this situation and maybe get these poor bastards home. Dornan and I want the president to know three things: first, there is a cover-up at DIA, second, what Garwood says is corroborated by a large amount of intelligence already in DIA files, and third, and most important, when viewed in its entirety the intelligence shows the Viets and the PL are holding not a few, but *hundreds* of prisoners."

Oglesby refused for the third time to agree to Hendon's proposal. The atmosphere grew charged, and, just as had occurred earlier in the day at the Pentagon, harsh words were exchanged. *Very* harsh words. Oglesby departed.

Oberst and Williams briefed the president in the Oval Office on December 7 as scheduled. Also present were McFarlane, Childress, and White House Chief of Staff James Baker III.

According to Williams's record of the meeting, he and Oberst first presented the "same briefing [that] is regularly given to members of Congress and their staffs." (Dornan and Hendon had each seen this briefing at least a half dozen times and knew that, since the departure of Tighe and Tuttle, the emphasis had been on dog tag reports and the recovery of remains rather than living POWs.) Then, as Hendon and Dornan had feared, Williams and Oberst informed the president that "information on hand at DIA does not corroborate Mr. Garwood's claims." Finally, according to Williams, "collaborator" Garwood and the "adversarial and vituperative" Hendon were roundly assailed by all in attendance, including the President himself.[60] (It is believed that what was said in the December 7, 1984, Oval Office briefing persuaded Ronald Reagan that the Americans cited in the postwar POW intelligence were all deserters or stay-behinds who had made their accommodations with the Communists and were living out their days in remote villages throughout Indochina. Perhaps the clearest indication of how convinced Reagan became of this came to light in March 1988, when Dana Rohrabacher, special assistant to the president and one of Reagan's favorite speechwriters, met with Reagan prior to leaving his White House post to run for the California congressional seat he now holds. Rohrabacher later explained that each departing member of the senior staff was customarily given five minutes with the president to thank him and say good-bye and to discuss whatever other matters he or she wished, and that on his last day at the White House he got his turn. "I asked him to help the Mooj [the Afghan mujahideen freedom fighters], help the contras, and get the POWs home," Rohrabacher later recalled. "Speaking specifically to my request about the POWs, to my complete surprise, the president said, 'Well, we know there are Americans there, but they are not really prisoners—they have families and are trying to live out their lives in private with their families, and it would be wrong for us to shine a spotlight on them.'" Rohrabacher, who as a civilian had traveled throughout Southeast Asia during the war and after the war had closely followed the POW issue, was speechless. "I immediately thought, Do I dare ask the president, *'Who says? Who says* these men have families and therefore are not really prisoners? *Who says this?* Have we talked to these men? Did the *men* tell us that? If not, how do we know?' But, of course, asking such questions would have been disrespectful, so I did not. But I immediately realized—*I knew*—knowing the way the White House works, that no one had talked to any of the MIAs, but rather, those close to the president had told him the men all had wives and families and should be allowed to live out their years in privacy, and the president had believed what he had been told.")[61]

Following the Oval Office briefing on the 7th, DIA passed official word to the military bureaucracy that "DIA doubts the validity of Garwood's information" and that his sightings "appear to be manipulations of other documented reportings which took place prior to the release of the POW'S," meaning they were based on *wartime sightings.*[62]

Griffiths, meanwhile, launched an attack on *The Wall Street Journal* for what she called the *Journal*'s "astonishing" decision to publish the Garwood article. In a three-page letter to Managing Editor Norman Pearlstein dated December 13, Griffiths, who as a principal member of the IAG had access to virtually all of the POW/MIA intelligence, charged that the publishing of Garwood's statements about POWs "without evidence of credibility" reflected "cruelty" and "inhumanity." She declared that "the WALL STREET JOURNAL's publication of the Garwood story demonstrates [a] mentality routinely found in the NATIONAL ENQUIRER, not a publication internationally accepted as responsible, factual and objective." She further informed Pearlstein that the League was solidly behind the Reagan administration's handling of the POW/MIA issue and declared that "[i]ndividuals who want to join in this quest are welcome unless their irresponsibility jeopardizes achieving the goals for which we have fought." Declaring that the Garwood article had caused "consternation" in the League's ranks, Griffiths told Pearlstein that to make things right, she needed to "arrange sensitive briefings with a responsible *Journal* reporter" and for that reporter to write "a valid and comprehensive report . . . about . . . current high level [Reagan administration] efforts" to account for the missing. She ended her letter on an ominous note, telling Pearlstein, "I hope you will take this letter in the serious vein in which it was written."[63]

## NEW YEAR'S RESOLUTIONS

The president's apparent satisfaction with what Williams and Oberst had told him notwithstanding, the Garwood revelations in the *Journal,* combined with Dornan's outburst in the Cabinet Room and word that Hendon and Dornan had been prohibited from attending the Oval Office briefing on the 7th, left some of the freshman Republicans stunned and angry. Three who were especially concerned were newly elected Representatives Bob Smith of New Hampshire, John Rowland of Connecticut, and Jim Saxton of New Jersey, all of whom soon approached Dornan and Hendon to suggest that a new effort be undertaken to free the prisoners and to demand that they be part of it.

In the days following their meeting with the president, the concerned freshmen met to discuss how best to proceed when Congress convened in January. They decided to focus their efforts on two areas. First, they would conduct a vigorous, no-holds-barred investigation of the Garwood sightings and all the other intelligence DIA had received on live POWs, and of the job DIA was doing analyzing that intelligence. At the same time, they would pressure the administration to shift its focus from the recovery of remains back to the recovery of live prisoners and would monitor the administration's actions carefully. Pledging to go to work the minute they were sworn in in January, they headed home to their individual districts for Christmas.

Down at the White House and the State Department, meanwhile, and over at the Pentagon, powerful people with a totally different agenda were making some New Year's plans of their own.

The cover-up that began in early 1983 and continued throughout 1984 continues to this day. For the authors' opinions on how it was structured and how it was sustained, see www.enormouscrime.com, Chapter 23.

# CHAPTER 24

# 1985

# "PROGRESS" IN THE SEARCH FOR
# REMAINS • FRESHMEN, STONEWALLED ON POWs, TURN
# TO PEROT • McFARLANE DROPS HIS GUARD

. . .

With war raging in Central America,[1] administration officials moved quickly in the first weeks of 1985 to minimize the damage caused by the Garwood revelations and blunt what they knew would be a strong attack on DIA by the freshman House Republicans. The administration's plan called for action on four fronts:

- First, mollify the families by showing progress in the hunt for remains. This was to be accomplished by conducting the first-ever postwar crash site excavation in Laos, which LPDR officials had agreed to in mid-1984, and purchasing remains for cash from the North Vietnamese, who as of 1985 would not allow crash site excavations in their country.
- Second, blunt the House freshmen's anticipated assault on DIA by conducting an "internal review" of the DIA Special Office for POWs/MIAs, issuing a "report" based on the "internal review" that praised the professionalism of the staff and the high quality of the work turned out by the office, and then using the report to deflect the congressional assault when it came.
- Third, work closely with the administration's point men in the House, Asian and Pacific Affairs Subcommittee Chairman Steven Solarz (D-NY), POW/MIA Task Force Chairman Gerald Solomon (R-NY), and POW/MIA Task Force Vice Chairman Benjamin A. Gilman (R-NY), to keep the intelligence bottled up and away from the freshmen.
- Fourth, stonewall any effort by the freshmen to go around the task force by refusing any and all requests for documents, intelligence, and/or assistance they submitted directly to DOD, DIA, CIA, State, etc.

## SHOWING PROGRESS ON REMAINS

The first postwar crash site excavation inside Communist territory occurred in early February at a remote site some twenty-five miles northeast of Pakse, Laos, where a USAF AC-130A Spectre gunship, call sign "Spectre 17," had crashed and burned on the night of December 21, 1972. The gunship had been hit while on a firing run over the Ho Chi Minh Trail in the southeastern panhandle of Laos and the crew had been attempting to return to their base at Ubon, Thailand, when fire had erupted on the left wing. After flying straight and level for several minutes with fire trailing behind the wing, the aircraft had exploded and plunged to the ground in hostile territory some twenty-five miles short of the Mekong.[2] Two crew members among the sixteen U.S. Air Force personnel on board had been rescued in Lao territory shortly after parachuting from the burning aircraft; the severed forearm of a third had been recovered by a search party the following day, but the remaining thirteen airmen could not be located and were subsequently listed as missing in action.

According to after-action reports filed by USAF personnel shortly after the crash and testimony later received from a captured Pathet Lao cadre who witnessed the crash and visited the crash site the following morning, here are the specifics of what occurred that evening and the following morning:

According to after-action reports, a black AC-130 Spectre gunship with sixteen crewmen aboard, call sign "Spectre 17," departed Ubon airfield, Thailand, at 5:39 P.M. on December 21, 1972, on an armed reconnaissance mission over Saravan, Laos.

The aircraft arrived in the target area without incident after a short 110-mile flight from Ubon. Once over the target area, crew members quickly located and began attacking three enemy trucks on the Ho Chi Minh Trail below. After destroying the first truck, they saw that antiaircraft fire was being directed toward their plane. As they attacked a second truck and began maneuvering the aircraft into position to silence the offending gun position, two additional gun sites opened up. At approximately 7:00 P.M., enemy gunners scored a direct hit on the plane's left wing.

The flight crew managed to keep the aircraft under control while putting out an emergency radio call that they had sustained serious battle damage and were returning to base. The crew radioed they were losing fuel at the rate of two thousand pounds per minute and had also lost the aircraft's utility hydraulic system. Hearing the transmissions from Spectre 17, other aircraft in the area responded with navigational information on the shortest route to Ubon field and began moving into position to escort Spectre 17 back to Thailand.

As the stricken aircraft headed toward Ubon, radio transmissions from the plane told of an increasingly perilous situation. One transmission described how fuel from the damaged left wing was now pouring into the cargo portion of the plane. As the cabin crew continued radio communication with nearby aircraft, other members of the crew began congregating near the rear exit ramp platform in anticipation of a bailout order. According to one of the two crewmen later rescued, at least five crew members were positioned on the ramp ready to bail out. In the words of the other surviving crew member, "Everyone was ready and waiting to jump."

At approximately 7:12 P.M., an explosion rocked the aircraft, causing it to burst into flames. Seconds later the left wing separated from the fuselage, sending the aircraft first into a hard left bank and then into a rapid, almost vertical dive toward the ground. One USAF eyewitness estimated the plane was at an altitude of seven thousand five hundred feet at the time of the explosion, another

estimated eleven thousand feet. The fact that it was dark at the time was believed to be the reason for the disparity between the two estimates.

The two crewmen who ultimately made it home that night were blown, fell,
or jumped from the rear ramp just prior to, at, or just after the moment the aircraft exploded. Both parachuted safely to the ground and were rescued uninjured by "Jolly Green 32" from Nakhon Phanom Air Force Base, the last of the
two at 9:21 P.M. Both were safely back at NKP by 11:00 P.M.[3]

The official summary of the captured PL cadre's testimony contained among
other information the following:

On approximately December 18 or 19 at about 1900 hours [7:00 P.M.]—a time
and date U.S. officials would later declare "correlated well to the loss of Spectre
17 on 21 December"—the cadre heard the approach of what he believed was a
"c-147." He then heard the aircraft explode, watched it descend in flames, and
from a distance observed the area of impact. The cadre said he immediately dispatched a squad to check the crash site area. He said the squad returned at approximately 2400 hours [midnight] and reported that they could not enter the
immediate area of the crash site because of large burning fires. Members of the
squad did, however, bring back five parachutes, all with the canopies deployed.
Two of these were partially charred; the other three showed no signs of char-
ring. The cadre decided he would wait until the wreckage cooled before going to
the crash site himself.

Soon after daylight, the cadre accompanied the squad members to the crash
site, which he estimated was located at map coordinates XC 087 086. He stated
that the crash site contained various heavily charred human remains and there
were no remains of entire bodies. He felt that there were at least five or six bodies but added that more bodies could have been in the aircraft and could have
been completely burned in the fire prior to or after the crash. He said that at his
direction, members of the squad dug a trench that was one meter long, one or
two meters deep, and sixty centimeters wide and placed all the remains in it and
covered them with dirt and rocks.

The cadre added that in addition to the five or six burned and dismembered
bodies, he and his men found two small piles of bloody bandages in the area of
the crash site.[4]

## EXCAVATION OF THE CRASH SITE BEGINS

On the morning of February 11, 1985, more than twelve years after Spectre 17
had gone down, U.S. experts arrived at the crash site to begin their work. The
excavation, hailed by U.S. embassy officials in Bangkok as "unprecedented,"
had attracted enormous press attention in the region. As a result, a host of reporters, including one network television crew from the United States, accompanied the team to record the event.

No sooner had members of the joint U.S.-Lao team begun their work than
reporters began dispatching in excruciating detail what they had found. UPI reported that the team had found flight helmets and other personal effects as well
as human teeth and bone fragments. Most of the bone fragments, UPI reported,
were "an inch or so in size."[5] The Associated Press quoted an official at the U.S.

embassy in Bangkok as saying, "We believe they [those remains] are Americans, [but] it's too early to know whether they are the remains of one or two people or three or four."[6] The *Bangkok Post* quoted the head of the search team as warning that "the remains had been 'very fragmented' by the force and heat of the crash and would be difficult to identify."[7]

When members of the search team finished their work, the American television crew filmed team members carrying five small bags of bone fragments away from the excavation site and reported that the bags were being sent to the U.S. Army's Central Identification Laboratory in Hawaii (CILHI) for examination and identification.[8] CILHI Commander Maj. Johnie Webb, USA, a member of the search team, told reporters the identification process would take "at least a month."[9]

## PURCHASING BONES FOR CASH FROM THE NORTH VIETNAMESE

Concurrent with their efforts at Pakse, administration officials moved in February to begin purchasing bones from the North Vietnamese. The administration plan called for payment to be made with cash provided secretly by either the CIA or wealthy individuals. The plan, approved by McFarlane, Armitage, Wolfowitz, and Shultz, among others, called for Childress and Griffiths to make the initial cash-for-bones offer to the North Vietnamese in Hanoi in late February.

In laying out the plan to Shultz in early February, Wolfowitz informed his boss that extraordinary measures had been put in place to ensure the undertaking remained secret. "The payment scheme is to be very closely held," Wolfowitz told Shultz, noting that "NSA [National Security Agency, the supersecret U.S. spy agency charged with intercepting enemy communications] has been instructed to severely limit the distribution of any intercepts of conversations on this subject" within the U.S. government.[10] (And with good reason, for, as Wolfowitz and the others knew, had the activist congressmen discovered that the administration was paying cash for bones, they would have immediately demanded that administration officials pay for the live prisoners first.)

## THE DIA "INTERNAL REVIEW"

On February 11, a task force made up of half a dozen top DIA analysts and managers began their "internal review" of DIA's Special Office for POWs and MIAs.

After "reviewing" the operation of the office for approximately two weeks, the task force issued its findings. Referring to the Special Office as either "DC-2" or "the PW/MIA Division," the task force declared among those findings:

- The unanimous response of those involved [in the internal review] is that DC-2 is a highly professional organization. . . .
- Members of the PW/MIA Division are extremely conscientious. . . .
- A review of collection and analytical processes of DC-2 left no doubt about the correctness of the procedures being applied. . . .

- The analysts in the PW/MIA Division are extremely thorough in their work, and it is apparent that they handle each case with the concerns of the PW/MIAs and the next of kin in mind.
- The fact that DC-2's personnel have continually performed at such a high level for a sustained period is probably directly attributed to the importance which they place on their mission.
- The quality of analysis, methodology and techniques used by DC-2 is very high.
- DIA management should consider greater recognition for the fine analytical work being done by DC-2.
- DC-2 approaches its mission in a positive manner, motivated by the humanitarian aspects of their tasks. . . .
- Despite a preponderance of false reports, a subtle but well orchestrated disinformation campaign, and unwarranted public harassment, DC-2 personnel maintain a positive and highly professional analytical approach to their mission.
- It is our judgment that the quality of analysis is very high. . . .
- Reports and testimony assessed to be false or deliberately fabricated are subjected to extensive investigation so that minute—and often irrelevant—points can withstand a test in a "court of law."
- It is our opinion that the methodology and analytical techniques developed and used by DC-2 personnel are unique and meet the highest standards of the Defense Intelligence Agency.
- The overall quality of the analysts is of high caliber.
- All analysts interviewed demonstrated a dedicated and high level of commitment to their job.
- Information received is assumed to be true and the approach taken is to methodically corroborate/confirm all aspects of the information provided by a given source.
- Analytic methodologies/techniques used to evaluate source and information are thorough and very impressive.
- There is much to be learned from DC-2 analysts on determining source reliability and information credibility.
- DC-2's analysts should be commended for their efforts to leave no stone unturned in search for facts.
- The quality of current refugee sources is extremely poor. . . .
- Flagrant fabrications are common and cause unnecessary dedication of valuable analytical assets.
- The perception in the refugee community is that providing information on PW/MIAs is the most expeditious means to enter the US. . . .
- [Two] members were very laudatory of Ms [Griffiths]. They say her approach is totally professional, and the experience which she brings from her work at the Leagues [sic] of Families has facilitated answering many requests.
- In summary, the . . . [review] team uncovered no major problems in the operations of DC-2. In this regard, each team member was extremely

impressed by the high quality of the operation being conducted. It is felt that the operation is among the most professional in DIA and the efforts of DC-2 in the areas of case documentation . . . [and] source follow-up . . . could be used as models within DIA as to how such operations should be conducted.[11]

The DIA official in charge of the review, Dennis M. Nagy, would rise through the ranks and later become the only civilian ever to head DIA, serving as acting director during late 1991.[12]

## STONEWALLING THE CONGRESSMEN

Soon after being sworn in, Hendon met with DOD officials and requested three things on behalf of Dornan, Smith, Rowland, Saxton, and a half dozen or so of his colleagues from his first term who had heard of the new push for live POWs and expressed an interest in joining in the effort. First, Hendon requested that copies of selected POW-related reports from his old Pentagon files be made available to his office. He further requested that DIA provide his office with the complete file of the refugee source who had seen the American POWs bathing and sunning themselves around a cistern in the military compound on Ly Nam De Street in Hanoi in 1978 and again in 1982 and who, though he passed two polygraphs, had been declared a fabricator. This report, which Hendon had monitored closely while working at the Pentagon, had taken on special significance when Garwood had told *The Wall Street Journal* that he had seen an emaciated American POW inside a military compound on Ly Nam De Street in 1978 and had been told that other American POWs were also being detained in the compound. Finally, Hendon requested that DOD fly the source of the Ly Nam De Street sightings to Washington so the members could interview him, compare his account to Garwood's, and judge for themselves whether or not he was a fabricator as DIA had said.

DIA denied Hendon's request for his Pentagon office files, saying they could not be located.[13] Childress, advised of Hendon's request for the complete case file of the refugee who had twice seen the American POWs on Ly Nam De Street, placed an "NSC hold" on the file and ordered that it not be forwarded to Hendon's congressional office "without clearance from the White House."[14] Deputy Secretary of Defense Will Taft, responding for Secretary of Defense Weinberger, declined Hendon's request that DOD fly the refugee to Washington for interviews. Taft explained that the refugee did not qualify for DOD-sponsored travel because "the Department of Defense has [already] interviewed [him] . . . and obtained from him the POW/MIA information he claims to have" and that "the information provided . . . has been determined to be a fabrication."[15]

Hendon made three more formal requests for his Pentagon files and the Ly Nam De Street sightings file.[16] When these requests were ignored, he and his colleagues appealed to the two senior Republicans on the POW/MIA Task Force, Chairman Gerald Solomon and Vice Chairman (and former chairman) Benjamin Gilman, for help. In a contentious meeting held in Solomon's office, the powerful Gilman—who had earlier warned Hendon during a meeting in his (Gilman's) office (also attended by members of Gilman's staff) that "if you don't stop pushing on the POWs you're going to destroy Cap Weinberger"—and Solomon, who would not so much as lift a finger unless Gilman and the administration approved of it, refused to help. When Hendon asked Solarz, the chairman of the House Foreign Affairs Committee's Asian and Pacific Affairs Subcommittee—the parent subcommittee of the POW/MIA Task Force—for help in getting the files, Solarz refused. When Hendon then asked Solarz to force DOD to fly the refugee to Washington by issuing a subpoena for the refugee, Solarz again refused.[17]

Stonewalled by the administration and by the chairman and vice chairman of the POW/MIA Task Force and the chairman of the Asian and Pacific Affairs Subcommittee, Hendon and his colleagues decided either to go to federal court in an attempt to force DOD to make the files available—a tactic Republican senators had recently employed when the CIA had refused to make documents available to them—or to introduce legislation to create an independent congressional commission to examine the intelligence and recommend to the Congress how best to get the POWs home. The congressmen's unanimous choice to head the commission: H. Ross Perot, the highly respected Texas businessman with a long history of support for the Indochina POWs.

Hendon approached a Washington attorney on behalf of his colleagues and requested that the attorney begin preparing the lawsuit. Concurrently, he asked Perot if he would he be willing to serve as chairman if Hendon and his colleagues decided to introduce legislation to create an independent commission. Perot told Hendon he would think about it and get back with a decision in the near future.

As the attorney went about his work and Perot pondered the offer to chair the independent commission, Hendon asked Garwood to come in to clarify the specifics of his sightings. During a meeting held in Hendon's office on February 8, Garwood impressed the several congressmen in attendance with his sincerity and remarkable recall, and in an electrifying move described and then drew from memory a sketch of the military compound on Ly Nam De Street where he had seen the emaciated American POW in late 1978—a sketch that matched exactly the compound where the refugee source had seen the POWs bathing around the cistern in 1978 and again in 1982. Garwood's sketch, in fact, showed that same cistern at the exact same place the refugee had said it was, which was the exact place it appeared in Buffalo Hunter reconnaissance photos of the compound.[18]

On February 12, Hendon contacted the White House and requested that he and the other congressmen be given a brief appointment with the president so they could convey the startling information Garwood had provided.[19] The request was ignored.

But then came even more corroboration of Garwood's sightings. In late March, a former ARVN lieutenant general who had spent seven years in reeducation, most of it in the Yen Bai area, came to Washington and told task force members that he had knowledge of American POWs being held in a camp on Thac Ba Lake, just north of Yen Bai. The general, who had served as commander of the Saigon Capital District until the city fell on April 30, 1975, told the members that he had refused to make the information available to DIA because he had been verbally abused by U.S. personnel during initial interviews in a refugee camp in Singapore.

The general said he had received the information about the Americans while he was confined to a reeducation camp near Thac Ba Lake in 1978. He explained that one of his men, a former ARVN captain, told him at the time that he had seen approximately forty American prisoners at a camp on Thac Ba. The general explained that the captain, who worked on a supply team that carried supplies to the various Yen Bai camps, reported he had seen the American prisoners on several occasions while delivering supplies to the American camp.[20]

When the congressmen told Solomon and Gilman of the general's testimony, the two advised the Special Office of the new information, asked that the analysts prepare a response, and scheduled a closed task force hearing to hear that response. Senior DIA analyst Robert Destatte, appearing before the task force on March 28, began by declaring that the lieutenant general was a "thoroughly unreliable reporter." He added that the lieutenant general's statement that he had been verbally abused during his initial interviews in the refugee camp in Singapore was "totally false" and "that such allegations are typical of unreliable sources." Then, to the further incredulity of the activist members present, Destatte declared that the report was a fabrication "conveyed by sources dispatched by an SRV security service for the purpose of misinformation." To repeat: Destatte testified this three-star ARVN general who had commanded the defense of Saigon and had later spent seven years in Communist reeducation camps was *a North Vietnamese agent* sent to trick the U.S. government into believing that POWs were still held (apparently so the United States would pay reparations to get them back). And because he was, in reality, a North Vietnamese agent, his report of POWs being held on Thac Ba Lake in 1978 was a fabrication. And because his report was a fabrication, it did not constitute corroboration of Garwood's sighting of POWs during the same year at what was almost certainly the exact same camp.[21]

In late March, Hendon's attorney had completed the necessary documents and was ready to file suit against DIA in U.S. District Court in Washington.[22] A short while later, Perot called Hendon and said that if the Congress saw fit to create the commission, he would be willing to serve as chairman.

For the congressmen, the choice between a lawsuit or a commission headed by Ross Perot was an easy one. Hendon quickly contacted the House legislative counsel and asked him draw up the necessary legislation. Given the need to maintain secrecy in the charged atmosphere that surrounded the POW issue at the time, Hendon asked the counsel to draw up language to "establish a commission to determine whether or not Dr. Josef Mengele," the infamous "Angel of Death" at the Auschwitz concentration camp during World War II—and who the press was reporting in early 1985 might still be alive and on the run in South America—"was [in fact] still alive and, should he be found to be alive, to report to Congress appropriate action the U.S. government should take to effect his capture." The congressmen planned, of course, to delete the reference to Mengele at the last minute; insert after the word *establish* the phrase "the Perot Commission on Americans Missing in Southeast Asia to determine whether or not United States prisoners of war are being held in Southeast Asia and to report to Congress appropriate action to effect the release of any prisoners of war found to be alive," and drop the bill in the hopper.

Hearing that *The Wall Street Journal* was planning to publish a hard-hitting follow-up to the Garwood story in late April, the congressmen decided to wait and introduce the Perot resolution in conjunction with that article.

On April 16, Hendon asked again for an appointment to convey to the president the important new information provided by Garwood and the former ARVN lieutenant general.[23] McFarlane would later deny the request.[24]

The *Journal* article appeared on April 24. The article quoted General Tighe—no longer silent—as saying the civilian analysts at the Special Office exhibited "a mindset to debunk" the intelligence about living POWs and that these analysts had been dismissing good reports about living POWs for so long "it had become habit-forming." The article further quoted Tighe as saying that "I continue to run into civilians [in the U.S. government] associated with this issue who tend to think that military personnel are expendable," and declaring that "it may be time for an independently sponsored presidential commission to examine the U.S. POW effort."[25]

That morning, Hendon introduced the Perot resolution as planned.[26] Speaking from the well of the House during the "One Minutes"—the one minute of floor time generally allowed each member at the beginning of the day's proceedings during which the member may discuss any topic of his or her choosing—Hendon declared the following:

> (Mr. HENDON asked for and was given permission to address the House for 1 minute and to revise and extend his remarks.)[27]
>
> Mr. HENDON. Mr. Speaker, quite often from this well I have quoted Lt. Gen. Eugene Tighe, former Head of the Defense Intelligence Agency, who says U.S. POWs are still being held in Southeast Asia. Today in the Wall Street Journal General Tighe says more. He says that analysts at DIA "show a mindset to debunk the intelligence they receive on our POW's," and that "they have been disclaiming good reports for so long it has become habit forming."
>
> General Tighe suggests that a Presidential Commission be appointed to examine the U.S. POW effort.
>
> Well, good luck, General; I requested such a commission over 1 year ago and my request was denied by staff.
>
> So today I am introducing legislation to create an independent Congressional Commission headed by Texas Industrialist H. Ross Perot, to determine once and for all how to get our men home.
>
> As the Wall Street Journal said today, "Getting these men back would demonstrate a moral commitment few nations possess." What better way to exhibit our commitment than to create this commission and what better man to head it than H. Ross Perot?

The resolution was given the official designation House Concurrent Resolution 129 and referred to the House Committee on Foreign Affairs.

The following day, Hendon sent a "Dear Colleague" letter to all House members explaining the rationale for the legislation and asking for their support and their cosponsorship.[28] Despite strong opposition from the administration;[29] from Solarz, Gilman, and Solomon;[30] and despite Griffiths later claim to her membership that HCR 129 was "the most irresponsible legislative proposal the League has seen in years" and had "little support,"[31] 265 members would sign on as cosponsors in the months ahead.[32] Among the GOP cosponsors would be all members of the House GOP leadership—Minority Leader Bob Michel (R-IL), Reps. Trent Lott (R-MS) and Jack Kemp (R-NY)—and Reps. Dick Cheney (R-WY), Ed Madigan (R-IL), Guy Vander Jagt (R-MI), Larry Craig (R-ID), Judd Gregg (R-NH), Dan Coats (R-IN), Hank Brown (R-CO), Connie Mack (R-FL), Pat Roberts (R-KS), Olympia Snowe (R-ME), Bob Smith (R-NH), Jim Jeffords (R-VT), Jim Broyhill (R-NC), John McKernan (R-ME), John Rowland (R-CT), Don Sundquist (R-TN), Tom Ridge (R-PA), Carroll Campbell (R-SC), Mickey Edwards (R-OK), Guy Molinari (R-NY), Bob Dornan (R-CA), Newt Gingrich (R-GA), Vin Weber (R-MN), C. W. (Bill) Young (R-FL), Chris Smith (R-NJ), Tom Loeffler (R-TX), Frank Wolf (R-VA), Dick Armey (R-TX), Tom Delay (R-TX), Bill Thomas (R-CA), Don Young (R-AK), Denny Smith (R-OR), Phil Crane (R-IL), Henry Hyde (R-IL), Bill McCollum (R-FL), Lynn Martin (R-IL), Floyd Spence (R-SC), Duncan Hunter (R-CA), David Dreier (R-CA), Jim Hansen (R-UT), Jim Saxton (R-NJ), Clay Shaw (R-FL), Joe Barton (R-TX), Hal Daub (R-NE), Helen Bentley (R-MD), Mike Bilirakis (R-FL), Dan Burton (R-IN), Jerry Lewis (R-CA), Bill Lowery (R-CA), Tom Hartnett (R-SC), Sherwood Boehlert (R-NY), John Kasich (R-IN), John McCain (R-AZ), and many other Republicans. Democrat cosponsors would include Reps. Tom Daschle (D-SD), Bill Nelson (D-FL), Bob Torricelli (D-NJ), Ron Wyden (D-OR), Harry Reid (D-NV), Barbara Mikulski (D-MD), Barbara Boxer (D-CA), Richard Shelby (D-AL), Byron Dorgan (D-ND), Tom Carper (D-DE), Timothy Wirth (D-CO), Jake Pickle (D-TX), Jack Brooks (D-TX), Bill Richardson (D-NM), Frank McCloskey (D-IN), Tony Coehlo (D-CA), Martin Frost (D-TX), Edward Boland (D-MA), Les Aspin (D-WI), Jim Jones (D-OK), Doug Applegate (D-OH), Buddy MacKay (D-FL), Billy Tauzin (D-LA), Vic Fazio (D-CA), Dan Glickman (D-KS), Beverly Byron (D-MD), Charles Stenholm (D-TX), Bruce Vento (D-MN), John Spratt (D-SC), Pete Stark (D-CA), Jim Oberstar (D-MN), Buddy Roemer (D-LA), Leon Panetta (D-CA), Marvin Leath (D-TX), Norman Maneta (D-CA), Marty Russo (D-IL), Marcy Kaptur (D-OH), Charlie Wilson (D-TX), Mickey Leland (D-TX), Dave McCurdy (D-OK), Ike Skelton (D-MO), Andy Jacobs (D-IN), Gary Ackerman (D-NY), Louis Stokes (D-OH), Bob Edgar (D-PA), Charles Bennett (D-FL), Lane Evans (D-IL), and a host of others.

Former I Corps Marine Mike Shelton, the *Orange County Register*'s editorial cartoonist—like thousands of other vets who closely followed the POW issue—was ecstatic at the news that Perot might head a new effort to get the POWs home. "Vietnam—It ain't over till it's over," Shelton declared in a haunting nationally syndicated editorial cartoon several days later. (See next page.) Still today one hears the phrase whenever Vietnam vets gather.

And then later in the month, over the Memorial Day holiday, the specter of American POWs abandoned in the jungles of Indochina further came alive as *Rambo: First Blood Part II* opened to packed theaters.[33] The film stars Sylvester

5/1    Distributed by King Features Syndicate

VIETNAM— IT AIN'T OVER TILL IT'S OVER

(COURTESY MIKE SHELTON, *THE ORANGE COUNTY REGISTER*)

Stallone as a Vietnam vet and former war hero John Rambo, who returns to Indochina after the war and single-handedly rescues a group of American POWs
from a prison camp in Laos.[34]

Though a number of Vietnam vets viewed John Rambo as a pathetic carica-
ture, the movie dramatically increased public interest in the POWs and spawned
renewed calls for action to get them home. Solarz responded by scheduling
hearings in June to question General Tighe about his latest comments in *The
Wall Street Journal* and to hear from administration witnesses about what they
were doing to address the live POW issue.

At the hearings, held on the 27th, Tighe, the star witness, repeated assertions he had previously made before the committee that living prisoners remained in captivity in Indochina. The intelligence that led him to that
conclusion, Tighe told the committee, "was among the most detailed of human reporting I have ever seen. . . . It is high quality human intelligence." He
then forcefully repeated his criticisms of the job DIA was doing in analyzing
that intelligence and said that though it would pain him to do so, he would be
in favor of extending diplomatic relations to Hanoi "to retrieve [even] one live
American."[35]

Following Tighe's testimony, the committee heard from a panel of administration witnesses led by Assistant Secretary of State Paul Wolfowitz. Under great
pressure to report progress on the live POW front—but unable to do so—
Wolfowitz was reduced to repeating the administration's "absolute commitment to the resolution of this issue" and, after characterizing the Spectre 17

excavation as "a major step" and an "encouraging success," to assuring the members that "our technicians at the CIL are using the latest in available technology to determine the identities of the [Spectre 17] remains" . . . and that "we will report the results to you as soon as the CIL's analysis is complete."[36]

Just in time for the League convention in July, CILHI rendered its verdict.

## SPECTRE 17, THE VERDICT

U.S. officials began notifying the Spectre 17 families of the Central Identification Laboratory's official findings in early July.

Anne Hart, wife of Spectre 17 navigator Capt. Thomas T. Hart III, USAF, and former vice chairman of the board of the League, remembers well the phone call she received from the Air Force Casualty Office. "They called me at home on Monday, three days before the fourth of July," Hart remembers, "and told me that Tommy's remains had been positively identified and would be available for burial in a matter of days. But having seen the tiny bags of bones on TV, I was stunned that they could have identified Tommy or anyone else with certainty, and so I asked them on what basis they had made the identification. They said they couldn't tell me. I then asked if they had been able to positively identify any of the other crewmen, and they said they couldn't tell me that, either. So I got off the phone and immediately started calling my friends whose husbands, brothers, and sons were on the plane with Tommy to see if they, too, had been notified. To my amazement, I found that all of us—all thirteen families—had been given the same message: 'positive ID.'"

Hart continued, "I remember saying to myself, 'Back in February I saw on this very television set here in my living room those five little bags of bone fragments being carried from the crash site. And now, presto, those fragments have become Tommy Hart and twelve other proud men? *The entire crew?*' I knew it just couldn't be possible."

Several days later, Hart received the official report on the identification of her husband from the Central Identification Laboratory in Hawaii. "The report said they had 'positively identified' Tommy from five tiny bone fragments, none bigger than a quarter," Hart said, adding that the identification had been made without the benefit of DNA analysis. "I was speechless, and then I thought, 'My God, if they did this to Tommy, they may have done the same thing to the others.' So I knew in my heart something was terribly, terribly wrong, and that I owed it to Tommy and the crew to find the truth."[37]

Hart began her quest for answers by refusing to accept the remains. Then, on July 5, she obtained a court order directing CILHI to allow an outside expert to examine the remains in order to render a second opinion. In response, CILHI personnel flew the remains from Hawaii to a U.S. facility in Oakland, California, where they were examined by an outside expert hired by Hart. The expert carefully examined both the remains CILHI experts had determined to be Captain Hart and the accompanying CILHI records. Following his examination, he filed an affidavit with the court stating the laboratory's determination that the remains were those of Captain Hart was "scientifically impossible, speculative and unreliable."[38]

When Hart received a copy of the affidavit, she contacted Hendon and the other congressmen and advised them of what the expert had found. She then called the other Spectre 17 families, told them of the results, and suggested that they also should consider second opinions. Two of the families, those of flight engineer M.Sgt. James R. Fuller, USAF, and 2nd Lt. George D. Macdonald, USAF, the plane's TV sensor operator, decided to do so; the others demurred. Hart and the families of Fuller and MacDonald agreed to meet at the National League of Families annual convention in Washington, DC, the following week to compare notes and plot strategy.[39]

The White House announced just prior to the League convention that the remains of all thirteen crew members from Spectre 17 had been positively identified.[40]

When Hart arrived in Washington, she found that the truth about her husband's "identification" had spread like wildfire among the POW/MIA families. As a result, she and the Fuller and MacDonald families received many offers of support and assistance. "We knew if the government could do that to Captain Hart, no U.S. serviceman was safe, not my son, not anyone's son," former League board chairman Earl Hopper later said.

One family member who did not offer support, however, was Griffiths, who, according to Hart, contacted her shortly after her arrival and warned that she should accept the government's identification and remain silent, and that if she did not, she would "destroy the credibility of the CIL." "That was bad enough," Hart says, "but later I had to listen to Vice President Bush tell the families what a wonderful job the administration was doing recovering and identifying the bodies and how they were planning to excavate *another* crash site in Laos! And all the while, up in my room were those two reports—the official report from the lab which claimed to identify every member of Tommy's crew from a pile of tiny bone chips, and the outside expert's declaration that Tommy's ID was a complete fraud. But there was the vice president, bragging about the great job they were doing! It was a devastating experience for a young military wife who believed strongly in our country and our system of government. It just tore me to pieces."[41]

## A RENEWED EFFORT TO GAIN ACCESS TO THE DIA FILES

Hendon and his colleagues, after talking to Hart's outside expert and realizing for the first time just how far administration officials were willing to go to show "progress" in their highly publicized hunt for remains, decided to launch another effort to gain access to the DIA files on live POWs. In mid-July, employing a technique used by antiwar congressmen and -women during the 1960s to pry sensitive information about the conduct of the war from a secretive Pentagon, Hendon and seventeen of his Republican colleagues filed a Resolution of Inquiry, a streamlined, nondebatable resolution that, once approved by the House Permanent Select Committee on Intelligence (HPSCI, pronounced "hip see"), would have required the secretary of defense to make available to the Congress within ten days "all case files complete with individual DIA analyses concerning reports of live Americans in Southeast Asia from the date of the release of the findings of the Woodcock Report on March 23, 1977, and ending on the date of the adoption of this resolution."[42]

As the congressmen awaited the Intelligence Committee's decision, in early September two former Green Berets—one of them a highly decorated former POW—filed a lawsuit in federal court in Fayetteville, North Carolina, charging Reagan administration officials and DIA Director James A. Williams with deliberately ignoring or discrediting reports about live POWs and violating U.S. law by not aggressively seeking the release or rescue of live POWs being held in Southeast Asia.[43]

On September 10, less than a week after the two Green Berets had filed their lawsuit, HPSCI Chairman Lee Hamilton (D-IN) reported to the House that he and the other members of his committee had rejected the congressmen's resolution of inquiry.

In his "Adverse Report," Hamilton explained that "the Committee staff had been directed to . . . assess the manning, funding, methodology, and operations of the DIA's POW/MIA Division . . . assess the professionalism and quality of the Division's finished analyses of POW/MIA-related intelligence . . . [and to examine] a representative sampling of POW/MIA 'live sighting' files." He pointed out that committee staff had received testimony from two DIA officials, Special Office chief Col. John Oberst, USAF, who had briefed the president back in December, and Oberst's new boss, Rear Adm. Thomas Brooks, USN, who held Admiral Tuttle's old position at DIA, and that he and the other committee members had received testimony and recommendations from Gilman, Solomon, and Solarz in executive session. Hamilton noted that Hendon had been allowed to meet with members of the committee's staff (but not with the members).

Continuing, Hamilton cited the following among the committee's findings:

- The Committee's review . . . convinces the Committee that DIA performs unbiased, professional, and thorough analyses of POW/MIA live sighting cases.
- DIA's POW/MIA Division personnel, most of whom are Vietnam veterans, thoroughly investigate and cross reference each report.
- DIA efforts are directed at impartial assessments of live sighting cases.
- The Committee . . . [agrees with Gilman's, Solomon's, and Solarz's] unequivocal rejection of suggestions that there had been a cover-up within the Administration or DIA of credible information about Americans held prisoner in Southeast Asia.[44]

Another good report card for DIA, the second, in fact, in six months. And this one filled out and presented by one of the most highly respected members of the House.

An angry Hendon and his equally angry colleagues—knowing that, as a direct result of Hamilton's actions, the abuse of the refugee sources and the cover-up of the intelligence would continue at least until they could get the Perot bill passed—put the word out to the press that the House Intelligence Committee was now a party to the cover-up and declared their intention to seek the files by whatever means necessary.[45]

*October*
## McFARLANE DROPS HIS GUARD

Washington, DC, like other national capitals, is two distinct towns: the one the public sees and hears about and the one known only to insiders. Given the allure and the special importance of what goes on in Washington, mechanisms have evolved over time to enable selected outsiders—for a fee, a political contribution, or whatever—to temporarily transition to insider status and catch a glimpse of what *really* goes on behind the city's closed doors.

One such mechanism in use during 1985 allowed outsiders—for the price of an admission ticket costing a mere $250—to spend the day listening to, questioning, and mingling with powerful government officials in relaxed forum-type settings in the Washington area. These daylong events were attended by movers and shakers from around the country who were willing to give up $250 and a day's time to get the unvarnished, unfiltered, and unspun truth from some of the nation's top leaders. And they usually got their money's worth, for the sessions were conducted on a strict off-the-record basis, which allowed the speakers the freedom to say things they would not otherwise discuss in a public forum lest their remarks end up in the press.

The speakers for the October 9, 1985, "Evans and Novak Political Forum" held at Washington's Madison Hotel were Senator Robert Dole (R-KS), New York Governor Mario Cuomo, President Reagan's chief of staff Donald Regan, and White House National Security Advisor Robert C. McFarlane. McFarlane was the last to speak, appearing in the afternoon after the others had completed their remarks and departed.

During the question-and-answer session that followed his prepared remarks, McFarlane was asked by former Rep. John LeBoutillier, who had worked with Hendon, McFarlane, and others on the POW issue during the early 1980s, and in 1985 headed a nonprofit POW advocacy group, about the possibility that POWs might still be alive in Southeast Asia. McFarlane stunned LeBoutillier and the fifty or so business executives and political operatives in attendance by replying, "I think there have to be live Americans there. There is quite a lot of evidence given by people who have no ulterior motives and no reason to lie, and they're telling things that they have seen." McFarlane then emphasized that he was expressing "how I really feel about it." According to LeBoutillier, after McFarlane finished answering other questions and departed, the moderators of the forum, columnists Rowland Evans and Robert Novak, remarked to the audience that they had been "shocked" by McFarlane's statements and that the presence of living prisoners of war in Indochina as outlined by the president's national security advisor was "big news."

LeBoutillier, who had seen a great deal of intelligence on live POWs during his service in Congress, agreed with McFarlane's assessment that prisoners were still alive and with the assessment of Evans and Novak that, given McFarlane's position, his remarks about POWs were indeed "big news." Eager to do whatever he could to help bring about the release of the prisoners,

LeBoutillier took a written transcript of an audiotape he had made during the forum to Bill Paul, *The Wall Street Journal* reporter who had written the Garwood and Tighe articles. (LeBoutillier had received permission from Evans to tape-record the entire proceedings. The tape recorder was in full view on the table in front of LeBoutillier.) LeBoutillier's account of what happened next offers enlightening insight into the remarkable world of Washington, DC, damage control.

> Paul agreed that McFarlane's statements were big news and decided to write a story. When he called the NSC for a comment, he was put in contact with Karna Small, the NSC's spokeswoman, who, incidentally, had attended the forum with McFarlane and had been present in the room when he made his statements about POWs. I know this, I saw her there.
>
> When Paul outlined what McFarlane had said and asked Small for a comment, she categorically denied that he had made such statements about POWs. Paul then told her that he was in possession of a written transcript of the remarks, but she replied that that was impossible and had to be a mistake because "Mr. McFarlane made no such statements." She then terminated the conversation.
>
> When Paul called me and told me what Small had said, I took the tape recording to him. He then called Small back and told her he was now in possession of a tape recording made at the forum and that McFarlane could be heard clearly uttering the statements in question. Small then said she would discuss the matter with McFarlane and call back. A short time later she called Paul back and said, "Whoever taped Mr. McFarlane's comments had no right to do so. The entire meeting was off the record. This account is a gross misrepresentation of Mr. McFarlane's views."
>
> Now, I understand a little bit about damage control—I myself often had to resort to it when I was a member of Congress. But I still am at a loss to understand how tape-recorded statements of a man making a statement and then confirming it by declaring "this is how I really feel" can be a "gross misrepresentation" of the man's views. But that's the way the spin doctors do it in Washington. Thank God, though, the *Journal* guys didn't believe them. They published a very accurate account of the event several days later.[46]

The *Journal* published McFarlane's comments on October 15 under the headline "McFarlane Believes Some U.S. POWs Are in Indochina." Follow-up articles quickly appeared in *The Washington Times, USA Today, The Washington Post*, and other newspapers throughout the country.[47] On the 16th, a Vietnam vet living in Kent, Washington, responded to McFarlane's remarks by going on what he said would be a two-month hunger strike designed to call attention to the plight of the POWs.[48] Two days later, Vietnam vets and relatives of MIAs chained themselves to the White House fence in response to McFarlane's remarks and DIA's mishandling of the intelligence and in support of the creation of the Perot Commission.[49]

## A BRIEF ENCOUNTER WITH MAJ. GEN. POWELL

In November, Hendon and a half dozen or so of his colleagues were asked to make a quick trip to Europe to help defuse a minor crisis that had developed among the United States' NATO allies. In preparation for the trip, Hendon and the others went to the Pentagon to meet with Secretary of Defense Caspar Weinberger and his senior military assistant, Maj. Gen. Colin Powell, USA. During the meeting in Weinberger's office, which Hendon's records show was held on November 19, the secretary and Powell briefed the group on the administration's objectives for their trip and offered guidance on how those objectives might best be achieved. A brief discussion followed, and then, as the meeting was coming to an end, Rep. Duncan Hunter (R-CA), the Armed Services Committee member who had been chosen to head the delegation, asked on behalf of all the congressmen present that Weinberger and Powell intervene and see to it that the refugee who had twice seen the American POWs on Ly Nam De Street (and whom DOD had earlier refused to fly in for congressional interviews) be brought to Washington at the earliest possible date so the members could interview him.

Powell, who had been extremely cordial to that point, stiffened at Hunter's request, and flashing what the Vietnamese call "a smile of anger," offered a curt reply, the contents of which Hendon cannot recall. Then, as Hendon attempted to pass to Weinberger a letter he had prepared that confirmed in writing Hunter's request concerning the refugee, Powell, clearly livid at what was taking place, indignantly snatched it away without comment.[50] Armitage, replying later for Weinberger, again refused to fly the refugee in for interviews as the congressmen had requested.[51]

## THE TRUTH ABOUT THE SPECTRE 17 IDS

On November 22, the Oklahoma City *Daily Oklahoman* printed an exposé on the Spectre 17 identifications that would prove even more embarrassing to the administration than *The Wall Street Journal*'s revelations about McFarlane's statements at the Evans and Novak forum. Citing documents received from DOD under the Freedom of Information Act and interviews the newspaper had conducted with various forensic experts, the article declared that remains from the Spectre crash site had been identified only from "small fragments of burnt, fractured and weathered bones"; that the procedure used to make the identifications "is not a means of positive identification"; and that "the families generally should have been told that a positive identification was impossible."

Then, as proof that the identifications of at least three of the crew members could not possibly have been made as CILHI and the White House had claimed, the newspaper published sketches showing the specific pieces of bone (in black) that had been used to "positively identify" three of the crew members, Capt. Thomas T. Hart III, USAF, M.Sgt. Rollie K. Reaid, USAF, and 2nd Lt. George D. MacDonald, USAF.[52]

Embarrassed Pentagon officials declined all requests for comment following the publication of the article, saying the information about the Spectre 17

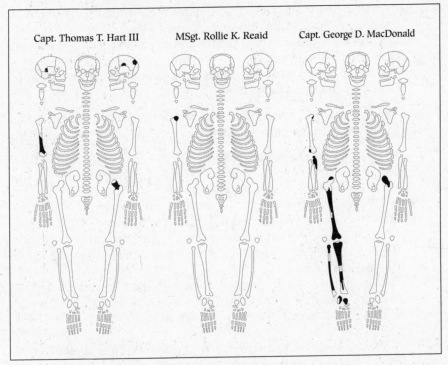

Capt. Thomas T. Hart III        MSgt. Rollie K. Reaid        Capt. George D. MacDonald

Three servicemen "positively identified" from black portions of bone. (DEPARTMENT OF DEFENSE, FROM FILES OF MRS. THOMAS T. HART III)

IDs had been released to the newspaper in violation of DOD policies. That these officials had been extremely concerned about the article's contents quickly became clear, however, when in early December they assembled a three-man team of outside experts and rushed them to CILHI to "review and analyze identification procedures and associated methods of documentation utilized there."[53]

The team, consisting of forensic anthropologists from the University of Maryland and the University of Florida and a forensic odontologist from New York, arrived at CILHI during the second week of December. After "three full days of inspecting the facilities, procedures and personnel involved in identification," team members declared the following in their eight-page report:

- Only two of the cases from Pakse, Laos could be identified by us with confidence.
- Some of the points of comparison were based on presumptive findings in badly fragmented and incomplete cases. These included the determination of sex and race based on knowledge of the occupants of the airplane rather than evidence from the skeleton itself.
- The mention of dental identification in an individual case where no teeth were present may have led to confusion in several cases.
- Most of the Pakse cases would not stand scientific scrutiny.

- We found that positive identification, or even tentative identification, was not possible in a majority of these cases.
- The credibility of the Army's Central Identification Laboratory, Hawaii, has been threatened and swift and decisive corrections are necessary.
- This failure to exercise proper standards of identification [of the Pakse remains] is of a blatant nature.[54]

In a subsequent article describing the Pakse "identifications" and the team's findings, *The Philadelphia Inquirer* would report that:

- After examining the Army's records, the scientists concluded that only deliberate distortions could explain why the Army made so many fundamental mistakes in its identification methods.
- A professor of anthropology at the University of Wyoming . . . [who had examined the evidence] . . . said . . . [that] "in the case of Mr. Fuller, no matter how much benefit of the doubt you give the Army forensic anthropologist, there are some things there that point very strongly at intellectual dishonesty.
- The anthropologists' . . . findings have buttressed broader accusations by POW-MIA organizations that the military is falsifying identifications to account for as many Vietnam-era MIAs as possible and close its books on the war.
- A Defense Department spokesman strongly denied the allegations, declaring that the Reagan administration was seeking "a full and complete accounting" of the 2,441 Americans unaccounted for in Indochina. "I would find any allegations of intentional distortions . . . to be totally absurd," said Lt. Col. Keith Schneider.[55]

In a similar article, *The Washington Times* would later

- quote Dr. Donald Parker, nephew of Spectre 17 crewman Sgt. James R. Fuller, as saying that "I inspected the remains and found them to be a handful of chips. . . . They fit in the palm of your hand. I took them to . . . the local county medical examiner. He determined they could not be identified. I took them to other anthropologists, and they said they could not be identified, even as to race."
- quote Dr. Michael Charney, the outside expert hired by Anne Hart, as saying, "What we're talking about here [in the case of Captain Hart] is a bone from which they claim you can tell race, age, height, weight and handedness. . . . There's no way those bones proved those things, yet CIL said they did."
- report that following its examination of CIL and its procedures, "the team issued a report with an unequivocal conclusion: The Army should consider a review of all recent cases processed by the laboratory, 'since this report may give rise to questions concerning previously closed cases.'"
- quote one of the commission analysts as declaring that "the forensic anthropologists at the CIL have been leaned upon to produce results. One

has the impression that rapid identification is one of the more important focuses for the Army."
- quote a DOD spokeswoman as saying that "the Army has full confidence" in the CIL findings and expressing "concern that experts in the forensic field, unfamiliar with military methods, can indeed review cases and come up with erroneous conclusions."[56]

But that would not be all. In a letter later written to Secretary of the Army John Marsh, one of the three experts who participated in the December 1985 investigation at CILHI would tell Marsh that "the issues of misidentifications, fraudulent identifications, lack of professional ethics and incompetence at CILHI are very serious matters" and that "many of the recent identifications from Pakse . . . are an insult to the Vietnam Veterans, their families and all Americans."[57]

Unfortunately, Marsh and other administration officials would remain unmoved by it all and would let the Pakse "identifications" stand. Nor would Griffiths be moved; she would continue for years to tell her membership and members of Congress and media representatives that "the excavation of the [Pakse] site resulted in the recovery of thirteen Air Force crewmembers missing in that incident" and that the White House announcement that the remains of all thirteen Air Force crew members whose remains were recovered in the joint excavation of the Pakse site "demonstrate the technical expertise of the Central Identification Laboratory."[58]

In the end, most of the Spectre 17 families, eager for closure, would side with Griffiths and the administration and accept the CILHI "IDs." Anne Hart, Sergeant Fuller's nephew Dr. Donald Parker, and the family of 2nd Lt. George MacDonald, however, would all eventually succeed in having the "identifications" of their loved ones overturned, only to be told that DOD's decision to rescind the identifications would not change their legal status, and that, in fact, their loved ones would continue to be carried on the Pentagon's books as "not unaccounted for."[59]

## THE PUBLIC DEBATE OVER LIVE POWs CONTINUES

The public debate over live POWs continued throughout December. On the 5th, the president himself weighed in when he called Gino Cassanova, the Washington State Vietnam vet who had gone on a hunger strike for the POWs the day after hearing what McFarlane had said at the Evans and Novak forum, and asked Cassanova to end his strike. According to *The Washington Post*, Reagan told Cassanova that he shared his concern about missing servicemen but that the many "rumors" about servicemen still alive had proved false when checked, the same thing the president had told Dornan and the freshman Republicans in the Cabinet Room almost a year earlier. The *Post* reported that Cassanova, talking to Reagan over a cellular telephone, agreed to the president's personal request that he come out of his cage and, after almost eight weeks, end his fast.[60]

Also on the 5th, Kissinger, asked about live POWs during an appearance at

Creighton University in Bellevue, Nebraska, declared that it would be "senseless" for the Vietnamese to have kept living American prisoners for the last dozen years. He then asked his questioner, "[W]hy would they do it?" He went on to characterize the situation in Central America as the " 'biggest danger' to U.S. foreign policy interests at this time."[61]

On December 15, CBS's *60 Minutes* aired a segment on the live POW issue. Appearing on behalf of the POWs were Tighe, Hendon, Garwood, and the two Green Berets who had filed suit against the administration; Armitage appeared as spokesman for the administration.

After Tighe, Hendon, Garwood, and the two Green Berets, former POW Maj. Mark Smith, USA, and Sgt. 1st Class Melvin McIntire, USA, made clear to correspondent Ed Bradley that DIA had long ago received convincing evidence that American servicemen remained captive in Indochina, Bradley asked Armitage if the U.S. government believed Americans were still held prisoner. Armitage responded with the stock answer that the administration assumed some were but declared, "We have not yet been able to prove their existence." Bradley pressed Armitage to declare just what type of evidence it would take to bring about some kind of action to get the POWs home. Would it take photographs, names, fingerprints?

Although the Ly Nam De Street sightings by Garwood and the refugee who had passed two polygraphs met the criteria he was about to describe, Armitage told Bradley, "[W]e would like to have a report which is current and specific, regarding the circumstances of the captivity. We would, if we had our way, like a second refugee report [or] something of that nature which basically stated the same set of facts under generally the same set of circumstances. Additionally, we would like to be able to, through one of our national technical means,[62] verify the report." Cutting quickly to Tighe, Bradley asked, "Have you seen reports that match all of those qualifications?" Tighe replied, "Yes, I have," and went on to say that whether the number of POWs remaining alive was "one or two hundred I want us to get them out."

Asked by Bradley how that might be accomplished, Tighe replied,

> I think you have to start [with] the diplomatic route. I think the Vietnamese are very, very interested in full recognition by this government. Primarily because they are economically in such bad straits. So it's a very self serving thing, but I think they are also interested in reconstruction money and the possibility of paying that in the past, and I understand it was part of our treaty with them that we would, has not been fulfilled and I think they'd like to see that fulfilled. Time means nothing to them, though. I think over and over again we have to learn that. They've got plenty of time. They're very patient people.[63]

Digesting the *60 Minutes* segment, Hendon and his friend and colleague Bob Smith, who had watched the broadcast together, concluded that even though General Tighe's strong performance would undoubtedly move a number of congressmen and -women to add their names to the growing list of cosponsors of the Perot Bill,[64] the segment would do little to convince the president that a cover-up was under way in his administration.

Little did Hendon and Smith know that, as a direct result of the program they had just watched, in fewer than three weeks they would be sitting in the Oval Office telling the president just that—that a cover-up *was* under way—and suggesting how he might go around his advisors and finally get the truth about the live POWs.

CHAPTER 25

1986

TRENCH WARFARE

. . .

Hendon and Smith were incredulous (Hendon now for the second time) at what the White House Secret Service agent was telling them. The agent, a Vietnam vet, had seen the *60 Minutes* piece and had been angered by Armitage's statement that the administration was unable to prove the Vietnamese were holding POWs. The agent had shown up unannounced at Hendon's office shortly after New Year's to tell Hendon that while stationed just outside the Oval Office in late January 1981, he had learned otherwise.

After hearing the agent's story, Hendon had called Smith, who was out of town at the time, and asked him to return to Washington right away to hear what the agent was saying firsthand. And so here they were in the first week of January, the agent, Hendon, and the just-off-the-plane Smith, in a bar in northern Virginia, going over—and back over, and then back over again—every detail of what the agent said he had seen and heard.

The following day, Hendon and Smith each called the White House and demanded they be given fifteen minutes with the president. Apparently moved by the urgency in the congressmen's voices, White House aides agreed to their request and set the meeting for the afternoon of January 9.

The day before the scheduled meeting, *The Washington Times* reported that Armitage, Wolfowitz, Childress, and Griffiths had just returned to Bangkok from talks in Hanoi and that Armitage, speaking at a news conference in the Thai capital, had declared that the U.S. government had no proof that American POWs were being held in Vietnam and had denied that a cover-up was under way. Hendon, reading the article in his office, tore it out and wrote in the margin, "Mr. President, if that's negotiating strategy then fine, I accept it, but if not, this is just an absolute lie." He placed the article aside for use the following day.[1]

*January 9, The Oval Office*
## "RESPECTFULLY, MR. PRESIDENT, IS IT TRUE?"

The president, Vice President Bush, National Security Advisor John Poindexter, and congressional liaison Oglesby all greeted Hendon and Smith as they entered the Oval Office. Following the general courtesies attendant with such meetings, Hendon showed Reagan *The Washington Times* article and, after conveying the message he had written in the margin, reached down and rubbed the yellow Oval Office rug and said, "I tell you honestly, Mr. President, your people are lying to you just like this rug is lying here on the floor of the Oval Office." The president chuckled and acknowledged that possibility, then asked how he might get more accurate information. Hendon pleaded with him to recall General Tighe to active duty and direct him to conduct a top-to-bottom review of the intelligence on live prisoners and the job DIA was doing analyzing that intelligence. Tighe, Hendon told Reagan, lived in nearby Virginia and could easily be contacted.

Hendon then apologized for what he was about to say and told the president that earlier in the week an unimpeachable source had informed him and Smith that in late January 1981, the administration had received an offer from the Vietnamese government to trade the American POWs they were holding in return for payment of some $4 billion. (The Secret Service agent had told Hendon and Smith that while stationed in the hallway just outside the Oval Office, Reagan, Bush, Casey, and National Security Advisor Richard Allen had emerged and, pausing in the hallway, had briefly discussed the offer and how the administration should respond to it. The agent said he had distinctly and clearly heard what the four men were discussing.) After briefly referring to the trips he and LeBoutillier had made to Laos for the president back in 1981 or 1982, Hendon asked Reagan, "Respectfully, Mr. President, is it true? Did the Vietnamese offer to trade the prisoners back for $4 billion?"

Hendon recalls that the president paused for a moment and replied softly, either "Well, I don't remember," or "Bill, I don't remember."

Hendon further recalls that after a long, uncomfortable pause, the vice president spoke up, saying that he did remember such an offer involving the figure of around $4 billion, but that to the best of his recollection it was for the return of *remains,* not living prisoners. The vice president then grew agitated and demanded to know who the source of the information was. Hendon and Smith apologized and said they could not name the source, and Bush began directing a stream of unpleasantries at Hendon. Hendon, who heretofore had enjoyed a very warm and cordial relationship with the vice president, was astounded by Bush's aggressiveness and the fury in his voice. The attack ended with Bush angrily telling Hendon that he would talk to former National Security Advisor Richard Allen and others about the reported offer and get back to him and Smith by phone.

A degree of cordiality returned when the president changed the subject and began offering his thoughts on why the Vietnam War had been lost (Congress), the quality of imagery acquired by U.S. spy satellites (extremely high), and several other topics. Then, exhibiting his trademark graciousness, Reagan promised to consider Hendon's and Smith's proposal that he recall General Tighe, apologized for having to adjourn the meeting, warmly thanked Hendon and Smith for coming, assured them that the vice president would be getting back to them shortly, and, along with Bush, escorted the two to the door.

*Monday, January 13*
## GOOD NEWS AND BAD NEWS

Hendon and Smith knew before breakfast the following Monday that they had hit a major nerve. The first indication came when Armitage, appearing on ABC's *Good Morning America* to report on his trip to Hanoi, declared publicly for the first time that "there may indeed be some Americans held against their will [in Indochina]."[2]

Then came the even more stunning statement about live POWs from Wolfowitz, who was appearing at the same time on the *Today* show over on NBC. "We've had over 800 reports of live Americans in Vietnam in the last 10 years," Wolfowitz declared. "We've checked out a lot of them. . . . There are roughly 100 that we believe hold up under this [*sic*] best scrutiny we can put to them."[3]

A response to what had occurred in the Oval Office, Hendon and Smith knew.

Then came the good news/bad news call to Hendon from Bush. The vice president first informed Hendon that he and the president had agreed to contact General Tighe and ask him to head a review panel to look at all the intelligence on live POWs and report his findings to the White House. Bush told Hendon that Tighe would begin work within a matter of several weeks and added he had informed the new Director of DIA, Lt. Gen. Leonard H. Perroots, USAF, about the decision to bring Tighe back in and Perroots had offered his wholehearted support.

Then, moving to the offer, Bush declared that he had talked to Dick Allen and that Allen could not recall the Vietnamese offering to sell back living POWs. Bush demanded again to know the source of the story, and when Hendon again respectfully declined to provide the source's name, Bush exploded, accusing Hendon of "coming down here and insulting the president of the United States" and warning Hendon that because Reagan could not recall any such offer, "if you continue to pursue this matter you will be questioning the personal integrity of the president." Astounded by Bush's threatening tone and the crystal-clear message he had just conveyed, Hendon, facing a tough reelection fight in the fall, pledged not to raise the matter of the offer again, thanked Bush for agreeing to bring Tighe back in, and assured him that he, Smith, and the other activist congressmen stood ready to assist Tighe and the administration in any and every way they could.[4]

On January 16, Perroots, whom Hendon had been working closely with for several months and greatly admired, wrote Tighe and officially invited him to return to DIA to "head a two or three person audit/inspection team to review all of the current [POW] case files and handling of those files."[5] Several weeks later Perroots advised Hendon that Tighe would begin his work in March, and that he had decided in the interim to conduct an investigation of the Special Office of his own, a hard-nosed baseline investigation, as Hendon recalls Perroots describing it. Perroots said he had assigned his top aide, an Air Force bird colonel named Kim Gaines, to conduct the investigation, and assured Hendon that the no-nonsense Gaines would vigorously investigate what was going on in the Special Office and that he and Gaines would let the chips fall where they might.

*February–March*
## "THE DIRECTOR'S PW/MIA TASK FORCE REVIEW OF THE PW/MIA DIVISION"

The Perroots Task Force, made up of the impressive Gaines, an equally impressive no-nonsense Army Ranger lieutenant colonel named Joe Schlatter, and three others, began its work on February 24. The task force members conducted a vigorous three-week-long investigation and then, on March 18, filed their report.

The task force report, officially designated the "Director's PW/MIA Task Force Report" but known as the "Gaines Report," left little doubt that what Tighe and the congressmen and the Vietnam vets and the activist families were saying was true—that the analysts and managers in the Special Office were intent on discrediting intelligence sources rather than analyzing the intelligence, and that as a result, DIA's findings relative to the intelligence on live POWs could not be believed. In a blistering indictment of the POW division, Gaines, Schlatter, and the others cited these among their findings:

- There exists a mindset to debunk . . .
- Within PW/MIA division, it [this mind-set] has evolved over time as an investigative technique, whereby intense effort is initially focused on the veracity of sources with a view toward discrediting them.
- When a case is being worked, . . . it is plainly evident that the emphasis is on the investigative side of the question in most cases, where the focus rests on debunking the source more than it does on analysis of the information itself.
- The existence of this sort of bias . . . can insidiously reduce the objectivity of analysis.
- There tends to be a strong moralistic bias at work which manifests as a preoccupation with everybody's motives and unrealistic expectations with regard to source accuracy.
- In the main, sources who volunteer information have no ulterior motive, especially those already relocated to the U.S. [Some] sources were very young when they observed the event; others were in dire straits as a result of the war; and in many cases, the "sighting" was a fleeting one. Therefore, sources should not be badgered when they come forward to volunteer information they do not recall well, in view of the long time interval involved.
- This is not a newly developed attitude, as review established that Adm Tuttle, a former supervisor, had noted it during his tenure through 1981, but was not able to reverse it before reassignment.
- Unfortunately, the mindset now permeates the division in other investigative matters, and it appeared during the review period that just

about any new idea on the PW/MIA issue is met with a negative response.

- Reinforcing the mindset is the investigative audit trail which has confirmed an inordinate number of originally promising sources to be fabricators.
- The data base is a wasteland. The data base, of course, is the central foundation for the entire DIA PW effort and why a recognized problem of such importance (and management admits to the "recognition") had gone unsolved simply boggles the mind.
- The PW division does not appear to function in the mainstream of the DIA collection system.
- All aspects of the staff element emerged as significantly deficient.
- PW analysts carry no credentials nor are they trained investigators.
- The division is woefully behind the rest of the agency in analyst training.
- All functions are carried out in a haphazard fashion.
- No disciplined, coherent, collection management was being performed.
- Given the existing discrepancies in the functional areas, the task force has no confidence that the current analytical process has adequately addressed all relevant factors or has drawn totally reliable conclusions.[6]

Stunned by what Gaines, Schlatter, and the others had found, and determined to fix the problems that plagued the Special Office, Perroots relieved Special Office chief Oberst of command and replaced him with Gaines.[7] To make sure Gaines would succeed in cleaning up the mess he had inherited, Perroots reassigned the respected Schlatter to serve as chief of the Analysis Branch at the Special Office. When word of these staff changes reached Capitol Hill, Hendon and his colleagues were ecstatic. Finally, they believed, competent, honest people would be calling the shots down in the trenches at the Special Office. And because of that, they further believed the POWs might soon be saved.

*Late May*
## THE TIGHE VERDICT

General Tighe and the five members of his task force—Lester McGee, a retired Army colonel who had served on Tighe's pre-Homecoming task force that had predicted that roughly twice as many POWs would return at Homecoming than were actually released; DIA's highly respected Far East Asia intelligence specialist and member of the National Strategic Warning Staff, John F. McCreary, JD; DIA's top security and counterintelligence expert, Vice Assistant Director of Security and Counterintelligence Arthur G. Klos; Maj. Gen. John S. Murray, USA (Ret.), who had served as chief of U.S. military interests in South Vietnam after Operation Homecoming; and former Navy personnel officer and DIA Management Specialist Roberta Carper Maynard—spent hundreds of hours during April and May reviewing the intelligence on live POWs and interviewing the Special Office analysts.[8]

When the members agreed on their findings and completed their final report, Tighe submitted it for comment to an official review panel he had convened.

Serving on the panel were Lyman Kirkpatrick, the former CIA inspector general; former SAC Commander Gen. Russell Dougherty, USAF (Ret.); former CENT-COM Commander Gen. Robert Kingston, USA (Ret.); and two former Vietnam-era POWs, Lt. Gen. John Peter Flynn, USAF (Ret.), who had commanded U.S. POWs in Hanoi, and the legendary Brig. Gen. Robinson Risner, USAF (Ret.). Perot had been invited to serve on the review panel, but with his close friend Risner already on board and the Perot Bill before Congress at the time, he had chosen not to participate.

After reviewing the Tighe Task Force's final report, titled "The Tighe Task Force Examination of DIA Intelligence Holdings Surrounding Unaccounted for United States Military Personnel in Southeast Asia" but known simply as the "Tighe Report," the review panel notified Tighe that the members had unanimously approved the report and agreed with its conclusions and recommendations.[9]

Tighe submitted the task force report to Perroots on May 27. In the letter of transmittal accompanying the report, Tighe and the other task force members informed Perroots they had found no "cover-up."[10] The remainder of their findings were set forth in the accompanying report. Among them were the following:

- There is evidence, even in our limited sample, that Americans remain alive in Vietnamese custody against their will.
- DIA holds evidence that establishes the probability that live American personnel are still held captive in Laos and Vietnam by the Socialist Republic of Vietnam.
- Vietnam . . . is waging a war of politics using the PW/MIA issue as the leverage for compelling the U.S. to pay a "blood debt"—a term used in [its] directives connected with POWs.
- The Vietnamese are acting out the role of victor with the vanquished supplicating for mercy. It is a centuries old display of oriental superiority played out on the world stage with all the pomp and ceremony that the U.S. and international press can provide. It is, in short, a ritual of victory.
- The refugee community that has provided the bulk of the eyewitness reports strikes us as possibly the finest human intelligence data base in the U.S. post-World War II experience.
- As a source of intelligence information, the refugee community is distinctive. By any measurement the refugees have remarkable powers of observation and memory. Eyewitnesses understand the significance of their observations and the importance of subtle differences in detail, behavior and confinement conditions. . . . In our review we measured their power of observation by the clarity and detail of the accounts. Their memory was also judged against correspondence of the account to real places, persons and events. Despite the passage of time, the accounts contained sufficient details to establish a high degree of plausibility and frequently correlate to known places or events. . . . The sources understand the importance of what they have observed, most often tell consistent stories . . . and leave themselves vulnerable to all sorts of

independent checks of their story. This is singular in itself, and highly probative.

- For the record we note that not all refugees are sincere . . . and [that] all sorts of charlatans, frauds, pirates and bandits have emerged to extort funds or other benefits based on PW/MIA'S information. . . . We consider these . . . groups troublesome but typical of the backwash of warfare. Despite the unsavory sources, the brazenness of the worst makes them easy to spot. . . . [These] unsavory characters and self-serving motives in no way obscure the overall quality of information coming from the refugee community.

- While some sources are inventive, self serving and consequently untrustworthy, others are eyewitnesses, military officers and peasants with no ulterior motives and in enough numbers to make one uneasy about discounting testimony that smacks of an authenticity that could satisfy a grand jury. . . . As a body, their reporting accuracy may exceed that of any comparable human source data base of which this task force is aware.

- Over the years the perceived mission of the PW/MIA center at DIA has changed, officially and unofficially, from analysis of the intelligence flowing into DIA on this issue to "resolving the issue" whereby doubt is cast on the veracity of the intelligence and it is discarded.

- Our investigation reveals that the greatest problem associated with this issue is the lack of professional analysis of the intelligence. . . . There is little evidence that any significant analysis of the intelligence received has been accomplished in recent years.

- Almost without exception the JCRC is requested to recontact the original source to provide additional details. . . . The files clearly show that more often than not the purpose of these subsequent contacts with the source is to challenge the veracity of the source and eventually discredit the substantive information provided.

- [The] task force has been unable to find evidence that the PW/MIA center has a method for following up such information other than to re interview the same source or others who might have known the person. This technique, in the cultural environment of Southeast Asia, has invariably, consistently and predictably resulted in the discrediting of the source. Consequently one tends to doubt every resolution of a case labeled as a fabrication. We find most of these judgments without meaning, and untrustworthy.

- DIA analysts measured the worth of intelligence reports on live POW's still held in Southeast Asia as "resolved," meaning "not to be believed," or "unresolved" meaning we haven't yet proved these intelligence reports false.

- The PW/MIA element simply lacks a concept for working with so-called unresolved cases except to try to routinely brand them as fabrications.

- Among the case files there appears a dominant emphasis on the negative. No accent on the positive. Balance of examination of the evidence is not apparent.

- We found evidence of a presumption of mendacity in every "case" file.

- Our review has uncovered a repeated pattern of mental closure. The files show a tendency by the analyst to make up his mind about the value of a report before his own inquiries are satisfied. Comments by the analysts and notes in the files suggest this practice is heavily influenced by a bias that all refugee reports are suspect unless proven otherwise. . . . A more basic problem is the bias in expectations that refugees are not reliable reporters unless proven to be so. This contradicts the assertion by PW/MIA center personnel that, "we treat all reports as valid unless discounted." We found precisely the opposite approach to be the truth over and over.

- Many at DIA have come to believe that all of the "live sighting" reports are hoaxes.

- The intelligence and legal professions have long ago developed the major criteria for source evaluation. The PW/MIA center evidently developed its own shorthand version, applying technology as a substitute for critical analysis. The use of . . . the polygraph . . . by the center has been indiscriminate, without sensitivity to its limitations. Evidence presented to the task force indicates the use of leading questions in the polygraph, cultural barriers in translation and understanding and no apparent awareness of the frailties of the test.

- Refusal to be polygraphed is not an indication of unreliability. Our Secretary of State has publicly refused a polygraph. The same exculpation entitlement goes to Laotian peasants, ex ARVN soldiers, and Khmer peddlers.

    Even in those cases where the polygraph results give reason to show that this source is not practicing deception, PW/MIA center continues to pursue leads in an attempt to discredit the source.

- One refugee declined to continue helping the PW/MIA center when it persisted in questioning his veracity despite his having passed two polygraph and one hypnosis test.

- The passing or not passing of a polygraph test, either way, is used against belief in the source.

- Despite the cynicism of interrogators and evidence of their hostility actually conveyed to the refugee sources, these people have persisted in coming forward to tell their stories. Most know what they saw, even though PW/MIA analysts concluded the opposite.

- The credibility of PW/MIA center's judgment that a refugee account is a fabrication must be considered low.

- [Reagan/Bush administration] policy about prisoners of war and missing in action is not supported by the behavior of government organizations charged with carrying [out] policy. . . . The issue has not been accorded the highest priority. Indeed national defense must at least compete strongly for the position of preeminence. But the distance between public policy and official practice suggests it is close to the lowest in fact. Dedicated intelligence and other governmental resources are minimal; interagency cooperation is more apparent than real; collection priorities are among the lowest; [and] claims on assets and monies are repeatedly denied in favor of routine agency operations.[11]

In fewer than one hundred pages, Tighe, his task force, and his review panel had demolished the administration's entire POW "effort." And to make matters worse, they had declared that the substantive portions of their report should be made public.

## June
## THE WHITE HOUSE MOVES TO CHANGE THE TIGHE REPORT

On the very day Tighe filed his report, Bud McFarlane and Ollie North were in Tehran, Iran, selling arms to the Iranian government in return for Iran's help in gaining the release of a small group of Americans held hostage by pro-Iranian Hezbollah terrorists in nearby Lebanon. The mission was part of a supersecret ongoing administration effort that, when discovered by the press later in the year, would explode into the Iran-contra affair.[12] And so it is not surprising that when North's suite mate in the Old Executive Office Building, NSC Asian Affairs Director Dick Childress, read the report, he moved quickly to change its findings.

In a two-page memorandum and eleven-page attachment written just after he had finished reading the report, Childress told Perroots:

> I have just finished my first reading of the Tighe report and must say I have never seen a document like it except for a few tracts at POW/MIA rallies. . . . It is a less than clever attempt to play on your need to publicly refute "cover-up," then proceeds to demonstrate cover-up without saying so in those portions of the report he expects to be made public. And the public will compare it with the administration's statements and say "cover-up." . . .
>
> How can they say that the files show a probability of prisoners being held today, then say there is no cover-up? It contradicts our own public statements.[13]

But Childress had only just begun. Expressing fear that the Tighe Report might "destroy the strategy" and "split this country again over Vietnam," and warning that a number of Tighe's findings would be perceived either as proof or evidence of "conspiracy and cover-up," and declaring that evidence that live POWs were being held had not yet been obtained, he directed that the Tighe task force be called back into session and made to change its findings. He then outlined for Perroots the specific findings he wanted changed.

Foremost on Childress's list was the matter of the task force's declarations about living prisoners. Citing the task force's finding that "there is evidence, even in our limited sample, that Americans remain alive in Vietnamese custody against their will," Childress warned Perroots that "this is the categorical statement that the Rambos have been waiting for" and suggested that Perroots demand of Tighe that the statement on live Americans, a finding Childress declared "has the most serious policy implications," "be proven or removed."

Childress went on to suggest that Perroots make a similar demand that Tighe "prove or remove" a number of other findings. Childress then made the incredible claim that "the credibility of the POW/MIA analysis [performed by DIA] is not low, but high" and warned Perroots that "if your troops do not receive an aggressive defense against this nonsense, they could justifiably walk and talk—I would!"[14]

Perroots, in a telephone conversation with Hendon several weeks later, spoke candidly of the order he had received to change the report. "The report states there is evidence of a probability of Americans in captivity," the director explained, "but the policy people have told me this is too hot and have directed me to scrub the report before it is released. They say this is simply not the kind of thing they want out on the street. They say it could be 'dynamite,' and that if it gets out in its current form we could have the families going down Pennsylvania Avenue. They have told me to take a different approach."[15]

Upon being informed by Perroots of the order he had received to change the Tighe Report's findings, an alarmed Hendon alerted a half dozen close friends who served with him on the POW/MIA Task Force. Moving quickly, the members dispatched a letter addressed jointly to the president, House Speaker Thomas P. "Tip" O'Neill Jr., Asian and Pacific Affairs Subcommittee Chairman Solarz, and POW/MIA Task Force Chairman Solomon informing them that they (the seven congressmen) had determined on the basis of "extensive classified briefings we have received and the volume and clarity of the information we have seen . . . [that] American POWs remain captive in communist prisons in Southeast Asia," and asking them to use their influence "to see to it that a bipartisan, independent commission, headed by H. Ross Perot, is created immediately by either Presidential or Congressional action to recommend ways to effect the release of these men."[16]

Perroots, angered by press accounts of the letter and its contents, immediately broke off all contact with Hendon and his colleagues.[17] As a result, it would not be until the U.S. Senate investigated the POW/MIA issue during 1991–1992 and most POW-related documents held by DOD were subsequently declassified that the congressmen would learn for sure how Perroots and those who served under him had reacted to the White House demand that the report's findings be changed.

## PERROOTS AND HIS MEN HEAD SOUTH, NEVER TO RETURN

DOD records declassified in the early 1990s show that Perroots and his men moved on several fronts in the summer of 1986 to comply with the directives outlined in Childress's June 18 NSC memorandum. Their actions included efforts to (1) morph the American POWs cited in the Tighe Report as being alive in Vietnam into deserters; (2) discredit human intelligence reports Tighe and members of his task force had cited as credible, thus undermining the task force's conclusions; and (3) pressure members of both the Tighe task force and the Tighe review panel to repudiate their support of the task force's findings relative to live POWs.

### Efforts to Morph the American POWs Cited as Being Alive in Vietnam into Deserters

Soon after receiving Childress's directive, Perroots sent a copy of the Tighe Report to Rear Adm. Thomas A. Brooks, USN, who at the time was DIA's deputy director for JCS support but who during 1985 had served in Tuttle's old position with direct line authority over the Special Office.[18]

After reading the report from "cover to cover," Brooks advised Perroots in early July that "the wording of the report . . . must be reworked to provide the preciseness required of an analytical document." He told Perroots among other things that:

> I would have no trouble supporting a statement to the effect that there is adequate evidence to indicate that there are still Americans in Viet Nam. But then a distinction must be made between the classic prisoner kept in a cell and individuals, like Garwood, who may have reached an accommodation with the Vietnamese and have an entirely different status. They are not considered prisoners by the Vietnamese (although they probably are not free to leave should they desire to do so) but, in the terms they used to describe French troops released some fifteen years after the termination of the French Indo-China War, they are "ralliers." . . . The study states that the key analytic question should be "whether Americans remain alive in Southeast Asia against their will." I would drop the "against their will" because it requires a judgment, and concentrate on determining whether they are there. . . . In the Summary, the statement is made: "there is evidence, even in our limited sample, that Americans remain alive in Vietnamese custody against their will." Again, the definition problem; what is "custody" and what does "against their will mean"? [sic] Both of these phrases conjure up images of bamboo cages and leg irons, but the most credible reporting from Vietnam portrays situations similar to Garwood's rather than RAMBO situations. . . . In the Conclusions section, the wording becomes even more intemperate where it states, "DIA holds evidence that establishes the probability that live American personnel are still held captive in Laos and Vietnam by the SRV." . . . [In reality,] [t]here is little evidence of Americans being held in a formal prison system.[19]

## Efforts to Discredit Human Intelligence Reports and Undermine the Task Force's Conclusions

Declassified records show that, concurrent with Perroot's and Brooks's efforts to morph the POWs Tighe said were held in Vietnam into "ralliers" and "Garwoods," an effort was undertaken by the managers and analysts at the Special Office to undermine the findings of the Tighe task force by discrediting the refugee sources whose testimony Tighe and members of his task force had cited as credible. The methods employed by the managers and analysts to discredit the testimony of just one of these sources—DIA Source 3562—would prove illustrative of their attitudes toward all the other sources Tighe and his task force had cited in their report.

DIA Source 3562, the reader may recall (www.enormouscrime.com chapter 23), was the third of three sources who reported seeing U.S. POWs being forced by their guards to pull plows in rice fields on the Plain of Jars in northern Laos long after the war had ended.[20] The first two sources, a former Royal Lao second lieutenant and his brother, a former Royal Lao captain, had both testified in 1984 that while undergoing seminar on the Plain of Jars, they had seen on two or three occasions between the years 1976 and 1979 two Caucasian prisoners identified as Americans, and that each time they had seen them, the Americans were being used in place of water buffalo and made to pull plows in the rice fields. Then, in 1985, Source 3562, this sixty-year-old former Royal Lao Special Guerrilla Unit (SGU) major, had testified that while being detained in seminar camp on the Plain of Jars, he had on two separate occasions during 1976 observed ten American pilots plowing the rice paddies in a state-owned rice field as water buffalo would, with two or three pulling the plow instead of the water buffalo and another in back guiding it. At the time of the Tighe investigation, the major had undergone two extensive interviews in Thailand, and both times had told the exact same story. The Tighe Report had cited his testimony as evidence that American POWs were being used as forced labor in farming activities.

Kicking off what appeared to be a clear attempt to undermine Tighe's findings, Lao desk analyst former Lao Gen. Soutchay Vongsavanh contacted the major at his new residence in St. Paul, Minnesota, on August 11 and interviewed him yet a third time about his two 1976 sightings of the ten American pilots. The major repeated the testimony he had twice given in Thailand without change. Soutchay noted in the record the major "maintained that he had seen 10 Americans."[21]

Following this third interview of the major, Soutchay contacted JCRC personnel in Bangkok and directed them to interview refugees who had been held on the PDJ and ask them if they had seen American POWs pulling plows in the rice fields there.[22] They reportedly elicited statements from several refugees who said *they* had not seen American POWs pulling plows on the Plain of Jars and dutifully reported those statements back to Soutchay.

Then, according to a report later authored by the chief of the Special Office and sent to Perroots, Soutchay, armed with the refugees' alleged statements, interviewed the major a fourth time at his home in Minnesota. In his report to Perroots, the chief wrote that Soutchay informed the major that the U.S. government had contacted other refugees who had been detained on the Plain of Jars and that "each . . . emphasized that they never saw nor heard of American POWs."[23] Two other sources, however—the Royal Lao lieutenant and the Royal Lao captain—had also seen American POWs pulling plows under guard on the Plain of Jars around 1976, which Soutchay should have known given his position as the principal Lao Desk Analyst at the Special Office.

No one other than Soutchay and the major know exactly what was said next, but according to the chief's report, upon being told that the other refugees had testified that no POWs had been held on the Plain of Jars after the war, the major allegedly recanted his testimony and "admitted that the claimed sighting was not true, that, in fact, he never observed any American PWs in Laos." (Think for a moment. Would having a Lao general officer with control over your and your family's future telling you that surely you were mistaken about what you saw such a long time ago back in your homeland move you to reconsider? Who among the newly arrived refugees would it *not* move?)

Informing Perroots that on the basis of the major's "admission," the case was now "resolved," the chief praised those involved for their fine work, declaring, "[T]he resolution of this important case represents an outstanding job by the Joint Casualty Resolution Center and [Soutchay]." Then, the chief declared, "[I]t also demonstrates the fragile foundation for some of the analytical conclusions reached by the Tighe Group."[24]

And so it went with every other piece of intelligence cited by Tighe in his report.[25]

### Efforts to Pressure the Tighe Task Force and Review Panel to Repudiate Their Support of the Findings Relative to Live POWs

Tighe and the members of his task force were called in in midsummer to discuss their findings with Perroots. Just as Hendon and Smith had been caught off guard by Bush's outburst in the Oval Office on January 9, Tighe and the members of his task force were similarly surprised by the reception they received from Perroots.

Perroots "absolutely went into a tirade," Tighe later testified. "He said that our report was 'absolutely going to tear this government apart' and demanded we make changes." It was, Tighe said, "a very fiery session."

Tighe later testified how surprised he and the others had been at the time that Perroots was so adamant in his demands. "There was just no ifs, ands or buts about it," Tighe said. "[But] we didn't bow to his mood at first at all, and, in my recall, the next-to-the-last draft of this whole thing [the rewritten report] said the same, exactly the same thing. It wasn't until the very end when he just absolutely demanded we change [the finding about live prisoners] or destroy the whole effort in DIA. And everybody in this place is very loyal to DIA. You've got to understand that, too. . . .

"[So] after we discussed the whole thing, we changed it [from 'probability'] to 'strong possibility.' "[26]

### DAMAGE CONTROL

Unable to extract anything more than this minor concession from Tighe and the members of his task force, Perroots and Childress declared that virtually all of the still-explosive report would remain classified. Perroots then scheduled a news conference and a Capitol Hill briefing to reveal the unclassified portions— but informed Tighe that he would not be allowed to attend either event.[27]

Tighe, an officer and a gentleman but no fool, countered by telling his side of the story to *The New York Times* before Perroots had time to convene his news conference and Capitol Hill briefing. The *Times* account, written by the paper's highly respected foreign affairs and national security reporter Rick Berke, appeared on September 30 under an unambiguous headline.

The same day the article by Berke appeared, Perroots countered with the

# P.O.W.'s Alive in Vietnam, Report Concludes

By RICHARD L. BERKE
Special to The New York Times

WASHINGTON, Sept. 29 — A Pentagon panel, after a five-month review of intelligence files, has concluded that American prisoners of war are still alive in Southeast Asia.

The head of the group, Lieut. Gen. Eugene F. Tighe, Jr., a former director of the Defense Intelligence Agency, said in an interview today that "a large volume of evidence points" to the likelihood that Americans are being held by the Vietnamese Government.

He said he doubted that the evidence was strong enough to give the United States added leverage to win the release of any prisoners. He suggested Vietnam might accept war reparations in return for the Americans.

The group's report, to be released at a briefing Tuesday at the Pentagon, found that there was no cover-up of evidence that there are still prisoners, according to General Tighe.

Last March, the current director of the Defense Intelligence Agency, Lieut. Gen. Leonard H. Perroots, told a House subcommittee on Asian and Pacific affairs that he had appointed General Tighe, as the request of Congress, "to come in for as long as necessary to get updated on follow-up actions" by the Government on missing servicemen. General Tighe said his task force

could not say how many missing Americans were alive. Government officials have estimated that the number could be at least 100.

General Tighe said the best evidence came from many reports by refugees who said they had seen Americans.

"There were as many differences as you could imagine," he said of the refugee reports. "They ran the gamut from first-hand sightings to hearsay. But when you have that large volume of evidence that points in those directions, why that's what you conclude. Lyman The review panel included Lyman Kirkpatrick, former inspector general of the Central Intelligence Agency; Gen. Russell Dougherty of the Air

Force, who is a former head of the Strategic Air Command; Gen. Bob Kingston of the Army, who is a former commander of the United States Central Command; Brig. Gen. Robbie Risner of the Air Force, who was a prisoner of war in Vietnam, and Lieut. Gen. John Peter Flynn of the Air Force, who was a leader of prisoners of war.

The actual search of intelligence files was conducted by Maj. Gen. John S. Murray of the Army, former chief of United States military interests in Vietnam; Col. Lester E. McGee Jr. of the Army, former intelligence specialist; John Francis McCreary of the national strategic warning staff, and Roberta Carper Maynard, a management specialist of the Defense Intelligence Agency.

---

# Report Says Americans May Be in Indochina

By RICHARD HALLORAN
Special to The New York Times

WASHINGTON, Sept. 30 — The Director of the Defense Intelligence Agency said today that there was a "strong possibility" that some Americans remain alive in Indochina 14 years after the Vietnam-American participation in the Vietnam war ended.

But in a news conference at the Pentagon, the Director, Lieut. Gen. Leonard H. Perroots, said that "I have no credible evidence, no strong compelling evidence" to sustain the possibility.

The general declined to speculate on whether the Americans were being

held prisoner or had remained in Indochina of their own will.

General Perroots appeared to be less positive than his assessment of the possibilities than Lieut. Gen. Eugene F. Tighe Jr. in an interview on Monday night.

General Tighe recently led a task force that reviewed all information pertaining to the issue of the missing Americans. He said last night that "a large volume of evidence" pointed to the conclusion that some Americans were still alive in Indochina.

The Pentagon said that 2,387 soldiers, sailors, marines and airmen, plus 42 civilians and 1 person from the

Coast Guard remain unaccounted for after the war in Vietnam.

General Perroots, an Air Force officer, said he was being cautious in his assessment "to avoid giving false hope to those who have placed their trust in us."

The issue of possible prisoners of war or people listed as missing in action still being in Indochina is among the most emotional questions remaining from the war in Vietnam.

Not only are some families still without definite word but some veterans organizations have asserted that the Government has not done all it could to determine the fate of those listed as

missing.

The group led by General Tighe, a former Director of the D.I.A., reported that "there was no evidence of a cover-up" by anyone in the Government, General Perroots said.

## 91 'Live Sightings'

He said the possibility that live Americans remained in Indochina was based on 91 "live sightings," mostly reported by Vietnamese refugees, over the last 14 years, 12 of which occurred from 1982 through 1985.

General Tighe also noted, General Perroots said, "that significant information remains in the hands of the Indochinese Governments." The United States does not have diplomatic relations with the Government of Vietnam. Among the recommendations from General Tighe's group were that more

analysts be added, that all files be automated, and that intelligence from all agencies be better integrated.

Basically, General Perroots said his statements today did little to advance American knowledge about possible prisoners or others living in Indochina. "I'm not sure that it has moved," he said.

But, he added, "actions to investigate live-sighting reports as well as other information will continue to receive necessary priority and resources based on the assumption that some Americans are still held captive."

---

*The New York Times* article, September 30, 1986. (COPYRIGHT 1986 *THE NEW YORK TIMES*. REPRINTED BY PERMISSION)
*The New York Times* article, October 1, 1986. (COPYRIGHT 1986 *THE NEW YORK TIMES*. REPRINTED BY PERMISSION)

administration's version at his Pentagon news conference and later on the Hill. Perroots's performance yielded an article in the *Times* the next day that offered a perspective quite different from Tighe's.

Perroots's statement that he possessed "no credible evidence" to sustain the possibility that POWs remained alive in captivity, and his inference that any Americans who might be alive in Indochina likely have remained there of their own free will, proved too much for Hendon and the other activist congressmen. Angered by what Perroots had said and done, Hendon called William Casey, the director of Central Intelligence, and invited him to come to the Hill for an emergency meeting on POWs. The meeting was scheduled for the afternoon of October 7.

*October 7, 1986*
## THE DCI'S CANDID ASSESSMENT

The meeting with Director Casey, held in Hendon's office and preceded by the customary security sweep for listening devices, was attended by Casey, a man Hendon did not know but assumed was Casey's deputy, Robert Gates, two other individuals from the CIA, Hendon, Smith, and perhaps a half dozen of the other activist congressmen. An affidavit later filed by Hendon, based on meeting notes he recorded on the morning following the meeting, indicates that the following transpired:

> On the 7th of October, at approximately 5:15 p.m., the Director of Central Intelligence, William Casey, along with a man I believe to be his Deputy, Robert Gates, and two CIA personnel, came to my Congressional office at 115 Cannon House Office Building in Washington, D.C. to discuss the issue of American prisoners of war in Southeast Asia. This meeting lasted approximately one hour. No contemporaneous notes were taken and to my knowledge no recordings were made of the conversations that took place. However, the next morning, on the 8th of October, 1986, I made notes concerning what was said during the course of the meeting. My notes reflect the following:
>
> After a general discussion of the issue of American prisoners remaining in Southeast Asia, I requested that Director Casey become as personally involved for the POWs as he had been in seeking the release of the hostages in Beirut. In reply, Director Casey complained about the lack of specificity of information regarding Americans still held in Southeast Asia and complained that LTG Eugene Tighe, USAF (ret), former Director of the Defense Intelligence Agency, along with me and several others who spoke out on the POW issue, always talked in generalities rather than specifics. What he needed to gain the release of the prisoners, Casey said, was specific information.
>
> He said,
>
> "If you'll give me specific information, I'll move, I'll send in Navy seal teams, the 82nd Airborne if necessary. But we don't have that kind of specific information."
>
> I then said,

"But Bill, at Rach Gia [Vietnam] we have nine reports of American servicemen being held captive in that one city. Two of those reports give the same name, rank and service information of an American prisoner, and three of the sources report they have touched and talked with that American by virtue of being in the very same cell with him. A half dozen refugees report seeing POWs being taken toward or into the prison, and a defecting guard from the same prison reports the presence of American prisoners in that prison. Some of these nine different reports were received as recently as the early 1980's. What in the world," I asked Casey, "does it take?"

Then Director Casey said to me,

"There you go again with your goddamn generalities. That's old stuff—it's of no use from an operational (military rescue) standpoint."

I pressed Casey,

"Just what does it take? How specific does the information need to be before the U.S. government will act, either militarily or diplomatically?"

Director Casey said,

"Two people seeing them."

And I asked,

"What kind of people? Boat people? Because if it's boat people, we have many instances where two or more Asian refugees have simultaneously seen the very same prisoners of war in captivity, with such reports occurring well into the 1980's."

Director Casey responded by saying,

"No, it takes two of <u>my</u> men." He then added, "but the problem is, we can't get our men into Vietnam." He continued, "Because the prisoners are being moved, we can't get timely information on their exact location." And he stated that this was the identical problem we faced in trying to get our hostages out of Lebanon.

There then followed a general discussion of the different standards of proof that are necessary for a military rescue versus a diplomatic initiative to free the POWs.

I pointed out to Director Casey that, given the fact that he did not consider our current intelligence on POWs specific enough to enable their rescue, surely a different standard of proof applied to diplomatic initiatives.

"Certainly," I said, "by any measure the evidence we currently hold is sufficient to launch an all out diplomatic effort to gain release of the prisoners."

Director Casey stated that he was not in the diplomatic side of things, but rather,

"I am in operations."

He went on to say,

"Look, the nation knows they (the POWs) are there, everybody knows they're there. You guys have written the President (advising him they are there), you're always talking about it, Gene Tighe is always talking about it, but there's no groundswell of support for getting the men out." He continued, "Certainly you are not suggesting that we pay for them, surely you're not saying we should do something like that with no public support." He concluded by saying, "look, we [screwed] up in 1973, we [screw] up all the time, and my job is to make sure that we don't [screw] up again. What do you want, another hostage crisis?"[28]

Hendon, ever mindful of the assistance Casey had provided during the period of the Lao Initiative in 1981 and 1982, revered the plainspoken, no-nonsense DCI in the same way and with almost as much gusto as he revered Reagan. So did all the others in attendance. But all, too, were deeply disturbed by what they had just heard. Frustrated and angry, they decided to go all out to force the Perot Bill, long bottled up in Solarz's subcommittee, to an immediate vote.

## ROSS PEROT, LONGTIME FRIEND OF THE INDOCHINA POWs

Ross Perot had played a key roll in wartime efforts to ensure that Americans held captive in Indochina received the benefits mandated for all POWs by the Geneva Convention. Perot had traveled to Laos to personally implore the Pathet Lao to treat the American prisoners they held humanely. Additionally, as outlined in a memorandum written to President Richard Nixon by the deputy secretary of defense several months after the war,

> In December 1969, Mr. Perot sponsored a flight to Paris for over 150 family members to enable them to personally protest to the North Vietnamese delegation their failure to comply with the Geneva Convention. He also flew around the world in a widely publicized attempt to deliver Christmas packages to our men held captive in Hanoi. In April 1970, Mr. Perot sponsored a flight for newsmen to South Vietnam to emphasize our adherence to the Geneva Convention regarding captured enemy personnel. Perhaps the most noteworthy and effective initiative by Mr. Perot resulted in the placement in the Nation's Capitol of displays portraying the rigors of captivity experienced by our men held in prison cells in North Vietnam and bamboo cages in South Vietnam.[29]

Just after Operation Homecoming, Perot had thrown a huge welcome home gala for the returning POWs and afterward had kept in close touch with many of them. Highly respected by the returnees and the families, and by government officials at all levels in Washington as well, Perot had soon become the de facto spokesman for all who had not returned at war's end.

As the years had passed and the boat people and land refugees had poured out of Indochina with stories of American servicemen still held captive, Perot, like Casey, had become convinced that American servicemen remained in Communist hands. Unlike the DCI, however, Perot believed the United States should forswear the military option and concentrate solely on negotiations to gain the prisoners' release. And given America's commitment under the Paris accords to rebuild war-torn Indochina and the references the Vietnamese and Lao frequently made to that commitment, Perot privately believed that as a last resort Uncle Sam might have to pay to get the men home.

And that, of course, would turn out to be the main reason the hard-liners in the administration had so vigorously opposed the legislation Hendon and the others had introduced.

The hard-liners' antipathy toward Perot was said to have had its origin in an interview the plainspoken Texan had granted *The Detroit Free Press* soon after HCR 129 had been introduced. The resulting article, published on July 14, 1985, and widely circulated among POW/MIA family members and veterans' groups and on the Hill, quoted Perot as saying that the time might be right to "cut a deal and pay" for the men. He was further quoted as saying that the Vietnamese and Lao are "patiently holding all the cards, [and] the thing to do is to find out what they want and make a deal." Paying for the men, Perot said, "may be the price of losing the war."[30]

Though Perot had earlier served as a member of President Reagan's Foreign Intelligence Advisory Board, administration hard-liners had seized upon his remarks in the *Free Press* as evidence he was now unfit to serve in any official capacity. Working with Griffiths, they had moved first to bottle up the Perot Bill in subcommittee and then had actively lobbied members of Congress not to sign on as cosponsors.

But then had come the appointment of Tighe and his task force, and with it an invitation to Perot from Tighe that he serve on the task force review panel. As previously noted, Perot had chosen not to participate, but things had changed in a big way when he had learned in early summer that the White House was demanding that Tighe change his findings. Approaching his fellow Texan the vice president, Perot had reportedly expressed strong concern about the demanded changes to the Tighe findings and had asked that he be granted belated access to the intelligence files so he could study them carefully and determine once and for all where the intelligence pointed, what it all meant. Bush, reportedly with the agreement of the president, had granted Perot's request, and for several months during the summer and early fall Perot had been visiting the Pentagon regularly to study the intelligence on live POWs case by case, document by document, line by line.

Though Perot has never publicly discussed the specific intelligence reports he examined, it is reasonable to assume that he focused at some point on the more current intelligence. A quick review of the declassified case files shows that, thanks to the fact that the refugee flow had continued at high levels during 1986,[31] there was a significant amount of reasonably fresh intelligence to be examined:

- In <u>mid-January 1986</u>, DIA had received two JCRC reports from separate and independent refugee sources telling of the detention of American POWs at the very same prison camp in Saravan Province, in the southeastern Lao panhandle. (Saravan Province lies just north of the southernmost province of Attopeu.) Both sources had described the prison as being located at the base of Phou Ngoua (pronounced "Poo [mountain] New-uh" [buffalo], i.e., Buffalo Mountain), near the village of Ban Kadon in extreme southern Saravan Province.

  The first of the two mid-January 1986 reports quoted a forty-seven-year-old former Royal Lao sergeant as saying he had first learned about the American prisoners in March 1976 while he and his brother were searching for medicinal herbs in the Ban Kadon area.[32] He explained that when he and his brother had asked villagers if they might find a certain type of herb in the nearby Phou Ngoua Valley, the villagers warned them that the valley was a restricted area and no one was allowed to go there. The sergeant reported that when he asked what was so important in the valley and why no one was allowed to go there, the villagers explained that there was a small prison camp located on the southeast slope of Phou Ngoua and that "27 former American pilots who were shot down in the war" were being detained there. (See map page 307, point 1.)

The sergeant reported that he and his brother ignored the villagers' warning and immediately set out for Phou Ngoua to see for themselves whether or not the villagers' story about the prison and the twenty-seven American pilots was true. He said they hiked partway up the mountain to a point where they could see into the valley below, and, looking down, saw the prison camp at the precise location the villagers had described. He said that because the camp was located approximately three kilometers from their vantage point, he and his brother were unable to discern whether or not American prisoners were being held inside.

The sergeant reported that after observing the prison, he and his brother headed back down the mountain and left the area. He said he never returned to the Ban Kadon/Phou Ngoua area but that his brother did return in 1983 and later told him that during this visit he had been told that the American prisoners were still being detained in the camp.[33] (See map page 307, point 2.)

The second of the mid-January 1986 reports quoted a sixty-two-year-old former Royal Lao colonel as saying he had personally observed more than twenty Caucasian American prisoners at a prison camp located at the base of Phou Ngoua in early August 1982, and a smaller number of American prisoners when he returned to the prison in September. (See map page 307, points 3 and 4.) The colonel explained that he had gone to the Phou Ngoua camp in August along with members of a food delivery team and had observed the Americans for a brief period while the food was being transferred. He said that he observed three Americans carrying firewood into the front gate of the camp and approximately twenty others farther inside. He said all of the American prisoners were Caucasian and recalled that the three entering the front gate were dressed in black clothing.

The colonel said that during his September visit, he observed two American prisoners carrying firewood into the camp, one of whom was tall and slender and had red hair. He said he also saw several other American prisoners inside the camp preparing the midday meal. Some were preparing food while others built a fire. The colonel said he saw yet another American making his way down to a nearby stream to get water. He recalled that some of the Americans were wearing straw hats to shield them from the sun.[34]

DIA analysts knew that in addition to corroborating one another, the two mid-January 1986 JCRC reports provided corroboration for an earlier report DIA had received that also told of U.S. POWs being detained at Phou Ngoua. This report, received by DIA in August 1984, had quoted a Lao refugee as reporting that as of March 1983, twenty American POWs were being held in a prison camp located at the base of Phou Ngoua.[35]

Combining the information contained in all three reports, it is clear that at the time Perot conducted his study, DIA had received intelligence indicating American POWs were confined at the Phou Ngoua (Buffalo Mountain) Prison near Ban Kadon, in southern Saravan Province Laòs, in March 1976, August 1982, September 1982, March 1983, and on an undetermined date sometime during 1983.

- On January 24, 1986, DIA had received a JCRC report that quoted a forty-six-year-old former Royal Lao Air Force second lieutenant as saying that over a four-day period between December 26 and 30, 1985, he and a friend had observed four American prisoners who were being detained at a Vietnamese military camp located just east of the village of Ban Don, near the Vietnamese border in eastern Savannakhet Province, Laos. (See map page 307, point 5.) The lieutenant said the Americans worked on the camp's four jeeps during the day and retired each night to an underground room adjacent to the area where the jeeps were parked. He said the first American was tall and thin and had burn scars on his chest; the second was tall, heavyset, and almost bald, and his right arm was withered and could not be used; the third was tall with black shoulder-length hair and full beard down to the chest; and the fourth was of average height and had long, dark brown hair and an abnormally thin left leg that caused him to walk with a limp. All four, he said, wore leg irons.[36] When the information about the four American prisoners reached DIA on January 24, fewer than thirty days had passed since they had last been seen by the lieutenant.

- On January 29, 1986, DIA had received a JCRC report that quoted a Vietnamese refugee as saying that in 1981, three high-ranking Communist officials stationed in Saigon had shown him 218 black-and-white pictures of individual American POWs whom the officials said had been transferred to the South during the Chinese invasion. According to the refugee, each American had a name board hung around his neck on which was recorded a name and a number. The refugee said he later decided that if he could determine where the Americans were being held, it might be possible to rescue them and "get them on board a ship for Thailand, as refugees do." He said he and other members of the resistance were later able to determine that the Americans were being held in a POW camp in Phu Khanh Province. He said the camp was located in a rubber tree area at a point approximately seventy kilometers west of Nha Trang.[37] (See map page 307, point 6.) He said he and a number of resistance fighters armed with small arms launched an attack on the camp in August 1983 in an effort to free the Americans but were driven back. He added that prior to the assault he had observed several of the American prisoners exercising inside the camp.[38]

- On February 3, 1986, DIA had received a JCRC report that quoted a thirty-eight-year-old former Royal Lao sergeant as saying that while in Kham Keut, Laos, on a mission with Lao resistance forces in December 1985, a

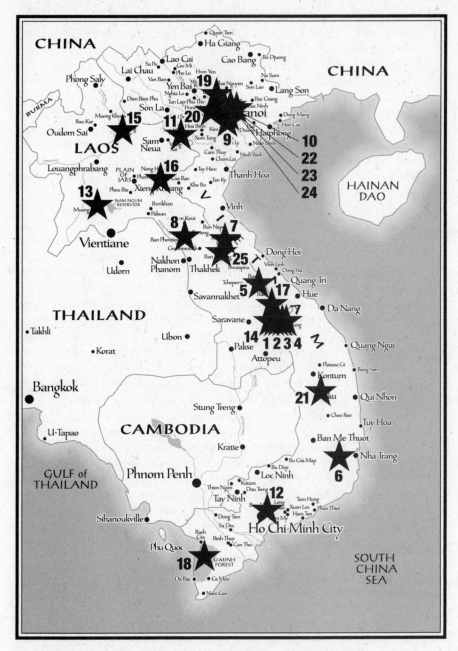

Selected reports of U.S. POWs received during 1986. (HENDON/ANDERER)

trusted old friend who lives there told him that earlier in December, he and about fifty other people had been sent by local officials to deliver food to a cave located in Vietnam at a point along Route 12 not far from the Lao border. The sergeant said the friend told him that he saw three American prisoners outside the cave, which he said was located in a valley near Route 12 just on the other side of the Vietnamese border.[39] (See map page 307, point 7.) The sergeant stated that he believed what his friend told him about seeing the three American prisoners at the cave because the two had been good friends during the war and he knew the man would not lie to him.[40] Lao National Route 12, DIA analysts knew, runs from the city of Thakhek, also called Khammouan, located on the Mekong River opposite Nakhon Phanom, Thailand, across the central panhandle to the Mu Gia Pass, where it enters Vietnam and becomes Vietnam National Route 15. When the information about the three American prisoners reached DIA on February 3, fewer than sixty days had passed since the sergeant's close friend had reportedly seen them outside the cave.

• On February 4, 1986, DIA had received a second report from this same Royal Lao sergeant, this one telling of a group of twenty-six American POWs the sergeant had personally observed while on another, earlier mission inside Laos. This report quoted the sergeant as saying that while leading his resistance unit on a reconnaissance patrol southwest of Kham Keut in April 1981, he and his men talked to a truck driver who told them he had recently transported twenty-six American prisoners to a mine located at a nearby cave called Tham Seua (Tiger Cave). The driver reported that the American prisoners had been moved to the mine because they possessed "technology experience" and could maintain the mine's rock-crushing machinery.

The Lao sergeant said that he became curious and asked the truck driver to take him to the mine so he could see the prisoners for himself. He said the driver agreed and subsequently took him and one member of his unit to the mine site, which was located near the village of Ban Phontiou. (See map page 307, point 8.) The sergeant said that once there he saw and counted twenty-six American prisoners dressed in villager-type clothing sitting and standing inside a fenced compound built around the mouth of the cave. He noticed that the Americans were being guarded by Pathet Lao soldiers. He said that one of the Americans seemed to be older than the rest, about fifty-five years of age. This prisoner, he recalled, had white hair and walked with a limp.

The sergeant said that soon after seeing the American prisoners at the mine, he and his men crossed back into Thailand and returned to their base. He said that when he informed his commander what he and the other member of his unit had seen, the commander ordered him and his men to return to Laos, attack the mine, and rescue the American prisoners. The sergeant said that in June he and his men crossed back into Laos to carry out their orders, but when they arrived at a village near the mine site they were told that all of the Americans had recently been moved to another location. He said that no one he and his men talked to was sure where the Americans had been taken.

The sergeant's February 4 report cited the specific names and map coordinates of a number of villages in the area and the map coordinates of the cave itself, and was accompanied by a memory sketch he drew showing the exact location of the cave. When Senate intelligence investigators later map-tracked the information contained in the report and in the memory sketch, they were convinced beyond any doubt that the sergeant possessed intimate knowledge of the area he had described and unquestionably had traveled through the area as he had testified.[41]

- On <u>March 19, 1986</u>, DIA had received a report that quoted a CIA source as saying an SRV Ministry of Interior colonel had told him that sometime between 1982 and 1985, some fifty to seventy American POWs were detained south of Hanoi at an MOI-administered prison designated "Camp 52." Subsequent interviews with the CIA source established that the prison in question was one located at Binh Da Village that had formerly been used as a detention facility for high-ranking South Vietnamese reeducation inmates, and that the Americans had been moved there from a detention facility located on Ly Nam De Street in Hanoi.[42] (See map page 307, points 9 and 10.) Both places of detention cited by the CIA source—the B-52 Prison at Binh Da Village and a detention facility on Ly Nam De Street in Hanoi—were well-known to DIA analysts at the time the CIA report was received.[43]

- On <u>March 26, 1986</u>, DIA had received a JCRC report that quoted a former Lao dental assistant as saying that he had learned from a Lao medical doctor that during the late 1970s, the king of Laos and two Caucasian American prisoners had been detained together in a cave near Sop Hao, in Sam Neua Province, Laos. (See map page 307, point 11.) The dental assistant reported that the doctor told him he had been assigned by the PL government to care for the three prisoners, and that he had done so for approximately two years before he himself had been arrested and imprisoned in late 1979. The doctor reportedly said the king was in poor health, but the health of the two Americans was good. The doctor also reportedly said that in spite of their good health, the two Americans suffered far more than did the Royal Lao prisoners confined to seminar camps in the area.[44]

- On <u>May 7, 1986</u>, DIA had received a JCRC report that quoted a South Vietnamese refugee who had formerly worked as a hunting guide on a sprawling PAVN military reservation just north of Bien Hoa as saying that he and two associates had almost been killed by PAVN troops during the summer of 1983 when they had stumbled into a small camp on the reservation where approximately fifty American prisoners of war were being detained. (See map page 307, point 12.)

The guide said the Americans, all of whom were under PAVN guard, were dressed in green PAVN clothing. He said that a Communist official with him at the time of the sighting later said that the PAVN troops in charge of the American prisoners fed them well to keep their weight up. This was done, the official reportedly said, because the Americans were a "gold mine," and because the government was "as wise as a grandmother" and knew well that "the death of one prisoner would be the same as losing thousands of dollars."

The guide described the camp as being near the Ma Da woods and said it had been camouflaged with bamboo trees to prevent it from being seen from the air. He drew a highly detailed memory sketch showing towns and villages in the area, and, within the military reservation itself, natural and man-made landmarks, roads, bridges, streams, PAVN and local force troop deployments, the exact location of the camp where he and his associates came upon and observed the Américan prisoners, the nearby Ma Da woods, etc.[45]

When Senate intelligence investigators later compared the guide's memory sketch to maps of the area just north of Bien Hoa, they found the sketch to be highly accurate. When they map-tracked the guide's travels on the military reservation, they determined beyond question that he had traveled through the remote area of the tightly guarded base just as he had described. The investigators found still more corroboration of the guide's account in an intelligence report DIA had previously received that had also chronicled the presence of approximately fifty American prisoners in the Bien Hoa area. This report, received by DIA on April 16, 1985, had quoted a South Vietnamese refugee as saying that a friend had told him that in October 1982, while undergoing reeducation in the Bien Hoa area, he had personally observed "about fifty Americans at the Suoi Mau reeducation camp in Bien Hoa," all of whom were wearing "very old" green military uniforms.[46] At the time they had received this report of the fifty American prisoners at Suoi Mau, DIA analysts had already learned a great deal about the Suoi Mau reeducation camp complex, which they knew was composed of at least three separate detention facilities located along QL 1 (National Route 1) in the Bien Hoa area.[47]

On May 29, 1986, DIA had received from the National Security Agency the transcript of an intercepted Pathet Lao radio transmission in which the PL were discussing the mid-May 1986 transfer of an unspecified number of "prisoners of war" between two points in Laos. The report quoted the PL as stating the POWs were transferred from the area around Muong Fuong to Nong Tha.

The NSA report cited the location of Muong Fuong as "1843N 10208E [UTM map coordinates:] SF 9772," just west of the Nam Ngum Reservoir in far northern Vientiane Province.[48] (See map page 307, point 13.) The report did not specify the location of Nong Tha, but Senate intelligence investigators would later determine that the village of Nong Tha, also known as Ban Daknong, is located at map coordinates 1514N 10708E, some nine miles southeast of Ban Kadon, in extreme southern Saravan Province.[49] (See map page 307, point 14.)

The author of the NSA report noted that though the PL had not specifically stated that the prisoners being moved were Americans, "the Lao do not normally refer to captured Thai soldiers or Lao expatriates as prisoners of war."[50] This, plus the fact that DIA had previously received reports telling of American POWs being detained in the vicinity of the Nam Ngum Reservoir during 1981, mid-1981, June 1984, October 1984, and October 1985,[51] and in the Ban Kadon area in extreme southern Saravan Province in March 1976, August 1982, September 1982, March 1983, and on an undetermined date sometime during 1983 (see mid-January 1986 reports above), makes it reasonable to assume that the POWs being transferred from the Muong Fuong area to Nong Tha in mid-May 1986 were, in fact, Americans.

When the NSA intercept reached DIA on May 29, approximately two weeks had elapsed since the POWs had reportedly been transferred from Muong Fuong to Nong Tha.

- On <u>July 29, 1986</u>, DIA had received a CIA report that quoted a Lao woman as saying she had seen three Caucasian prisoners near Muang Ngoy in northern Laos in mid-April 1986. The CIA report quoted the woman as telling relatives and friends that she had observed the three Caucasians and their PAVN guards as she was traveling along the main road east of Muang Ngoy at a point some eight kilometers from town.[52] (See map page 307, point 15.) She reportedly said that when she first saw the three Caucasians, she thought they were Soviet advisors but became unsure when she noticed that two of the three were wearing leg irons. She reportedly said that local residents later told her the three Caucasians she had seen were American prisoners who had been captured prior to 1972.[53] When the information about the three American prisoners reached DIA on July 29, just over ninety days had elapsed since the woman had reportedly seen them just east of Muang Ngoy.

- On <u>September 8, 1986</u>, DIA had received a JCRC report that quoted a former Vang Pao militiaman as saying he had been held in a cave prison complex south of Nong Het, Laos, from 1976 until October 1985, and that during the entire period of his incarceration, five American POWs had also been held in the complex. The militiaman said the prison complex was located a three-days' walk south of Nong Het in a remote area near the Vietnam border not served by roads. He drew a map of the area showing Nong Het and the nearby prison that closely matched U.S. military maps of the region.[54] (See map page 307, point 16.)

    The militiaman said the complex consisted of three caves located at the base of a sheer karst formation. He said the caves faced east and that the morning sun provided the occupants with the day's only illumination. He said a total of approximately one hundred prisoners were detained in the three caves, and that five of them were Caucasian Americans. He said the Americans were housed in "the second of the three caves."

    The militiaman said that all prisoners detained at the facility—Asian and American alike—were required to participate in work details outside the caves every day. He said these details generally involved either working in the camp's large garden plot, located about one kilometer east of the caves, or cutting wood in the surrounding forests. He said that as a result of the camp's requirement that all prisoners participate in these daily work details, he had been able to observe the American prisoners every day over a period of eight years. He added, however, that he had never had the opportunity to communicate with them because he and the other Asian prisoners were never allowed in the immediate area where the Americans were working.

    The militiaman described two of the American prisoners as tall and the other three as noticeably shorter. He said all were in average health and that all had skin browned from working outside every day. He said all had closely cropped brown hair but added that the hair on the oldest of the five, whom he estimated to be about forty-five to fifty years old, was beginning to gray.

He estimated the ages of the other four Americans to be between thirty-five and forty. He said the Americans always wore green prison uniforms with long sleeves and long pants and, like the Asian prisoners, sandals made of cut-up rubber tires.

The report concluded with the militiaman's statement "that he would be glad to do anything he could if it might provide the Americans an opportunity to be freed since he felt sorry for them" and his offer "to go back to obtain evidence—photographic, signature or otherwise—of the Americans' presence at the cave-prison." When the information about the militiaman's repeated sightings of five American prisoners at the cave-prison complex south of Nong Het reached DIA on September 8, approximately eleven months had passed since he had last seen the Americans confined there, two days since he had made his offer to U.S. officials in Thailand to return to the complex and attempt to obtain evidence that they were still there.[55]

• On <u>September 20, 1986</u>, DIA had received a report from CIA describing the reported June 1986 transfer of a group of 226 American prisoners from an unspecified location in Vietnam to a prison camp in Songhon District, Savannakhet Province, Laos, and the reported sighting of some of those American prisoners at the camp soon after their arrival.[56] (See map page 307, point 17.) The brief report stated that a member of the PL guard unit assigned to the camp had told his brother about the newly arrived American prisoners and that the brother had come to the camp and had personally observed an undetermined number of these Americans being detained inside the heavily guarded facility.[57] When the CIA report was received at DIA on September 20, approximately ninety days had elapsed since the transfer of the 226 American prisoners from Vietnam to the prison camp in Songhon District, Savannakhet Province, Laos, had reportedly taken place. Less time, of course, had elapsed since the reported sighting of some of those prisoners inside the camp.

• On <u>October 8, 1986</u>, DIA had received a JCRC report describing the reported sighting of three American prisoners and the reported presence of 180 others in the upper U-Minh Forest in extreme southern Vietnam. (See map page 307, point 18.) The report quoted a South Vietnamese teacher as saying that a woman who lived in the upper U-Minh had told him in late 1984 or early 1985 that she had recently encountered three Americans cutting wood in a forest clearing near her home and that during a conversation with the three they had identified themselves as Americans and had told her there were 180 other Americans in the area. She reportedly said that during their conversation she asked them, "Why are you still here?" and the Americans had replied in Vietnamese, "The Americans won't come back for us. We will depend on Uncle Ho's rice to live." The woman also reportedly said she heard from other people in the upper U-Minh that cultivated fields appeared from time to time in the area and she surmised these fields might be the fields the 180 Americans were using to support themselves.[58]

All the while Perot was studying the intelligence, the activist congressmen, the activist Vietnam vets, and the activist families were hard at work signing up cosponsors for the Perot Bill. When the list reached 265 members in early October, Solarz was forced to schedule hearings. Solarz advised the members of his subcommittee that Tighe, Perot, Griffiths, and a senior representative from DIA would testify and then an up-or-down vote on the legislation would be held.

## October 15
## THE VOTE ON THE PEROT BILL

Tighe led off the October 15 hearings by testifying that he was even more convinced than he had been in 1981—when he had first testified before the subcommittee that POWs remained alive—that American POWs remained captive in Indochina. "After the passage of five years and review of an almost entirely new, different and convincing set of reports which I recently reviewed," Tighe declared, "my opinion—my conviction on this issue has not changed, but is reinforced—stronger now, by far, than in 1981."[59]

Tighe went on to suggest that the Vietnamese were seeking both reparations and diplomatic recognition in return for the prisoners. "You see evidence in the data base that they consider the economic value of prisoners of war," Tighe told the subcommittee. "A pilot was worth so much to them in terms of reward. Another type of individual captured was worth so much and so forth. . . . In my view, the Vietnamese feel strongly that they should get reparations from the United States and feel somehow deprived of that."[60] On the related matter of diplomatic relations, Tighe stated, "I spent 4 years in the South Pacific during World War II. I couldn't conceive that we would ever have diplomatic relations with Japan, and I drive a new Toyota. I would suggest that the inevitability of at least de facto recognition of the Hanoi government would hasten our ability to resolve this issue, and it is my recommendation that we stop trying to avoid this and try to move it forward to the point where it could be a centerpiece in our resolution of the issue."[61]

Perot followed Tighe to the witness table. He began by assuring the subcommittee that "every member of this [Tighe] commission will come in here and under oath say what General Tighe said, only most will say it in much stronger and more colorful language, because General Tighe tends to understatement. So you are not looking at a one man minority position." Perot then went on to say that he had originally been asked to be a member of the Tighe review panel but his "business schedule" had prevented him from participating. He continued by saying that later, when the commission had finished its work, he had been asked by President Reagan and Vice President Bush to conduct an individual study of the matter. "Both the Vice President and the President wanted me to get to the bottom of this, come to them and tell them what I have found," Perot said, adding that he was "midflight in that study now."[62]

Perot said that one of the two major problems he had uncovered was the fact that, as one senior official had admitted to him, "We set the screen so tight that nothing can get through."[63] The other major problem was the administration's unwillingness to negotiate for the release of the men. "I have had any number of senior people in our government say, 'we will never bend, negotiate,'" Perot said, "and I say, 'then there is only one thing to do—declare them live casualties of the war and write them off.' " He continued:

> These people are trained in their military background to gather information to a sufficient level to rescue someone. That requires many times the order of magnitude of knowledge over, "Is there anyone there?" . . . We have people trying to find enough information so that we can mount a rescue. Believe me, gentlemen, we cannot rescue these people with military force. There is no way to do it, and I can spend as much time as you want on that. . . .
>
>   How would you like to be in charge of 25 or 30 simultaneous rescues in a place where we have no military presence. Because if you don't get them all at once, they are going to move them, kill them. . . . We are not psychologically equipped to do anything but win a war [but] we didn't win this war. We want to relieve Bataan and just take our people out. We can't do that, so we have with the best of intentions avoided facing the real issue.[64]

Following Perot's testimony, Solarz, employing strategy worked out in advance with Childress, Griffiths, Gilman, and Solomon, moved in for the kill. Questioning in very reasonable terms the wisdom of creating a commission to *negotiate* for the release of the prisoners, Solarz told Tighe and Perot that "if your analysis is accurate that there are men being held there against their will and that it is impossible for us to rescue them and that the only way to get them out is through a process of negotiation, it is not clear to me what useful purpose the establishment of a commission would serve. A commission cannot conduct negotiations. Only the President of the United States, or his designees, can conduct negotiations. If there is a solution to the problem, it seems to me it lies not in establishing a commission . . . but in having the President embark on these negotiations." Continuing, Solarz said, "[T]he answer lies not in conducting additional investigations . . . but in inducing the President to muster the will to engage in negotiations. That, in my judgment, would not require a commission. All it requires is the President of the United States, who has the responsibility for our foreign policy, to do it."[65]

Hendon and his colleagues all knew that no one could question what had just been said. But how clever of Solarz first to concede the presence of live POWs and then use the administration's inaction on the issue as the primary reason not to *pass* the Perot Bill but to *defeat* it!

Following testimony in opposition to the resolution by DIA's Brig. Gen. James Shufelt, USA, who chaired the POW/MIA Interagency Committee (IAC), and POW/MIA Interagency Group (IAG) principal member and League executive director Griffiths—and the adoption of two minor amendments—Solarz called for a voice vote. When those in favor of the resolution appeared to prevail, he called for a recorded vote and, producing sufficient Democratic proxies, defeated the resolution on a four–four tie vote.[66]

The activist Vietnam vets and the activist POW/MIA family members in attendance, many of whom had been working the Hill for weeks lining up cosponsors, were enraged and vowed vengeance. Perot, more sanguine, thanked the congressmen who had voted in support of the commission and privately assured them, the vets, and the distraught family members that he would press on with his independent study. Childress, for his part, returned to the White House to e-mail the results of the vote to his boss, National Security Advisor Poindexter. First telling Poindexter that "Ann Griffiths made all the right policy points as usual," Childress then described how Solarz, after giving "the most eloquent defense yet of the President's commitment" and persuading "one of his colleagues [to] walk and lining up proxies for others, . . . secured a tie vote and killed the commission." Childress went on to say that had it not been for Solarz, "We would have had a commission voted out that would . . . certainly advocate normalization or reparations publicly to gain Vietnamese cooperation."[67]

## ANOTHER HOSTAGE RELEASED IN LEBANON • A CLOSE ELECTION • IRAN-CONTRA EXPLODES IN THE PRESS

On November 2, hostage David Jacobson, former administrator of the American University Hospital in Beirut, was released after spending seventeen grueling months in captivity in Lebanon.[68] Two days later, *The Washington Post* reported that upon his arrival at a U.S. base in Wiesbaden, Germany, Jacobson had made an impassioned plea that the administration do whatever was necessary to gain freedom for the remaining hostages. "Those guys are in hell. We've got to get them home," the *Post* quoted Jacobson as saying in a front-page story.

For the president, Casey, Poindexter, McFarlane, North, and the others, Jacobson's release had been good news, indeed. But on page A15 of the *Post* that same morning was some very bad news as well. The ominous headline "Beirut Magazine Says McFarlane Secretly Visited Tehran" was the first public hint stateside that the administration's top secret arms-for-hostages operation might be in trouble.

In the midterm elections held that same day—November 4—the Democrats regained control of the Senate for the first time since Ronald Reagan had swept them from power in 1980. Over on the House side, the Republicans lost only a handful of seats; the new House, a *Post* headline declared, would be "a Near Carbon Copy" of the old. Hendon was one of the House GOP casualties, losing his bid for reelection 50.7% to 49.3%.[69] A postelection analysis in his district's leading newspaper would declare that his opponent's victory "was forged around his charge that Hendon was misleading Western North Carolinians with assurances that a proposed nuclear waste repository in the mountains was 'dead.' "[70] (Back in mid-January, just as Hendon's reelection campaign was getting under way, the administration had announced that the Department of Energy was studying a plan to build the nation's eastern nuclear waste repository under a portion of the most populous county in Hendon's congressional district. The announcement and the ensuing public outcry had rocked the campaign and many believed forced Hendon into a defensive posture from which he never recovered.)

The day after Election Day, a second hint the administration's arms-for-hostages operation was in trouble appeared in an article on the front page of the *Post* that suggested McFarlane's secret visit to Tehran had been related to the American hostages held in Lebanon.[71] On the 6th, the *Post* reported in yet another front-page story the stunning news that "the release of three American hostages in Lebanon over the last 14 months followed a series of shipments of military cargo to Iran after secret discussions between top White House envoys and representatives of the Tehran regime."[72]

And with that, the horse was out of the barn.

Smelling blood, House and Senate Democratic leaders on the 9th called for hearings to probe the administration's reported arms deal with Iran, decrying it as an attempt to circumvent the will of the Congress.[73] Then, one syndicated columnist after another weighed in. "Ronald Reagan . . . shook hands with the Devil," the *Post*'s Mary McGrory declared on the 11th, "and made tapioca of his own credibility, his Middle East policy and relations with the European allies he has so often lectured on the folly of giving in to terrorist blackmail."[74] "The administration has responded to disclosures of its extraordinary, and on the face, duplicitous, hypocritical and self-destructive trading with Iran of arms for hostages . . . [with] open defiance," Haynes Johnson declared in the *Post* on the 12th. "Not since the Nixon days," he wrote, "has the Washington political climate been so poisoned by an air of partisan confrontation."[75] "A Whiff of Watergate?" Daniel Schoor asked on the *Post*'s opinion page that same day—right under Charles Krauthammer's piece titled, "Somebody Should Resign," and just above an Evans and Novak column about the Reagan NSC titled, "Like 'a Shadow CIA.'"[76]

Soon, the president found that not only was his judgment being questioned, but his integrity as well. On the 14th, the *Post* reported on Reagan's address to the nation the previous evening in which he had denied the U.S. had "paid 'ransom' to Iran for the American hostages held in Lebanon"—and then, in an adjoining article—reported that Reagan himself had "ordered secret arms shipments to Iran last spring after being told that it was the only way to get Tehran's help in freeing five U.S. hostages then held in Lebanon by pro-Iranian terrorists." Reagan, the popular "softhearted hard-liner"—the heretofore much admired "Teflon president" to whom very little criticism seemed to stick—was for the first time in his presidency in deep, deep trouble.[77]

Damaging revelations continued one after another for ten days. Then, on the 24th, the *Post* published a sobering front-page news analysis by their highly respected writer Robert Kaiser. Under the headline "Iran Operation's Fallout Humbles White House," Kaiser declared that in the period of just a few days, "President Reagan's inner circle appears to have lost the deference of the American political establishment." "With stunning speed," Kaiser wrote, "the most popular—and most resilient—president of modern times has been humbled by a sequence of events unlike any in his presidency: the revelation of a profoundly unpopular secret policy, a presidential speech to the nation and a news conference on its heels that—according to polls—made matters worse, followed by an extraordinary display of backstabbing among his aides that has left Reagan by himself in the eye of the storm." After declaring that "[p]olitical Washington is rarely so unanimous as it was this weekend in its perception of Reagan's difficulties," Kaiser reported that "[h]ardly a voice could be heard speaking up for him or praising his handling of the last two week's events."

The following day, the 25th, all hell broke loose when Attorney General

Edwin Meese III announced at a White House press briefing that a portion of the profits from the sales of arms to Iran had been diverted to the contras, this during a period when Congress had cut off U.S. military aid to the rebels and had prohibited the administration from helping them in any way. The headline in the *Post* on the 26th was terrible for the president and his men: "Iran Arms Profits Were Diverted to Contras; Poindexter Resigns, NSC Aide North Is Fired." The one that appeared the following day, Thanksgiving Day, was even worse: "Justice Dept. Launches Criminal Probe of Iran Arms Fund Transfer to Contras."

It was, Perot told Hendon in a telephone conversation shortly after Thanksgiving, "a bad time to be a hostage."

## IN THE MIDST OF THE MAELSTROM, THE INDOCHINA POWs ARE NOT FORGOTTEN

Notwithstanding the Iran-contra revelations and the fact that it was, indeed, a very, *very* bad time to be an American hostage, interest in the Indochina POWs and the administration's failure to do anything substantive to recover them remained high throughout November and December.

In an unprecedented swipe at Reagan, America's leading Roman Catholic prelate—and longtime Reagan friend and admirer—New York's conservative Cardinal John Joseph O'Connor, had called on the president just before Veterans Day to mark the holiday by clearing up questions that had arisen about his handling of the POW/MIA issue and launching "a new national commitment to finding and freeing the hundreds of U.S. military men believed to be alive in Southeast Asia."

In an article appearing in the *New York Post* on November 10 under the headline, "O'Connor Prods Prez on MIAs in Asia," the popular O'Connor, who, as a Navy chaplain, had landed with the Marines in the early days of the Vietnam War, earned the Legion of Merit with Combat "V" for service in I Corps, and had later gone on to serve as chief of chaplains for the Navy with the rank of rear admiral,[78] had declared his hope that Reagan would use Veterans Day "to remind the entire country and the world of his continuing commitment to set them [the POWs] free." Quoting O'Connor as saying that Vietnam vets are "still in anguish over the fact that we still have several hundred [missing in action] in Laos and Vietnam," the *Post* had gone on to underline the respected cardinal's obvious displeasure with the administration's handling of the issue and with the mixed messages about live prisoners coming out of Washington. Saying O'Connor felt the "conflicting Pentagon statements about MIAs and PWs do not help their [the prisoners'] cause," the *Post* quoted O'Connor as saying, "I would hope the President can dissipate the ambiguity and make clear his own convictions." The *Post* added that O'Connor was heartened by recent negotiations that had led to the release of American hostages in Lebanon and had voiced hope that similar secret negotiations might be undertaken with the Vietnamese and Lao. "We have clearly learned . . . that the government uses a variety of methods to bring this about," O'Connor was quoted as saying. "I can only hope the President has his own means of bringing about [the release of the POWs and MIAs in Southeast Asia]."[79]

The president, who by Veterans Day had just begun taking fire for the arms-for-hostages deal, had not responded publicly to Cardinal O'Connor's plea and instead had passed up Veterans Day ceremonies in Washington and headed for California to devise a strategy to deal with the unfolding Iran-contra crisis. The activist Vietnam vets and the activist POW/MIA families, meanwhile, had gathered at the Vietnam Veterans Memorial in Washington to plot strategy of another sort. And over on K Street at American Legion Headquarters, legion officials, angry over the changes to the Tighe Report and the administration's strong opposition to the Perot Bill, had decided to demand that the White House send a high-level representative to the legion's upcoming annual Washington conference in February to explain the administration's actions and state what, if anything, was being done to get the live POWs home.

Perot, for his part, stuck to his word and went back to work studying the POW intelligence. Among the reports received at DIA since he had temporarily suspended his work to prepare for the October hearings were the following:

- On October 14, 1986, the day before the vote on the Perot Bill, DIA had received a report quoting a Vietnam refugee as saying that a former ARVN officer who had been held in the Vinh Quang Reeducation Camp near Phu Tho City northwest of Hanoi had told him that he had observed several American POWs in an underground bunker complex near the camp during 1980 or 1981, and that the officer had subsequently learned that a total of about twenty American prisoners were being detained there. (See map page 307, point 19.) According to the refugee, the former officer explained that he had come upon the bunker containing the American prisoners while chasing cattle that had broken away from the herd he had been assigned to tend. The officer reportedly said that when he saw them from a distance of several meters, the Americans, four or five in number and all Caucasian, were sunning themselves inside a secured, fenced compound built around the front of the bunker. The officer reportedly said the Americans were "tall and fair and were wearing 'VC uniforms.'" He also reportedly said he also saw the forms of other prisoners inside the darkened bunker.[80]

- On October 28, 1986, DIA had received a JCRC report that quoted a refugee who had recently escaped from prison in Vietnam as saying that from 1976 to 1986 he had periodically observed a large number of American POWs who were being detained at a prison west of Son Tay. The refugee explained that he had been arrested for espionage in North Vietnam in 1954 and had been detained at six different prisons in the North over a thirty-two-year period before escaping from a facility in Thanh Hoa Province in May 1986 and fleeing Vietnam.[81]

  The refugee said he had seen the Americans during the ten years he had been confined to the K-2 prison west of Son Tay. He said he saw them when he delivered vegetables to their prison, Son Tay K-3, which he said was located just west of K-2 and just south of Bat Bat Prison at a point near the base of Mt. Voi. (See map page 307, point 20.) He noted that K-3, like Bat

Bat, was under the control of the Ministry of National Defense and not the Ministry of Interior (Bo Noi Vu), which controlled K-2, where he was confined.[82] (See map page 320.)

The refugee explained that he had been assigned to pick vegetables and to deliver them twice daily by oxcart to K-3. He said that on almost every trip he had been met at the front gate by a handicapped American prisoner who helped him unload the vegetables and then took them into the prison. The refugee described the American as tall and thin, in his fifties, with a slightly dark complexion, short reddish-brown hair, and brown eyes. He had a pronounced right-legged limp and his right arm was permanently bent inward at the elbow. The American was always dressed in a solid gray prison uniform with a long-sleeved collarless jacket that had "TCT 07" printed on the back, and long pants. He also wore rubber tire sandals and a *non la,* the Vietnamese conical hat.

The refugee explained that except for times when he or the American was sick, they saw each other twice a day for almost ten years. He said he and the American did not speak at first, but some time later they began talking in hurried whispers when the guards were not too close. The refugee explained that their first conversations were simple greetings, but later the American, speaking in Vietnamese he said he had learned in prison, began asking about things "on the outside. Like the Chinese invasion." The refugee recalled that he had asked the American in 1980 how long he had been a prisoner, and that he had replied "over 10 years." The American later said his name was "UY-STON"[83] and that his arm and leg had been injured when he had parachuted out of his plane and landed in trees and then struck the ground. According to the refugee, "UY-STON" further said that because of his injuries he did not work with the other American prisoners held at the K-3 prison but instead was a cook. He then reportedly told the refugee that the other American prisoners worked repairing airplanes at a nearby air base.

The refugee reported that in 1980 the amount of vegetables he was required to pick and deliver to K-3 increased from twenty-five to seventy kilograms twice daily, and that at that time he began to notice more American prisoners in and around the camp. He saw these Americans primarily when they were taken in groups of approximately twenty to twenty-five to a nearby stream to bathe. He said there were no blacks, only Caucasians, and that though they appeared very thin, all seemed to be in good health. The refugee said that he asked one of the guards, whose name was Dinh, about the increased number of Americans at K-3, and that Dinh replied only, "They owe a blood debt to the people. They must stay behind to help."

The refugee said that by 1984, he and "UY-STON," whom he described as intelligent and having a gentle, soft-spoken demeanor, began to speak more often. He said it was then that "UY-STON" told him, "If you should ever be released, tell the USG there are 123 of us still here." The refugee said that from that day forward, each time they met, "UY-STON" would remind him of this by saying, "Remember, won't you?" and he would always reply, "I won't forget."

The refugee reported that he continued seeing "UY-STON" and the other

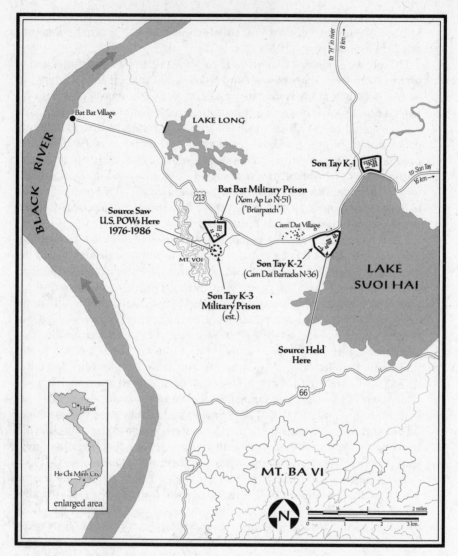

Reported locations of Son Tay K-2, Bat Bat, and Son Tay K-3. (HENDON/ANDERER)

American POWs at Son Tay K-3 until May 1, 1986, when he was transferred to a new camp in Thanh Hoa Province. He said he escaped from a work detail at the new camp three weeks later and ultimately made his way to Malaysia where, in October, he approached U.S. officials with his story.

The refugee expressed confidence to JCRC officials that as of the date of their meeting in Malaysia the Americans were still at the Son Tay K-3 camp. At the conclusion of the interview, he vigorously protested the harsh treatment he had received from U.S. officials during the interview process and signaled an end to his cooperation by declaring, "I have now completely fulfilled my responsibilities toward 'UY-STON.' "[84]

When the information about "UY-STON" and his fellow POWs reached DIA on October 28, less than six months had passed since the refugee had last seen them at Son Tay K-3.

- On December 19, 1986, DIA had received a JCRC report that quoted a Khmer refugee as saying he had personally observed two American prisoners in 1981 as they were being escorted out of a prison compound located on the south side of Route 19 in the vicinity of what U.S officials immediately recognized was Camp Holloway, the former U.S. base located just east of Pleiku in the Central Highlands.[85] (See map page 307, point 21.) The refugee, who said he was working as a tobacco vendor at the time of the sighting, explained that he had been riding in the back of a truck with other vendors and some PAVN soldiers when the truck driver took a twenty-minute rest stop at a point just outside the main gate at the facility. He said it was during this rest stop that the two American prisoners, both of whom were Caucasian, came out of the prison camp compound under the escort of several security personnel wearing yellow uniforms.

  The vendor told U.S. officials that he and his fellow travelers watched the prisoners and the security personnel come up onto the highway, turn left (west), and begin walking down the highway toward Pleiku. The vendor said that as the group walked past the truck, one and perhaps more of the PAVN soldiers riding in the truck with him said the two Caucasians were American prisoners.

  The vendor described the two Americans as being over thirty and wearing dark blue short-sleeved shirts with round Oriental-type collars and white vertical stripes on the back and dark blue trousers. He said that a round metal disk with red numbers on it was fastened to the breast of each man's shirt but added he could not recall the numbers on either disk. He said that as he and the others watched, the two Americans and their security escorts headed on down the road toward Pleiku and he never saw or heard about them again.[86]

- Also on December 19, 1986, DIA had received a JCRC report that quoted former North Vietnamese Public Security Service (PSS) counterespionage officer as saying he had seen an American POW at a Ministry of Interior hospital in Hanoi in September 1981, and another, different American POW at the same hospital in April 1985.[87] (See map page 307, points 22 and 23.)

  The officer told U.S. officials in Hong Kong that he was undergoing treatment at the hospital for malaria at the time the first sighting occurred. He explained that he had just exited his room on the fourth floor when he noticed a guard standing in the hallway outside a nearby room. He said he became curious and walked over to see who the guard was guarding. Peering into the room, he saw a Caucasian man wearing a brown and white striped pajama-type uniform sitting on the bed. The officer said the man was about five-seven and stocky and had hairy arms and a hairy chest, light brown hair, and blue eyes. The officer recalled that the uniform the man was wearing had alternating vertical brown and white stripes on both the shirt and long pants. The officer said that soon after he saw the Caucasian, one of the hospital doctors explained that the man was an American prisoner who had been brought to the hospital from a prison camp for treatment of malaria. The officer said the doctor did not mention the name or location of the camp.

The officer went on to say that after being admitted to the same hospital in April 1985 for an adenoids operation, he saw a guard standing in the hallway outside the same room as before, and that when he went over to the doorway and looked in, he saw another, different American prisoner sitting on the same bed. This American was similar in appearance and garb to the first but had a larger head.

The officer reported that in addition to the two American prisoners he had personally observed at the hospital, a PAVN lieutenant colonel who was a distant relative had told him in 1985 that a number of American prisoners were being detained at the time inside the Ministry of Defense Citadel compound in downtown Hanoi.[88] (See map page 307, point 24.)

• Finally, also on December 19, 1986, DIA had received a report from CIA stating that certain individuals in Khammouan Province, Laos, were hiding an American MIA and that, as of November 19, 1986, PL authorities were conducting searches for the American in and around villages near Napang ([UTM] map coordinates WE 775 300), some twenty to twenty-five miles south of the Mu Gia Pass. According to the CIA, one of those villages was located at WE6513, the other at WE6612.[89] (See map page 307, point 25.)

When the CIA report was received at DIA on December 19, the information about the American MIA was exactly thirty days old.

With the receipt of the three reports on the 19th, the tally of individual, seemingly credible accounts of American POWs held after the war that had been received by DIA during 1986 rose to twenty-five, twenty-three of which had told of servicemen being detained during the 1980s. (In order of receipt during 1986, these reports had told of Americans held prisoner in 1976, 1983, 1982, 1982, 1985, 1983, 1985, 1981, 1982–1985, 1982–1985, late 1970s, 1983, 1986, 1986, 1986, 1976–1985, 1986, 1985, 1980–1981, 1976–1986, 1981, 1981, 1985, 1985, and 1986.)

In total, about one account every other week for the entire year.

But with the cover-up firmly in place and, as Perot had noted, "the screen set so tight nothing could get through," nothing did get through—and not one of the twenty-five aforementioned accounts about live POWs received during 1986 was believed.

## PEROT CONCLUDES HIS STUDY AND PREPARES HIS RECOMMENDATIONS

The president, having been warned by Republican leaders in late November that he "must move quickly to repair his tarnished credibility or risk long-term damage to his administration and his party,"[90] had responded by replacing National Security Advisor John Poindexter with longtime Washington insider Frank Carlucci, and, at Carlucci's request, had appointed Lt. Gen. Colin Powell, USA, to be Carlucci's deputy. Both men were on board by mid-December.[91]

Just before Christmas, as Perot was wrapping up his study and putting the final touches on his recommendations for the president and vice president, it was reported in the press that under the new Carlucci/Powell regime, Oliver North's old office—the NSC's now-infamous Office of Politico-Military Affairs— would be abolished.[92] News of the move quickly lifted the spirits of the activist Vietnam vets and the activist family members, who believed that Childress, North's suite mate, might find himself swept out in the housecleaning, and that somehow Perot might move into the vacuum and get things back on track. But that hope evaporated when Griffiths passed the word that rather than fire Childress—who had been instrumental in the selection and entombment of the "Unknown" Soldier in 1984, who had been party to the "identification" of the Spectre 17 remains in 1985, who had ordered the Tighe Report findings changed, and who had engineered the defeat of the Perot Bill earlier in 1986— Carlucci and Powell had chosen to embrace him and leave him in day-to-day control of the NSC's POW/MIA "efforts."

Perot, surveying the chaos that had ensued in the wake of the Iran-contra revelations—and knowing it was "a bad time to be a hostage," knowing what had happened to the Tighe Report, knowing what DIA was doing to the intelligence on live prisoners, seeing that his patron, the vice president, was showing less and less interest in the live POW issue, and seeing Carlucci's and Powell's embrace of Childress—had to have known that what he was about to propose to the president and the vice president would not go down easy.[93]

## CHAPTER 26

### 1987

## PEROT TO HANOI • A BOMBSHELL FROM GENERAL VESSEY • NO EVIDENCE?

. . .

On January 9, 1987, DIA received a report from CIA stating that the American serviceman reportedly being hidden from Lao authorities during November and December in the area just south of the Mu Gia Pass had been discovered by Lao People's Army troops and taken into custody. According to the CIA report, the American, a Spectre gunship pilot named Stephenson, who had reportedly been captured in the Sepone area during the war, had been apprehended by LPA troops who had raided the village of Napang on [date redacted] December. According to the report, the villager who had been harboring Stephenson, a man named [name redacted], had also been apprehended. The report stated that shortly after being taken into custody, both Stephenson and the villager had been taken to an undisclosed location in nearby Boulapha District.[1]

In February, aware of the growing revolt at the American Legion, the White House dispatched three speakers to the legion's annual Washington conference. The speakers were the administration's ambassador to the United Nations, retired army lieutenant general and former Deputy CIA Director Vernon "Dick" Walters, Childress, and Griffiths.

According to an account of his speech published in *Stars and Stripes*, Walters told the legionnaires that no American POWs were alive in Vietnam and that sources who claimed to have seen live American prisoners had submitted to polygraph examinations and had failed the tests. Walters also "noted that it would be detrimental for the Vietnamese government to surface a live American twelve years after the Paris Accords brought an end to American involvement in Southeast Asia."

According to the *Stars and Stripes* account, Childress later took to the podium and, after requesting that television photographers turn off their cameras, "decried individuals and groups who have accused the U.S. government of coverups, circulated claims about sightings of live POW/MIAs, and spread false reports that have come out of Thailand and Laos." The paper reported that Griffiths then spoke on "current developments"—but several in attendance would report that she had spent almost her entire allotted time praising Childress and the other members of the administration's POW/MIA team for the fine work they were doing on behalf of her brother and all the other MIAs, and stressing how strongly the League of Families supported the Reagan administration's dedicated search for the POWs and MIAs.[2] As was almost always the case after a Childress/Griffiths tag team presentation, most in the audience came to believe that the issue was one of KIAs and not MIAs, and as a result, talk of revolt cooled.

In early March, five activist family members and one of the leaders of the activist Vietnam vets, distressed at how quickly and effectively Childress and Griffiths had handled the legionnaires—and convinced that no progress could ever be made on the live POW issue as long as Griffiths remained in power at the League—took over the League's Washington office by force, barricaded themselves inside, and vowed to remain until Armitage, Wolfowitz, Childress, and Griffiths were replaced. The standoff ended quickly, however, when DC police stormed the office, arrested the six, and took them away to jail.[3] Griffiths, in reporting the attempted takeover to her membership some days later, ridiculed the effort and the call for her to step down, telling the families that her position on the IAG "provides [me] the vehicle for access to highly sensitive information" and "guarantees that the families have the most current, objective and factual information available."[4]

Perot, meanwhile, was hard at work trying to get the president and vice president to adopt the one major recommendation that had come out of his study of the POW issue, a recommendation he had earlier conveyed to Bush but upon which Bush had not yet acted. If he and the president wanted to get the POWs back, Perot had told Bush, they should appoint a presidential emissary on POWs, give him broad powers, and send him to Indochina at once with orders to negotiate for as long as was necessary to gain release of the prisoners.

Perot would later state that he had felt strongly that the appointee had to be an "ongoing direct representative of the President of the United States to resolve this issue, as opposed to these one-time things that start and stop and haven't produced results." He would explain that

> We always wade in on a three-day soiree, complete with television crews, and then come home and declare it over. That's the history of the investigatory process. If we just really hunkered down and stayed on the ground and stayed there and worked with them and negotiated with them, and the presidential emissary has the broad authority he needs to get it done, and if we have as an objective to get whoever's alive back, . . . then that's the environment where you get it done. . . .
>
> But you can't ping pong it; you have to go and stay.[5]

The appointment of a presidential envoy, then, with broad authority and the ability to remain on station in Indochina until he got the job done, Perot had told the vice president, was a surefire way to get the POWs home. (Implicit in Perot's recommendation, of course, was the fact that he believed himself totally qualified for the position. Though he never requested to be appointed, no one doubted at the time that he would have willingly served had he been asked.)

Perot still had not heard back from Bush when, on March 19, the Vietnamese ["suddenly"] invited him to come to Hanoi at once "to exchange points of view and discuss issues of our mutual concerns."[6]

When Perot advised the White House of the invitation and sought the president's and vice president's approval for the trip, Powell, the Deputy National Security Advisor, vigorously objected. Later explaining that Perot had "made it clear that his interest had to do with finding live Americans, not just accounting for dead Americans, and . . . that . . . he believed there were live Americans . . . and that was what he was interested in, bringing home the live ones," Powell indicated that he had strongly opposed the trip primarily out of fear that Perot might give away the store in an attempt to get the POWs back. Perot, Powell explained, was "more willing to offer things to the Vietnamese in the way of potential economic benefits . . . or changes in the political and diplomatic situation between our two countries than the President and the administration was willing to do."[7] And there was this additional problem: Discussing his objections to the trip with the vice president's chief of staff at the time, Powell cautioned that the Vietnamese had denied holding American POWs for the last fourteen years and that "if they were to [now] produce live people, can you imagine what will be asked for?"[8]

From Powell's perspective, then, a twin calamity loomed: The price for the POWs might be very high, and Perot might be willing to pay it.[9]

Powell's strong objections notwithstanding, in the end the decision was made to approve the Perot trip, subject to several conditions. According to what Perot would later tell Senate investigators, Howard Baker, the president's recently arrived chief of staff, explained that the White House would go along with the trip so long as Perot understood he was going to Vietnam as a private citizen and not as an official representative of the president. Perot said that Baker then proceeded to tell him that the president had decided to appoint a special emissary on POWs just as Perot had suggested. Retired Joint Chiefs of Staff Chairman Gen. John W. "Jack" Vessey, USA, would be appointed to the post, and the president requested that Perot put in a good word for Vessey during his upcoming talks in Hanoi.[10]

It was, of course, a stunning rebuke of Perot, one clearly designed to so embarrass the proud Texan that he would cancel the trip rather than suffer the humiliation now attendant on making it. But Perot ignored the bait, assured Baker he would travel as a private citizen as requested, and agreed to the president's request that he put in a good word for Vessey during his visit.

In a matter of hours, Perot's advance men were winging their way toward Vietnam. Several days later, Perot himself followed.

## *Late March, Hanoi*
## THACH AND PEROT

Private citizen Perot arrived in Hanoi and went right to work. His first stop: a meeting with Vietnamese Foreign Minister Nguyen Co Thach, Hanoi's veteran point man on the POW/MIA issue who had served as Le Duc Tho's principal deputy at the Paris peace negotiations during the war.

Perot would later recount how the seasoned Thach had led off their first meeting, held on March 25, with his standard line that Vietnam held no American POWs, and how in response he, fresh from his study of the intelligence, had replied, "Don't embarrass yourselves, I know too much." Whereupon, Perot says, Thach started laughing and said, "We were told that you were direct, but you're even more direct than we were told you are. But we will get along well because we are direct, too." With that, Perot says, he and Thach began what would be a series of cordial discussions about the POW issue and how it might be resolved.

During these discussions, Thach expressed what Perot characterized as "deep, deep fear" about how it would look if any POWs were ever released. Perot said he responded by suggesting prisoners might be "found" in Laos, thus minimizing embarrassment to the Vietnamese.

Perot said he informed Thach of the pending Vessey appointment and assured him the retired general enjoyed his, the president's, and the American people's strongest support. Perot said the Vietnamese were pleased at the appointment and expressed hope that in Vessey they might find relief from the rude treatment they had been receiving from the current team of U.S. negotiators. Perot said the Vietnamese went on to emphasize that as victors in their war with America, they felt they should be afforded respect, but instead, America's negotiators were "rude and arrogant." Perot later explained that "we are always asking them to do things for the U.S. and we are unwilling to do anything for them," and as a result, "they do not trust the U.S. government [and] pointed out several times we haven't kept our promises, and their favorite [example] is the Nixon reparations."

Perot would later characterize the U.S. negotiating strategy as "rough them and stiff-arm them," and said the Vietnamese "were basically telling me that this was not a productive strategy. And anybody who watched them during the war knows that they are a tough, resolute people and probably the best way to deal with them is not to bounce them around and rough them up."

Perot later said his three days of talks ended with the Vietnamese reiterating that they were "very positive" about Vessey's appointment and would work diligently with him to address the problems that continued to divide the two countries. His work complete, Perot departed for the United States to report his findings to President Reagan and Vice President Bush.[11]

## DALLAS

Perot returned to the United States, incorporated his trip report into the package of findings and recommendations from his earlier study of the intelligence, and asked for an appointment to brief the president. When he was told the president would not see him until early May, a chagrined Perot reportedly phoned the vice president for help. When none was offered, unpleasantries were exchanged. Several similar conversations followed, each resulting in bruised feelings and an increasing level of distrust between the two men. All the while Perot, chafing at not being able to personally present what he considered critically important information to the president, waited.

In his report, which he had incorporated into a letter addressed to the president, Perot told Reagan the United States had left POWs in Indochina after the war; we don't know exactly where they are currently being held; it would be unrealistic to attempt a military rescue to retrieve them; negotiations offer the only realistic chance of gaining their release; that General Vessey was an excellent choice as envoy and would have Perot's full support, but that to be effective, Vessey must have a broad charter that would enable him to discuss not only POW/MIAs but also other matters of importance to the governments of Vietnam, Laos, and Cambodia. Perot also informed the president that he had, at Baker's request, strongly endorsed General Vessey to the Vietnamese and that their reaction had been very positive. Perot concluded his report by stating, "the principal obstacle in obtaining the release of these men since the end of the war has been a lack of diligence and follow-through by our government. Choosing a man of General Vessey's stature, giving him a broad mission, supporting him with whatever resources he needs, and having him report directly to you is the strongest possible approach to gaining the release of these men."

These formal findings and recommendations having been listed, Perot went on in his letter to offer the president his personal and professional assistance in helping launch a new era of reconciliation with the Vietnamese. If the administration would lift its travel restrictions governing Vietnamese diplomats attending the United Nations, Perot said, he would personally accompany Foreign Minister Thach on a private trip to points of interest all across the United States. Similarly, if the administration would allow legendary Vietnamese general Vo Nguyen Giap to visit the United States as a private citizen, Perot would introduce him to the members of the Joint Chiefs of Staff, arrange for Giap to lecture at the National War College, and personally accompany him to points of interest in the United States. If the administration would reconsider its earlier denial of a visa for a famed Vietnamese pianist who had sought to tour the United States, Perot would handle all arrangements for the pianist's tour. If the administration would allow a small number of Vietnamese to visit the United States to study our economic system,

Perot again would make all the arrangements. And, he added, if the president approved, he would be willing to underwrite a similar mission of economists and businessmen to Vietnam to assist the Vietnamese in rebuilding their economy.[12]

Rather than mail the letter, Perot planned to present it to the president and explain its contents during their meeting.

## MEANWHILE, THREE NEW INITIATIVES AIMED AT GETTING THE POWs HOME

During April, as Perot waited to see the president, Hendon and an old friend and his now-former colleagues on the Hill were all hard at work implementing new initiatives designed to get the live POWs home.

Following his departure from Congress in January, Hendon had gone to work at the American Defense Institute, a conservative, pro-defense Washington think tank headed by his longtime friend Capt. Eugene "Red" McDaniel (USN, Ret.), a highly decorated Navy pilot who had spent almost six years in captivity in North Vietnam. In April, the two had launched a new effort which, if it worked, would force the administration into negotiating for the unlisted, unreturned POWs. Their plan was simple: (1) they would establish a $1 million reward to be paid to the first citizen of Vietnam, Laos, or Cambodia who escaped or defected from Communist territory with an American POW and turned that POW over to the U.S. government; (2) they would immediately begin publicizing the reward in Vietnamese-language publications and on the ground in Southeast Asia, knowing that (3) if the reward worked and an American POW was indeed freed, public opinion would force the administration to enter good faith negotiations to secure the release of the remaining prisoners.

To underwrite the reward, Hendon and McDaniel first each pledged $100,000, to be paid once the freed American was in U.S. custody and it had been confirmed that he was, in fact, a bona fide prisoner of war, and then Hendon went to the Hill and collected similar $100,000 pledges from eight of his former GOP colleagues.[13] A million dollars worth of pledges in hand, Hendon and McDaniel then scheduled a news conference at the Charlotte Motor Speedway, whose owner had long been concerned about the POWs, to announce the reward.

On the day of the news conference, April 27, Hendon and McDaniel rented $1 million in cash and two guards from a local bank, flew in five of the eight congressmen who had helped underwrite the reward, and, in the presence of the money and the guards; speedway officials, including the owner, who at the last minute had decided to pledge $100,000 himself toward the reward; a group of activist family members, activist Vietnam vets, and former POWs; and a contingent of press, formally announced that the reward had been created and that it would soon be advertised not only in Vietnamese-language publications but also on the ground in Southeast Asia. Wire service accounts and photos of the congressmen and the cash appeared in the following days in newspapers throughout the United States and, of particular importance to all in attendance at the news conference, in newspapers in Southeast Asia as well.[14]

Shortly after returning to Washington from the news conference at the

Charlotte Motor Speedway, Hendon's close friend and reward contributor Rep. Bob Smith (R-NH), who was convinced, as were all of the activist congressmen, that if the American people could see the intelligence on live POWs currently in the files at DIA they would pressure the administration into immediately entering good faith negotiations to gain the prisoners' release, introduced legislation directing the Department of Defense and other government agencies to immediately declassify all postwar reports of sightings of captive Americans in their possession, and to make those reports available to the public. Smith's legislation, introduced on April 30, was assigned the title "House Resolution 2260" and referred to the Armed Services and Foreign Affairs and Intelligence Committees.[15]

Also on April 30, another of Hendon's closest friends, activist congressman Rep. Frank McCloskey (D-IN), introduced H. Con. Res. 114, a bill designed to completely overhaul the administration's POW/MIA bureaucracy by doing away with Childress's and Griffiths's powerful fiefdom, the POW/MIA Interagency Group (IAG), and assigning many of its duties to a high-level State Department official with rank similar to that of presidential envoy. Unless Congress intervened and made this fundamental structural change, McCloskey told colleagues, Griffiths and Childress would remain in power and the cover-up would continue with no end in sight.

## May 6, 1987
## WASHINGTON • AMBUSH IN THE OVAL OFFICE

When a smiling Perot, briefcase in hand, was finally ushered into the Oval Office on May 6 to present his findings and recommendations, he found White House Chief of Staff Howard Baker, National Security Advisor Carlucci, Deputy National Security Advisor Powell, and the president in attendance, but no Bush. Following the initial handshakes and banter with Baker, Carlucci, and Powell at the door, Baker led Perot across the office to shake hands with the president.

When the men took their seats, the president, reading from three-by-five index cards he held in his lap and motioning—almost lecturing, really—with his left hand, conveyed to Perot the crystal-clear "thanks but no thanks" message Carlucci, Powell, and Baker had prepared. Carlucci would later say the president told Perot " 'we appreciate your interest and the help you've tried to give us . . . [W]e now think we've gotten an excellent negotiator in Jack Vessey, . . . and I think it's important that you support Jack . . . and that we have Jack as the channel, and we would appreciate it if you would tell the Vietnamese that henceforth . . . General Vessey is going to be the channel.' "[16] One administration official would later characterize the president's tone as "deliberately cool."[17] Carlucci would later say the whole thing had been worked out in advance in the hope that Perot would bow out of the process altogether.[18]

Perot, embarrassed and more than a little bit taken aback by the treatment he was receiving, moved quickly to extricate himself from the ambush he had walked into. He told the president he would abide by his wishes, would support General Vessey, and would have no further contact with the Vietnamese. A

The Oval Office, May 6, 1987. *Left to right:* White House Chief of Staff Howard Baker, President Ronald Reagan, Ross Perot, National Security Advisor Frank Carlucci, Deputy National Security Advisor Colin Powell. (COURTESY RONALD REAGAN LIBRARY)

courteous disengagement followed, and with that the meeting—and the eight-month effort by private citizen Henry Ross Perot of Dallas, Texas, to help the Reagan/Bush administration get the POWs home—came to an end.

(Though he had been roughed up pretty badly by the president, Baker, Carlucci, and Powell in the Oval Office that day, when all was said and done Perot came to believe he had been treated even more shabbily—hung out to dry, in fact—by his old friend the vice president. It would turn out that the vice president's actions during this period would stick in Perot's mind—and, unfortunately for Bush, deep in Perot's craw as well—from the spring of 1987 until late in the evening of the Tuesday following the first Monday in November in 1992.)

## THE ADMINISTRATION REACTS TO THE NEW INITIATIVES

Responding to increasing public pressure that something be done to get the POWs home—pressure that had spiked dramatically in the wake of all the publicity about the reward and Smith's bill to declassify the intelligence and McCloskey's to abolish the IAG—administration officials began in the spring to aggressively play down the possibility that any POWs might still be alive. In late May, Vice President Bush himself, replying to a California woman's letter expressing concern that the administration was not acting on the many reports of live POWs and her support for the reward and for Smith's bill, reminded the woman that "our policy is to assume live American prisoners remain in Southeast Asia until proven otherwise," but then he went on to declare unequivocally that "despite sensational reports to the contrary, we have no evidence that a single American is being held captive in Southeast Asia."[19] Other officials, meanwhile, usually speaking on background, also began passing definitive word there was no evidence POWs remained alive. One such statement appeared in an article on Laos in *National Geographic,* in which the author of the article, after noting that "552 Americans, mostly USAF and Navy fliers," remained unaccounted for in Laos, asked rhetorically, "[C]ould any of these Americans still be alive and held against their will?" and then quickly dismissed the possibility by stating, "[P]rivately, [U.S.] experts say no."[20] Soon, similar background sessions with members of the press would become the order of the day.

As pressure for action on the live POW front continued to build, the White House dispatched Childress and Griffiths to Hanoi in late May to seek Vietnamese approval of a formal agenda for any future visit by Vessey. In their meetings with Vietnamese officials, Childress and Griffiths informed their hosts that before the president would agree to send Vessey, Vietnam must agree to an agenda that would allow discussion of only "humanitarian" issues, i.e., POW/MIAs and Vietnamese immigration to the United States, and not "political matters," i.e., reparations/postwar reconstruction aid. The Vietnamese, of course, quickly saw this for what it was—the old one-way street they had seen so many times before—and would have no part of it. Bristling with indignation, they told Childress and Griffiths that Vietnam would reserve judgment on even receiving Vessey until the U.S. side agreed to open the agenda to Vietnam's main concern—reconstruction aid—and warned that "if the U.S. envoy comes only to discuss the MIA, the visit would be unsuccessful."[21]

Troubled by the U.S.-proposed agenda that would not allow any discussion of the issue most important to them, the Vietnamese soon responded with several hard-hitting public statements outlining what the SRV expected from any future Vessey visit. A classified CIA analysis of public statements made in mid-June by Thach and Communist party chief Nguyen Van Linh—and the enormous significance these statements held for the U.S. side—read in part as follows:

> Hanoi has revived its pre-1978 hard line linking a U.S. aid commitment to resolution of the question of American servicemen missing in action during the Vietnam war. Speaking at a press conference in Hanoi on 18 June, SRV Foreign Minister Nguyen Co Thach stressed that Vietnam is "many times more concerned about healing its own wounds of war"—a common formulation routinely used before 1978 to refer to the U.S. economic aid commitment to Vietnam under article 21 of the 1973 Paris Peace Accords—than with the MIA issue. Strongly signaling that the two questions are linked, he warned that "no results" can be achieved in solving outstanding "humanitarian" issues if there is "only a one-way" exchange. The question of a U.S. aid commitment to Vietnam also received attention from party chief Nguyen Van Linh in an interview carried by the Italian paper *L'Unità* on 21 June, which thus far has not been replayed by Vietnamese media. The United States, Linh noted without elaboration, "has failed to honor" the pledges it

made in the Paris Accords and is "not paying the more than $2 billion in war compensation" due Vietnam.[22]

In early July, Thach repeated once again Hanoi's requirement that aid be on the agenda during any talks with Vessey. This time, the Vietnamese leader, meeting with a group of American academics and war veterans in Hanoi, pointedly declared that Vietnam required economic assistance from the United States before it would help resolve the fate of missing American servicemen. He explained that U.S. aid would help persuade Vietnamese peasants to cooperate in the hunt for missing Americans and told his guests, "If you wish the cooperation of the people, [the United States] must give humanitarian aid to help heal the wounds of war." Thach was further quoted as declaring that "we are expected to help heal the wounds of war in the United States, but they have no responsibility to help us in Vietnam? No way."[23]

## July, Washington
## SHULTZ REJECTS A "TWO WAY STREET" • VESSEY DEPARTS FOR HANOI

The administration's public response to Thach's latest demand for aid was firm and, given the continuing fallout over the Iran-contra affair, highly predictable. Addressing the annual convention of the League of Families in Washington on July 18, Secretary of State George Shultz, who in recent months had publicly scorned his own president for paying for the hostages in Lebanon, warned the families in unmistakable language that America would not under any circumstances pay for their loved ones in Southeast Asia. "Recent press reports," Shultz told the families, "indicate that Vietnam is raising the concept of humanitarian cooperation as a 'two way street, including economic assistance.' Humanitarian reciprocity is one thing," he continued, "but any attempt to trade information on our missing men for economic aid is another. We cannot agree to this." Shultz went on to warn the families that "we must face the possibility that we will not be able to move the issue forward" and to declare that "the answers to the questions so important to us are to be found in Hanoi and Vientiane, not Washington."[24]

Shultz's speech to the League had a twofold effect: it lowered the expectations of the families that anything substantive would come out of a future Vessey trip, and "prepped the battlefield" for Vessey if and when he visited Hanoi. Accordingly, on the 24th, the White House announced that all arrangements for Vessey's trip had been completed and that he and members of his delegation would travel to Hanoi to conduct talks on the MIA issue and other humanitarian concerns *of the United States* in early August.[25]

## August 1–3, 1987
## HANOI

General Vessey arrived in Hanoi on August 1 and immediately went into a private session with Thach. In a cable dispatched a short while later to Washington, Vessey described what occurred:

In the private session Thach said he hoped that my trip could be a success for both countries. He said that he understood the importance of the POW/MIA problem to the US, and that he acknowledged the need to solve it on a humanitarian basis. He said that VN also had great wounds from the war and that she needed reciprocal humanitarian help. I thanked him for the welcome and his understanding. I told him that my mission was POW/MIA resolution and the discussion of other US humanitarian concerns and that if there were movement on resolution of our problems there was some flexability [sic] to address VN humanitarian concerns. I told him that recognition, aid and trade were political issues outside my charter, but that I would listen to VN concerns on any issue and take to President Reagan. Thach told me that he understood and would not raise political issues at all, but if I had any messages on political issues he would listen. He then said we needed to address both sides of the problem; how to solve the POW/MIA issue and how to display humanitarian reciprocity to VN. He said that he was severely criticized in 6th party congress for giving in to the US on POW/MIA without getting help for VN humanitarian problems . . . We then bandied a bit about the chicken and the egg before proceeding to the plenary session.[26]

Vessey would later report that in the plenary session that followed, "I stressed our understanding that the talks were to focus on POW/MIA and other humanitarian issues and that these issues should not be linked to broader political questions that separate us," and pointed out that "absent a Vietnamese withdrawal from Cambodia, there could be no progress toward normalization of diplomatic or trade relations or any talk of economic aid."

Vessey reported that the Vietnamese led off with their usual categorical denial that they held any American prisoners, but that he replied that there were many questions that must be answered before the American people, and especially the families of the missing, could accept such an assurance. Vessey went on to say that he told Thach that "most Americans did not believe Vietnam was being truthful on the POW/MIA issue and that many, many Americans believe that Vietnam still held live prisoners."[27]

Continuing, Vessey said he then outlined America's humanitarian interests, which he said were (1) the return of any live Americans; (2) the resolution of discrepancy cases as well as the "died in captivity list"; (3) crash site excavations; (4) the repatriation of remains; and (5) the fullest possible accounting of our POW/MIAs.

Vessey said that in reply, Thach said that he, too, had humanitarian concerns stemming from the war that he wished to discuss. "They said they had 1.4 million war-disabled, 500,000 orphans and many destroyed schools and damaged hospitals," Vessey later recalled, and "they stressed that these, too, would have to be addressed if there was to be progress on the humanitarian concerns of the U.S. side."[28]

Vessey said he responded by saying the United States would consider "the possibility of cooperation in certain specific humanitarian areas," specifically artificial limbs for the war wounded and assistance for children orphaned by the war. He said he also told Thach that because current U.S. law prohibited any direct financial participation by the U.S. government, funding for any such effort must come solely from private charities and other nongovernmental organizations (NGOs).

Thach, clearly insulted at the thought that any of the postwar aid he had helped win at Paris—even the tiny amount outlined by Vessey—might come from charities and NGOs and not from the U.S. government, warned Vessey that if the U.S. side persisted in its plan to have NGOs handle aid, he would direct that Vietnamese NGOs handle the search for missing Americans.[29]

Unmoved, Vessey warned Thach that in return for the artificial limbs, the United States would expect Vietnam to help account for some seventy American servicemen who were believed to have been captured by the Vietnamese but who had not returned at Operation Homecoming.

And on and on it went—thrust, parry; bob, weave; advance, retreat; chicken, egg; egg, chicken—through two more plenary sessions and three more private meetings. When it was over, neither man, neither side, neither country, had much to show for the effort. So little substantive progress had been made, in fact, that a veteran *New York Times* reporter with intimate knowledge of the region who was accompanying the American delegation would file a story on the way out of Hanoi declaring there had been "no progress reported in three days of talks on Americans missing since the Vietnam War" and that indications were that "cooperation between Hanoi and Washington on accounting for the missing has not recovered even the momentum it had achieved two years ago, when the two sides had begun to meet regularly."[30]

*August, Washington*
## VESSEY DROPS "LIVE MIA" BOMBSHELL

Vessey returned to the United States and, on August 10, briefed the president at the White House on his trip. The Vietnamese had agreed to renew their efforts to find MIAs, Vessey told Reagan, and in return the United States had agreed for the first time to allow NGOs to provide Vietnam with prosthetic devices and other rehabilitative equipment.

Following his brief meeting with the president, Vessey proceeded to the White House Press Room and, after briefing members of the press on what he had accomplished in Hanoi, dropped a bombshell on the issue of live Americans. "The Vietnamese have acknowledged that there are some wild parts of their country," Vessey declared, and "the suggestion is that it is possible for there to be live Americans in Southeast Asia, not under the control of the Vietnamese government." The Vietnamese had not actually told him Americans were alive in these remote areas, Vessey explained, but "that is the inference I draw. . . . I don't know if there are any there, but there is evidence some might be," he told the stunned press corps.[31]

What in the *hell* was going on, official Washington asked. Was there maybe something to this "MIA thing" after all?

## A BIG DOSE OF COLD WATER FROM LANGLEY: • "NO CREDIBLE EVIDENCE OF LIVE POWs," CIA RESPONDS, NO "PLAUSIBLE MOTIVE" FOR HANOI TO KEEP THEM

In a move some in the intelligence community later came to believe was prompted by Vessey's August 10 revelation about possible live MIAs, the CIA published a classified fourteen-page report in early September declaring there was "no credible or convincing evidence that any live American POWs remain in Indochina" and that there was "no plausible motive" for Hanoi to have retained any. The agency distributed the report throughout the government during September.

In the report, a Special National Intelligence Estimate or SNIE (pronounced SNEE) titled "Hanoi and the POW/MIA Issue," the report's authors—after acknowledging that a large number of sighting reports had been received since war's end and that these "sighting reports continue to be received and analyzed"—declared that not one of the postwar reports "has yet proved to be the sighting of an American still held captive." Rather, the report's authors declared, "65 to 70 percent were sightings of Americans who are accounted for (for example, returned POWs, missionaries, civilian detainees, USMC deserter Robert Garwood); . . . 15 to 20 percent were determined to be fabrications [and] . . . 10 to 20 percent are, at any particular time, still under analysis." And that was not all. The report's authors went on to make clear that each of these three findings—there was no credible or convincing evidence that any live American POWs remained in Indochina, there was no plausible motive for Hanoi to have retained any, and none of the sightings received had involved Americans in a captive environment—represented the official position of the U.S. intelligence community.[32]

Had Smith's bill to declassify all the intelligence already become law, no one at CIA or anywhere else in the U.S. intelligence community would have dared publish such a document. This because—forget all the intelligence on live POWs received in past years—the intelligence reports received from *January to mid-September 1987 alone* made a mockery of the SNIE's findings. Here is what just some of that intelligence said:

- The reader will recall that back on January 9, CIA had reported to DIA that the American MIA Stephenson had been apprehended by LPA troops in Ban Napang the previous month and taken to an undisclosed location in nearby Boulapha District. (See map page 337, points 1 and 2.)
- On March 23, 1987, DIA had received a JCRC report that quoted a former ARVN officer as saying that while accompanying two friends to a remote area of the Ca Mau Peninsula on Vietnam's southern tip in late April 1984 to arrange a boat escape from Vietnam, he had had a chance encounter with an escaped American POW. According to the report, the ARVN officer reported that the encounter had occurred near Nam Can and "sketched a map of the location which bears a strong resemblance to the vicinity of [map coordinates] WQ 088711."[33] (See map page 337, point 3.)

The ARVN officer had told JCRC interviewers in Malaysia that the encounter with the escaped American had occurred when he had left his party at a small canal-side coffeehouse located near a ranger station and walked up a trail searching for a place to relieve himself. He explained that after finding a suitable place, a clump of bushes located just off the trail, he had entered the bushes and squatted down and was in the process of relieving himself when he heard a voice say once and then again in English, "Who are you?" He said that when he turned to his right rear to see who was talking, he saw a male Caucasian emerging from the brush with an upraised hatchet in his right hand. He said the man, seeing that he was in an embarrassing situation, halted about two meters from him. The ARVN officer said the man was about six feet tall, big boned and thin, and wearing a black peasant outfit, a straw hat, and a head scarf that left only his face visible. He said that because the man's head was covered he could not determine the color of his hair but saw that he had a scraggly reddish mustache and, on the left side of his face, a long scar that ran diagonally from high on the cheekbone down across both lips and ended on his chin. The man was missing several teeth on the upper and lower jaws on the left side of his mouth, as if the wound that had produced the scar had also knocked out the teeth. His eyes were blue and deeply sunken as if from worry. The ARVN officer noticed that both of the man's hands had what appeared to be burn scars on them and that he was barefooted and several of his toenails were missing. The peasant outfit, the officer told JCRC interviewers, was the largest he had ever seen but was still too small for this man.

The ARVN officer told U.S. investigators that with the hatchet still held high, the Caucasian asked him, "Can you speak English?" and he replied, "Yes, but who are you?" He said the Caucasian then asked, "Can I trust you?" and he replied, "Yes, you can," and explained that he was former ARVN. He said that upon hearing that, the Caucasian said, "I am an escaped U.S. prisoner-of-war" and continued with several phrases he did not understand. The ARVN officer said he had been surprised to hear this, as he believed that no Americans remained in Vietnam, and fearing he might have misunderstood the Caucasian, he asked, "[A]re there any American prisoners left in Vietnam?" He said the Caucasian appeared angered by the question but answered nevertheless, "Nearly a hundred."

The ARVN officer told JCRC interviewers that he and the escaped American were able to continue conversing for some time. He said that when the American asked him what he was doing in such a remote area and he replied that he had come there to arrange a boat escape, the American implored him to arrange passage for him on the boat as well. He said he told the American that he would first have to ask permission from the boat captain, but the American seemed to suspect he was shrugging him off and so he assured him by saying, "I promise I will come back for you today or tomorrow." The ARVN officer said he then asked the American his name and age, but the American replied, "When we get on the boat, I'll tell you everything." The ARVN officer said he and the American then went about working out a series of signals and passwords to be used when he returned to pick the American up. He said that when the plans were finalized, he

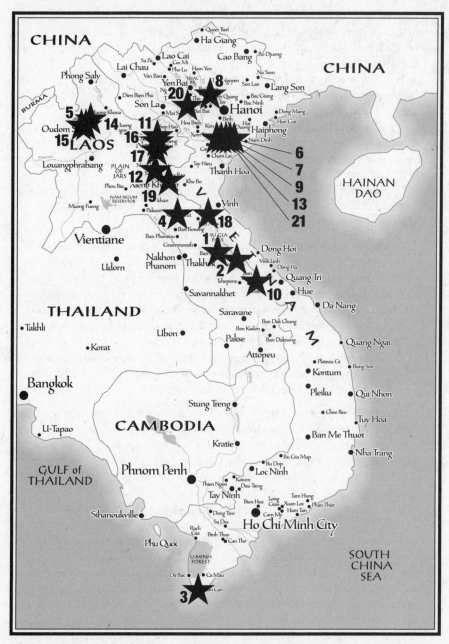

Selected reports of U.S. POWs received during 1987. (HENDON/ANDERER)

gave the American some money and a pack of Dalat cigarettes and was preparing to depart when a Vietnamese man came walking down the path toward the ranger station and saw them and eyed them suspiciously as he passed. He said that, alarmed, he bid the American a hurried farewell and headed back to join his party. He said that as he was leaving, the American uttered a long phrase in English that he did not understand and that when he glanced back he saw that the American was staring at the cigarettes and money he had given him.

The ARVN officer told JCRC interviewers that he returned to the coffee-house and rejoined the members of his party and soon after they left the area. He said that a short time later the person making arrangements for his and the others' escape told him he could not depart as planned because he did not possess the required "legal papers." More than two and one half years elapsed, he said, before he successfully booked passage on another boat and finally escaped to Malaysia.

Commenting on the ARVN officer's testimony that he had collected during two days of interviews held in Malaysia on February 27–28, 1987, the JCRC interviewer wrote:

> Comment: Source was very cooperative throughout the interview, presenting his information in a straightforward and apparently spontaneous manner. He speaks with a [redacted] accent, and supplemented his Vietnamese with occasional English terms and expressions during the interview. His English is accented but clear. Source stressed that he had come forward with his information out of a sense of moral obligation to the alleged American prisoner, and did not do so in hope of resettlement. Despite close and pointed questioning of some of the more improbable and embarrassing aspects of his story, source remained cheerful. The information presented in his written statement does not differ significantly from that presented in the interview.[34]

The ARVN officer's sighting of the escaped American POW near Nam Can in late April 1984, DIA personnel knew, tended to corroborate two earlier postwar sightings of American POWs in the Nam Can area. These sightings, both made by a former ARVN commando in June 1977 and reported to DIA in late 1981, involved two separate groups of American POWs. The first group, reportedly totaling 120 men, was said to be detained at a former South Vietnamese naval-base-turned-prison-camp in the Nam Can area; the other group, reportedly 47 in number, was reportedly held at another former naval base nearby. According to the former ARVN commando, the American prisoners "look skin and very old now."[35]

• On March 27, 1987, CIA had sent DIA a report that quoted a sensitive source as saying that during the mid-1970s he had heard an official assigned to the Vietnamese embassy in East Germany state that "the Americans would have to pay the SRV reparations for the war because the SRV had U.S. POW'S and therefore this matter would be easily enforceable." The CIA reported that the source recalled hearing the official make this statement sometime during 1975–1976.[36]

• In late April 1987, DIA had received a letter from a former Lao refugee living in the United States who said friends in Laos had informed him that "Morgan Jeferson Donaho/D.O.B. 2nd May 1944/Airplane AC-123/No. 32931 and 5 others unknown" were being held prisoner in Laos and that the information "was very urgent because my friends in Laos are afraid the live prisoners will be killed or moved [but] if we hurry maybe we can rescue them."[37] In a telephone interview conducted by Special Office analysts on May 12, the former refugee reportedly refined the name of the American prisoner to "Morgan Jeferson Donahue" and reported that Donahue was being detained in a prison at Baytong Mountain, near Kham Keut, in Khammouan Province.[38] (See map page 337, point 4.)

DIA analysts immediately recognized that Morgan Jeferson Donahue was missing USAF Lt. Morgan Jefferson Donahue, who had been aboard a C-123K that had crashed on December 13, 1968, after colliding with another U.S. aircraft during night operations over central Laos. According to the pilot of Donahue's plane, who parachuted from the stricken C-123K and was rescued soon after daylight, both the copilot and Donohue, one of the navigators, had parachuted out before he did. The pilot also reported that as he drifted toward the ground in the darkness, he saw the parachute of another crewman descending below him. DOD records show that the pilot was the only member of the seven-man crew rescued. DOD records also show that the birthdate provided by the former refugee correlates with that of Lieutenant Donahue and the type of aircraft reported matches the aircraft Donahue was aboard.[39]

• On April 29, 1987, DIA had received a JCRC report that quoted a member of the Lao resistance as saying that a relative of his who was a guard at a seminar prison in Oudom Sai City, Laos, had informed him during the last half of 1986 that twenty-one American prisoners were being held in a separate part of the facility. (See map page 337, point 5.) According to the guard, the Americans were forced to work from morning until evening as electricians and as repairmen for "old machines of every type" and were "very weak because they work hard and do not have enough food."

The official at Lao resistance headquarters who provided the guard's account to JCRC noted that "it is believed that these people who are military men and Americans are probably still at the seminar prison at Muang Udomxai . . . [and that] . . . the OPL [Lao resistance organization] is reporting this matter so that all parties can attempt to obtain additional details . . . [and that] . . . if the United States feels it is appropriate for us to [do] anything quicker than this, please come to meet with me."[40]

• On April 30, 1987, DIA had received a report from JCRC that quoted a recently arrived Vietnamese refugee as saying that he had heard about a group of American POWs who were seen in Ha Nam Ninh or neighboring Hoa Binh (Ha Son Binh) Province in northern Vietnam during the early 1980s. (See map page 337, point 6.) The JCRC report quoted the refugee as saying that while attending an acquaintance's "welcome home from reeducation celebration" in 1983, the acquaintance, a former ARVN psychological warfare officer held in the North, told him that he himself had seen the American prisoners a short time before his release. According to the refugee, the acquaintance said he and some of his fellow soldiers had been moved out of their camp because a foreign delegation was coming to inspect the facility, and that while en route by truck to a new camp located near the Laotian border they came upon the Americans. The refugee said the acquaintance told him the Americans, all dressed in brown and black prisoner clothing, were walking along the road under guard. The refugee added that he was convinced the acquaintance was telling the truth, in part because he had worked with Americans for a long time and knew very well what they looked like.[41]

- On May 18, 1987, CIA had sent DIA a report indicating the presence of American POWs in Ha Nam Ninh Province in northern Vietnam during early 1986. According to the CIA report, persons alleged to be American prisoners of war were reportedly still being detained in an interrogation center located "in an area in the southwest quadrant, from Ninh Binh City [located at map coordinates] (XH 0340), of Ha Nam Ninh Province."[42] (See map page 337, point 7.)

- On May 27, 1987, DIA had received a report from JCRC that quoted a recently arrived refugee as saying his father, a former ARVN infantry major who had undergone reeducation at the Vinh Quang reeducation camp complex northwest of Hanoi, had personally observed five or six Caucasian American POWs near the camp during 1981 or 1982. (See map page 337, point 8.) The refugee said his father explained that he and members of an ARVN work party were being marched to a labor detail when they came upon a shed with a guard posted out front, and when they walked past the shed, they saw that there were five or six Caucasian American prisoners inside. The father said the Americans were dressed in khaki uniforms and appeared to be working on some type of machine. He added that shortly after seeing the Americans, a member of his work party asked a member of the camp staff about what had just occurred. The father said the staff member replied, simply, "American prisoners in Vietnam are specialists."

The refugee concluded by telling JCRC interviewers that his father had told him and other members of his family about his encounter with the American prisoners on many, many occasions. Explaining why his father had told the story so often, he said that whenever his father heard the Vietnamese government's official position that Vietnam does not hold any American POWs broadcast on the radio, he would exclaim "Xao" (liars), and repeat his own experience for all the family to hear.[43]

DIA analysts knew, or should have known, that the report of the major's sighting of the American prisoners at Vinh Quang during 1981 or 1982 tended to corroborate the report they had received back on October 14, 1986, that described an ARVN inmate happening upon a group of American POWs being detained in an underground bunker complex near the Vinh Quang camp in 1980 or 1981, and subsequently learning that a total of about twenty American prisoners were being detained in the Vinh Quang camp system.

- On June 1, 1987, DIA had received a report from JCRC that quoted a former Buddhist nun as saying her brother had told her upon his return from reeducation in 1982 that he had seen many American prisoners housed in a compound adjacent to his reeducation camp in Hanoi. The nun said her brother, a former Buddhist monk who had been accused by the Communists of being in the employ of the CIA, told her he had seen the Americans during 1979.[44] In a subsequent interview with CIA personnel, the nun reported that at JCRC's request she had contacted her brother in Saigon for additional information about the American prisoners, and he had informed her that he had, in fact, seen the Americans during 1979, but not in Hanoi as she had recalled, rather in Ha Nam Ninh Province south of Hanoi.[45] (See map page 337, point 9.)

- On June 7, 1987, DIA had received a report from JCRC that quoted a former ARVN private as saying that following his capture by PAVN forces shortly before the fall of Saigon, he and a group of approximately one hundred other ARVN prisoners were being marched to a Communist POW camp near Lao Bao, the town that straddles the Vietnam/Lao border on Route 9 in far western Quang Tri Province, and that as they neared the town they came upon a group of American prisoners performing forced labor on a road construction project. (See map page 337, point 10.) The ARVN private told JCRC interviewers that he and his fellow POWs passed within about fifty meters of the Americans, whom he said appeared to be part of a large workforce that included PAVN soldiers and a civilian labor force of Vietnamese men and women. He said the Americans, ten or eleven in number, were all Caucasians. Some, he said, were wearing light-colored prison uniforms with wide vertical burgundy stripes; others wore undershirts that appeared to have been white when new but were now yellow from dirt and perspiration. He recalled that during the time he and his fellow POWs passed by, the Americans were either standing and leveling the road with hoes or sitting down resting. He further recalled that some were very tall and others shorter but still taller than the average Vietnamese.

  At the conclusion of his interview, the ARVN private opined that the Americans were being forced to work on the roads because the PAVN wanted revenge for the damage they had caused by their bombing.[46]

- On June 19, 1987, CIA had sent DIA a report outlining information on POWs the agency had recently acquired from a former PAVN junior officer. A DIA recap of the CIA report, distributed on June 25, showed that the PAVN officer had

> stated to [CIA] interviewers that he was privy to the conversation of two unidentified Northern Vietnamese personages in July 1986 in Haiphong in which the two discussed the continued holding of a certain class of U.S. PWS after the release of other PWS in 1973. [Source] related a hearsay description of this extended detention of quote U.S. Air Force officers . . . , the children of upper class and capitalist families unquote as part of an important Vietnamese economic strategy to obtain U.S. $7 billion in war reparations. {Note: the figure of $7 billion is unusual; the common amounts bruited by those who would support Socialist Republic of Vietnam (SRV) aims are the A) $3.25 billion in

grant aid, and B) other forms of food and commodity aid up to an amount of $1.5 billion, totalling $4.75 billion, that are alluded to in the 1 February 1973 Nixon letter to Prime Minister Pham Van Dong as an extension of a hoped-for honorable implementation of the Paris Peace Accords.][47]

• On July 2, 1987, DIA had received a report from JCRC outlining information JCRC interviewers had recently acquired about American pilots being detained in two separate prisons in northern Laos from early 1973 until February 1978. The report stated the information about the Americans had come from a former lieutenant colonel in the Royal Lao Police who had been released from seminar in February 1987 and had recently fled to Thailand.

The report quoted the lieutenant colonel as saying he had learned from one of his guards that four American pilots had been imprisoned during early 1973 in a cave prison in the vicinity of Ban Eun (Ban Na Eune, map coordinates VH 2385) in Sam Neua Province; that one of those Americans, identified as an F-105 pilot captured late in the war, had been shot in the face during a dispute between two guards and had died; and that the three remaining pilots had subsequently been transferred to another cave prison, this one near Nong Hed (Nong Het), a town situated on Route 7 just inside the Lao-Vietnamese border at map coordinates UG 9455. (See map page 337, points 11 and 12.) The lieutenant colonel was further quoted as saying that he had received word from another source that a total of at least ten American pilots, including the three transferred from Ban Eun, were being detained in the cave prison at Nong Hed (Nong Het) as of February 1978. He further reported that this prison was controlled by both North Vietnamese and Laotian personnel, and that to gain entrance, one reportedly had to have the signature of "the highest level Laotian government officials."[48]

• On July 30, 1987, DIA had received a report from its new operations center at the U.S. embassy in Bangkok that operated under the code name "Stony Beach" that told of "white-skinned prisoners wearing Vietnamese-style clothing working with hand farming implements in the fields" around a reeducation camp in Ha Nam Ninh Province in northern Vietnam. According to the report, the prisoners were said to have been seen frequently from 1975 until early 1979 by a former South Vietnamese naval officer undergoing reeducation at the Ha Nam Ninh camp. The naval officer reportedly said he never got close enough to the white-skinned prisoners to determine their nationality by speech but surmised they were Americans or French. (See map page 337, point 13.) He reportedly added that he had been transferred out of the camp when the Chinese attacked Vietnam in early 1979 and did not know what happened to the white-skinned prisoners after that time.[49]

• On August 21, 1987, DIA had received another report from Stony Beach, this one containing several items of recently acquired information about Americans being detained in the SRV. First among those items was the following:

1. In late May, 1975, ARVN Col. [name redacted], former [redacted] I ARVN Corps, reported for interrogation and re-education at the Tran Hoang Quan School, Cho Lon. There, he met a PAVN Colonel, name unk. The PAVN Col. told Col. [name redacted], "You must declare everything [in making your personal history statement] in detail. If you do, sooner or later you will be released; otherwise, you will be held forever. There are even some U.S. pilots whom we are still holding so as to demand reparations in the future."[50]

- On <u>August 24, 1987</u>, DIA had received yet another report from Stony Beach, this one telling of the recent sighting of two American POWs in northern Luang Prabang Province, Laos. According to the report, the sighting had taken place near the village of Ban Long Kat (Ban Kat, map coordinates SH 973997) on June 9, 1987, some two and one half months earlier.[51] (See map page 337, point 14.) Citing the testimony of an eyewitness, the report stated that a Lao police sublieutenant and twelve troops were transporting the two American prisoners and that the group had stopped in Ban Kat for a meal. The eyewitness described the two Americans as wearing blue Vietnamese-style cotton work uniforms and blue hats. He said both could speak the local Lao dialect, and that one told him that all his friends had died and that he had been forced to leave his pigs and chickens after being with them for eight years and four months and that he missed them. The eyewitness said the sublieutenant told him that two days earlier PL officials in Vientiane had issued an order to Oudom Sai Province to immediately remove all American POWs and transport them to Sam Neua Province. (See map page 337, points 15 and 16.) The order cited the U.S. embassy in Vientiane's questioning of the Lao government about the presence of POWs in Oudom Sai as the reason for the relocation.[52]
- On <u>September 8, 1987</u>, DIA had received still another report from Stony Beach, this one indicating the presence of American pilot prisoners in southern Sam Neua Province, Laos. The American pilots cited in this report, reportedly twelve in number, were said to have been confined to a cave prison in the southern part of the province as recently as January 1985.[53] (See map page 337, point 17.) An earlier JCRC report had reported the presence of twelve American prisoners in 1982 at a military camp located east of Sam Neua Province town near the village of Nong Co (Nong Kou, map coordinates VH 1958).[54]
- On <u>September 15, 1987</u>, CIA had sent DIA a report that quoted a CIA source as saying that two separate groups of American POWs were being held in Nghe Tinh Province in northern Vietnam during 1986. The source reported that members of first group of Americans, thirty-five in number, were held in a cave prison near Sadoi, which the source said was approximately a day's walk inside Vietnam toward Vinh from the Lao/SRV border near Nape, Laos. (See map page 337, point 18.) The source reported that members of the other group, which numbered fifteen, were detained in a cave prison located near Binh Hoei (Ban Hoei), approximately one day's walk inside Vietnam on Route 7 from Nong Het, Laos, near the Lao/SRV border.[55] (See map page 337, point 19.) In a similar report of the same two

sightings filed by Stony Beach several days earlier, DIA interviewers had quoted the source as saying the American prisoners had been held at both locations since at least 1980 and that they were fed twice daily and allowed outside twice daily as well as to exercise and to cultivate vegetables.[56]

• Also on September 15, 1987, DIA had received a report from a U.S. military intelligence detachment in Korea outlining testimony of a recently arrived refugee who reported the existence of a large underground prison reportedly located inside a mountain near Hung Hoa, northwest of Hanoi, where some three hundred Americans were being detained as late as 1984. (See map page 337, point 20.) The report read in part:

> Source: [Name], a refugee staying at a Vietnamese refugee camp in Pusan, Korea, who acquired the information from a Vietnamese army officer. Reliability of the source and subsource have not been established.
>
> Summary: Possible underground detention facility for U.S. POW's is located in the area of Hung Hoa //geocoord: 2115N/10518E//, Phu Tho Province, North Vietnam. The facility is said to house approximately 300 U.S. POW's.
>
> Text: 1. Location: A detention facility housing some 300 U.S. POWs is located within a mountain approximately 50 kilometers (km) west of Phuc Yen //geocoord: 2114N/10542E//, Vinh [Phu] Province. The approximate location of the prison is geocoord: 2116N/10516E; UTM: 48QWJ270520. The area is mountainous and the Hong [Red] River //geocoord: 2017N/10634E// flows nearby.
>
> 2. Security at the facility:
>
> B. Three defensive perimeters surround the mountain, with each defensive line spaced two kilometers apart. Vietnamese army units are deployed along each defensive line. The only access road to the area is narrow and extends from an unknown road.
>
> C. Check points are located at each entrance to the first and second defensive lines, and are encountered upon entering the site. All personnel and cargo are thoroughly inspected prior to entry into the area. Vehicle loading compartments are covered and secured before given access to the area. Supplies are also transported into the area by 200 and 300 ton boats using the Hong River.
>
> D. Officers and enlisted personnel are deployed along the first defense line zone. Only officers are deployed along the second and third defensive lines. Individuals are allowed to enter only the perimeter area where they are assigned (field comment: subsource was assigned to the second defensive line). The third defensive line is the zone in the center of the area (field comment: subsource heard from members assigned to the third defense line that there were approximately 300 U.S. POW's living in the underground facility of the mountain). Once assigned to the area, no one is authorized to communicate with anybody outside of the area.
>
> 3. The POW's have a daily one-hour sunbath period within the underground facility through a specially designed sun bath system. POWs are provided Western style meals, baths, and enjoy recreational facilities.
>
> Comments: 1. Prior to leaving Vietnam in Feb 87, source frequented the home of the subsource, Vietnamese Army Captain [name] in Haiphong City.

The captain's sister-in-law, named [name], is a close friend and old schoolmate of the source.

2. In 1982, subsource was a member of Headquarters, 350th Security Command, Vietnamese Army in Haiphong with the rank of first lieutenant. In Dec 82, subsource suddenly disappeared from his home without any notice. In Dec 84, he returned home wearing the rank of captain and was reassigned to the same unit. During his two year absence, subsource's unit of assignment and location were unknown to his family.

3. After his return in Dec 84, Captain [name] related the above data to source and added the following information: in Feb 82, he and nine other army officers in his unit were selected for a special assignment and were transferred to Hanoi along with an unknown number of army officers from various other units. They were not allowed to inform their families of their location. The following day, they traveled to Viet Tri //geocoord: 2118N/10526E//, Phu Tho Province by train. At Viet Tri they boarded army trucks and moved to the assigned area.

4. Subsource surmised that the tight security around the detention area was to prevent a rescue operation similar to the Son Tay raid.

5. Source volunteered the information in this report. Based on the demeanor of the source, the debriefer feels he was sincere and relating what he understood to be the truth. Source is 36 years old, an auto mechanic by trade and a high school graduate. . . . Source is available for further debriefing. Departure to a third country is not expected in the immediate future.[57]

DIA analysts knew, or should have known, that the report from Hung Hoa appeared to corroborate an earlier report of a prison located deep inside a mountain somewhere in the Hoang Lien Son Mountain Range. That report, received in mid-1981, had quoted a drunk PAVN soldier as saying he had served as a guard at the facility, which he reportedly said held five hundred to one thousand prisoners, all either "important RVN military or American POWs." The soldier reportedly said the place where the prisoners were confined was "down near the bottom of the mountain with entrances gained by a road up the mountain," and that to reach the area where the prisoners were kept "it was necessary to go down through the inside of the mountain."[58] As previously discussed, it was earlier believed that this prison, if it actually existed, was located closer to Yen Bai, near the center of the Hoang Lien Son Range, than to Hung Hoa, near the range's southeastern terminus.

By any objective measure, the intelligence on live POWs received during the first eight and a half months of 1987 alone had destroyed each of the findings set forth in the SNIE. But with all of it being classified—and with Smith's bill bottled up in Solarz's subcommittee—who would know?

Then would come what would arguably be the most intriguing of all the 1987 reports. This report, received by DIA from Stony Beach on November 3, described the reported March 1987 escape of an American POW from the detention facility in Ha Nam Ninh Province just south of Hanoi. (See map page 337, point 21.) According to this report, a Communist party official who had recently fled

Vietnam reported that while visiting Ha Nam Ninh Province on official business in March 1987, he had learned that the day before he arrived, two guards at a detention facility in the province had released an American POW while he was outside for his daily sun bath and the three together had attempted to flee. The official further reported that he had been told that all three men had been apprehended and returned to the detention facility, and that while they were being apprehended one of the guards had been wounded in the leg. The official told Stony Beach interviewers he had learned of the escape when a Communist official he was visiting asked him over lunch if he had heard "the hot news story in town" and then proceeded to describe the escape.[59]

Given that DIA had previously received at least thirteen reports of American POWs being detained in Ha Nam Ninh Province after the war, including three and perhaps four received in 1987 alone (see map page 337, points 6, 7, 9, and 13), this fourteenth report from the province appeared plausible.[60]

Given the plausibility of the report, it must be said that few who know Ross Perot doubt that had the "hot news" from Ha Nam Ninh Province reached him while he was in Hanoi for talks with Nguyen Co Thach in late March, the outcome of his trip—and the history of America's postwar relations with the Socialist Republic of Vietnam from late March 1987 on—would have been very, very, *very* different.

## THE NGOs TAKE CENTER STAGE

Just prior to Veterans Day, the head of one of the America's largest Vietnam veterans' organizations, the thirty-thousand-member Veterans of the Vietnam War (VVnW), declared that his organization was convinced that five hundred to six hundred American servicemen remained captive in Southeast Asia and called on President Reagan to fly immediately to Vietnam to personally press for their release. "If he did that, they'd all be home by Thanksgiving," National Commander Mike Milne, a former infantryman in Vietnam, told the Associated Press.[61]

The White House, however, chose not to schedule the presidential trip to Vietnam Milne had requested, but instead in mid-November set in motion plans to dispatch a team of officials from several different NGOs to Vietnam to begin implementing the prosthetics initiative Vessey and Thach had agreed on back in the summer, and create a small NGO of its own—to be headed by Griffiths—to provide small amounts of assistance to the Vietnamese over and above that to be provided by existing NGOs.

In mid-December, a team of officials from several of the established NGOs traveled to Vietnam to begin implementing the administration's new prosthetics initiative. After a week-long visit, team members contacted the press to tell of their accomplishments and outline their plans for the coming year. One of these officials, David Elder of the American Friends Service Committee, told UPI that he and representatives from four other charities had visited five rehabilitation centers in both the North and South and had received "a good reception." Then, acknowledging that in the past many donors had been reluctant to send aid to the Vietnamese because of a lack of U.S. government support for such aid, Elder said that now, with President Reagan being personally behind the effort, aid for Vietnam's disabled would begin to increase. "The big difference now is the presidential encouragement," he said, citing a December 7 letter to the group's leader from Reagan in which he stated he was "deeply grateful" for the group's plans to visit Vietnam and declared, "[Y]our voluntary effort will help accelerate a process of healing that, despite our continued political differences with Vietnam, is much needed."

"The president's letter," Elder said confidently, "will mean a lot to corporate donors who might wonder whether this is a legitimate exercise."[62]

Perhaps. But as Elder and his associates—and those in the administration who had devised the "charities only" aid plan would soon find out—a letter from Ronald Reagan to the head of an American NGO was not what Nguyen Co Thach was looking for. What he and his countrymen wanted, Thach would soon declare for the umpteenth time, was for the U.S. government—repeat, the U.S. *government*—to fulfill its commitment as set forth in an earlier presidential letter, this one sent by Richard Nixon way back on February 1, 1973. Only when this was done, Thach would say, could there be any substantive progress in the hunt for missing Americans.

CHAPTER    27

1988

"JUST TWO BAR OF SILVERS FOR EACH MAN"

. . .

*The New York Times* reported just after New Year's that the U.S. State Department had issued "a report detailing Vietnam's need for charitable assistance and encouraging private organizations to provide the help." The article went on to note that in spite of the fact that U.S. officials have consistently "resisted Hanoi's pleas for direct Government aid or reparations," those same officials privately expressed hope that by encouraging private aid in the form of prosthetics for Vietnam's 60,000 amputees, "the Vietnamese will be more cooperative on the issue of missing servicemen."[1] In a related article on the matter, the Associated Press quoted a State Department spokesman as denying emphatically that the administration's call for assistance was in any way related to U.S. efforts to persuade Vietnam to account for missing American servicemen.[2]

On January 6, *USA Today* reported that three of the activist congressmen— Reps. Frank McCloskey (D-IN), Bob Smith (R-NH), and John Rowland (R-CT)— were currently en route to Vietnam to search for American MIAs and that prior to their departure, the State Department had denied their request to take Robert Garwood along to show them where he had seen POWs in captivity after the war.[3] In denying the congressmen's request, Secretary of State George Shultz had declared Garwood's inclusion in the delegation "would be inappropriate and potentially harmful to our foreign policy interests in the region."

Vietnam's response to the publicity surrounding the U.S. report on charitable assistance and the conflicting statements by U.S. officials as to what the report represented were predictable. Thach, speaking to reporters in Ho Chi Minh City on January 18, rejected the U.S. plan out of hand, calling it "inadequate" and "not correct" and declaring as he had so many times in the past that a major portion of any aid his country received from the United States must come from the U.S. government. "Otherwise," Thach said, sounding his old refrain, "my people will ask why the United States refuses to give Government aid to Vietnam while Vietnam gives Government aid to the U.S. [by searching for American MIAs]."[4]

Thach's negative public response to the administration's proposed aid plan drew a predictably negative response from Washington, where State Department spokesman Chuck Redman officially rejected Vietnam's demand for U.S. aid and called Hanoi's action on last year's pledge to help resolve the cases of missing Americans "disappointing."[5]

Chicken? Egg? Egg? Chicken? "Appropriate?" "Inappropriate?" "Disappointing." "Not disappointing." As usual, the *Orange County Register*'s Mike Shelton, who continued to monitor the POW issue closely, knew exactly what it all meant.

(COURTESY MIKE SHELTON, *THE ORANGE COUNTY REGISTER*)

*April*

## HEARINGS HELD ON SMITH'S BILL TO DECLASSIFY THE POW INTELLIGENCE

On April 20, Solarz held a public hearing on HR 2260, Bob Smith's bill to declassify the POW intelligence. In a hearing room packed to the walls with activist family members, activist Vietnam vets, and representatives of scores of small grassroots lobbying organizations that had sprung up all across the country in support of the POWs, Griffiths, who had earlier declared she and the League opposed the bill because it "appears aimed at generating domestic pressure against our own government,"[6] repeated her strong opposition, saying this time that "no viable rationale exists for publicly releasing intelligence information." Schlatter, now head of the Special Office, agreed and warned ominously that public release of the intelligence "would show the extent of our collection capability and our investigatory and analytical techniques . . . and would reveal our degree of knowledge about the location, infrastructure and facilities which might hold U.S. prisoners." According to *The Washington Times,* when Solarz sided with Griffiths and Schlatter and declared, "'The real problem lies in Hanoi, not in Washington,' a loud series of coughs and grumbles nearly drowned him out."[7] In the end, Solarz and members of his subcommittee did nothing, which, of course, in a town where doing nothing often is doing something, was just what the administration wanted.

Several days after the hearing, Griffiths further explained to her membership that her opposition to HR 2260 was rooted primarily in the fact that release of the intelligence on live POWs "would jeopardize serious efforts now ongoing to return our missing relatives, alive or dead." She went on to reject the allegation made by the activists that a cover-up was under way and declared forcefully, "It is important that current priority assets, particularly within the Defense Intelligence Agency, are no longer wasted on responding or reacting to such unfounded allegations."[8] The families were comforted and relieved. So, of course, were Powell and Childress over at the NSC, Shultz and Wolfowitz at State, Carlucci and Armitage at Defense, and Schlatter and his team at the DIA Special Office. But perhaps especially Powell, who would later write that an overriding fear at the time was that "Reagan would have gone for another hostage-freeing scheme at the drop of a Hawk missile."[9]

Vietnam vets crossing Memorial Bridge during first Rolling Thunder rally, Memorial Day weekend 1988. (COURTESY *ROLLING THUNDER MAGAZINE* AND ROLLING THUNDER 2001 BOARD OF DIRECTORS: ARTIE MULLER, CHAIRMAN; DANNY "GREASY" BELCHER, PRESIDENT; WALT SIDES, DIRECTOR; TED SAMPLEY, DIRECTOR)

Uncomforted and unrelieved, however, were the biker vets, several thousand of whom descended upon the Vietnam Veterans Memorial in Washington over Memorial Day, engines roaring, huge black POW flags flying, to protest the abandonment of their brothers. They named their protest Rolling Thunder, and pledged to return every Memorial Day until the POWs came home.

## July
## REAGAN TO FAMILIES: WE WILL NOT PAY FOR LIVE PRISONERS, BUT WE WILL ACCELERATE THE SEARCH FOR BONES

With only months left in the Reagan presidency, administration officials met on several occasions during late spring and early summer to develop a work plan for the rest of the year and a strategy for handing off the poisonous live POW issue to the new president, whom almost everyone now believed was going to be Vice President Bush.

By July, the work plan and handoff strategy were complete. Reagan would address the POW/MIA families for the last time during the League's annual convention in Washington in late July. There, he would lay out the administration's work plan for the remainder of his term, thank the families for their support over the years, and say his good-byes. Outlining the work plan, the president would cite Communist intransigence on the matter of postwar aid as the reason for a lack of progress on the live POW issue and would forcefully repeat his administration's refusal to swap aid for prisoners. He would then reassure the families by announcing that a new series of crash site excavations would be conducted in northern Vietnam in the near future. Additionally, he would announce that his administration was preparing a voluminous study outlining everything that had been accomplished on the POW/MIA issue since 1981—as well as those things that still needed to be done—and declare the study would be presented to the incoming president to ensure there would be no interruption in the government's effort to achieve "the fullest possible accounting" of those still missing in Indochina. It was decided that Childress and Griffiths would be the principal authors of the study, assisted by their superiors and other members of the POW/MIA IAG.

When the president arrived at Washington's J. W. Marriott Hotel on the morning of July 29 to address the families, he was greeted by shouts from a small group of protestors who believed his administration was spending too much time looking for remains and not enough trying to find and repatriate live POWs.

A *New York Times* article later quoted one of the protesters, Londa Chandler of Uniondale, New York, as saying, "I think we should go to Vietnam and say: 'We know you have live guys. What do you want for them?'" and noted Chandler had made the comment after "recalling that the Reagan Administration allowed the sale of arms to Iran in an attempt to free American hostages held in Lebanon." The article went on to identify Chandler as a member of the Forget-Me-Not Association, "which considers the National League of Families to be too moderate, an 'arm of the Government, not an adversary,' as another protester put it." The article also quoted another member of the Forget-Me-Not Association, Dana Chwan, as saying most members of the association consider the administration's latest talks with Vietnam an "attempt by the Government to write the issue off."[10]

The president stuck to the script prepared by his aides. He first praised the leadership of the League for "resist[ing] simplistic solutions." He then praised the charitable organizations that were assisting Vessey with the prosthetics initiative and declared defiantly that his administration would never "weaken in our resolve to resist attempts to use this humanitarian issue for political gain."

What his administration *would* do, the president then said, was send teams to the SRV in the near future to begin a new series of joint U.S.-Vietnamese crash site excavations. Alluding to a new agreement on joint excavations that had been completed only hours earlier in Hanoi, the president promised that these excavations would begin as soon as possible and continue for the remainder of his term, and that the agreement to allow them raised hopes that a "break-through" might be in the offing. Finally, to the applause of most of those present, the president announced he had directed that a comprehensive study on the POW/MIA issue be prepared, "detailing our efforts, accomplishments, and what remains to be done," and that this study be presented to his successor.[11]

"We love you, Mr. President," a woman shouted from the audience as Reagan prepared to leave the hall. "All signs give us great hope," League chairman George Brooks told a reporter after the president's speech, citing the new crash site search agreement with the Vietnamese as the primary source of his encouragement.[12]

Reagan's enormous popularity, the applause, the woman's shouted praise, and Brook's encouragement and hope notwithstanding, it began to dawn on more and more of those present that day that the administration actually might not *want* the live POWs back, and for two obvious reasons. First, if administration officials really wanted the live prisoners back, they would simply take the political heat and trade aid for them as the Vietnamese were literally begging them to do. The president, however, had just declared he would not do this. And second, having now gained unfettered access to the crash sites, had administration officials had any interest whatsoever in live prisoners, they would have demanded they be taken to the nearby prisons where intelligence indicated living POWs were being held.[13]

And so, for the activist families, the popular president's prepared remarks that morning had not offered great hope; to the contrary, they had extinguished any remaining hope they had that Ronald Reagan, now in the last months of his presidency, would make one more effort to get the live POWs home.

*November 11, 1988*
## NORTHEAST THAILAND

The JCRC's veteran Thailand-based interviewer, SMSgt. William Gadoury, USAF (pronounced GAD ree), was spending a portion of his Veterans Day listening to yet another story about American POWs being detained by the Communists in

Laos. Gadoury, a fixture around the river towns and refugee camps of northeast Thailand, had interviewed and reinterviewed and reinterviewed again hundreds of Lao and Thai—and loved to boast that he had never found even one whom he believed to have credible information about live POWs. Disliked by the refugees for his heavy-handed tactics and hated by the activist families and vets for his ridiculing of the intelligence, Gadoury, through acts of commission and omission, had in the minds of many done incalculable harm to the effort to repatriate live POWs from Laos. Today, Veterans Day, 1988, he would outdo himself.

The source Gadoury was interviewing, a Thai man employed at the hospital in Sakon Nakhon, a small city west of Nakhon Phanom in the far northeast, told Gadoury that within the past month he had been in contact with a Lao man who told him about and showed him proof of American prisoners held inside Laos. The Thai explained that the Lao man had recently crossed into Thailand to inform him that he had personally observed a location in rugged mountains in the tri-border area (Laos, Vietnam, Cambodia) where 260 Americans are being held. The Lao told him that 270 Americans had previously been held there, but 10 had died. He repeated that he had gone to the area himself and had seen some of the prisoners being held in a cave at the foot of a large karst mountain. To prove what he said was true, the Lao had reportedly produced six recently shot color photographs that showed eight or nine of the American prisoners at the cave prison. According to the Lao, the prison was located in a valley served by only a single road, and the entrance to the valley was well guarded and only resupply trucks were allowed in. The Lao further explained that he was related to one of the guards, and that guard had expressed an interest in helping the American prisoners return to freedom if he and his men could be accommodated. Concluding, the Thai told Gadoury that he was willing to cooperate with U.S. authorities and the Lao intermediary and the guard in a joint effort to free the American prisoners, but before he would agree to do so he wanted to know the terms of the $2.4 million reward he had heard about in the news.

Given his vast experience in the region and his unparalleled knowledge of the postwar intelligence from Laos, it is almost inconceivable that Gadoury did not recognize the similarities between what he was hearing from the Thai man and information contained in two earlier reports that had told of American POWs being detained in a similar prison in the tri-border area. The first report had described a prison located just east of the village of Dak Chung where 250 to 300 American and Thai POWs were reportedly detained during 1976.[14] The second, which Gadoury himself had filed after interviewing a source in 1986, had described a cave prison located four to five kilometers east of the village of Dak Chung and the sighting of American POWs confined to that prison during November 1983. According to this second report, the cave where the Americans were being detained was located at the base of a steep face of a mountain.[15]

Notwithstanding these reports, according to a report he would later file, Gadoury responded to the source's current query about the reward by informing him that "the U.S. government was not offering a reward" and "did not support the private group who is advertising the reward," and after "point[ing] out that many people have been inquiring recently about the reward . . . cautioned [the] source not to be too quick to believe every rumor he hears."[16]

*November 11, 1988*
## WASHINGTON

Surely unaware that one of his own men had only hours before instructed a potential rescuer in Thailand not to pursue a plan designed to rescue American POWs reportedly being held in Laos in return for the reward the Republican congressmen were offering, Ronald Reagan spent a portion of his last Veterans Day as president at the Vietnam Veterans Memorial in Washington.

*The Washington Post's* Michael York, one of the reporters covering the president's visit to the memorial that Veterans Day, filed an account of the visit that captured the emotion surrounding the MIA issue in a manner not often seen in print journalism. York's account appeared the following morning on the *Post's* front page under the headlines "Reagans Pay Emotional Visit to Vietnam Veterans Wall, *Fate of the Missing Haunts Ceremony.*" Next to the article was a striking picture of the president and Mrs. Reagan standing alone, hand-in-hand at the Wall as Mrs. Reagan reached out to touch some of the names.

York wrote that just as the first lady was touching the names on the Wall, "[s]uddenly, the quiet was broken, when one of more than 10,000 people attending the Veterans Day ceremony shouted a protest of administration policy toward those still listed as missing in action. 'Mr. President, when will you bring my father home?' the woman shouted."

York explained that several minutes before, the president had delivered a "rousing, patriotic speech in which he declared America's cause in the war 'just,'" and that the crowd had responded with vigorous, sustained applause. But, York wrote, when Reagan had later mentioned negotiations with the Vietnamese over the return of remains, the crowd had heckled him loudly. When he had tried to calm the crowd by noting the National Park Service "now flies the white-on-black POW-MIA flag [here] at the Wall on Veterans Day and Memorial Day," he was again interrupted by the shouts of protesters. "Bring them home so we won't have to fly it anymore," York quoted a man in Army fatigues as shouting. York wrote that Reagan ignored the man and the shouts and signs of others saying "Free American POWs" and "No more lies."

York went on to report that "many of those who did not join the shouting were nonetheless drawn to the ceremony by their concerns about those still missing" and cited as examples Vietnam vets Pete Clancey and Kevin McGonigle, who told him they had driven to Washington from New Jersey to register support for new efforts to determine the fate of the MIAs. "I think there are a lot of unanswered questions," McGonigle, a newly elected City Council member in Fanwood, N.J., told York. "Vietnam refugees have said they have seen Americans there, [and] [t]hese questions need to be answered."

What, one wonders, would those in the crowd have said or done had they known of the Veterans Day message Gadoury had delivered just hours before in Thailand?

The president's last public appearance on behalf of the Vietnam POWs and

MIAs now in the history books, those responsible for setting and implementing administration policy—Powell, his deputy for Asian affairs Childress, Griffiths, and the others on the IAG—went about *their* last task: completing their study of the POW/MIA issue and the administration's effort to resolve it and having the study ready for presentation to President-elect George Bush upon his inauguration in January.

## THE REAGAN ADMINISTRATION'S FINAL REPORT ON THE POW/MIA ISSUE

Senate investigators combing the intelligence files in 1991 and 1992 would discover that credible intelligence about live POWs had continued pouring into DIA throughout 1988. They would also find that in accordance with long-established practice, the NSC's Childress had received an official copy of each intelligence report. They would further find that much of the intelligence received during 1988 tended to corroborate other prior reporting. Additionally, they would find that during the last quarter of the year—the period when Childress, Griffiths, and the others were putting together the administration's comprehensive final report, the flow of intelligence had been especially heavy and its credibility especially high.

A brief synopsis of selected intelligence reports received by Childress during 1988 shows that:

- On January 5, 1988, Childress had received a hearsay Stony Beach report that quoted a guard who worked at the Tay Hieu State Prison/State Farm in the far northwestern reaches of Nghe Tinh Province in northern Vietnam as saying American POWs were being held at the prison during 1978 and 1979. (See map page 356, point 1.) According to what the guard reportedly said, the Americans had been captured during the war "from the southern Laos front."[17]

    Given that previous reports had indicated American POWs were being detained in Nghe Tinh Province during the same time period, the report seemed plausible.
- On January 15, 1988, Childress had been advised that a former Lao refugee residing in California had contacted DIA about an effort he said was under way to repatriate four American POWs reportedly being held in a cave north of Paksan, Laos. (See map page 356, point 2.) According to a report filed by DIA analyst Gen. Soutchay Vongsavanh, who had interviewed the former refugee,

    [The former refugee] said his brother in law came to see him on december [*sic*] 1987. [The brother-in-law] has arrived U.S. just 4 months ago and has information about 4 American POWS in the area of Paksan but he did not see by his own eye, but only hearsay, from a fellow of the Hmong communist in Laos.

    [Name redacted] stated that his brother in law . . . said while working with the resistance . . . inside Laos at Paksan province he . . . has met with Hmong communist who have guarded 4 American POWS and several Laotians and Hmong prisoners, they were separated from the American room, these Hmong communists have told [the brother-in-law] we are Hmong ethnic so we do not need to shoot each other, now I am guarding 4 American POW in the cave and I am sick and tired to keep them too long for over 10 years already and they (Americans) became old aged so I would like to get rid of them to give you, if you have money just two bar of silvers for each man and I'll tell my boss that I have killed them because they (Americans) have tried to escape from the prison.

The Hmong communist also said these American POWs have moved from [redacted] province long times ago; unfortunately [the brother-in-law] did not have any of silver bars to give to the guards at the cave. The location of the cave was north of Muang Paksan. During the conversation, [the brother-in-law] has asked [the man being interviewed by DIA, the former refugee living in California] to contact with the American official, because [the brother-in-law] would like to have American official to hire him . . . to go back Laos to get Americans POWS back to United States, if he . . . fails to do the job he does not need anything from U.S. and he would pay by himself for the trip from U.S. to Thailand for round trip, if he . . . could bring out the American POWS from Laos to Thailand U.S. must pay him.[18]

U.S. officials later declined to participate in the proposed effort to liberate the four American prisoners.[19]

• On <u>February 2, 1988</u>, Childress had received a Stony Beach report describing the sighting in mid-March 1987 of three emaciated American POWs who were reportedly confined to a cave prison on Katon Mountain just west of Sepone (Tchepone) in the Laotian panhandle.[20] (See map page 356, point 3.) According to the report, at around midday on March 15, 1987, a ten-man Lao government research team performing geological tasks in an area just west of Sepone reportedly came upon a large cave guarded by Pathet Lao soldiers armed with AK-47s. According to what one of the geologists reportedly told a relative, the team approached the cave and introduced themselves to the soldiers. In the ensuing conversation, the geologist said the soldiers informed the group that they were guarding American POWs who were held inside the cave. They further said they were tired of guarding the Americans and would like to release them. According to the report, at that point one of the geologists asked if he could see the Americans, and one of the guards consented and invited him to step inside the cave. This geologist later said that once inside the cave, he stood and watched as the guard ordered the prisoners to move to the front of the cave. The geologist said that three Americans then came forward and stopped about ten feet away from where he was standing. He described the three as all being tall, thin, and sickly. All had long hair and beards and were dressed in very old clothes. They seemed to lack food and medical supplies, and it appeared they slept on the ground. The geologist said he studied the American prisoners for approximately two minutes before the guard ordered the prisoners back into the rear of the cave.

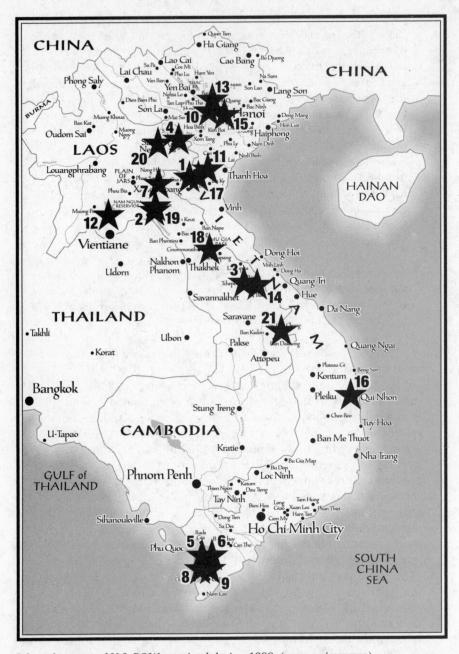

Selected reports of U.S. POWs received during 1988. (HENDON/ANDERER)

In reporting what the geologist had reportedly seen, the source of the Stony Beach report offered to help in any way he could to get the three American POWs out of Laos. Declassified records show that his offer had not been accepted and that no further investigation of the reported sighting had taken place.[21] Senate investigators would later consider this lack of follow-up especially egregious, because some sixteen months earlier, DIA, Childress, and other addressees had received a report from the exact same area quoting a group of Pathet Lao soldiers as saying they had been guarding three American prisoners there for a long time and were very poor and wanted to find a way for them and the Americans to escape to Thailand and sought help for such an escape. Just as with the current case, no such help had been offered.[22]

- On <u>February 22, 1988</u>, Childress had received a JCRC report concerning the detention during early 1985 of nine American prisoners in a cave south of Sop Hao, in the "gorilla's eye" in eastern Sam Neua Province, Laos. (See map page 356, point 4.) The Sop Hao area, everyone familiar with the postwar intelligence knew, had been the focus of large numbers of reports about American POWs being held there in the postwar period. According to the source of this latest report—a member of the Lao resistance—the Americans were kept in the cave at night and were required to work on construction details during the day. The source told U.S. officials that when senior resistance officials had learned where the Americans were being detained, they had ordered a rescue operation be mounted, but the operation had failed and at least two of the potential rescuers had been captured and executed.[23]

- On <u>February 27, 1988</u>, Childress had received a JCRC report from Thailand quoting a recently arrived refugee as saying that one day before his departure from Vietnam on January 7, 1988, several friends had visited him in Ho Chi Minh City and told him they knew for certain "many" American prisoners were being held in the U-Minh Forest region of the Ca Mau Peninsula and asked him to contact members of "the American delegation in Bangkok" and convey that information to them. (See map page 356, point 5.) The refugee, a former official in the RVN Ministry of Finance, told JCRC officials he had known two of the friends for more than fourteen years and believed their story.[24] Those familiar with the postwar intelligence knew, of course, that a number of other sources had also reported that U.S. POWs were being detained after the war in the U-Minh.

- On <u>April 5, 1988</u>, Childress had received another JCRC report telling of American prisoners being detained in the U-Minh. (See map page 356, point 6.) This report quoted a forty-eight-year-old former ARVN second lieutenant as saying that when he had told a friend in mid-1986 that he intended to enter refugee channels, the friend had replied that he had some important information he wanted him to pass to the U.S. government and had related the following: "Sometime during 1985, [name redacted] (U/I) observed 25 male and one female Caucasian Americans who were being held by Communist authorities in Forest 390 (Rung 390). Forest 390 was located in Minh Hai Province between the Upper U Minh (Thoung) and Lower U Minh (Ha) areas. The female prisoner was acting as a doctor and providing medical treatment to the other 25 male American prisoners."[25]

The second lieutenant had gone on to report that [name redacted] had asked for nothing in return for his information and had said that his only purpose in providing the information was to help the Americans return home.

• On <u>April 22, 1988,</u> Childress had received a report from Stony Beach in Bangkok describing the presence over time of four American POWs in a prison camp/cave complex southeast of Nong Het, Laos, and the possible presence of two of those Americans at the camp at the time the Stony Beach report was prepared. (See map page 356, point 7.) The information about the Americans, Stony Beach reported, had recently been received from "a controlled asset of proven reliability with excellent access who obtained the information from [name redacted], a Lao People's Army officer and alleged member of the Lao People's Revolutionary Party, with purported good access, whose reliability is unknown." The relevant portions of the report follow:

2. In 1981, . . . source observed four U.S. PW detained in a mountain basin located approximately 10 km southeast of Nong Het //UTM coords UG 946550//, Laos. The prisoners were detained in a mountain basin in a non-wooded area about two or three rai [approximately 2 acres] in size, surrounded by mountains. A cave, located on one side of the entrance to the basin, had been converted into a living shelter where beds were placed. The detention facility did not have a fence. Co-located with the alleged U.S. PW were former FAR [Forces Armée Royales, the Royal Lao] government officials and military officers who were undergoing political rehabilitation. These FAR officials were considered by the new government to be the most dangerous and "hard headed" officers, and possessed the worst records. Source opined that these officials probably would never be released. One of the Lao officers who was detained at this facility was General [name redacted], the former chief of staff, who was later killed while trying to escape.

3. In 1984, source returned to the same detention facility where he observed, at close range, two PW. They were the only U.S. PW located there at the time. When source asked the whereabouts of the other two PW, the security guards informed him that the other two PW, formerly held at this location, were transferred to Vieng Xai //approx geocords 2025N 104 02E// to prevent all the PW from escaping at on[e] time. Sometime prior to 1984, some of the security guards were arrested for attempting to help prisoners escape. The remaining prisoners, in order to preclude escape, had no duties other than general cleaning of the area in which they lived. Source, who did not pay much attention to the two PW, could only describe them as being between 35 and 40 yoa in 1984.

4. Source believes that the two U.S. PW are still detained at the above location because personnel who work or visit that area would have told him had the prisoners been relocated.[26]

Those familiar with the postwar intelligence knew that another source, a former inmate, had earlier reported that he had observed five American prisoners being detained in a camp of similar description in the same general area from 1976 until October 1985 (see Chapter 25).

• On <u>May 11, 1988</u>, Childress had received a report from JCRC stating that a Vietnamese refugee had told JCRC interviewers in the Philippines that he "knew for a fact" that 150 Americans were living in the U-Minh Forest and had volunteered to lead an expedition to find them.[27] (See map page 356, point 8.)

• On <u>May 18, 1988</u>, Childress had received a second Stony Beach report quoting the controlled source who had reported in April about the four/two U.S. POWs at the camp southeast of Nong Het (see above). In this latest report, the source reported among other things that:

> 1. During the war in Indochina, Lao policy stated that all Communist units had the responsibility to capture U.S. servicemen. Once captured, the prisoners were turned over to the representative of the party secretary general of each province. The Communist party policy was to keep these prisoners as a tool for political bargaining. However, those prisoners apprehended by village defense forces or irregular (Kong Lon) units were usually killed due to the problem of escorting them from remote areas to the provincial secretary general.
>
> 2. The current Lao government policy concerning the retention of U.S. PW results from past LPRP central committee meetings in which the Lao government accepted the principle agreed to by the other Indochinese governments of Vietnam and Kampuchea to retain prisoners for political reasons. Laos would keep U.S. PW to force the U.S. government to pay war reparations needed for reconstruction in Laos. Kampuchea would retain prisoners to force the USG to recognize the Heng Samrin government as the only lawful government of Kampuchea in the United Nations. The three Indochinese governments also agreed to move the remaining U.S. PW "around" to serve their needs.[28]

• On <u>May 20, 1988</u>, Childress had received another hearsay report telling of American POWs being detained in the U-Minh Forest in far southern Vietnam. The source of this latest report, a recently arrived former resident of Ho Chi Minh City, told U.S. officials that two days before his scheduled departure from Vietnam, a female friend told him she had some POW/MIA information she would like him to pass to the U.S. government. The refugee told U.S. officials that among the information the woman wanted passed was the fact that her brother had personally observed a group of American POWs being escorted under guard in the U-Minh Forest area of the Ca Mau Peninsula sometime during January 1988.[29] (See map page 356, point 9.)

• On <u>June 22, 1988</u>, Childress had received a Stony Beach report describing a conversation about American POWs a refugee reported he had overheard in Ho Chi Minh City in December 1986. According to the refugee, he had overheard one retired field-grade PAVN officer tell another that perhaps 280 to 300 American POWs were still being held behind three rings of security in a prison in the Ba Vi Mountain area west of Hanoi and that a few of those Americans were being held in an underground facility there.[30] (See map page 356, point 10.) Those familiar with the postwar intelligence quickly noted the similarity between this report and information earlier provided by another Northerner about some three hundred American POWs reportedly being held in an underground prison located behind three rings of security in the mountains just south of Hung Hoa, in an area just west of Ba Vi Mountain, during 1984. (See Chapter 26.)

- On July 9, 1988, Childress had received a hearsay report from JCRC that indicated American prisoners were being detained at a prison camp in Thanh Hoa Province in northern Vietnam during 1986. (See map page 356, point 11.) The report, provided to JCRC by a Vietnamese refugee who said he had learned about the Americans from his father, described how a group of South Vietnamese prisoners had reportedly been tasked by their captors to deliver food to a prison camp in Thanh Hoa Province and upon arriving at the small camp had found it occupied by Caucasian prisoners with long beards. According to the father, the South Vietnamese delivering the food had decided that, based on their appearance, the Caucasian prisoners "had to be Americans."[31] Though hearsay in nature and lacking specific detail other than the information concerning the appearance of the Caucasian prisoners, given the high volume of previous reporting about American POWs being held in Thanh Hoa Province during the late 1970s and early to mid-1980s, the July 9 report of American prisoners being detained there in 1986 appeared plausible.[32]

- On August 10, 1988, Childress had received a hearsay report from Stony Beach telling of the presence of American POWs at a camp located south of the Nam Ngum Dam in the far northern reaches of Vientiane Province, Laos. (See map page 356, point 12.) According to the source of the Stony Beach report, he and his uncle, who lived in the area, were traveling by bus along a main road south of the dam in March 1985 when they passed a side road that was closed off by a wooden-framed barbed-wire gate that was manned by LPLA (Lao People's Liberation Army) sentries. The source said that after they passed, he asked his uncle what lay down the road behind the gate and his uncle replied the road led to a site named Houay Khong where American soldiers were imprisoned. Source said he had expressed incredulity at this, but his uncle replied he was certain American prisoners were currently being detained at the site.[33] Inasmuch as map tracking shows that the source had accurately described highway numbers, bridges, and the general topography in the vicinity of the reported camp, and given that the DIA had received earlier reports indicating American POWs were being detained in areas just south and west of the dam from 1981 until May 1986, this latest report of American servicemen reportedly being detained in the area during March 1985 appeared plausible.

- On September 7, 1988, Childress had received a hearsay account from Stony Beach indicating that fifteen to sixteen prisoners who were presumed to be Americans had been seen sometime around 1984 in the vicinity of the Vinh Quang Reeducation Camp northwest of Hanoi. (See map page 356, point 13.) The report quoted a former captain in the RVN National Police who had been detained at Vinh Quang as telling a fellow former National Police captain that he had personally observed fifteen to sixteen prisoners whom he assumed were Americans while he was out of the camp on a work detail. The captain who had reportedly seen the Americans described them as all being thin and dressed in the same blue uniforms ARVN inmates wore. He also said the Americans did not speak to him or to one another during the period he observed them, but did communicate through hand signals. It was unclear from the report whether the captain meant the Americans had used hand signals to communicate among themselves, with him, or both.[34] Given that two independent sources had placed American POWs in the vicinity of the Vinh Quang Reeducation Camp System during the early 1980s, the former police captain's reported statements that he had seen fifteen to sixteen prisoners whom he presumed to be Americans outside his camp around 1984 appeared plausible.

- On <u>September 8, 1988</u>, Childress had received a Stony Beach report that had provided the names, ranks, and military services of five Americans and a highly detailed sketch of the prison camp just north of Route 9 in eastern Savannakhet Province, Laos, where they were reportedly being detained. (See map page 356, point 14.) Stony Beach officials stated they had received the information from a "high ranking Royal Thai Navy intelligence officer who gained access to the information in the course of his duties." The Royal Thai Navy officer, a captain, had reported the American prisoners "were reportedly seen by resistance forces (both Kampuchean and Laotian)" and that he had received the information about them from members of the resistance elements he was in contact with.

According to the Royal Thai Navy captain, the names, ranks, and services of the five Americans were

| Tommy Hart | Capt | USAF |
| Eddy Mercer | T/Sgt | USAF |
| Joe Berch | Capt | USAF |
| Jim Fuller | T/Sgt | USAF |
| Morgan Donahue | Capt | USAF |

"All names," Stony Beach officials declared in their report, "crosschecked with valid MIA cases."[35]

Given the specificity of the information about the Americans, the highly detailed sketch map of the camp where they were reportedly held, the fact that the names of the five Americans "crosschecked with valid MIA cases," and the fact that a number of other sources had also reported the presence of American POWs in eastern Savannakhet Province after the war, the report appeared plausible.

- On <u>November 16, 1988</u>, Childress had received a Stony Beach report quoting an eyewitness as saying he had seen two American pilots being detained at the Bang Liet/Thanh Liet Prison in the southwest Hanoi suburbs as recently as June 1988, some five months earlier. (See map page 356, point 15.)

The maximum security Bang Liet/Thanh Liet facility was well-known to U.S. officials because American POWs had been held there during the war. Though located within the small village of Thanh Liet, wartime officials had named the prison "Bang Liet" after another nearby village and had assigned it the official designation "Bang Liet PW Camp N-125." The facility had been subjected to almost continuous aerial surveillance throughout the war. When the American POWs who had been held there during the war were released at Operation Homecoming, they reported that they had called the facility "Skidrow."[36]

The source of the November 16 account, a former Ministry of Interior informant who himself had been imprisoned at Bang Liet/Thanh Liet/ Skidrow, had told U.S. officials after escaping from Vietnam that he had seen two American prisoners at the prison as recently as June 1988. He had explained that he had seen the two Americans daily when he cleaned their cells, and had said a camp cadre told him the two Americans were pilots and that eleven other Americans were also being held at the facility.

The informant had described the Americans as being about forty-seven years old, tall, and very thin with sallow skin, blue eyes, short gray hair, and stubble beards. They wore solid color gray two-piece prison uniforms that had two pockets in the lower front of the shirts. One of the pilots, the taller of the two, had a large burn mark covering his entire left cheek from the eye down to his lower jaw. The informant had said that though the American pilots were in adjacent cells, they were not allowed to speak and thus had no contact with each other or with anyone else.

The informant had said that he saw the two American pilots twice a day when he cleaned their waste bowls and brought them water. He said the pilots were either seated in their chairs or exercising when he entered their cells, and that they always looked "very sorrowful." He said they would often gesture with their right hands in what he believed was an expression of their religious beliefs. With the right hand, the informant said, each pilot would touch his own forehead, right shoulder, then left shoulder.

The informant had told U.S. officials that the Americans were fed very poor rice, salt, peanuts, and small amounts of fish, pork, chicken, eggs, and bananas. This diet, he said, was reserved for foreign prisoners, while the diet of reeducation subjects was far more restricted. According to the informant, other foreigners held at the prison in addition to the thirteen Americans included Cambodians, Chinese, Thai, and an approximately seventy-year-old Japanese Buddhist monk.

The informant had further told U.S. officials that in spite of Vietnam's policy that any inmate who disclosed information about what he had seen at the maximum security Bang Liet/Thanh Liet/Skidrow prison could be imprisoned for an additional three to five years, he would be willing to return to Vietnam and assist the U.S. government in mounting a rescue of the Americans he believed were still being held at the facility.[37]

• On December 8, 1988, Childress had received a hearsay JCRC report that described the March 1987 sighting of three groups of American POWs totaling an estimated 180 men being force-marched under guard along a jungle path some forty kilometers west of the southern coastal city of Qui Nhon. (See map page 356, point 16.) According to the source of the report, a fifty-four-year-old former South Vietnamese police officer, a friend had approached him in mid-August 1988 prior to his departure from Vietnam and had asked him to relay the details of the sighting to U.S. authorities. According to the police officer, his friend had told him his two sons had personally observed the Americans while searching for sandalwood in the jungle. The sons reportedly described the Americans as being dressed in green uniforms and tied together hand to hand, and had reportedly overheard guards discussing the fact that the prisoners had been transferred to the South due to the Chinese attack on Vietnam. After telling U.S. officials what the friend had told him, the police officer had offered to contact the friend and communicate further about the American POWs using a prearranged code, but U.S. officials had declined his offer and warned him of the danger to individuals in Vietnam who dealt in the POW/MIA issue.[38] Map tracking would show that the area of the reported sighting lay just south of National Route 19 near the former U.S. air base at Ben Cat.[39]

- On December 22, 1988, Childress had received a hearsay Stony Beach report that described the late-January 1985 sighting of six to seven prisoners who appeared to be Americans in a mountain area in the extreme northwest of Nghe Tinh Province in northern Vietnam. (See map page 356, point 17.) According to the report, a recently arrived Vietnamese refugee had told U.S. officials in Hong Kong that a confidant of his—a construction contractor who performed work for the Public Security Service in central and northern Vietnam—had told him he had personally observed the prisoners as they exercised in a clearing near his worksite. The contractor reportedly said the Americans were wearing two-piece prisoner-type uniforms with alternating reddish and gray stripes and were performing various random exercises, not in unison. He also reportedly said the sighting had been brief because PSS personnel had apparently seen him looking at the Americans and had ordered him to leave the immediate area.[40]

Given the previous reporting from Nghe Tinh Province, including the earlier January 5, 1988, report telling of American POWs being detained during 1978 and 1979 at the Tay Hieu State Prison/State Farm in the far northwestern reaches of the province (see above), the December 22 report appeared plausible.

- On December 23, 1988, Childress had received a hearsay Stony Beach report quoting a PL guard as declaring that twelve American POWs were currently being detained in a cave near Ban Khilek in Khammouane Province in the central Laotian panhandle. (See map page 356, point 18.) According to what the guard reportedly said, the cave was called "Tham Kaeb" (*Tham* means "cave"; *Kaeb* is the name of the cave, i.e., "Kaeb Cave") and the Americans had been detained there for seven or eight years. Stony Beach officials reported that Ban Khilek was located at map coordinates WE 2446 in Nhommarath District of Khammouane Province.

Inasmuch as Stony Beach had reported that the information about the twelve Americans had been collected by "a controlled asset of proven reliability who obtained the information from a . . . [Thai intelligence] asset with demonstrated access and reliability," and inasmuch as map tracking showed the area of the sighting to be as described by the source, and inasmuch as DIA had received other reporting telling of American POWs being detained in the area, the December 23, 1988, report quoting the PL guard as saying the twelve American POWs were currently being detained at Tham Kaeb appeared plausible.[41]

• Also on <u>December 23, 1988</u>, Childress had received another Stony Beach report, this one quoting a Thai merchant who arranged sales of foodstuffs to military clients in Laos as saying he had observed four American POWs at a quarry north of Paksan, Laos, three times a month from February 1988 through mid-August 1988, some four months earlier. (See map page 356, point 19.) The merchant had explained that he had seen the Americans while making calls on Lao military clients based at the quarry.

The merchant told U.S. officials that he had seen the four American POWs and approximately twenty Lao prisoners during each of his fifteen or more visits to the site from February until mid-August 1988. He said the American and Lao prisoners were no longer capable of productive work due to age and infirmities but were still required to perform eight hours of labor daily in the quarry. The merchant described the Americans as being haggard and emaciated and dressed in ragged, dark-colored Lao military uniforms and sandals made from vehicle tire treads. All four of the Americans, he said, had had their left hand intentionally maimed by their captors.

The merchant said that on one occasion he had been able to talk briefly with one of the Americans, whom he believed to be the senior man of the four. The conversation, he said, was in the Lao language. According to the merchant, the prisoner stated he had been a pilot and had been captured about 1973 or 1974. The American said his name was Jay, but the merchant told U.S. officials he did not know whether this was the man's actual name or just an initial. The merchant described Jay as being approximately six feet tall with gray hair and blue eyes. He had a jagged, stitch-marked scar from the ear down the left cheek from a wound sustained when his aircraft was shot down.

The merchant said that he did not attempt to obtain additional details about either Jay or the other three Americans because it would have been imprudent to show too much interest in them. He could therefore not provide detailed descriptions of the other prisoners, saying only that they were of differing heights, all were haggard and emaciated, one was blond, and one walked with the aid of a cane or stick. The merchant told U.S. officials he believed the others were enlisted men since they deferred to Jay.

The merchant told U.S. officials that he believed a trader could easily gain access to the site for reconnaissance and/or that a small rescue force could easily approach the quarry without detection. He added that he considered the entire guard force ripe for bribes.[42]

Given that map tracking of the information provided by the merchant proved conclusively he had visited the area north of Paksan that he had described, and given especially that on January 15, 1988, DIA had received a report from a former Lao refugee living in California stating that four American POWs were currently being detained in a cave north of Paksan, Laos (see above), the merchant's sightings of the four American POWs at a quarry north of Paksan from February until August 1988 appeared plausible.

• Finally, throughout most of the month of December, Childress and other administration officials had examined, discussed, analyzed, and reanalyzed stunning satellite imagery taken back in January that showed the letters "USA" and a classified USAF/USN escape and evasion code in a dry rice paddy 5.2 kilometers southwest of the Sam Neua, Laos, airfield. Though the imagery had been acquired in January, imagery analysts had discovered the "USA" and the E&E code only in early December. (See map page 356, point 20.)

The three letters "USA," which had been dug out of the bottom of the rice paddy, appeared to be partially filled with water. DIA imagery analysts determined each of the three letters was approximately twelve feet tall and together they stretched over a distance of some thirty-seven feet. The analysts estimated that based on weather conditions and farming practices employed in the area, the letters had been constructed sometime between October 1987 and January 1988.

Just below the "USA" was a huge version of the secret USAF/USN ground to air distress symbol $K$, apparently fashioned from rice straw. The analysts determined this $K$ was approximately twenty-four feet tall and nineteen feet across.[43]

The telltale $K$, U.S. officials knew, was the same secret ground-to-air pilot distress code seen in the garden plot at Gnommorath in 1980 and—in Morse code form—on the roof of one of the interior lockups at the Dong Vai (Dong Mang) Prison in northern Vietnam in 1975–1976. This Sam Neua $K$, however, was unique in that, in accordance with instructions issued to some aircrewmen during the war, it had been modified with an appendage—in this case a "foot" on its "left leg," a modification that made it a "walking K" or "walking kilo." Though this "foot" was readily apparent in the imagery, due to its highly classified nature at the time, the foot was omitted from a less highly classified line drawing of the imagery that was circulated among top U.S. officials.[44]

Final tally for the year: at least twenty-one seemingly credible reports, including the previously discussed Thai hospital employee's account of the Americans reportedly being held near Dak Chung, Laos, that Gadoury had received on Veterans Day. (See map page 356, point 21.) When added to the seemingly credible accounts received the previous year, *and* those received in 1986—*and* all the other reports received during the Reagan years, *and* all the reports received during the Carter years, *and* those received during the Ford years, *and* those received during the postwar Nixon years, the volume of intelligence was truly staggering.

It was in this context, in this environment, with these numbers on the table,

# NORTHERN LAOS NEAR SAM NEUA
## JANUARY 1988

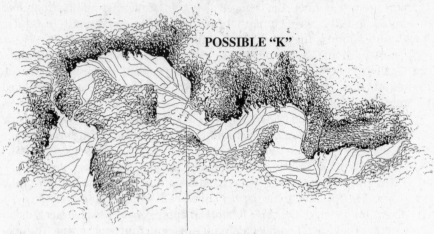

**POSSIBLE "K"**

**"USA" CLEARLY VISIBLE**

(INVENTORY OF THE RECORDS OF THE SENATE SELECT COMMITTEE ON POW/MIA AFFAIRS, 102ND CONGRESS [1991–1992], NATIONAL ARCHIVES)

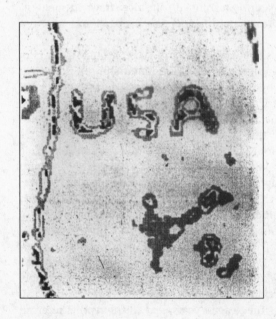

(INVENTORY OF THE RECORDS OF THE SENATE SELECT COMMITTEE ON POW/MIA AFFAIRS, 102ND CONGRESS [1991–1992], NATIONAL ARCHIVES)

that Childress, Griffiths, and the others set about completing the Reagan administration's final report on the POW/MIA issue and submitting it to their superiors for approval. As previously noted, once approved, the report would be presented to the new president upon his inauguration.[45]

# CHAPTER 28

## 1989

## ". . . THE STATUTE OF LIMITATIONS HAS BEEN REACHED"

. . .

Congress . . . has changed in our time. There has grown a certain divisiveness. We've seen the hard looks and heard the statements in which not each other's ideas are challenged but each other's motives. And our great parties have too often been far apart and untrusting of each other. It's been this way since Vietnam. That war cleaves us still. But, friends, that war began in earnest a quarter of a century ago, and surely the statute of limitations has been reached. This is a fact: The final lesson of Vietnam is that no great nation can long afford to be sundered by a memory.
—PRESIDENT GEORGE H.W. BUSH, Inaugural Address, January 20, 1989

The biggest surprise was that Bush used yesterday's state occasion to attempt to exorcise the devilish legacy of the Vietnam war.
—"GEORGE BUSH Sworn In as 41st President, Declares He Will 'Use Power to Help People,'" *Washington Post,* January 21, 1989

Some called it just more of the same, just another cover-your-ass work of fiction by administration officials intent on keeping the plight of the unlisted, unreturned POWs secret. Others called it the best housewarming gift George H. W. Bush could ever have hoped for. Those familiar with how Washington goes about its work knew, of course, it was both, and that its impact on the effort to repatriate the unlisted, unreturned POWs would be devastating.

And indeed, the historic *Final Interagency Report of the Reagan Administration on the POW/MIA Issue in Southeast Asia*—which had been circulated around the bureaucracy during early January and released to the public late in the day on January 19, the day before Bush's inauguration—was a damning document. The report essentially found that no POWs had been left behind at Operation Homecoming and that virtually all of the postwar sightings of American prisoners had been correlated to "specific individuals returned in Operation Homecoming," i.e., the returnees, and not to POWs detained after Operation Homecoming.[1]

A *Washington Post* account of the report's findings appeared on the 21st, the first full day of the Bush presidency. The headline read, "U.S. Doubts POWs Still in Vietnam, *Reagan Administration Releases Final Report on Missing Americans.*" The first sentence read, "In one of its last official acts, the Reagan administration said it found no evidence that North Vietnam held American prisoners of war after 1973."

## RATCHETING UP THE REWARD

Deeply concerned by the content of the final report—and alarmed by statements made by the new president in his Inaugural Address that "the statue of limitations [on the Vietnam War] has been reached" and that America "can [not] long afford to be sundered by a memory [of that war]," and alarmed further that these two events raised the specter of a calculated effort by the new administration to end the debate on live POWs once and for all—Hendon and his colleagues and the activist families and vets moved quickly to ratchet up their efforts to advertise the $2.4 million congressionally sponsored reward.

Prior to early 1989, the group had publicized the reward primarily by taking out advertisements in Vietnam-language publications, handing out thousands upon thousands of reward leaflets in Thai villages and at numerous border crossings and checkpoints located along the Thai-Lao border, sending reward leaflets into Laos by courier, dumping sealed plastic sandwich bags containing reward leaflets into the Mekong at several points in northeastern Thailand in hopes the bags would wash ashore downstream in Laos or even farther downstream in Cambodia or Vietnam, and conducting periodic press conferences in Thailand. But now, a new effort was clearly needed.

In early February, Hendon and three family members chartered a small trawler that had once brought refugees from Vietnam to Hong Kong and, accompanied by several members of the press, sailed from Hong Kong into the South China Sea and launched on the prevailing winds toward Vietnam and Laos hundreds of large balloons with reward leaflets hanging in sealed plastic bags beneath them. Though it was not known for sure whether any of the balloons ultimately reached their target or any of the plastic bags ultimately washed ashore in Vietnam, word of the voyage and the reward poured into Indochina by the Voice of America, BBC, Radio Australia, Philippine-based Radio Veritas, and print media outlets.[2] To the consternation of officials in Washington, Hanoi, and Vientiane, similar voyages and balloon launches would be repeated several times in the months ahead.

*March, Vientiane and Washington*
## MORE "CONSTERNATION"

Sixty days into George H. W. Bush's presidency, the top diplomat at the U.S. embassy in Vientiane, Laos, Chargé d'affaires Harriett Isom, cabled the State Department in Washington with what she characterized as "startling information." Isom wrote that she had just learned of a "colony of American servicemen" currently living in a high mountain valley just east of Phou Bia ("Poo Bee-uh," i.e., Mt. Bia), Laos's highest peak, located northeast of Vientiane at a point some sixty kilometers northeast of the Nam Ngum Reservoir.

Isom reported that the information about the Americans had originated with a "foreign businessman" working in Laos who had learned the information during a recent conversation with an official in the LPDR Ministry of Industry in Vientiane. The businessman said that he had petitioned the Lao government to grant his company a minerals lease in the Mt. Bia area, and the Lao official had responded that this would not be possible because American servicemen were in the area. The businessman, Isom said, had been "most struck by the matter-of-fact tone with which this startling information was passed along."

Isom went on to say that the Lao official had reportedly explained that the Americans had been living in the area since the war and were "not POWs"; rather, he said, they "had settled in the area, the site of a former special forces camp on the slopes of the Phu Bia massif and were quietly living there as part of the village."

Isom expressed surprise and skepticism that the businessman's story could be true, in spite of the fact that several years earlier the embassy had received a report from a different, independent source who had told of the detention of American POWs at Mt. Bia. That report, dispatched from the embassy to Washington on October 29, 1984, had quoted a Pathet Lao intelligence officer as saying he had recently seen approximately thirty American POWs at Mt. Bia, and that they were being detained in a cave under combined Vietnamese/Lao guard. He said that during the day the American prisoners worked under guard outside the cave cooking, farming, and performing other tasks. He reported it was during one of the periods when the American prisoners were outside the cave that he had observed them.[3]

After expressing surprise and skepticism about the businessman's report, Isom, despite the earlier report, and despite the ease with which an indigenous agent could have been dispatched to the area to see if the Americans were actually there (as two independent sources had now reported), sought permission from her superiors in Washington to turn over the businessman's information to Lao government officials and ask them to send a team to Mt. Bia to check it out.[4]

When the Special Office received its copy of the explosive Isom telegram, Col. Joseph Schlatter, USA, now chief of the office, moved quickly. Immediately composing a memorandum for his boss, the deputy director of DIA, Schlatter declared, "We have just received the attached message from American Embassy, Laos." Then, after briefly outlining the message's salient points and two perfunctory steps he had taken to "investigate" the report, Schlatter—in spite of the fact that the earlier report of thirty American POWs being held at Mt. Bia during October 1984 was in the Special Office files and, in fact, still "under analysis"—informed the deputy director that "we have no previous reporting of Americans in this area under any circumstances." Then, addressing Isom's mind-boggling request that she be given permission to turn over the information about the Americans to Lao government officials and ask *them* to send a team to Mt. Bia to check it out, Schlatter asked that he be allowed to "contact State and concur with her suggestion."[5]

Two days later, on March 23, Secretary of State James Baker informed Isom by cable that her request to approach the Lao had been approved.[6] Within hours, Isom went to the Foreign Ministry and met with Bounkeut Sangsomsack, the director of the ministry's Department Two, the American Affairs Department. According to Isom's official report of the meeting, she told Bounkeut:

—I have a very delicate matter to take up with you.

—A foreign investor in Laos learned recently from a Lao government official in the Ministry of Industry, who related the information in the most matter-of-fact way, that a "colony" of Americans are living in a locale of northern Vientiane Province on the slopes of Phu Bia.

—The Lao official, in answer to the investor's query, denied that the men in question [were] POW's but did assert that they were living there of their own accord. He also noted that these were not Mennonites or Quakers or NGO's, but Americans who had stayed behind from the war. They were neither pro-tected nor living in custody and lived in a village. They did not want to be disturbed, the Lao official stated.

—The United States government would be surprised, in light of the Lao gov-ernment's frequent statements that there are no Americans or POW/MIA's in Laos, if this assertion were true. I need not tell you the consternation such information, founded or unfounded, could cause in the United States.

—I request that you investigate this allegation with the greatest discretion and let me know as soon as possible what you find.

Isom reported that after hearing her presentation, Bounkeut replied "he just could not believe such a story could be true" but assured her he "would pass the story immediately to his superiors and an effort would be made to investigate it."[7]

To characterize Isom's actions and statements—and those of Baker, Schlatter, and other officials in Washington as well—as utterly shameful surely does not begin to adequately describe what had occurred. Regardless, *within the space of fewer than five days,* Isom, Baker, Schlatter, and the others had "resolved" the Phu Bia sightings—and "consternation" had been avoided.

*June–July, Washington*
## THE MT. BIA OUTRAGE IS ECLIPSED

In early June, administration officials received word that American POWs had again been seen alive inside Bang Liet/Thanh Liet/Skidrow prison in the south-west Hanoi suburbs, this time as recently as January 1989, some five months be-fore. These POWs had reportedly been seen by a sixty-five-year-old Japanese Buddhist monk who had been released by the North Vietnamese earlier in the year after spending thirteen and a half years in Vietnamese prisons. The monk, hospitalized since his return to Japan and still very ill, had revealed the infor-mation about the POWs during discussions with his thirty-seven-year-old daughter, who had then passed it first to officials at the U.S. embassy in Tokyo and subsequently to a Kyodo News Service reporter.

The Kyodo reporter had published his story about the American prisoners on June 7. According to the reporter's story, the monk, Iwanobu Yoshida, said he had been held with American prisoners of war in four different prisons during his thirteen and a half years of confinement. Yoshida was quoted as saying that the five or six American POWs held with him in Hanoi during the last seven years of his captivity had called him "Jap" and that one had helped him when he had fallen ill and had difficulty walking. He further said the Americans were forced to engage in construction work.

Kyodo reported that officials at the U.S. embassy in Tokyo had been given Yoshida's information by the daughter and quoted one of those officials as saying, "The reports are not unbelievable, there is no reason to doubt her story and her attitude." The official was further quoted as saying the monk's information was "very interesting" and that it would be sent immediately to Washington "to be studied by experts."[8]

The day after receiving the Kyodo report, the Special Office received an official report of Yoshida's sightings from DAO officials at the U.S. embassy in Tokyo. This report read in part:

Yoshida currently is living outside Sapporo and continuing to recover from the illnesses incurred during his imprisonment. . . . The following information was reported by Takatsuka [his daughter] based on her conversations with her father since he returned to Japan.

. . . For about the last six or seven years of his imprisonment, Yoshida was kept in a cell that held 7–8 prisoners. He stated two or three of these individuals were Americans, who said they were U.S. military officers. Three years before his release Yoshida had a stroke, which largely rendered him bedridden. The Americans in the cell reportedly assisted him during this ordeal, helping him with bodily functions and keeping clean. As a youth, Yoshida graduated from Sophia University, Tokyo's international university, where he majored in English literature. While that was some time ago, he still remembered enough English to talk with the American prisoners.

. . . Prior to his stroke, Yoshida and the other prisoners left the prison building each day to work at a farm. He was involved in raising poultry and growing rice. He stated other prisoners were engaged in "civil engineering" projects. . . . The prison was a concrete building near a small town in the suburbs of Hanoi. The prisoners slept on straw mats and were given identical Oriental clothing.[9]

Everyone in the Special Office who read the Kyodo and DAO reports immediately sensed that this Japanese Buddhist monk—sixty-five-year-old Iwanobu Yoshida—and the "approximately 70-year-old Japanese Buddhist monk" the Ministry of Interior informant had reported seeing along with the two U.S. pilots inside Bang Liet/Thanh Liet/Skidrow prison in the Hanoi suburbs during June 1988, exactly one year before, had to be the same man (see Chapter 27).

But that is not what Schlatter would tell his superiors, members of Congress, and others. Instead, in a memo he wrote to his superiors the day he received the DAO report, Schlatter declared:

DIA has interviewed over 10,000 sources from Indochina, primarily Vietnamese refugees. Most of these were imprisoned by the communists for varying lengths of time in various prisons. We have developed a clear picture of the Vietnamese prison system, including the criminal, political and re-education

prison systems. The conclusions from the body of reporting on the prison system are: (1) no U.S. PWs were in that system after Operation Homecoming,
Spring 1973; and, (2) Americans have been in prison in Vietnam as recently as
mid-1988, possibly still now. These Americans have been arrested for various
misadventures and alleged violations of Vietnamese codes, primarily violation of Vietnamese territorial waters. We have, in almost every case, identified
these Americans by name; others we have identified only as Americans/Aus-
tralians/Europeans/etc. . . .

. . . We can draw no conclusions without further details but my suspicion
at this point is that Yoshida did have contact with American prisoners at one
or more times. [However], these Americans were not U.S. PWs; instead, they
were individuals who had been arrested for violation of Vietnamese codes.
His mental condition and the general publicity about the U.S. PW-MIA issue
has resulted in embellishment of his possible contacts with arrested Americans.[10]

And so it came to be that the American POWs Yoshida saw were now, quickly
and officially, American, Australian, and/or European yachtsmen, drug runners,
and/or other civilians—not American POWs. The prisoners couldn't possibly be
American POWs, Schlatter declared, because no American POWs had been held
anywhere in the Vietnamese prison system after Operation Homecoming.

Schlatter's statements and declarations notwithstanding, news that Yoshida
had seen the American POWs up until just before his release back in January appeared prominently in *The Washington Post* on June 10.[11] When members of
Congress from both sides of the aisle demanded answers, DIA again declared
that the prisoners were "yachtsmen," not POWs.[12] When the congressmen demanded proof, Schlatter and his analysts verbally provided them with a list of
seven "best cases." The list, later provided in written form, was composed of a
West German civilian, an American civilian who had been detained at Bien Hoa
and Saigon after the fall of the South, a British civilian yachtsman, three American male civilian yachtsmen, and an American civilian yachtswoman.[13]

On June 12, DIA received additional information from Japan that made the
administration's "yachtsman defense" even more farcical. That day, the DAO reported that Yoshida had now been personally interviewed by U.S. officials and
had provided additional information. According to this new report, Yoshida told
officials he believed two hundred to three hundred Americans had been held with
him outside Hanoi in addition to those he had shared a cell with, and reported
that a Vietnamese security official who spoke fluent Japanese had told him just
prior to his release that a total of seven hundred to eight hundred Americans were
being held by the Hanoi government.[14]

In mid-June, administration officials turned the information Yoshida had
provided over to Vietnamese authorities and requested they investigate it and report back what they found.[15] They then spent the balance of June and the entire
month of July publicly assailing Yoshida's motives, character, physical and mental health, etc., and dismissing at every opportunity the credibility and value of
the information he had provided. The effort proved devastatingly effective, and
by the time administration officials appeared at the League of Families annual

convention in late July to assure the families that Yoshida had seen yachtsmen and not POWs, the activist families were reduced to circulating an interview with Yoshida published in the *National Enquirer* as the only evidence they had that Yoshida had, in fact, seen American POWs back in January and the Vietnamese had told him seven hundred were still being held. Though the interview would later prove to be an almost perfect match of what Yoshida had told U.S. officials during interviews in Japan—and with credible intelligence the U.S. later received—administration officials had a field day ridiculing the tabloid's account.[16]

Soon after the League convention, Schlatter ended the debate on the Yoshida case by telling a special forum on POWs/MIAs convened by the American Legion that Yoshida's testimony about live POWs had been proved to be "absolute nonsense."[17] Later, in their final report on the case, he and his analysts would state definitively that the Americans Yoshida had seen and been held with up until January 1989 were—officially—"American civilians who were detained for various violations of Vietnamese codes and later released."[18]

## WHAT TO DO?

By late summer it was clear to almost all the activist families and vets that President Bush and members of his administration were friends of the unlisted, unreturned POWs in name only—and, many believed, not even in name. First had come the well-timed and very damaging Reagan final report on POWs/MIAs released on January 19. Then Bush himself had decreed fewer than ten minutes into his presidency that the Vietnam War was officially over and the American people should no longer be sundered by its memory. Next the Mt. Bia reporting had been received and, though corroborated by the earlier testimony of the PL intelligence officer, had been turned over to the Communist authorities for "investigation." After that, the Japanese monk Yoshida had come forward in June with his startling testimony about the American POWs being held with him at Bang Liet/Thanh Liet/Skidrow prison in January—testimony corroborated in precise detail by an earlier eyewitness, the MOI informant—and in response Bush officials had morphed the American POWs into yachtsmen and a yachtswoman, given this intelligence Yoshida had provided to Communist authorities for "investigation," and then publicly savaged both Yoshida and his daughter. Finally, to add insult to enormous injury, though the intelligence about the Americans at Mt. Bia and those at Bang Liet/Thanh Liet/Skidrow outside Hanoi had been turned over to Communist authorities in Vientiane and Hanoi, respectively, for "investigation," administration officials had refused to make that very same intelligence available to the activist members of Congress, the activist families, vets, and the press—claiming it was "classified."

Undeterred, the activist families and vets approached two of their oldest allies on the Hill, North Carolina Sen. Jesse Helms, the ranking minority member of the Senate Foreign Relations Committee, and Sen. Charles Grassley (R-IA), and requested their assistance. Helms quickly responded by introducing legislation to allow taxpayers to check off a box on their income tax forms to contribute to a reward fund payable to any Asian who rescued a live American POW. He then directed the Foreign Relations Committee's minority staff to conduct an in-depth investigation of all postwar intelligence reports received by the DIA that indicated American POWs had been held prisoner after Operation Home-coming.[19] Grassley quietly launched a similar investigation. Both investigations began with little fanfare in October.

The activist families spent late September and early October revisiting a matter they had been debating since Bush had taken office back in January: whether or not they should attempt to meet with Bush personally, show him intelligence they had received from DIA over the years—including several intelligence reports telling of specific, named POWs alive in captivity within the last year—and try to convince him to restart the pre-1983 effort to recover living prisoners.[20] Some of the newer members of the activist group felt strongly that the president was being misled by those under him and pushed the group to request a meeting. Others among the family group, mostly old-timers who subscribed to the storied Wash-ington axiom, "The heavies always know," believed asking for such a meeting would be a total waste of time.

And then came the Loma Prieta earthquake that devastated the San Fran-cisco Bay Area in mid-October, and in its wake a unanimous decision by the group—old-timers, newcomers, and everyone in between—that they must try to see the president at once.

## A PERSONAL PLEA TO THE PRESIDENT

On October 17, some sixty-two thousand fans packed into Candlestick Park to see game three of the 1989 World Series. Just after 5:00 P.M., a massive earth-quake rocked the Bay Area and "shook the ballpark like a dog would a rag."[21]

A team of reporters at the *San Francisco Examiner* later described the scene at the "Stick":

> The stadium clock read 5:05 and pre-game World Series ceremonies were just commencing when the quake hit Candlestick Park.
>
> It began with a low rumble that sounded as though thousands were stomping their feet to greet the players' entry onto the field.
>
> Then the vibrations intensified and suddenly the huge canopy over-handing [sic] the upper deck began to ripple. The light towers swayed back and forth like straws in the wind and the right field foul pole whipped like the top of a fishing rod. Chunks of dirt and concrete show-ered down on those sitting beneath the upper deck.
>
> A stunned hush fell over the crowd of 62,000.
>
> For about 30 seconds, the stadium shook wildly until the shocks sub-sided. A great roar erupted from the crowd. . . .
>
> Within minutes, the public address system directed fans to move to lower levels of the stadium. Some, though, were confused by the an-nouncement, unsure if an evacuation had been ordered. Most stayed in their seats. A few moments later, all power went out.
>
> There were isolated instances of panic as a few fans began moving toward

the exits. [Then] [n]ervous laughter broke out in a great collective emotional release as people realized they had survived a major earthquake.[22]

Others in the Bay Area were not so lucky. One section of the upper deck of the Oakland Bay Bridge collapsed onto the lower deck, causing an unknown number of unsuspecting motorists to drive off into the chasm and be killed. In San Francisco's Marina district, dozens were killed and injured as buildings collapsed and fires fed by ruptured gas lines ravaged entire city blocks. At least one area of Fisherman's Wharf, one eyewitness said, "looked like Hiroshima."[23]

Across the bay, attention was focused on a mile-and-a-half-long double-decked section of I-880 in West Oakland known as the Cypress Freeway. Here, the quake had dislodged portions of the upper deck and sent them pancaking onto rush hour traffic below. The *Examiner* reported that rescuers had rushed to the scene and worked feverishly to extricate the injured. One six-year-old boy was saved after an Oakland physician amputated one of his legs to free him from a crushed car. Another child was found alive in a car with his dead parents. One motorist was pried alive out of a pickup truck that had been crushed to a height of two and one half feet. Rescuers told of other vehicles crushed to a height of four inches. "You know what you imagine how things look after the world ends," one paramedic said, "that's the way it looked."

The *Examiner* reported further that by midnight, "Dozens believed to be dead lay trapped in the collapsed freeway in sliver sized automobiles as more than 100 medical professionals lingered in an emergency command post set up at the site." The paper quoted one doctor as expressing pessimism about the chance of finding any remaining survivors Wednesday morning when the search was to resume. "There may be a guy out there who's going to write his Reader's Digest story in three days. But I doubt it," the doctor said. "You can't drop that much concrete on a car and have people get out."[24]

Rescue operations at the collapsed freeway resumed on schedule Wednesday and continued throughout the day and on into Thursday. Officials reported that bodies had been recovered from some thirty-one vehicles and estimated it would be another week before all the dead could be removed and the process of rebuilding the Cypress could begin.

On Friday, as what the *Examiner* called "the dreadful extrication process" resumed, President Bush, accompanied by federal, state, and local officials, visited the site to personally inspect the damage and thank the rescue crews for their efforts. The president, standing beside the wreckage of the freeway at Cypress and Twentieth Street, appeared deeply moved by what he saw. One of the workers who briefed the president on the cleanup effort later told reporters Bush "acted like he was in shock, like we did when we first got here. He got out of the car and walked over to me and he was without words for a while. He asked me if I had found any bodies, and I, of course, had to tell him yes. He was pretty much in dismay about what he saw."[25] A *Washington Post* reporter accompanying the president wrote that Bush "looked up, stared for a moment at the expressway, and said simply, 'Jesus.'"[26]

Following his visit to the collapsed freeway, the president traveled by helicopter to the Presidio for a briefing and then on to Santa Cruz, near the quake's epicenter, where he received yet another briefing and conducted a walking tour of a damaged shopping mall. He boarded Air Force One late in the evening and returned to Washington.

A remarkable scene unfolded at the Cypress early the next morning. The *Examiner* reported that at about 6:00 A.M., Caltrans engineer Steve Whipple was crawling around inside the "great death trap" [at a point some four blocks up the freeway from where the president had stood only hours before] when he came upon a small cavern that had been formed by a huge collapsed concrete beam. Inside the cavern was a small, silver-colored Chevrolet Sprint. Inside the Sprint was a man. Alive.[27]

Whipple immediately summoned rescuers, who began cutting their way to the man. Word spread like wildfire that someone had been found alive and a crowd quickly gathered. Reuben Perez, twenty-five, of Berkeley, heard the news on the radio and drove to the site. "We wanted to see this guy cut out of his concrete tomb alive," he told the *Los Angeles Times*. "It's a thrill to know someone is still alive," added Alfred Anderson, a sixty-three-year-old construction worker helping with the cleanup effort. "We had no hope for anybody, seeing the things we've seen up there."[28]

By 8:00 A.M., paramedic Diana Moore was able to reach the trapped motorist. "When am I going to get out of here?" the man asked. The answer would come three hours later when rescuers using the Jaws of Life finally freed Buck Helm, a fifty-seven-year-old longshoreman, from the silver, wheeled casket he had occupied for the last three and a half days.[29] Helm was carried to the edge high up on the wreckage at 11:27 A.M. As he was being slowly lowered to the ground in a wire basket, loud cheers and applause broke out among rescue workers and bystanders.[30] As rescuers placed Helm in an ambulance, a Red Cross worker drove his truck along the rope line restraining the crowd, shouting, "He's alive! He's alive! He's alive!"[31]

Monday, two days after the dramatic rescue in Oakland, coauthor Stewart hand-delivered a letter to the White House on behalf of the activist families:

Dear Mr. President,
When we saw the rescuers on television lowering Mr. Buck Helm from the wreckage of I-880 in Oakland, we knew we must share with you personally, as soon as possible, devastating information about our loved ones who are reportedly trapped half a world away in the rubble of Southeast Asia. The men we speak of are U.S. prisoners of war; the source of our information is the U.S. Department of Defense.

Your advisors, including most recently Secretary of Defense Richard Cheney, are saying—in spite of fresh intelligence to the contrary—that our relatives and all other U.S. servicemen missing in action in Southeast Asia are dead. There is no way, they say, that any of those men could have survived. Mr. President, that's exactly the same thing they told you about Buck Helm as you walked near the ruins of that freeway: "They are all dead, no chance, no hope that any survived." They told you that and you believed them and left the scene, unknowingly leaving Mr. Helm and perhaps others trapped alive in the wreckage only a few yards from where you stood. You took the word of the experts, the career bureaucrats, those who know the most about earthquakes, survivability and human endurance. They were advising you in good faith—but they were wrong.

Mr. President, the Department of Defense has provided us with intelligence documents reporting a number of American servicemen alive in captivity within the last year. Among the men reported recently held prisoner are relatives of many of the undersigned. Some were identified by their familiar name, rank and service, along with a map of the camp where they were reportedly held. In spite of the fact that there are a number of corroborating intelligence reports from the same general area, DOD bureaucrats have told us—and we assume they have told you—that there is nothing to any of these reports—that all the men are dead. Please, Mr. President, don't believe them any longer. We implore you, reject their flawed arguments and allow us to personally show you what those who flee Southeast Asia are saying about our relatives and the many other Buck Helms trapped there.

We respectfully request a ten minute "bureaucrat free" appointment with you at the earliest possible time. We believe that the lives of perhaps hundreds of captive Americans hang in the balance.[32]

## *December*
## THE WHITE HOUSE RESPONDS

Six weeks passed before a National Security Council official replied to Stewart and the families on behalf of the president. Citing the president's earlier pledge to "do all a government can" to resolve the fate of the missing, Peter Watson, the director of Asian affairs on the NSC, assured Stewart and the others that Bush and members of his administration would continue to press the Vietnamese and Lao governments for answers, and declared that cooperation with those governments was the key to obtaining the fullest possible accounting. Then, after noting that "we will continue to pursue this issue as the humanitarian one it is, separate and distinct from political differences"—i.e., "we will not trade aid for prisoners"—Watson offered the families the following advice concerning the intelligence reports they had received from DIA. Underlining for emphasis, he declared, "We . . . firmly believe that those most interested in this issue should exercise care not to confuse reports of sightings with evidence of American prisoners from the Vietnam War." He went on to point out that 68 percent of all such reports received to date "have been resolved through correlation with Americans who were in Indochina but have since returned to the United States," 24 percent "are known or suspected fabrications by the source," and the remaining 8 percent were unresolved and "under continuing high priority investigation in an attempt to confirm the information."[33]

Reading the letter, the families saw that with the exception of the underlined portion, there was nothing new here. They had, after all, heard the pledges of the government's strong commitment to the live POWs cited repeatedly since the cover-up had begun in earnest back in mid-1983. They had also repeatedly heard officials cite various versions of the "percentage breakdowns" but had come to find out that the reports officials claimed were unresolved at any given time would almost all soon be "resolved" and moved into either the "returnee" or "fabrication" category. Then new reports that had been received in the meantime would take their place in the "unresolved" category, and every one of *these* reports would also be "resolved" and placed in either the "returnee" or "fabrication" category—and the process would then repeat itself over and over and over again. Clever, but nothing new.

What was new, of course, was this stunning assertion by the Bush White House that testimony of eyewitnesses should no longer be considered evidence. The activist families were dumbfounded. If Bush had applied this logic during his visit to the Cypress Freeway, if rescuers had come running out of the rubble shouting that Helm lay trapped alive inside, Bush would have said he didn't consider their testimony to be evidence that Helm really *was* alive and would have left and gone on to the Presidio and Santa Cruz and then on back to Washington. (*Webster's New World Dictionary* defines *evidence* as "**1**. something that makes another thing evident; sign **2**. a statement of a witness, an object, etc., bearing on or establishing the point in question in a court of law . . .").

CHAPTER 29

1990

SABOTAGING THE HELMS/GRASSLEY INVESTIGATIONS •
THE BUSH FINAL REPORT ON POWs • THACH'S
HISTORIC VISIT TO WASHINGTON

. . .

DIA officials moved boldly in early 1990 to head off Helms, Grassley, and their investigators.

First, they began clearing the decks of approximately a dozen "troublesome" eyewitness accounts that were still officially "unresolved." These reports—among the highest profile and most credible of the surviving postwar reports—had remained in the "unresolved" status up to now because of their obvious credibility and the fact that each had attracted scrutiny from Capitol Hill and/or the activist families, the activist vets, and the press. Because of that scrutiny, DIA had feared that controversy would erupt if any less-than-credible debunking of these reports were attempted. Better to leave these high-profile sightings languishing in the "under investigation" category, the thinking had been, rather than risk debunking them and having members of Congress, the activist families/vets, and/or the media loudly contest the decision. But now, with

Helms and Grassley banging on the door, these reports *had to be* debunked, lest the senators discover them and cite them as convincing evidence POWs had been or were being held.[1]

Second and concurrent with their "deck-clearing" operation, DIA officials set about preparing a Bush administration "final report" on the live POW issue— this one to be far more damning than the Reagan administration final report, this one designed to end forever the debate about live prisoners.

Third, and also concurrent, these officials moved to block Helms, Grassley, and their investigators from gaining access to the eyewitness accounts and the analysts' working files.

The thinking was that by doing all three of these things—clearing the decks of the unresolved high-profile and obviously credible eyewitness accounts, preparing a damning Bush administration "final report," and keeping Helms and Grassley and their investigators at bay—the administration would be able to publish the lethal "final report" before Helms and Grassley could get into the files. Thus, if and when the senators did gain access, they would find no credible eyewitness testimony still on the books.

## CLEARING THE DECKS

The deck-clearing operation involved approximately a dozen especially credible eyewitness reports that heretofore had defied DIA's best efforts to debunk them—and one startling new eyewitness account about several hundred American POWs being detained during the war in an underground prison located down inside a mountain in a mountainous area south of Hung Hoa and west of Son Tay, the same area where other sources had reported large numbers of American POWs detained after the war in a similar down-inside-a-mountain-type prison.

The deck-clearing operation claimed its first victims in early February when the analysts suddenly "resolved" a troublesome eyewitness account that had been on the books since the late 1970s. The source of this report, DIA Source 0447, was a Lao refugee who had worked for the Royal Lao as a truck driver during the war. He had first reported by letter from Thailand in 1979 that while being detained in a prison near Vieng Sai City in Sam Neua (Houaphan) Province, Laos, during late 1975–early 1976, he had seen five American pilots confined to a cave prison located close to where he was being detained. The refugee had said in his letter:

> On 30 December 1975, I had [first] seen 5 American pilots unknown names in the jail, which is 15 km. in the north of Viengxay. The said jail is just 400 meters from the jail where I was. I can not know the 5 American pilots because we are not in the same jail. The American jail is in the hole of the foothill. The meal and other that the communists gave the prisoners of war are better than Laotians.
>
> I wonder why the communists do not send them back to their country because the war has already ended. According to the chief of the jail, he said that they would keep 5 American pilots here to work because they have good background of the machine.

... Request your government to force ... the Priminister [sic] of Laos to [send] 5 American pilots back to their country so that they can meet their wives childrens [sic] and their parents.[2]

Later, when the refugee had reached a new home in America, he had filed a sworn affidavit about his sighting and had passed a private polygraph test. In his affidavit, the refugee had declared the following, among other things:

I saw five Caucasian prisoners being held in the cave. I was told by my guard that these prisoners were American pilots. All five of the prisoners were quite tall—approximately six feet in height. . . . I noticed a gold ring on one of the prisoners [sic] hands. . . .
    When I was interrogated I was brought down to the cave, approximately ten yards from the entrance, and interrogated in bamboo huts. . . . During the interrogation the guards would point to the American prisoners and ask me if I had helped Americans. They also would question the American prisoners while they were questioning me and I could see the American prisoners shaking their heads when they pointed to me. . . .
    The Americans wore a light green uniform that appeared to be a Soviet uniform. They wore pieces of car tires tied to their feet for shoes. I also saw a pink towel which the Americans used to wash themselves when they were taken to the stream to wash. All five of the American prisoners were quite skinny; however, they all appeared to be uninjured. I did notice that when the American prisoners were sitting down that I could see a red rash on the lower part of their ankles.[3]

Subsequently, the refugee had been interviewed and repolygraphed by U.S. officials. According to DIA records, DIA analysts had requested the polygraph "for the purpose of verifying information related by [source name redacted] regarding the possible imprisonment of U.S. citizens within Laos during 1976." The source had passed the polygraph, thus verifying the information he had provided about the five American pilots.[4] It was at that point that the debunking process began.
    The analysts first appealed the ruling of the USAF polygraph examiner, saying they were sure the results were flawed and the source was lying. The appeal was denied, however, and the polygraph results allowed to stand.[5] Rebuffed but not dissuaded, the analysts launched a withering assault on the source, first on his background and bona fides, next his character, then his motives, etc. Several months into the debunking in late 1981, then-Congressmen Hendon and LeBoutillier were tipped off by a friend inside the Special Office about what was going on and intervened—forcefully warning DIA officials that any further effort to assail this refugee or his testimony would have to withstand the closest congressional scrutiny. "He's fair game, so fire away," the congressmen had told DIA, "but you better be able to back up your final decision on this case with facts and solid analysis." The civilian managers and analysts backed off, and nothing substantive had been done to debunk the report until the deck-clearing operations began in earnest in early 1990. By that time DIA had

received scores of additional intelligence reports of American POWs being detained in Sam Neua (Houaphan) Province after the war, including SIGINT and IMINT.

In February 1990, Joe Schlatter and his deck-clearing team reopened their "investigation" of Source 0447's sighting and quickly issued their "final evaluation":

EVALUATION: [Source name redacted] was never able to pinpoint the area of the sighting, other than it was near Viengsay, in Houa Phan Province. If he had traveled north of Viengsay for 15 kilometers as he stated initially, he would have been close to Sam Neua City, the base camp area of the Soviets. There is some doubt as to where the sighting occurred, whether in a jail, a cave, or near a mountain and some doubt as to why he was in the area of the sighting, i.e., being held in a prison, a jail, or travelling [sic] through in a truck. It should be noted that determination was made early on that [source name redacted] lied as to why he was arrested by the Pathet Lao and why he was in the area of Viengsay. On the other hand he passed a polygraph examination when he stated he observed Caucasian prisoners and when he claimed that the guards told him that the Caucasians were American.

Based on information from the large number of Lao sources who were held or lived near Viengsay, that there were no American PWs in that area, while Soviets were often seen in the province, it is highly probable that [source name redacted] observed Soviet advisors working in Houa Phan Province. [Source name redacted's] sighting information is similar to many previous refugee reports received by DIA/PW-MIA in which the refugee source claimed to have seen Caucasian prisoners and to have been told by Pathet Lao guards that the Caucasians were American. The majority of these former reports were determined to have been sightings of either American Mennonite or United Nations Development Program teams, Soviet advisors, or other Europeans detained in a specific area or travelling [sic] in the area with armed escorts. In this instance, [source name redacted] probably observed Soviet advisors working out of a base camp somewhere near Houa Phan Province.

DATE OF EVALUATION: February 1990

PW-MIA CATEGORY: Nationality Undetermined, not U.S.[6]

## DIA SOURCE 0995

Source 0447's sighting disposed of, Schlatter and his men turned their sights on DIA Source 0995, a Lao refugee who had resettled to New Mexico in 1980. He had told his English teacher shortly after his arrival that he had seen six emaciated American POWs under guard inside a POW camp in far northern Lao province of Phong Saly in the late 1970s.[7] The teacher had passed word of the sighting to a local USAF officer who had forwarded it to DIA.

When interviewed by Special Office personnel in mid-1981, the refugee said that while he and two coworkers were delivering a truckload of supplies to a PL camp near Muong Khoua, they saw six manacled, emaciated Caucasian prisoners being escorted to a camp bath point under guard. He said he asked a Pathet Lao soldier at the camp who the prisoners were and the soldier replied they were American pilots and that fifty of them were being held in the camp. When the refugee subsequently passed two polygraphs—and satellite imagery confirmed the existence of a camp that matched his description in every detail at the exact location on Route 19 west of Muong Khoua where he said he and his friends had seen the Americans—DIA requested that CIA dispatch a ground reconnaissance team to the camp to confirm whether or not the American prisoners were still being held there. The DIA request was passed to CIA two days after Christmas 1982, at the height of Reagan administration interest in the live POW issue.[8] Unfortunately, the story of Gritz's and the other former Green Berets' abortive raid into Laos broke in the press several weeks later, in late January 1983, and the reconnaissance mission was scrapped.

Hendon, who had monitored developments in the case closely during his first term in Congress, was a consultant at the Pentagon at the time the mission was scrapped. Before resigning his Pentagon post in June 1983, he attempted to get the operation to Muong Khuoa laid back on, but failed. After reclaiming his congressional seat, he again sought to have the mission to Muong Khoua reinstated, but this request, too, was denied. All the while, the refugee source himself repeatedly asked DIA for a camera and permission to return to the Muong Khoua to photograph any Americans still held there, but these requests were also denied.[9]

Frustrated by the administration's post-1983 attempts *not* to find and try to rescue the emaciated American prisoners seen at the Muong Khoua camp, Hendon, after he had been defeated for reelection in 1986 and soon after he and the others had established the $2.4 million reward for the return of a living POW, cited unclassified portions of the Muong Khoua sighting at a press conference in Washington. In the days that followed, a woman in Minnesota who had learned of Hendon's comments wrote to her local newspaper and to her congressman, Rep. Gerry Sikorski (D-MN), demanding to know why the administration had not moved to rescue the prisoners Hendon had spoken of. Sikorski forwarded her query to the chairman of HPSCI, Rep. Louis Stokes (D-OH),[10] who in turn forwarded it to the Pentagon for an answer.

On December 14, 1988, Schlatter replied to Stokes:

The report Mrs. Zuettel cites, which was printed in the "Letters to the Editor" section of the <u>St. Paul Pioneer Press Dispatch,</u> does not appear to be based upon intelligence information in the possession of the U.S. government. It does, however, bear a strong resemblance to a claim made in an August 1987 speech by former Congressman Bill Hendon during a news conference in front of the Lao Embassy in Washington, D.C. In his prepared remarks, which were printed and widely distributed, Mr. Hendon said:

"Fifty held at a camp near Muong Kua in northern Laos, where a Laotian delivering rice to a military camp passed within arms length of 5 U.S. POWs, all thin, handcuffed, wearing ankle chains and tied to one another with rope. 'Those are American POWs,' the guard said, 'we have 50 of them in this camp.' (Double polygraph confirmed)"

We have nothing to substantiate the validity of Mr. Hendon's report, nor has he offered any evidence to back it up.

Regretfully, claims such as those made by Mr. Hendon give the American people the erroneous impression that we possess hard evidence of U.S. PWs in Indochina and that we are ignoring it. As you know, this Agency takes very seriously the priority the President has placed on the PW/MIA issue and our obligation to pursue an accounting for the missing American servicemen and civilians. If compelling evidence of prisoners is developed, efforts to bring our men back will proceed immediately from that point.

Sincerely,

JOSEPH A. SCHLATTER
Colonel, USA
Chief, Special Office for Prisoners
of War and Missing in Action[11]

When Hendon learned of Schlatter's reply, he sent word that he had personally interviewed the refugee source and if necessary would make a videotape of that interview available to Congressmen Sikorski and Stokes. Schlatter quickly penned another response to Stokes, this one saying that DIA had, in fact, received similar information from a Lao refugee, but the information had been determined to be a fabrication. Schlatter's second response, dated December 27, 1988, read as follows:

This is to follow up on our letter of 14 December which responded to a query from Representative Gerry Sikorski regarding the alleged sighting of U.S. PWs in Laos.

Further research had revealed that over seven years ago we received a report which contained some elements similar to the claims Bill Hendon made at the news conference to which I referred in my previous letter. Although the source was polygraphed twice, the results of which indicated no deception, the individual is a heavy drug user and was using drugs at the time, which would invalidate the polygraph examination results. He has also been convicted and jailed on rape charges in California.

Nevertheless, the source's record aside, his claim to have seen six Caucasians in mid-1977 in Laos is considered to be without substance. Other sources in the same area at the time report an absence of Americans in any capacity; however, they do report the presence of Soviet advisors, which may account for the source's reported sighting of "Caucasians."

I hope this additional information will be of assistance to you and Congressman Sikorski in responding to his constituent.

Sincerely,

JOSEPH A. SCHLATTER
Colonel, USA
Chief, Special Office for Prisoners
of War and Missing in Action[12]

Accompanying Schlatter's letter was a copy of DIA's official evaluation of the refugee's sighting. The evaluation, dated February 16, 1988, read in part:

ANALYSIS: In 1986 DIA was advised [source name redacted] was imprisoned in California on criminal charges. Merced County police authories [sic] determined . . . [source name] was a drug addict since the 1970's.

[Source name redacted], when interviewed by DIA, was noted as heavily tattooed. They [sic] types and locations of tattoos are unique among criminals in Laos. . . .

DIA has reviewed the results of [source's] criminal/drug background against the results of . . . [the] polygraph. His background precludes the use of the polygraph in measuring [source's] truthfulness and reliability. . . .

EVALUATION: [Source name redacted] may have some hearsay knowledge of the [presence] . . . of Soviet advisors in Phong Saly Province, but did not make the sighting as claimed. . . .

VO-PW CATEGORY: Fabrication.[13]

When Bob Smith, leader of the fight for the unlisted, unreturned POWs in the House at the time, was advised of Schlatter's letter and accompanying February 16, 1988, "evaluation," he came down hard on Schlatter and his analysts, ridiculing their "analysis" and "evaluation" and demanding that the case be reopened. Stung by Smith's attack and fearing further congressional intervention, Schlatter reluctantly agreed; he rescinded the evaluation of "fabrication" and returned the case to "unresolved" status. There the matter had lain until Helms and Grassley came knocking.

Clearing the troublesome Muong Khoua sighting from the books in early February 1990, Schlatter and his team ruled that Source 0995, the loathsome dope-smoking, tattooed rapist they had earlier ruled a fabricator, was now, upon reconsideration, a truthful, credible witness—only he was confused about what he had seen. Yes, *he had been* to the prison at Muong Khoua, Schlatter and his men now acknowledged, and yes, *he had seen* manacled, emaciated Caucasian prisoners being detained there under guard, but these prisoners weren't American pilots as he had been told by a guard—they were Soviet advisors. "DATE OF EVALUATION: February 1990. PW-MIA CATEGORY: Non U.S.; Soviets."[14]

## A QUICK TRIP TO THE HILL TO BUY TIME

In April, as Schlatter and his analysts went about their work, Grassley, after months of being rebuffed by DIA officials in his attempt to gain unfettered access to the DIA files on live POWs, sent a formal, written demand to DOD that he, Helms, and members of their staffs be granted immediate and unencumbered access to all eyewitness accounts of live American POWs and the analysts' working files for each account. (As previously stated, prior to Grassley's and Helms's announcement back in October 1989 that they intended to examine these files as part of their effort to investigate the U.S. government's handling of the live POW issue, access had been blocked to everyone in the legislative branch, even senators and congressmen with jurisdiction over the POW/MIA issue.)

Responding to Grassley's April demand, administration officials dispatched Griffiths to Grassley's office to buy time. Grassley would later declare on the floor of the Senate that during his meeting with Griffiths in his office, "[S]he told me . . . that she had read [all of the] . . . eyewitness accounts and that they show no evidence that American citizens were left behind in Southeast Asia after the war in Indochina."[15] Griffiths performed her assigned task well, and Grassley acquiesced.[16]

Valuable time having been bought, Schlatter and his team went back to work clearing the decks and completing their final report, the findings of which would be presented at the League annual convention in mid-July.

## GARWOOD'S FIVE SIGHTINGS
## SIGHTINGS #4979, 4980, 4981, 4982, AND 4983

Robert Garwood's five sightings of American prisoners held after the war in northern Vietnam had been on the books since December 1984.[17] Though roundly assailed by administration officials when they had first surfaced, by 1990 all five were still officially "under analysis" and "unresolved," because of continuing, intense scrutiny from Bob Smith and retired DIA Director General Tighe, both of whom had personally interviewed Garwood, declared him a credible witness, and warned DIA that any attempt to debunk his sightings without cause would be met with a strong response.

But now, in 1990, with Helms and Grassley breathing down their necks, Schlatter and his analysts quickly and officially "resolved" all five sightings. They declared that two of Garwood's sightings—his nighttime sighting of the U.S. POWs getting down out of the railroad boxcar at Yen Bai in 1977 (#4979) and his later sighting of these and other American POWs at the camp on nearby Thac Ba Lake in 1978 (#4980)—were "fabrications." They declared that his sighting of the emaciated U.S. POW inside the military compound on Ly Nam De Street in late 1978 (#4981) was not of an American POW moved from the Chinese border as Garwood had been told, but of "an unidentified Caucasian . . . possibly an American non-detainee." They declared that his periodic sightings between 1973 and 1979 of American prisoners working at a prison warehouse complex in Gia Lam village across the river from Hanoi (#4982) were sightings of "unidentified Caucasians at Hanoi area airfields." Finally, they declared that Garwood's periodic sightings during the summer and fall of 1973 of approximately twenty U.S. POWs being detained at the military prison at Bat Bat, west of Son Tay (#4983), were sightings of "American POWs released at Operation Homecoming."[18] Garwood, then, officially, was lying twice and telling the truth three times; but in the three instances where he was telling the truth, he was confused about what he had seen and had not actually seen American POWs detained after Operation Homecoming.

## THE REMAINING EYEWITNESS SIGHTINGS FROM HA NAM NINH BA SAO/ROCKPILE • DIA SOURCES #8666 AND #10721

With Garwood now out of the way, the analysts moved to "resolve" the last two remaining eyewitness accounts of American POWs being held at the Ba Sao/Rockpile Prison Camp in Ha Nam Ninh Province, the hotbed of sightings just south of Hanoi.

The reader will recall (Chapter 26) that by the end of 1987, the U.S. government had received at least fourteen reports telling of American prisoners being detained long after the war at the Ba Sao/Rockpile Camp in Ha Nam Ninh Province, or at or near one of the several Ba Sao/Rockpile subcamps, or at other nearby locations in the province. The reader will further recall that one of those fourteen reports had involved an American POW and his two guards who had reportedly escaped around the time of Ross Perot's late-March 1987 visit to Hanoi.

Ha Nam Ninh reports 15 and 16—the ones Schlatter and his analysts were now clearing out of the active case files, both involved testimony from eyewitnesses who said they had seen American POWs inside the main Ba Sao/Rockpile Camp during the early to mid-1980s. By 1990, these were the only eyewitness accounts from Ba Sao/Rockpile that had not yet been debunked by DIA.

The first eyewitness (DIA Source 8666), a former truck driver who lived in Hanoi prior to his escape from Vietnam, had told U.S. officials in early 1989 that he drove his truck to the camp in early September 1983 to pick up a load of crushed rock from the prison quarry. He told U.S. officials that while waiting for ARVN prisoners to load the rock, he climbed the hill behind the quarry and, after reaching the ridgetop, squatted down to rest and smoke a cigarette. He said that when he looked down into the prison agricultural area, which lay in the huge karst-enclosed valley below, he saw at the base of the hill a group of American prisoners milling around inside a small triple-perimeter, barbed-wire encircled compound.[19]

He said the compound containing the Americans was composed of three small buildings, a latrine, and a large bulletin board that was positioned inside the compound near the interior fence line.

The truck driver said he observed the Americans from his seated or crouched position for approximately an hour and a half. He said he counted seventeen Americans, all Caucasians, some with beards, all dressed in two-piece prison uniforms with large stripes of alternating dark and light shades of gray and numbers printed on the trousers as well as the shirts. He said that after he had observed the Americans off and on for the one and a half hours, one of the camp guards walked to the bulletin board and called out loudly in a foreign language. He said that upon hearing the guard's command, the Americans, carrying picks and shovels, came out of the buildings or moved from their places in the compound and assembled before the bulletin board. The truck driver said the guard then moved among the Americans, and just as the guard and other guards were beginning to accompany them out of the barbed-wire enclosure, another, different guard spotted him crouching on the ridgetop and ordered him out of the area. He said he quickly left his position and returned down the eastern slope of the mountain to the quarry. He said that when his truck was fully loaded, he departed for Hanoi.

The truck driver rendered two hand-drawn sketches for U.S. officials, one of the general layout of Ba Sao Prison showing the quarry, the hill, the main prison compound, the small barbed-wire compound where the American prisoners were being detained, nearby guard towers, etc., and the other a detailed, primitive sketch of the interior of the American compound. He also informed U.S. officials that he had learned from a Vietnamese prisoner who had escaped from Ba Sao in 1987 that the Americans were still being held there at the time the man had escaped (1987).[20]

The second eyewitness (DIA Source 10721), a former North Vietnamese Public Security Service officer in his mid-thirties who had been based in Haiphong before fleeing Vietnam, had told U.S. officials in August 1989 that while visiting the Ba Sao Prison on official business during June 1984, he personally observed at least four Caucasian prisoners just inside the prison's main gate.[21] He had gone on to say that he was told moments later by another PSS officer the prisoners were Americans.

The August 1989 report chronicling the PSS officer's sighting had read in part:

At approximately 2300 hours on an unrecalled date in Jun 84, source observed an enclosed truck (Soviet ¾ ton type with bed enclosed in canvas) carrying four to six foreign prisoners out of camp Ba Sao, Ha Nam Ninh Province. Source recalled that the prisoners were Caucasians with light brown hair. He saw them through the openings of the truck only for a few minutes. The truck passed slowly from a parked position about 100 meters within the front gate past source, who was relieving himself behind the guest house to the right of the gate. Source claims he was able to see six guards seated on the side benches within the truck and four Westerners seated in the space between the guards. This truck was preceded by a three-wheeled vehicle (motorcycle with sidecar) carrying two guards and followed by two similar trucks, one empty followed by one full of Public Security personnel.

. . . Thinking that the prisoners had been Soviets, source commented to his friend when he returned to the guest house, that he had been surprised to see Soviets incarcerated in Ba Sao Prison. His friend . . . asserted that the prisoners had not been Soviets, but Americans recently moved into the camp and now being transferred to another one.[22]

On July 7, Schlatter and his analysts issued their final evaluations of both the truck driver's sighting from the ridgetop overlooking the prison agricultural area (#8666, Ha Nam Ninh report 15) and the PSS officer's sighting just inside the front gate (#10721, Ha Nam Ninh report 16). They first ruled that the truck driver's sighting was a "fabrication." "Frequent, consistent, reliable reporting over the last 10 years from multiple sources, including former inmates, open press, and several American and other friendly Western visitors," they declared, "confirms no Americans were held at Ba Sao after Operation Homecoming in 1973."[23]

They then declared that the PSS officer's sighting of American POWs just inside the main gate was also a "fabrication." This was the case, they declared, because "frequent, consistent, reliable reporting over the last 10 years from multiple sources, including former inmates, open press, and several American and other friendly Western visitors confirms no Americans were held at Ba Sao after Operation Homecoming in 1973."[24]

## MEANWHILE, STUNNING NEW INTELLIGENCE ON AN UNDERGROUND PRISON NORTHWEST OF HANOI

During late spring and early summer, as the analysts were working to clear the decks and complete their final report on the POW/MIA issue in time for the League's mid-July convention, the Special Office received what was surely one of the most important eyewitness accounts of live American prisoners acquired during the postwar period.

The essential elements of the startling new intelligence, which DIA received from a U.S. intelligence detachment in the Far East on June 21, read as follows:

P 211421Z JUN 90 . . .
[RETRANSMISSION OF] P 210100Z JUN 90
FM DET 32 PSAA SEOUL KOR//CC// . . .

SUBJ: IIR 1 512 0218 90/UNDERGROUND DETENTION FACILITY FOR U.S. PW'S IN NORTH VIETNAM

Source: [Source name redacted], is a Vietnamese refugee who acquired the information by virtue of having lived in the northern section of Vietnam. Source's reliability has not been established. . . .

Summary: [redacted] This is a Stoney Beach report. In May, 1972, source visited an underground facility in the northern section of Vietnam where it was purported that approximately 200 U.S. servicemen were beig [sic] detained.

Text: 1. During training to become a public prosecutor in North Vietnam, prosecutor trainees visited prisons. During one such visit in May 1972, an underground facility was visited in which approximately 200 U.S. servicemen purportedly were imprisoned. The facility was said to house only U.S. servicemen. Among the prisons visited, this was the only underground prison facility which held U.S. servicemen. The facility was located approximately 30 kilometers west of Son Tay City //geocoord: 2108N/10530E//. The approximate location of the facility is //geocoord: 2110N/10520E//. (Field comment— Although source tried to pinpoint the location he was unable to do so.) The detention facility was located in a heavily forested and uninhabited area.

2. Visitors to the facility were required to use a mountain path to access the area. Vietnamese Army guards were posted around the facility. There were an unknown number of wooden buildings above ground which appeared to be barracks, a kitchen and guard shacks for the security guards. All visitors were

required to identify themselves at the guard shack before entering the under-ground facility.

3. There were three flights of steps to the lower level of the underground fa-cility. Each flight of steps consisted of 10 to 15 steps. The inside of the facil-ity was lined with concrete. Public Security Police were responsible for security within the facility. Visitors to the facility received a briefing that dis-closed that there were approximately 200 U.S. servicemen detained in the fa-cility and that the majority of them were pilots. After the briefing, visitors were shown the U.S. PW's. The U.S. PW's could be observed through the iron-bar doors of the cells.

4. Each cell was three meters long, two meters wide and 2.5 meters high and housed three to five persons. A list of cell occupants was posted on the wall of each room. (Field comment—Source could not remember any of the names.) Some blacks were seen among the inmates. The group visiting the facility were [sic] given the opportunity to observe four or five cclls [sic]. (NFI) [no fur-ther information].

Comments: (Field comment)—1. Source was intelligent and cooperative. He volunteered the information in this report and is available for further debrief-ing. From 71 to 73 source underwent training to become a public prosecutor in North Vietnam. In May 1972, he was among a group of trainees that vis-ited the underground facility described in text. Source's group stayed overnight at the facility and left at 0700 hours the following morning. In 1979, source was fired from his position as a public prosecutor because he had married a Chinese woman in 1977. In 1980, he and his wife escaped from Vietnam to China, where they joined a group of Vietnamese refugees whose destination was South Korea. Source arrived in South Korea in Jun 1988.[25]

When map tracking showed that the prison the former prosecutor had de-scribed was located in the mountains near the Black River and south of Hung Hoa—the exact area where during the early-mid 1980s a PAVN guard had re-portedly helped guard a prison located inside a mountain where three hundred American POWs were reportedly being detained[26]—Schlatter and his analysts had to have known that in all likelihood they had just been afforded a glimpse inside one of the crown jewels of Vietnam's second-tier prison system—the su-persecret system where American POWs were periodically detained in large numbers during the war but from which no prisoner ever returned. Yes, there had been many reports of other second-tier prisons, but this one, everyone who read it had to have known, had to be one of the most important. Proof? Of course not. But what a bonanza this new report was: The information was cor-roborated by other independent testimony, and the source (the former prosecu-tor) appeared credible and was available in Korea for immediate reinterview, polygraph, and further exploitation. Two hundred American prisoners reported held at this prison late in the war—perhaps three hundred in the early-mid 1980s. It was, by any measure, a stunning development.

Schlatter and his analysts worked the case for ten days and then, on July 1, issued their final evaluation. That evaluation read in its entirety:

### DIA EVALUATION OF PW/MIA INFORMATION
### PROVIDED BY VIETNAMESE REFUGEE SOURCE
### [SOURCE NAME REDACTED]

SUMMARY: Source reported he saw U.S. prisoners in an underground facility west of Son Tay City in 1972. He was told the facility held 200 prisoners.

DETAILS: In May 1972, source states that he visited a prison as part of his training to become a public prosecutor. He said the facility was located underground about 30 kilometers west of Son Tay City in what is now Hanoi Municipality. He was unable to pinpoint the facility location on the map but said it was located in a forested, uninhabited area. According to the source, the above ground portion was comprised of wooden buildings and guard shacks and was accessed by way of a mountain path. The underground portion was lined with concrete, accessed by three flights of stairs and housed 200 U.S. PWs.

ANALYSIS: Son Tay City lies 30 kilometers northwest of Hanoi in what is now Hanoi Municipality. Source claimed that the prison he visited in 1972 was located 30 kilometers west of Son Tay City. Imagery of this area and time frame indicates neither the presence of an above-ground facility such as he described, nor evidence of the logistics and support that would have been required to sustain an inmate population of 200.

Although no camp is located 30 kilometers west of Son Tay, many former Vietnamees reeducatees and U.S. PWs, alike, have reported on the several confinement facilities located at other distances west and northwest of Son Tay. None of these reports support this source's claims. Reeducatees commonly were allowed to communicate freely with one another. However, to prevent or disrupt subversive prisoner organizations, inmates were frequently transferred from one subcamp to another. Hence, many became intimately familiar with many aspects of their surroundings. From information supplied by these former reeducatees, and by former U.S. PWs, much is known about the physical characteristics and inmate populations. Some of these camps never housed any American prisoners. Of those that did, no one camp in the vicinity of Son Tay Municipality ever held 200 U.S. PWs throughout the entire war, much less 200 at one time. And by July 1970, all U.S. PWs had been moved out completely, relocated to facilities in other parts of the country. All U.S. PWs known to have been incarcerated in these camps have been accounted for. Analysis determines that Source has fabricated this story.

EVALUATION: Source [source name redacted] fabricated this report.

DATE OF EVALUATION: 01 July 1990

PW/MIA CATEGORY: Fabrication.[27]

There was no reference to map tracking. No reference to the PAVN guard's reported statements about the three hundred or so American POWs being held in an underground prison in the same area during the early to mid-1980s. No suggestion this was a second-tier prison. No follow-up interview of the source. No polygraph. And no demand levied on the SRV that U.S. officials be allowed to search the area at once.[28]

## THE BUSH ADMINISTRATION FINAL REPORT

The long-planned Bush administration final report on the live POW issue was completed just before the families arrived in Washington for their annual convention in mid-July. The report's major findings, portions of some underlined by the report's authors for emphasis, included these:

- After the war, refugees became the primary source of intelligence on this issue, but we have also questioned defectors from Vietnam's intelligence and security services and its Ministry of Foreign Affairs. National technical systems [SIGINT, COMMINT, IMINT] have also provided information on these matters. . . . Despite this extensive collection effort, we have yet to identify in past or current holdings any pattern of evidence that confirms that any American servicemen might have been held against their will after the war. We have instead identified a positive pattern indicating that no U.S. military personnel remained in captivity after Operation Homecoming (1973).
- Persons sighted by refugees have been returned prisoners, Westerners detained by communist authorities for various reasons, and Westerners residing in Indochina, such as technicians, aid workers, or missionaries. Refugee sources who report truthfully on the Indochina prison system universally report the absence of U.S. PWs after early 1973.
- A thorough review of the results of more than a decade of refugee reporting leads to the conclusion that the refugees have not seen U.S. PWs held after 1973.
- DIA analysts developed a collection and analytic strategy to search for evidence of any pattern of directives, organizations, activities and facilities needed to administer, secure, house, feed, provide medical care for and exploit U.S. PWs. This analysis developed clear evidence of a system for handling U.S. PWs during the war, but no such system is in evidence after 1973.[29]

The Reagan report released in January 1989, the reader will recall, had declared there were no POWs held after 1973. The Bush report released in July 1990 now repeated that earlier finding and further declared there was no prison system for holding American POWs after 1973.

Though the Bush report would remain essentially classified, its unclassified findings were trumpeted to the families at the League's annual convention in mid-July. Schlatter, distilling the report's findings, told the families, "if we look at everything we collected [in intelligence] during the war and everything we've collected since the war, we don't find any evidence" of captive Americans. (Schlatter would soon depart for a new DIA posting in Japan. He would return in July 1993 and serve as deputy director of the reconstituted Defense POW/MIA Office until his retirement on April 1, 1995.)[30]

## SHOVING, SHOUTING MATCH BREAKS OUT AT LEAGUE CONVENTION • COURTS-MARTIAL EFFORT BEGINS

As if Schlatter's pronouncement to the families about no live POWs wasn't bad enough, the activist families learned during the League convention that their darkest fears about their government's reaction to the $2.4 million congressionally sponsored reward were true: The JCRC's Gadoury and other U.S. officials had long been instructing persons living in Vietnam, Laos, and Cambodia not to attempt to free live American POWs and return them to U.S. control for the reward.

Hendon had first gotten word that such an effort was afoot in late 1989 and had notified the congressional sponsors.[31] When several congressmen had complained to DOD, they had been assured the United States would never do such a thing; there must have been a mistake in translation, transmission, etc. But now had come a new report—and a stunning admission to the families by JCRC officials that JCRC personnel were, as a matter of official policy, telling potential rescuers that they should cease and desist in their attempts to free American POWs for the reward the congressmen were offering.

The new report, which precipitated a near brawl at the convention the day after Schlatter's speech, involved a missing Army warrant officer named William P. Milliner. Milliner, a Cobra gunship copilot, had been lost when his ship went down in the area of the Lao/South Vietnam border during Lam Son 719 operations in early 1971. Nothing had been heard from Milliner or about him until mid-October 1989, when a Thai businessman had approached JCRC personnel in Thailand with word that Milliner was alive in Laos and could be brought to the Lao/Thai border for the reward. Gadoury had handled the case.[32]

Because Milliner had been reported alive by name, DIA, as required by law, had forwarded the report to Milliner's parents in Kentucky. When the parents had asked DIA what had been done about the report, authorities had refused to say. Suspicious, the Milliners had come to the League convention seeking answers.

In a reception area outside the main meeting hall, the Milliner family, Hendon, a number of family members and supporters, and several of the activist Vietnam vets found Gadoury and demanded to know what action he had taken on the Milliner report. Gadoury responded defiantly that he had personally informed the source of the report—the Thai businessman—that there was no reward and that he and his associates inside Laos should drop their plan to free Milliner. Gadoury went on to say that he had made those statements in the course of his official duties and in compliance with official U.S. government policy and would continue making similar statements to other prospective rescuers until ordered by his superiors to stop doing so.

Gadoury's statements and attitude had enraged those who had assembled to support the Milliners. Pushing and shoving ensued; harsh words and threats were exchanged. It ended only when Gadoury's Hawaii-based boss, Lt. Col. Joe

Harvey, USA, head of JCRC, pushed his way through the crowd and announced that Gadoury had, in fact, been following orders when he had told the Thai businessman to stop trying to free Milliner for the reward. Harvey then ordered Gadoury out of the area. When the crowd turned its wrath on him, Harvey declared he had nothing more to say and exited the area.[33]

Genuinely angered at what had transpired, Hendon, Stewart, the Milliners, and others decided to immediately lodge formal courts-martial charges against Harvey, Gadoury, and his on-scene commander, the chief of the JCRC office in Bangkok, Air Force Lt. Col. James D. Spurgeon. When word of their effort spread among those attending the convention, other family members signed on as complainants. Some 50 signed on during the convention, and within several weeks approximately 140 of the activist family members had joined in the effort.

(In mid-August, in an attempt to limit the damage Gadoury was doing on the ground in Indochina, Hendon and Jim Stewart, coauthor Stewart's eldest brother, flew to northeast Thailand to distribute more reward flyers and attempt to reassure as many people as possible that, contrary to what JCRC officials were telling them, the $2.4 million reward was alive and well and would be paid as promised to anyone who brought an American POW to freedom. The two then returned to Bangkok and announced at a news conference that requests for courts-martial were being filed against the three JCRC officials.[34] The situation, they hoped, stabilized for the moment, Hendon and Stewart returned to the United States.)

Hendon filed his and the families' complaint against Gadoury, Spurgeon, and Harvey with the USAF Office of Special Investigations at Bolling Air Force Base in suburban Washington in mid-September. (Harvey being Army, Hendon requested that AFOSI officials forward the complaint to the U.S. Army's Criminal Investigation Division [CID] so officials there could conduct a separate investigation of Harvey's conduct.) Alleged violations cited in the complaint included making false statements, conspiracy, and indifference to death. Hendon and the family members stated in their complaint that they believed the findings of the investigations would lead to courts-martial proceedings being brought against the three men.[35]

In October, Hendon and the families learned from press accounts that no formal investigations into Gadoury's, Spurgeon's, and/or Harvey's actions would be conducted. The requests for investigation had been denied, an AFOSI official told one reporter, because the three men had been "stating policy as standard procedure and there is no need to investigate somebody who's doing his job." A Pentagon spokesman voiced strong support for the AFOSI decision, declaring that "the U.S. government is absolutely opposed to and absolutely discourages such activities" [freeing an American POW for the reward] because they "not only may be a violation of host country and U.S. law, but they seriously impede U.S. government efforts to resolve the POW-MIA issue." The fact that twenty-two current and former congressmen had pledged $100,000 each to the reward, the Pentagon spokesman said, was "irrelevant." "It is not a U.S. government reward. [T]he U.S. government is opposed to rewards."[36]

## NGUYEN CO THACH MAKES UNPRECEDENTED VISIT TO WASHINGTON, DECLARES *AGAIN* THAT AMERICANS MAY BE ALIVE IN WILD AREAS OF HIS COUNTRY • HELMS ISSUES EXPLOSIVE INTERIM REPORT

As it turned out, the news in October would not be all bad for the unlisted, unreturned POWs and those working to gain their release. First, while in Washington at midmonth for discussions on the POW/MIA issue, Vietnamese Foreign Minister Thach would again declare that Americans might be alive in isolated areas of his country. Thach's comments would prompt *The Washington Post* to suggest that if the administration would approach the matter of live POWs in a slightly different way, perhaps progress might be possible. Then, at month's end, Helms would release an interim report on his investigation of the live POW issue that would send shock waves throughout Washington and the entire country. Taken together, Thach's pronouncement and Helms's findings would lift the spirits of the activist families and vets to heights not seen since the Reagan administration had attempted in earnest to repatriate live prisoners during 1981 and 1982.

Indochina watchers knew that in the context of U.S.-Vietnamese relations, Thach's mid-October visit was historic, representing the first time since the fall of the North in 1954 that a Communist diplomat of Thach's rank had been allowed to travel to the American capital. Calling the trip "unprecedented" and "ground-breaking," the Associated Press reported on the 17th that Thach traveled to Capitol Hill to confer with members of the Senate Foreign Relations Committee and later to the Army-Navy Club near the White House for a meeting with Vessey, Griffiths, and other administration officials. AP reported that following several hours of discussions, Vessey told a joint press conference that the two sides had "agreed to new levels of cooperation to resolve the fates of the missing in action in Southeast Asia." AP also reported that Thach pledged to cooperate with the United States in the hunt for missing Americans, "expressed eagerness for normal relations with the United States" and "offered assurances there are no American servicemen in Vietnamese custody, but allowed for the possibility that some might still be alive in a remote region without the knowledge of the government."[37]

Was the wily Thach, standing this time just across Lafayette Park from the White House, sending the same "the ox is slow but the earth is patient" signal to Bush he had sent via Vessey to Reagan from Hanoi back in the summer of 1987? At least one editorial-page editor at *The Washington Post* seemed to sense he was, and offered a possible solution to the dilemma the two countries faced. Writing in a *Post* editorial published on the 19th, the editor declared that "no aspect of Vietnam's conduct has produced more bitterness among Americans than its toying with the MIA/POW issue over the years." He then went on to explain that "[a]t first it seemed (and to some it still does) that Hanoi was playing this card against delivery on American pledges of reconstruction aid—pledges that Washington considered voided by Vietnamese violations of the Paris peace accords," and "[t]hen it seemed the issue was caught up in internal Vietnamese wrangling." He then declared "Questions linger about whether some live Americans remain behind—Vietnam denies it," and asked, "Would it help, as some suggest, to devise categories of 'unregistered' POWs or 'deserters' to skirt Hanoi's insistence that no American 'prisoners' remain 'under its control'?"[38]

Some ten days passed and then Helms released his blockbuster interim findings.[39] *The Washington Times* reported that Helms's investigators had unearthed a secret U.S. government report stating that "several hundred" Americans were being held captive in 1974, one year after Operation Homecoming. The existence of that one report, one investigator told the *Times*, "undercuts 17 years of official denials that POWs remained in captivity." Helms's investigators told the *Times* that based on that 1974 report and their analysis of a number of postwar intelligence reports that told of living American POWs, the U.S. government's stance that there is no evidence of American POWs in the region "cannot be supported."[40] AP reported among other things that the Helms report accused the Defense Department of (1) reaching a negative conclusion about missing Americans and then undermining contrary evidence, (2) discrediting—often in error—live sighting reports about U.S. personnel from hundreds of refugees, and (3) intimidating these refugees and dismissing their testimony on technicalities. AP went on to quote Helms himself as stating that the report's major story may have been that "there was a deliberate effort by certain people in the government to disregard all information or reports about living MIAs-POWs."[41]

"POW-MIA Cover-Up Charged, GOP Senate Committee Members Say Defense Dept. Undermined Evidence," the *Manchester Union Leader* proclaimed in a huge front-page headline on October 30.

## November and December
## CIRCLING THE WAGONS

With the dreaded C-word in newspapers and reverberating through VFW and American Legion halls from coast to coast—and even through the ranks of the fiercely pro-administration League of Families, as well—administration officials moved in November and December to shore up their defenses. First, they greatly accelerated efforts already under way to open a POW/MIA office in Hanoi. Nothing, they knew, would put a lie to Helms's charges faster than the sight of American servicemen fanning out over the countryside to "search" for the long-lost MIAs. But they also knew that opening the new office might take months, and so to provide some immediate evidence of the administration's commitment during the period of negotiations about the new office, they decided to lay another "good report card, self-administered" on the Special Office and its employees.

On December 4, the director of Central Intelligence announced that the National Intelligence Meritorious Unit Citation was being awarded to the civilian analysts at the Special Office in recognition of their "exemplary performance, consistent excellence, and superior professionalism"—and that the nation's highest individual intelligence honor, the National Intelligence Distinguished Service Medal, was being bestowed upon the recently departed Schlatter for his outstanding work at the office.

The Unit Citation read:

Special Office for Prisoners of War and Missing in Action, Defense Intelligence Agency, is hereby awarded the NATIONAL INTELLIGENCE MERITORI-
OUS UNIT CITATION in recognition of its exemplary performance, consistent
excellence, and superior professionalism from January 1986 to June 1990. As
the sole Intelligence Community office dedicated to the issue of unaccounted-
for Americans in Southeast Asia, the Special Office operates in an environment
of political policy demands, intelligence activities, emotional sensitivities,
and public relations attention. The accomplishments of the Special Office
have consistently earned the highest praise, commendation, and expressions
of support from Executive and Legislative Branch policymakers, other citizens, and veterans' groups. The trust gained by the Special Office from individuals across the political, public, and intelligence fields is worthy of
acclamation. That trust is testimony to the dedicated professionalism and
personal commitment of all members of the Special office [sic], past and present. The continued contributions of the Special Office reflect great credit on
each of its members, the Defense Intelligence Agency, and the Intelligence
Community.[42]

Griffiths rushed news of the awards and a scathing attack on Helms's interim
findings to the League membership on December 6.[43] A majority of the families
were duly impressed, and another crisis was averted.

Decidedly *unimpressed*, however, was Schlatter's replacement at the Special
Office, an Army bird colonel named Mike Peck.

# PART V

# CHAPTER 30

1991

# ONE LAST CHANCE TO SAVE THE UNLISTED, UNRETURNED POWs

. . .

I consider [the POW/MIA issue] to be a cruel and tragic hoax.
—STANLEY KARNOW, Pulitzer Prize–winning
author of *Vietnam: A History*

I found no evidence while I was in Vietnam [for a brief visit in the summer of 1989] to support the missing-in-action theory one so often encounters in the United States that Vietnam continues to hold American prisoners.
—NEIL SHEEHAN, Pulitzer Prize–winning
author of *A Bright-Shining Lie*

There has yet to be any credible evidence that any prisoners were withheld in Indochina, and even if some were held, their number could not have been more than a few dozen at the very most. . . . This handful of cases is the foundation on which the colossal structure of the POW/MIA myth has been built.
—H. BRUCE FRANKLIN, author of "The POW/MIA Myth: How the White House and Hollywood Combined to Foster a National Fantasy"

There came to exist in America . . . in the years that followed the Vietnam War, a small cottage industry made up of swindlers, dime-store Rambos, and just plain old conspiracy nuts who preyed on the emotions of the families and on the attention of officials who were dedicated to the search for our missing. They had helped convince many of the families and a few members of Congress that the U.S. government had knowingly abandoned American servicemen in Vietnam and that five successive presidential administrations had covered up the crime. It was among the most damaging and most hurtful of all the lies about the Vietnam War that I ever encountered.
—SENATOR JOHN MCCAIN (R-AZ), in *Worth the Fighting For*, with Mark Salter

Col. Millard "Mike" Peck, USA, had served three wartime tours in Vietnam, earning the Distinguished Service Cross, three Silver Stars, three Bronze Stars for valor, two Purple Hearts, a Defense Meritorious Service Medal, an Army Meritorious Service Medal, nine Air Medals, an Army Commendation Medal for valor, and a number of campaign ribbons and foreign decorations. An infantry officer with Ranger and airborne qualifications, he had trained with the French Army and had served as an assistant professor (language) at West Point. Before taking over from Schlatter in July 1990, he had worked in DIA's Current Intelligence

Section providing intelligence watch and current intelligence support for the Joint Chiefs of Staff. Prior to that, he had been duty director for intelligence (DDI) in the National Military Intelligence Center, serving both as chief, Eastern Division and chief, Asia Division.[1]

It was during his service on the Joint Staff that Peck had first seen the flow of intelligence from Indochina telling of American prisoners still alive in captivity. When he had discussed this intelligence with his colleagues, a number of them had informed him that a cover-up was under way in DIA's Special Office for POWs/MIAs, an office that Peck at the time knew nothing about. The POW office, Peck's colleagues told him, was a black hole into which much went but from which nothing ever returned.

The more intelligence Peck had read, the more concerned and vocal he had become. Then, in the spring of 1990, Peck's boss and mentor, the director of the Joint Staff, Rear Adm. Edward D. Sheafer, USN, had been notified that he would be appointed deputy director of DIA, a job with direct chain-of-command authority over the Special Office. Sheafer, knowing Peck's concern for the missing and the outstanding work he had done for him at the Joint Staff, approached Peck and asked him to come with him to DIA to head up the Special Office. Peck jumped at the offer, later saying that both the opportunity to continue working for Sheafer and the chance to find out what was really going on in DIA's black hole were key reasons for taking the job. Peck would later say he and his boss had figured, "Hey, we've got a problem here, so maybe Sheafer and Peck can fix it."[2]

When Peck had taken over the Special Office in July 1990, he had quickly seen that the "black hole" rumors were true. Responding in his typical style, he had assembled the staff and informed them that things were going to change, and quickly. From now on, Peck had declared, the office was going to aggressively pursue every one of the reports on living prisoners. He was going to be very proactive and very operationally oriented.

Hearing of Peck's pronouncements and sensing that in Sheafer and Peck they had a latter-day Tighe/Tuttle tag team on their hands, administration officials had moved quickly to sabotage the new effort. The Sheafer/Peck team was on the job only a matter of weeks when word came down that the Special Office had been removed from Sheafer's chain of command and that Peck would henceforth report directly to the civilian executive secretary of DIA rather than to Sheafer. His lifeline to Sheafer cut, Peck was doomed.

True to his word to be very proactive and very operationally oriented—and perhaps unaware at the time what he faced—Peck had pressed on, calling for immediate no-notice inspections of Vietnamese prisons and even proposing that the United States take the Israeli approach to the problem and grab a high Vietnamese diplomat and hold him until the Vietnamese came to the table and began negotiations for a prisoner swap. When these and other recommendations were denied, he had informed his civilian superiors that the Special Office was a disaster area. When asked to explain, he had replied that he could best describe the situation by simply signing the 1986 Gaines Report, because nothing, he said, had changed in the five years since the report had been written.

By January 1991, word began circulating at the Pentagon that the troublemaker at the Special Office would be reassigned. Aware of the rumors, Peck took his case directly to Lt. Gen. Ed Soyster, USA, in the form of a flip-chart briefing outlining the problems and deficiencies he had uncovered at the Special Office. After seeing Peck's briefing, Soyster informed Peck that things were "just not working out" and offered him a new job that Soyster said would be more in line with his skills—a liaison position with the French Army in Germany. Astounded, Peck declined Soyster's offer, returned to his office, and began preparing a memorandum outlining the improprieties he had earlier put forth in his complaints to his civilian bosses and had just presented to Soyster. In the memorandum, which he delivered to Soyster on February 12, Peck cited the following among the numerous improprieties he had discovered while serving as chief of the Special Office:

- The mindset to "debunk" is alive and well. It is held at all levels, and continues to pervade the POW/MIA Office.
- Practically all analysis is directed to finding fault with the source.
- Rarely has there been any effective, active follow through on any of the sightings, nor is there a responsive "action arm" to routinely and aggressively pursue leads.
- That national leaders continue to address the prisoner of war and missing in action issue as the "highest national priority" is a travesty. From my vantage point, I observed that the principal government players were interested primarily in conducting a "damage limitation exercise" and appeared to knowingly and deliberately generate an endless succession of manufactured crises and "busy work" . . . with little substance and no real results.
- It appears the entire issue is being manipulated by unscrupulous people in the Government or associated with the Government. Some are using the issue for personal or political advantage and others use it as a forum to perform and feel important, or worse. . . . The entire charade does not appear to be an honest effort, and may never have been.
- The policy people manipulating the affair have maintained their distance and remained hidden in the shadows, while using the Office as a "toxic waste dump" to bury the whole "mess" out of sight and mind in a facility with limited access to public scrutiny.
- Many of the puppet masters play a confusing, murky role. For instance, the Director of the National League of Families occupies an interesting and questionable position in the whole process. Although assiduously "churning" the account to give a tawdry illusion of progress, she is adamantly opposed to any initiative to actually get to the heart of the problem, and, more importantly, interferes in or actively sabotages POW-MIA investigations. . . . She was brought from the "outside" into the center of the imbroglio, and then, cloaked in a mantel [sic] of sanctimony, routinely impedes real progress and insidiously "muddies up" the issue. . . . As the principal actor in the grand show, she is in the perfect position to clamor for "progress," while really intentionally impeding the effort.
- From what I have witnessed, it appears that any soldier left in Vietnam, even inadvertently, was, in fact, abandoned years ago, and that the farce

that is being played is no more than political legerdemain done with "smoke and mirrors" to stall the issue until it dies a natural death.

Noting that "any military officer expected to survive in this environment would have to be myopic, an accomplished sycophant or totally insouciant," Peck concluded his memorandum with a request that Soyster relieve him of his duties at the Special Office and assist him in being retired immediately from active military service.

## March
## A NEW INITIATIVE IN THE U.S. SENATE

In early March, several weeks after Peck sent his memorandum to Soyster, now-Senator Bob Smith, the former congressman and longtime POW advocate and DIA critic, got wind of the memorandum and the enormous consternation it was causing inside the administration. When Smith sought a copy of the memorandum from DIA, his request was denied. Disgusted, he took to the floor of the Senate on March 14 and introduced legislation to create a Senate Select Committee on POW/MIA Affairs. Too much about the live POW issue was being kept secret, Smith charged, and it was time for the Senate to exercise its authority and thoroughly investigate the issue once and for all. Helms and Grassley, still being denied complete access to all of the intelligence on live POWs, joined Smith on the Senate floor to speak in favor of his bill.[3]

## A MESSAGE ON THE OFFICE DOOR

On March 28, Peck received word from Soyster that his request that he be relieved of command had been granted. Shortly after reading Soyster's reply, Peck stapled a copy of his February memorandum to his office door and walked out of the Special Office suite, never to return.

Knowing the fuse had been lit and the Peck bomb could go off at any minute, Vessey rushed to Vietnam to do whatever it took to break the ongoing impasse over the Hanoi office. On April 20, he announced that negotiations had been successfully completed and that the office would be up and running in a matter of weeks.[4]

In mid-May, as U.S. officials worked feverishly to get the new office opened in Hanoi, word of Peck's explosive memorandum and his unorthodox departure from DIA finally reached the mainstream press. First reported in *U.S. News & World Report* and *The Washington Times,* the story soon appeared from coast to coast under damning headlines. "Ex-Official's memo calls U.S. MIA effort a charade, travesty," blared the *Orange County Register*. "Pentagon Official Resigns, Alleges Cover-Up On MIAs," the *Los Angeles Times* reported. Even *The Washington Post* unlimbered the politically incorrect "C-word," declaring "Ex-Official Alleges Administration Coverup On POW/MIA Issue." *The New York Times* laid the matter squarely at the feet of the president himself, declaring "Bush Is Said To Ignore the Vietnam War's Missing." *The Washington Times,* in a follow-up article that appeared under the headline "Colonel Says Support-Group Leader Hinders

Search for Vietnam POWs," highlighted Peck's allegations that Griffiths played a key role in the cover-up.[5]

## THE HELMS FINAL REPORT

Much to the administration's discomfort, it turned out that the Peck revelations were only the first wave of what would become a frontal assault on the administration's POW policy during the spring and summer of 1991. Within days of the publicity surrounding Peck's resignation, Helms released the final report of his investigation of the government's handling of the POW issue and the drumbeat began anew.[6] Under the damning headline, "Report: Government Leaves MIAs to Rot in Prison," the *Sacramento Union* quoted Helms spokesman Dan Perrin as saying, "The government sticks with its official position that there are no POWs or MIAs. We say that is ludicrous."[7] *USA Today* offered the shocking revelation that "the U.S. Government has tried to sabotage efforts to find any of the 2,276 Americans still listed as missing in Vietnam, a report out Thursday charges."[8] Half a world away, the *Bangkok Post* quoted the national commander of the Veterans of Foreign Wars as telling President Bush in a letter that he should appoint an independent commission to investigate the charges leveled by Peck and Helms. "These are serious allegations from very credible sources," the VFW leader was quoted as saying. "They call into question the integrity of the United States Government and cast serious doubt as to whether the POW/MIA issue has ever truly been 'of highest national priority.' "[9]

Rather than appoint an independent panel to investigate what now had all the makings of a full-blown scandal, Defense Secretary Dick Cheney directed that DIA itself investigate the Peck charges. In June, Cheney announced that that inquiry "has concluded there is no foundation to support" charges that the Defense Department is ignoring or covering up reports of live sightings of U.S. prisoners of war in Southeast Asia and that "no further action is required in this case."[10] Cheney, who enjoyed broad, bipartisan support in the Senate, was further quoted as saying he hoped "this incident has not added to the burden of the families of our missing personnel. They have my personal commitment that resolution of the issue of prisoners of war and missing in action is a matter of the highest national priority."[11]

Thanks to the findings of the DIA inquiry and to the popular Cheney's personal assurances of his commitment to the missing and to resolving their fate, Senate lawmakers cooled to the thought of embracing the controversial legislation Smith had introduced. By early summer, the chances of Smith's bill passing appeared to be slipping away.

## A DOD INFORMANT'S DUBIOUS PHOTOGRAPH TURNS THE TIDE

It was into this environment that word came out of Cambodia that a DOD informant[12] had provided the United States with a photograph said to be of three American POWs. When the photo made its way into the press, the impact was similar to a cup of gasoline being thrown on a struggling campfire; before the explosion subsided, the photo appeared in virtually every major newspaper in America, on every major nightly television newscast, even on the cover of *Newsweek*. Thousands of letters poured into congressional offices demanding an end to the "cover-up" and immediate action to get the POWs home. Surveying the landscape, the *Chicago Tribune* declared on July 21 that "at perhaps no time since the end of the Vietnam War, has the Government's credibility on this issue been more suspect."[13]

On July 26, National Security Advisor Brent Scowcroft moved to stanch the flow by declaring he was convinced no American POWs remained alive.[14] Rather than allay fears, Scowcroft's widely reported statement served only to fan the flames. Senate Minority Leader Bob Dole (R-KS), when asked on NBC's *Meet the Press* about the national security advisor's statement, replied, "I don't know [if any are alive], and I don't think Brent Scowcroft knows." Dole then called on Bush to appoint a presidential commission to investigate the POW/MIA issue from top to bottom.[15]

The administration went to a full-court press following Dole's nationally broadcast call for a presidential commission. On July 30, the Pentagon announced with much fanfare that Cheney had signed an order increasing the number of investigators working on the POW/MIA issue from 134 to 222 and authorizing the creation of a new high-level post at the Pentagon—that of deputy assistant secretary of defense for POW/MIA affairs—to oversee the government's expanded effort to find POWs and MIAs.[16] Simultaneously, Cheney traveled to the Hill to meet with Dole and other key senators to lobby against the formation of either a presidential commission or the proposed Select Committee on POW/MIA Affairs. The secretary and his associates attempted to explain away Colonel Peck's charges by stating that Peck "did not understand substantive intelligence process" and had "tried to change U.S. policy." Peck's allegations, Cheney flatly declared, were not supported by the facts. Cheney and his associates went on to say that though minor problems might have existed at the Special Office, these problems would be solved by the addition of the new investigators.[17] Cheney was emphatic: He and the president were committed to resolving the POW/MIA issue and needed no help whatever from either a presidential commission or a new Senate committee.

But a "perfect storm" had developed, and even Cheney couldn't stop it. Things came to a head on Friday, August 2. First, that morning, *The Wall Street Journal* reported that 69 percent of those surveyed in a new *Wall Street Journal*/NBC News poll believed that Americans were still being held prisoner in Southeast Asia. Three-quarters said the government wasn't doing enough to get them out.[18] Later in the day, when Bush himself was asked by a reporter how he felt about the possibility that some POWs might still be alive, the president dug in his heels, declaring that "as General Scowcroft said the other day, and I back him fully, there's no hard evidence of prisoners being alive." Bush then invited anyone with hard evidence to "please bring it forward."[19]

By day's end, even the administration's strongest supporters on Capitol Hill had seen and heard enough. Having read with great care Peck's letter and Helms's report and the newspaper headlines and their mail and the polls, that evening members of the Senate unanimously approved Smith's bill creating a new Senate Select Committee on POW/MIA Affairs.[20]

# ONE LAST CHANCE TO SAVE THE UNLISTED, UNRETURNED POWs

As passed by the Senate, Smith's legislation called for a committee of twelve senators, six chosen by Majority Leader George Mitchell (D-ME) and six by Minority Leader Dole. Because the Senate was controlled by the Democrats in 1991, a Democrat would serve as chairman and a Republican as vice chairman. The committee was empowered to subpoena documents and witnesses and was given approximately eighteen months to complete its investigation.

Mitchell picked his team within hours of the bill's passage. Chairing the committee would be Massachusetts Senator John Kerry, the decorated Vietnam War veteran who had later become an articulate spokesman in the antiwar movement. First elected to the Senate in 1984, Kerry had made a name for himself as chairman of the Subcommittee on Terrorism, Narcotics and International Operations, where he had conducted hard-hitting investigations of some of the world's most notorious drug lords and money launderers. To serve with Kerry, Mitchell chose Vietnam veterans Bob Kerrey of Nebraska, a former Navy Seal who had won the Congressional Medal of Honor in Vietnam, Charles Robb of Virginia, Tom Daschle of South Dakota, Harry Reid of Nevada, and Dennis DeConcini of Arizona. DeConcini would decline the post and be replaced by Herb Kohl of Wisconsin.

Dole would choose Vietnam veterans Smith, McCain, and Hank Brown of Colorado, and Grassley, Helms, and Nancy Landon Kassebaum of Kansas. The minority leader would not initially choose his vice chairman, being torn between Smith, the chief sponsor of the bill creating the committee, and former POW McCain. Kerry wanted McCain and lobbied hard behind the scenes for his appointment.[21] Perhaps for this very reason, Dole ultimately chose Smith.

Kerry had been chairman barely ten days when he announced to the press that he was leaving immediately for Indochina to investigate what he called "hot leads" on living POWs. Simultaneously raising the hopes of the POW/MIA families and surprising his critics who said he had no real interest in living prisoners, Kerry told *USA Today* before his departure, "I approach this with an absolute judgment of possibility somebody is alive. There's a solemn obligation every single one of us feels. . . . We've got to resolve this."[22]

And move to resolve it he did. After a series of meetings with Vietnamese leaders, Kerry returned to the United States and announced at a news conference that he strongly doubted there were any prisoners being held by the Communist governments of Southeast Asia. While conceding that MIAs might have fallen into the hands of groups beyond the reach of the governments and could still be alive, Kerry said, "I think the likelihood that a government is formally holding somebody is obviously tiny."[23]

Smith and his staff were speechless. It was as if Earl Warren, days after having been appointed to investigate the assassination of President John Kennedy, had taken a cab ride through Dealey Plaza, publicly declared his findings, and then convened his commission to "carefully weigh" the evidence. How the hell could the intelligence possibly get a fair hearing, the vice chairman and his men wondered, now that the chairman himself had already publicly dismissed it?

At the request of the horrified activist families, Hendon met with Kerry soon

after his press conference to tell him of the huge volume of intelligence showing American POWs being held after the war by the Vietnamese and Lao governments and to inform him exactly where the intelligence files were being
stored and to request that he see to it that all of that intelligence be delivered to
the committee so he and his fellow senators and members of the Select Committee staff could examine it. At the meeting, held in Kerry's Russell Senate Office Building office and attended by Kerry, his foreign affairs assistant Nancy
Stetson, and the person Kerry had chosen as staff director of the Select Committee, Frances Zwenig, Hendon made his pitch.

Following a brief overview of the intelligence and where it was located, Hendon asked Kerry if he could show him some examples of the intelligence reports
that Hendon had acquired in declassified form over the years. Kerry thanked
Hendon for his offer but said his schedule was tight and that it might be better
if Hendon and Zwenig adjourned to an adjoining conference room to go over
the material; Zwenig, Kerry assured Hendon, would fill him in on all the details
later. Hendon thanked Kerry for his time and his concern for the missing and, as
the chairman had suggested, adjourned to the conference room with Zwenig.

To Hendon's surprise, he was into only his second or third declassified intelligence document when an obviously agitated Zwenig blurted out, "Listen,
there is no need for us to go over these reports. The committee is not going to
have time to go through all of this type of information. Our job is to put the war
behind us and normalize relations. So there is no need to go over all this. But
thank you for your interest and for taking the time to come by."[24]

Hendon covered the route from Kerry's office in Russell to Smith's in the
Dirksen Senate Office Building in record time. First, Hendon told his old friend,
had come Kerry's "hot leads" stunt—and now this!

Deeply concerned by what Zwenig had said, Smith contacted Kerry and demanded that he join him in ordering the administration to provide the committee with copies of every piece of POW-related intelligence in the U.S.
government's files. Kerry agreed to take the matter under advisement and get
back to Smith.

Kerry reported back that he had decided to go along with Smith's request that
the intelligence be provided to the committee. He then informed Smith of his
desire to add Sedgwick "Wick" Tourison, the former chief of analysis at the DIA
Special Office, to the Select Committee investigative staff and, as required under
committee rules, requested Smith's approval to do so. Tourison, Smith knew all
too well, was one of the most notorious debunkers ever employed at the Special
Office (the authors suggest that readers see www.enormouscrime.com, Chapter
23). Additionally, Tourison had recently written a book titled *Talking With Victor
Charlie* in which he had declared, "I was satisfied [after leaving the Special Office
in 1988] that there were no live United States POWs in Southeast Asia and that
there hadn't been any since Operation Homecoming in early 1973."[25] Given all
that, Smith understandably vetoed Kerry's request, and Tourison was not hired.

Kerry, however, refused to give up, and simply bided his time until Smith
needed a similar okay from him on some aspect of the committee's work. Weeks
passed, and when such an occasion arose, Kerry initially refused Smith's request
and then again asked that he be allowed to hire Tourison. Smith countered that

Kerry could hire Tourison on two conditions: First, he must agree that Tourison not be allowed to participate in any way in the intelligence portion of the committee's investigation, and second, he must agree to allow Smith to hire Hendon as a member of his personal staff and delegate him to the committee as a full-time intelligence investigator to assist in the investigation of the POW intelligence. Kerry agreed to both conditions, and Tourison and Hendon were soon brought aboard.

(To some, it seemed outrageous that Tourison would be allowed to participate in the committee's deliberations, even with the proviso that he not be allowed to play any role in the investigation of the intelligence; to others, it appeared equally outrageous that Hendon would be allowed anywhere near the intelligence he had for so long been accusing the government of covering up. But such is the give-and-take that characterizes life in the U.S. Senate, where one must give something to get something; where, as they say, "One man's fat is another man's lean.")

Smith, his top aide Dino Carluccio, and Hendon quickly began developing an investigative work plan and assembling a team of intelligence investigators. Chosen to lead the effort was DIA intelligence officer and attorney John Francis McCreary, the highly respected former member of the Tighe Task Force and principal author of the task force's final report. McCreary knew the POW issue inside and out and came highly recommended by Tighe, who told Smith that McCreary was one of the nation's finest and most accomplished intelligence officers. Working with McCreary would be two retired army colonels, William "Bill" LeGro, who had served as chief of intelligence at the U.S. embassy in Saigon during the period 1973–1975 and had been among the last of the Americans evacuated when the city fell, and Harold "Nick" Nicklas, who had just completed a distinguished career in Special Operations. Also serving would be civilians Robert "Bob" Taylor, a distinguished Middle East intelligence analyst formerly assigned to the Office of the Secretary of Defense (International Security Affairs); John Holstein, Ph.D., a former House Foreign Affairs Committee Indochina expert and former director of Asian affairs for the Agency for International Development (AID) and Hendon.

By Thanksgiving, the investigative plan was almost complete. Smith and his men would request access to all intelligence (HUMINT, SIGINT, IMINT) relating to captured Americans received after January 27, 1973, by either the CIA, DIA, JCRC, the various military intelligence services, defense attaché offices worldwide, NSA and/or DEA, including those agencies' analysis of each individual report; and all postwar POW-related staff memoranda, decision memoranda, action memoranda, background papers, policy briefs, minutes, operations orders, National Security directives, "Tank Briefs," "Morning Summary Reports," "Weekly Activity Reports," and/or similar items generated by the Department of Defense, the Department of State, and the National Security Council.[26]

All agreed it would be a massive undertaking. When word was received in December that a former KGB Major General identified as Oleg Kalugin had recently stated on Australian TV that the Soviets had interviewed three U.S. POWs in Vietnam long after the war had ended, all agreed, also, *that it was time to get to work.*

# CHAPTER 31

# 1992

# THE FRAGGING

. . .

Senator Kerry and Sen. McCain chaired the country's most thorough investigation into the fate of the POW/MIAs in Southeast Asia. . . . His closest friends
told him the issue was too volatile, the political dangers too ominous, but Senator Kerry insisted that "It's something you do as a soldier, you don't leave anyone behind."

—"VETERANS," JohnKerry.com

The old controversy over American soldiers abandoned in Vietnam was
reawakened when newspaper front pages and then the cover of *Newsweek* displayed a photograph purportedly showing three American POWs still in captivity. Lurking below this issue, as always, was the war that had not yet ended.
"I set out literally to bring that ending about," Kerry told me. "I knew as a matter of policy that it should take place, and I think John [McCain] felt the same
way." McCain lent Kerry his unimpeachable integrity on the question of the
war that each wanted to end. Kerry drove the process, but only McCain could
have enabled him to drive it home.

—JAMES CARROLL, "A Friendship That Ended the War"

Mr. McCain described most POW/MIA activists as "ethical people," but said
others had "managed to advance the utterly ridiculous contention that Americans were knowingly abandoned at the war's end by their government."

—"MCCAIN ON 'ONE FINAL MISSION,'" *Washington Times*

Deeply committed to reestablishing U.S. diplomatic relations with Vietnam, in
Zwenig's opinion the war was not officially over. "We still had a lot of unfin-
ished business to do," she recalled. "Until we cleared up the POW/MIA issue it
was impossible for the Bush administration to embrace Vietnam in any way.
And the Republican right, including Bob Smith, were convinced, wrongly so,
that American POWs were still being held captive."

—DOUGLAS BRINKLEY, *Tour of Duty: John Kerry and the Vietnam War*

"Nobody wanted to be on that damn committee," Bob Kerrey said. "It was an
absolute loser. Everyone knew that the P.O.W. stories were fabrications, but no
one wanted to offend the vet community."

—JOE KLEIN, "The Long War of John Kerry"

The year 1992 began with a flurry of press accounts suggesting the presence of
American POWs in Vietnam and Laos long after Operation Homecoming.

The first appeared on New Year's Day when the Oklahoma City *Daily Oklahoman* published an editorial on the POW/MIA issue titled, "It Has To Come
Out." The editorial, based on an interview the editors had conducted with Senate

Intelligence Committee Chairman David Boren (D-OK), outlined Boren's on-the-record and quite remarkable assessment of how the matter of the Indochina POWs had been mishandled by every administration since 1973, and how embarrassing it was going to be when the Senate Select Committee finally got to the bottom of the mess and publicized what had occurred. In the editorial, the highly respected Boren first predicted the new committee would discover that more prisoners than previously thought had been left in Laos. He then stated his belief that when the Paris accords were signed, "there were people involved that didn't want all the questions raised at that time" and that "[o]nce they decided not to disclose it at the time of the agreement, the next year, they decided it was too embarrassing [and] the longer it went the more embarrassing it got to be." That thought process, Boren said, was evident "in administrations in both parties." Boren explained further that "they always thought 'Well, I [will] hand this on to the next guy to admit we really made a big mess,' [and as a result] those who knew the truth kept handing it on." "There are people, obviously, in the military and otherwise, in the foreign policy establishment," Boren said, "who feel they are going to be embarrassed if this comes out. And so, they keep it secret." He concluded by saying "It has to come out, and it will."[1]

Then, on the 2nd, the entire front page of the New York *Daily News* was consumed by the banner headline "Ex-KGB Spy: Viets Held U.S. POWs After '73", and an accompanying picture of Maj. Gen. Oleg Kalugin, the former KGB general who had appeared earlier on Australian TV. Inside, a long article outlined Kalugin's personal account of how the Soviets had interviewed the three American POWs in Vietnam during 1978.[2] Dozens of similar articles about Kalugin's revelations appeared in other American newspapers in the days that followed.[3]

Like the tree that fell in the forest but made no noise because no one was there to hear it fall, Boren's remarks to his small home state newspaper would almost certainly have gone unnoticed in Washington had they not been picked up and distributed by a Capitol Hill think tank specializing in defense matters. The head of the think tank, Frank Gaffney, who had served in the Pentagon during the Reagan years and who heretofore had shown little interest in the POW issue, was stunned by Boren's remarks and, noting that they had gone "unremarked by the national media," quickly went to work faxing the chairman's comments to congressional offices and policy makers throughout the government. Calling Boren's statements "mind-boggling," the highly respected Gaffney declared that "for the first time, a senior, serving official of the United States government—one who, by dint of his committee responsibilities, is in a position to know—has said the unsayable about U.S. prisoners of war and missing in action in Southeast Asia: a cover up, perpetrated by both Democratic and Republican administrations, has been underway for decades aimed at concealing the fact that American servicemen remained incarcerated at the end of the Vietnam War." Gaffney noted that "as politically explosive revelations go, Sen. Boren's pronouncement represents a *high megatonnage blast*."[4]

A high megatonnage blast, indeed, Smith and his men knew. But, of course, those on the other side of the issue—both in the Bush administration and on the committee—knew it as well, and soon signs began appearing they were working hard to counter its effects. First came two stunning personnel changes at the committee that dramatically altered the landscape and quickly tipped the scales away from the unlisted, unreturned POWs. And then came revelations by Tourison and Kerry that tipped them even farther. By early February, it became clear to Smith & Company that all was not well along the Potomac and that they faced the fight of their lives in their effort to expose what Boren and Gaffney had so correctly stated was a long-running bipartisan effort to cover up the fate of the unlisted, unreturned POWs.

## THE JANUARY PERSONNEL CHANGES

In January, just as the committee's investigation was getting under way, two critical personnel changes occurred at the committee, one involving the addition of a new personal designee to the staff by Senator Helms, the other involving the departure, after only ninety days or so on the job, of the committee's deputy staff director.[5] The reasons that reportedly lay behind these personnel changes—and the effect they would have on the outcome of the committee's investigation—offer a sobering glimpse into Bush administration efforts to keep the committee investigation from succeeding.

The facts surrounding the appointment of Helms's new designee, a retired Navy rear admiral named James "Bud" Nance, who Helms had recently hired following a staff shake-up at the Foreign Relations Committee and had then assigned to the POW/MIA Select Committee as his personal designee, were laid out for all the world to see in an "Inside the Beltway" column that appeared in the January 10 edition of *The Washington Times*. In the widely read and always politically charged column, columnist John Elvin wrote that day that the "State Department and Bush White House have longed to hush Jesse 'Senator No' Helms in his crusades over wasted foreign aid, ignored POWs and MIAs, and a host of other issues, and that with the hiring by Helms of former White House National Security Advisor James W. 'Bud' Nance, a retired Navy Admiral . . . [a] number of observers believe the mission has been accomplished." Elvin explained that earlier in the week Helms had fired "most of his longtime conservative committee aides on the recommendation of consultant Nance, whom the Senator then appointed new Republican staff director." Elvin said that following his appointment, Nance "promptly telephoned the White House to tell his old friend Brent Scowcroft, Mr. Bush's national security advisor, "I want to help you any way I can."

Elvin went on to explain that Helms and his wife had both been ill recently, and that those illnesses had "taken their toll on the senator's attention to Senate duties." "It was into that void," Elvin said, "that Adm. Nance moved to wipe out hard-line conservative Helms aides—with apparent backing from some staff dissidents and Senate Republican moderates who argued that Mr. Helms' frequent disagreement with the administration had 'isolated' him within the Senate." Elvin went on to say that "to those for whom Mr. Helms has stood as a last bastion of traditional, chivalrous conservative thought and action, the knives in the backs of hard-line staffers mark the end of an era. They view the alliance between Adm. Nance and Gen. Scowcroft as the induction of Mr. Helms into the New World Order."[6]

"New World Order" aside, Smith and his team were devastated by the Nance developments, for they knew that as far as their investigation was concerned, they had lost not only the expertise of the Foreign Relations Committee staffers who had produced the two earlier Helms reports—staffers with whom they had planned to consult frequently in the months ahead—but a powerful and badly needed ally on the committee as well: the powerful Helms himself, the very man who for years prior to the formation of the Select Committee had, along with Sen. Strom Thurmond (R-SC), led the fight in the Senate to bring the POWs home.

Smith was still reeling from the Helms/Nance developments when he was hit in mid-January by what had all appearances of another Bush administration inside deal, this one apparently involving Cheney and Wolfowitz and the committee's deputy staff director, Alan Ptak (pronounced puh-tack). Though different in nature from the Nance matter—the Ptak case involved the departure of a powerful staff member rather than the appointment of one—what happened with Ptak would prove no less damaging to Smith's efforts on behalf of live POWs in the months ahead.

The history of the Ptak case was this: The reader will recall that back in July 1991, a political firestorm had developed in the wake of the Peck resignation, the release of Helms's final report, and the emergence from Cambodia of the dubious photograph of the three alleged American POWs. Cheney, in what was to many an obvious attempt to head off the formation of the select committee, had announced a massive increase in the number of personnel being assigned to the hunt for POWs and MIAs and the creation of a new high-level Pentagon position, that of assistant secretary of defense for POW/MIA affairs, to oversee the "newly-energized U.S. effort." The person appointed to the newly created position, Cheney announced, would report directly to Cheney's deputy secretary of defense for policy, Paul Wolfowitz. Despite Cheney's assurances, however, the Senate, bowing to public pressure, had created the select committee anyway in early August.

Soon after the select committee was created, Ptak, who had worked for the CIA and under Anthony Principi at the Senate Veterans Affairs Committee, and in mid-1991 had just begun working at the Senate Select Committee on Intelligence, abruptly resigned his position at the intelligence committee and took a job as deputy staff director of the newly created POW/MIA committee. Working closely with Zwenig and others, he had participated in virtually every aspect of the committee's work throughout late 1991, acquiring along the way close associations with subordinates and a wide and detailed knowledge of the committee's plans, strategies, policies, etc. Over at the Pentagon, meanwhile, the newly created position of ASD/POW-MIA remained unfilled.

Now comes January 1992. The committee's investigative work plans and strategies are complete and the investigation is about to begin in earnest. Suddenly, at midmonth, Ptak abruptly resigns *this* position, cleans out his desk, and departs. Days pass, and then, in late January, Cheney announces that the president has decided to name Ptak the nation's first assistant secretary of defense for POW/MIA affairs, reporting directly to the undersecretary of defense for policy, Paul Wolfowitz, and, ultimately, to himself (Cheney).[7]

Smith, incredulous, wonders how this all could be happening. Older, wiser heads tell him that no one ever suggested that Bush, Scowcroft, Cheney, and Wolfowitz weren't damn good at running a government.

## THE TOURISON REVELATIONS AND THE CHAIRMAN'S ROAD MAP

More trouble for Smith surfaced at a committee staff meeting held in Nance's conference room on January 24. At the meeting, Tourison announced that Kerry had named him the committee's "numbers guy" and assigned him the task of determining exactly how many men were unaccounted for at the conclusion of Operation Homecoming in 1973. To the amazement of those present who were familiar with the history of the POW/MIA issue, Tourison then stated that his early research indicated there were not really some two thousand and four hundred POW/MIAs as DOD had steadfastly reported since the end of the war, but probably far, far fewer. Then Tourison dropped the second shoe, declaring that in the course of his research he had already "discovered" a heretofore unknown list of 890 Army "known deserters" whose existence had never before been reported.[8]

As 890 deserters was in such stark contrast to the five Vietnam War deserters DOD had consistently reported since 1976,[9] Hendon and McCreary voiced immediate objections. When Mark Salter, McCain's top aide, came to Tourison's defense and charged Hendon and McCreary with trying to stifle Tourison's pursuit of the truth, Smith's men knew for sure something very bad was afoot. Far *fewer* POW/MIAs than previously reported? Eight hundred and eighty-five *more* "known deserters"?

In early February, the *Boston Globe Magazine* published a lengthy article written by the *Globe's* highly respected Washington reporter Jack Farrell that chronicled Kerry's long history in dealing with the Vietnam War and its aftermath and what Farrell called Kerry's "ardent involvement" in the POW/MIA issue. Near the conclusion of the article, which covered everything from Kerry's service in Vietnam during the war to other investigations he had conducted in the U.S. Senate to the persistent buzz that he was planning a run for the presidency, Farrell wrote that Kerry was working to steer members of his POW/MIA committee to three conclusions: (1) yes, a few men were indeed left behind, and (2) yes, the Pentagon bureaucracy had exhibited a mind-set to debunk the reports about live POWs, but (3) no, none are still alive and therefore it is time to put the issue to rest.[10]

Smith and his investigators, reading this *second* version of what Kerry expected the committee to find—this one somewhat different from the first that Kerry had outlined after his "hot leads" trip to Indochina but still no less threatening to the unlisted, unreturned POWs—were both stunned and angry. With Smith leading the way, they ratcheted up their demands for the intelligence reports, which had not yet been delivered due to the Bush administration's insistence that before the senators or the intelligence investigators would be allowed to see the reports, the names of the sources and, tellingly, the names of the DIA analysts and JCRC interviewers handling each case had to first be redacted.

In a matter of days the first copies of the DIA working files began arriving at the Office of Senate Security in the Capitol. Hundreds would soon follow. Finally, for the first time ever, U.S. senators and their investigators would have an opportunity to see what the U.S. government *really* knew about living POWs.

## THE INVESTIGATION OF THE INTELLIGENCE BEGINS AT LAST • THE HOWS, WHYS, AND WHEREFORES

Smith's intelligence investigators began their analysis of the postwar intelligence by analyzing DIA's previously classified computerized printout of all HUMINT reports on missing Americans received by the U.S. government since the end of the Vietnam War. The list, unearthed by LeGro, contained 16,814 numbered reports and covered 231 pages. Known as the "SI (pronounced "sigh") Report," it included reports of crash sites, grave sites, prisons, and, of primary importance to the investigators, living Americans.[11] After analyzing the report, the investigators refined their focus and ordered a second printout containing only those intelligence reports relating to live Americans. This printout, which ran 59 pages and contained 4,287 entries, would become the investigators' most valued tool, their Bible, their Rosetta stone.[12]

Analyzing their streamlined version of the SI Report, the investigators saw that approximately seven hundred of the postwar reports described wartime events involving live POWs, i.e., the actual shootdowns and captures of American fliers and/or details of their subsequent incarcerations. Most of these accounts came from North Vietnamese or Pathet Lao refugees who had lived or operated in enemy territory during the war.

In analyzing these wartime sightings, investigators found that in many cases more than one refugee had reported seeing or hearing about the same wartime event. The investigators found, for example, that at least four refugee sources had independently described the August 5, 1964, shootdown and capture near Hon Gai of Lt. Cmdr. Everett Alvarez, USN, the first American pilot shot down and captured over North Vietnam.[13] They found that at least eleven had independently described events surrounding the shootdown of another Navy pilot, Lt. Cmdr. Edwin Tucker, near Hon Gai on April 24, 1967.[14] In the case of a third Navy pilot, Lt. Cmdr. John S. McCain III, the investigators found that at least five refugees had in one form or another independently described his October 26, 1967, shootdown over Hanoi, his landing in Truc Bach Lake just northwest of the Ministry of Defense Citadel, and his subsequent capture.[15] And on and on and on the wartime sightings went.

Moving to the reports of Americans seen or reported alive in communist territory after the war, the investigators found that often, as with the wartime reports, more than one refugee had reported seeing or hearing about the same person or event. More than three hundred, for example, had described seeing or hearing about that same single American living freely near Yen Bai in northern Vietnam from 1976 to 1979—clearly Robert Garwood.

The investigators found that hundreds also had reported seeing or hearing about American servicemen in captivity after the war, and that in a number of cases the refugees had reported Americans being detained in the same general area or even in the same prison. Two refugees, for example, had reported seeing American POWs being detained at a certain prison during 1976, two more said they had seen American POWs there in 1978, another reported he had seen Americans POWs being held there in 1981, three had reported the presence of American POWs there in 1982, etc. The more the investigators combed the intelligence, the more examples they found of refugees independently reporting American POWs being held after the war in the same general area, or at the same specific prison, at the same time or over a period of time. These reports, McCreary and Hendon determined, would be the focus of the investigation, for the obvious reason that the reports tended to corroborate one another, and, as both men knew, when it comes to analyzing human intelligence, absent IMINT and/or SIGINT and/or the ability to conduct an on-site investigation, corroboration by other human sources is the best lie detector ever devised by man.

That corroboration is, in fact, the best lie detector in determining a witness's truthfulness on a given matter is hardly worthy of debate. Consider these examples: If, during graduation week, the local 911 operations center gets a call from a kid on a cell phone who says Central High School is on fire, officials at the center will immediately sense a trick, as they should. But if the principal, his administrative assistant, two teachers, the football coach, and a passing motorist all call in in the next minute or so with the same story, these same 911 officials know there is a degree of probability approaching certainty that something very bad is happening over at Central High. Or suppose a man who lives on Maple Avenue reports to police that crack cocaine is being sold out of the house at 239 Maple. In the absence of other reports of drug dealing at that address, this man's report will almost certainly be viewed with caution. Maybe the source has a long history of false reporting; maybe he has had a dispute with the owner of 239 Maple over loud music emanating from the house and has contrived the drug story to settle a score; maybe he is confused and it is 932 Maple instead of 239—or maybe 239 Oak.

But suppose the school crossing guard assigned to the intersection of Maple and Third, the prostitute who works the corner after hours, the postman, a UPS delivery man, three school kids who live on the block, a plumber, a real estate salesperson, the hairdresser who runs the shop across the street at 242 Maple, a pizza delivery man, a Jehovah's Witness volunteer who has evangelized in the neighborhood, a dog walker, two junkies, and the chairwoman of the Maple Avenue Community Watch all report drug deals going down at number 239. What then? The answer, of course, is obvious: There is a degree of probability approaching certainty that 239 Maple is, in fact, a crack house. Granted, the police will never know this for sure until they raid the place and find the proof. But even in the absence of such a raid, given the number of independent sources reporting the same thing at the same place at the same time or over a period of time, few could honestly doubt what was really going on behind that ugly purple front door at 239 Maple.

In the intelligence business, attempting to determine the veracity of a HUMINT report by checking for corroborative reports and comparing them as to event, location, time, circumstance, etc., with the information provided by the HUMINT source is called pattern analysis. The more a definite pattern develops in the reporting, i.e., same event, same place, same time/period of time etc., the more likely it is that the sources are telling the truth. An extension of pattern analysis, cluster analysis, a tool as old as intelligence analysis itself, involves the plotting of locations provided by sources on a map to test for corroboration. As common sense would indicate, if large numbers of reports from independent sources cluster around any given location (239 Maple Avenue), there is a high degree of probability that the event the sources reported did in fact occur. And, correspondingly, a high degree of probability that the individual sources are credible, truthful reporters of that event. (Granted, individually these sources may include drug dealers, prostitutes, thieves, and other unsavory characters, but because these people independently reported that the same event was taking place at the same location at or around the same time or over a period of time, there is a high probability they are reporting truthfully about that event and are, therefore, credible witnesses to that event.)

McCreary and Hendon knew well that during the war, U.S. military intelligence officials had used cluster analysis frequently and effectively in Indochina. They knew, for example, that after wartime officials had received a mere handful of reports that American servicemen were being deployed as human shields at the Hanoi Thermal Power Plant, U.S. officials had declared, "In consideration of these reports, it is reasonable to conclude that PWs were being worked within the plant in order to deter aircraft from attacking it."[16] Likewise, they knew that in the early 1980s DIA had, on the basis of just seven refugee reports, confirmed the presence of "an American [obviously Garwood] living and working in cooperation with the Vietnamese during the period 1975–1978 near the town of Yen Bai." "Based upon the volume and consistency of the reporting [the seven reports]," DIA had declared, ". . . there is sufficient evidence to conclude that a currently unidentified American was living with the Vietnamese at Yen Bai between 1975–1978."[17] But McCreary and Hendon also knew—for reasons they were convinced could only be bad—that DIA had consistently refused to subject the postwar reports of live prisoners to cluster analysis, choosing instead to "analyze" and "investigate" each as if it were the only report ever received and then, in every case, rule that the source was either lying or had actually seen Russians, missionaries, etc.[18] Knowing *all* of that, McCreary and Hendon chose cluster analysis as a way of showing that DIA's position could not possibly be valid.

McCreary, Hendon, LeGro, and Holstein, with periodic assistance from Nicklas, spent more than twenty-seven hundred hours vetting the postwar HUMINT.[19] In the process, they found some 925 refugee reports they believed plausible and then began posting them with color-coded plastic flags and pennants on a large map of Indochina—a square flag for each eyewitness report, a triangular pennant for each hearsay report; a blue flag or pennant for a sighting in the '70s, a red flag or pennant for sightings in the '80s, and a yellow flag or pennant when the date of the postwar sighting had not been stated or could not be accurately determined.

The plotting of the flags and pennants had barely gotten under way when small plastic forests began appearing on the landscape.[20] Mostly blue flags and pennants sprung up in the Chinese border provinces of Lao Cai, Tuyen Quang, Cao Bang, and Lang Son, suggesting that Americans had been held in those areas but prior to 1980. Mixed clusters of blue, red, and yellow sprung up at various other locations throughout the North, signifying either continuous or intermittent detention of American prisoners at those locations over an extended period of time. By the time all the flags and pennants had been posted, the Hanoi area was blotted out completely under a canopy of both flags and pennants, many of which had "subclustered" at the specific prisons in the Hanoi area.

In the South, clusters had developed in the Central Highlands, Ho Chi Minh City, areas to the northwest, northeast, and east of the city, and the U-Minh Forest at Vietnam's southern tip.

In Laos, Sam Neua Province, the old guerrilla stronghold, sported ninety flags and pennants, representing twenty-three eyewitness accounts and sixty-seven hearsay reports telling of American POWs held there from 1973 until 1989. In adjoining Xieng Khoang Province, the entire area of the Plain of Jars and portions of Route 7 near the Vietnam border could not been seen under the dense canopy of plastic. Farther south, Route 8 between Kham Keut and the Vietnamese border looked like a parade route. Another cluster stood near Gnommorath, some thirty miles down Route 8 from Kham Keut. Farther south still, in Savannakhet Province, the area around Route 9 near Tchepone disappeared completely from view.

Along various roadways, trails, footpaths, and waterways in both countries, meanwhile, flags and pennants periodically appeared, indicating sightings of American POWs in transit.

Looking at the map, the investigators saw that from Cao Bang to the Ca Mau in Vietnam and from Oudom Sai to Attopeu in Laos, the reports clustered and clustered and clustered again. The refugees, the clusters said, were telling the truth.

## THE APRIL 9, 1992, INTELLIGENCE FINDING

The select committee was scheduled to convene on April 9 in closed session to receive the investigators' comprehensive briefing on the postwar intelligence. McCreary and Hendon would brief the HUMINT, Taylor the IMINT. At Kerry's insistence, a dry run for staff was scheduled for the evening of the 8th.

On the morning of the 8th, McCreary sat before the map putting the finishing touches on the investigators' briefing:

Our task, as I stated at the onset, is to examine what the substantive intelligence indicates about the possibility of American prisoners of war remaining in Southeast Asia. We posted flags only for those entries that indicated Americans in a captive environment after Operation Homecoming. This means we looked for the presence of guards; weapons; chains and shackles; prison features and confinement; and so on. . . .

We did not post flags for:

A. Clearly outrageous, inflated, exaggerated, or impossible reports—such as numbers in the thousands.

B. Several hundred sightings that equated to Robert Garwood; sightings of Emmet Kay, Arlo Gay, Tucker Gougelman; and other known U.S. personnel who have since returned, whether dead or alive.

C. We did not post flags for reports of dogtags, remains, crash sites, grave sights [*sic*].

D. We rejected reports that plausibly equated to French, Australian, Soviet, Greek, or other foreign nationals.

E. We rejected reports of Americans living freely, or with wives and children or those we assessed to not be in confinement at the time of the sighting.

F. We rejected for posting a number of reports that we equated to sightings of stragglers.

G. We did not accept reports of yachtsmen, adventurers, and drug- and other smugglers.

H. We also excluded sightings equated to Americans detained during and after the fall of Saigon and later released.

The end product of this process is this map which contains 928 flags. . . . There are 215 blue and red square flags, signifying eyewitness accounts; 484 blue and red pennants and 229 yellow pennants, signifying hearsay accounts. . . .

### ANALYTICAL TECHNIQUE

We used a cluster analysis technique to investigate possible consistency and redundancy in **all** of the intelligence, both hearsay and eyewitness. We wanted to see what all of the intelligence indicated—to see how the content of the reporting clustered. This is a longstanding and proven method of analysis used by the US intelligence community. I want to stress that this is the same method of analysis used by the U.S. intelligence community to track scud missile firings by Iraq during the Gulf War. As you recall, missile basket areas were identified, defined, and then targeted. A similar process also is used in tracking SS-25 mobile missile units in the Commonwealth of Independent States. This is a longstanding and proven analytical technique in the US intelligence community.

We want to emphasize that in this cluster analysis we have chosen to focus on the **information content** that the refugees and other sources have provided during the past 19 years. The information trends which are reflected on the map are not dependent on one or even a handful of individual reports. Rather, the trends and patterns reflect the redundancy and the consistency in the total volume of intelligence reporting in the period under investigation.

To recap our procedure,

1. We took the DOD . . . List of over 16,000 [reports] and filtered out reports before Homecoming.

2. Next we filtered out all reports that we felt did not equate to Americans in a captive environment after Operation Homecoming.

3. Finally, we plotted what was left over on the map to see what it showed about the total volume of intelligence reporting from all sources. The clustering effects . . . are the output of this process.

I have labored to explain our data and our technique because our findings disagree with those of the DIA. . . .

We concur with the findings in the Gaines report.

We also wish to state clearly our analytical conclusion.

**The intelligence indicates that American prisoners of war have been held continuously after Operation Homecoming and remain in captivity in Vietnam and Laos as late as 1989.**

**The intelligence indicates that no American prisoners of war have survived in Cambodia.**[21]

Compared with the many intelligence findings he had helped develop during his twenty-two years at DIA, McCreary felt that backing up these would be a simple task. Using the map, he and Hendon would first present an overview of each cluster of sightings. Then, using overhead transparencies of the actual intelligence reports, they would go through each cluster, report by report and line by line, for all the senators to see.

A veteran of countless hours spent briefing DOD officials, McCreary looked forward to this briefing like none he had ever presented. Never before had he seen better intelligence. Never before had he been more confident of his findings.

That evening, he and Hendon presented their dry run briefing as Kerry had directed. Present were Zwenig, senior staffers from the individual senators' offices, and two of Kerry's top foreign affairs specialists. At the conclusion of the briefing, the three Kerry staffers and Salter of McCain's office voiced strenuous objections to the investigators' findings regarding both the validity of the Gaines Report's findings and the fact that POWs remained alive as late as 1989.

## April 9, 1992
## U.S. CAPITOL

The select committee convened at 1:30 P.M. on April 9 in the U.S. Capitol's highly secure intelligence tank, Room S-407. Ten of the twelve committee members were in attendance, many accompanied by staff. A copy of the briefing text sat at each senator's place on the raised dais. The atmosphere was charged, fueled by the presence of several officials from DIA who had been invited by Kerry and McCain.

Kerry had no more than gaveled the meeting to order when McCain bolted from his chair and began waving a copy of the classified briefing text in the air and shouting, "Mr. Chairman, this briefing has been leaked by the investigators!" When Smith demanded that McCain prove his charge, McCain demurred, declaring instead that if the briefing proceeded, the information imparted to the committee surely would be leaked, and for this reason the briefing should not go forward.

Kerry, exhibiting what one investigator later called "all the spontaneity of a NASA rocket launch," joined McCain in professing profound concern over the possibility of "leaks" and then declared that because of that concern, he had decided that no findings of any kind could be presented or discussed, including the findings stated in the briefing text. Kerry addressed the investigators directly and declared that anyone who discussed the investigators' printed findings outside of

S-407 "would wish he had never been born." Kerry then told the stunned Mc-Creary to proceed.[22]

McCreary had barely begun his presentation when McCain retook the floor and began hectoring the twenty-two-year DIA veteran. Questioning McCreary's credentials and professional judgment, the Arizona senator repeatedly and loudly proclaimed that the DIA Special Office analysts were correct [in their assertion that all the intelligence sources were liars or had seen Russians or other foreigners and not POWs] and that a cluster of refugee reports telling of live American servicemen being held at a given prison in Vietnam or Laos had no more value than "a cluster of flying saucer sightings in Texas." "When you get a bunch of flying saucer sightings in the same area, does that prove there are flying saucers?" McCain mockingly demanded of McCreary and the investigators.[23]

McCreary made a game attempt to continue, but McCain had made it an adversarial contest—the old "witness doing the unspeakable, arguing with a United States senator" scenario McCain so often employed in other hearings—and it was a contest McCreary simply could not win. After briefly presenting some of the intelligence and how it clustered, he turned the floor over to Hendon, who briefed for a short while and in turn recognized Taylor for his short briefing on satellite imagery. Kerry then declared that anyone who drew any conclusions from the three investigators' presentations "ought to have his head examined" and, before leaving for another appointment, directed that all copies of the classified briefing text held by the investigators or provided to the senators be passed to Kerry's staff so they could be counted, placed in burn bags, and destroyed. No copies, Kerry told all present, were to leave the room.

"Welcome to Capitol Hill," Hendon told his much embarrassed and very angry comrade-in-arms as he and McCreary began gathering up the hundreds of overhead transparencies and files and placing them on carts for the return trip to the investigators' secure office in the basement of Russell.

Zwenig shadowed the investigators' return to their office and, once all were inside, declared that Kerry had directed her to collect any extra copies of the briefing text in the investigators' safes. She also announced that Kerry had "directed that all computer records relating to the briefing be destroyed in my presence." "So let's do it," she declared. Each investigator—McCreary, Hendon, LeGro, Holstein, and Nicklas—complied by deleting all files related to the briefing from their individual computers and showing Zwenig they had done so. Professing satisfaction, the staff director departed.

The classified briefing texts were delivered by committee staff to the Office of Senate Security for destruction the next morning.[24] Hearing the destruction had taken place, Smith's disgusted investigators took the weekend off, their first in months.

## "WHO'S GOING TO KNOW? IS SOMEBODY GOING TO LEAK IT?"

When the investigators returned to the Hill on Monday, they found that only Smith, Grassley, and Smith's chief staffer, the committee's deputy staff director,

Dino Carluccio, shared their outrage over what had occurred at the briefing and afterward. Kerry and his staff, acting as if nothing untoward had taken place, were lighthearted and happy as they went about preparing for their long-scheduled fact-finding trip to Southeast Asia slated to begin at week's end. The trip was an especially important one for Kerry, who had persuaded C-SPAN to accompany the delegation and videotape the senators as they went about their work and then air the tape during the upcoming Memorial Day weekend.

As preparations for the trip continued, word began filtering out of the investigators' office that the investigators were contemplating a full-scale walkout to protest what had occurred during and after the April 9 briefing. Alarmed at the prospect of this occurring just prior to his crucial and highly anticipated fact-finding mission, Kerry sent committee counsel Bill Codinha to calm the waters.

Codinha met with the investigators in their office on Thursday afternoon, one day before the committee's scheduled departure. Smooth, savvy, and, to Hendon at least, quite likable—but totally misreading the depth of indignation felt by those assembled—Codinha began the meeting with a surreal discourse about the "progress" the committee had made to date, Kerry's plans for future hearings on matters such as the Paris Peace Accords, Nixon administration efforts regarding POWs, and the like, and other mundane topics. Ignoring any mention of what had happened only days before, Codinha told the investigators that he could now see "light at the end of tunnel" for the committee and its work.

Seeing that Codinha had no intention of addressing what had occurred during and after the intelligence briefing, Hendon spoke up. "I am concerned, Bill," he said, "that I might not make it to the end of the tunnel, because I may well find myself in jail before we get there. I say this because, upon reflection, I fear, and the others here have similar fears, that we may have committed felonies by participating in the destruction of the classified briefing text and the computer records."

"Who's going to know?" Codinha snapped. "It's all classified. Anyway, who is the aggrieved party?"

"Maybe the 2,494 MIA families?" Hendon replied.

"How are they going to find out?" Kerry's old friend from the Middlesex County DA's Office asked. "It's classified, committee confidential. Is somebody going to leak it?"

With that, the gentleman's gentleman among the investigators, himself a lawyer, literally exploded. "For God's sake, what the *fuck* is going on here?" Mc-Creary roared. "There is a higher measure than getting caught! For Christ's sake, this is a matter of right and wrong!"

Hendon jumped back in, "Listen to me, Bill, goddamn it, I want a legal opinion that what we were directed to do by Senator Kerry was legal. I want legal counsel on this. . . . I *demand* a legal ruling that absolves me and the rest of us of any wrongdoing for following the chairman's order to destroy those documents. I *demand* my name be cleared. Do you understand me, Bill: I *demand* it."

"You're making a mountain out of a molehill," Codinha told Hendon and McCreary. Then, perhaps sensing the rage that was building in the room, his voice changed and he said, "but seeing as how you all seem to feel this strongly about this, maybe you should put in writing what you want and I will take a look at it."[25]

## THE CHAIRMAN'S STRANGE, NEWFOUND INTEREST IN THE CLUSTER BRIEFING

John Kerry panicked when he heard what had happened in the investigators' meeting. He quickly put out a memorandum directing the investigators to meet with him the following evening just prior to the committee delegation's 11:30 P.M. departure for Southeast Asia. The memorandum read:

MEMORANDUM

TO: Investigators
FROM: The Honorable John F. Kerry, USS, Chairman
THROUGH: Frances Zwenig, Staff Director, *Frances* [handwritten]
DATE: April 15, 1992

(1) Senator Kerry has requested that all Investigators, the Staff Director, the Deputy Staff Director, and the Chief Counsel attend a meeting in his office (SR-422) at 7:30 p.m. tomorrow (April 16, 1992).

This meeting is mandatory, and there can be no excused absences.

(2) Senator Kerry has further requested that those investigators working on the Laos and Vietnam plan provide to him the following:

(a) A portable version of the cluster map;
(b) The collective recommendation of the Laos/Vietnam Investigators of the five (5) strongest locations of clusters (or locations within clusters) with background information for each cluster in the Hanoi area;
(c) The collective recommendation by the Laos/Vietnam investigators of the five (5) strongest locations of clusters (or locations within clusters), with background information for each cluster in the Saigon/Ho Chi Minh City area;
(d) The collective recommendation by the Laos/Vietnam investigators of the five (5) strongest location(s) of clusters (or locations within clusters), with background information for each cluster in the Laos area.

This information is required for the trip and will be used by the Senators in requesting to go to certain areas. It is essential that it be provided by close of business (5:00 p.m.) April 16, 1992.[26]

The investigators were astounded. Suddenly, the senator who had ordered the destruction of the cluster briefing only one week before had acquired a newfound interest in its contents, telling his investigators, "give me your best leads, tell me the best clusters, and I will go and personally check them out myself." Oh, sure, they said, recalling Kerry's "hot leads" trip back when the committee had first been formed.

Knowing well what was going on, the investigators voted unanimously to refuse every one of Kerry's requests and, in an attempt to prevent their chairman
from checking out "hot leads" on his own, demanded that at least one intelligence investigator be allowed to accompany the delegation to ensure that any
"on site investigations" the chairman might carry out would be conducted in a
professional manner. Additionally, they sent Codinha a formal request signed
by all six calling for the appointment of an independent counsel to "clear us of
any potential wrongdoing in connection with our participation in the destruction of committee staff documents ordered and carried out on 9 April 92."[27]
Several hours later, in a memorandum to Kerry, Smith, through Carluccio, confirmed his support of the investigators' refusal to provide the information Kerry
had requested.[28]

At the meeting the next evening, held just hours before the delegation's departure from nearby Andrews Air Force Base, Kerry vehemently denied any
wrongdoing in the matter of the destruction of documents and this time demanded rather than requested that the investigators provide him with the map
and their choices of the best "targets" in Hanoi, Ho Chi Minh City, and Laos.
When the investigators again refused but suggested they might provide the information if at least one of them was allowed to accompany the delegation,
Kerry said there was no room on the plane. With that, the meeting descended
into name-calling, threats, and insults. When the analysts refused for the final
time to provide the intelligence unless at least one could accompany the delegation, a seething Kerry and his staff departed for Andrews to meet the other members of the delegation.[29]

Shortly before midnight, Kerry, Smith, Robb, Grassley, and Brown, along
with ten staff members and the delegation's military escort boarded their sixty-
three-passenger C-137, the Air Force's workhouse version of the Boeing 707.
With most of its seats empty, the plane departed on schedule for Hawaii and
points west. One passenger later described the atmosphere aboard as charged,
polarized, and uncomfortable, with Kerry, Robb, and McCain's ally Brown in
one camp and Smith and Grassley in the other.

*Bangkok*
## SENATOR KERRY DRIVING THE PROCESS

Initial press reports of the delegation's arrival in Southeast Asia confirmed the
investigators' worst fears about their chairman and cast a pall over the investigative office. These first reports, received by the investigators from the committee's public affairs shop, indicated that Kerry, speaking to reporters at the
delegation's first Southeast Asia stop in Bangkok, had declared the matter of
deserters "a significant one" and had suggested that many of the reports the
U.S. government had received about POWs being held captive after the war actually involved deserters, not prisoners. The headlines were dreadful: "Senator
Links Reports Of M.I.A.'s to Deserters" (*New York Times*), "Kerry cites desertions
as factor in MIA reports" (*Boston Globe*), "Sightings might be deserters" (*Washington Times*), "Kerry: MIA sightings may actually be deserters" (*Boston Herald*).[30]

"So that's what Tourison's 'never-before-reported' list of deserters was all about," one of the investigators said. Now themselves seething, they held their breath as Kerry approached Hanoi.

*Day One*
## HANOI

"Dino's on the phone," someone said. "He's on the plane headed into Vietnam and needs to talk to you pronto." Hendon took the phone. He could hear the concern in his close friend's voice, even over the considerable static. "I'm with Senator Kerry and Senator Smith here on the plane, and Senator Kerry asked that I call you and tell you one last time that he wants that information on the prisons and the consequences are going to be severe if you don't provide all of it, right now." Hearing Kerry's voice in the background telling Carluccio to say something more, Hendon interrupted and said, "Dino, I want you to put your hand over the phone and look that sorry son of a bitch right in the eye and say, 'Senator, Billy says you can go fuck yourself, the investigators have decided to take the intelligence and conduct their own prison visits,' and come back and tell me what he says." "Billy, this is serious, I'm serious, what should I tell Senator Kerry?" Carluccio said. "Tell him just what I said," Hendon replied. "I'm sorry, Dino. I know you're in a tight spot there, but that's the investigators' position and it ain't gonna change, now or ever."[31]

The delegation's sleek USAF C-137, "United States of America" emblazoned on its blue and white fuselage and an American flag on its tail, arrived at Hanoi's Gia Lam Airfield around midmorning on Tuesday the 21st. Delegation members were greeted by Nguyen Xuan Phong, deputy director of the MFA's (Ministry of Foreign Affairs) Department of Americas, and other midranking Vietnamese officials. Following a series of interviews with members of the waiting press corps—all dutifully filmed by members of the C-SPAN crew who had flown in earlier to cover the senators' trip—the delegation proceeded to Hanoi's Thang Loi Hotel for check-in.

Senators and staff members then joined Vietnamese officials in a hotel conference room for the obligatory welcoming ceremony/agenda meeting. The meeting was closed to all press but was taped by C-SPAN.

Following a warm welcome by Le Van Bang, acting director of the Department of Americas, Kerry, with assistance from Zwenig and Brig. Gen. Thomas Needham, USAF, and his staff from the Joint Task Force/Full Accounting (JTF/FA) office in Hanoi, went over the proposed schedule line by line with Bang, Phong, and other Vietnamese officials. When Kerry found the schedule somewhat crowded and suggested several adjustments, Bang assured his guest he would attempt to accommodate all the proposed changes. Several changes were discussed, and, when agreement had been reached, Kerry announced the delegation would depart immediately for downtown Hanoi for lunch, then attend a meeting with a group of ambassadors and later visit the war museum.

## Day Two
## HANOI

The next morning—Wednesday—the delegation, accompanied by Needham and his staff and a large contingent of media representatives including the C-SPAN crew, attended a series of meetings with high-level Vietnamese officials. The first was with the minister of interior, the official with authority over most of Vietnam's prisons. The delegation then paid a courtesy call on the minister of national defense, who exercised control over military prisons, and then finally traveled to the Presidential Palace for a private audience with Communist Party General Secretary Do Muoi, Vietnam's most powerful official.

At the conclusion of the meeting with Do Muoi, Kerry and the other senators stepped outside to announce a historic breakthrough in U.S.-Vietnamese relations. Do Muoi, they declared, had just agreed to allow the delegation to visit a prison in the Hanoi area on a "no-notice" basis. As excited reporters stood pen in hand, Kerry declared: "We are going to put it [Do Muoi's commitment] to the test this afternoon. We have asked for a person from the Ministry of Interior to be assigned to us. They are going to meet us at lunch. They do not know where we are going to ask to go at this point in time. And we are going to ask to go somewhere and see if we can get in and it's a place we have been denied access to previously. So we'll see where we wind up."[32]

After an intermediate stop at Ho Chi Minh's tomb to pay their respects, members of the delegation went to the Interior Ministry. There, Kerry informed officials of his desire to lead an immediate live sighting investigation to Bang Liet/Thanh Liet/Skidrow prison just southwest of town. This, of course, was the prison where the monk and a number of other sources had reported American servicemen being held as recently as 1989.[33] Having made his request, Kerry, who one observer later described as incredibly cool given the tremendous sense of excitement and anticipation that prevailed at that moment, calmly led the delegation to a luncheon hosted by Foreign Minister Nguyen Manh Cam.

Following the luncheon with Cam, Kerry and his delegation, accompanied by Phong and his staff, Needham and his staff, and the C-SPAN crew and a host of print reporters, departed by car for Skidrow. Horns blaring, the delegation motorcade barreled through Hanoi's crowded streets for perhaps twenty to thirty minutes before reaching the facility.[34]

Kerry led the delegation through the outer gate and approached a crowd of Vietnamese officials standing in the inner parking lot. After a brief exchange, the delegation was escorted into a nearby conference room. Addressing the group, Col. Nguyen Cong Nhuan declared through an interpreter, "We were just informed you were coming!" Kerry responded with a number of general questions about the prison and requested that the delegation be allowed to immediately inspect the facility and talk to some of the prisoners held there.

Nhuan declined, telling his visitor, "We are not allowed to satisfy all your requirements. I can show you where the U.S. POWs were held [during the war], but there are other places you cannot be allowed."

Seemingly taken aback by Nhuan's refusal, Kerry protested to another Ministry of Interior official seated nearby. The tension became palpable when the second official sided with Nhuan and they together denied Kerry's request. With that, Kerry stood up and led the group and the press corps out into the parking lot to regroup.

Once outside, Needham approached Phong and began berating him and his interpreter in full view of the press. As the C-SPAN cameras rolled and the reporters watched, Needham declared, "You have all this American press, you must show them around or you will lose all the gains." Towering over the tiny Phong and gesturing forcefully with his hands, Needham told him, "You must call Minister Cam and order him to show these senators around! If you don't, everybody here is going to believe there is somebody in there! You must get on the phone and call and let these people see, even if it's just the senators and no press." Then, shaking his finger in Phong's face, Needham issued a stern warning: "If you don't solve it, it's going to be very bad. You understand?"

The press corps was aghast, for seldom in face-conscious Asia does one hear of, much less witness, such a public pillorying of an important government official. Everyone in the parking lot—Vietnamese and American alike—stood in stunned silence waiting for Phong to react. Then, to the amazement of some and the relief of all, Phong acquiesced. Calls were quickly placed seeking the permission Kerry and Needham had sought. While waiting for a reply, the Vietnamese allowed the senators and their staffs to tour the portion of the prison where American servicemen had been held during the war.

When word came back that permission for a complete inspection of the prison had been granted, the Vietnamese excused the press and escorted the delegation through the entire facility. Kerry and the senators then stepped outside the front gate to inform the press that they thoroughly searched the prison and had found neither American prisoners nor any evidence any had been held there after the war.

It was a stunning victory for Kerry. Zwenig, who would later state that her boss "knew the way . . . [to normalized relations with Vietnam] was through the vets," instantly knew the footage would become the centerpiece of the upcoming C-SPAN broadcast.[35] And great press, no doubt, back in America in the days ahead.

And did Zwenig ever have it right. *Boston Herald* reporter Christopher Cox, traveling with his home state senator, filed a glowing report of the Kerry-led "Senate raid on Thanh Liet village." Cox quoted Kerry as saying the committee's destination was a closely guarded secret and that ninety minutes' notice had been given "so that people don't greet you at the door with AK-47s." "There has to be some modicum of order to this process," Cox quoted Kerry as saying. "We saw every cell that we wanted to," Cox further quoted Kerry as saying after the "snap visit." "Any cell that was locked was unlocked in our presence," Kerry said, "and we were able to go in and see who was in it." Cox added that while the committee found no evidence of live POWs, Kerry said the visit was "significant" in that it tested the process of cooperation promised by Do Muoi, general secretary of the Communist Party, in a ninety-minute morning meeting with the committee.[36]

The *Los Angeles Times* later carried a similar story filed by the Associated Press bureau in Hanoi. Appearing under the headline "Vietnam Allows 4 U.S. Senators to Search Prison," the AP story declared in part that "four U.S. Senators scoured a Vietnamese prison camp Wednesday for signs of American captives in a test of Hanoi's willingness to resolve the issue of servicemen missing from the Vietnam War" and noted the senators had given Vietnamese authorities ninety minutes' notice of their desire to visit before traveling to the camp . . . near Hanoi. "The camp commander," AP said, "initially balked at the visit, but he later got new orders."[37]

*The Washington Post* reported from Hanoi that, "in an unprecedented concession from the Vietnamese government, a team of U.S. Senators was allowed today to tour a Vietnamese prison on the outskirts of Hanoi that once housed American prisoners of war." The *Post* quoted Kerry as saying, "I think it's very significant that on an hour-and-a-half's notice we were able to walk in here and look around. This was the best way to test a promise, and it shows the way we can work to allay the fears and suspicions of conspiracy theorists."[38]

## *Late April*
## WASHINGTON

John Kerry returned to Washington triumphant, exultant. Addressing a news conference shortly after his return, he characterized his short-notice inspection of the Thanh Liet Prison as "a real and significant breakthrough" and declared his sense "that this tortured long chapter with respect to Vietnam could possibly be brought to a close in the next months."[39] Later, meeting with POW activists and families, he proclaimed a "new level" of cooperation from the Hanoi government. All the while, follow-up stories appeared in various publications trumpeting the delegation's successful no-notice inspection of Thanh Liet.[40]

His leadership now unquestioned, Kerry sent word to the investigators that if they would withdraw their request for a special counsel he would allow them again to brief the senators on the intelligence. The investigators, of course, jumped at the chance and—the negative results from Thanh Liet notwithstanding—began putting together a second briefing they believed would convince the senators beyond any doubt that POWs were still held in large numbers.

In the briefing, held on May 12, the investigators reviewed some of the intelligence reports that clustered both in general areas and at specific prisons in northern Vietnam, including one heretofore unknown, supersecret underground prison that multiple sources had reported was located between the Ho Chi Minh Mausoleum and the MND Citadel in Hanoi and connected to both and to other nearby government buildings by tunnels. Based on the intelligence, the investigators were convinced that upward of several hundred American POWs had been detained in this prison in the postwar period.

The briefing, which lasted just over three hours, was marked early on by assertions of support for DIA by McCain and, when McCain took particular offense at something that was said, his departure for Senate business and his subsequent refusal to return. (The dustup had occurred during a portion of the briefing that involved sources who had passed one, two, and, in one case, three polygraphs and were still not believed by DIA. Hendon, briefing at the time, had raised as an example of DIA bias the case of the prized Ministry of Interior defector who reported to CIA agents in Malaysia in 1984 that he had seen some twenty to thirty American POWs getting off a Prisons Management Department bus inside the Xuan Loc K-4 Prison northeast of Saigon in 1979.[41] When Hendon noted that DIA officials, upon reading the portion of the initial CIA report that said the defector had passed a polygraph, had written in the margin, "Oh, hell, we better re-poly this guy!" McCain had shouted, "What's wrong with *that*?" Things had deteriorated from that point.)

In the end, the investigators ignored McCain's support for the DIA analysts and the work they had performed and, stating again their agreement with the findings of the Gaines and Tighe reports—and their agreement as well with the findings set forth in another internal DIA review of the Special Office, this one a highly critical 1985 critique known as the Brooks Report[42]—stuck to their earlier findings that DIA had totally mishandled the intelligence on live POWs and declared again their unanimous finding that "the intelligence indicates that American prisoners of war were held continuously, up until 1989, in Laos and in Vietnam."[43]

Kerry, unlike before, accepted the investigators' findings in a civil manner but then raised an objection that quickly sent the investigators' warning flags from half-mast back to the top of the flagpole. How could there be hundreds of POWs alive as the intelligence indicates, Kerry wondered, when only a much smaller number, say, one hundred or so, actually survived? "That means that your available universe for people who have potentially been captured is smaller than these one hundred or two hundred that are in these reports," he said. ". . . It's a physical impossibility to have two hundred or three hundred [American POWs being held] if your available universe is less than one hundred. It's impossible to have more people held prisoner than there are in the universe that could be held prisoner." A reasonable position, most present nodded. Trouble, the intelligence investigators suspected, cooked up by the chairman and his "numbers guy" for the upcoming public hearings Kerry had scheduled to establish the "baseline" number of POW/MIAs left behind at Operation Homecoming.

Walking back to their office, McCreary and Hendon discussed their fears that, Kerry's gutsy no-notice inspection of Skidrow notwithstanding, he might be up to his old tricks. "No matter what the intelligence says, he just isn't buying," McCreary said. "Looks like he really is going to rule that only a few were left—and then say that because only a few were left, none of the intelligence reports showing more than a few alive after the war can be believed."

"The [*Boston*] *Globe* road map lives," Hendon told McCreary.

## MEMORIAL DAY

After weeks of heavy promotion, C-SPAN aired *Vietnam Revisited* throughout the entire Memorial Day weekend. The centerpiece of the program—the segment about Kerry's trip back to Vietnam and the exciting footage of the no-notice in-spection of Thanh Liet Prison—was repeated several times and seen by perhaps hundreds of thousands of Vietnam vets.

In an interview that preceded the airing of the Kerry trip segment, Zwenig, who had participated in the snap inspection of Thanh Liet, told viewers her boss had "pushed the edge of the envelope" at Thanh Liet and had given the Vietnam-ese "next to no notice."[44] The videotape report of Kerry's trip then began, first with coverage of the delegation's arrival at Gia Lam Field on Tuesday morning and then of the agenda meeting, which had taken place immediately after the delegation arrived at their hotel from the airport. In the videotape of the agenda meeting, which showed Kerry and Zwenig, other senators and other staffers, Needham and his staff, and Bang and Phong and their staffs discussing the dele-gation's proposed agenda, Kerry is seen and heard telling Bang and Phong of his desire to visit the Thanh Liet Prison the following day, Wednesday. Apparently unaware he is being taped [the meeting was officially closed to the print press but was taped by C-SPAN], Kerry tells Bang, "Originally tomorrow there had been a visit to the prison at Thac Ba. . . . What I would like to request is if we could change that and go to the Thanh Tri area. Could we go down tomorrow? . . . It's, uh, Thanh Liet." Bang replies, "We will ask. We will inform the Interior Ministry." Bang then suggests that Kerry and his delegation might visit Thanh Liet "after the meeting with the . . . minister of interior at half past eight [the next morning]." Kerry first replies, "We could go straight there, conceivably," but moments later, after further discussions with Garnett E. "Bill" Bell, a member of Needham's staff, realizes the schedule for the following morning is too cramped to accommodate the trip to Thanh Liet and tells Bang and Phong the delegation would have to go to the prison after the planned meeting with Do Muoi.[45]

Hendon, watching the broadcast with friends, froze. Kerry's "snap visit" to Skidrow, the tape proved, had been a fraud from the beginning. From Kerry's press conference outside the Presidential Palace when he announced to the world's press he would "test" Do Muoi's promise, to his declaration at that press conference that "they do not know where we are going to ask to go at this point in time," to his delivery of the "short notice" to officials at the Ministry of Inte-rior after the press conference, to the "frenzied" motorcade roaring through Hanoi to the prison, to Colonel Nhuan's "refusal" to allow a thorough inspec-tion of the prison, to Needham's dramatic "dressing-down" of Phong in the prison parking lot, to Phong's "caving in" to Needham's "demands," to Kerry's repeated postinspection declarations to the press at the prison of "short notice," to his repeating those statements ad nauseam to the American press and his col-leagues upon his return to the United States, to Zwenig's declaration to viewers only moments before that Kerry had given the Vietnamese "next to no notice"—the tape proved the entire episode a contrived lie.

Hendon replayed the exchange at the agenda meeting over and over again. There was no mistaking what had occurred: Kerry had personally informed the Vietnamese of his desire to inspect Thanh Liet Prison at the closed agenda meet-ing held before lunch on Tuesday; the inspection had taken place after lunch on Wednesday, the following day.

This, Hendon knew, was how you ask the last man to die in Vietnam.

## THE INVESTIGATORS RESPOND WITH THREE NEW INITIATIVES: CONDUCTING ON-SITE PRISON INVESTIGATIONS THEMSELVES, BRIEFING THE "McCAIN CLUSTER," AND OFFICIALLY ESTIMATING THE NUMBER OF POWs STILL ALIVE IN VIETNAM AND LAOS

Responding to Kerry's faked "no notice" investigation of Thanh Liet Prison, Hendon dusted off the plan to have the intelligence investigators conduct their own no-notice inspections of prisons in both Vietnam and Laos and quickly began selecting targets.[46]

At the same time, Hendon, responding to McCain's strong show of support of the work done by the DIA analysts and his continued belittling of both the intelligence on live POWs and the investigators' use of cluster analysis to analyze patterns and help assess source credibility, decided to order up the five postwar reports concerning McCain's shootdown that were cited in the SI Report and brief these reports to the assembled senators. (McCain, the reader will recall, was shot down over Hanoi in October 1967 while attacking the Yen Phu Thermal Power Plant in northwest Hanoi. Grievously injured during ejection (both of his arms and his right leg had been broken), he parachuted into Truc Bach Lake, just west of the power plant, and almost drowned before he was pulled from the lake by a group of bystanders. After being beaten by an angry mob as he lay injured on the ground, he was taken away by Vietnamese authorities and imprisoned at Hoa Lo Prison (the "Hanoi Hilton").)

THE PLANNED BRIEFING ON THE "McCAIN CLUSTER" WAS NEVER PRESENTED. HAD IT BEEN, IT would have gone something like this:

Hendon, briefing, with annotated map of Hanoi:

"Senators,

"DIA Source 11352, a high school student residing in Hanoi during 1967–1968, told U.S. officials that at approximately 11:00 A.M. on an unrecalled day in April or May of 1967 or 1968, he had heard on the school's public address system that a U.S. aircraft that had bombed the Yen Phu electric power plant in Hanoi had been shot down and the pilot had landed in Truc Bach Lake. The source said he went to the lake and observed several police officers pulling the pilot from the lake. He said he heard from others in the area that the pilot had parachuted out of the aircraft under a red parachute and had landed in the water. The source described the pilot, whom he saw from a distance of about ten to twenty meters for a period of about five minutes, as Caucasian, over two meters tall, and weighing approximately one hundred kilograms. The source recalled the pilot was wearing a gray one-piece flight suit, a white helmet, and high-topped black boots. His right leg had been injured and he could not walk when pulled ashore. The source believed that based on the pilot's reaction to his injury he had broken his right femur."[47] (See map page 430, point 1.)

"DIA Source 3814, an electrician prior to fleeing northern Vietnam in 1985, told U.S. officials that he was on a pleasure outing in Hanoi during the summer of 1968 when he observed the shootdown of a U.S. jet aircraft and the capture

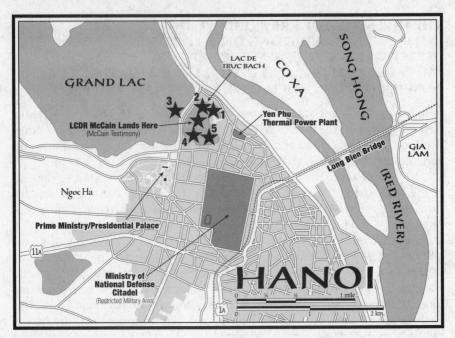

Shootdown and Capture of Lt. Cmdr. John S. McCain III, USN, Hanoi, DRV.
(HENDON/ANDERER)

of the pilot. The source said that around midday he saw seven or eight American jets flying around Hanoi. He further said that as he was observing one particular aircraft—this one flying from the area north of Ho Tay (West Lake, Grand Lake )— he saw that it was being attacked by a PAVN Air Force MiG. He said that after the attack he saw one pilot eject from the American aircraft and descend under a fully deployed red parachute into Truc Bach Lake (also called White Bamboo Lake). The source went on to say that after the pilot landed in the water, a Public Security Service officer and a man who had been fishing from the shore of the lake waded out and captured the pilot and brought him back to the shore, where he was held for about fifteen minutes. The source said the pilot was Caucasian, between thirty-three and thirty-five years of age, and wearing a dark flight suit and a pilot's helmet. The source recalled the pilot was injured and had numerous lacerations. He said after about fifteen minutes the pilot was taken away in a covered command car in the direction of downtown Hanoi. The source said that some of the spectators said he was a major, while others said he was a lieutenant colonel. The source added he also heard the pilot was in the U.S. Navy."[48] (See map above, point 2.)

"DIA Source 8147, a Hanoi tailor before fleeing to Hong Kong in 1987, told U.S. officials that at about 1:00 P.M. on an unrecalled day in the late 1960s, he saw a red parachute descending a kilometer or so northeast of where he was standing on Hang Bot Street in Hanoi. The source said he later heard that the pilot had landed in Tay Lake (West Lake, which adjoins Truc Bach Lake) and had been captured."[49] (See map above, point 3.)

"DIA Source 7984, a table tennis instructor who lived in Hanoi prior to fleeing to Thailand in 1987, told U.S. officials that he witnessed the capture of an American pilot who had parachuted into Truc Bach Lake in Hanoi City sometime during 1971 or 1972. The source said he was home during the afternoon that day when the general air raid alert sounded. He said that after hearing the sounds of several aircraft attacking the Hanoi area, he stepped out of his house, which was located about fifty meters from the edge of Truc Bach Lake, and looked up and saw one fully deployed parachute descending toward and then into the lake. He said that after the pilot landed in the water, he watched one of his neighbors swim out and capture him and bring him to shore. The source said he observed the pilot from a distance of approximately two hundred meters. He described him as Caucasian and said he appeared to be injured in one leg and hobbled along assisted by a Vietnamese man on both sides as he walked to a military vehicle. The source speculated the pilot was taken to Hoa Lo Prison."[50] (See map page 430, point 4.)

"DIA Source 5454, an architectural student in Hanoi during the war who later fled to Malaysia, told U.S. authorities that the talk around his Hanoi neighborhood one afternoon was that an American pilot had just parachuted out of his aircraft and landed in Truc Bach Lake. The source said he was at home at the time and did not actually see the pilot or the aircraft and was uncertain even as to the exact year the incident had taken place. He did recall, however, that 'the neighborhood talk said that the pilot had broken his leg and that he was the son of a US Admiral.'"[51] (See map page 430, point 5.)

Hendon, continuing:

"Our differences aside, John, I extend my hand in friendship and respect and ask you: a flying saucer, or a brave American pilot in desperate straits? Liars, cheats, charlatans, fast-buck artists and con men, or, because these sources had independently reported the same event taking place at the same location during the war, five men whose credibility as reporters of that event, in fairness to all concerned, should not be subject to ridicule or further question?"

FINALLY, THE INVESTIGATORS RESPONDED TO KERRY'S FAKED "SNAP VISIT" TO SKIDROW BY DOING something they had heretofore refused to do—file official estimates of the number of American POWs they believed, based on their examination of the intelligence, were currently being held by the Vietnamese and Lao governments. Voting by "secret ballot" on June 3 (and with no prior discussion among themselves), the investigators made the following estimates: Colonel Nicklas, who had spent the least amount of time of the five investigators working on the HUMINT and most of his time on special projects,[52] estimated that more than a hundred POWs remained alive as of June 3, 1992, and declared himself unqualified to say specifically where they were being held.

Colonel LeGro, who, given his previous posting as chief of intelligence at the DAO in Saigon, had chosen to concentrate primarily on the HUMINT that told of American POWs being detained after the war in the South, estimated that 150 American POWs remained in captivity in southern Vietnam and 50 were still held in Laos; he declared himself unqualified to estimate the number being held in northern Vietnam. Holstein, McCreary, and Hendon, all of whom had worked the HUMINT from both northern and southern Vietnam and from Laos, made the following estimates (again, without any discussion among themselves or any comparing of notes, etc.):

| INVESTIGATOR | VIETNAM | LAOS | TOTAL EST. ALIVE 3 JUNE 1992 |
|---|---|---|---|
| Holstein | 300 | 350 | 650 |
| McCreary | 500 | 350 | 850 |
| Hendon | 350 | 300 | 650[53] |

## CHAOS

The select committee descended into chaos when John Kerry found out what the Smith forces were up to. In mid-June, Kerry first revoked Hendon's security clearance, allegedly because, as Kerry later told *The Washington Post,* Hendon "was suspected of leaking classified information," and then Carluccio's, allegedly for the same offense.[54] Hendon, knowing he would be unable to proceed with the no-notice prison inspections, the McCain cluster briefing, or any other activity that required access to the intelligence, gave Smith notice of his intention to resign and began cleaning out his office.[55] Within a week he was out the door. Carluccio, facing similar hurdles in carrying out his duties, cleaned out his office at the committee's headquarters suite in the Hart Building and moved back into Smith's suite of offices in Dirksen.

Deprived of the services of his two trusted aides, Smith, in a move that sent shock waves through the committee, angrily resigned his post as vice chairman, advising Dole of his decision by letter on the 19th.[56] When Grassley reportedly threatened to follow suit, Dole reportedly convened a meeting of the two and declared his strong desire that they continue to serve. Acknowledging both men's concerns about the direction Kerry was taking the committee and Smith's outright disgust at the way Kerry and McCain were denigrating credible intelligence on live POWs, Dole reportedly pledged that if the two would stay on he would personally assist them in their effort to get all of the postwar intelligence on live POWs into the public domain, something the Bush administration was actively opposing.[57] Respectful of Dole's wishes and encouraged by his pledge of assistance with the declassification process, both men agreed to press on.[58]

Returning to work, Smith and Grassley redoubled their efforts to force the administration to declassify all the POW-related intelligence. Concurrently, Smith and McCreary began preparing for a series of public hearings on the intelligence that were slated to begin in August, where Smith planned to make public for the first time some of the intelligence his investigators had presented to the senators back in April and May—intelligence both he and McCreary believed proved convincingly that large numbers of POWs remained alive in captivity in both Vietnam and Laos up until 1989.[59] So intent was Smith on putting the intelligence before the public that he publicly threatened that if the administration did not agree to declassify the intelligence in time for the August hearings, he would release it himself.[60]

*June 24–25*
## JOHN KERRY, DRIVING DOWN THE NUMBERS

Kerry convened his much-anticipated "Numbers Hearings" on June 24. Moving quickly to his point, he announced in his opening statement that only 133 of the some 2,400+ Americans still unaccounted for in Southeast Asia could possibly have ever been prisoners. Explaining how he had arrived at this figure, Kerry declared:

> Our committee has compiled a list . . . of 244 Americans who did not return at Operation Homecoming but who were or should have been recorded prior to Operation Homecoming as in captivity. One hundred and eleven of those people are accounted for as having died in captivity by virtue of the debriefings of those prisoners who did return during Operation Homecoming, leaving you with a potential universe, according to our analysis of DOD's and DIA's documents, . . . [of] . . . 133 people at the end of Operation Homecoming about whom we should have been asking questions. . . .
>
> . . . Our purpose in doing . . . this has been . . . to build the foundation upon which subsequent hearings on the Paris peace accords, on Laos and on live sighting reports may be held.[61]

One of the few members of the audience that day who understood the true significance of Kerry's announcement was Vietnam vet Ted Sampley of Kinston, North Carolina. Sampley had served two tours in Vietnam with the Green Berets and published a Vietnam veterans' newspaper highly critical of the U.S. government's handling of the live prisoner issue. "We had seen Kerry's faked prison raid on C-SPAN over Memorial Day, and the bogus 'charges' he had lodged against [Hendon] and Dino when [they] challenged him on it," Sampley later said. He added:

> I remember sitting in the audience that day and how perfectly clear it was to me what he [Kerry] was up to. I guess the best way to describe it is that it was just like the inflated enemy body counts in Vietnam, except backwards, because here, Kerry was fraudulently *reducing* the numbers, rather than inflating them, in an effort to get the answers he wanted.
>
> The reason he did this, of course—he even said so—was to set the stage for his upcoming hearings on the intelligence on living prisoners. That intelligence, we later found out, showed that hundreds and hundreds of our men had remained in captivity in Vietnam and Laos long after the war. Kerry, of course, knew what those reports showed, and that's why up front he reduced the number of missing to only 133 men. He did it so that when those intelligence reports were made public they would look crazy, exaggerated, faked.
>
> "How can you possibly have five hundred being held prisoner when only one hundred are missing?" he asked? To those unfamiliar with the issue, it seemed very logical. But in reality, it was just like the prison visit we had seen on C-SPAN, a complete fraud, a total scam, a big lie, government at its very worst. I can still recall the rage I felt as I sat in the audience that day and

watched it all unfold. But that turned out to be nothing compared to the rage we all felt when we saw Kerry's and McCain's performance at the intelligence hearings.[62]

## THE INTELLIGENCE HEARINGS BEGIN

In late July, President Bush, bowing to a ninety-six–zero Senate vote calling on him to declassify the postwar intelligence, did so.[63] Now having received the green light from the White House, the committee finalized plans for a series of public hearings on the intelligence. The HUMINT relating to live prisoners would be the subject of hearings to be held in August and September; the IMINT would be addressed in a hearing scheduled for early October.

By the first days of August, Smith and McCreary were ready to discuss for the first time in public some of the best postwar HUMINT relating to live prisoners. Their focus would be an underground prison in Hanoi reportedly located between the Ho Chi Minh Mausoleum and the nearby Ministry of Defense Citadel and connected to each by a large tunnel. Approximately twenty intelligence reports comprised this "Ho Chi Minh Mausoleum/MND Citadel" cluster, and based on that intelligence, Smith and the investigators believed that during the 1980s several hundred American POWs had been detained either in the underground facility proper or aboveground inside the connected, heavily guarded MND Citadel compound.

The Senate Select Committee's "Big Four." *Left to right:* John Kerry, McCain aide Mark Salter, Kerry aide and former chief of analysis at the DIA Special Office for POW/MIAs Sedgwick Tourison, John McCain. (COURTESY *U.S. VETERAN DISPATCH*)

Also ready to speak in opposition to Smith and McCreary were Kerry, Mc-Cain, and a large contingent from DIA, including the director of DIA himself, Lt. Gen. James R. Clapper, Jr., USAF.

Kerry opened the first intelligence hearing on August 4 with a stunning announcement: Working with DIA, he said, committee staff (i.e., Tourison) had conducted additional reviews of the 133 cases of Americans believed left behind at Homecoming—Kerry's "universe of possible prisoners"—and as a result of those reviews had determined that the "universe" was not 133 as previously believed, but was actually only 43 men. Kerry explained:

> Last month we held hearings concerning lists of POWs and MIAs compiled by the Department of Defense. For the first time we analyzed, as an outside group, those lists. And our committee reconstructed those lists.
>
> Both the committee and the Defense Department agree . . . that you still have valid questions remaining today about [only] 43 of those who were on the committee's . . . [initial] list. [This] is the universe of people about whom there remain the most serious questions. . . . It is in this context that we . . . begin this morning . . . 2 days of really rather extraordinary hearings . . . [and] for the first time in the history of this issue, vent [*sic*] the live sighting reports, the live sightings of American prisoners in Southeast Asia.[64]

Kerry's remarkable recalculation of the numbers put Smith and McCreary totally on the defensive, for now, under the chairman's and Tourison's "guidelines," any report or combination of reports citing more than 43 POWs could not be believed.

Smith, seemingly undeterred by Kerry's opening gambit, began with an overview of cluster analysis and then addressed several of the intelligence reports that comprised the Ho Chi Minh Mausoleum/MND Citadel cluster. Alluding to McCreary's upcoming briefing on all the reporting from this cluster, Smith informed the DIA witnesses sitting before him that he expected each of them to declare on the record, under oath, "whether or not there is a detention facility there, underground, at the Citadel, near Ho Chi Minh's tomb. Is there or is there not?"[65]

At that point McCain weighed in to "strongly caution" the committee and the public not to reach any conclusions about the veracity of the intelligence until everyone had had the opportunity to hear how DIA had evaluated each report and each source. Offering a preview of the DIA's evaluations, McCain suggested that the sources were either (1) untruthful, (2) confused about what they had seen, (3) individuals who offered misinformation for sale, (4) individuals who had pursued fraudulent means to emigrate from their country, (5) individuals who had sought financial rewards for their information on living POWs, or (6) individuals who had, in the end, recanted their testimony about living American prisoners. Nowhere was there a suggestion by McCain that *any* of the sources might be telling the truth.[66]

As McCain stood to depart for another meeting, Grassley, Smith's only ally on the committee, wondered out loud how "out of thousands of accounts about seeing or hearing about live American prisoners that not one, not one is deemed valid. . . . Statistically," Grassley said, "that is remarkable."[67]

## THE HO CHI MINH MAUSOLEUM, THE UNDERGROUND PRISON, AND THE MND CITADEL

The Ho Chi Minh Mausoleum sits along the western edge of historic Ba Dinh Square in northwest Hanoi, where Ho had ascended a platform on September 2, 1945, to declare his country's independence.

Twenty-four years later, to the day, on September 2, 1969, Ho had died.[68]

Though Ho had requested that his body be cremated, at the Politburo's direction his remains were preserved by Russian experts and placed in a secret crypt near Son Tay until an imposing mausoleum could be built.[69] One of the Russian experts who visited the secret temporary crypt in 1971 would later tell a remarkable story: "I was taken through the jungle to a place near Chantai, a small town about thirty kilometers from the capital," the Russian later wrote. "Nestling among the trees was a building of light-brown brick: the tomb of Ho Chi Minh. It was a faithful replica of Lenin's mausoleum, though smaller—only 60 square meters. It looked like a toy."

The Russian said that when he was taken into the temporary mausoleum, he observed Ho Chi Minh's preserved remains and "a corridor ten meters deep leading to a concrete chamber to which the body was removed during air raids."

He went on to say that in the spring of 1971 an American helicopter was observed following the course of the Red River at a point approximately one and a half kilometers [approximately one statute mile] from the mausoleum, and that some other U.S. helicopters then arrived and landed on the opposite bank. The Americans, he said, "were looking for some of their compatriots who had been kept in a camp nearby, [b]ut the place had been deserted long since, and the para[trooper]s had to go away empty-handed."

The Russian then revealed that the episode involving the helicopters "was enough to make the North Vietnamese generals decide to strengthen the security around the mausoleum." "Ho's body," the Russian explained, "was regarded as sacred, and they knew that its capture or destruction would deal a fatal blow to the morale of their troops. 'If the Yankees ever did get hold of it,' the Russian quoted a North Vietnamese general as saying at the time, 'we'd be prepared to hand over all our American prisoners in exchange for it.' "[70]

The permanent mausoleum was built with Soviet assistance and took more than five years to complete. It was dedicated on August 29, 1975, some four months after the fall of Saigon.[71] Then, on September 2, Vietnamese National Day—the day Ho had proclaimed independence in the square thirty years earlier—tens of thousands of Northerners from all walks of life thronged into the square to celebrate the opening of the mausoleum and the recent conquest of the South. Press reports chronicled Vietnam's top leaders and hundreds of dignitaries from throughout the Communist world standing on the east front of the mausoleum to review the seemingly endless parade of military might and citizenry passing through the square below.[72]

As the following declassified DOD line drawing derived from satellite imagery in 1992 shows, the square, now called Ba Dinh Park by some, is bounded by the Presidential Palace on the northwest (1), Communist Party Headquarters on the north (2), and on the east by the historic Ba Dinh Conference Hall

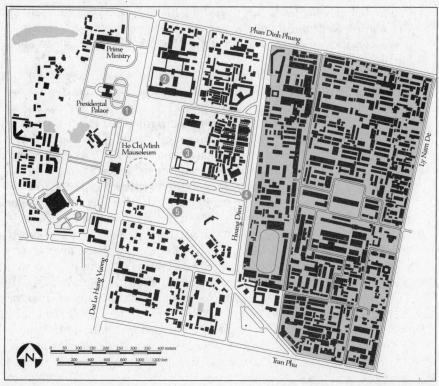

Ministry of National Defense Citadel and Ho Chi Minh Mausoleum Complex, Hanoi, SRV, with authors' annotations. (DIA/SENATE SELECT COMMITTEE ON POW/MIA AFFAIRS)

(3), a portion of the west wall of the MND Citadel (4), and the Ministry of Foreign Affairs (5).

Smith told those in attendance that in late 1985–early 1986, DIA had received the first of what would become a steady stream of intelligence telling of American POWs being detained in a secret underground prison in Hanoi. Some of the sources reported that the prison was located just to the east of the mausoleum and connected to it and to the nearby MND Citadel by a large underground tunnel or tunnels. Among the intelligence sources reporting on this facility were workers who had helped construct the mausoleum and/or the tunnel(s) and security personnel and others who had been inside the underground prison and/or the tunnel(s).

Among those reports, Smith knew, were the following:

• DIA Source 8682, a nephew of Cambodian leader Heng Samrin, fled his country to neighboring Thailand in late 1985–early 1986. He told U.S. officials soon after his arrival that while attending a study course in Hanoi in September 1984, he and seventeen other Lao and Vietnamese officials attending the course were taken on a tour of a large underground prison in Hanoi and that while inside the prison he and the others observed approximately three hundred American POWs being detained there. He explained that Vietnamese Premier Pham Van Dong had permitted the visit because "he wanted to demonstrate the bravery of Vietnamese troops and [the] power of Communism by showing how the Vietnamese were able to humble the Americans."

The Cambodian explained that on the morning of September 12, he and the other officials left the Hanoi Central Party Committee office and drove for about fifteen minutes. He said the officials' eyes were covered during the entire trip and remained covered until the group was inside the underground facility. He described the prison as being 100 by 100 meters in size and said he was told it contained a total of thirty-eight cells. He said he and the others personally observed the Americans in three of these cells, approximately a hundred to a cell. He said the Americans appeared to be in their late thirties and were "very slender and pale with long beards." Some were bald. All were dressed in blue civilian clothes and some used canes.[73]

• DIA Source 5633, a fisherman who fled northern Vietnam to Hong Kong in 1986, reported that he had learned from a North Vietnamese Public Security Service officer in 1979 that an unspecified number of American pilots were being detained in a secret underground prison located in the area of the Ho Chi Minh Mausoleum in Hanoi. The source reported the facility is known as the "Ly Nam De Secret Jail," and is connected to the tomb of Ho Chi Minh by a concealed underground tunnel. He reported that entry to the underground prison is gained through a residential dwelling located in a restricted area [inside the MND Citadel] open only to high-ranking military officers. The source said one has to pass three checkpoints to get into the restricted residential area, which he said is used as living quarters for VIPs.[74]

• DIA Source 7591, a Northerner who fled to Korea in 1987, reported that in 1970, the Vietnamese government constructed an underground detention facility in Ba Dinh Park adjacent to Ho Chi Minh's tomb, and that a rumor circulating among college students in Hanoi and Haiphong indicates that until 1985 the facility had been used intermittently to hide American prisoners of war. The Northerner, who said he first heard the rumor while attending the Vietnam National Shipping School in Haiphong in 1980, reported that the underground detention facility was constructed at the same time Ho Chi Minh's tomb was being constructed. He said that like the detention facility, most of the tomb itself was also constructed underground. He said that civilian construction workers selected by the Vietnamese government to participate in the construction of the tomb underwent background investigations that covered their families for three generations. Word of the presence of the underground detention facility, he said, originated with these construction workers.

The source said the tomb proper consists of a 100-meter by 100-meter by 50-meter granite aboveground structure and three underground floors. He said a company-sized special unit stationed seventy to eighty meters west of the tomb provides security. He further said that access to the tomb is allowed to all tourist groups, and individual Vietnamese citizens can visit the tomb either with permission from the local police station or during periods when foreign tourists are visiting the tomb.

The source told U.S. officials that while visiting Hanoi in 1985, five years after first hearing about the underground detention facility from friends at the National Shipping School in Haiphong, he heard the same information from friends who lived in Hanoi. He said that many of the Vietnamese general populace believe some American prisoners of war are still detained in a very secret place and are to be used in future negotiations with the U.S. government. He said he believes that the rumor is true because "most rumors that circulate among the general populace have proved to be true in the past."[75]

- DIA Source 8113, a classified CIA source, stated in October 1988 that as of late July 1988, two hundred American POWs were reportedly detained in an underground prison in Hanoi.[76]
- DIA Source 8621, a former civilian technician and practitioner of traditional Oriental medicine, told U.S. officials after escaping from Vietnam in late 1988 that he had been assigned to work on the Ho Chi Minh Mausoleum during 1970 and that there was an underground prison located beneath the mausoleum. The technician, who said he had installed lighting and ventilation systems in two rooms of the mausoleum, reported that the underground prison complex included a tunnel that ran between the mausoleum and the nearby Ministry of Defense Citadel. He told U.S. officials that extensive security measures were in place at the monument during the construction phase, that a number of local streets had been blocked off, and that two regiments of security forces had been deployed to protect the facility. He reported that when arriving for work, all workers were escorted to a changing room where they changed into work uniforms and deposited all personal property in assigned lockers. They were then escorted to their individual worksites. Workers were not allowed to enter any rooms other than those in which they worked, and were always escorted. The technician stated that these security measures seemed very excessive for a monument. He went on to quote one worker, a Mr. Cong, as saying that his workstation was down in the tunnel that ran east to a point under the MND Citadel compound. The technician reported that Mr. Cong was later accepted for employment with an oil-drilling company in Vung Tau.[77]
- DIA Source 10675, a former North Vietnamese PSS officer who fled Vietnam in 1990, reported that on two separate occasions—in February 1977 and again in September 1984—he had participated in search activities to recapture American POWs who had escaped from SRV detention facilities. The PSS officer reported that as a result of his participation in the September 1984 search, he learned from a fellow officer that an undetermined number of American POWs were to be transferred from a prison camp in Thanh Hoa Province to a prison located "beneath the Ho Chi Minh mausoleum on Hung Vuong Street." The source told U.S. officials that the prison beneath the mausoleum had been built at the same time as the surface structure and said he learned in late 1986 that American POWs were still being detained in the facility.[78]
- DIA Source [number unknown], a recent defector from Hanoi, had reported to select committee investigators—and the information had been forwarded to DIA—that there was a secret underground facility underneath the Min-

istry of Defense Citadel/Ho Chi Minh Tomb complex that was "the size of a football field." The facility, the defector reported, served as a prison for American POWs but would also be used by Vietnam's leaders as a nuclear bomb shelter in the event war broke out anew with either America or China. The defector reported there were underground tunnels in the area so large that "they can drive cars and trucks through them."[79]

What had emerged from the intelligence, Smith knew, was a picture of a structure not unlike the supersecret U.S. Government Relocation Facility buried deep beneath one wing of the Greenbrier Hotel in White Sulfur Springs, West Virginia. This facility, code-named "Greek Island," had been constructed during the late 1950s and early 1960s and until mid-1992 had served as the bomb shelter/relocation center for members of the U.S. Senate and House of Representatives in the event of a nuclear attack on the United States. Just as had the combination bomb shelter/prison facility reportedly constructed deep underground at the Ho Chi Minh Mausoleum, the Greenbrier facility had also remained secret until mid-1992, when its existence had been revealed by famed investigative reporter Ted Gup in *The Washington Post Magazine*.

The world-famous Greenbrier Resort, White Sulfur Springs, West Virginia, circa 1962. The newly completed West Virginia Wing sits on the hill behind the main facility. (COURTESY OF THE GREENBRIER)

Writing in the May 31, 1992, edition of the *Post Magazine*, Gup had quoted several local workers who had helped construct the facility and one former government official "whose familiarity with the facility dates back to its origins" as describing the underground facility in detail—two-foot-thick concrete walls, dormitory filled with hundreds of metal bunk beds, infirmary complete with operating table, shower rooms, numerous offices, radio and communications room, telephones and cryptographic machines, kitchen and adjoining large dining hall featuring false windows complete with wooden frames and country scenes painted on them, two self-contained diesel generators, and many other features, all secreted behind a huge blast door that, when opened, allowed access into a long tunnel that led into the hillside and ultimately into to the facility located deep beneath the hotel.

Gup had also quoted numerous officials involved in the day-to-day operation of the facility, however, as denying flat-out that it existed. Additionally, he had quoted James A. Searle Jr., a spokesman for the company that owned the Greenbrier, as saying, "There's no bomb shelter, no government facility [here]. I can tell you what I know is the truth and that is the end of it." Gup had also quoted the president and managing director of the Greenbrier, Ted Kleisner, as declaring reports that such a facility existed under the hotel's West Virginia Wing were " 'bizarre,' 'fantastic' and utterly untrue." When Gup had accompanied Kleisner to one of the secret doorways inside the hotel that reportedly led to the underground facility and had requested that he be allowed to enter, Kleisner had refused, declaring the doorway led only to an equipment area and saying, "We just don't need to go back there." When Gup had persisted and demanded to know why he could not enter, Kleisner had again refused. Gup had written that Kleisner had later asked him, "Do you honestly think that if there was imminent global nuclear war that Congress would be sipping tea and listening to concerts at the Greenbrier?"[80]

Searle's, Kleisner's, and the many other officials' categorical denials notwithstanding, Gup's exposé had quickly led to an official admission by U.S. officials that "Greek Island" did in fact exist, and an explanation by the patriotic Kleisner that "our country asked us to do something extraordinary and our company didn't question it." The federal government canceled its lease shortly after Gup's article appeared and began decommissioning the facility.[81]

## ONE HELL OF A CLUSTER

When the reports indicating the presence of an underground prison at the Ho Chi Minh Mausoleum and the suggestion that American POWs were being detained there during 1979, 1980, 1984, 1984, 1985, 1986, 1988, and at some other undetermined date after the war were viewed in the context of the reporting from the nearby highly secure MND Citadel compound—where human intelligence sources had reported American POWs being detained in 1974, 1977, 1978, 1978, 1978, 1978, 1979, 1980, 1981, 1982, 1982–1985, 1985, 1986, 1986, and 1988[82] in areas the intelligence indicated were directly connected by tunnel to the underground prison near the mausoleum and to the mausoleum itself, the

combined Ho Chi Minh Mausoleum/MND Citadel Cluster became one of enormous significance.

Smith knew then (and, of course, so did DIA) that as of the date of this first
intelligence hearing, August 4, 1992, the combined reports from the two,
interconnected sites that comprised this cluster indicated American POWs were
being detained there at least during 1974, 1977, 1978, 1978, 1978, 1978, 1979,
1979, 1980, 1980, 1981, 1982, 1982–1985, 1984, 1984, 1985, 1985, 1986, 1986,
1986, 1988, 1988, and at some other undetermined date after the war. No one in
their right mind, Smith believed, would dare venture to deny publicly that
American POWs had been held at the combined facility after the war.

But DIA Director James Clapper and his team of briefers from the Special Office, clearly having been given the green light by Cheney, Wolfowitz, Ptak,
Kerry, and McCain, would do just that, and with a shocking display of contempt
for the sources of the intelligence, the information the sources had provided,
and the senator who was determined to make that information public.

Moving to the witness table, Clapper and his men told the committee—just
as McCain had suggested—that they considered the intelligence sources all to
be liars, charlatans, agents of the North Vietnamese, persons who were confused
about what they had seen, persons who were mentally unstable, persons who
were seeking immigration assistance or cash favors, or persons who had later re-
tracted their accounts voluntarily. Not *one* eyewitness, the DIA witnesses testified, had actually seen American POWs in, around, or under the Ho Chi Minh
Mausoleum/MND Citadel Complex after the war. Then, having assailed the
sources to their satisfaction, analyst Gary Sydow, chief of analysis at the Special
Office, and Robert Destatte, the long-serving senior Vietnam analyst, proceeded
to ridicule the very thought that an underground prison facility existed near the
mausoleum or anywhere in Hanoi. Openly mocking Smith's, McCreary's, and
the intelligence sources' assertion that such a facility existed, Sydow and
Destatte testified under oath, one after another, that:

I must say that when I visited Ho Chi Minh's tomb, I didn't see any signs of
an underground prison.

That particular area is open to the public. It is in an area that is the major
park. The communist headquarters is . . . right on the edge of the big plaza
there. The government headquarters is across the street. Two major tourist at-
tractions are to the left of the memorial and [at] the Ho Chi Minh tomb, you
have thousands of people in that area every day. The likelihood that they
would be holding American prisoners in an area like that, I would hold is low.

We have asked the Vietnamese [government] if there is a prison there several
times and each time they said no.

There are only a handful of reports that mention an underground facility.

This is not a significant level of reporting.

We don't find the corroborating of this kind of reporting of an underground prison to be sufficient.

There is no reporting that would corroborate the construction of any underground facility.

He describes an underground tunnel system which leads up to or incorporates an underground prison facility underneath the Ho Chi Minh mausoleum. We don't find the corroborating of this kind of reporting of an underground prison to be sufficient to find this report credible.

He's describing POWs . . . in a place I wouldn't find underground facilities; in a compound where corroborating reporting doesn't support him.

We find no evidence to sustain a belief that there was a prison there, and certainly the underground prison that this fellow described never existed.

It is not possible to build an underground facility of the nature that you have described.

Restrictions imposed by some of the soil conditions there relate to the unlikelihood that there would be an underground facility of any sort in that area.

The city of Hanoi has a very high water table. . . . To propose that there might be an underground facility in Hanoi means to propose that you would have a water evacuation system that would entail a great deal of construction; certainly something that we would have been aware of with the coverage we had of that area. I don't consider this report probable.

I spoke to a French engineer and he finds it incomprehensible that there would be an underground facility.

I suspect that some of the speculation about a tunnel derives from a newspaper of a few years ago when they were renovating the Dong Xuan market, the main market in northeastern Hanoi city. Some of the excavation work that was going on attendant to the reconstruction or the renovation, they had to go into one of the sewer lines. And they, according to the newspaper report, found the remains of a communist soldier who had died—for some reason had been down in there and died during the war against the French. It's only a guess on my part, but I suspect that the kernel of truth in some of these stories about a tunnel are rumors that have grown from that one particular newspaper report.

The only thing that would qualify for a tunnel in that area is the sewer system.

I can't find any evidence that there is even a basement in any building anywhere in that country.

We can find no evidence to sustain a belief that there is an underground prison in Hanoi.

[There is] a higher priority for me than will-o'-the-wisp reports that there is an underground facility in an area of Hanoi that we know very well. That's not a priority. It's very unlikely that 200 POWs would be kept underground.

In my judgment, we have adequate evidence to make, with good confidence, a judgment that the underground facility doesn't exist.

Then, for good measure, Sydow and Destatte added this about the intelligence relating specifically to the MND Citadel:

All the reporting we have from this area doesn't suggest to us that there are POW facilities of any kind within the MND (Citadel).

If there were any American POWs held in that compound after 1973, I am confident, totally confident, that I would have uncovered some indication of that in my conversations with the local residents.

I have walked and ridden my bicycle around the perimeter of the citadel area several times. I have yet to find anyone who has not scoffed at the idea that American POWs were held there after the war. By the way, I have chatted with guards at the gate to the Citadel.[83]

All told, it had been some performance by the men charged with analyzing the postwar intelligence on living POWs. In a mere half day's testimony, the DIA chief and his team had stated or implied under oath that (1) all eyewitness intelligence sources were either lying, confused, or worse; (2) there was "no evidence to sustain a belief" that the that American POWs were held above or below ground in the Ministry of Defense/Ho Chi Minh Mausoleum complex after Operation Homecoming; (3) no tunnels could possibly have been constructed beneath Hanoi due to the high water table; (4) reports of the underground prison with a connecting tunnel to the mausoleum and the Ministry of Defense Citadel compound were probably based on rumors that had grown from a single newspaper report about the remains of a Vietminh soldier being found in the Hanoi sewer system; and (5) bike rides around the Citadel compound by Destatte and a visit by U.S. officials to the mausoleum to view the remains of Ho, coupled with statements by Vietnamese guards and denials by Vietnamese officials that any underground prison is located in the area of the mausoleum, were considered "adequate evidence to make, with good confidence, a judgment that the underground facility doesn't exist." Without ever inspecting the site, they had declared with authority: "It is not possible to build an underground facility of the nature . . . described."

"Pentagon doubts reports of Hanoi holding POWs in underground jail," *The Washington Times* declared the next morning.[84] The *Los Angeles Times* reported the same day that though Smith had declared that "the presence of a secret underground facility for American POWs in Hanoi at the Citadel is the only rational explanation for all these sightings and reports over the years, . . . a panel of senior Pentagon officials and analysts, including Lt. Gen. James R. Clapper Jr., director of the Defense Intelligence Agency, disputed Smith's assertion, saying most of the reports have turned out to be false, with many of them [being] fabrications by refugees seeking financial rewards or help in immigrating to the United States."[85] Reuters reported from Vietnam on the 6th that a senior Vietnamese official had "ridiculed claims that Vietnam held missing U.S. servicemen in an underground detention center beside the tomb of Ho Chi Minh until the late 1980's, calling the charges 'a funny story.' "[86] Several days later, Radio Hanoi declared that the entire POW/MIA controversy had been concocted by the American movie industry, and that movies like *Uncommon Valor, Missing in Action,* and especially the second installment of the Sylvester Stallone Rambo films, *First Blood,* had caused "the story about American prisoners being left behind in Southeast Asia . . . [to] become a top-hit myth in the United States." The real MIAs, the announcer declared derisively, are the "thousands of homeless Vietnam war veterans now living on the streets of the United States . . . [the] missing in America."[87]

For Smith, Grassley, and McCreary and his investigators, a grand opportunity seemed to be slipping away in a sea of negative press.

But then the Smith forces got four unexpected back-to-back breaks during mid–late August and the pendulum began to swing back. The first involved inadvertent statements made by the Russian ambassador to Vietnam, the second were statements made by officials at the U.S. Defense Nuclear Agency, and the third were statements made by an ARVN refugee during routine screening in Thailand. The fourth, incredibly, involved the discovery of a coded message sent by a living American prisoner of war detained in northern Vietnam. When decoded, the message stated: "I'm alive! Get me the hell out of here!"

*August 15, Hanoi*
## THE RUSSIAN AMBASSADOR

On August 15, Russia's ambassador to Vietnam, Rashid Khamidouline, was asked about the matter of the underground prison during an interview with Reuters and BBC correspondents in Hanoi. The ambassador said that he had been involved in the region for thirty years and had never heard of any American prisoners being held after the war by the Vietnamese and certainly none had been held beneath the Ho Chi Minh Mausoleum. But he then went on to state that the mausoleum had been built with the assistance of Soviet experts and that there was a restricted underground area beneath it. "There is a lot of equipment, a cooling device. When we built that we put in a triple generator system in case of an electricity black-out," the ambassador said. "The whole area around Huong Vuong (Street) was rebuilt," he continued. "They cut into the Soviet ambassador's residential yard. They redid the whole complex. . . . They redid the whole Ba Dinh square, so that trucks could go past without shaking the ground. It had to be very solid. . . . It (the construction) had to be very secret because the war was still going on. It was very controlled."[88]

In reporting Ambassador Khamidouline's remarks, Reuters added that the Russian "said it was basically sacrilegious for the Vietnamese to hear of reports of Americans supposedly being held prisoner near the mausoleum." "It [the mausoleum]," Reuters quoted Khamidouline as saying, "is sacred for them."[89]

## August 21, Washington
## THE DEFENSE NUCLEAR AGENCY

At Smith's insistence, the Defense Nuclear Agency, the U.S. government's premier specialists in detection of hidden underground facilities, launched a "quick look" study of the Ho Chi Minh Mausoleum area three days after Clapper's, Sydow's, and Destatte's testimony. The primary purpose of the classified study was to determine the feasibility of constructing such a facility in the Hanoi area and if such a facility might be located specifically in the area of the Ho Chi Minh Mausoleum/MND Citadel.

On August 21, based on information previously gathered by DNA and a "quick look" at soil conditions, water tables, etc., in the Hanoi area as well as SR-71 photography of the mausoleum area itself, DNA published its findings. Among those findings were the following:

Underground facilities are constructible in virtually any environment under the earth's surface to reasonable depths.

. . . The depth of the water table [in the Hanoi area] should be two to four meters but may vary seasonally.

Underground and below water table surface excavation in the Hanoi area would require "soft ground" excavation techniques. Relatively deep surface excavations would have to be dewatered and supported by "tie backs" or bracing. Tunneling would be accomplished with shields. These techniques have been routinely employed since the 1960's.

The former Soviet Union expertise in soft ground tunneling is well known; there is no reason to believe that this expertise was not available to the North Vietnamese.

Construction of an underground facility employing standard techniques would not have disrupted existing facilities such as utility and water lines and sewage and storm sewers.

In terms of technical feasibility, the North Vietnamese could have constructed either underground cut-and-cover facilities or a tunnel system in the environs of Hanoi during the time period of interest.

Analysis of available [imagery/photography] indicated a below ground infrastructure far more elaborate than what one would expect from simply a mausoleum. The infrastructure includes the approximately 30 ft and 20 ft wide interconnecting buried passageways between structures, facade type annex structures which are actually windowless buildings, matching square structures which may or may not be part of a ventilation or emergency egress system, and what appears to be alternate entrances to the facility.

It is interesting to note that the public is not allowed on the backside of the tomb area where the majority of these ancillary features are located, and the latest [imagery] indicates that this rear area is still secured by fences, walls and foliage and controlled by guard houses.

The Ho Chi Minh Mausoleum,
Ba Dinh Square, Hanoi, 1994.

The conclusions from this quick look assessment are: (1) that it was entirely feasible for the North Vietnamese to have constructed underground facilities in the environs of Hanoi, (2) portions of the Tomb's ancillary structures are buried, and (3) the function of certain features at the Tomb are unknown and warrant further investigation.

Included in the DNA report was a copy of an SR-71 reconnaissance photo taken from directly over the mausoleum on December 2, 1974, some nine months before the mausoleum was dedicated. The photo, a revealing close-up of the mausoleum itself, showed the infrastructure described above and the area immediately behind the mausoleum. It showed virtually none of Ba Dinh Square, however, the vast area in front of the mausoleum beneath which the underground prison and associated tunnel/tunnels were said to have been constructed.[90]

## August 27
## EXPLOSIVE NEW HUMINT ON THE UNDERGROUND PRISON AND THE MAN WHO REPORTEDLY SUPERVISED ITS CONSTRUCTION

Just as the DNA report had spelled big trouble for DIA personnel and their supporters on the select committee, so too had an explosive HUMINT report that arrived at the Pentagon in the early morning hours of August 27.

This new report, filed by DIA's Stony Beach office in Bangkok and identified as "IIR 6 024 0534 92/Alleged Captive Americans in Ho Chi Minh Mausoleum, Hanoi, Vietnam," cited the testimony of a recently arrived former ARVN NCO who had "tested positive on POW" in early August when he had been asked by U.S. officials in Thailand if he had any knowledge of American POWs being held in Vietnam after the war. At the time, he was undergoing routine screening while en route from Vietnam to his new home in the United States.

Stony Beach reported that the former ARVN soldier explained that he had talked at length with a member of the Communist party who had worked as an architectural draftsman on the Ho Chi Minh Mausoleum construction project. The ARVN soldier said the draftsman told him that "under the tomb is a long tunnel containing many rooms." This tunnel, the draftsman said, is buried twelve meters underground and has walls constructed of concrete. The drafts-man said the interior partitions between the rooms are made of welded thick steel sheets and noted that the people working in one room couldn't see the people who worked in the adjoining rooms. The draftsman stated that the rooms were used by the Vietnamese government to print money and also were intended for use as defense headquarters during time of conflict.

The draftsman further stated that approximately three hundred Russians had participated in the construction of the tomb, and that they and other workers were transported to the tunnel in well-covered vehicles. The design of the tun-nel, the draftsman said, is such that a unit of Russian-made T-54 tanks can be driven above it during military reviews without any adverse effects on the tun-nel structure. He also said that Do Muoi [in 1992 the SRV's most powerful offi-cial] had served as chief inspector of the tunnel's construction.

Stony Beach officials in Bangkok, surely cognizant of the controversy swirling around the mausoleum at the time, suggested in their report that the ARVN soldier be put under surveillance by the FBI upon his arrival in the United States. They also recommended that "analytical research be conducted to assess the plausibility of Do Muoi serving as construction supervisor of Ho Chi Minh's mausoleum." "Good IIR (Intelligence Information Report). Needs to be evalu-ated," someone wrote on the cover sheet of the report after its arrival.[91]

Coming as it had on top of all the other HUMINT from the Ho Chi Minh Mausoleum/MND Citadel area—and just after DNA's findings—of course it was a good report! And as to the need for conducting "analytical research . . . to as-sess the plausibility of Do Muoi serving as construction supervisor of Ho Chi Minh's mausoleum," none was required, for the U.S. intelligence community had long known that Do Muoi had served during the war as vice premier and chairman of the State Capital Construction Committee and from the period of the American withdrawal until 1977 as vice premier and minister of construction—and had stood with other Communist leaders from throughout the world and watched PAVN tanks rumble by not only during the massive cel-ebration marking the opening of the mausoleum on September 2, 1975, but many times since as well.[92]

## THE CODED MESSAGE FROM LIEUTENANT COLONEL SEREX

In late August 1992, the deputy director of the U.S. Air Force Joint Services SERE Agency (JSSA)—the agency responsible for survival, evasion, resistance, and es-cape (SERE) training for U.S. pilots—informed Smith's investigators that while studying recent (June 5) satellite imagery of the Dong Vai (Dong Mang) Prison north of Hon Gai, he and one of his associates discovered a valid USAF/USN escape and evasion code in a field just west of the prison and above it the name of a missing USAF flight officer. The deputy director, twenty-six-year veteran Robert G. Dussault, would later testify formally what he and his associate had seen:

A. . . . I saw up at the CIA, very clearly to me there was the name S-E-R-E-X.

Q. Capital letters?
A. Yes, and it was in a field just outside the . . . [Dong Vai Prison], and there was a number above it and there was the name SEREX, and below it, as I remember now, 72/TA/88.[93]

Q. How many digit number [*sic*] was above the SEREX?
A. I'd say roughly nine or ten. I don't remember. I'd say roughly nine or ten. It could have been a Social Security Number or just my imagination. But the thing that struck me as interesting is that—and I didn't know this at the time, I just wrote that stuff down, and when I got back Al checked the list of people that are unaccounted for, and there was an individual still unaccounted for by the name of Serex. . . .

Q. Okay, so you saw on a June 5, 1992 photograph of the Dong Mang [Dong Vai] prison camp that you looked at at the CIA this year . . . you saw SEREX with the nine to ten digit number above and the 72/TA/88 beneath it?
A. Mmm-hmm. [Yes.]

Q. How do you interpret the 72/TA/88?
A. Well, this is a guess, but the way I would look at it would be that the guy went down in 72—my first reaction would be that he went down in 72, the TA would be his monthly followed by his long term E&E symbol, followed by the year he arrived at the location. That's all speculation.

Q. Was A a backup symbol?
A. Yes.

Q. Do you know when?
A. In the—according to my recollection, in the 72 timeframe . . .

A. . . . What I did with the CIA [personnel] is I circled it for them to look at.[94]

For both the administration and the Kerry/McCain forces on the committee, news that the name of a missing Air Force flight officer with a valid USAF/USN E&E code beneath it had been found in current imagery was a *really* high-megatonnage blast. Seeing the danger they faced, officials quickly developed a program to assail, ridicule, attack, and discredit the imagery so forcefully and thoroughly that its intelligence value would be destroyed.[95] But how does one assail and ridicule a current satellite image showing a valid USAF/USN E&E code and a missing U.S. Air Force flight officer's name in a field next to a prison in North Vietnam? And what about the 1975 imagery that showed pilot distress codes at this same prison? And what about the half dozen postwar HUMINT reports that had told of U.S. POWs being detained at the prison both during and after the war, including reports of fifty to sixty American POWs seen inside the prison in 1976, perhaps thirty seen there again in mid-1979, and three to four dozen taken there by truck in 1982?[96]

No matter. They would have to find a way. The June 5, 1992, satellite imagery simply could not stand. And neither, of course, could the June 1975 imagery from the same facility. Nor could any of the other imagery survive.

The joint, all-out assault on the crucial IMINT was about to begin.

## THE JOINT BUSH ADMINISTRATION/SENATE SELECT COMMITTEE ASSAULT ON THE POSTWAR IMAGERY

For those who do not believe that during the summer and fall of 1992 the Bush administration was intent on destroying the credibility of all postwar intelligence on live POWs—especially the satellite imagery and *most* especially the current satellite imagery—consider the following remarks delivered by Deputy Assistant Secretary of Defense for POW/MIA Affairs Alan C. Ptak, the former deputy staff director at the select committee who in mid-1992 served as titular head of the administration's POW/MIA effort, during POW/MIA Recognition Day ceremonies held on September 18. Speaking to U.S. Army personnel, Ptak, according to an official Pentagon transcript, declared the following:

> Today is a day we recognize our POWs and MIAs. . . . Today is a day to re-member that over 70,000 Americans remain unaccounted for from World War II, 8,000 from Korea, and over 2,000 from Vietnam.
>
> Today I want to talk about one very basic truth about those Americans un-accounted for, and I want to talk about one very basic lie. The basic truth is this: your government, from the President of the United States on down is fully committed to accounting for these Americans.
>
> [Regarding those unaccounted for from Vietnam], let me give you a short report of the steps we have taken, all within the past year. The President cre-ated the office I now occupy. This is the first time that our government has had a Deputy Assistant Secretary of Defense to focus exclusively on POW-MIA issues. We have begun one of the largest declassifying operations in gov-ernment history. We have already released 82 thousand pages of previously secret and top secret documents relating to POW and MIA matters. Last year we had 150 men and women working POW/MIA issues. We have increased that number to over 400. We have put Americans on the ground in Vietnam, Laos, and Cambodia. We are working full time to account for our missing be-cause we see it as a sacred obligation that we owe these Americans and their families.
>
> And that brings me to the basic lie I mentioned earlier. The basic lie is that the U.S. Government knowingly left Americans behind and is now covering this up. If this lie lives, then it will tear at the very guts of our military. If fu-ture Americans become convinced their country won't stand behind them when the chips are down, then they won't stand on the front lines for their country. So let me start here, today, with you, to bury this lie.

First, though hundreds of investigators have been through millions of pages of documents, not one shred of evidence, solid evidence, has been found to support any part of this lie. The next time you hear somebody talk about coverup, think about this: Most of the 400 men and women working to account for our POW/MIAs are men and women in uniform. Like you, they take pride in their military service. Like you, they would not let their buddies down. Like you, they would be the first to speak out at the first hint of footdragging or coverup.

Yes, there are questions about our missing and unaccounted for Americans. But the answers aren't in American files. The answers are in Vietnam, in Laos, [and] in Cambodia. . . . The answers are slow in coming, but we will not rest until we're certain we have them.

Thank you. God bless you . . . God bless the United States Army . . . and God bless the United States of America.[97]

The first indication that the Administration would help "bury" the "basic lie" by destroying the value of the postwar imagery came shortly after POW/MIA Recognition Day when Dussault, preparing his testimony for the upcoming select committee imagery hearings scheduled for mid-October, met with CIA photo interpreters to review all the postwar imagery relating to POWs and to further discuss the Serex imagery in detail. This meeting took place at the National Photographic Interpretation Center (NPIC) (pronounced "N-pick"), a joint CIA/DIA command located at the Navy Yard near Capitol Hill. Dussault later told Senate investigators that to his amazement, the CIA photo interpreters informed him during the portion of the discussion relating to the June 5, 1992, imagery of the Dong Mang (Dong Vai) Prison that the "SEREX 72/TA/88"—all of which he had circled on the photograph up at Langley—had now *disappeared*.

Q. You say that you then met again with CIA photo interpreters . . . ?
A. Right. . . . When we went to NPIC, the CIA guys were there and they briefed us. . . . They said look, we saw the numbers. They admitted seeing the same numbers I did. When I circled it they were right there and they said yeah, we saw it. But . . . at NPIC, they briefed the fact that they . . . did a digital on this thing, looked at it on a light table, and it wasn't there, and [they said] it must have been an anomaly, [a] photographic anomaly.

I don't understand photographic anomalies, I wouldn't know how to explain one if somebody asked me to. . . .

. . . When someone tells me that that's a photo anomaly that SEREX would occur on a photo—and they say that happens, a SEREX would appear on a photo and would be a result of the photographic process, I think that's unusual, but I've got no way to argue with them.[98]

But, of course, Dussault did have a "way to argue with them," and that was by bringing his case to Smith and his investigators, which he did soon after his meeting at NPIC. Smith, deeply concerned, quickly moved to have Dussault and his assistant testify before the committee in closed session. Some of Smith's investigators—no longer trusting anyone other than Smith and Grassley to do the right thing—leaked what had occurred along with several unclassified versions of line drawings of some of the postwar satellite imagery to a *Dateline NBC* correspondent, who began preparing a story.

During the closed briefings, held on October 2 and 5, Dussault explained to the senators what the CIA personnel had said about the June 5, 1992, "SEREX" imagery, offered JSSA's analysis of the other imagery relating to live POWs, and then stunned those present by declaring that, while recently reviewing 1988 imagery of Laos, he and his associates had discovered nineteen four-digit numbers that matched the four-digit authenticators of known MIAs, each laid out or constructed on the ground in remote areas along Lao National Route 4 southeast of the Plain of Jars, and had discovered the name of a missing USAF pilot and an accompanying four-digit number laid out or constructed beside a road east of the Sam Neua Valley.[99]

When Dussault completed his testimony, DIA officials present launched into what Grassley later called "a full court debunking" of the imagery, especially the nineteen four-digit numbers in the 1988 imagery of Laos that matched the four-digit authenticators of known MIAs. These four-digit numbers were not really authenticator numbers constructed by missing air crewmen, DIA officials testified, but were naturally occurring shadows and vegetation.[100]

Smith and Grassley, understandably enraged by the DIA officials' testimony—and reportedly disgusted by a comment Kerry made to Smith that the "symbols could have been made by dancing girls"—responded by demanding that the committee hire a team of unbiased outside experts to examine *all* of the imagery—the June 5, 1992, "SEREX" imagery, the 1988 imagery showing the nineteen four-digit authenticator numbers, the 1988 imagery of the "USA/Walking K" E&E code, and all of the other postwar imagery—and report their findings to the committee. To calm a situation that was rapidly getting out of control, Kerry agreed to have the committee hire two such experts, one to be chosen by him, the other by Smith, and have them begin their examination of the imagery as soon as possible.

*October 6, 1992*
## A DISCUSSION OF THE SAM NEUA "USA/WALKING K" E&E CODE ON *DATELINE NBC*

The *Dateline NBC* segment on satellite imagery aired October 6. A portion of the discussion involving correspondent Jon Scott, Senator McCain, and former SSC intelligence investigator Hendon went as follows:

> SCOTT: (Voiceover) DATELINE has obtained this computer-enhanced photograph, taken by an American spy satellite in January, 1988, In a rice paddy in Northern Laos, the letters U-S-A are clearly distinguishable. But what is chilling to some Pentagon analysts is the symbol below.
> (Document showing rudimentary U-S-A spelling)
> MR. BILLY HENDON: Underneath it is unquestionably what is known as a walking K, and the foot on the K. Again, the foot is the key.

SCOTT: Ex-Congressman Bill Hendon is a controversial POW hunter. A former advisor to the Pentagon and Senate investigators, he had access to
some of the government's most sensitive POW files.

MR. HENDON: And I have talked to the people in charge of the compart-
mented program that—that deals with the escape and evasion symbol that
was in the satellite photography. And they say, "Hey, no question. That's
an American flier."

SCOTT: This is a list of distress signals American flyers were told to display on
the ground if shot down—simple alphabet letters, but with modifications
only pilots knew. The symbols are so secret that the Pentagon still blacks
out the alterations.

(Footage of secret distress signals)

MR. HENDON: That can only be a US pilot telling you, "Get me out of here."
That's all it can mean.

SCOTT: And he's saying that in January of 1988?

MR. HENDON: Absolutely.

SCOTT: (Voiceover) In the past, Hendon has been accused of exaggerating his
evidence. But independently of Hendon, Dateline has obtained evidence
that supports his assertions about the walking K. This memo was prepared
by the JSSA, a secret intelligence unit in charge of training American pilots
how to use distress symbols. Its conclusion: "Although it is possible for
someone other than an American being held against his will could have
made these signals, JSSA believes these signals must be considered valid
until we know otherwise. The 'USA' appears to be the more recently made.
The 'K' appears to have faded by time. If the crew member received no response to his 'K' signal, it is reasonable to expect them to make progres-
sively more blatant signals, including a 'USA.' If it works, he goes home."

(Footage of Hendon and Scott reviewing a map; declassified documents;
memo)

SCOTT : You were a pilot.

SENATOR MCCAIN: Yes.

SCOTT : You were given the same kinds of [di]stress codes.

SENATOR MCCAIN: Yes, we were.

SCOTT : When you see this K, the walking K, doesn't that catch in your throat
a little bit?

SENATOR MCCAIN: Oh, it caught in my throat enormously. I would also say
[though] that my experience and knowledge of prison camps is that the
guards do not generally allow prisoners to go out and stamp out U-S-A in
large letters so that it can be photographed [by] satellite or by airplane.
That's not their habit.[101]

John Kerry had not liked what he had seen on Dateline—not the leaked, unclassified line drawings of the imagery Scott had presented, not Hendon quoting
the JSSA experts as telling what it all meant, not even his friend McCain's pouring
cold water on the imagery of the USA/Walking K E&E code at Sam Neua in 1988,
which Kerry had considered too weak a response. And so Kerry called DOD the
following day with instructions that DOD witnesses "come on strong—appalled"

at the upcoming hearings and bring photos that have been blown up to "show that the K is not a K and that it does not have walking feet," and that Mr. Gadoury [JCRC Bangkok] should "explain how the USA could have been made" [that is, that it had not been constructed by a POW]. Kerry told DOD it was time to "demonstrate reality" and "put a lie to it," and added that unless DOD personnel "answer this attack directly the leakers will win and they will be able to claim 'everybody knows' it was made by a POW." To prevent exactly that from taking place at the upcoming imagery hearings, Kerry again urged that the DOD witnesses scheduled to appear "come on strong—appalled."[102]

## THE OCTOBER 15 IMAGERY HEARINGS

When the committee convened in public session on the morning of October 15 to discuss the postwar imagery, only three senators, Kerry, Smith, and Grassley, were in attendance. Following an opening statement by each, Kerry turned the floor over to Assistant Secretary of Defense Duane Andrews.

As Andrews began to speak, a scene eerily reminiscent of Kerry's earlier slashing of the universe of POWs and MIAs from more than two thousand four hundred men to only forty-three developed, and in a matter of moments Andrews reduced the number of postwar photos and satellite images that might conceivably relate to American POWs to two. Only the July 1973 reconnaissance photo showing the "1973 TH" pilot distress code near the Plain of Jars (see www.enormouscrime.com, Chapter 23) and the 1988 imagery of the "USA/K" near Sam Neua, he declared, were worthy of analysis. The others, he said, were for various reasons not related in any way to American POWs or MIAs.

When Andrews finished and Kerry attempted to seize on what he had said, combat broke out between Kerry and Smith:

> KERRY [to Andrews] . . . Just so the record is very clear, there are only two images that are currently in the possession of DIA or DOD or any entity that we are still trying to analyze and understand, is that correct?
> SMITH [interjecting] Mr. Chairman, there are many images in dispute. I certainly do not want to be included in the we. I do not agree that there are only two. . . .
> KERRY: . . . Let us be really careful. The American public is listening really carefully and a lot of POW activists are listening very carefully. And if we pretend to them that something is a symbol when it is not, we are falsely raising hopes.
> SMITH: . . . I am not pretending anything.
> KERRY: There is no trained person that has yet determined them to be a symbol, Senator. . . . I will not be party to falsely raising hopes. There are no symbols that have yet been determined to be person made symbols that are in front of the committee. That is just a fact. I do not know why we are struggling with this unless it is of great interest to have everybody hyped up over some imaginary symbols.
> SMITH: Well, let each Senator speak for himself, Mr. Chairman. I do not agree with that conclusion. I think the evidence is very compelling. I think the

laws of probability would indicate to you that if there are a series of numbers that identify with an individual or individuals who are missing in action in Southeast Asia and those numbers correlate with individuals, the laws of probability would tell you that it is a very high probability that those people are in fact, identified with those numbers.

KERRY: But no one, Senator, has yet determined—no one has determined—that those are, in fact, real, man-made symbols. Is that correct, Secretary?

ANDREWS: That's absolutely correct. In fact, we've determined that we do not believe they are. And when I say we, this is not [only] the Defense Intelligence Agency position. They are a very professional part of our government. It's also the Central Intelligence Agency and the Department of Defense's position based on the best analysis that we have to date.[103]

With that, Andrews moved on to explain why DIA had rejected the other imagery. Dong Vai, site of the possible 1975/1976 rooftop distress signal, Andrews declared, was "not a facility that housed American prisoners," and it was therefore "highly unlikely that the symbols were consciously placed on the roof structure as a signal." Regarding the 1992 "Serex" imagery from the same prison, Andrews declared flatly, "When we looked at the imagery, it [SEREX] was not there."

The "52K" symbol imaged at Gnommorath [Fort Apache] in central Laos in late 1980 and again in early 1981, Andrews told the committee, was most probably a combination of shadows and "the irregular furrows of many individual garden plots." Regarding the nineteen four-digit authenticator codes that had been so hotly contested during the October 2 and 5 briefings, Andrews stated that since those briefings, all nineteen numbers had disappeared from the imagery. "When we looked at the imagery [again] we did not see the numbers," he declared.[104]

Moving to the "USA/Walking K" imagery—one of the two images DIA considered worthy of further study—Andrews, ignoring the fact that JSSA had officially declared fewer than four months earlier that the "USA" and the attached "Walking K" imaged in the rice paddy near Sam Neua on January 22, 1988, "should be considered valid ground signals until proven otherwise," declared that "we have no reason to believe at this time that it is, in fact, an evader symbol."[105]

And on and on it went. When it was over, only the "Buffalo Hunter" reconnaissance photo of the "Flying Tango Hotel" E&E code taken just northeast of the Plain of Jars in 1973 was still standing. But just barely—for as Andrews had noted at one point during his testimony, "It [the E&E code] is not what we would expect to be used by an unaccounted for U.S. military person."[106]

For the unlisted, unreturned POWs, October 15 had been another very rough day. Predictably, the 16th would prove rough as well: "Experts can't link spy photos to MIAs" (USA Today), "Most Symbols Explained, POW-MIA Panel Is Told, Defense Official Rejects Coverup Charges" (Washington Post), "Satellite Photos Dismissed in Hunt for U.S. POWs in Southeast Asia" (Los Angeles Times). Several weeks would pass before the Arkansas Democrat Gazette's Vic Harville offered the most definitive account of what had occurred:

(VIC HARVILLE, COURTESY *ARKANSAS DEMOCRAT-GAZETTE*)

The potentially ruinous imagery disposed of, Kerry entered the home stretch of the committee's investigation with only a handful of major items remaining on his to-do list. One was to "prove" there was no underground prison located under or adjacent to the Ho Chi Minh Mausoleum in Hanoi. Another was to find some way to defuse a major controversy that was developing because of Smith's insistence that the Secret Service agent who said that in 1981 he had heard President Reagan and others discussing a Vietnamese offer to sell POWs back for reconstruction aid be brought before the committee to testify. A third was to hold one final series of public hearings to establish indelibly in the minds of the public that, though a few POWs might have been left, there had been no conscious attempt by the government to cover up their existence and, sadly, none still remained alive. A fourth was to craft a final report acceptable to all members of the committee—a tough row to hoe given Smith's and Grassley's feelings. And then, of course, when it was all over, he would cite the committee's findings as the principal reason the United States should change its policy toward Vietnam and move quickly toward normalized relations.

## November 3
## ELECTION DAY

The presidential election was held on November 3, and though few observers thought much of it at the time—and perhaps fewer still have thought of it since—the unlisted, unreturned POWs played a pivotal, seminal role. Their contribution: third-party candidate H. Ross Perot himself, who had entered the presidential race in the spring amid a flurry of press reports indicating he had done so because of mistrust between him and President Bush that had developed during 1986 and 1987 when Perot had conducted his investigation into the POW issue. The press had had a field day with the story. "Is Perot After the Presidency—Or the President?" *Business Week* had asked in its April 6, 1992, edition; "MIA Issue Shaped Perot's View of Bush," *The Washington Post* had declared in a front-page story on April 18; "Perot Stand On Prisoner Issue Left Bush With Bitter Feeling," *The New York Times* had reported on its front page on May 12, but Perot had brushed off the reports and had become an instant sensation. In late May, a *Washington Post*–ABC News poll conducted nationwide had shown him leading in a three-way race against Bush and former Arkansas Governor Bill Clinton, 34 percent to Bush's 31 percent to Clinton's 29 percent.[107]

Then, in mid-July, in one of the strangest twists in American political history, Perot had abruptly dropped out of the race, citing alleged Bush campaign dirty tricks. He had reentered the race on October 1, and, though badly wounded by the controversy surrounding his decision to withdraw, ended up playing a defining role on Election Day, garnering 19 percent of the popular vote to Clinton's 43 percent and Bush's 38 percent.[108] Political pundits agreed that had Perot not been in the race, those who voted for him would have supported Bush over Clinton by a wide margin.

*November–December*
## THE ENDGAME

Undoubtedly pleased that he would soon have a friend in the White House who shared his strong desire to normalize relations with Vietnam, Kerry flew to Hanoi in mid-November with Daschle and Brown to tackle the lingering problem of the underground prison at the Ho Chi Minh Mausoleum. Brown would later say that after requesting access to the area beneath the mausoleum, the group was taken to the mausoleum, escorted down several levels, and allowed to enter a large room. Brown said the room contained several large generators, one of which he noticed was American-made, large, exposed pipes, and a number of large doors. Brown said that these doors remained closed throughout the group's brief time in the room and added that neither he, Kerry, nor Daschle requested they be opened.[109] For Kerry, it was proof enough, and upon the group's return he entered a statement into the official record declaring that he and Daschle and Brown had learned conclusively during their trip that no such underground facility existed.[110]

Unconvinced, Smith resolved to go to Hanoi in the days ahead to see for himself.

## THE LINGERING MATTER OF THE SECRET SERVICE AGENT

Smith and Grassley had been trying hard to get John Syphrit before the select committee for months. Though Syphrit, the Secret Service agent who had told

Smith and Hendon in 1986 about Hanoi's offer to sell back the American POWs they held to the United States for reconstruction aid, was a willing witness, for the last five months the White House, the Secret Service, Kerry, McCain, and attorneys of every stripe had blocked the move. Now, in the waning days of the committee's investigation, Smith had demanded that Syphrit be heard.

Declassified committee records show that Smith had almost succeeded in getting Syphrit's testimony on the record way back in July. In fact, Syphrit had been en route from his then-current posting at a Treasury Department laboratory near Chicago to Washington to be deposed by committee investigators when White House National Security Advisor Brent Scowcroft intervened with Kerry to stop him from testifying.[111] The following day, Kerry had gone to the White House and met alone with Scowcroft to discuss the Syphrit matter.[112] Then had come the letter from Secretary of the Treasury Nicholas Brady urging all members of the committee to "reconsider your action" [to hear Syphrit's testimony],[113] followed by the not-so-veiled threat from the director of the Secret Service warning the senators that if they persisted in their efforts to depose Syphrit, potentially embarrassing statements made by U.S. senators who had in the past been afforded Secret Service protection might also become public. "Many of your fellow Senators can attest not only to the professionalism of the Secret Service, but also to their confidence and trust in its employees," Director John Magaw had warned each member of the select committee by letter on July 24. "They will also tell you how important it was for them to be able to speak freely and candidly while our agents were in close proximity to them and their closest advisors. Before the Select Committee takes this step we ask that you consult with those Senators who have received Secret Service protection."[114]

Unquestionably swayed by the administration's fierce counterattack, the committee had decided in late July to suspend its attempt to depose Syphrit and try instead to locate other witnesses who might have knowledge of the Vietnamese offer. According to a memorandum circulated by Codinha at the time, the thinking was that if other credible witnesses could be found, there would be no need to hear from Syphrit and the controversy over whether or not he should testify would simply go away.[115]

But then had come a remarkable series of events in August, which together had given rise to a dramatic increase in media interest in Syphrit's story and renewed calls that he be brought before the committee. The first of these events had occurred on the 7th, when the *Los Angeles Times,* quoting a "retired official who held a senior intelligence position" during 1981, reported that "soon after taking office in January 1981, the Ronald Reagan Administration received an offer from Vietnamese officials, transmitted through Canadian diplomats . . . [stating that] they reportedly were willing to free an unspecified number of prisoners in return for reconstruction aid they believed that President Richard M. Nixon had promised when the Paris Peace Accords were signed in 1973."[116] The second had occurred on the 11th, when *The Washington Times* had quoted Syphrit himself as saying in a recent interview that he had overheard the Vietnamese offer being discussed during a January 1981 conversation among Reagan, Bush, Casey, and National Security Advisor Richard Allen and that, as he recalled it, Casey had said during the conversation the offer "had come through China and Canada from the Vietnamese."[117] The third had occurred a short while later when Smith had contacted his longtime friend and supporter Max Hugel, Casey's former confidant who had served as deputy director for operations (DDO) under Casey during 1981 and was now living in New Hampshire, to ask Hugel if he was the "senior intelligence official" referred to in the *Los Angeles Times* article and, if not, to find out what, if anything, Hugel knew about the reported offer. According to Smith, Hugel had told him that he had not talked to the *Times* and suggested the official who had was probably [authors' redaction of CIA official's name], a retired high official Hugel said was currently working in Los Angeles for a defense contractor. Then, to Smith's surprise, Hugel had proceeded to say that the story about the Vietnamese offer was true: Yes, it had been received by the Reagan administration on January 26, 1981, to be exact, and it involved payment of $4 billion for U.S. POWs being held by the Vietnamese in Laos. Hugel had also told Smith that China was somehow involved in the matter, and that when Reagan had learned of the offer, he had gone "ballistic" and had told Casey to 'Get 'em—find 'em and get 'em.'" Hugel had also told Smith that around the time it was received, the Vietnamese offer had been common knowledge among senior intelligence officials and, at the CIA at least, had been the subject of a great deal of "water fountain talk." [Though no longer a member of Smith's staff, Hendon had continued to unofficially offer advice and assistance to his beleaguered friend throughout the summer and fall. During one particularly hectic August weekend, Smith, unable to reach Hugel to inquire about the offer, had called Hendon and asked him to help locate Hugel and arrange a time he and Smith could talk. Hendon had found Hugel that afternoon at a racetrack in southern New Hampshire and had told him to please stand by, that Smith needed to talk to him at once. Hendon had advised Smith, who then called Hugel and asked him about the Vietnamese offer. After the conversation, Smith had called Hendon back and gone over with him what he and Hugel had just discussed. In a later conversation, Smith had offered additional details to Hendon. What Smith told Hendon during both conversations is reflected in Hendon's handwritten notes of the first conversation titled "Max Hugel to Bob Smith [illegible mark] call ___ Aug '92," and later handwritten additions that together form the basis for the above account. (Hendon's handwritten phone notes, with redaction by Hendon, from Hendon files.) Smith would later place a similar version of what Hugel told him in the official record of the select committee. Hugel would later give sworn testimony that he had no knowledge of any offer, nor did he remember telling anyone he had.][118]

Though one might have expected the August revelations to move the committee to break with Scowcroft and the administration and bring Syphrit in, no such thing had occurred. In fact, there had been no movement at all on the matter until November, when Smith had again attempted to arrange for Syphrit's testimony, and, when the Secret Service had successfully blocked this attempt,[119] had then forced the issue to a head by calling for an up-or-down vote. Would the committee subpoena the Secret Service agent and hear his testimony about the 1981 offer, the objections of Kerry, McCain, Scowcroft, Brady, Magaw, and the others notwithstanding, or would they not, yes or no? Smith demanded.

Ballots were sent to each senator with instructions they must be returned to the clerk by 5:00 P.M. on November 23.[120]

Smith called Hendon soon after the members convened to vote. The initial count, he said, had gone like this: Smith: "Yes." Grassley: "Yes." McCain: "No." Brown: "No." Kassebaum: "No." Helms: "Abstain." Reid: "No." Robb: "No." Kerrey: "No." Kohl: "No." Then, and only then, Smith said, with the subpoena already doomed by a seven–two vote, Kerry and Daschle had each voted "Yes." Final vote: seven–four against hearing Syphrit, with one member abstaining.[121]

*The Washington Times* confirmed the committee's decision the day before Thanksgiving under the headline, "MIA Panel Won't Call Secret Service Agent." Grassley, speaking for himself and undoubtedly for Smith as well, told the *Times* that the committee's decision was "troubling in the extreme" and declared, "[I]t is a highly extraordinary act when a committee of Congress . . . refuses to take legitimate, relevant testimony—hearsay or otherwise—from any witness. This is just one more instance in which this committee . . . has caved in to the desires of the executive branch it was established to investigate."[122] Pulitizer Prize–winning author and columnist Sydney Schanberg would write some weeks later that "A Kerry ally, Sen. John McCain, who though a former POW himself has oddly scorned all evidence of men left behind, lobbied hard with committee members against subpoenaing the former Secret Service man."[123]

His to-do list growing shorter and shorter, his goals as set out in the *Globe* road map now clearly within reach—and knowing that in Washington, perhaps more than almost any other place in the world, the endgame is the only game— Kerry focused all his efforts on the final set of public hearings he had scheduled for early December. He and McCain had assembled an impressive array of witnesses, most of them Vietnam veterans, all eager to testify that there was nothing to the postwar intelligence, there had been no cover-up, and that, sad as it was, no POWs remained alive. The "Wrap-Up Hearings," as Kerry and members of his staff called them, would begin on December 1.

## December 1–4
## THE FINAL HEARINGS

On December 1, a stream of current and former officials who had help run the government's postwar POW effort appeared before the committee to pat themselves on the back for a job well done and declare in one fashion or another that no cover-up had taken place and that in spite of their Herculean efforts to find evidence of living POWs, sadly, no such evidence had been found. Appearing were DIA Director Jim Clapper; his deputy, Dennis Nagy; former DIA directors Jim Williams and Lennie Perroots; former DIA assistant deputy director (and later director of naval intelligence) Tom Brooks; senior DOD intelligence official Ron Knecht, POW/MIA Special Office Chief Bob Sheetz; former Special Office chiefs Kim Gaines and Joe Schlatter; and current and former POW/MIA IAG members Dick Childress, Ann Griffiths, Carl Ford, and Ken Quinn.[124] Not surprisingly, all agreed with McCain that the select committee's intelligence investigators' approach to analyzing the HUMINT had been fallacious and that there was nothing in the imagery that indicated any POWs had survived.

Then came a day-long hearing dealing with the activities of various veterans' groups and POW/MIA advocacy organizations, a number of which, Kerry and McCain charged, were guilty of "fraud" for raising money to help recover "non-existent POWs." Kerry cited as one example one activist organization's recent fund-raising appeal that implied that the committee believed 650 POWs were still alive. Kerry called the claim "fraudulent . . . , disingenuous . . . and grotesque on its face." A representative of the company that drafted the appeal, however, knowing that the number 650 had come from the intelligence investigators' own estimates made back in June, stuck to his guns, calling the number "a correct statement of fact." An Associated Press account of the hearing would quote committee members as accusing several POW advocacy groups of "exaggerating or fabricating claims that POWs were known to be alive in order to generate funds," and McCain specifically as declaring that "the people who have done these things are not zealots in a good cause, [but instead are] . . . criminals . . . some of the most craven, most cynical and most despicable human beings to ever run a scam."[125]

Next, the committee received testimony about the live prisoner issue from, among others, former POW and retired Vice Adm. James B. Stockdale and his wife, Sybil, who had founded the National League of Families during the period her husband had been held prisoner in North Vietnam. Both testified that no POWs remained alive.[126] Then members met in public for the last time to receive testimony from various officials involved in current DOD efforts to account for the missing. Witnesses included presidential envoy Gen. Jack Vessey; JTF/FA's Maj. Gen. Tom Needham, who had assisted Kerry with the "no-notice inspection" of Thanh Liet Prison back in April; Deputy Assistant Secretary of Defense (POW/MIA) Al Ptak, who had laid out the administration's policy on live POWs so forcefully during his "basic lie" speech back on POW/MIA Recognition Day; POW/MIA IAG members Griffiths, Ford, and Quinn; POW/MIA Special Office Chief Bob Sheetz and his analysts Bob Destatte, Gary Sydow, and Warren Gray; JCRC's Thailand-based representative Bill Gadoury; and a number of others.[127]

"All P.O.W.'S Freed, Ex-Admiral Says," *The New York Times* reported after Stockdale testified, declaring that the former POW's testimony "may help debunk persistent reports that American soliders [sic] or aviators were left when the United States withdrew."[128] "Panel Finds No Data on Live U.S. POWs," *The Washington Times* reported, quoting Vessey as telling the committee that "all of the evidence gathered points toward death" at crash sites or when captured, and declaring that the idea the Vietnamese would hold POWs for twenty years "is almost beyond the realm of comprehension."[129] *The Washington Post*, in an article accompanied by a large picture of McCain and Vessey laughing together in the hearing room just prior to Vessey's testimony, quoted Vessey and other senior military officers as saying "they are convinced that Hanoi is not holding any live prisoners, does not have any large numbers of remains it could deliver promptly and has made a sincere commitment to cooperate with Pentagon MIA investigators." The *Post* went on to say that "besides saying that Vietnam holds no living prisoners and does not have any warehouse of POW remains, senior officers and Defense Intelligence Agency analysts testified that . . . there is no underground prison in Hanoi where Americans might be concealed, there never has been, and the DIA did not mislead the committee about such a facility" and that the "huge 'USA' letters photographed by a spy satellite in a remote rice field in Laos in 1988 were a boy's artwork, copied off an envelope, not a distress signal from a U.S. prisoner."[130] The *Post* added almost in passing that "the hearing, the last before the committee issues a final report, was structured to allow Defense Department witnesses to challenge or rebut some of the most persistent theories put forward by family members and MIA activists who believe Hanoi is concealing the truth. Although the issues have been thrashed out at length in previous hearings, Kerry said 'these things are hanging out there, folks,' and creating doubt where there should be none."[131]

Game, set, match, Senators Kerry and McCain.

The hearings over, Kerry appeared to believe that the only major thing still "hanging out there and creating doubt where there should be none" was the underground prison at the Ho Chi Minh Mausoleum. He apparently further believed that a quick trip to Hanoi with Smith and another quick visit to the generator room would end that doubt. And so, in mid-December, it was off to Hanoi for one last visit, then a speedy return to Washington to oversee the preparation of the committee's final report.

## *Mid-December*
## A TRIUMPHANT RETURN TO HANOI

Kerry biographer Douglas Brinkley would later declare in *Tour of Duty: John Kerry and the Vietnam War* that "an entire book could be written about Kerry's journeys back to Southeast Asia between 1991 and 1993."[132] Though Brinkley discussed several of those trips in detail, strangely, he would not chronicle Kerry's infamous April 1992 trip to Thanh Liet Prison, nor would he dig deeply into what had taken place during Kerry's trip back to Hanoi with Smith in mid-December.

Kerry returned to Hanoi triumphant on December 18, and from the moment he arrived he was accorded folk-hero status. Smith, taken aback by the fawning, lay back, even choosing at one point to forgo the "Vice-Chairman's seat" next to Kerry during a photo op staged by Vietnamese officials.[133]

Then came the ritual "big breakthrough," with Kerry declaring after a private meeting he and Smith had with SRV Foreign Minister Nguyen Manh Cam that the Vietnamese leader had made available "crucial information" on missing Americans and documents containing "very interesting information." In fact, Kerry added, "more documents than we have requested." Asked by members of the press to describe the contents of those documents, Kerry declared, "[T]hey had shootdowns, dates of deaths, places of burial, and this is the critical information we are looking for." Literally gushing over what Cam had given him, Kerry declared, "[T]he minister could not have been more forthcoming."[134]

But, of course, "crucial . . . critical information" on "shootdowns, dates of deaths, places of burial" was not what Smith had come for. And so, soon after the press conference, Smith and Kerry quietly slipped off to inspect the underground area beneath the Ho Chi Minh Mausoleum.

Kerry's account of what occurred at the mausoleum was first revealed publicly in 2004 by Brinkley in *Tour of Duty*. "The most difficult part of Kerry's job,"
Brinkley wrote, "was pronouncing *definitely* that no American POWs were being
held captive in Vietnam" (Brinkley's italics). Brinkley then explained that
"[e]very time Bob Smith's Senate office got a lead about a POW, no matter how
questionable, Kerry was forced to check it out, and [t]he most difficult rumor to
bat away was that U.S. servicemen were being held hostage under Ho Chi
Minh's tomb in Hanoi." Brinkley said that in an effort to "bat away" this rumor,
Kerry had insisted during the mid-December visit to Hanoi that he and Smith be
allowed to conduct an "on-the-spot investigation" of the tomb. According to
Brinkley, "the two senators [soon] found themselves being escorted all over the
dark subterranean underground of Hanoi." "It was weird," Brinkley quoted
Kerry as saying. "We were forced to keep it quiet. But there we were inspecting
these musty catacombs and crazy tunnels." Brinkley wrote that Kerry and Smith
found no evidence of an underground prison and as a result Smith's suspicions
were placated. "That was a big hurdle," Brinkley quoted Kerry as saying. "By giving us that kind of special access, it proved they weren't hiding anything. There
were no POWs under Ho Chi Minh's tomb. Bob Smith was starting to come
around."[135]

"Totally false, it never happened," Smith would later say when told of Kerry's
claim that the two had been allowed to inspect an underground tunnel or tunnels in the vicinity of the Ho Chi Minh Mausoleum. "Why, if that *had* happened, who in their right mind believes I would have remained silent, especially
after DIA had trumpeted so loudly and so publicly and so *contemptuously* that no
such tunnel or tunnels existed, that no tunnels or underground structures could
be built under Hanoi because the water table was too high? Catacombs? Tunnels? It's just not true. We were never allowed to go into any catacombs or tunnels, and John knows it."[136]

What actually occurred, Smith would later say, was that he and Kerry were
taken down into the basement area beneath the mausoleum and escorted into a
"great big room" containing a number of very large pipes. Smith would further
say:

I asked the Vietnamese what the pipes were for, and they said they were
used to ventilate the tomb, and I said, "those are pretty big just to ventilate
this small mausoleum." We saw several doors leading out of this big room,
and I asked, "Can we go through those doors" and the Vietnamese said "No,
it is not allowed." It was clear to me the pipes were headed somewhere behind those doors but we were not allowed to go there—we were not allowed
to open *any* of the doors. My assumption was the tunnel the intelligence
sources had told us about was through one or more of those doors, but I repeat: *they would not let us open the doors*. To say that we did open them—and
that we then went into some tunnel or tunnels or catacombs—is totally and
completely false. I know. I was there with John. I repeat, we did not go into
any tunnel or tunnels, any underground passageway, any "catacomb" or
any other underground structure that day or any day. We simply walked
into the big room with the big pipes and a bunch of doors and walked

around inside the room and, after my requests that we be allowed to look behind each door were *denied,* we left the room by the same door we had entered and went back upstairs. That is what happened that day and nothing more.[137]

Weird? What was *really* weird was what was going on down in Ho Chi Minh City at the *exact time* Kerry says he and Smith were "inspecting [the] musty catacombs and crazy tunnels" near the mausoleum and coming up empty-handed on POWs. As reported by the business news network "Business Wire" on December 21, 1992:

### COLLIERS INTERNATIONAL OPENS OFFICE IN VIETNAM

HO CHI MINH CITY (DEC 21) BUSINESS WIRE—Anticipating the lifted U.S. trade embargo, Colliers International opened an office this week in Ho Chi Minh City and was awarded the first real estate license to operate in Vietnam. The new office represents the only international real estate operating network in the country and one of the first American-based companies to invest in Vietnam since the war.

Stewart Forbes, CEO of Colliers International, who just returned from Vietnam, indicates the sheer determination and productivity of the people, in addition to the region's natural resources, such as oil reserves, will attract sorely needed capital. . . .

Colliers International, based in Boston, Mass., is one of the largest real estate federations in the world.[138]

Stewart Forbes is Sen. John Forbes Kerry's cousin.[139]

*Christmas Break*
## WASHINGTON

Smith returned to Washington to find that the imagery expert he had hired had discovered another pilot distress signal in the June 5, 1992, imagery of Dong Vai Prison. According to the expert, Col. Lorenzo "Larry" Burroughs, USAF (Ret.), who had once served as acting director at NPIC, the signal was the two-letter USAF/USN E&E code "G/Walking X," followed by the four-digit authenticator "2527." Burroughs would later report with a "100 % level of confidence" that he had seen the "GX 2527" in the imagery and added that "JSSA has . . . confirm[ed] and match[ed] this number as a valid authenticator code against a known MIA."[140] Kerry's outside expert, as Smith expected, disputed Burroughs's findings, saying the "G/Walking X" E&E code and the four-digit authenticator "2527" Burroughs had seen in the June 5, 1992, imagery were in reality "natural shadings in the field and . . . not man-made intentional symbols." The fact that the four-digit authenticator matched that of a missing American flight officer, Kerry's expert declared, was simply a "coincidence."[141]

But none of that mattered now, for the battle was over, the senators had long since made up their minds, and it was time to put the finishing touches on the final report and move on. Smith, sickened by what he had seen and heard over the past year, and knowing well that Kerry and McCain had the votes to write anything they wanted into the final report, decided to fight hard for his positions but sign it no matter what it said—and then make a run for the White House and try to correct what his colleagues had wrought. "Don't do either— don't sign and don't run for president," a close friend advised Smith, adding that Kerry and McCain would use his signing to validate everything they had done, and that because Smith was "a workhorse, not a show horse," he would never succeed in a presidential race.

The committee's final report, signed by all twelve members, would be sent to the printer just after New Year's.

CHAPTER 32

1993–1995

# "THE VIETNAMESE KNOW HOW TO COUNT"

. . .

Kerry had carefully studied photographs, analyzed reports, and tracked down rumors. . . . [W]ith McCain's constant support, [he] tackled every allegation presented. Together they were walking a political minefield, careful not to make a misstep. All the Vietnam veterans in America were watching them with a close eye. There was, however, something extremely reassuring about the hawk (McCain) and the dove (Kerry) determined to find closure on the thorniest issue still remaining between the United States and Vietnam.
—DOUGLAS BRINKLEY, *Tour of Duty: John Kerry and the Vietnam War*

Kerry's work as head of the POW/MIA committee was bitterly divisive, pitting true believers against hardened skeptics like Republican John McCain. "People now think it was easy to do," says Bob Kerrey, the former Democratic senator. "But I heard people say to John McCain and John Kerry: 'You are traitors. There are a lot of people dead because of you.'" Kerry brought together the warring sides in both parties to do what most veterans and senators thought was impossible: write a final report that won unanimous support. Kerry and McCain did more than just debunk the myth of living POWs; they opened the door to normalizing relations with Vietnam.
"KERRY BY THE BOOK," *Newsweek*, October 25, 2004

Tourison, Kerry's "numbers guy" on the committee staff and former chief of analysis at the DIA Special Office for POWs/MIAs, had boasted around the Hill over the Christmas break that he was one of the principal authors of the committee's final report.[1] In early January, Tourison treated nervous vets and family members to a taste of what was coming by publicly declaring in *New York Newsday* that the POW/MIA issue was "a hoax."[2]

But then came the public unveiling of the final report and the *really* bad news: The three goals Kerry had laid out for the committee in the "*Boston Globe* Roadmap" almost a year before had been achieved. The *Globe,* the reader will recall, had reported in February 1992 after interviewing Kerry that he planned to steer his new POW/MIA Committee to three conclusions: (1) yes, a few men were indeed left behind, (2) yes, the Pentagon bureaucracy had exhibited a mind-set to debunk the reports about live POWs, but (3) no, none are still alive and therefore it is time to put the issue to rest.[3] And now it had all come to pass.

According to the committee's official final report released by Kerry on the 13th, regarding the matter of a few men being left behind,

> [On] the question of numbers . . . , part of the pain caused by this issue has resulted from rumors about hundreds or thousands of Americans languishing in camps or bamboo cages. The circumstances surrounding the losses of missing Americans render these reports arithmetically impossible.
>
> The Committee emphasizes that simply because someone was listed as missing in action does not mean that there was any evidence . . . of survival. We may make a presumption that an individual could have survived, and that is the right basis on which to operate. But a presumption is very different from knowledge or fact, and cannot lead us—in the absence of evidence—to conclude that someone is alive. Even some of the cases about which we know the most and which show the strongest indication that someone was a prisoner of war leave us with certain doubts as to what the circumstances were. The bottom line is that there remain only a few cases where we know an unreturned POW was alive in captivity and that we do not have evidence that the individual also died in captivity.[4]

In regard to the alleged "mindset to debunk," the report declared:

> Allegations have been made in the past that our government has had a "mindset to debunk" reports that American prisoners have been sighted in Southeast Asia. Our Committee found reason to take those allegations seriously.[5]

And finally, in regard to the critical matter of living POWs, the report stated:

> Today, the U.S. spends at least $100 million each year on POW/MIA efforts.
>
> Still, the families wait for answers and, still, the question haunts, is there anyone left alive? The search for a definitive answer to that question prompted the creation of this Committee.
>
> As much as we would hope that no American has had to endure twenty years of captivity, if one or more were in fact doing so, there is nothing the Members of the Committee would have liked more than to be able to prove this fact. We would have recommended the use of all available resources to respond to such evidence if it had been found, for nothing would have been more rewarding than to have been able to re-unite a long-captive American with family and country.

Unfortunately, our hopes have not been realized. This disappointment does not reflect a failure of the investigation, but rather a confrontation with reality. While the Committee has some evidence suggesting the possibility a POW may have survived to the present, and while some information remains to be investigated, there is, at this time, no compelling evidence that proves that any American remains alive in Southeast Asia.

The Committee cannot prove a negative, nor have we entirely given up hope that one or more U.S. POWs may have survived. As mentioned above, some reports remain to be investigated and new information could be forthcoming. But neither live-sighting reports nor other sources of intelligence have provided grounds for encouragement . . . particularly over the past decade. The live-sighting reports that have been resolved have not checked out; alleged pictures of POWs have proven false; purported leads have come up empty; and photographic intelligence has been inconclusive, at best.

In addition to the lack of compelling evidence proving that Americans are alive, the majority of the Committee Members believes there is also the question of motive. These members assert that it is one thing to believe that the Pathet Lao or North Vietnamese might have seen reason to hold back American prisoners in 1973 or for a short period thereafter; it is quite another to discern a motive for holding prisoners alive in captivity for another 19 years. The Vietnamese and Lao have been given a multitude of opportunities to demand money in exchange for the prisoners some allege they hold but our investigation has uncovered no credible evidence that they have ever done so.[6]

In addition to those three principal findings, the report stated that the members had also examined the matter of a "cover-up" and had "found . . . a 'mindset to accuse' [the government of a cover-up] that has given birth to vast and implausible theories of conspiracy and conscious betrayal." Those theories, the members had declared, were "without foundation." The report went on to state that the members felt that:

The POW/MIA issue is too important and too personal for us to allow it to be driven by theory; it must be driven by fact. Witness after witness was asked by our Committee if they believed in, or had evidence of, a conspiracy either to leave POWs behind or to conceal knowledge of their fates—and no evidence was produced. The isolated bits of information out of which some have constructed whole labyrinths of intrigue and deception have not withstood the tests of objective investigation; and the vast archives of secret U.S. documents that some felt contained incriminating evidence have been thoroughly examined by the Committee only to find that the conspiracy cupboard is bare.[7]

And on the matter of cluster analysis, the report stated that the members had voted ten–two to declare such analysis "meaningless" when used to determine if live POWs remained captive.[8]

The committee's findings were reported throughout the nation the next day: "No sign MIAs alive, Senate panel reports" (*Boston Globe*), "Senate Panel Finds 'No Compelling Evidence' of POWs in Indochina" (*Washington Post*), "Senate Study on Vietnam-War Captives Concludes No U.S. POWs Remain Alive" (*Wall Street Journal*), "Senate report: Government didn't 'abandon' prisoners" (*USA Today*), "'Most exhaustive' study says no POWs were left in Asia" (*Washington Times*).

"My God, how could they have done this?" wives, sons and daughters, mothers and fathers, grandmothers and grandfathers, brothers and sisters, aunts and uncles, and countless other relatives of the MIAs asked.

"Some of the most craven, most cynical and most despicable human beings to ever run a scam," Vietnam vet Sampley declared.

## JANUARY 25, UNITED STATES SENATE

Lest anyone might have misunderstood the committee's findings, Kerry took the floor of the Senate on January 25 to restate them in his own words. Declaring that the information contained in his committee's report was "as close to the full truth as we could hope to come," Kerry told his colleagues:

> Although the Committee . . . uncovered evidence that a small number of Americans may have survived in captivity after Operation Homecoming, there is, in my view, no reason to believe that any Americans remain alive today. Yes, the possibility exists that a prisoner or prisoners could be held deep within a jungle or behind a locked door under conditions of greatest security. But there is no evidence of that, and it is hard to conceive of a reason for it. Moreover, the nations of Vietnam and Laos are becoming more and more open. Foreign businessmen, diplomats, tourists and aid workers have poured into both countries, especially Vietnam. But neither these foreigners, nor any of the thousands of individuals who have worked in the Lao or Vietnamese prison systems have come forward with a confirmed report that an American not yet accounted for is being held alive. Moreover, the Select Committee conducted an exhaustive review of files, records, photographs and other materials without developing a single, solid lead indicating that an American is currently being held in captivity. We are operating, and we should continue to operate, on the presumption that one or more Americans may still be held alive, but we cannot say that we have found evidence in the form of live-sighting reports, signals or imagery intelligence or other sources that makes us optimistic about that today.[9]

Hendon, watching Kerry's performance on C-SPAN, wondered, "Was he talking about Stewart Forbes when he mentioned all those foreign businessmen pouring into Vietnam?" Dismissing the thought for what it was—a mean-spirited reaction to all that had occurred—he found it quickly replaced by another, this one more measured and of far greater significance. The Vietnam War, Hendon realized, had just come to an end—before his very eyes—and, remarkably, at the exact same place and in the exact same manner it had begun.[10]

## THE UNLISTED, UNRETURNED POWs DO NOT GO QUIETLY

National Security Council official Nancy Soderberg had been on the job only a few days when on February 2, 1993, she received the startling memorandum about the unlisted, unreturned POWs from Richard Bush, a Democrat staffer and Asia expert employed by the House Asian and Pacific Affairs Subcommittee. Given the historical significance of Bush's memorandum, and what happened after it was received at the NSC, the entire document, absent handwritten notations on it at the time it was later declassified and released by the NSC, is presented below.

TO      Nancy Soderberg
FR      Richard Bush
DA      February 2, 1993
RE      Urgent Matter Regarding POW/MIAs in Vietnam.

### SUMMARY

I have received what appears to be credible information about American POW/MIAs in Vietnam. The information suggests that Americans may have been held alive by Hanoi <u>after</u> 1973.

I am bothering you about this because without your intervention, public release of the information is probably inevitable. That would put the Administration badly on the defensive on the POW/MIA issue, something that neither of us wants. Properly handled, you can use this to advantage with the Vietnamese and with the American public.

### BACKGROUND

The information comes by way of Steven Morris, a researcher at Harvard's Center for International Affairs and a public supporter of Clinton in the campaign. Steven is working on a history of the Vietnam War, and has recently had a chance to do research in selected Russian archives.

During the course of that research, he accidentally came upon a Russian-language copy of a September 1972 speech by a Vietnamese deputy chief of staff to the Politburo. In the speech, the general discussed how Vietnam should use the American POWs under its control in its negotiations with the Nixon Administration. In the course of his discussion, he provided data on the number of Americans that Vietnam held at that time, broken down by:

-the location of their capture (North Vietnam, South Vietnam, Laos, Cambodia)
-type (fliers, saboteurs, or other—presumably ground personnel)
-rank
-political outlook ("progressive, neutral, and reactionary")
-the number of prisons in which the men were held.

*As far as Steven or I know, this is the only case where an official Vietnamese source provides Hanoi's accounting of the number of Americans under its control. As such, it is an important benchmark against which to judge Vietnamese claims.*

Preliminary Analysis of the Numbers

I have taken Steven's information and compared (a) the Vietnamese figures regarding the number of POWs whom they had controlled who had been captured in North or South Vietnam and (b) the American numbers for Americans lost somewhere in Vietnam. (The same could be done for Laos and Cambodia). The results are as follows:

(a) As of September 15, 1972, Hanoi believed it controlled 1,097 POWs, including fliers shot down in North and South Vietnam, saboteurs captured in North Vietnam, and soldiers taken in South Vietnam. (Obviously, this figure does not include Americans shot down in the Christmas 1972 bombing).

(b) Based on current American data, the US government believes that that [sic] Vietnam could have had as many as 1,046 live Americans captured in North and South Vietnam before the end of the war. This figure includes:

-definitely, the 582 men returned in Operation Homecoming;
-definitely, 61 men who were known to have been alive at the time they were lost and who have since been determined to have died;
-almost definitely the 268 men whose remains have been returned (alternatively, these remains could be from soldiers classified as "killed in action, body not recovered").
-perhaps 135 "discrepancy cases," men who probably [were] alive at the time they were loss [sic] but whose death has not been satisfactorily verified.

The similarity between the two totals is remarkable.

Assuming the Vietnamese figures are correct (and there is no reason not to), it is hard to avoid the conclusion that on September 15, 1972 Hanoi held 515 Americans who had been captured in North Vietnam and South Vietnam but who were not returned at the time of Operation Homecoming. What happened to these men?

-They may have died from natural or unnatural causes during the September 1972–March 1973 period;
-They may have been held beyond Operation Homecoming and died from natural causes;
-They may have been held beyond Operation Homecoming and executed at some point, perhaps because the Americans did not provide aid to Vietnam or failed to meet some other expectations.
-They may still be alive.

## WHAT HAPPENS NOW

At the time Steven called me with this information on Sunday evening [January 31], his intention was to provide the New York Times with a translation of the document. Because I thought the White House should have an opportunity to decide how this information should be used, I encouraged him to think about cooperating with the Administration in a less public way. My justification was:

-If anyone is still held, going public might result in their quick death.

-If [we] catch the Vietnamese in a lie, they have shown themselves more likely to respond in the right way if we have approached them privately.

-As Steven points out, there may be more information in the Russian archives, particularly the Presidential archives; we are more likely to access if we raise the issue privately.

What I did not tell Steven was that I did not want the Clinton Administration to be hit with a public bombshell on the POW/MIA issue in its early weeks. You should be able to develop a strategy for using this information—and any further information we can get out of the Russians—against the Vietnamese in a way that maximizes results for the MIA families, does not inevitably create a new obstacle to normalization, and demonstrates the Administration's diplomatic skill.

However, as much as Steven wants to do the right thing, he does not trust the bureaucracy. If he were told just to turn over his information to DIA, he would probably say "No, thanks," and head for the Times. If he is handled properly, however, I think it will work to your advantage.

## PROPOSAL

I would suggest the following:

-that Tony [Lake, the national security advisor] or Sandy [Berger, the deputy national security advisor] meet with Steven, as evidence both of high-level interest and of your intention to maintain White House control over the response to this information.

-that Steven be hired on as a consultant to do further research in Russian archives, with perhaps some help from the Administration in getting broader access. The fact that he is working on a history of the Vietnam War gives him a decent cover.

Please let me know how you wish to proceed. Steven is waiting for me to provide some sort of answer.[11]

Richard Bush was highly respected in intelligence and foreign policy circles—he would move on to serve as national intelligence officer for East Asia at the National Intelligence Council during 1995–1997 and would later hold the Michael H. Armicost Chair in Foreign Policy Studies at the Brookings Institution—and so his analysis of the information Morris had discovered and his recommendations to Soderberg about what she and her colleagues should do about it carried weight.[12] But now, in early February, with the POW issue just having been put to rest and the move to normalize relations with the SRV rapidly gaining steam, what were Soderberg, Berger, Lake, and the president to do? Though Bush had suggested they should "develop a strategy for using this information . . . against the Vietnamese in a way that maximizes results for the MIA families [and] does not inevitably create a new obstacle to normalization," they surely knew that the two goals were now mutually exclusive: the administration could not possibly achieve both. And so, after just days on the job, Bill Clinton faced perhaps his first foreign policy crisis and the painful choice that came with it. Whom would he look to for guidance—his idol John F. Kennedy, or his friend and recent bene-factor John F. Kerry? What was it going to be, MIAs or normalized relations?

On February 11, Berger met with Morris and begged for time so administra-tion officials could acquire a copy of the Russian document and analyze its con-tents. Morris agreed.[13] U.S. officials in Moscow eventually acquired a copy of the document, translated it into English, and, on March 22, dispatched both ver-sions to Washington.[14] Documents in hand, the Clinton team finalized their strategy.

The first public indication of what that strategy would be came on March 31, when Winston Lord, formerly Kissinger's top aide at the Paris peace talks and now Clinton's nominee for the State Department's top Asia policy post, that of assistant secretary of state for East Asian and Pacific affairs, told the Senate For-eign Relations Committee the new administration was considering moving quickly toward improved relations with Hanoi. According to *The Washington Times*, Lord told the committee that "the U.S. stance toward Vietnam is 'under urgent and intensive review'" and "made clear the administration is consider-ing an acceleration of its predecessor's policy of improving ties slowly."[15]

Whether or not Lord's testimony pushed Morris to release the Russian docu-ment to *The New York Times* as he had originally intended is not known for sure, but something did, and on April 12 the "political bombshell" Bush had warned about went off. "Files Said to Show Hanoi Lied in '72 On Prisoner Totals," the *Times* reported that day in a lengthy front-page account filed from Moscow. The first several paragraphs of the story alone were staggering. The article first stated that "a document described as a top secret report written by a senior Vietnamese general and delivered to the Communist Party Politburo in Hanoi in September 1972 says that North Vietnam was holding 1,205 American prisoners of war at a time when North Vietnamese officials were saying that the number was only 368," and then went on to quote the author of the report, Gen. Tran Van Quang, the deputy chief of staff of the North Vietnamese Army, as saying "1,205 American prisoners of war located in the prisons of North Vietnam—this is a big number. Officially, until now, we published a list of only 368 prisoners of war, the rest we have not revealed."

The article noted that 591 American POWs had been released from North Vietnamese prisons at war's end, and then quoted Steven J. Morris, the forty-four-year-old researcher for the Harvard Center for International Affairs and the Russian Research Center at Harvard who first found the document in January, as saying that "[o]n the basis of this, we can conclude that more than 700 Americans had been held back by the Vietnamese at the time of Operation Homecoming." Morris was further quoted as saying: "this is the biggest hostage-taking in the his-tory of American foreign policy and we still don't know where the hostages are, what happened to them, if they are still alive."

The *Times* revelations would stun—*stun*—official Washington and prompt a furious and predictably mean-spirited debate. Charges about the Russian docu-ment's authenticity and accuracy and even about the character and motives of Morris himself would be raised, answered, and then raised again. The debate would rage white-hot for three days. Then, on the 15th, Clinton would move to end it by issuing an astonishing, historic directive to Vessey. Vessey would carry out the president's directive swiftly and efficiently, and by the 25th the window of opportunity Steven Morris had opened would be closed.

## THE FURIOUS THREE-DAY DEBATE OVER THE RUSSIAN DOCUMENT

U.S. officials, on full alert for weeks in anticipation of the Russian document becoming public, quickly declared that the document should not be believed, for a variety of reasons. Robert Sheetz, director of the DIA Special Office for POWs, declared in a memorandum dated the 12th, the day the *Times* article appeared, that "DIA believes the number 1205 could be an accurate accounting of total prisoners held, including American, ARVN, and Thai POWs . . . [but that the] numbers in this document cannot be accurate if discussing only U.S. POWs." He went on to reiterate that "DIA believes that this document is referring both to U.S. POWs and to allied POWs, particularly ARVN commandos," and suggested that the "confusion" about the prisoners' nationalities had resulted from an inaccurate translation.[16] Kerry, mysteriously, came up with the same response, telling *The New York Times* that he wondered "whether all of the 1,205 prisoners mentioned . . . were really Americans, or whether some of them might have been Lao, Thai or Korean and lumped in with the Americans because they were allies of the Americans."[17] Other unnamed U.S. officials, meantime, informed *The Washington Post* that the Russian document was riddled with erroneous statements.[18]

On the morning of the 13th, the pendulum swung back when *The New York Times* published large portions of the Russian document. The article appeared under the headline, "Vietnam's 1972 Statement on P.O.W.'s: Triple the Total Hanoi Acknowledged," and was accompanied by a picture of Morris and his declaration that the document represented a "smoking gun." Reading the text of the document for the first time, readers saw General Quang's chilling statement to the Politburo that "The question of the American prisoners of war, as is well known, we intend to resolve in the following manner: . . . Nixon must compensate North Vietnam for those enormous losses which the destructive war caused."[19] That evening, the pendulum swung even farther when, as previously noted at the beginning of this book, former Carter national security advisor Zbigniew Brzezinski and former Nixon national security advisor and secretary of state Henry A. Kissinger appeared together on the *MacNeil/Lehrer NewsHour* and characterized the document as "sustainable" and "authentic."

Then, on the 14th, the pendulum began to swing back when the *Times* reported in a dispatch from Bangkok that Vietnam's senior diplomat dealing with American affairs had declared the Russian document a "clear fabrication," because, he said, the alleged source of the information about the 1,205 Americans, PAVN General Quang, had been assigned to South Vietnam during 1972 and could not possibly have authored the report as the document had stated.[20] Then came Tourison, Kerry's former "numbers guy," who told *The Washington Post* that the number of American POWs cited in the Russian document (1,205) was "not consistent with the known facts" and (as Sheetz and Kerry had earlier suggested) actually included South Vietnamese commandos, Taiwanese commandos, and Thais captured in cross-border operations. Tourison explained that the South Vietnamese commandos, some 450 of whom he estimated had been lost on covert missions in North Vietnam during the war, were "consistently defined by the Vietnamese as 'American commandos,'" and that fact "has quite often misled people to think they were Americans when actually they were South Vietnamese who worked for us."[21] What Tourison did not tell the *Post* was that during 1985, while an analyst at DIA's Special Office for POWs and MIAs, he himself had written:

> "Vietnamese commandos were also called 'American' commandos (biet kich my) although the term 'American' was seldom used by the commandos themselves. It was used only to denote the American training given to the commandos and not intended to suggest that the commandos were Americans."[22]

## CLINTON'S HISTORIC DIRECTIVE TO VESSEY

On the 15th, the day Tourison's "explanation" received wide play in the *Post,* Vessey went to the White House to meet with the president and his top advisors. The topic: Vessey's upcoming trip to Hanoi and the crucial fork-in-the-road talks he would have with Vietnamese leaders about the explosive "1205 document." It was during this White House meeting, according to a senior official of unimpeachable integrity who was present, that Clinton, speaking directly to Vessey and issuing what the official said were obviously "marching orders," told Vessey in these exact words, "[I do] not want the 1205 document to get in the way of normalization of relations with Vietnam."[23]

A cavalier, imperious, and callous dismissal of perhaps the best single piece of intelligence ever received about American POWs being held by the North Vietnamese? Of course. But no one would know, because as is often the case in Washington, a far different account of what had been said would be prepared for public consumption. Reporting under the headline "Clinton Bars Thaw With Hanoi Until Fate of POWs Resolved," Reuters filed this story shortly after the Clinton-Vessey meeting had ended:

> WASHINGTON, April 15, Reuters—President Bill Clinton gave retired General John Vessey final instructions on Thursday on his mission to Vietnam and reaffirmed there can be no thaw in relations until the fate of U.S. war prisoners is fully resolved.
>
> Clinton told Vessey during a meeting to inform Vietnamese officials next week that unanswered questions about the fate of former U.S. servicemen missing since the Vietnam War ended in 1975 must be cleared up, a White House spokesman said.
>
> Spokesman George Stephanopoulos said the president sought Vietnam's response to a document that suggests it lied about how many American prisoners Hanoi held during the war as well as the return of remains and access to military archives.
>
> "The president stressed that he wanted the fullest possible accounting and said that only when we have that can we even consider any changes in our policy towards Vietnam."

Like any military subject, the prisoner of war/missing in action (POW/MIA) issue is sensitive for Clinton, who is politically vulnerable for having opposed the Vietnam War and avoiding service in that conflict.

The controversial document, dismissed as a fake by the Vietnamese·government, will be "the first thing General Vessey will bring up to the Vietnamese," Stephanopoulos said. . . .

On Tuesday the Pentagon urged caution over the document, which was found in Moscow archives earlier this year by a Harvard University researcher.

Asked if Clinton had made a judgment on the validity of the document, Stephanopoulos said: "We don't have any final determination. We're going to wait until we hear" what Vessey learns.[24]

## VESSEY CARRIES OUT HIS ORDERS

Morris, perhaps by now sensing what was up, made one last effort to salvage his priceless find by penning an op-ed piece for the *Post*. The piece, which appeared on the 18th, was titled simply, "The Vietnamese Know How to Count."[25] But of course, it was too little, too late—the books had long since been cooked, the president had already given his marching orders to Vessey, and Vessey had already departed for Hanoi to carry them out. One needed only to read the headlines—not the articles—that appeared in *The Washington Post* on the 20th and the 22nd to know that Vessey, the "Soldier's Soldier," had carried out those orders with stunning speed and efficiency and that, as the president wished, the "1205 document" would not become an impediment to improved U.S./SRV relations.

- "Doubts on MIA's," "U.S. General Questions Alleged POW Document," "U.S. General Expresses Doubts About Alleged POW Document," the *Post* declared in three separate headlines on the 20th.[26]
- "Vessey Faults Russian Paper On U.S. POWs, *Emissary Calls Document Inaccurate, Highly Inflated*," the *Post* declared on the 22nd.[27]

The fragging of the survivors of the seven hundred American POWs cited in the Russian document having been carried out—by the president of the United States and a retired U.S. Army four-star general, no less—administration officials moved quickly to restart their previously announced multistep plan to normalize relations with the SRV.

## THE ROAD TO NORMALIZATION

On July 2, the president announced that his administration would no longer oppose the refinancing of Vietnam's $140 million debt to the International Monetary Fund. Press reports stated that this move cleared the way for millions of dollars in potential multilateral (U.S. and other countries) aid to the SRV. He then dispatched the highest-ranking delegation to visit Vietnam since the war to Hanoi for a new series of talks. The delegation, led by Assistant Secretary of State Lord, Deputy Secretary of Veterans Affairs Herschel Gober, and Lt. Gen. Michael Ryan, USA, a top assistant to Joint Chiefs Chairman Gen. Colin Powell,

USA, provided the Vietnamese with a huge collection of captured wartime North Vietnamese documents, which delegation members suggested would help the Vietnamese find some of their own missing soldiers. "We've asked the Vietnamese to provide documents, and they've been responsive, and now we're attempting to be responsive," one U.S. official explained.[28]

Five months passed, and then Lord returned to Hanoi. According to Reuters, Lord used the occasion to praise the Vietnamese for their "extremely good" cooperation on the POW/MIA issue and to declare "as conclusively as anyone can" that no U.S. POWs remained alive in Vietnam. Reuters further quoted Lord as saying that there were no sightings in U.S. files that required further investigation and that "there has never been evidence uncovered of someone being held alive."[29] Lord then returned to the United States and, citing Hanoi's cooperation on the POW/MIA issue, recommended that the U.S. trade embargo be lifted.[30]

Clinton ordered an end to the trade embargo in early February 1994. The president's decision, front-page news all over the world, appeared in *The New York Times* under the headline, "Clinton Drops 19-Year Ban on U.S. Trade With Vietnam; Cites Hanoi's Help on M.I.A.'s."[31]

In July 1994, Lord and Gober returned to Vietnam to participate personally in a crash site excavation in the southern part of the country. Both again praised the Vietnamese for their outstanding cooperation on the POW/MIA issue.[32] Other high-level administration officials who followed in late 1994 and early 1995 and participated in similar crash site excavations in the North heaped similar praise.[33]

In late April 1995, administration officials were jolted when legendary Vietnamese general Vo Nguyen Giap called on the United States to provide reconstruction aid to Vietnam as part of the normalization process. Kyodo News Service reported on the 29th that Giap, interviewed by a Kyodo reporter in Hanoi prior to the twentieth anniversary of the fall of Saigon, declared that "the United States retains a 'moral and legal' responsibility . . . to help Vietnam recover from the war's lingering effects," and that he considered normalization a "wise policy" that offered "a chance [for the United States] to help ease the losses caused by the United States to Vietnam." Kyodo further reported that Giap drew attention during the interview to the requirement in the January 1973 Paris Peace agreements that the United States contribute to Vietnam's postwar reconstruction and noted that then "U.S. President Richard Nixon, in a secret letter to then North Vietnamese Premier Pham Van Dong, [had] put forward a target figure of 3.25 billion dollars of grant aid over five years, plus up to 1.5 billion dollars in 'other forms of aid.'" Kyodo wrote that Hanoi has long "pointed to Nixon's written pledge that the aid would be implemented 'without any political conditions,'" and declared "Vietnam's initial demand that the pledge be implemented was partly responsible for the failure of the two countries to normalize relations in 1977."[34]

Mortified by Giap's comments—and surely fearing that those comments might presage additional demands for reconstruction aid similar to those made by Hanoi during the 1977 normalization negotiations—Clinton officials moved quickly.

In mid-May, the obligatory "leaks" that usually precede major diplomatic pronouncements took place and articles began appearing in the press stating that Clinton's aides were pushing him to bite the bullet and normalize.[35] The obligatory cooling-off period that usually follows such articles then ran its course and the president convened the nation's leaders at the White House to hear his historic decision.

Standing before a packed audience in the East Room on July 11, 1995—with Kerry, McCain, Vessey, and other dignitaries assembled immediately behind him—Clinton declared it was "time to bind up our own wounds" and announced he would extend full diplomatic relations to the Socialist Republic of Vietnam.[36]

Most media reaction was positive.

Some was not.

# New York Times

**Late Edition**

New York: Today, mainly sunny, warmer. High 88. Tonight, clear, warm. Low 72. Tomorrow, hazy, hot and humid. High 92. Yesterday, high 84, low 64. Details are on page D19.

NEW YORK, WEDNESDAY, JULY 12, 1995          $1 beyond the greater New York metropolitan area.          60 CENTS

# U.S. GRANTS VIETNAM FULL TIES; TIME FOR HEALING, CLINTON SAYS

Associated Press

President Clinton announced at the White House the extension of full diplomatic recognition to Vietnam. Looking on, from left, Senators John Kerry, John McCain and Charles Robb and retired Gen. John Vessey.

## CONGRESS DIVIDED

### Move Draws Criticism and Support From Veterans' Groups

**By ALISON MITCHELL**

WASHINGTON, July 11 — Saying the time was at hand to "bind up our own wounds," President Clinton today extended full diplomatic recognition to Vietnam 22 years after the American withdrawal from a bitterly divisive war that still scars the national psyche.

Mr. Clinton, the one-time student protester who avoided serving in a war he once said he "opposed and despised," announced the normalization of relations in a brief ceremony in the East Room attended by military figures, the families of those still missing in action and members of Congress who were veterans of the war and prisoners of the Vietnamese.

"This moment offers us the opportunity to bind up our own wounds," the President said, evoking words used by Lincoln at the end of the Civil War. "They have resisted time for too long. We can now move onto common ground."

"Let this moment," he said, "in the words of the Scripture, be a time to heal and a time to build." [Excerpts, page A9.]

But the decision drew criticism as well as support from legislators, veterans' groups and families of missing servicemen.

Mr. Clinton said the United States would continue to press Vietnam for a full accounting for the 2,202 United States service personnel officially listed as missing in Southeast Asia. He said that in the months since he lifted the United States trade embargo on Vietnam in February 1994, the remains of 29 more missing Americans had been identified and Hanoi had turned over hundreds of pages of documents.

"We will keep working until we get all the answers we can," Mr. Clinton said. "Our strategy is working."

Vietnam's Prime Minister, Vo Van Kiet, responded positively to Mr. Clinton's decision in a statement broadcast Wednesday morning, Hanoi time. He pledged to continue Vietnam's cooperation in helping to account for missing Americans.

Mr. Clinton's announcement of full diplomatic relations completed a process begun by the Bush Administration in 1991 when Washington and Hanoi agreed on a detailed series of steps that would lead to recognition. Recognition was sought as eagerly by American business groups as it was bitterly opposed by the American Legion and some relatives of Americans missing in the war.

But the move was particularly risky for a President whose efforts

*Continued on Page A8, Column 4*

## Finally, Opening the Door All the Way

**By R. W. APPLE Jr.**

WASHINGTON, July 11 — The wonder is not that the United States is establishing normal diplomatic relations with Hanoi, two full decades after the fall of Saigon; the wonder is that it took so long.

**News Analysis**

Presidents have come and gone since those final apocalyptic scenes of a long, wretched war — the American Ambassador fleeing from Saigon with the embassy's flag folded under his arm, the fevered scramble for the last seats on the last helicopter out. Neither Gerald R. Ford nor Jimmy Carter nor Ronald Reagan nor George Bush could bring himself to recognize the government that Washington had demonized for so long, though Bush started down the path.

Instead, fate chose an unlikely pair of men: Bill Clinton, liberal Democrat, who like many thousands of his contemporaries managed to avoid fighting in a war that never won the full-hearted support of the American people, and John McCain,

### After a Losing Fight, U.S. Shakes Hands

conservative Republican, son and grandson of admirals, who not only fought as a Navy pilot, but, shot down, spent more than five years in an enemy prison camp.

President Clinton provided the political impetus, Senator McCain of Arizona the political cover without which Mr. Clinton might have feared to act.

There were other key players as well, notably American business, eager for its share of the riches that Vietnam, its talented people and its offshore waters seem to promise, and American diplomats, who see friendship with Vietnam as an important asset for the United States as it seeks to counter Chinese influence in Asia.

The conventional explanation for the delay was the difficulty in accounting for the Americans still carried on military rolls as missing in

action. According to the Pentagon, there are 2,202 of them if you count all of Southeast Asia, 1,618 if you count only Vietnam. Of that total, only 55, by official tally, are known to have been seen alive in captivity at some stage.

But the real reason lay much deeper within the national consciousness.

Far, far more Americans are listed as missing in the Korean War (8,170) and in World War II (78,750). Yet no one ever suggested it would be possible to account for more than a handful of them — not to mention the hundreds of thousands of north

*Continued on Page A8, Column 1*

### A Range of Emotions About Closer Ties

President Clinton's announcement that the United States would establish relations with Vietnam provoked emotions as divided as feelings about the Vietnam War itself.

Among families of servicemen still classified as missing in action, there was a sense of betrayal. For many Vietnamese refugees who have begun new lives in America, it was a day colored with sadness. In Ho Chi Minh City, many Vietnamese were hopeful that the new status would bring economic benefits. American executives hailed the announcement, but cautioned that diplomatic ties alone would not unleash an investment boom.

*Articles, pages A8-9.*

## Cancer Link Contradicted By New Hormone Study

**By GINA KOLATA**

Just one month after a study found that women who took hormone replacement therapy after menopause had an increased risk of breast cancer, another study has found no such effect.

The new study, being published today in The Journal of the American Medical Association, compared some 500 women aged 50 to 64 who had newly diagnosed breast cancer with a similar group of healthy women. The authors found no link between use of the hormones and breast cancer. In fact, they found that women who had used hormones for eight years or longer had, if anything, a lower risk of breast cancer than those who had never taken them.

therapy increased the risk of breast cancer by 30 to 70 percent.

Researchers say the conflicting results of the two highly regarded studies underscore the fact that this is science in progress: they are nowhere near obtaining a completed picture of the risks and benefits of taking hormone replacement therapy after menopause.

Other researchers are sharply divided in their interpretation of the studies. Some think the cancer risk from hormone therapy is nonexistent, or virtually so. Some, on the other hand, are convinced that the hormones do slightly increase the risk of breast cancer. But, they say, because this increase is small, as a

## INSIDE

**Files Show How U.S. Broke Soviet A-Bomb Spy Ring**

Newly declassified Government documents revealed how the United States, using a small team of codebreakers, found the first clues that the Soviet Union sought to steal the blueprints for the atomic bomb in World War II. Page A10.

**Battle of East 13th Street**

(COPYRIGHT 1995 *THE NEW YORK TIMES*. REPRINTED BY PERMISSION)

(COURTESY STEVE KELLEY, COPLEY NEW SERVICE AND THE *SAN DIEGO UNION-TRIBUNE*)

(BY PERMISSION OF STEVE BENSON AND THE CREATORS SYNDICATE, INC.)

CHAPTER 33

1995–2005

"WAR LEGACIES"

. . .

The Long Bien Bridge, which crosses the Red River 600m north of the new Chuong Duong Bridge, is a fantastic hodge-podge of repairs dating from the American War. US aircraft repeatedly bombed the strategic Long Bien Bridge (which at one time was defended by 300 anti-aircraft guns and 84 SAM missiles), yet after each attack the Vietnamese somehow managed to improvise replacement spans and return it to road and rail service. It is said that when US POWs were put to work repairing the bridge, the US military, fearing for their safety, ended the attacks.

—ROBERT STOREY AND DANIEL ROBINSON, *Vietnam,*
Lonely Planet Tourist Guide, 1997

Behind thick concrete walls and iron doors, Ho Chi Minh and other top North Vietnamese leaders hid out in secret underground tunnels [beneath the MND Citadel] during U.S. B-52 bombing raids and plotted key military strategies that led to America's defeat in the Vietnam War.

For the first time, Hanoi has opened the bunker, . . . where the 1968 Tet offensive and the fall of Saigon were planned from about 30 feet below the surface. . . .

Vietnam's Defense Ministry occupied the property until recently, relocating to another site and turning the area over to the city of Hanoi. Only a small underground section of the bunker was opened to the public, with most of the tunnels remaining closed and classified.

"No one knows how long (the tunnels are)," said professor Le Van Lan, a historian with in-depth knowledge of the site. "It's a secret. There's many legends that they go to Ho Chi Minh's mausoleum."

—"Vietnam Opens Bunker Used by Ho Chi Minh,"
Associated Press, Hanoi, 2004

The Vietnamese continued to raise the issue of postwar reconstruction aid after normalization. They raised it when U.S. Secretary of State Warren Christopher and Assistant Secretary Winston Lord traveled to Hanoi in August 1995 to formalize the normalization process and participate in ceremonies marking the opening of a new U.S. embassy.[1] They raised it again just before National Security Advisor Anthony Lake visited Hanoi in July 1996.[2] They raised it again just after America's first ambassador to the SRV, former Vietnam War POW and U.S. congressman Douglas "Pete" Peterson, arrive for work in Hanoi in May 1997.[3] They raised it *again* just prior to Secretary of State Madeleine Albright's June 1997 visit to Hanoi,[4] and *still again* several weeks after her departure.[5]

In early April 2000, General Giap raised the issue once again during a news conference held in advance of the twenty-fifth anniversary of the fall of Saigon. AP accounts of the news conference, held at the Government Guest House in Hanoi, included these statements:

> The Vietnamese general who orchestrated military victories over the French and Americans said today that Washington has an obligation to help Vietnam rebuild and must take the initiative in further normalizing relations.
>
> Americans are not only welcome back, said the white-haired general, but they have an obligation to return and rebuild the impoverished nation. . . .
>
> "We can put the past behind, but we cannot completely forget it," Giap said. "As we help in finding missing U.S. soldiers, the United States should also help Vietnam overcome the extremely enormous consequences of the war." . . .
>
> The United States has avoided the issue of war reparations, although negotiations are under way on sharing research into the effects of Agent Orange and other toxic defoliants that U.S. planes sprayed to strip away cover for communist forces.[6]

And finally, just prior to President Clinton's historic November 2000 visit to Hanoi—the first ever by a seated U.S. president—the Vietnamese raised the issue once more. The matter came up when a Foreign Ministry spokeswoman was briefing foreign correspondents in advance of Clinton's visit and was asked, "What is Viet Nam's position on compensation for war damages afflicted on Viet Nam by the Americans?" The spokeswoman responded, "The pains and losses which have been suffered by the Vietnamese people in the aftermath of the American war of aggression are heavy and huge. Solving war legacy including the effects of Agent Orange is a humanitarian imperative. It is our view that the United States should fulfill its spiritual and moral duty, make real contributions to solving war legacy."[7] "Vietnam demands war reparations," Agence France-Presse declared in a dispatch from Hanoi.[8]

The wounds of war heal slowly in the Socialist Republic of Vietnam.

And, of course, in America as well.

Where the Vietnam Veterans Memorial—the black granite "Wall" with the names of those killed and those still missing etched into it—is Washington, D.C.'s most visited memorial. And where, from coast to coast, black-and-white POW flags fly at U.S. Post Offices and at other federal facilities; at state capitols and thousands of other state and local government buildings and facilities; on the floor of the New York Stock Exchange; at airports, at manufacturing plants, and small businesses; at ball fields, stadiums, and arenas, including major league baseball fields, NFL football stadiums, and NBA basketball arenas; at NASCAR and other racetracks and sports venues; at local war memorials, union halls, VFW and American Legion halls and other places where veterans congregate; and at many private residences, especially in rural areas. And are displayed on many a semi; many a pickup truck; many an automobile; many a motorcycle—and many a motorcyclist.

And where, incredibly—or *inevitably,* as some historians see it—the Vietnam

War continues to play a key role in national politics. It did in the 2000 presidential election, when J. Thomas Burch Jr., chairman of the nation's largest POW advocacy group, the never-say-die National Vietnam and Gulf War Veterans Coalition, took the stage with Texas governor George W. Bush during the critical South Carolina GOP presidential primary and blasted Bush's opponent, John McCain, for having abandoned Vietnam vets, both those who had returned at war's end and those still missing.[9] The Arizona senator, fresh off an eighteen-point victory over Bush in the New Hampshire primary and surging in the polls at the time, was staggered. *The Washington Post* reported that Burch's comments "infuriated McCain, tapping into his combative instincts and baiting his campaign into a negative spiral." McCain never recovered and lost the state by eleven points. Bush went on to capture the Republican nomination and the presidency.

And it did again in the 2004 presidential race, when a group of former Vietnam-era Navy swift boat vets and former POWs who called themselves Swift Vets and POWs for Truth savaged Democrat nominee John Kerry with a barrage of hard-hitting television ads questioning his wartime service in Vietnam and his antiwar activities in the United States after his return.[10] The ads, which ran only in selected states but reverberated throughout the country, proved pivotal. Kerry lost to Bush in a close race.

And it may yet again, because shortly after the 2004 election, Kerry and McCain both served notice they planned to seek their party's nomination for president in 2008.

THE LONG BIEN BRIDGE . . . THE STILL-SECRET TUNNELS RUNNING FROM THE MINISTRY OF Defense Citadel to the Ho Chi Minh Mausoleum . . . reparations . . . "the Wall" . . . POW flags and the brave men they represent . . . U.S. presidential elections.

War legacies all.

# EPILOGUE

## A PROPOSAL FOR PRESIDENT BUSH

· · ·

Question [addressed to Melvin E. Richmond, chief of staff, Defense Prisoner of War/Missing Personnel Office at a DPMO briefing on POWs/MIAs, held in suburban Washington, DC, in early 2005]: How many live sighting reports have you received in the last three years?

Response: A firsthand live sighting report is one in which the individual reporting the information claims he or she has personally seen the alleged POW. Since January 1, 2002, DPMO has received 293 reports of live prisoners of war in Southeast Asia. Of these reports, 45 are firsthand live sighting reports. The remaining 248 reports are hearsay reports . . . in which the individual reporting the information heard it from someone else, and did not personally see a live American.

Of the 45 firsthand reports, 24 of the sightings were reported to have occurred during the war years, 1 was reported to have occurred during the 1976–1985 time frame, and 20 were reported to have occurred between 1986 and 2005.

Of the 248 hearsay reports, 80 were reported to have occurred during the war, 16 during the 1976–1985 timeframe, and 132 during the 1986 to 2005 timeframe. No timeframes were specified for 20 of the hearsay reports.

All reports of live Americans being held captive are analyzed and pursued accordingly.

"Responses to Follow-on Questions," DPMO, January 26, 2005

Between March 2005 and July 6, 2006, we received 63 additional reports of Americans sighted in Southeast Asia. Of the 63, 17 are firsthand reports, which we are currently analyzing. At least 9 of the 17 first hand [sic] reports are wartime sightings referring to purported Americans seen during the Vietnam War. The remaining 46 reports are hearsay. Assessing the validity of the hearsay reports is particularly difficult because it is often difficult to track down the original sources of the information.

—ROBERT J. NEWBERRY, Acting Deputy Assistant Secretary of Defense, POW/Missing Personnel Affairs, in a July 20, 2006, letter to Mrs. Dolores Alfond

When will it all end, this awful war that noted presidential historian Robert Dallek has so correctly labeled "the worst foreign policy disaster in the nation's history"?[1]

"Get real, it ended a long time ago, and it's long since past time to acknowledge that fact and move on," government officials on both sides of the Pacific and virtually all Indochina experts will tell you. But ask the activist families, the activist Vietnam vets, and perhaps many who only now for the first time have been exposed to the postwar intelligence on live POWs, and they'll tell you, "Not yet, or at least not until former Nixon national security advisor and secretary of state Henry Kissinger and members of his Paris negotiating team—current Bush Administration official John Negroponte, current assistant secretary of defense Peter Rodman, former assistant secretary of state Winston Lord, and the others, along with Generals Alexander Haig and Brent Scowcroft, who held down the fort in Washington—get on a plane and head for Hanoi and Vientiane to set right that which went so wrong. And to stay and negotiate, as Ross Perot suggested to Ronald Reagan that any U.S. negotiator should, "for as long as . . . necessary to gain release of the prisoners."

And not until, the activist families and vets will tell you, the surviving members of the Montgomery Committee and the Woodcock Commission make the same trek.

And not until President and Nobel Peace Prize winner Jimmy Carter and the surviving members of his late 1970s POW/MIA team go—former national security advisor Zbigniew Brzezinski, former secretary of defense Harold Brown, former assistant secretary of state Richard Holbrooke, and Holbrooke's deputy James Rosenthal, who served as the late Leonard Woodcock's chief of staff during the critical negotiations with Phan Hien in Hanoi in early 1977.

And not until those who served on President Ronald Reagan's POW/MIA team go as well—George Schultz, Richard Armitage, Paul Wolfowitz, Robert Mc-Farlane, Frank Carlucci, Gens. Colin Powell and John Vessey.

And not until President George H. W. Bush, his secretary of defense Dick Cheney, his secretary of state Jim Baker, and other members of the Bush/Quayle POW/MIA team also go.

And not until President Bill Clinton and those who served on his POW/MIA team—Anthony Lake, Samuel Berger, Madeleine Albright, Bill Cohen, Herschel Gober, Ambassador Pete Peterson[2]—all go.

And not until John Kerry and members of his Senate Select Committee on POW/MIA Affairs—John McCain, Harry Reid, and the others—all go as well.

"Getting the men back would demonstrate a moral commitment few nations possess," *Wall Street Journal* reporter Bill Paul wrote way back in 1985.[3] Surely that still applies today.

To exhibit America's commitment, President George W. Bush should immediately create a new negotiating team and appoint all of the above-named former officials to serve as its members. Bush should personally inform the leaders of both Vietnam and Laos that the full power and prestige of his presidency and the goodwill of the American people are behind his new team and their effort to repatriate live POWs, and should then dispatch the members to Hanoi and Vientiane with instructions to stay and negotiate for as long as is necessary to gain release of the prisoners.

A foolish suggestion, an effort doomed to failure before it even begins? Maybe. But maybe not. After all, the Vietnamese *do* know how to count! And John Kerry's partner in the infamous contrived "snap inspection" of Thanh Liet Prison, former SRV minister of construction and former Communist party general secretary Do Muoi, the underground-prison-building "counter in chief" who knows everything about live POWs, is still around as an "advisor" to the Vietnamese Communist party. So are PAVN generals Giap and Quang and a host of other high officials with intimate knowledge of the American POWs held by the SRV. Over in Laos, Khamtay Siphandone, who as supreme commander of all PL forces personally ran the American POW effort both during and after the war, now holds the country's most powerful post, that of president and chief of state of the Lao People's Democratic Republic.[4] And Souboun Srithirath, long one of the most important players on the POW front, holds the powerful position of minister to the president's office. And Dr. Ponemek Daraloy, who over twenty years ago served as vice minister of public health and in that capacity reportedly personally provided health care to some of the U.S. POWs the LPDR was holding, now serves as minister of public health.[5] First question for Ponemek: Still making your rounds, Doctor?

Fertile ground, indeed, in both countries. But ground that must be carefully cultivated if it is to become productive. And cultivated soon.

So, when *will* this awful war end? For many Americans, either when all the remaining POWs are returned safely to their homeland, or when all possible avenues for their release have been explored—forthrightly, honestly, and thoroughly—by what would be, by any measure, the most powerful and knowledgeable U.S. negotiating team ever assembled.

That's when the Vietnam War will end for many Americans. And not a minute sooner.

President George W. Bush alone can make it happen. But he must act now, before the tapping from deep inside the wreckage of Indochina finally stops.

We close by asking the reader not to accept the simplistic answers some U.S. officials will undoubtedly offer in an effort to avoid having to confront the intelligence presented in this book. Many such answers will be offered; we ask especially that you accept neither of these:

The North Vietnamese and Pathet Lao have not, as some will immediately claim, taken out all the American prisoners described in the postwar intelligence and executed them, or dynamited their underground prisons with them inside, or starved them all to death or withheld medical care until they all died. Anyone who knows the North Vietnamese and Pathet Lao knows they would never do these things. It is not in them. It is not their way. They have not killed our men, and will not; to the contrary, all available evidence shows they have gone to great lengths and incurred huge costs and risks to keep them alive.

"If some Americans are still held prisoner as you claim," other officials will say, "then we demand that you tell us where they are being held at this very moment, and if you can't then there's nothing to any of this." We respectfully reply: Only through negotiation, not military action, can these American prisoners ever be freed, so what does it matter, what difference does it make *where* they are currently being held? The North Vietnamese and the Pathet Lao know, and that is all that can matter. For now, location-wise, the only thing U.S. officials need to know is, where is the *negotiating table*?"

WE HAVE NOW COMPLETELY FULFILLED OUR RESPONSIBILITIES TOWARD "UY-STON." WE PRAY for him and for all the other brave Americans abandoned in Southeast Asia, and especially for those who, at great personal risk, held up signs saying "Come get us now." And waited. And waited. And, with the others, wait still.

Anybody here seen my old friend John?

—BILLY HENDON
—BETH STEWART
Winter 2007

**PREFACE**

   1. Bill Hendon telephone interview with Mr. Richard Fiske, 1995.

**INTRODUCTION**

   1. The events of the Bay of Pigs invasion and its aftermath were reported extensively in all major newspapers and magazines throughout the United States. See, e.g., *New York Times, Los Angeles Times, Washington Post, U.S. News & World Report* from April 1961 to July 1963. Also see www.enormouscrime .com, Introduction.

**CHAPTER 1. THE POW HOSTAGE PLAN AND ITS IMPLEMENTATION**

   1. Michael R. Beschloss, ed., *Taking Charge, the Johnson White House Tapes, 1963–1964* (New York: Simon & Schuster, 1997), p. 493.
   2. Edwin E. Moise, *Tonkin Gulf and the Escalation of the Vietnam War* (Chapel Hill: University of North Carolina Press, 1996), pp. 73–93. The torpedo tubes from the deck of one of the attacking North Vietnamese torpedo boats are on display at the Central War Museum in Hanoi.
   3. Stanley I, Kutler, ed., *Encyclopedia of the Vietnam War*, Macmillan Library Reference (New York: Simon & Schuster Macmillan, 1996), pp. 213–14; Beschloss, *Taking Charge,* pp. 200n, 493–515; Harry G. Summers, Jr., *Historical Atlas of the Vietnam War* (Boston: Houghton Mifflin, 1995), pp. 94–95. Almost all historians now agree the reported August 4, 1964, attacks did not occur. (See examples at "Vietnam War Intelligence 'Deliberately Skewed,' Secret Study Says," *New York Times*, December 2, 2005, and "Analysis Casts Doubt on Vietnam War Claims," Associated Press, December 2, 2005.)
   4. CIA NVN DOI 1964–68 SGN 16 Feb 71, Vietnam-Era POW/MIA Database, Library of Congress. (Hereafter POW/MIA.)
   5. CIA 10 Oct 67 DOI 1966, SGN 7 Oct 67, POW/MIA.
   6. CIA 10 June 71, NVN, DOI 1965–June1967; CIA IIR CS-311/06253-71, NVN, both POW/MIA.
   7. CIA 18 Apr 69 DOI 66 to Feb 68 SGN 1 Apr 69, POW/MIA.
   8. Ibid.
   9. RAND Corporation, Memorandum RM-5729-1-ARPA, January 69, "Prisoners of War in Indochina (U)," POW/MIA.
   10. DOD IIR 6 029 0584 71; DOD IIR 6 029 0606 71, both POW/MIA.
   11. DCI to DIRDIA 7 Dec 1971, POW/MIA.
   12. CMIC US 972-67, POW/MIA.
   13. CIA CS-311/03552-70, POW/MIA.
   14. DOD IIR 6 029 1015 70, POW/MIA.
   15. DOD IIR 1516 0356 71, POW/MIA.
   16. DOD IIR 1516 0115 70, POW/MIA.
   17. NIC 1479/67; DOD IIR 1516-0038-69; DOD IIR 6028 5594 68, both POW/MIA.
   18. Lt. Gen. Harold G. Moore, USA (Ret.) and Joseph L. Galloway, *We Were Soldiers Once . . . and Young* (New York: Random House, 1992), p. 185. Also CIA 814462; CIA NVN/LAOS, 6 July 67, DOI Feb 66; radio intercept 8 April yy unk; DOD report 4 184; CIA Vientiane 140950Z, all POW/MIA.
   19. US PWs in SEA 31 Aug 70 28-page report, p. 2, POW/MIA. *U.S. Army Photo
   20. Ibid.

21. *Field Manual, Counterintelligence Operations,* HQ Department of the Army, January 1972, Fig. B-10, DA Form 568.

22. DOD IIR 1516 0566 70, POW/MIA.

23. *Americans Missing in Southeast Asia: Hearings Before the House Select Committee on Missing Persons in Southeast Asia,* 94th Cong., part 3, March 17, 1976, p. 120.

24. Sedgwick D. Tourison Jr., *Talking With Victor Charlie: An Interrogator's Story* (New York: Ballantine Books, 1991), p. 114.

25. DOD IIR 6-075-5086-67, POW/MIA.

26. DOD IIR 6 017 0139 68, POW/MIA.

27. DOD P250812Z NOV 67 ZEX, POW/MIA.

28. NIC 1591/67, POW/MIA.

29. DOD IIR 1516 0023 70, POW/MIA.

30. CMIC US 1220-67, POW/MIA.

31. DOD IIR 1516 0061 72; NIC 1483/67, both POW/MIA.

32. NIC 1147/67; DOD IIR 1516 0823 70, both POW/MIA.

33. USMACV *Command History,* 1970, vol. II, p. X-29, POW/MIA.

34. DOD IIR 6 027 0139 68, POW/MIA.

35. CMIC US 1052-68, POW/MIA.

36. USMACV *Command History,* POW/MIA.

37. DOD IIR 6 029 0141 70, POW/MIA.

38. USMACV *Command History,* POW/MIA.

## CHAPTER 2. HANOI BOUND

1. See map titled "Binh Tram Locations," POW/MIA.

2. *The NVA B3 Front Rear Services System,* files of Bill Hendon.

3. CMIC US 422-67, POW/MIA.

4. NIC 296/68, POW/MIA.

5. CMIC US 562-68, POW/MIA.

6. NIC 1562/67, POW/MIA.

7. CMIC US 291-68, POW/MIA.

8. CMIC US 562-68, POW/MIA.

9. DOD IIR 1516 0631 70, POW/MIA.

10. Ibid.

11. CMIC US 485-67, POW/MIA.

12. CMIC US 753-67, POW/MIA.

13. NIC 531/68, POW/MIA.

14. CMIC US 074-67, POW/MIA.

15. CIA IIR TDCS-314/13598-67, POW/MIA.

16. CMIC US 2321-68, POW/MIA.

17. CIA IIR TDCS-314/01659-67, POW/MIA.

18. NIC 1591/67, POW/MIA.

19. CMIC US 594-68, POW/MIA.

20. CIA MFR 1 July 1968, POW/MIA.

21. Headquarters, 6499 Sp Acty Gp, Report No. 1516 0788 70, p. 27, POW/MIA.

22. CIA SGN 090433Z JUN 71, POW/MIA.

23. See examples at DOD IIR 1516 0954 70; DOD IIR 1516 0003 71; DOD IIR 6-026-0115-67; DOD IIR 1516-0194-69; DOD IIR 1516-1707-69; CIA CS 317/09060/71, all POW/MIA.

24. See examples at DOD IIR 6 029 0851 70 and DOD IIR 6 029 0394 72, both POW/MIA.

25. See example at CIA CS-311/03566-72, POW/MIA.

26. DOD IIR 1516 0045 71; CIA IIR 14 June 1971, both POW/MIA.

## CHAPTER 3. AMERICAN POWs CAPTURED BY THE PATHET LAO

1. DOD IIR 1 775 0016 72, POW/MIA.

2. CIA 471643 18 Nov 71, POW/MIA.

3. CIA 488817 9 Dec 71, POW/MIA.

4. DOD IIR 6 856 0371 71, POW/MIA.

5. CIA TDCS-314/00505-67, POW/MIA.

6. CIA Laos, Vientiane, October 8, 1971, POW/MIA.

7. CIA IIC 14699-123 DOI April–June 65; R 200628Z JAN 73; P 260830Z JAN 73, All POW/MIA.

8. See examples at CIA TDCS-314/00624-66; CIA TDCS-314/17426-67; CIA TDCS-314/08455-

68; CIA TDCS-314/11944-67; CIA TDCS-314/14907-67; CIA IN 30903; CIA TDCS-314/17292-67; CIA TDCS-314/08450-68, all POW/MIA.

9. CIA CS-311/01685-69, POW/MIA.

10. CIA TDCS-314/09796-69, POW/MIA.

11. CIA IN 65565, POW/MIA.

12. Two annotated (DOD annotations) declassified DOD reconnaissance photos taken October 11, 1969, of Ban Nakay Teu Cave Prison complex, showing American POWs (in white T-shirts) and other personnel in and about the cave complex itself and on volleyball court located just northeast of the cave complex, National Archives via Rich Daly. See also [DIA] Directorate for Intelligence, Imagery Analysis Division, Imagery Analysis Memorandum C-07-73399-79/DB-5C, to DB-4H [redacted], from DB-5C, July 17, 1979, subject: PW Camp Photography—Sam Neua Area, Laos (U); May 6, 1986, document concerning the photo titled "Appendix, Photo Evidence," both National Archives via Rich Daly.

13. CIA TDCS-314/00217-70, POW/MIA.

14. "P.O.W. Issue in Laos Linked to Bombing," *New York Times,* April 23, 1972.

15. CIA CS-311/01685-69, POW/MIA.

## CHAPTER 4. AMERICAN POWs IN NORTH VIETNAM

1. NIC 759/67, POW/MIA.

2. See examples at DOD IIR 6 029 1079 71; CIA IIR 9 NOV 72; DOD IIR 1 516 0272 72; CIA IIR 6 Dec 72; CMIC US 411-67; CIA 66388; DOD IIR 6 029 1354 70; DOD IIR 1516 0648 70, all POW/MIA.

3. CIA IIR 3 Dec 70, POW/MIA.

4. DOD IIR 1516 0169 71, with photo, POW/MIA.

5. NIC 1227/67; CMIC US 1397-68; DOD IIR 1516 0332 71; photo; unnumbered document on nine reports, all POW/MIA.

6. CMIC US 503-68; CMIC US 142-68; DOD IIR 6 028 0942 68; photo, all POW/MIA.

7. CIA IIC 15781-78, POW/MIA.

8. CIA IIC 15603-42, POW/MIA.

9. CMIC US 1076-67, POW/MIA.

10. CIA map, Reel 412; photo, both POW/MIA.

11. CIA TDCS-314/05799-68, POW/MIA.

12. DOD IIR 6 029 0466 71, POW/MIA.

13. DOD IIR 6 029 0574 71, POW/MIA.

14. CMIC US 322-68, POW/MIA.

15. DOD IIR 1516 0788 70, POW/MIA.

16. CIA IIRs 11 August 1971, 4 August 1971, all POW/MIA.

17. CIA IIC 22 July 66, POW/MIA.

18. CIA IIC 10 Oct 67, POW/MIA.

19. CIA IIC 26 Aug 68, POW/MIA.

20. "NVN Master Target List by JCS Target Number," February 27, 1967, Lyndon Baines Johnson Library, Austin, Texas.

21. DIA message 242356Z MAY 68, POW/MIA.

22. Annotated reconnaissance photo titled "North Vietnam, Ha Noi Thermal Power Plant 21 02 35N 105 50 51E," Johnson Library.

23. DOD IIR 1516-1140-69, POW/MIA.

24. CIA 280823z AUG 68, POW/MIA.

25. COMUSMACV Command History, Vol. II, 1969, pp. x-16–x-18; photo, both POW/MIA.

26. CMIC US 2082-68, POW/MIA.

27. NIC 951/68, POW/MIA.

28. CMIC US 1809-68, POW/MIA.

29. NIC 326/69, POW/MIA.

30. NIC 040/69, POW/MIA.

31. DOD IIR 6 075 0098 68, POW/MIA.

32. CIA IIR 21278, POW/MIA.

33. CIA IIR 21245, POW/MIA.

34. CIA IIC IN 20695, POW/MIA.

35. CIA IIC TDCS DB-315/03134-67, POW/MIA.

36. IIC TDCS DB-315/03191-67 photos of facility, POW/MIA.

37. Memorandum from Richard Helms to Robert S. McNamara, August 10, 1967, subject: American Prisoners in North Vietnam, with Attachments: Four Photographs, POW/MIA.

38. "Jets Hit Hanoi Bridge," *Pacific Stars and Stripes,* August 13, 1967, p. 6; Dana Bell, *Air War over*

*Vietnam,* Vol. III (Harrisburg, PA: Arms and Armour Press, 1983), photo 28; "Battle at the Bridge," *Airman,* December 1969, p. 31.

39. Portion of unnumbered, undated CIA memorandum approved for release September 23, 1983, POW/MIA. Also annotated DOD reconnaissance photo titled "Hanoi RR/HWY Bridge (Doumer Bridge)," Johnson Library.

40. Jeffery Ethell and Alfred Price, *One Day in a Long War* (New York: Random House, 1989), p. 10.

41. "U.S. PWs and PW detention sites in North Vietnam, 1 February 1968," p. 4, POW/MIA.

42. CIA IIR 20 June 1972, POW/MIA.

43. NIC 1165/68, POW/MIA.

44. DOD IIR 6 029 0980 70, POW/MIA.

45. DOD IIR 6 029 0004 71, POW/MIA.

46. CIA IIR CS-311/03332-72, POW/MIA.

47. CIA IIR CS-311/07801-71, POW/MIA.

48. CIA IIR 5 Feb 73, POW/MIA.

49. CIA IIR CS-311/103759-72, POW/MIA.

50. Authors' annotated CIA map of events and locations described ibid.

51. DOD IIR 1516-1508-69; CIA IIR 5 Nov 71; CIA IIR 7 July 72, all POW/MIA.

52. DOD IIR 1 516 0641 71, POW/MIA.

53. Prewar map of Hanoi town plan, POW/MIA.

54. Archimedes L. A. Patti, *Why Vietnam?* (Berkeley: University of California Press, 1980), p. 174.

55. See the "March Coup," pp. 41–42, 57, 72–75.

56. DOD 2 222 1393 66, POW/MIA.

57. Ibid.

58. DIA reconnaissance photograph titled "Ha Noi Detention Installation Citadel N-62, 21 02 09N 105 51 02E," POW/MIA.

59. DIA reconnaissance photograph titled "North Vietnam, Hanoi PW Camp, MND, N-67, 21 02 16N 105 51 00E," POW/MIA.

60. DOD IIR 6028 0544 68; CMIC US 236-68, both POW/MIA.

61. 5th Counterintelligence Team Interrogation Report 5CIT/32/68, POW/MIA.

62. 5th Counterintelligence Team Interrogation Report 5CIT/6/68, POW/MIA.

63. Inclosure [*sic*] 1, CMIC U.S. 1192-68, POW/MIA.

64. 5th Counterintelligence Team Interrogation Report 5CIT/6/68, POW/MIA.

65. Ibid.

66. Ibid.

67. NIC 777/68, POW/MIA.

68. DOD IIR 1516 0788 70, p. 11, POW/MIA.

69. CIA IIR 10 Dec 70, with source's sketch, POW/MIA.

70. DOD IIR 6029 0114 69, POW/MIA.

71. DOD IIR 1516 0797 70, POW/MIA.

72. CIA memo 2 Aug 68, POW/MIA.

73. Ibid.; authors' annotated map.

74. *Vietnam Courier,* September 29, 1969, p. 3; *Life,* March 22, 1968, p. 31; Harrison E. Salisbury, *Behind the Lines—Hanoi* (New York: Harper, 1967), p. 192.

75. North Vietnam Photo Intelligence Briefing Notes on Briefing Board NO. 8-68-7, August 19, 1968; Defense Intelligence Agency, *Basic Report, Military Logistics North Vietnam, Ha Noi Barracks and Storage and Possible PW Camp N-63,* February 1973, both POW/MIA.

76. Three DIA reconnaissance photos of N-63, two annotated, one unannotated, POW/MIA.

77. DOD IIR 6028 6029 68, POW/MIA.

78. CIA memorandum, May 4, 1972, subject: Possible Location of an Additional Prisoner of War Enclosure in the Hanoi–Bac Mai Area, POW/MIA; authors' annotated map.

79. DOD IIR 1516 0788 70, p. 24, POW/MIA.

80. "NVN Master Target List by JCS Target Number."

81. DOD IIR 6028-5768-68, POW/MIA; authors' annotated 1:50,000 map of Nam Dinh area.

82. "NVN Master Target List by JCS Target Number."

83. DOD IIR 1516 0788 70, pp. 23–24, POW/MIA.

84. "NVN Master Target List by JCS Target Number."

85. Authors' annotated 1:50,000 map of Thai Nguyen steel mill/Luu Xa village area and reported location of POW camp.

86. DOD IIR 1516 0566 70, POW/MIA.

87. CIA IIC TDCS-314/15074-69, POW/MIA.

**88.** DOD IIR 1516-1118-69, POW/MIA.

**89.** "NVN Master Target List by JCS Target Number."

**90.** Authors' 1:50,000 annotated map of reported location of POW camp near Phuc Yen air base.

**91.** See Chapter 2 and www.enormouscrime.com.

**92.** DOD IIR 1516 0644 70, POW/MIA.

## CHAPTER 5. 1972: THE WAR DRAWS TO A CLOSE

**1.** "U.S. Bombs Dike Gates, Hanoi Says," *Washington Post,* July 4, 1972, p. 1.

**2.** *Quan Doi Nhan Dan Viet Nam 1944–1979* (Hanoi, 1979), pp. 162–63, 184, 222–23, 245; Samuel Lipsman, Stephen Weiss, and the editors of Boston Publishing Company, *The Vietnam Experience: A False Peace* (Boston: Boston Publishing Company, 1985), p. 63; Edward Doyle, Samuel Lipsman, Stephen Weiss, and the editors of Boston Publishing Company, *The Vietnam Experience: America Takes Over* (Boston: Boston Publishing Company, 1982), p. 133; Marvin E. Gettleman, ed., *Vietnam: History, Documents, and Opinions on a Major World Crisis,* 2d ed. (Greenwich, CT: Fawcett, 1965), pp. 421ff.

**3.** For a detailed analysis of the damage the North Vietnamese say was caused by the first sixty days of Linebacker raids, see FBIS, Asia and Pacific, July 19, 1972, North Vietnam, K1.

**4.** FBIS, Asia and Pacific, June 28, 1972, North Vietnam, K12.

**5.** FBIS, Asia and Pacific, June 23, 1972, North Vietnam, K9; June 26, 1972, North Vietnam, K25; July 3, 1972, North Vietnam, K22; July 12, 1972, North Vietnam, K26; July 12, 1972, North Vietnam, K25.

**6.** "Hanoi Attacks Near Hue Continue for Ninth Day," *Washington Post,* June 28, 1972.

**7.** FBIS, Asia and Pacific, July 17, 1972, North Vietnam, K26; July 20, 1972, North Vietnam, K16; July 18, 1972, North Vietnam, K19; July 21, 1972, North Vietnam, K22; July 24, 1972, North Vietnam, K24.

**8.** To their great pleasure, U.S. officials later learned that as a result of these bombing attacks, North Vietnamese cadres reportedly began claiming that Fonda "had been an agent of the U.S. government sent to acquire intelligence for targeting purposes." airgram A-29, to SECSTATE WASHDC [and multiple addressees], from Amembassy Kuala Lumpur, subject: 16 years detention in North Vietnam [source name redacted], p. 12, DIA Source file 1610/4232/4233/4234, POW/MIA.

**9.** Luu Van Loi and Nguyen Anh Vu, *Le Duc Tho–Kissinger Negotiations in Paris* (Hanoi: The Gioi Publishers, 1996), pp. 254–256.

**10.** John Negroponte recalls that the number of PAVN troops allowed to stay in the South under the October 8 proposal was ten divisions. (Select Committee on POW/MIA Affairs, United States Senate, Deposition of John Negroponte, p. 51.) Wartime CINCPAC Adm. U. S. Grant Sharp stated in his 1978 critique of the war that the figure was 210,000–220,000 PAVN (Admiral U.S.G. Sharp, *Strategy for Defeat* [San Rafael, CA: Presidio Press, 1978], p. 260.) Maj. Gen. John E. Murray, USA, U.S. defense attaché in Saigon during 1973 and 1974, later estimated the number of communist troops remaining in the South to be 250,000. (Stephen Weiss, Clark Dougan, David Fulghum, Denis Kennedy, and the editors of Boston Publishing Company, *The Vietnam Experience: A War Remembered* (Boston: Boston Publishing Company, 1986), p. 144.) South Vietnamese President Thieu repeatedly stated that the figure was 300,000.

**11.** Henry Kissinger, *White House Years* (Boston: Little, Brown, 1979), pp. 1345–49.

**12.** Marvin Kalb and Bernard Kalb, *Kissinger* (Boston: Little, Brown, 1974), pp. 356, 357.

**13.** Ibid., p. 357.

**14.** Kissinger, *White House Years,* pp. 1356–57.

**15.** Ibid., pp. 1345–46.

**16.** H. R. Haldeman, *The Haldeman Diaries* (New York: Putnam, 1994), pp. 515–17.

**17.** "A Deal With Hanoi, a Duel With Thieu," *Newsweek,* October 30, 1972, p. 24.

**18.** Kissinger, *White House Years,* p. 1366.

**19.** Seymour M. Hersh, *The Price of Power: Kissinger in the Nixon White House* (New York: Summit Books, 1983), p. 585.

**20.** Nguyen Tien Hung and Jerrold L. Schecter, *The Palace File* (New York: Harper, 1986), p. 83.

**21.** Ibid., p. 85.

**22.** Kissinger, *White House Years,* p. 1370.

**23.** Kalb and Kalb, Kissinger, p. 364.

**24.** Hung and Schecter, *Palace File,* p. 90.

**25.** Kalb and Kalb, Kissinger, pp. 366–68.

**26.** Ibid., p. 369.

**27.** Ibid., p. 372.

**28.** Kissinger, *White House Years,* p. 1382.

29. Oriana Fallaci, *Interview with History* (New York: Liveright, 1976), p. 48.

30. Kissinger, *White House Years*, p. 1382.

31. Ibid., p. 1385.

32. Hung and Schecter, *Palace File*, p. 103.

33. Ibid.

34. Kissinger, *White House Years*, p. 1386.

35. Hung and Schecter, *Palace File*, p. 104.

36. Ibid., p. 105.

37. Ibid.

38. Richard M. Nixon, *RN: The Memoirs of Richard Nixon* (New York: Grosset & Dunlap, 1978), p. 702.

39. Hung and Schecter, *Palace File*, p. 105.

40. "Thieu Assails Peace-Plan Terms, Asks Guarantee, Hanoi Pullout," *New York Times*, October 25, 1972.

41. Hung and Schecter, *Palace File*, pp. 104–05.

42. " 'Peace at Hand,' Matter of Weeks: Kissinger," AP/UPI in *Pacific Stars and Stripes*, October 28, 1972, p. 1.

43. Hung and Schecter, *Palace File*, pp. 383–84.

44. Kissinger, *White House Years*, p. 1412.

45. Larry Engelmann, *Tears Before the Rain* (New York: Da Capo Press, 1997), pp. 185–86.

46. Hung and Schecter, *Palace File*, p. 126.

47. Ibid., pp. 126–27.

48. Kissinger, *White House Years*, p. 1415.

49. " 'The Cowboy . . . on His Horse,' Kissinger Talks About Peace and Kissinger," *Sunday Star and Washington Daily News*, November 19, 1972, p. 1.

50. "Saigon Senate Backs Thieu," *New York Times*, November 21, 1972.

51. Kissinger, *White House Years*, p. 1417.

52. Ibid.; Loi and Vu, *Tho-Kissinger Negotiations*, p. 358.

53. Loi and Vu, *Tho-Kissinger Negotiations*, p. 359.

54. Ibid., p. 363.

55. Ibid., pp. 365–67.

56. Ibid., p. 366.

57. Kissinger, *White House Years*, p. 1418.

58. Ibid.

59. Loi and Vu, *Tho-Kissinger Negotiations*, p. 380.

60. Ibid., pp. 380–82.

61. Ibid.

62. Kissinger, *White House Years*, p. 1422; Nixon, *RN*, pp. 722–23.

63. Kissinger, *White House Years*, p. 1424.

64. Nixon, *RN*, p. 723.

65. Kissinger, *White House Years*, p. 1425.

66. Haldeman, *Haldeman Diaries*, p. 542.

67. Nixon, *RN*, pp. 723–24.

68. Kissinger, *White House Years*, p. 1426.

69. Ibid.

70. White House memorandum, "The President's Meeting with the Joint Chiefs of Staff," Thursday, November 30, 1972, 10:15 A.M., the Oval Office, National Archives.

71. Nixon, *RN*, p. 724.

72. Loi and Vu, *Tho-Kissinger Negotiations*, p. 388.

73. Kissinger, *White House Years*, pp. 1428–29.

74. Nixon, *RN*, p. 731.

75. Kissinger, *White House Years*, p. 1444.

76. Ibid., p. 1443.

77. Loi and Vu, *Tho-Kissinger Negotiations*, p. 418.

78. Kissinger, *White House Years*, p. 1444.

79. Loi and Vu, *Tho-Kissinger Negotiations*, p. 419.

80. Memorandum from Central Intelligence Agency, Office of the Director, to Director, Defense Intelligence Agency, October 18, 1972, subject: ICC Official's Comments on Enemy Exploitation and Deployment of U.S. POWs; and on the Alleged Deaths of Several, with attached intelligence report P 270358Z OCT 72, both POW/MIA.

**81.** Karl J. Eschmann, *Linebacker: The Untold Story of the Air Raids Over North Vietnam* (New York: Ivy Books, 1989), pp. 217–21.

**82.** "Twelve Days of the Aerial Dien Bien Phu," *Nhan Dan*, n.d., Library of Congress.

**83.** John T. Smith, *The Linebacker Raids* (London: Arms & Armour Press, 1998), pp. 123–24.

**84.** Loi and Vu, *Tho-Kissinger Negotiations*, p. 419. In truth, the B-52s did not strike targets in the port of Haiphong in force until the night of December 22. (Brig. Gen. James R. McCarthy and Lt. Col. George B. Allison, *Linebacker II: A View From the Rock* (Maxwell Air Force Base, AL: Air War College, 1979); Eschmann, *Linebacker*; Smith, *Linebacker Raids*; Marshall L. Michel III, *The Eleven Days of Christmas* (San Francisco: Encounter Books, 2002).

**85.** Larry Guarino, *A POW's Story: 2801 Days in Hanoi* (New York: Ivy Books, 1990), pp. 328–29.

**86.** Kissinger, *White House Years*, p. 1447.

**87.** "Nixon Halts Bombs; Hanoi to Negotiate," AP in *Pacific Stars and Stripes*, January 1, 1973, p. 1; Kissinger, *White House Years*, pp. 1458–59; Loi and Vu, *Tho-Kissinger Negotiations*, p. 422.

## CHAPTER 6. JANUARY 1973: PEACE AT A VERY HIGH PRICE

**1.** "The Pressures on Hanoi," *Newsweek*, February 26, 1973, p. 13.

**2.** "The Late December 1972 U.S. Blitz on North Viet Nam," DRVN Commission for Investigation of the US Imperialists' War Crimes in Viet Nam, January 4, 1973, POW/MIA.

**3.** Nixon, *RN*, pp. 744–45.

**4.** Ibid., pp. 743–744.

**5.** Defense Intelligency Agency, January 3, 1973, Memorandum for the Chairman, Joint Chiefs of Staff, subject: Information on PW Camps, with enclosures and appendices including DOD Bomb Damage Assessment Photograph mission BH Q225, 22 Dec 72, POW/MIA; authors' annotated map.

**6.** Loi and Vu, *Tho-Kissinger Negotiations*, pp. 424–25.

**7.** Deposition of William Sullivan, Select Committee on POW/MIA Affairs, United States Senate, July 20, 1992, pp. 102, 131, Inventory of the Records of the Senate Select Committee on POW/MIA Affairs, 102d Cong. (1991–1992), National Archives.

**8.** Deposition of George H. Aldrich, Select Committee on POW/MIA Affairs, July 14, 1992, p. 40, ibid.

**9.** Kissinger, *White House Years*, p. 1464.

**10.** Loi and Vu, *Tho-Kissinger Negotiations*, p. 327.

**11.** Deposition of Henry Alfred Kissinger, Select Committee on POW/MIA Affairs, September 14, 1992, p. 28, Inventory of the Records of the Senate Select Committee on POW/MIA Affairs.

**12.** Report by SACSA [Special Assistant for Counterinsurgency and Special Activities] to the Joint Chiefs of Staff, *Ransoming U.S. and Other Free World Prisoners of War in North Vietnam,* October 19, 1966; memorandum for the secretary of defense, subject: Ransoming of US and Other Free World Prisoners of War in North Vietnam, JCSM-683-66, Oct. 22, 1966, both POW/MIA.

**13.** *Americans Missing in Southeast Asia*, Part 5, July 21, 1976, p. 40.

**14.** Loi and Vu, *Tho-Kissinger Negotiations*, pp. 112–16.

**15.** Ibid., p. 179.

**16.** Ibid., p. 186.

**17.** Ibid., p. 204.

**18.** Kissinger, *White House Years*, p. 1035.

**19.** Loi and Vu, *Tho-Kissinger Negotiations*, pp. 263–64.

**20.** Ibid., p. 264.

**21.** Kissinger, *White House Years*, p. 1355.

**22.** Loi and Vu, *Tho-Kissinger Negotiations*, p. 439.

**23.** "31. Zhou Enlai and Pham Van Dong, Beijing, 13 April 1968," Cold War International History Project, Woodrow Wilson International Center for Scholars, Washington, DC, virtual archive.

**24.** Kissinger, *White House Years*, pp. 1461–62.

**25.** Kissinger cable Z 112000Z JAN 73, FM PARIS HAKTO 21 TO THE SITUATION ROOM, POW/MIA; Loi and Vu, *Tho-Kissinger Negotiations*, p. 439.

**26.** Loi and Vu, *Tho-Kissinger Negotiations*, p. 440.

**27.** Memorandum of conversation, participants: Prime Minister Souvanna Phouma, Vice Prime Minister; General Alexander M. Haig, Jr., Vice Chief of Staff, United States Army; Ambassador Godley; John Negroponte; NSC Staff, Thursday, January 18, 1973, 2:30–4:00 P.M., Souvanna Phouma's Residence, Vientiane, files concerning Kissinger's later February 1973 trip to Thailand, Cambodia, Laos, and Vietnam, National Archives.

**28.** Memorandum of conversation, participants: President Lon Nol; Prime Minister Hang Thun Hak; General Alexander M. Haig, Jr., Vice Chief of Staff, United States Army; Ambassador Emory

Swank; John Negroponte; NSC Staff, Thursday, January 18, 1973, 10:00. A.M.–12 noon, President
Lon Nol's Residence, Phnom Penh, ibid.

29. Kissinger, *White House Years,* p. 1470.

30. Loi and Vu, *The-Kissinger Negotiations,* pp. 444–45.

31. Ibid., p. 445.

32. Deposition of Henry Alfred Kissinger, p. 131.

33. National Security Council, January 29, 1973, memorandum of conversation, participants:
Mr. Henry A. Kissinger and 22 Representatives of the National League of Families of American Pris-
oners and Missing in Southeast Asia . . . [and others, including, briefly, the President], Roosevelt
Room, the White House, January 26, 1973, 11:00 A.M.–12 noon, subject: U.S. Prisoners of War in
Southeast Asia, National Archives.

34. P R 300040Z Jun 70, POW/MIA.

35. October 8, 1970, memorandum, subject: [redacted] North Vietnam List of U.S. PW's,
POW/MIA.

36. Undated memorandum from the Secretary of Defense, "Memorandum for the Secretaries of
the Military Departments," subject: December 1970 PW List from NVN, with attached document
"Guidance for Use in Response to Queries by PW/MIA Families," POW/MIA.

37. Ibid.

38. R 112218Z JUN 69 FM DIA TO RUFDWP/USDAO PARIS FRANCE, POW/MIA.

39. Deposition of Eugene F. Tighe, Jr., Select Committee on POW/MIA Affairs, February 27, 1992,
p. 47; Inventory of the Records of the Senate Select Committee on POW/MIA Affairs.

40. Deposition of Thomas Hinman Moorer, Select Committee on POW/MIA Affairs, April 22,
1992, p. 162, ibid.

41. Deposition of Eugene F. Tighe, Jr., p. 51; also Defense Intelligence Agency, "Americans Missing in Indochina: An Assessment of Vietnamese Accountability," prepared by Defense Intelligence
Agency Special Office for Prisoner of War and Missing in Action, pp. 35–36, POW/MIA.

42. Deposition of Henry Alfred Kissinger, pp. 37–38.

43. Deposition of Winston Lord, Select Committee on POW/MIA Affairs, May 12, 1992, p. 22,
Inventory of the Records of the Senate Select Committee on POW/MIA Affairs.

44. Ibid., pp. 69, 64–66.

45. Ibid., p. 66.

46. "Vietnam Peace Pacts Signed; America's Longest War Halts," *New York Times,* January 28, 1973.

47. "Agreement on Ending the War and Restoring Peace in Vietnam," in *Treaties and Alliances of
the World* (Detroit: Gale Research Co., 1981), pp. 377–79.

48. Ministry of National Defence Democratic Republic of Vietnam, "U.S [*sic*] Pilots Captured in
the Democratic Republic of Viet Nam," Inventory of the Records of the Senate Select Committee on
POW/MIA Affairs.

49. Provisional Revolutionary Government of the Republic of South Viet Nam, "List of U.S [*sic*]
Military Personnel Captured in South Viet Nam," ibid.

50. Provisional Revolutionary Government of the Republic of South Viet Nam, "List of Civilian
Personnel of the United States and Other Foreign Countries Captured in South Viet Nam," ibid.

51. Z 271956Z JAN 73 ZFF-6, FM USDEL FRANCE TO RUEKJCS/NMCC PENTAGON WASHDC
FLASH, POW/MIA.

52. "Message from the President of the United States to the Prime Minister of the Democratic Republic of Vietnam, February 1, 1973," Gerald R. Ford Library, Ann Arbor, MI.

53. Memorandum for the Chairman, Joint Chiefs of Staff, March 21, 1973, subject: Information
Pertaining to PW/MIA Situation in Laos, enclosure: Personnel on the 1 February 1973 Pathet Lao
List, POW/MIA.

54. Abstract of Deposition of Mr. Rodman, Select Committee on POW/MIA Affairs, pp. 77–78,
Inventory of the Records of the Senate Select Committee on POW/MIA Affairs.

55. *POW/MIA'S,* p. 147.

56. Deposition of Eugene F. Tighe, Jr., pp. 45–53.

57. O 020400Z FEB 73 FM THE SITUATION ROOM TO COLONEL GUAY PARIS, authors' files.

58. CIA Memorandum for Dr. Henry A. Kissinger, February 2, 1973, quoted in CIA Memorandum
for Dr. Henry A. Kissinger from Office of the Director, dated March 20, 1973, paragraph 1, POW/MIA.

59. Three intercepts of enemy radio traffic, dated in order of presentation, 7 Feb 73, 5 Feb 73 01
58z, and 6 Feb 73 00 12z, POW/MIA.

60. DOD map titled "Binh Tram Locations," with authors' annotation, POW/MIA.

61. Memorandum for Henry A. Kissinger, from Brent Scowcroft, subject: Forthcoming Trip, February 6, 1973, National Archives.

## CHAPTER 7. FEBRUARY 1973: A HISTORIC JOURNEY TO HANOI

1. Daily Report Supplement, "Asia and Pacific, the Agreement and Protocols on Ending the War and Restoring Peace in Vietnam (24 January 1973)," FBIS, January 31, 1973, No. 21, Supp. 5.
2. "Say Hanoi Claims Victory Over U.S. in Vietnam War," *Nhan Dan,* quoted by AP in *Pacific Stars and Stripes,* January 26, 1973.
3. "VWP CC Issues Slogans Greeting People's Victory," FBIS, Asia and Pacific, January 29, 1973, North Vietnam, K10.
4. "VNA Reports Activities in Hanoi on First Day of Peace," FBIS Asia and Pacific, January 29, 1973, North Vietnam, K24.
5. Hanoi Domestic News Service, February 1, 1973 in FBIS, Asia and Pacific, February 5, 1973, North Vietnam, K18.
6. FBIS, Asia and Pacific, January 30, 1973, North Vietnam, K9.
7. FBIS, Asia and Pacific, January 29, 1973, North Vietnam, K12.
8. "VNA Describes Hanoi on First Tet After War Years," FBIS, Asia and Pacific, February 5, 1973, North Vietnam, K16.
9. "Return to Hanoi," FBIS, Asia and Pacific, February 6, 1973, North Vietnam, K14.
10. Ibid.
11. Z 100233Z FEB 73 FM THE SITUATION ROOM TOHAK 60, National Archives.
12. Henry Kissinger, *Years of Upheaval* (Boston: Little, Brown, 1982), p. 23.
13. Z 101825Z FEB 73 FM HENRY A. KISSINGER HAKTO 22, National Archives.
14. O 111627Z FEB 73 FM HENRY A. KISSINGER HAKTO 30, National Archives.
15. Kissinger, *Years of Upheaval,* p. 29.
16. Ibid., pp. 33–34.
17. Deposition of William Sullivan, p. 210.
18. Z 120010Z FEB 73 FM HENRY A. KISSINGER HAKTO 33, National Archives.
19. Ibid.
20. Gia Lam Field, located just across the Red River and just southeast of the eastern terminus of the Long Bien Bridge, was Hanoi's main wartime civilian airport. Gia Lam was the point of departure for all American POWs released in Hanoi at Operation Homecoming. It should not be confused with the outlying military airfield where Kissinger had landed, the Phuc Yen MiG base, which is located near Noi Bai, some ten miles north of the city. After the war, Phuc Yen was converted to partial civilian use and renamed Noi Bai International Airport.
21. Z 122025Z FEB 73 FM HENRY A. KISSINGER HAKTO 44, National Archives.
22. O 140900Z FEB 73 FM HENRY A. KISSINGER HAKTO 59, National Archives.
23. Z 122025Z FEB 73 FM HENRY A. KISSINGER HAKTO 44.
24. Howard and Phyllis Rutledge, with Mel and Lyla White, *In the Presence of Mine Enemies* (Charlotte, NC: Commission Press, 1977), p. 105.
25. Rear Admiral Jeremiah A. Denton Jr., *When Hell Was in Session* (Washington, DC: Morley Books, 1997), p. 240.
26. Everett Alvarez Jr. and Anthony S. Pitch, *Chained Eagle* (New York: Donald I. Fine, 1989), p. 256.
27. Denton, *When Hell Was in Session,* p. 240.
28. "VNA Reports Hanoi Release of 116 U.S. POW'S." FBIS, Asia and Pacific, February 12, 1973, North Vietnam, KG.
29. Capt. Jim Mulligan, *The Hanoi Commitment* (Virginia Beach, VA: RIF Marketing, 1981), p. 283.
30. Z 122025Z FEB 73 FM HENRY A. KISSINGER HAKTO 44.
31. Ibid.
32. Ibid.
33. Kissinger, *Years of Upheaval,* p. 42.
34. Z 122025Z FEB 73 FM HENRY A. KISSINGER HAKTO 44.
35. O 201020Z FEB 73 FM HENRY A. KISSINGER HAKTO 111, National Archives.

## CHAPTER 8. FEBRUARY–MARCH 1973: THE "MOST TORTURED" ISSUE, "THE TOUGHEST SALE"

1. North Vietnamese copy of communiqué: "Hanoi Releases Communique on Kissinger's Visit," FBIS Asia and Pacific, February 15, 1973, North Vietnam, K1; U.S. copy: O 131005Z FEB 73 FM H. A. KISSINGER HAKTO 47 COR CY, National Archives.
2. Quoted in O 151403Z FEB 73, FM THE SITUATION ROOM TOHAK 189, TO LORD/RODMAN FOR DR KISSINGER . . . subject: Morning News Summary, National Archives.
3. "Scott Predicts N. Viet Aid Despite Opposition," *Pacific Stars and Stripes,* February 18, 1973, p. 6.

4. "Mills Says President Can Impound Funds," *Washington Post,* February 11, 1973, p. A25.

5. "The 'Post-Vietnam' Period Begins," *Washington Post,* February 15, 1973, p. A20.

6. Haldeman, *Haldeman Diaries,* p. 579; also Memorandum of Conversation, participants: President Nixon; H. R. Haldeman; Lt. Gen. Brent Scowcroft, Deputy Assistant to the President for National Security Affairs, February 15, 1973—Thursday, Oval Office, National Archives.

7. Memorandum of Conversation, participants: President Nixon; Elliot Richardson, Secretary of Defense; Joint Chiefs of Staff; Major General Brent Scowcroft, Deputy Assistant to the President for National Security Affairs, Thursday, February 15, 1973, 1:00 P.M., Pentagon, National Archives.

8. Memorandum of conversation, participants: President Nixon; Vice President Agnew; Christopher Soames, EC Commissioner; William P. Rogers, Secretary of State; George P. Shultz, Secretary of the Treasury; Roy L. Ash, Director, Office of Management and Budget; Elliot L. Richardson, Secretary of Defense; James T. Lynn, Secretary of Housing and Urban Development; Peter M. Flanigan, Assistant to the President; Brent Scowcroft, Deputy Assistant to the President for National Security Affairs; Friday, February 16, 1973, 9:30 A.M., Cabinet Room, White House, National Archives.

9. "Special National Assembly Session Marks Victories," FBIS, Asia and Pacific, February 21, 1973, North Vietnam, K1.

10. Text of Pham Van Dong Feb 20 Report to National Assembly, FBIS, Asia and Pacific, February 22, 1973, North Vietnam, K6.

11. "Special National Assembly Session Marks Victories."

12. "Hanoi Reports Other Speakers at Special Assembly, FBIS, Asia and Pacific, February 22, 1973, North Vietnam, K14; "National Assembly Unanimously Approves Paris Agreement," ibid., K4.

13. "Report on Closing Session of National Assembly," FBIS, Asia and Pacific, February 23, 1973, North Vietnam, K4–K7.

14. Ibid.

15. Message of the Prime Minister of the Democratic Republic of Viet Nam to the President of the United States of America (February 23, 1973), Gerald R. Ford Library.

16. "Rogers: Don't Bar N. Viet Aid," *Pacific Stars and Stripes,* February 23, 1973, p. 1.

17. Fulbright: "Fulbright: I'll Back Hanoi Aid In Return for Cuts of Military," AP in *Pacific Stars and Stripes,* February 20, 1973; Kennedy: "On Providing Aid to Yesterday's Enemies," *Time,* March 5, 1973, p. 16; Stevens: UPI in O 200736Z FEB 73 FM THE SITUATION ROOM TOHAK 283, National Archives; Scott: "And Now, Reconstruction," *Time,* February 26, 1973, pp. 17–19.

18. Richard F. Newcomb, *A Pictorial History of the Vietnam War* (Garden City, NY: Doubleday, 1987), p. 277.

19. Rowland Evans and Robert Novak, "Direct Aid for North Vietnam?" *Pacific Stars and Stripes,* March 16, 1973 p. 10.

20. "And Now, Reconstruction."

21. "Kissinger: Hanoi Aid is Investment in World Peace," AP in *Pacific Stars and Stripes,* February 24, 1973, p. 9.

22. "Kissinger: N. Viets Won't Hide POWs on Us," AP in *Pacific Stars and Stripes,* February 28, 1973, p. 3.

23. "Nixon: Hanoi Aid Won't Cut Domestic Funds," UPI in *Pacific Stars and Stripes,* March 4, 1973, p. 21.

24. "No Aid to Hanoi if They Violate Pact—Richardson," UPI in *Pacific Stars and Stripes,* March 7, 1973, p. 2.

25. USDEL JEC PARIS 06507, 1973 MAR 15 PM 6 57Z to SECSTATE WASHDC IMMEDIATE, subject: US-DRV Joint Economic Commission—Opening Session, files of Gareth Porter.

26. USDEL JEC PARIS 06761 1973 MAR 19 PM 6 06 Z to SECSTATE WASHDC IMMEDIATE, subject: US-DRV Joint Economic Commission—Second Session, ibid.

27. USDEL JEC PARIS 06876 1973 MAR 20 PM 5 37 to SECSTATE WASHDC, subject: Initial Comments on Performance of the DRV Delegation, US-DRV Joint Economic Commission, ibid.

28. USDEL JEC PARIS 07210 to SECSTATE WASHDC IMMEDIATE, subject: US-DRV Joint Economic Commission—Third Session, ibid.

29. USDEL JEC PARIS 07335 1973 MAR 23 PM 6 44 Z to SECSTATE WASHDC IMMEDIATE, subject: US-DRV Joint Economic Commission—Fourth Session, ibid.

30. Ibid.

## CHAPTER 9. MID- TO LATE MARCH 1973: THE RETURNEE DEBRIEFS TELL OF HUNDREDS OF AMERICAN POWs HELD BACK

1. Memorandum for Dr. Henry A. Kissinger, Assistant to the President for National Security Affairs, from Office of the Director, Central Intelligence Agency, March 20, 1973, subject: Indication

that the Communists are Holding Previously Unlisted U.S. POW's As a Future Bargaining Tool, POW/MIA.

2. O R 220948Z MAR 73 FM AMEMBASSY VIENTIANE TO SECSTATE WASHDC, National Archives.

3. Naval message R 231035Z MAR 73, subject: PWs in Laos: Swedish TV Crew Returns From Samneua. The passage about U.S. POWs read, specifically, "SEOM USPWS" POW/MIA.

4. "U.S. Fears Laos POWs will be Used as 'Pawns,'" UPI in *Pacific Stars and Stripes,* March 25, 1973.

5. Department of State telegram 056484 272320Z MAR 73, subject: PW'S—Walter Cronkite, National Archives.

6. See examples in "Homecoming (Egress Recap) Summary of all Non-Returnees Reported and Candidate DIA Identifier, PW/MIAs Not Listed to Be Returned," 24 APR 1973; "Homecoming (Egress Recap) Casualty Resolution Report, Name Known," 02 SEP 1977, pp. 78, 130; Naval Message P 020053Z 73; ONI 53-1A, all POW/MIA. Also see Deposition of Robert George Dussault, Select Committee on POW/MIA Affairs, October 8, 1992, pp. 37–38, Inventory of the Records of the Senate Select Committee on POW/MIA Affairs.

7. "Highlights of Operation Homecoming," U.S. Department of Defense, undated 55-page report on Operation Homecoming, POW/MIA.

8. *Hearings Before the House Select Committee on Missing Persons in Southeast Asia,* Part 3, pp. 317–18.

9. "Thermal Power Plant (TPP) PW Camp Complex," undated twelve-page DOD working paper; two-page portions of debriefs of returnees Lt. Cmdr. Tschudy and Lt. Cmdr. Galanti, all POW/MIA.

10. For returnees' unclassified descriptions of the trip up the trail, see Frank Anton with Tommy Denton, *Why Didn't You Get Me Out?* (Arlington, TX: Summit Publishing Group, 1997), pp. 109–21, and Zalin Grant, *Survivors* (New York: Da Capo Press, 1994), pp. 236–49.

## CHAPTER 10. SPRING 1973: "A 'CANCER' ON THE PRESIDENCY"

1. Nixon, *RN,* p. 791.

2. Ibid., pp. 791–99.

3. Ibid.

4. Haldeman, *Haldeman Diaries,* p. 13. To hear the actual audiotape, go to www.HPOL.org.

5. Nixon, *RN,* p. 799.

6. Haldeman, *Haldeman Diaries,* p. 13.

7. Full text of McCord letter in "McCord: Members of My Family . . . Fear for My Life," *Washington Post,* March 24, 1973, p. A10.

8. "Watergate Perjury, Pressure Charged," ibid., p. 1.

9. Haldeman, *Haldeman Diaries,* p. 610.

10. G. Gordon Liddy, *Will: The Autobiography of G. Gordon Liddy* (New York: St. Martin's Press, 1980), p. 408; *Washington Post,* March 24, 1973, p. 1.

11. *Washington Post,* March 24, 1973, p. 1.

12. Nixon, *RN,* p. 806.

13. "McCord Lists More Names In Watergate," *Washington Post,* March 26, 1973, p. 1.

14. Nixon, *RN,* p. 806.

15. Ibid.

16. "M'Cord Says Dean, Magruder Knew in Advance of Bugging," *Los Angeles Times,* March 26, 1973, p. 1.

17. Haldeman, *Haldeman Diaries,* pp. 602–03.

18. Nixon, *RN,* p. 807.

19. "McCord Charges Backed," *Washington Post,* March 27, 1973, p. 1.

20. Nixon, *RN,* pp. 808–09.

21. Haldeman, *Haldeman Diaries,* pp. 610–11.

22. Nixon tapes of March 27, 1973, POW/MIA'S, p. 886.

23. "Hanoi Radio Attributes Remarks to Former POWs," Hanoi International News Service, FBIS, Asia and Pacific, IV, March 30, 1973, North Vietnam, K8.

24. "Address to the Nation About Vietnam and Domestic Problems," March 29, 1973, Public Papers of the Presidents, Richard Nixon, 1973, pp. 234–38, National Archives.

25. Monica Crowley, *Nixon in Winter* (New York: Random House, 1998), p. 266.

26. Ibid., p. 265.

27. "Viets Claim Additional POWs Held," AP in *Pacific Stars and Stripes,* April 9, 1973, p. 6.

28. "Chicagoan Tells of Seeing Missing Son in Cambodia," *Chicago Tribune,* April 9, 1973, p. 5.

29. "Woman Says Son Is P.O.W. in Cambodia," AP in *New York Times,* April 9, 1973, p. 4.

30. "She 'Saw' POW Son," *Evening Star and Washington Daily News,* April 9, 1973, p. 1.

31. *POW/MIA'S,* p. 97.

32. Draft, "Conversation 893–13, Conversation between the President and Roger Shields, Manolo Sanchez enters during the conversation," Oval Office, April 11, 1973, 12:04–12:29 P.M., p. 2, National Archives.

33. Ibid., p. 11.

34. Ibid., pp. 14–15.

35. Ibid., pp. 15–16, 23.

36. *POW/MIA'S,* p. 97.

37. 011035Z JUN 73, FM AMEMBASSY SAIGON TO SECSTATE WASHDC IMMEDIATE 2984 LIMITED OFFICIAL USE SAIGON 10389, Hendon files.

38. "Told to Attack Peace Units, Alleged Defector Reports," AP in *New York Times,* June 9, 1973.

39. Untitled transcript of statements by John Marsh declassified November 13, 1992, from [former State Department POW/MIA official Frank] Seiverts Files, POW/MIA 9203138, Box 14, Inventory of the Records of the Senate Select Committee on POW/MIA Affairs. Seiverts told Hendon that this transcript was from an oral history Marsh had provided.

40. *POW/MIA'S,* p. 94.

## CHAPTER 11. SPRING, SUMMER, AND FALL 1973: THE COLLAPSE OF THE JEC TALKS • THE COLLAPSE OF THE PARIS PEACE ACCORDS

1. Henry Kissinger, *Years of Renewal* (New York: Simon & Schuster, 1999), pp. 1059–60.

2. Kissinger, *Years of Upheaval,* p. 416.

3. "Rogers: Don't Bar N. Viet Aid," *Pacific Stars and Stripes.*

4. Deposition of Winston Lord, pp. 276–77.

5. "Communique Signed at Paris on Implementation of Viet-Nam Agreement," *Department of State Bulletin,* July 9, 1973, pp. 45–53.

6. Telegram from chief of the U.S. Delegation to the Joint Economic Commission Maurice J. Williams to Rogers, June 18, 1973, in Gareth Porter, *Vietnam: The Definitive Documentation of Human Decisions* (Stanfordville, NY: Earl M. Coleman Enterprises, 1979), Vol. 2, p. 638.

7. USDEL JEC PARIS 16859, 1973 JUN 19 PM 518Z to SECSTATE WASHDC IMMEDIATE, subject: US-DRV Joint Economic Commission: Tenth Session, June 19, 1973, files of Gareth Porter.

8. USDEL JEC PARIS 17226, 1973 JUN 22 PM 133Z to SECSTATE WASHDC IMMEDIATE, subject: US-DRV Joint Economic Commission: Discussions on Third-Country Procurement and Possible Multilateral Assistance, Gareth Porter files. Given the negotiating history relating to a cease-fire in Cambodia, it is clear that Williams was simply playing the Kissinger "game." Kissinger had raised the matter of a Cambodian cease-fire repeatedly in his past talks with Tho, but according to Kissinger aide George Aldrich, "The Vietnamese told us they couldn't produce it. . . . They would say quite earnestly that they would do everything possible. But they couldn't commit themselves to a settlement." (Gareth Porter, "The Broken Promise to Hanoi," *The Nation,* April 30, 1977, pp. 520–21.) According to another Kissinger aide, Peter Rodman, "The North Vietnamese were in good faith when they said they had no control over their Cambodian comrades. . . . I think in good faith they did make an effort to get a ceasefire in both Laos and Cambodia . . . it's one of those occasions in which they were not lying to us . . ." (Deposition of Peter Rodman, pp. 125, 127, 167.) According to Kissinger himself, Tho, unable to convince the Khmer Rouge to quit fighting, had suggested that Kissinger meet personally with Cambodian leader Prince Norodom Sihanouk in an attempt to arrange a cease-fire, but Kissinger had rejected this idea. (Z 122025Z FEB 73 FM HENRY A. KISSINGER HAKTO 44.) When Chinese Premier Chou En-lai had made the same suggestion, he had again refused. (Memorandum for the President, from Henry A. Kissinger, February 16, 1973, National Archives.)

9. USDEL JEC PARIS 17256, 1973 JUN 22 PM 446Z to SECSTATE WASHDC IMMEDIATE, subject: US-DRV Joint Economic Commission: Twelfth Plenary Session, June 22, 1973, files of Gareth Porter.

10. USDEL JEC PARIS 17978, 1973 JUN 29 PM 631Z to SECSTATE WASHDC IMMEDIATE, subject: US-DRV Joint Economic Commission: 14th Plenary Session and Expert-Level Meeting, June 29, 1973, ibid.

11. USDEL JEC PARIS 17862, 1973 JUN 28 PM 1744Z to SECSTATE WASHDC IMMEDIATE, subject: US-DRV Joint Economic Commission: Present Status of Negotiations, ibid.

12. USDEL JEC PARIS 18478, 1973 JUL 5 PM 657Z to SECSTATE WASHDC IMMEDIATE, subject: US-DRV Joint Economic Commission: 15th Plenary Session and Expert-Level Meeting, July 5, 1973, ibid.

**13.** USDEL JEC PARIS 19330, 1973 JUL 13 PM 2003Z to SECSTATE WASHDC IMMEDIATE, subject: US-DRV Joint Economic Commission: Negotiating Situation as of July 13, ibid.

**14.** USDEL JEC PARIS 19617, 1973 JUL 15 PM 641Z to SECSTATE WASHDC IMMEDIATE, subject: US-DRV Joint Economic Commission: Negotiating Situation as of July 17, ibid.

**15.** USDEL JEC PARIS 19623, 1973 JUL 17 PM 654Z to SECSTATE WASHDC, subject: Proposed First Year Program, ibid.

**16.** Telegram from U.S. Chief of Delegation Williams to Rogers, July 23, 1973, in Porter, *Vietnam,* Vol. 2, pp. 639–40.

**17.** USDEL JEC PARIS 19877, 1973 JUL 19 PM 914Z to SECSTATE WASHDC, subject: Progress in Negotiation of Proposed First Year Program of Reconstruction Assistance, files of Gareth Porter.

**18.** "DRV Delegation Issues Statement on DRV-U.S. Economic Talks," FBIS, Asia and Pacific, IV, July 26, 1973, North Vietnam, K1.

**19.** Hanoi Radio Comment, FBIS, Asia and Pacific, IV, July 26, 1973, North Vietnam, K1.

**20.** "U.S. in No Rush To Talk About Aid With North Viets," AP in *Pacific Stars and Stripes,* July 29, 1973, p. 7.

**21.** Kissinger, *Years of Renewal,* p. 478.

**22.** Kissinger, *Years of Upheaval,* p. 29.

**23.** Porter, "Broken Promise to Hanoi," p. 521.

**24.** "Reportage on Airport Ceremony, Welcoming Banquet for Castro," FBIS, Asia and Pacific, IV, September 13, 1973, North Vietnam, K4–K8; "Castro-Led Delegation's Activities in DRV Reported," FBIS, Asia and Pacific, IV, September 17, 1973, North Vietnam, K2–K10.

**25.** "Reportage on Airport Ceremony, Welcoming Banquet for Castro"; "VNA Carries Text of Le Duan, Castro 12 Sep Banquet Speeches," FBIS, Asia and Pacific, IV, September 4, 1973, North Vietnam, K1–K8.

**26.** "Castro-Led Delegation's Activities in DRV Reported."

**27.** Authors' color map titled "Locations in Quang Tri Province, RVN, Visited by Premier Fidel Castro, 15 Sept 1973"; "Castro Activities in Liberated Area Reported," FBIS, Asia and Pacific, IV, September 19, 1973, South Vietnam, L1–L4; photo, "Workers in June 1973 restore the lines in the southern town of Dong Ha, now administered by the Provisional Revolutionary Government," in Nguyen Khac Vien, *Tradition and Revolution in Vietnam,* Indochina Research Center, May 1975, Fall Collection, Howard University Library, Washington, DC. The statement that the famous bridge at Dong Ha had "fallen" into the riverbed was only partially accurate. For an excellent account of how U.S. Marines and ARVN soldiers heroically blew the bridge and sent it crashing into the Cua Viet River during the 1972 Easter Invasion, see John Grider Miller, *The Bridge at Dong Ha* (Annapolis, MD: Naval Institute Press, 1996).

**28.** "Text of Castro's 15 Sep Speech in Liberated Area," FBIS, Asia and Pacific, IV, September 18, 1973, South Vietnam, L4–L7; "Castro, Le Duan Address Hanoi Banquet Given By Cubans," FBIS, Asia and Pacific, IV, September 18, 1973, North Vietnam, K1–K7; "RVN Spokesman Ridicules Castro's Quang Tri Visit," FBIS, Asia and Pacific, IV, September 18, 1973, South Vietnam, L7–L8.

**29.** "Castro Activities in Liberated Area Reported."

**30.** "Text of Castro's 15 Sep Speech in Liberated Area."

**31.** Photo with description, "raising the NLF flag among PLAF fighters in Quang Tri province (South Viet Nam)," "Fidel Castro in Viet Nam," *Nhan Dan,* no. 17, October 1973, p. 5; "Castro Activities in Liberated Area Reported."

**32.** "Castro Activities in Liberated Area Reported."

**33.** Ibid.

**34.** Peter Macdonald, *Giap* (New York: W. W. Norton, 1993), p. 333.

**35.** General Van Tien Dung, *Our Great Spring Victory* (New York: Monthly Review Press, 1977), p. 10.

**36.** See three photos of General Dung in Bernard Fall, *Hell in a Very Small Place* (New York: Da Capo Press, 1985), and one in Philip Gutzman, *Vietnam: a Visual Encyclopedia* (London: PRC Publishing, 2002), p. 413; three photos of General Dung at Trung Gia in a "Shadowy Foe in the Flesh" *Life,* July 19, 1954, pp. 18–19; and one photo at Paul Doumer Bridge in Stanley I. Kutler, ed., *Encyclopedia of the Vietnam War* (New York: Simon & Schuster Macmillan, 1996), p. 140.

**37.** Macdonald, *Giap,* p. 333.

**38.** Richard Nixon, *No More Vietnams* (New York: Arbor House, 1985), p. 183.

**39.** "People's Liberation Armed Forces Command Order," FBIS, Asia and Pacific, October 15, 1973, South Vietnam, L2–L3, in Porter, *Vietnam,* Vol. 2, p. 641.

**40.** Kissinger, *Years of Upheaval,* p. 371.

**41.** Quoted in Kalb and Kalb, *Kissinger,* p. 435.

**42.** Robert C. McFarlane and Zofia Smardz, *Special Trust* (New York: Cadell & Davies, 1994), pp. 150, 155, 159, 188–89, 257, 331.

**43.** Deposition of Robert C. McFarlane, Select Committee on POW/MIA Affairs, June 5, 1992, pp. 4, 52–55, Inventory of the Records of the Senate Select Committee on POW/MIA Affairs.

**44.** Oliver L. North and David Roth, *One More Mission: Oliver North Returns to Vietnam* (Grand Rapids, MI: Zondervan, 1993), p. 67.

**45.** Kalb, *Kissinger,* p. 434.

**46.** Nixon, *RN,* p. 968.

## CHAPTER 12. 1974: THE END OF THE LINE FOR RICHARD NIXON

**1.** The White House, Memorandum of Conversation, participants: Secretary Henry A. Kissinger, General Brent Scowcroft, Sven Kraemer, NSC, 20 members of the Executive Board of the National League of Families, February 9, 1974—12:10 P.M.–1:00 P.M., the Roosevelt Room, Inventory of the Records of the Senate Select Committee on POW/MIA Affairs.

**2.** Nixon, *RN,* p. 975.

**3.** "Former Nixon Aides Indicted In Cover-up of Watergate Case," *Washington Post,* March 2, 1974, p. 1.

**4.** "Jaworski Appeals to Supreme Court," *Washington Post,* May 25, 1974, p. 1.

**5.** "Court Orders Nixon to Yield Tapes; President Promises to Comply Fully," *Washington Post,* July 25, 1974, p. 1.

**6.** "Judiciary Panel Formally Begins Historic Debate," ibid.

**7.** "Judiciary Committee Approves Article to Impeach President Nixon, 27 to 11," *Washington Post,* July 28, 1974, p. 1.

**8.** "2d Impeachment Article Voted," *Washington Post,* July 30, 1974, p. 1.

**9.** "Article III Approved by Panel," *Washington Post,* July 31, 1974, p. 1.

**10.** Nixon, *RN,* p. 1057.

**11.** "Nixon Resigns," *Washington Post,* August 9, 1974, p. 1; "Nixon Resigns," *New York Times,* August 9, 1974, p. 1.

**12.** Nixon, *RN,* pp. 1086–90.

**13.** "Ford Gives Pardon to Nixon, Who Regrets 'My Mistakes,'" *New York Times,* September 9, 1974, p. 1.

**14.** "Watergate 25," a June 1997 package commemorating the 25th anniversary of the Watergate burglary, www.washingtonpost.com.

**15.** "4 in Watergate Break-in Given Freedom by Sirica," *Washington Post,* July 12, 1975, p. 4.

**16.** "McCord Parole," *Washington Post,* May 28, 1975, p. 10.

**17.** "Watergate 25."

## CHAPTER 13. JANUARY-APRIL 1975: THE END OF THE LINE FOR SOUTH VIETNAM

**1.** Dung, *Our Great Spring Victory,* p. 25.

**2.** Ibid., pp. 23–24.

**3.** Ibid., pp. 35–42.

**4.** Military History Institute of Vietnam, *Victory in Vietnam: The Official History of the People's Army of Vietnam, 1954–1975,* trans. Merle L. Pribbenow (Lawrence: University Press of Kansas, 2002), pp. 370–72.

**5.** Dung, *Our Great Spring Victory,* pp. 71–72.

**6.** Ibid., p. 77.

**7.** Allen Dawson, *55 Days: The Fall of South Vietnam* (Englewood Cliffs, NJ: Prentice-Hall, 1977), pp. 57–58.

**8.** General Cao Van Vien, *The Final Collapse* (Washington, DC: Center of Military History, United States Army, 1983), pp. 77–78.

**9.** Harry G. Summers Jr., *Historical Atlas of the Vietnam War* (Boston: Houghton Mifflin, 1995), p. 196.

**10.** Dung, *Our Great Spring Victory,* p. 100.

**11.** Ibid., pp. 119–20.

**12.** Summers, *Historical Atlas of the Vietnam War,* p. 198.

**13.** Dung, *Our Great Spring Victory,* pp. 151–52.

**14.** Ibid., pp. 152–53.

**15.** Ibid., p. 215.

**16.** Military History Institute, *Victory in Vietnam,* p. 419.

**17.** Dung, *Our Great Spring Victory,* p. 251.

**18.** Tiziano Terzani, *Giai Phong! The Fall and Liberation of Saigon* (New York: St. Martin's Press, 1976), p. 175.

**19.** "Le Duc Tho Speech," Saigon Domestic News Service, FBIS, Asia and Pacific, IV, May 16, 1975, South Vietnam, L6.

**20.** "Le Duc Tho Speech," Saigon Domestic News Service, FBIS, Asia and Pacific, IV, May 19, 1975, South Vietnam, L2.

## CHAPTER 14. MAY–DECEMBER 1975: "CUBA SUGGESTED TO US TO KEEP THEM BACK" • CONGRESS INVESTIGATES THE FATE OF THE POWs AND MIAs

**1.** "Fleeing Planes Crash," "74 Planes to U-Tapao Base," *Bangkok Post,* April 30, 1975, p. 1; "Flight to RP" (photo), *Manila Bulletin Today,* May 1, 1975, p. 1.

**2.** "RP Refugee Ship Due Today from Vietnam," *Manila Bulletin Today,* May 1, 1975, p. 1; "3,000 Refugees Due," *South China Morning Post,* Hong Kong, May 4, 1975, p. 1; "Rescue Vessels Bring in 27,000 [to the Philippines]," *South China Morning Post,* Hong Kong, May 5, 1975.

**3.** See FBIS, Asia and Pacific, IV, South Vietnam, May 8–June 3, 1975.

**4.** Memorandum dated 25 May 1983, "My Two Year Reeducation Camp Activities," Katum Camp File, POW/MIA.

**5.** Document LN 182-82, DIA Source file 0941, POW/MIA.

**6.** In neighboring Laos, the Pathet Lao had begun capturing and imprisoning pro-U.S. military officers and government officials by employing the same methods the North Vietnamese had used so successfully in the conquered South. First, PL authorities announced in the press that high-ranking soldiers and officials of the Royal Lao government should pack their clothes and report to local schools for a brief "seminar." Like their allies the South Vietnamese, the unsuspecting Royal Lao had willingly complied, but once inside the schools, they had been arrested and, following indoctrination sessions, had been taken to jungle prisons for long-term imprisonment. By year's end, tens of thousands of former Royal Lao soldiers and officials, including virtually the entire officers' corps, would be confined under the most brutal conditions imaginable in Pathet Lao "seminar" camps throughout the country. Many would not survive; many who did would not be released until the mid- to late 1980s. ("Lao Govt Ready for US Property Talks," *Bangkok Post,* July 6, 1975, p. 1; "The Pathet Lao Armed Forces—A Paper Tiger?" *Bangkok Post,* November 10, 1975, p. 6; R 181024Z Feb 88, subject: IIR 6 024 0210-88/List of Former Ranking RLAF Officers in Seminar Camp #6, Mouang Het (D); R 201416Z Nov 87, subject: IIR ◇◇6 024 0106◇◇ 88/Security Officer in Seminar Camp Numbers 4, 6 and the Mouang Poua Labor Camp; R 031400Z Mar 88, subject: IIR 6 024 0249-88/Ranking Royal Lao Officers (U); R 190618Z Nov 87, subject: IIR 6 024 0093 88/Royal Lao Officers in Seminar Camp 6; R 140720Z Sep 87, subject: IIR 6 024 0155 87/Seminar Camp at Phone Hong and Muang Het Districts, Laos; excerpts from R 061923Z Feb 87, subject: POW-MIA: Absence of American POWs at Reeducation Camps in Attopeu Province, Laos From August 1975 to September 1986; Locations of Reeducation Camps in Attopeu Province; CIA FIR dated April 21, 1982, subject: Reeducation (Seminar) Camps in Xieng Khouang, Attopeu, Phong Saly, Savannakhet and Vientiane Provinces [DOI: 1975–1981]; R290351Z Nov 86, subject: Absence of Americans From September 1975 to September 1986 at Four Reeducation Camps in Sepone District, Savannaket Province; Conditions and Location of Four Reeducation Camps in Sepone District; R 181232Z May 83, subject: Indochinese Refugees: Lao "Seminarians," all from Laos Seminar Camp Files, POW/MIA.

**7.** "Pham Van Dong Speech," FBIS, Asia and Pacific, IV, June 4, 1975, North Vietnam, K3–K11.

**8.** "Reports Mark National Assembly Session 4 Jun," "Nguyen Duy Trinh Report," FBIS, Asia and Pacific, IV, June 5, 1975, North Vietnam, K1–K3; also CIA speed letter, February 25, 1976, subject: Americans Missing in Action as a Result of the Vietnam Conflict, CIA Files, POW/MIA.

**9.** "Hanoi Radio Commentary Connects U.S. Aid to MIA Issue," FBIS, Asia and Pacific, IV, June 11, 1975, North Vietnam, K1.

**10.** "11 Jun NHAN DAN Commentary," FBIS, Asia and Pacific, IV, June 11, 1975, North Vietnam, K2.

**11.** Robert Kaylor, UPI dispatch, "MIA 6-11," Shields Files, POW/MIA.

**12.** "White House Openly Scraps Paris Agreement, Hanoi Says," "Attitude 'Unacceptable,' Station Commentary: Erroneous Statements by the United States," FBIS, Asia and Pacific, IV, June 16, 1975, North Vietnam, K1–K2.

**13.** "White House Openly Scraps Paris Agreement, Hanoi Says."

**14.** For a copy of the letter, see "Pham Van Dong Replies to U.S. Congressmen on MIA's," FBIS, Asia and Pacific, IV, July 8, 1975, North Vietnam, K1–K2.

**15.** "Hanoi links MIA search to US aid," *Bangkok Post,* July 8, 1975.

16. *Americans Missing in Southeast Asia, Summary, Conclusions, and Recommendations,* December 1976, p. 1.

17. Excerpt from Press, Department of State, September 16, 1975, No. 481-A, "Question and Answer Session Following the Informal Remarks by the Honorable Henry A. Kissinger, Secretary of State, Before the Southern Governors Conference," p. 6, Department of State Library, Washington, DC.

18. *Hearings Before the House Select Committee on Missing Persons in Southeast Asia,* Part 2, p. 93. This claim, made earlier to the POW/MIA families at the White House, would become Kissinger's stock response when asked about the possibility that POWs might be alive in Vietnam. "Why would they hold them?" he would ask. "There is no reason for them to hold them," he would declare. But, of course, those familiar with the issue knew that, rather than "Why would they hold them?" in the absence of the North Vietnamese receiving the reconstruction funds Kissinger himself had promised them at Paris and in Hanoi, the more appropriate question was, "Why would they give them back?"

19. Ibid., Part 5, pp. 47, 56; undated "report on November MIA Committee meeting with Kissinger," quoting J. Angus MacDonald, Select Committee staff director, with accompanying note, both Gareth Porter files. Also "U.S., Vietnam Hold Two-Hour Paris Meeting," *Washington Post,* November 13, 1976, p. A8.

20. Memorandum for the record, December 6, 1975, Paris, France, House Select Committee on Missing Persons in Southeast Asia, p. 9, Gareth Porter files.

21. "Hopes of US-Hanoi Friendship in Talks," UPI in *Bangkok Post,* December 9, 1975.

22. Memorandum for the record, subject: Meeting with the President of the United States, December 17, 1975, pp. 1–2, Gareth Porter files.

23. "Chairman Montgomery's Opening Remarks, Conference with DRV Officials, Hanoi, North Viet Nam, 21 December 1975," p. 4, Gareth Porter files.

24. Meeting notes of D. Gareth Porter, pp. 25–27, Gareth Porter files.

25. Ibid., p. 27.

26. *Americans Missing in Southeast Asia, Final Report Together With Additional and Separate Views of the Select Committee on Missing Persons in Southeast Asia,* December 13, 1976, Appendix I, pp. 249–53.

27. Meeting notes of Gareth Porter, pp. 27–28.

28. *Hearings Before the House Select Committee on Missing Persons in Southeast Asia,* Part 3, p. 130.

29. Ibid., p. 99. The CIA's Foreign Broadcast Information Service offered a slightly different account of what had transpired at the meeting. In an article appearing in the December 24, 1975, edition of *FBIS Trends,* FBIS analysts, quoting the VNA, first stated that Dong had "assured the delegation that 'responsible DRV organs' would continue searching for information on American personnel still missing, but at the same time he repeated Hanoi's demand for U.S. aid." Then, again quoting the VNA, the FBIS analysts went on to write that "the U.S. Congressional delegation 'also saw the U.S. responsibility . . . and obligation to heal the wounds of war in Vietnam.'" ("Trends in Communist Media," FBIS December 24, 1975, p. 17, Vietnam, "DRV Releases American Bodies; Pham Van Dong Sees Congressmen.")

30. "Communists Take Over in Laos," *Bangkok Post,* December 4, 1975, p. 1.

31. "Hanoi to Send Goods, Fuel by Road to Laos," *Bangkok Post,* December 9, 1975, p. 1. Other press accounts at the time offered other interesting insights into the mind-set of the PL and the way they intended to do business. According to "Laos Barters People for Petrol" in the *Bangkok Post* on December 6, the Pathet Lao, three days after taking power, had traded two hundred Thai businessmen and shop owners they had detained to the Thai government for twenty Laotians the Thais were holding and two thousand two hundred liters of gasoline. The *Post* reported that terms of the exchange were "a strong indication of the petrol shortage which Laos has been suffering, along with a scarcity of other necessary commodities, since the closure of the border in the middle of last month."

32. *Americans Missing in Southeast Asia,* Part 2, p. 99.

33. "Hanoi Pledge to US," *Bangkok Post,* December 24, 1975, p. 1.

34. Letter dated October 20 1978, beginning "Dear Mrs Anh," DIA Source file 0287, POW/MIA.

35. P 050517Z FEB 86, JCRC Report T86-034, DIA Source file 3893, Inventory of the Records of the Senate Select Committee on POW/MIA Affairs.

## CHAPTER 15. 1976: MONTGOMERY CONTINUES HIS INVESTIGATION • AMERICAN POWs SEEN IN CAPTIVITY IN BOTH NORTH AND SOUTH VIETNAM

1. *Americans Missing in Southeast Asia, Final Report,* p. 115.

2. National Security Council memorandum for Brent Scowcroft, from Thomas J. Barnes, Les Janka, subject: Congressional Request for Copies of the Nixon–Pham Van Dong Exchange of Correspondence, March 19, 1976, Gerald R. Ford Library.

**3.** Department of State Memorandum of Conversation, subject: Missing in Action in Indochina, March 12, 1976, 8:00 A.M., the Secretary's Dining Room, p. 8, Gerald R. Ford Library.

**4.** *Hearings Before the House Select Committee on Missing Persons in Southeast Asia*, Part 5, p. 180.

**5.** Ibid.

**6.** "Radio Scores U.S. for Neglecting Commitments," FBIS, Asia and Pacific, IV, April 16, 1976, North Vietnam, K1.

**7.** "Former President Nixon's Message to Prime Minister Pham Van Dong," *Department of State Bulletin,* June 27, 1977, pp. 674–75.

**8.** *Americans Missing in Southeast Asia*, Part 2, Appendix, pp. 103–31.

**9.** Ibid.

**10.** Navy pilot John S. McCain III had been shot down over Hanoi in October 1967 while attacking the Yen Phu Thermal Power Plant in northwest Hanoi. Grievously injured during ejection (both of his arms and his right leg had been broken), he parachuted into Truc Bach Lake, just west of the power plant, and almost drowned before he was pulled from the lake by a group of bystanders. After being beaten by an angry mob as he lay injured on the ground, he was taken away by Vietnamese authorities and imprisoned. (Summary Report of LCDR John S. McCain III's Experience in North Vietnam, Mission and Shootdown, DIA Source file 7984, POW/MIA.) Following a brief period of initial detention at Hoa Lo Prison (the "Hanoi Hilton") and subsequent hospitalization for treatment of his injuries, McCain had been deployed for two years as a human shield at the "Plantation" POW camp, the converted film studio located directly across the street from the MND Citadel compound in Hanoi (target JCS 57). He had been transferred back to Hoa Lo, then to Bang Liet/Thanh Liet Prison just southwest of Hanoi (which the returnees called "Skidrow"), back to Hoa Lo, back to "Skidrow," back to Hoa Lo once again and, in the closing days of the war, back to the "Plantation." He had been released from the "Plantation" on March 14, 1973. (John McCain with Mark Salter, *Faith of My Fathers* [New York: Random House, 1999]; also *Places and Dates of Confinement of Air Force, Navy and Marine Corps Prisoners of War Held in North Vietnam 1964–1973, a Technical Report*, Headquarters USAF Analysis Program, Southeast Asia Prisoner of War Experience, Series 800-2, June 1975, pp. 43–45, and multiple declassified U.S. government documents, all Bill Hendon files.)

**11.** *Americans Missing in Southeast Asia*, Part 3, February 18, 1976, pp. 39–43.

**12.** Ibid.

**13.** *Americans Missing in Southeast Asia*, Part 3, March 3, 1976, p. 106.

**14.** Al Santoli, *Everything We Had* (New York: Random House, 1981), p. 234.

**15.** "Mac's Facts no. 45 (Room 7, Hanoi Hilton)" at http://www.eos.net/rrva/nampom/room _7.html; Defense Prisoner of War/Missing in Action Office Reference Document, "U.S. Personnel Missing, Southeast Asia [and Selected Foreign Nationals] [U] Alpha, Chronological and Refno Reports," June 1995, p 27; John McCain with Mark Salter, *Worth the Fighting For: A Memoir* [New York: Random House, 2002], p. 11; "McCain and Salter, *Faith of My Fathers*, p. 307.

**16.** Ernest C. Brace, *A Code to Keep* (New York: St. Martin's Press, 1988), and McCain and Salter, *Faith of My Fathers*.

**17.** *Americans Missing in Southeast Asia*, Part 3, March 31, 1976, p. 175.

**18.** Ibid., p. 183.

**19.** Department of Defense Intelligence Information Report 2 240 5013 79, "Alleged Sighting of US Persons in the SRV," date: 790924, with enclosure "Report of Interview, Subject: Interview With Vietnamese Refugee Re: US Persons in VM," September 18, 1979, Shields Files and NLF Files, POW/MIA.

**20.** P 151537Z May 87, subject: IIR 6-014-0017-87/Long Binh Area Sighting; P 242002Z Nov 87, subject: IIR 1 517 0034 88/Sighting of Live Americans in Vietnam, both DIA Source file 6244, POW/MIA.

**21.** JCRC I81-004, 7 March 1981, subject: Refugee Report, Alleged Sighting of Two Caucasians Near Re-Education Camp, DIA Source file 0953, POW/MIA.

**22.** R 270945Z SEP 88, Subject: JCRC RPT T88-463; Observation of Four Male Caucasians Believed to be US PWS IN DONG NAI, DIA Source file 5679, POW/MIA.

**23.** DIA Source file 0941, POW/MIA.

**24.** Testimony of former RVNAF Captain in R 260956Z Feb 88, DIA Source file 6556, Inventory of the Records of the Senate Select Committee on POW/MIA Affairs.

**25.** Statement of unknown reeducation camp inmate in RUEOFUAO834, paragraphs 5 and 6, February 24, POW/MIA; relevant portions of 1981 report of DIA Source 10029, with cover letter of March 6, 1981, to Mr. Lance Downing, DIA Source file 10029, POW/MIA.

**26.** May 25 1983, statement of unknown former reeducation inmate in Katum Camp File, POW/MIA.

**27.** See example at R 260812Z JUL 89, subject: IIR 6 024 0298 89/Caucasian Working at Camp Group 1, Hoang Ling Son in Jul 76, DIA Source file 10601, POW/MIA.

**28.** Report of official debrief of Vietnamese refugee Thai Phi Long, May 5–7, 1981, American Embassy, Copenhagen, Denmark, DIA Source file 0941, POW/MIA.

**29.** R 070550Z Sep 88, subject: JCRC Report T88-458, Firsthand Sighting of 60 to 70 Alleged US PW Held in Northern Vietnam During June 1976, DIA Source file 8432, POW/MIA.

**30.** JCRC M81-019, 20 August 1981, subject: Refugee Report, Caucasian Prisoners Sighted Near Son La, DIA Source file 1072, POW/MIA.

**31.** See examples at R 211207Z Apr 86, subject: JCRC Report T86-141, Caucasian Seen in Vietnam, and P 240359Z Apr 85, subject: JCRC Report I85-016, Live Sighting of American in Yen Bai Reed, both DIA Source file 3150, POW/MIA.

**32.** JCRC M80-015, 31 January 1980, subject: Refugee Report, Alleged Sighting of Caucasians in Captivity, NVN, DIA Source file 0558, POW/MIA.

**33.** JCRC HK82-020, 13 July 1982, Subject: Refugee Report, Alleged Sighting of Caucasians on Work Crew; R 250923Z Apr 83, subject: Refugee Report . . . , both DIA Source file 1351, Inventory of the Records of the Senate Select Committee on POW/MIA Affairs. The motor grader operator's description and hand-drawn sketch of the area where his sightings occurred place the sightings less than two miles southeast of a prison and a group of associated subcamps located at Coc Mi, near the Red River town of Pho Lu in Lao Cai Province. (Authors' color map.) The North Vietnamese called this prison complex Phong Quang or Central Prison #1. The main prison, located at UTM coordinates VK183737, and its five nearby subcamps were known to U.S. officials during the war as the "Coc Mi Possible PW Camp N-34," after the nearby village. (Defense Intelligence Agency, *Basic Report, Military Logistics, North Vietnam, Coc Mi Possible PW Camp N-34*, February 1973, "Miscellaneous PW Files, Possible PW Camps," POW/MIA. Also DIA reconnaissance photo with schematic and annotated map titled "[Illegible] Etnam [*sic*] . . . Poss PW Camp, N-34, [illegible] 104 12 16E" and "North Vietnam, Poss Satellite Compounds to Coc Mi Poss PW Camp, N-34, [redacted]", [redacted] Memorandum to [redacted], from [redacted], September 7, 1972, subject: Coc Mi Poss PW Camp, N-34, with six photographs, all from Hendon files.) Though wartime U.S. officials had considered it possible that American POWs were being held at Coc Mi N-34 and/or its subcamps during the war, no American prisoners returned by the North Vietnamese at Operation Homecoming reported they had been held there. In 1979, however, a Vietnamese refugee would report to U.S. officials that he had been held at the prison on a subversive operations charge during 1971 and had observed approximately two hundred American POWs being held there. He would explain that he saw the Americans only once as they were leaving the prison complex on a labor detail. He would also say that the guards told him the prisoners he had seen were Americans. (Color DIA map titled "Location of Possible PW Camps [In North Vietnam], Hendon files; *Places and Dates of Confinement of Air Force, Navy and Marine Corps Prisoners of War Held in North Vietnam 1964–1973*; JCRC M79-177, 24 July 1979, subject: Sighting of U.S. POWs in North Vietnam, JCRC Archival Files, POW/MIA; *Gazetteer of Vietnam*, Vol. I (A–K) [Washington, DC: Defense Mapping Agency, 1986], p. 185, "Bao Thang.") In addition to the motor grader operator who reported seeing the American POWs on the work gang in the summer of 1976, other independent sources would report the presence of American prisoners at or in the vicinity of the Phong Quang (Coc Mi) complex after 1976. These accounts are given in the text in chronological sequence.

**34.** CIA memorandum, 20 May 1977, subject: Reported Sightings of Caucasian/American Prisoners in North Vietnam, FIR-317/09161-77, pp. 1–2, CIA Files, POW/MIA.

**35.** Ibid., pp. 2–3.

**36.** P081145Z JUN 87, subject: JCRC Report T87-253, Hearsay of 30 US POWs in Hoang Lien Son (P), 1976, DIA Source file 6471, Inventory of the Records of the Senate Select Committee on POW/MIA Affairs.

**37.** P 211412Z JUN 90, subject: IIR 1 512 0221 90/Movement of U.S. PW's Within North Vietnam, Inventory of the Records of the Senate Select Committee on POW/MIA Affairs.

**38.** R 270621Z FEB 90, subject: IIR 6 024 0355 90/Alleged Americans Held in Cave at Cao Bang, Aug 76–Jun 77, with source's hand-drawn sketch, (DIA Source file 11363/40874, POW/MIA.) U.S. POWs had, in fact, been held at this prison at Bo Djuong Village in Cao Bang Province during the latter months of the war. U.S. officials had named the prison "Loung Lang PW Camp N-124," after a nearby village, and had photographed it frequently during the last months of the war. (Military Logistics, North Vietnam, Loung Lang Possible PW Camp N-124, [redacted] February 1973, Camp Files, POW/MIA; annotated black-and-white DOD reconnaissance photo with date redacted titled "North Vietnam, Loung Lang PW Camp N-124, 22 28 21N 106 24 45E," with schematic and map, Hendon files.)

At war's end, U.S. officials had learned from the returnees that just over two hundred of them had been moved to the prison from Hanoi in mid-May 1972 and been held in the aboveground portion of the facility until mid-January 1973, when they were returned to Hanoi. All of these POWs, including Maj. Douglas B. Peterson, USAF, were returned or accounted for at Operation Homecoming. "Armand J. Myers et al., *Vietnam POW Camp Histories and Studies,* Vol. I, *Professional Study No. 5169* (Air War College, Air University, United States Air Force, Maxwell Air Force Base, Alabama, April 1974), pp. 9, 439–50; color DOD map titled "Camps from Which U.S. POWs Returned at Operation Homecoming," Hendon files; *Places and Dates of Confinement of Air Force, Navy and Marine Corps Prisoners of War Held in North Vietnam 1964–1973;* P 191518Z Mar 73 Operation Homecoming/Air Force Message Special Report No. 52, March 15, 1973, subject: Dogpatch, Returnee: Peterson, Douglas B., Camp Files, POW/MIA.

Peterson and the other returnees from Loung Lang N-124 told Homecoming officials they had named the prison "Dogpatch." ("Myers, *Vietnam POW Camp Histories,* and unannotated black-and-white DOD reconnaissance photo titled "Dogpatch," both Hendon files.) One returnee reported that when he and the other two hundred or so Americans first arrived at "Dogpatch" in May 1972, they "found some writing, some of it very despondent, in English, on a wall or two indicating the camp held some Americans prior to that time." (P 222202Z MAR 73, subject: Dogpatch, DIA Archives File 373-84-0088, POW/MIA.) Other returnees reported that these messages contained the phrases "Laos 66" and "Texas Tech." Many returnees reported that the aboveground portion of the prison had been constructed in 1969. ("Loung Lang Prisoner of War Camp," Inventory of the Records of the Senate Select Committee on POW/MIA Affairs.) Given all these statements by the returnees, it must have been obvious to all concerned that the despondent messages had to have been written by American prisoners confined to the prison between the date the facility was opened in 1969 and the time the group of just over two hundred POWs arrived there from Hanoi in May 1972. These facts take on special significance when one considers that not one of the POWs who returned from North Vietnam during or after the war reported that he had been held at "Dogpatch" at any time prior to the arrival of the two hundred or so Americans in May 1972. *(Places and Dates of Confinement of Air Force, Navy and Marine Corps Prisoners of War Held in North Vietnam 1964–1973.)*

Of additional special significance is the fact that a number of other wartime and postwar sources would tell U.S. officials about the cave where the electrician had encountered the American POWs during late 1976 and early 1977. First word of this cave had come from one of the "Dogpatch" returnees, who reported that he and the other POWs detained there had "observed a cave located about 75 yards southeast of the [main] compound to which NVA personnel were seen to take light machineguns" and that "radio equipment was observed [being] taken into the cave." (O 021742Z MAR 73, Confinement Chronology Report No: 2, Returnee name: Chapman, Harlan, Rank: LTCOL, DIA Archives File 373-84-0088, POW/MIA.) Later in the postwar era, the existence of this cave would be reported by at least three other independent sources. One of these sources would describe the cave and draw a sketch showing it at the exact location cited by the returnee. (JCRC HK84-063, 20 June 1984, subject: Refugee Report, Possible U.S. Remains at Dong Khe, Cao Bang, Camp Files, POW/MIA.) Two others would report—just as the electrician had—that American POWs were housed in the cave after Operation Homecoming. The more descriptive of the two reports is discussed at length in Chapter 18. The other, presented herein, is Department of State, "Translator's Summary of Communication," Language: Vietnamese, Date of communication: December 16, 1980, Addressed to: The President, Name and address of writer: Mr. [redacted] and attached translation LN 336-81, both DIA Source file 0972, POW/MIA.

39. Correspondence of Gillespie V. Montgomery, Chairman, U.S. House of Representatives, Select Committee on Missing Persons in Southeast Asia, to the Honorable George H. Bush, Director, Central Intelligence Agency, February 16, 1976, Shields Files, POW/MIA.

40. *Americans Missing in Southeast Asia,* Final Report, December 13, 1976, pp. 25, 27.

41. *Hearings Before the House Select Committee on Missing Persons in Southeast Asia,* Part 3, p. 132.

42. "Unresolved Current Allegations Concerning Possible American PWs in Vietnam," CIA Files, POW/MIA.

43. Central Intelligence Agency, Memorandum for Director of Central Intelligence, from [redacted], Deputy Director for Operations, subject: Re-evaluation of PW/MIA Information, August 13, 1976, CIA Files, POW/MIA. For examples of reports held by the agency at the time that quoted North Vietnamese and Vietcong officials as saying the DRV was still holding American POWs, see "United States Government Memorandum To Chief, Domestic Collection Division, Attn: [redacted], From [redacted], DATE: [redacted], subject: [redacted], and FIR-317/09153-76, COUNTRY: Vietnam, DOI: September 1975–January 1976, subject: Americans Remaining in South Vietnam and Detention of Americans in North Vietnam," both CIA Files, POW/MIA.

**44.** Authors' annotated map, annotated line drawing of imagery, copy of imagery, CIA Files, POW/MIA and Hendon files.

**45.** Central Intelligence Agency, Directorate of Intelligence, July 6, 1976, memorandum for [redacted], subject: Dong Mang Prison Camp, NVN; Central Intelligence Agency, Directorate of Intelligence, Imagery Analysis Service, July 9, 1976, Memorandum for the record, subject: Briefing to DOD on North Vietnamese Prison Camp, both CIA Files, POW/MIA.

**46.** July 9 NOTE FOR Mr. Bush, copy [illegible], CIA Files, POW/MIA.

**47.** *Americans Missing in Southeast Asia,* Summary, Conclusions, and Recommendations; Letter of Transmittal, Major Conclusions and Recommendations.

**48.** Ibid.

## CHAPTER 16. 1977: A NEW PRESIDENT ADDRESSES THE MATTER OF THE UNLISTED, UNRETURNED POWs

**1.** Memorandum for the record, July 24, 1994, subject: Live Sighting, Dec 76–Feb 77, Lai Chau, DIA Source file 18919, POW/MIA. During the war, U.S. officials had discovered a large prison located just west-northwest of Lai Chau that exhibited all signatures associated with a maximum security prison for POWs. This prison, which officials named "Lai Chau Possible PW Camp, N-101," lay in a small, isolated streambed just north of the Black River. None of the POWs released at Operation Homecoming reported that they had been held at Lai Chau N-101. (Color DIA map titled "Location of Possible PW Camps [in North Vietnam]," Hendon files; Defense Intelligence Agency, basic report, Military Logistics, North Vietnam, Lai Chau Possible PW Camp N-101, "Miscellaneous PW Files, Possible PW Camps," POW/MIA; North Vietnam intelligence briefing notes, July 10, 1972, installation: Lai Chau Possible PW Camp, N-101; annotated DIA black-and-white wartime reconnaissance photo titled "North Vietnam, Lai Chau Possible PW Camp N-101, 22 04 22N 103 09 04E" with schematic and map, 20 Sep 71, Hendon files; *Places and Dates of Confinement of Air Force, Navy and marine Corps Prisoners of War Held in North Vietnam 1964–1973.*)

**2.** R 221751Z Dec 88, subject: IIR 6 024 0033 89/Hearsay of 18 Alleged Americans Incarcerated in North Vietnam as Late as July 1977, DIA Source file 8279, Inventory of the Records of the Senate Select Committee on POW/MIA Affairs.

**3.** R 010745Z Oct 86, subject: JCRC Report T86-403, Two Caucasians Seen Near Katum Re-education Camp in January 1977, Katum Camp Files, POW/MIA; authors' annotated color map titled "Locations Near Cambodian Border Where Southerners Reportedly Encountered U.S. Prisoners During 1977," point 1.

**4.** JCRC M82-039, 17 July 1982, subject: Refugee Report, Hearsay of Americans at Tay Ninh, DIA Source file 1356, POW/MIA; map, "Locations Near Cambodian Border Where Southerners Reportedly Encountered U.S. Prisoners During 1977," point 2.

**5.** DOD IIR 2 240 5005 79, Alleged Sighting of US Persons in the SRV, DIA Source file 2411, POW/MIA; map, "Locations Near Cambodian Border Where Southerners Reportedly Encountered U.S. Prisoners During 1977," point 3.

**6.** Statements of DIA Source 9183 in P 100200Z JUN 87, subject: JCRC Refugee Report RP87-005, Hearsay of Possible American Prisoners in Vietnam in 1977, DIA Archives files, POW/MIA; map, "Locations Near Cambodian Border Where Southerners Reportedly Encountered U.S. Prisoners During 1977," point 4.

**7.** Presidential Commission on Americans Missing and Unaccounted for in Southeast Asia, *Report on Trip to Vietnam and Laos March 16–20, 1977, I, Mandate of the Commission,* POW/MIA.

**8.** O 231816Z FEB 77, Fm Amembassy Paris to Secstate Wash DC Immediate 9986, subject: US-VN Relations: SRV Fonmin's Reply to Secretary's Letter, Jimmy Carter Library, Atlanta.

**9.** Nyan Chanda, *Brother Enemy* (San Diego: Harcourt, 1986), p. 147.

**10.** Memorandum for the president From Cyrus Vance, Subject: Your Meeting with Presidential Commission on MIA's, March 11, 1977, p. 2, Jimmy Carter Library.

**11.** Deposition of Richard Holbrooke, Select Committee on POW/MIA Affairs, October 7, 1992, p. 18, Inventory of the Records of the Senate Select Committee on POW/MIA Affairs.

**12.** Deposition of Zbigniew Brzezinski, Select Committee on POW/MIA Affairs, November 5, 1992, pp. 14, 17, 20, 21, Inventory of the Records of the Senate Select Committee on POW/MIA Affairs.

**13.** Central Intelligence Agency, 8 Mar 1977, memorandum for Mr. James D. Rosenthal, Director, Vietnam, Laos, and Cambodia, Bureau of East Asian and Pacific Affairs, Department of State; Mr. Frank A. Sieverts, Deputy Coordinator for Prisoner of War and Missing in Action Matters, Department of State; Bruce L. Heller, Commander, USNR, Chief, Prisoner of War/Missing in Action Branch,

Resources and Installations Division, Directorate of Intelligence (Research Center), Defense Intelligence Agency; [and one additional redacted addressee] from William W. Wells, Deputy Director for Operations, subject: Comment by Socialist Republic of Vietnam (SRV) Embassy Employee in Bonn on Possibility of U.S. Prisoners Being Held by the SRV for Use in Negotiations on Aid from the U.S. for the SRV, FIR-317/09157-77, CIA Files, POW/MIA.

14. Richard H. Growald, "Missing," UPI 03-16 [09238] AES, Jimmy Carter Library; also "MIA Search Is Pledged by Hanoi, But Says U.S. Must Honor Rebuilding Commitments," UPI in *Washington Star,* March 17, 1977, p. A-7, CIA Files, Reel 405, POW/MIA.

15. Recorded Views and Minutes of Dr. Roger Shields, Department of Defense Staff Representative to the Woodcock Commission, Inventory of the Records of the Senate Select Committee on POW/MIA Affairs.

16. Ibid.

17. Central Intelligence Agency, 16 Mar 1977, memorandum for Mr. James D. Rosenthal, Director, Vietnam, Laos, and Cambodia, Bureau of East Asian and Pacific Affairs, Department of State; Mr. Frank A. Sieverts, Deputy Coordinator for Prisoner of War and Missing in Action Matters, Department of State; Bruce L. Heller, Commander, USNR, Chief, Prisoner of War/Missing in Action Branch, Resources and Installations Division, Directorate of Intelligence (Research Center), Defense Intelligence Agency; Raymond Vohden, Captain, USN, Principal Advisor for Prisoner of War and Missing in Action Affairs (International Security Affairs), Office of the Secretary of Defense from William W. Wells, Deputy Director for Operations, subject: Comments of the Indonesian Ambassador to Hanoi on American Prisoners of War Remaining in Vietnam, FIR-317/09160-77, POW/MIA.

18. Hendon telephone interview with Woodcock, 1987; Hendon attempts to meet with Phan Hien in Washington (1991) and Hanoi (1993).

19. Aide-mémoire, March 18, 1977, attachment included in 3/23/77 White House memorandum for the president FROM Zbigniew Brzezinski, subject: Woodcock Commission Report, Jimmy Carter Library.

20. *Report on Trip to Vietnam and Laos March 16–20, 1977,* p. 15.

21. Ibid., pp. 19–20.

22. UPI 03-23 12:29 PES, POW/MIA.

23. Public Papers of the Presidents, Jimmy Carter, 1977, pp. 489–90, National Archives. Presidential Commission on Americans Missing and Unaccounted for in Southeast Asia, Remarks at a News Briefing on the Results of the Commission's Trip to Vietnam and Laos, March 23, 1977, pp. 489–90.

24. Letter from Jimmy Carter to Leonard Woodcock, March 25, 1977, Jimmy Carter Library.

25. *Administration of Jimmy Carter, 1977,* March 24, 1977, pp. 499–500.

26. *U.S. MIA's in Southeast Asia: Hearing Before the Committee on Foreign Relations, Report of the Presidential Commission on U.S. Missing and Unaccounted for in Southeast Asia,* April 1, 1977, p. 5.

27. Ibid., p. 16.

28. "U.S., Vietnam Turning to Aid Issue," with photo of Hien and Holbrooke, *Washington Star,* May 5, 1977, CIA Files, Reel 405, POW/MIA; Deposition of James D. Rosenthal, Select Committee on POW/MIA Affairs, October 27, 1992, p. 45, Inventory of the Records of the Senate Select Committee on POW/MIA Affairs.

29. Deposition of Richard Holbrooke, pp. 39, 20.

30. Ibid., pp. 26, 21, 17, 18, 23, 22, 24.

31. *POW/MIA'S,* p. 373.

32. "U.S. Won't Bar Hanoi From U.N.; Vietnam to Press Hunt for Missing," *New York Times,* May 5, 1977, p. 1.

33. "U.S. Drops Opposition to Vietnam U.N. Seat," *Washington Post,* May 5, 1977, p. 1.

34. Ibid.

35. "House Action: Ban on Vietnam Reparations Added to State Authorization," *Congressional Quarterly,* May 7, 1977, p. 884.

36. Deposition of Richard Holbrooke, pp. 30–31.

37. "Nhan Dan Commentary Scores 'ERRONEOUS' U.S. Policy Toward SRV," FBIS, Asia and Pacific, IV, May 11, 1977, Vietnam, K1.

38. "Quan Doi Nhan Dan Cites Terms for U.S. Relations," FBIS, Asia and Pacific, IV, May 16, 1977, Vietnam, K1–K2.

39. "Radio Stresses U.S. 'Obligation' Toward Vietnam," FBIS, Asia and Pacific, IV, May 18, 1977, Vietnam, K1–K2.

40. "Nhan Dan Commentator on U.S. 'Obligation' to Vietnam," FBIS, Asia and Pacific, IV, May 23, 1977, Vietnam, K8–K10.

**41.** National Security Council, memorandum for: Zbigniew Brzezinski from Michel Oksenberg, May 25, 1977, subject: Forthcoming Paris Negotiations with the Vietnamese, Jimmy Carter Library.

**42.** Memorandum for: the President from the Secretary of Defense, May 26, 1977, subject: Status Reviews for Servicemen Missing in Southeast Asia, Jimmy Carter Library.

**43.** "Vietnam Gives U.S. Data on 20 War Dead, 2d Round of Talks Ends in Paris—Money Issue Stalls Progress," *New York Times*, June 4, 1977, p. 1; "VNA Reports on SRV-U.S. Talks in Paris 2–3 Jun," FBIS, Asia and Pacific, IV, June 6, 1977, Vietnam, K1.

**44.** White House, memorandum for: the President from Zbigniew Brzezinski, June 15, 1977, subject: MIA Status Reviews; White House, memorandum for the Secretary of Defense, June 16, 1977, subject: Status Reviews for Servicemen Missing in Southeast Asia, both Jimmy Carter Library.

**45.** Quoted in *National League of Families of American Prisoners and Missing in Southeast Asia, Newsletter* CB-11, August 30, 1977, files of Elizabeth Stewart.

**46.** JCRC T80-053, 11 July 1980, subject: Refugee Report, Caucasian Captives at Binh Thuy; R 080757Z Nov 80, subject: Reinterview of Refugee [name redacted], both DIA Source file 0799, POW/MIA.

**47.** R 010745Z Oct 86, subject: JCRC Report T86-403, Two Caucasians Seen Near Katum Re-education Camp in January 1977, Katum Camp Files, POW/MIA; authors' annotated color map titled "Locations Near Cambodian Border Where Southerners Reportedly Encountered U.S. Prisoners During 1977," point 5.

**48.** Memorandum for the record, January 19, 1982, subject: Report of Interview—[source name redacted] (0118), DIA Source file 0118, POW/MIA; authors' map.

**49.** "Summary," DIA Source file 0945, Inventory of the Records of the Senate Select Committee on POW/MIA Affairs; five-page excerpt from letter from Source 0945 to the National League of Families refugee coordinator, Hendon files. The ethnic Chinese political prisoner (DIA Source 0945) escaped from Quyet Tien in 1978 and fled across the border to mainland China and then on to Hong Kong. He related his information about the American POWs to CIA agents in Hong Kong shortly after his arrival and informed them that a Taiwanese commando who had been held at Quyet Tien with him and had also escaped would confirm his story. When CIA agents located the commando in another Hong Kong refugee camp and debriefed him, he confirmed Source 0945's story, stating that he too had seen the American POWs at Quyet Tien. The commando also told CIA officials that another Taiwanese commando detained with him at Quyet Tien spoke English and had been able to talk with the Americans. (Undated CIA memorandum, subject: Alleged Sighting of U.S. Prisoners of War in North Vietnam, DIA Source files 0945 and 1311, Inventory of the Records of the Senate Select Committee on POW/MIA Affairs.) U.S. officials would later learn that yet another Taiwanese commando had reportedly escaped from the Quyet Tien complex and, while making his way toward the nearby Chinese border, had come upon a small prison compound that housed Americans. This facility was believed to be one of a number of scattered subcamps that, together with the large main prison compound, made up the Quyet Tien Prison complex. (Memorandum for the record, subject: Interview with [name redacted], 2 July 1985; undated memorandum for the record, Subject: Taiwanese Commandos at Quyet Tien Prison, SRV, both DIA Source file 2460, POW/MIA.) U.S officials would later receive word that yet *another* Chinese commando who had been held at Quyet Tien after the war had reportedly said that he too had encountered American prisoners at Quyet Tien and that he had communicated with them by tap code. (R 250318Z Jul 85, subject: JCRC Report I85-049, Commandos, Chinese Held in Prison in NVN, Camp Files, POW/MIA; R 081104Z Oct 85, subject: JCRC Report I85-049A, Reinterview of Vietnamese Refugee [name redacted], DIA Source file 2460, POW/MIA.)

**50.** JCRC T83-014, 10 March 1983 subject: Refugee Report, Hearsay of Death of American Prisoners in Vietnam, Inventory of the Records of the Senate Select Committee on POW/MIA Affairs, National Archives.

**51.** JCRC HK82-013, 24 May 1982, subject: Refugee Report, Alleged Sighting of Americans at Lao Cai in 1977, DIA Source file 1591, POW/MIA; authors' map.

**52.** Defense Prisoner of War/Missing in Action Office, memorandum to files from Dave Rosenau, February 16, 1996, subject: Interview with Mr. Tran Tu Thanh [DIA Source 42612], with cover letter dated April 8, 1997, from James W. Wold, deputy assistant secretary of defense (POW/Missing Personnel Affairs) to Honorable Robert C. Smith, United States Senate, files of Senator Bob Smith; authors' map. DIA Source 42612, refugee Tran Tu Thanh, would later be among those persons featured in Paul Hendrickson's best-selling book on the Vietnam War, *The Living and the Dead: Robert McNamara and Five Lives of a Lost War* (New York: Alfred A. Knopf, 1996).

**53.** JCRC HK83-020, 26 April 1983, subject: Alleged American Prisoners Held at Quyet Tien Prison, DIA Source file 1603, Inventory of the Records of the Senate Select Committee on POW/MIA Affairs; authors' map.

**54.** JCRC HK82-013, with source's hand-drawn sketch, DIA Source file 1591, POW/MIA; authors' map.

**55.** Handwritten letter from DIA Source 2455 to Mr. and Mrs. John Devine, DIA Source file 2455, POW/MIA.

**56.** DIA interagency brief, 13 June 1980, RADM J. O. Tuttle, USN, POW/MIA.

**57.** Three-page translation of redacted debriefing of DIA Source 0059, dated February 8, 1979, DIA Source file 0059, POW/MIA. The Tan Lap–Phu Tho prison complex was composed of a main, walled prison compound, located at coordinates 21°31'50" N and 104°54'30" E, UTM VJ906806, near the village of Xom Giong, and a series of a half dozen or so smaller prisons and subcamps located throughout the nearby countryside. During the war, U.S. officials had strongly suspected that American POWs were being held in the main compound, which the officials had designated as "Xom Giong Possible PW Detention Installation N-54." To these officials' great surprise, none of the Americans who returned at Operation Homecoming reported ever having been detained at Xom Giong N-54 or any of its associated subcamps. (Defense Intelligence Agency, basic report, *Military Logistics, North Vietnam, Xom Giong Possible PW Detention Installation N-54,* February 1973, "Miscellaneous PW Files, Possible PW Camps," POW/MIA; color DIA map titled "Location of Possible PW Camps [in North Vietnam]; annotated DIA reconnaissance photo titled "North Vietnam, Xom Giong Possible PW Detention Installation, N54, 21 31 50N 104 54 30E, BE NO 0616-03474," with schematic and map; "Imagery Interpretation Memorandum," to [redacted] from [redacted], August 1, 1972, subject: Xom Giang [sic] Poss PW Detn Instal, N-54 w/1 photo; *Places and Dates of Confinement of Air Force, Navy and Marine Corps Prisoners of War Held in North Vietnam 1964–1973,* all from Hendon files.) DIA records show that as the North Vietnamese began moving tens of thousands of Southerners to the North for long-term confinement in 1976, the Tan Lap–Phu Tho Prison complex was expanded and used both as a reeducation camp for newly arrived Southerners and, according to a number of independent sources, as a place of confinement for American POWs as well. North Vietnamese officials⁺ and Southerners detained in the Tan Lap–Phu Tho prison complex called the main prison compound near Xom Giong "Tan Lap–Phu Tho K-1," and the various subcamps "Tan Lap-Phu Tho K-2," "Tan Lap-Phu Tho K-3," etc. Several additional reports of American prisoners being held after the war in or in the vicinity of the Tan Lap–Phu Tho prison complex follow in the text in chronological sequence.

**58.** Typewritten debrief of DIA Source 1260, May 16, 1981, paragraph 5, with source's hand-drawn sketch of prison, DIA Source file 1260, Inventory of the Records of the Senate Select Committee on POW/MIA Affairs. The prison just north of Son La province town was known to U.S. officials during the war as the "Son La Possible PW Detention Installation, N-29." Though U.S. officials considered it possible that American POWs were being held at Son La N-29 during the war—and had therefore ordered that it be photographed on a regular basis—no American prisoners returned at Operation Homecoming reported they had been held there. (Authors' annotated 1:250,000 map of Son La area; Defense Intelligence Agency, basic report, *Military Logistics, North Vietnam, Son La Possible PW Detention Installation N-29,* February 1973, "Miscellaneous PW Files, Possible PW Camps," POW/MIA; color DIA map titled "Location of Possible PW Camps [in North Vietnam]; annotated wartime DIA reconnaissance photo, dated 25 Nov 65, titled "North Vietnam, Poss PW Detention Instl N-29, Son La 21 21N 103 55E," with schematic and map; "[redacted] Memorandum" to [redacted] From [redacted], February 14, 1972, subject: SonLa [sic] Poss PW Detn Instal, N-29 with attached photograph; *Places and Dates of Confinement of Air Force, Navy and Marine Corps Prisoners of War Held in North Vietnam 1964–1973,* all from Hendon files.)

**59.** Statement of DIA Source 0123 in letter titled [redacted], Boat No. 132, Kota Baru, Date of arrival 27 October 1978, with handwritten notations by U.S. officials reading "REF: M79-106, 24 May 79," DIA Source file 0123, POW/MIA; authors' annotated color map titled "Locations Near Cambodian Border Where Southerners Reportedly Encountered U.S. Prisoners During 1977," point 6.

## CHAPTER 17. 1978: THE SIGHTINGS OF THE UNLISTED, UNRETURNED POWs CONTINUE • THE REFUGEE EXODUS BEGINS

**1.** "Report," received from [redacted] on 11 Oct 78; DOD IIR 2 240 5002 80, both DIA Source file 0057, POW/MIA. Tran Phu Prison in downtown Haiphong was well-known to U.S. intelligence officials due to the fact that it had been used as a temporary detention facility for U.S. pilots shot down in the Haiphong area during the war. (Annotated wartime reconnaissance photo labeled "North Vietnam [redacted] PW Camp N-41, 20 51 07N 106 40 32E," Reel 7, Series 92-302, POW/MIA.) Debriefs of POWs released at Operation Homecoming indicated that ninety-six of the returnees had been held at the facility at one time or another between 1965 and 1973. All had subsequently been transferred to Hanoi and released or otherwise accounted for. (DIA analysis "[source name redacted]," IR 2 240 5002 80, p. 1, DIA Source file 0057, POW/MIA.). The postwar intelligence telling of American POWs at Tran Phu would be limited but compelling. In addition to the sighting of the four pilots by Source 0057 just prior to Tet in 1978, U.S. investigators would later learn from a cargo boat pilot whose ship had docked at Haiphong during April 1977 that while on the way to the market to buy some soap he observed two Caucasian prisoners waiting to be taken into the prison. They were dressed in Communist fatigues and wearing handcuffs, and were sitting in a cage mounted on the back of a pickup truck. Both were thin and had grayish beards. The boat pilot told U.S. officials that he had asked a police guard who the prisoners were and the guard had replied that they were American pilots who were being taken to the prison hospital. (JCRC M79-059, subject: Sighting of Americans in Captivity, DIA Source file 0198, POW/MIA.) Later, U.S. imagery experts analyzing postwar satellite imagery of the prison would discover classified pilot distress signals spelled out in laundry on the prison roof. This imagery of Tran Phu, which was shown to Hendon and his colleague John LeBoutillier by DCI William Casey at Director Casey's office at CIA headquarters at Langley, Virginia, in 1982, is similar to the imagery of Dong Mang Prison taken in 1975. Unlike the Dong Mang imagery, however, the Tran Phu imagery cannot be found in the declassified postwar intelligence. The only suggestion in the declassified intelligence holdings on file at the Library of Congress and the National Archives that the imagery of the distress signals crafted in the laundry on the roof of Tran Phu even exists involves a map showing the two prisons—Dong Mang and Tran Phu—where pilot distress signals are known by the authors to have been imaged on the roofs. (Untitled DOD annotated map of North Vietnam showing only Dong Mang and Haiphong prisons, POW/MIA.)

2. JCRC T80-057, 11 July 1980, subject: Refugee Report, Sighting of Caucasians in North Vietnam, DIA Source file 0802, POW/MIA. The Ba Sao prison complex near Phu Ly was well-known to U.S. intelligence analysts due to the fact that American POWs had been detained there during the war. The Americans held at Ba Sao, all of whom were released or accounted for at Operation Homecoming, were confined to a small walled compound that was one of a half dozen separate subcamps that comprised the sprawling Ba Sao complex. U.S. officials called the small prison where the wartime American POWs were held "Noi Coc PW Camp N-129" after the nearby village of Noi Coc. (Annotated black-and-white 1:50,000 DIA map showing location of "Noi Coc PW Camp," JCS Files, POW/MIA; and annotated black-and-white DOD reconnaissance photo titled "Noi Coc PW Camp N-129," Hendon files.) Returnees who had been held at this small camp inside the Ba Sao complex called it "Rockpile." (Color DOD map with authors' added title, "Camps from Which U.S. POWs Returned at Operation Homecoming, and annotated black-and-white DOD reconnaissance photo titled "Rockpile," both Hendon files.) The North Vietnamese, in addition to calling the sprawling prison complex "Ba Sao," refer to it as "Dam Dun" and/or "Nam Ha." The February 1978 nighttime sighting of the two Caucasian prisoners being force-marched along the road near the prison would turn out to be one of perhaps fifteen separate reports received by DIA that told of American POWs being held after the war in the Ba Sao/Noi Coc/"Rockpile"/Dam Dun/Nam Ha complex, its subordinate subcamps, or the surrounding area. These reports are discussed in later chapters.

3. Swedish map titled "BaiBang Guide," DIA Source file 0248, POW/MIA.

4. "Report of Americans Working on Roads North of Hanoi," *Jakarta Sinar Harapan*, December 6, 1980, p. 4; "MIAs May Be Slaves Working in Vietnam," UPI in unnamed newspaper; R 081448Z DEC 80, subject: Norwegian Reports on PWs; Embassy of the United States of America, Bangkok, May 6, 1981, to JCRC [redacted], subject: Swedish Source on MIA Information from Vietnam, all DIA Source file 0248, POW/MIA. Though Vietnamese authorities were quick to deny that the American prisoners had been seen on the road gang near Ham Yen, at least three sources—two British citizens employed as schoolteachers at the paper mill and one other Swedish technician—reported to U.S. authorities that they had learned while in Vietnam that the sighting had, in fact, occurred. In addition, U.S. officials would receive a number of other reports of American POWs being detained in the Bai Bang–Ham Yen area during the late 1970s. One of these reports quoted Vietnamese drivers employed at the paper mill as saying that there were "special places" nearby where "Nixon people" were imprisoned. Another involved the testimony of two Swedes employed at the mill who told U.S. authorities that they had been riding their motorbikes north of the mill in an area near Thac Ba Lake and had come upon a camp containing American prisoners. Yet another report quoted a Swedish employee of the mill as saying that he had been arrested near the mill by Vietnamese security forces, and that members of the security force told him they had arrested him because they believed he was an escaped American prisoner, adding, "We have some of them in our prisons." Finally, a West German engineer formerly assigned to the mill would report that he had seen two American POWs at Bai Bang in late 1979 in what many would consider the most remarkable circumstances imaginable. The West German's account follows in the text in chronological sequence. ("VNA Denies VOA Report on Captured Americans in SRV," . . . Hanoi VNA in English 1557 GMT 5 Dec 80; JCRC T79-025, 4 June 1979, subject: Report of "European-looking" Prisoners in North Vietnam; R 120431Z NOV 81,

subject: 1978 Alleged Sighting of POW's in Vietnam, all POW/MIA; untitled DIA document beginning, "In June 1978, DIA/DC-2 learned from an Australian journalist . . . ," Inventory of the Records of the Senate Select Committee on POW/MIA Affairs.)

5. JCRC RP81-0013, 20 July 1981, subject: Sightings of Live U.S. POW's in Vinh Phu Province; VM; 272130Z Jul 81, subject: Refugee Reports, both DIA Source file 0966, POW/MIA.

6. O 011611Z SEP 87, from CIA to [multiple addressees], subject: POW/MIA; Debriefing on Live Sightings of American Prisoners in North Vietnam in 1978, DIA Source file 7114, POW/MIA.

7. Map showing location of camp and source's hand-drawn sketch of facility, DIA Source file 1328, POW/MIA.

8. Typed "interview notes" with handwritten date 6 Aug 82, ibid.

9. R 181131Z AUG 81, subject: Refugee Report [redacted], DIA Source file 0998, POW/MIA.

10. JCRC M79-246, 6 December 1979, subject: Refugee Report, Seven Caucasians Sighted on a Labor Detail, with two maps, DIA Source file 0591, POW/MIA.

11. JCRC M79-132, 29 June 1979, subject: Refugee Report, Caucasians Held Captive in Loc Ninh Area, DIA Source file 0197, Inventory of the Records of the Senate Select Committee on POW/MIA Affairs.

12. JCRC M79-010, 23 February 1979, subject: Refugee Report, Sighting of Live Americans; Defense Intelligence Agency, "DIA Evaluation of PW/MIA Information Provided by Vu Van Xuong, both from "Uncorrelated Information Relating to Missing Americans in Southeast Asia," Department of Defense, December 15, 1978, pp. 3 595–3 396.

13. JCRC I80-016, subject: Refugee Report, Rumor of 30 Caucasians Near Bu Gia Map, DIA Source file 0830, POW/MIA. The account stating the woman was en route to visit her nephew rather than her husband was almost surely the more accurate, given that by 1978, all ARVN general officers held by the North Vietnamese had almost certainly been transferred to the North for long-term imprisonment.

14. P 200319Z MAY 87, subject: JCRC Refugee Report RP87-039, Hearsay of Two American Prisoners in Tay Minh [sic] Province in 1978, DIA Source file 9139, POW/MIA.

15. JCRC T80-074, 17 November 1980, subject: Refugee Report, Hearsay Information Concerning Live Americans in Tay Ninh, DIA Source file 0862, POW/MIA; authors' map.

16. P 301801Z JUL 87, subject: IIR 6 517 0356 87/Possible Americans in POW Camp, USAF Intelligence Files, POW/MIA.

17. "Report on the American POWs in Vietnam," July 5, 1982, declaration by DIA Source 1309, DIA Source file 1309, Inventory of the Records of the Senate Select Committee on POW/MIA Affairs; authors' three annotated maps of area.

18. R 110635 Z NOV 87, subject: IIR 6 024 0075 88/American Incarcerated in Tan Lap Re-education Camp, DIA Source file 7114, POW/MIA. The official DIA record of U.S. personnel missing in Southeast Asia provided to the U.S. Senate Select Committee on POW/MIA Affairs in 1991 would show that as of March 28, 1991, four U.S. servicemen named "Jackson" remained unaccounted for: Capt. Carl Edwin Jackson, USAF, Capt. James Terry Jackson, USAF, Lance Cpl. James W. Jackson Jr., USMC, and Capt. Paul Vernon Jackson III, USAF. (Defense Intelligence Agency, "U.S. Personnel, Southeast Asia (and Selected Foreign Nationals), Alpha and Chronoligical Reports, DIA\POW-MIA," Vol. 1, April 1991, Hendon files.)

19. Unnumbered, undated CIA memo, subject: Allegation of U.S. POW'S in the K-1 Prison West of Hanoi, DIA Source file 2060, POW/MIA.

20. Authors' annotated 1:50,000 map of area.

21. "The Tighe Task Force Examination of DIA Intelligence Holding[s] Surrounding Unaccounted for United States Military Personnel in Southeast Asia," May 27, 1986, p. 45, Tighe Task Force Files, POW/MIA.

22. Charles Benoit, "Vietnam's 'Boat People,'" in The Third Indochina Conflict, edited by David W. P. Elliott (Boulder, Co: Westview Press, 1981), p. 144.

23. "Trade Policy Implemented," FBIS, Asia and Pacific, IV, March 27, 1978, Vietnam, K11.

24. "Bourgeois Tradesmen Must Shift to Socialist Production," ibid., K9.

25. "Chinese Killed by Vietnamese Soldiers," South China Morning Post, Hong Kong, May 4, 1978, p. 1.

26. "Hanoi Feels Backlash of Chinese Exodus," New York Times News Service in South China Morning Post, August 10, 1979.

27. "Chinese Killed by Vietnamese Soldiers," South China Morning Post.

28. Barry Wain, The Refused: The Agony of the Indochinese Refugees (New York: Simon & Schuster, 1981), p. 89.

29. Map, "Countries of First Asylum for Indochinese Refugees, 1975–1982," in Jeremy Hein, From Vietnam, Laos, and Cambodia: A Refugee Experience in the United States (New York: Twayne, 1995).

**30.** For example, "Chinese Woman from VN Tells of Persecution," *South China Morning Post,* June 2, 1978, p. 4; "Evacuation Talks End in 'Complete Failure,'" *South China Morning Post,* July 1, 1978, p. 1; "China Hints of Further Retaliation," *South China Morning Post,* July 2, 1978, p. 1. News accounts would later report that so many ethnic Chinese fled the North during this period that their departure caused serious disruptions in many facets of life, including the day-to-day operation of the central government bureaucracy in Hanoi. It was also reported that the departure of the nation's ethnic Chinese physicians had left some areas of the country completely devoid of doctors. ("Hanoi Feels Backlash of Chinese Exodus," *South China Morning Post.*)

**31.** Wain, *The Refused,* pp. 89–90.

**32.** "The 'Refugee Racket,'" *Bangkok Post,* November 10, 1978; Wain, *The Refused,* photo caption. According to the DIA, fifty-two separate refugee camps would eventually be established in the first-asylum countries of Thailand, Malaysia, Singapore, Indonesia, Hong Kong, and the Philippines alone. (Undated briefing, "Stony Beach DIA PW-MIA Team, Hendon files.)

**33.** Brian Eads, "Boat People: Where and How Soon Will They Go?" *New Straits Times,* Singapore, December 5, 1978.

**34.** P 090019Z OCT 79, subject: Collection of Casualty Resolution Information from Indochinese Refugees, Shields Files, POW/MIA.

**35.** Later, when refugees began arriving in the United States in large numbers, a fifth pipeline developed. This one involved information about missing Americans being acquired within the continental United States by officials of various government agencies, relief organizations, resettlement agencies, churches, charities, etc., and forwarded to the Special Office. In most of these cases, the Special Office analysts themselves would contact the refugee directly, interview him or her by phone or in person, write up a report of the interview, and analyze the information provided.

## CHAPTER 18. 1979: A PRISON SYSTEM IN CHAOS • CONVINCING EVIDENCE FINALLY REACHES WASHINGTON

**1.** R 201920Z AUG 84, subject: Request for Assistance, DIA Source file 1538, Inventory of the Records of the Senate Select Committee on POW/MIA Affairs; drawing of camp and cave from HK84-063, POW/MIA.

**2.** Ibid. The reported sighting of the American POWs being evacuated from "Dogpatch" in early 1979 brought the postwar intelligence there full circle: Six or seven trucks said to hold American POWs were seen *heading to* the prison in 1976, American pilots were seen *inside* the underground portion of the prison in late 1976, and now these POWs were seen being *moved out* of the underground portion of the facility and *evacuated from* the prison in 1979. "Dogpatch," as previously noted, had been home to just over two hundred U.S. POWs during the last months of 1972 and during early to mid-January 1973. All, including Maj. Douglas B. Peterson, USAF, who would later become America's first postwar ambassador to Vietnam, were released or accounted for at Operation Homecoming in 1973.

**3.** A South Vietnamese commando who had been held at the provincial prison in Kim Boi District from February until June or July in 1978 later reported that during that time the North Vietnamese were busy setting up their alternative capital in the area in anticipation of possible PRC attacks on Hanoi City. (R 121445Z JUL 85, subject: Report of Interview, DIA Source file 5763, POW/MIA.)

**4.** LN 728-85, DIA Source file 1270, Inventory of the Records of the Senate Select Committee on POW/MIA Affairs.

**5.** Ibid.; LN 341-85; typed copy of original debrief of Source 1270 in refugee camp with date stamp "[unreadable number] JUN 1982" and beginning "In February 1979, approximately one hundred American prisoners were being . . ." with source's hand-drawn map and explanation of map points, both DIA Source file 1270, Inventory of the Records of the Senate Select Committee on POW/MIA Affairs; authors' map.

**6.** JCRC RP81-023, 13 July 1981, subject: Sighting of U.S. POW's and Clergymen in NVN (Hearsay), DIA Source file 1027; R 240931Z AUG 87, subject: IIR 6 852 0192 87/Possible POW/MIA's in Vietnam, USAF Intelligence Files, POW/MIA. During the war, U.S. officials received several hearsay accounts of American POWs being imprisoned in the Lao Cai area. After conducting aerial reconnaissance over the area, they discovered the existence of a maximum security prison in an isolated location approximately one kilometer east of the city. They named this prison, which lay at a point approximately one kilometer south of the Chinese border and just east of the main rail line that ran along the east bank of the Red River, "Lao Cai Possible PW Camp, N-80." Though wartime U.S. officials believed it possible that American POWs were being detained at Lao Cai N-80—and had therefore ordered the facility photographed throughout the war—none of the American prisoners returned at Operation Homecoming reported they had been held there. (Defense Intelligence Agency, "Basic Report, Military Logistics, North Vietnam," "Basic Report, Military Logistics, North

Vietnam, Lao Cai Possible PW Camp N-80," February 1973, both "Miscellaneous PW Files, Possible PW Camps," POW/MIA; North Vietnam Intelligence Briefing Notes, December 21, 1972, installation: Lao Cai Possible PW Camp, N-80; wartime DIA reconnaissance photo dated August 25, 1972, titled "North Vietnam, Lao Cai Possible PW Camp, N-80, 22 29 58N 103 58 49E," with map and schematic; "[redacted] Memorandum" to [redacted], from [redacted], December 11, 1972 subject: Lao Cai (Kay) Poss PW Camp, with attached collage of three photographs; "[redacted] Memorandum" to [redacted] from [redacted], January 22, 1973, subject: N-15, N-46, N-80, N-85, N-104, with attached photograph [of N-80]; "*Places and Dates of Confinement of Air Force, Navy and Marine Corps Prisoners of War Held in North Vietnam 1964–1973,* all Hendon files.)

7. Ibid.

8. Letter dated January 29, 1987, from Hoang Xuan Lam, alias Hai [DIA Source 8395] to Chairman of the Joint Vietnamese-American Veteran Association, DIA Source file 8395, POW/MIA; authors' map.

9. R 100509Z JUL 88, JCRC Report M88-077, Limited Hearsay of 35 American POWs In Hoa Lo Prison, DIA Source file 6816, Inventory of the Records of the Senate Select Committee on POW/MIA Affairs.

10. Official debrief of Vietnamese refugee Thai Phi Long, May 5–7, 1981, DIA Source file 0941, POW/MIA. The following documents contain information regarding a sighting by a CIA source carried in DIA records as Case "42635 POW-F/H 3 AM Pilots 'Hanoi Hilton' 1979," which remained classified as of mid-2003; letter from J. Thomas Burch, Jr., Chairman, National Vietnam & Gulf War Veterans Coalition, to Hon. Robert L. Jones, Deputy Assistant Secretary of Defense (POW/Missing Personnel Affairs), October 14, 1998; letter from Robert L. Jones, Deputy Assistant Secretary of Defense (POW/Missing Personnel Affairs), to J. Thomas Burch, Jr., Chairman, National Vietnam, Persian and Gulf Veterans Coalition, December 1, 1998; facsimile from William M. Hendon to Russ Thomasson [Office of Sen. Bob Smith], July 11, 2001 with handwritten chronological phone notes added by Hendon, all from Hendon files.

11. P 030825Z JAN 80; P 140800Z JAN 80, both DIA Source file 0503, Inventory of the Records of the Senate Select Committee on POW/MIA Affairs; authors' map.

12. John S. Bowman, ed., *The Vietnam War Day by Day* (New York: Mallard Press, 1989), p. 217; "China Troops Pour Across VN Border," *Bangkok Post,* February 18, 1979, p. 1.

13. "The terrible faces of war," *Bangkok Post,* February 25 1979, p. 1.

14. *Quan Doi Nhan Dan Viet Nam 1944–1979,* map p. 295.

15. R 092000Z JUN 82, subject: IR 1 517 0199 82/Vietnam/US Prisoners of War In Vietnam, DIA Source file 1168, POW/MIA.

16. R 3007577 NOV 79, subject: THIS IS IR 6 895 0289 79, JCRC Archival Files, POW/MIA.

17. JCRC T84-047, March 14, 1984, subject: Refugee Report, Alleged U.S. Prisoners Observed at Gia Lai–Kontum in 1979, with source's hand-drawn map, DIA Source file 2134, POW/MIA.

18. Letter dated September 22, 1983, to [name redacted], publisher of *Trang Den* magazine, Los Angeles, CA., with date stamp OCT 4 1983, DIA Source file 1817, POW/MIA; and one-page document 03 PP paragraph 4, DIA Source file 2134, POW/MIA.

19. JCRC T83-135, November 4, 1983, subject: Refugee Report, Hearsay Information of 200 Live Americans, DIA Source file 1672, POW/MIA microfilm collection; authors' map of Da Nang area.

20. This reference to a prisoner exchange, coupled with the reported statement by the guard in charge of the fifty or so American prisoners at the cave near Mai Son (see page 191) that "in the near future our government will return them to their country," led to speculation that the North Vietnamese may have developed some sort of plan to use the American POWs as an insurance policy against total defeat at the hands of the Chinese.

21. authors' map of Da Nang area.

22. R 190419Z JAN 81, subject: Request for Interview of Vietnamese Refugee, DIA Source file 0881, POW/MIA; translation of letter dated December 28, 1980, to Mrs. Le Thi Anh from Vietnamese refugee [name redacted]; DIA Evaluation of PW/MIA Information Provided by Vietnamese Refugee [name redacted]; typed Analyst's Desk Memorandum, paragraph 5, all DIA Source file 0881, POW/MIA.

23. R 200159Z APR 86, subject: JCRC Report T86-140, Report of American Prisoners at Sop Hao Re-ed Camp, Houaphan Laos, DIA Source file 5102, Inventory of the Records of the Senate Select Committee on POW/MIA Affairs. Intelligence reports received from former inmates and other human sources and from satellite imagery would later indicate that there were six main seminar camps in the Sam Neua (Houaphan) Province Seminar Camp System. These were (1) a headquarters facility known as "Sam Neua Seminar Camp #1," which was located in the area of Viengsai town (coordinates 20°25' N, 104°14' E, UTM VH2058); (2) several maximum security prisons and camps located in

the "Guerrilla's Eye" near Sop Hao (20°33' N, 104°27' E, UTM VH435735), which collectively were known as "Sam Neua Seminar Camp #2"; (3) a camp and work area located near Ban Soppane/Muong Poua, collectively known as "Sam Neua Seminar Camp #3" (20°29' N, 104°14' E, UTM VH2065); (4) a camp located just south-southwest of Muang Et town, which was called "Sam Neua Seminar Camp #4" (20°48' N, 104°01' [US. 00'] E, UTM UJ9700); (5) a camp originally located at Sam Teu (20°00' N, 104°38' E, UTM VH6212) but later moved to Ban Sop Pheua (Sop Phua, Sop Feua) (20°07' N, 104°51' E, UTM VH837255), which was known as "Sam Neua Seminar Camp #5"; and (6) a camp located just northeast of Muang Et at 20°50' N, 104°01' E, UTM UJ9804, known as "Sam Neua Seminar Camp #6." (Authors' color 1:1,000,000 PL/French map of Sam Neua (Houaphan) Province, Laos, titled "The Postwar Sam Neua (Houaphan) Province Seminar Camp System," and authors' color 1:250,000 map showing movement of Seminar Camp 5 from vicinity of Sam Teu to vicinity of Sop Feua titled "Sam Neua Seminar Camp #5 Sam Teu/Sop Pheua (Sop Feua)," both created from the following: handwritten notes by Lao Desk Analyst Soutchay Vongsavanh, a former Lao Army general officer employed at the DIA Special Office for POWs and MIAs, titled "S[illegible]mneua Province, Houaphan (P) LA.2" and beginning "Seminar camp Muangviengxay HQ. (20°25' N-104°14' E)"; "Viangxai Seminar Camp Histories," pp. 25–36; R180915Z APR 88, subject: IIR 6 024 0305-88/Reply to -VOP-05158; R 180507Z AUG 87, subject: IIR 6 024 0073 87/Re-education Camp Number 3, Ban Soppane, Laos; R 070336Z MAR 88, subject: IIR 6 024 250-88/Hearsay Regarding Live Sighting of American PW In Sam Neua (P), LA, all from Camp Files, POW/MIA; and R 101739Z AUG 88, subject: IIR 6 024 0422-88/Sop Feua Seminar Camp, DIA Source file 8324, POW/MIA.)

The camp where the Royal Lao lieutenant colonel said he saw the 111 Americans arrive in September was a subcamp of the "Sam Neua Seminar Camp #2" near Sop Hao, the most secure and brutal of the six Sam Neua seminar camps. Housing the royal family and the most senior and despised officials and soldiers of the former government, Seminar Camp #2 was composed of some seven subcamps. These subcamps, numbered 1–7, were "Sop Hao Prison Camp #1," located northeast of Na Ka Village at approximately 20°34' N, 104°29' E, UTM VH455745; two camps, reported to be "Sop Hao Prison Camps #2 and #3," located just inside Vietnam in the "Gorilla's Eye" (approximately 20°31'00" N, 104°29'30" E, UTM VH472693 and 20°31'30" N, 104°28'30" E, UTM VH465700, respectively); a camp with unknown designation (possibly either "Sop Hao Prison Camp #4" or "Sop Hao Prison Camp #6"), located approximately one kilometer northwest of Sop Hao airfield at approximately 20°33'50" N, 104°26'30" E, UTM VH425735; "Sop Hao Prison Camp #5," located northeast of Sop Hao town at approximately 20°35' N, 104°29' E, UTM VH455770; "Sop Hao Prison Camp #7," located northeast of Sop Hao town at approximately 20°35' N, 104°27'30" E, UTM VH4477; and the prison camp located near Ban Na Keo, some six kilometers south of Sop Hao town, where the Royal Lao lieutenant colonel said he saw the 111 American POWs being brought into the camp in September 1979. This camp near Ban Na Keo, which intelligence indicates was colocated with a Pathet Lao or PAVN battalion HQ located at approximately 20°30'20" N, 104°24'30" E, UTM VH3866, and which U.S. analysts sometimes referred to as "Company 2," was believed to be either "Sop Hao Prison Camp #4" or "Sop Hao Prison Camp #6." (Authors' color 1:250,000 map of "Gorilla's Eye" region of Sam Neua (Houaphan) Province, Laos, titled "Reported Locations of Sop Hao Prison Camps, aka 'Sam Neua (Houaphan) Seminar Camp #2,' Sam Neua (Houaphan) Province, Laos," and authors' black-and-white 1:50,000 map of Sop Hao area with same title, both created from the following: handwritten notes by Soutchay Vongsavanh; Defense Intelligence Agency, Directorate for Research, [redacted] Division, [redacted] memorandum, [redacted]-05-59078-86, to VO-PW [redacted] from [redacted] (Frank Meehan), June 2, 1986, subject: Sop Hao Possible Re-education Camp; Defense Intelligence Agency, Directorate for Research, [redacted] Division, [redacted] memorandum, [redacted]05-59080-86, to VO-PW [redacted] from [redacted] (Frank Meehan), June 2, 1986, subject: Sop Hao Possible Seminar/Re-education Camp; Defense Intelligence Agency, Directorate for [redacted] Exploitation, [redacted] memorandum, [redacted]-08-58356-88, July 25, 1988, subject: Sop Hao Reeducation Camps #1, #2, #3 and #7 Na Ka, Laos, to VO-PW (Attn: Bob Hyp); Defense Intelligence Agency, Directorate for Research, [redacted] Division, [redacted] memorandum, [redacted] 1-56282-85, to VO-PW [redacted] from [redacted] (Cpt. Robert X. Gonzalez), November 14, 1985, subject: [redacted] Search for Possible Seminar Camps in Sop Hao Area–Sam Neua Province Laos; Defense Intelligence Agency, Directorate for Research, [redacted] Division, [redacted] memorandum, [redacted] -04-56513-84- [redacted], to DC-2B [analyst name redacted] from [redacted] (Cpt. Robert X. Gonzalez), April 25, 1984, subject: [redacted] Search for Possible Seminar Camps in Sop Hao Area–Sam Neua Province Laos; R 292212Z OCT 86, subject: <><>Absence of Americans <><>at Political Reeducation Camps in Houa Phan Province, <><>Laos<><>; R 142314Z MAR 88, subject: IIR 6-014-0020-88/Prison Management in Houa Phan Province: 1975–86; R 160835Z SEP 88, subject: Last Group of Viengsay Political Prisoners Reportedly Released; 88.08.02 (pgm=reclist,(4)), [unreadable] Number 1, fac number=4400; 88.08.02 (pgm=reclist,(4)), [unreadable] Number 1, fac number=4401; 88.08.02 (pgm=reclist,(4)), [unreadable] Number 1, fac number=4402; 88.08.02 (pgm=reclist,(4)), [unreadable] Number 1, fac number=4406; 88.08.02 (pgm=reclist,(4)), [unreadable] Number 1, fac number=4409..B, all from Camp Files, POW/MIA; P 170910Z OCT 89, subject: IIR 6 814 0072 90/Traveler Obtains Possible MIA Information, DIA Source file 11026, POW/MIA; R 051020Z FEB 88, subject: JCRC Report T88-012, Firsthand Sighting of a Caucasian Under Military Escort in Northern Laos, DIA Source file 7658; POW/MIA; R 191836Z FEB 88, subject: IIR 6 024 0208-88/Alleged Live Sighting of American at Ban Naka, Sop Hao District, Sam Neua Province, Laos (LA), DIA Source file 7658, POW/MIA; R 060904Z FEB 87, subject: Hearsay of Americans in Houaphan, Laos, DIA Source file 5945, POW/MIA; R 310849Z JAN 89, subject: IIR 6 024 0104-88/Sighting of Three Caucasian Prisoners Near LA/VM Border and R 010402Z APR 94, SUBJECT: IIR 6 023 0025 94/Information on a Detention Facility Located Near Ban Sop Hao, LA (U), with source's memory sketch, both "Miscellaneous PW Files," POW/MIA; DIA annotated maps titled "Sop Hao Area Map, L7015 Sheet 5850 II, 1/50000, Encl: SNF 05-59078-86/DX 5D2" and "Sop Hao Area Map, 1:50,000 L7015 5850 II, Encl:SNF 05-59080-86/DX 5D2," both DIA Source file 5102, Inventory of the Records of the Senate Select Committee on POW/MIA Affairs.

24. P 080417Z MAY 86, subject: JCRC Report T86-182, Seventy American Prisoners on a Train in Long Khanh, Vietnam in 1979, DIA Source file 5115, POW/MIA; authors' map.

25. JCRC T82-022, June 11, 1982, subject: Refugee Report, Hearsay of Americans at Xuan Loc, Vietnam, DIA Source file 1319, POW/MIA; authors' map. It has not been determined if the group of seventy old, bearded American POWs reportedly seen getting off the train in Long Khanh Province in late 1979 and being marched off to a nearby POW camp was, in fact, the same group of (eighty) American POWs reportedly observed arriving at the prison camp at Xuan Loc in Long Khanh Province sometime in 1979 after their earlier evacuation from Lang Son near the Chinese border. Nor has it been determined where in the Lang Son area the eighty Americans had reportedly been held. Officials later postulated, however, that they may have been held at a prison located on the outskirts of Lang Son that had long been of interest to U.S. intelligence personnel. This prison, located just over 1.5 kilometers west-southwest of the city center, had been known to U.S. intelligence personnel during the war as the "Lang Son Possible PW Camp, N-104." Though wartime officials had considered it possible that American POWs were being held at Lang Son N-104—and had therefore ordered that the prison be photographed on a regular basis—none of the American prisoners returned at Operation Homecoming reported they had been held there. (Defense Intelligence Agency, Basic Report, Military Logistics, North Vietnam, Lang Son Possible PW CAMP N-104, January 1973, "Miscellaneous PW Files, Possible PW Camps," POW/MIA; "Possible/Suspect Prisoner of War Camps and Briefing Boards/Notes," black-and-white DIA map titled "Location of Possible PW Camps [in North Vietnam]"; "North Vietnam Photo Intelligence Briefing Notes on Briefing Board No. DI-8-72-751 (U)," October 4, 1972; low-quality annotated undated wartime DIA reconnaissance photo titled "North Vietnam, Lang Son Possible PW Camp, N-104, 215037N 1064505E, all from pp. 15–185, 15–186, 15–233, and 15–234 of unknown DOD publication, and high-quality annotated wartime DIA reconnaissance photo dated June 11, 1972, titled "North Vietnam, Lang Son Possible PW Camp, N-104, 215037N 1064505E," with schematic and map; *Places and Dates of Confinement of Air Force, Navy and Marine Corps Prisoners of War Held in North Vietnam 1964—1973,* all from Hendon files.)

26. JCRC HK84-040, April 11, 1984, subject: Refugee Report, Alleged Americans Held Near Hanoi; relevant excerpt (paragraph 3, subparagraphs A–C) from R 1208547 JUN 85, subject: Hong Kong Refugees Reporting Live Sightings of Americans, and source's hand-drawn sketch of building where he said he filmed the two American POWs, labeled "Sketch 'A,' " all DIA Source file 2197, POW/MIA; authors' map.

27. U.S. officials would quickly recognize that this was the same film studio that had been part of a multicompound prison facility that housed several hundred American POWs during the war. This prison compound, located just south of the Nga Tu So intersection at a point along the western boundary of Bach Mai Airfield, was known officially as "Cu Loc N-53," after a nearby village. The American POWs held there during the war called the main compound area of the prison the "Zoo," and an adjoining, smaller compound "Zoo Annex." (Annotated wartime DIA reconnaissance photo dated June 22, 1970, titled "North Vietnam, Ha Noi PW Detention Installation, Cu Loc, N-53, 21 00 08N 105 49 30E," with schematic; annotated wartime DIA reconnaissance photo with date redacted titled "North Vietnam . . . [redacted] . . . N-53 [redacted], 21 00 08N 105 49 30E," with schematic and map and number "2 1545" stamped in upper right-hand corner, both POW/MIA; R 231046Z JAN 90, subject: JCRC Report HK89-328, U.S [*sic*] POW's Observed in Hanoi City and Defense Intelligence Agency, "DIA Evaluation of PW/MIA Information Provided by Vietnamese Refugee Source [redacted] (40153)," both DIA Source file 11319, POW/MIA; annotated, untitled DIA map showing locations of

eight confirmed wartime prisons in the Hanoi area and pages 0001 and 0004 only of O 140643Z JUN 92, with handwritten notation "Film Studio @ Zoo" in upper right-hand corner of page 0001, all from Hendon files.)

**28.** Central Intelligence Agency, Memorandum for Assistant Vice Director for Collection Management, Department of Defense; Principal Advisor for Prisoner of War, Missing in Action Affairs (International Security Affairs); Director, Vietnam, Laos and Kampuchea, Bureau of East Asian and Pacific Affairs, Department of State, subject: Interviewing of Alleged U.S. Prisoners of War in Hanoi Circa November 1979," Hendon files, with additional, similar copy containing CIA document FIR-317/09237-84, DIA Source file 2231, POW/MIA. U.S. officials would receive other reports of American POWs being filmed by the North Vietnamese after the war. One such report that would prove especially useful in helping U.S. officials determine what the films were being used for would come from a Vietnamese woman who had served as a shipping and receiving clerk at the southern port of Qui Nhon after the war. This woman would tell U.S. officials that in March or April 1977, she and her fellow workers were shown a film about American POWs who were still held captive by the North Vietnamese government. The woman said that the film, which she and her coworkers were told had been shot in North Vietnam after the war and was being shown only to SRV government workers, contained footage of different groups of five to ten American POWs dressed in red striped pajamas. She said that during the film the narrator identified these American prisoners as pilots who had been shot down over North Vietnam. She also recalled the narrator stating that the prisoners shown in the film were being detained in North Vietnam. She further recalled that the narrator also berated the "American imperialists" and urged the audience to hate the United States and declared that the United States must pay "retribution" for the damage it had caused during the war. (Department of Defense Intelligence Information Report 2 240 5017 79, US PW's/MIA's in the SRV, date: 791204, with attached "Report of Interview," IAGPC-OPS, December 3, 1979, subject: Interview with Vietnamese Refugee Re: US PW's in the SRV, Shields Files, POW/MIA.)

**29.** Hendon's handwritten notes of interview with DIA Source 3560 (the West German engineer), on Hotel Continental stationery, dated 23 feb '93, beginning with "The Videotape—A 50 minute debrief of . . ." and accompanied by Source 3560's annotated hand-drawn sketch of the "Bai-Bang Papermill . . ." and the nearby Swedish administrative compound "Little Sweden," dated 21 February 1993, and signed by source. This sketch was prepared in Hendon's presence at Guayaquil, Equador. Handwritten notes in upper right-hand corner relating to "Olaf Svenssen" added by Hendon during source's preparation of sketch, Hendon files.

**30.** Hendon's videotaped interview of DIA Source 3560, the West German engineer, conducted at Guayaquil, Ecuador, February 23, 1993. The interview was necessitated by the fact the substantive portions of the original DOD interview of the source were not included in the source's file when it was declassified in late 1992. (R 311129Z OCT 85, subject: Report of Possible American MIA in Vietnam, with Hendon's handwritten note on page 2 stating "P.3+Missing from National Archives—Hendon, 10 feb '93," and source's original sketch map of "Compound at Bai-Bang, N. V.," redrawn on October 28, 1985, at Kano, Nigeria, by personnel from the U.S. Defense Attaché Office, U.S. Embassy, Lagos, with cover letter [redacted]-172-85 dated November 15, 1985, from Thomas E. Leverette, Colonel, USA, Defense Attache, Embassy of the United States of America, U.S. Defense Attache Office, Lagos, Nigeria, to Defense Intelligence Agency, Attn: VO-PW/ Mr. [name redacted], Washington, D.C., subject: Report of Possible American MIA in Vietnam; and R 011658Z OCT 85, subject: Report of Possible MIA in Vietnam, all DIA Source file 3560, Inventory of the Records of the Senate Select Committee on POW/MIA Affairs.)

**31.** Swedish map titled "BaiBang-Guide," acquired by Hendon from former officials of WP System/Bai Bang Paper Mill Project in Stockholm, Sweden, March 1993. Corrected location provided to Hendon by a confidential source whom Hendon considers reliable.

**32.** Names of the two Americans provided to Hendon by a confidential source whom Hendon considers reliable. Declassified DOD records show that around 9:00 A.M. on June 9, 1968, 1st Lt. Walter R. Schmidt Jr., USMC, was shot down while leading a flight of two A-4Es attacking North Vietnamese trucks hidden along a road leading into the northern end of the A Shau Valley, west-southwest of Hue in South Vietnam. ("File Record Summary" and annotated DOD 1:50,000 black-and-white map of shootdown site, Schmidt, W.R., Jr., Casualty Files, POW/MIA; authors' color 1:250,000 map of area titled "Shootdown and Probable Sighting of Lt. Walter Roy Schmidt, USMC, A Shau Valley RVN, June 1968.")

According to his FAC, who witnessed the shootdown and subsequent events, Schmidt successfully ejected from his stricken aircraft and landed in some low bushes about ten meters from the road. The FAC called in rescue helicopters and then established radio contact with Schmidt. Schmidt said he had a broken right leg and possibly a broken right arm and would need a medic on the ground. The rescue helicopters soon arrived and, according to the FAC,

> I escorted the first jolly green in three times, but each time he was driven off by ground fire. We continually expended ordinance on all the enemy positions observed, even when the jolly green was attempting to hover, but enemy ground fire came from all around, and drove the helicopter off each time. After the third attempt, both the helicopter and my O-2 were so low on fuel we had to return to our bases. While I was gone, another FAC escorted another jolly green into the downed pilot. This jolly green's engine was shot out and it crashed killing the crew. When I returned, numerous fighters were expending anti personnel ordinance all around the downed pilot. We still had radio contact with him, and hesaid [sic] that there were no enemy in his immediate vicinity. The next jolly green to attempt a pick up, was also hit in an engine, and was just barely able to make it into Khe Sanh for an emergency landing. After this, contact with the pilot on the ground was lost. Rescue was attempted until nightfall, but the enemy small arms fire continued to be too heavy for the helicopters to get in. The next morning, the pilot and chute were both gone. (Statement of Captain Charles Heckman USAF [Trail 36], from REFNO 1205-1-01, Schmidt.)

Marine Corps records indicate that Schmidt's wingman later offered additional details of what had taken place during the period from the 9:00 A.M. shootdown until darkness fell:

> The other pilot on the . . . mission stated that Lt Schmidt's parachute drifted into some trees but [he] managed to get to the ground. He was however unable to move from vicinity of parachute. Radio contact lost twice during the day. Believed Lt Schmidt uncon_scious [sic] at these times. At end of day enemy troops observed within twenty meters of Lt Schmidt's position. Next morning there was no evidence of the parachute, any personal gear, or . . . Lt Schmidt. (CO VMA-121 MAG-12 1STMAW INVES RPT 1:WDS:DC OVER 3040 OF 4JUL68, from "REFNO 1205-1-01, SCHMIDT.)

Declassified records state that though Schmidt was initially listed as "missing in Action," his status was quickly changed to "captured." The Marine Corps record describing the change in status states:

> Command decision made to change status to captured because of the following facts:

> The mountainous terrain would impede evasion: his self diagnosed injuries coupled with several sightings in_dicating [sic] he had not moved from his original position, tends to indicate his inability to do so: [sic] and that . . . just prior to darkness enemy troops observed within . . . 20 meters of Lt Schmidt. And that in the morning there was nothing left of the flight gear parachute or Lt Schmidt. Reinforced by the fact that the NVA are prone to taking POW's. (Ibid.)

On or about July 4, 1968, Schmidt's parents were formally advised that their son was being carried in "captured" status. (Ibid.)

On June 9, 1972, the fourth anniversary of his shootdown, Marine Corps officials in Washington reviewed the information surrounding [now Captain] Schmidt's "disappearance" and "directed that he be continued in his present status ("Captured"). (Department of the Navy, Headquarters United States Marine Corps, Washington, D.C., DNA-6-gas, 9 Jun 1972, memorandum signed "R.P Holt.)

On December 12, 1972, a Marine Corps casualty officer delivered a Christmas poinsettia to the home of Schmidt's parents. A portion of the Marine Corps memorandum describing the visit states that "only [Captain Schmidt's sister] Miss Helen Schmidt was home who accepted on behalf of her family. She stated that her father is now working and they are all becoming excited that Capt Schmidt may be home soon. Their hope is apparently built around the news media reports." (Page of memorandum signed by G. B. Kruczkowski, Capt, REFNO 1205-1-01, Schmidt.)

Captain Schmidt's name did not appear on any of the prisoner/died in captivity lists turned over by the Communists in January 1973 (see Chapter 6). Still, at the conclusion of Homecoming, Schmidt remained officially a "prisoner of war." (Draft letter to the Honorable Lester L. Wolff, REFNO 1205-1-01, Schmidt.) Until September 10, that is, six months after Homecoming, when Marine Corps officials changed Captain Schmidt's status from "prisoner of war" to "deceased." (Department of the Navy, Headquarters United States Marine Corps, Washington, D.C., MSPA-1-6-wah, 10 SEP 1973, subject: Determination of death; case of Captain Walter R. Schmidt, Jr., REFNO 1205-1-01, Schmidt.) The change in status having been made, the commandant of the Marine Corps sent the following message to Schmidt's parents in September 1973:

> I deeply regret to confirm that the status of your Son, Captain Walter R. Schmidt, Jr., has been changed from prisoner of war to deceased, body not recovered. Based on a review of your son's

case, it was determined that he died on 9 June 1968. On behalf of the United States Marine Corps I Extend our heartfelt condolences in your bereavement.
R. E. Cushman, Jr., General, USMC, Commandant of the Marine Corps. (REFNO 1205-1-01, Schmidt.)

But then, some sixty days later, the wheel ran off when suddenly and embarrassingly on December 14, 1973, it became apparent to U.S. officials that Schmidt had in all likelihood been captured alive and taken from the A Shau Valley as everyone had surmised in the first place. The news of Schmidt's apparent capture came from a captured Communist officer being debriefed during the continuing combat in Indochina. He reported that on an unrecalled day in June 1968, he observed a U.S. POW under guard in the A Shau Valley. The Communist officer said that he had seen the prisoner alongside a stream on the side of Route 548, the main north-south road leading through the valley. He cited the exact location as being in the vicinity of map coordinates YC425958. (Authors' annotated color 1:250,000 map titled "Shootdown and Probable Sighting of Lt. Walter Roy Schmidt, USMC, A Shau Valley RVN, June 1968.") The Communist officer said that one of the soldiers guarding the prisoner told him the POW was an officer and a pilot who had been captured in the A Shau Valley approximately fourteen to seventeen kilometers away. The officer estimated the POW to be twenty-six to twenty-eight years old. (Memorandum for the record, INTC-THM-dtf-3461, DEC 14 1973, subject: Captain Walter R. Schmidt, Jr., REFNO 1205-1-01, Schmidt.) In subsequent analyses of the sighting, DIA officials would state that (1) the details [of the captured Communist officer's sighting] "are consistent with 1st Lt. Walter R. Schmidt and, in fact, are in complete congruence with only Schmidt"; (2) "Schmidt became captured is strongly indicated by the close proximity of enemy troops . . . [and] this report adds weight to our assessment that he was likely captured"; and (3) the "report . . . , all details of which is [sic] consistent with Lieutenant Schmidt, indicates he was transported from the A Shau Valley area to an unknown location in June 1968." (Defense Intelligence Agency, memorandum [redacted]-1072/PW-MIA, 19 SEP 1989, from Joseph A. Schlatter, Colonel, USA, Chief, Special Office for Prisoners of War and Missing in Action, to Commander, Joint Casualty Resolution Center, Naval Air Station, Barbers Point, HI, subject: Wartime Interrogation Report Related to 1st Lt. Walter R. Schmidt Jr., with attachment titled "Case 1205: First Lieutenant Walter R. Schmidt, Junior, both REFNO 1205-1-01, Schmidt, W.R., Jr.)

Todd Melton, the other American prisoner reportedly returned to the Vietnamese by the Swedes, was one of the four Air Force Security Service "backenders" believed captured by the Pathet Lao after *Baron 52*, the USAF EC-47Q electronic surveillance aircraft, was shot down near Binh Tram #44 on the Ho Chi Minh Trail in southern Laos on February 5, 1973 (see Chapter 6). The aircraft Melton was aboard was basically a C-47 with a rear cargo compartment outfitted with banks of consoles containing top secret electronic eavesdropping equipment. The crew consisted of four officers—a pilot, a copilot, a "third pilot," and a navigator up front—and four enlisted men from the USAF Security Service—the "backenders"—who manned the consoles and collected the intelligence.

According to the official history of *Baron 52*'s unit, the 6994th Security Squadron, the *Baron 52* crash site was located on February 8 and a rescue/security force was sent in the following day "to investigate the crash site and recover any bodies and/or classified material that might have been left." Quoting from the official history:

> TSgt Schofield and Sgt Keen of the 6994th Security Squadron accompanied the rescue force to aid in the recovery of all classified material and equipment that was on board. TSgt Schofield was the third man on the ground, preceded by two pararescue men who established a perimeter. It was observed by TSgt Schofield that the main cabin must have suffered intense heat because all of the consoles were completely burnt. Of the remains of the three bodies found at the site, none were believed to be those of the Security Service crew. The USAFSS crew was listed as MIAs until 23 February 1973 when their status was changed to killed in action in spite of the fact that certain intelligence reports [redacted] had reported the capture of four fliers in the vicinity of the Baron 52 crash site. (Vietnam War Internet Project Documents Relating to POW/MIAs, "The Baron 52 Shootdown, USAF Oral History Interview," p. 3, www.vwip.org.)

33. Hendon's numerous conversations with Lieutenant General Tighe.
34. "POWs Won't be Found Without Cost," *Wall Street Journal*, April 24, 1985. Tighe would later cite the cases of former Marine Corps Private Robert Garwood and a young American civilian named Charles Dean (brother of Dr. Howard Dean) as the most glaring examples of how the analysts and managers at the Special Office chose to believe the postwar sightings of American stay-behinds and civilians but refused to believe any of the sightings of American POWs in captivity after the war. Garwood, who, as previously noted, chose to remain in North Vietnam at war's end, was the subject of a

number of refugee reports, virtually all of which the analysts believed. Dean, who had been active in the antiwar movement in the United States and had what DIA analysts called a "hippie-like" appearance, had been captured by Pathet Lao forces in September 1974 while floating down the Mekong River on a sightseeing trip with an Australian friend. Some sixteen independent human sources—many of whom later became refugees and told what they had seen or heard—reported details of Dean's and his friend's capture, their transfer to a PL prison facility, their imprisonment there, their subsequent transfer to another prison facility, statements they had reportedly made while in captivity, etc. Choosing to believe virtually all of these reports, DIA personnel had officially declared after the war that Dean and his companion had, in fact, been captured and imprisoned by the PL and had remained alive in captivity during the period of the reporting. (Hendon discussions with Lieutenant General Tighe; Defense Intelligence Agency, "Summary of Information Concerning the Case of Mr. Charles Dean, U.S. Civilian, and Mr. Neil Sharman, Australian Civilian," with photos, in *Americans Missing in Southeast Asia, Hearings Before the House Select Committee on Missing Persons in Southeast Asia*, Part 3, pp. 283–86.)

35. Biography of Jerry O. Tuttle, www.sei.cmu.edu/about/bov/tuttle.html.

36. Statement of Jerry O. Tuttle, memorandum for the record, December 6, 1991, subject: POW/MIA Discussions, Inventory of the Records of the Senate Select Committee on POW/MIA Affairs.

37. Hendon's telephone interview with Tuttle, February 5, 2001.

38. Hendon's telephone interview with Tuttle, February 5, 2001; Hendon's handwritten notes of conversation with Tuttle, Tuttle's office, the Pentagon, March 4, 1986.

39. Ibid.

40. Tighe had enormous respect for Tuttle and backed him to the hilt. (Tighe proudly referred to Tuttle as "my hot admiral.") Predictably, however, strong resentment toward Tuttle quickly surfaced in the Special Office. In the bureaucratic backstabbing that followed, the civilian managers and analysts tried repeatedly to sabotage Tuttle's initiatives and, making little effort to conceal their contempt for their new boss, put the word out all over Washington that he was trying to force them to say that POWs were alive when in fact none were. To this day, the civilian managers and analysts still derisively refer to the period as "the Tuttle era." (Hendon's numerous conversations with analysts and members of management team at the Special Office.)

41. For example, United States government memorandum, December 20, 1979, subject: PW/MIA Daily Report, DIA Files, POW/MIA.

42. From untitled DOD chart dated August 14, 1980, Reel 20, Series 92–302, DOD POW/MIA Microfilm Collection, Library of Congress, with authors' adjustment to reflect August total.

43. Memorandum for the Secretary of Defense from Jerry O. Tuttle, Rear Admiral, USN, Assistant Deputy Director for Defense Intelligence, subject: Sightings of Americans in Vietnam—Information Memorandum, November 2, 1979, DIA Source file 0412, POW/MIA.

44. Defense Intelligence Agency, U-4242/DI-E2/[redacted]/31 MAY 83/50501/mpk, from James A. Williams, Lieutenant General, U.S. Army, Director, to Honorable Gillespie V. Montgomery, House of Representatives, Washington, D.C., DIA Source file 0412, POW/MIA.

45. Message dated [redacted] NOV 79 from DIA Washington DC//DI to USDLO Hong Kong, for Captain Kully and LCOL Jordan from RADM Tuttle, subject: Refugee [name redacted], DIA Source file 0412, POW/MIA.

46. Selected pages of DIA Report of Interview with [source's name redacted], DIA Source file 0412, POW/MIA.

47. Handwritten letter from DIA Source 0405 with dateline "Bourges, October 20, 1979" to Miss Ann Mills Griffiths, National League of Families of P.O.W./M.I.A., Washington, D.C., DIA Source file 0405, POW/MIA.

48. Authors' color map titled "25–30 American POWs Seen in October and Again in November 1978 at Logging Camp SE of Loc Ninh."

49. Source's hand-drawn memory sketch titled "Sketch Map, PW Camp Located Near LOC NINH, VM," with handwritten notation "Incl #1," in Report of Interview with [source name redacted], 17 December 1979, Defense Intelligence Agency, Directorate for Defense Intelligence, Plans and Policy Division, PW/MIA Branch, DIA Source file 0405, POW/MIA.

50. P 091540Z NOV 79, subject: THIS IS IR 6 832 0294 79, US POW/MIA Sighting—Loc Ninh, South Vietnam (pp. 1–3 only, unknown number of subsequent page(s) omitted from declassified file), DIA Source file 0405, POW/MIA.

51. P 091547Z NOV 79, subject: OPS Data, DIA Source file 0405, POW/MIA.

52. Project assignment instructions, 1[illegible] November 1979, Possible Prison Camps/Detention Facilities in South Vietnam, DIA Source file 0405, POW/MIA.

**53.** Later reference to the CIOP in Central Intelligence Agency, 2 DEC 1980, memorandum for Director of Collection Management, Defense Intelligence Agency, Department of Defense, Attention: Colonel Franklin D. Mastro, from: John H. McMahon, Deputy Director of Operations, subject: Update of Clandestine Intelligence Operational Proposal (CIOP)—Socialist Republic of Vietnam, DIA Source file 0405, POW/MIA.

**54.** Analyst's 1:50,000 map, with handwritten annotations, DIA Source file 0405, POW/MIA.

**55.** Justification for Current Loc Ninh Recon Within [redacted], DIA Source file 0405, POW/MIA.

**56.** "Final Report of Interviews with Le Dinh," Defense Intelligence Agency, Directorate for Defense Intelligence, Plans and Policy Division, PW/MIA Branch, all from Reel 17, Series 92-300, POW/MIA.

**57.** Embassy of the United States of America, Defense Attaché Office, Paris, France, U-2081, to Defense Intelligence Agency, Attn: DI, Washington, D.C., October 19, 1979, subject: *Le Matin* Article with enclosure and "Defector Reports on Soviet Missile Bases in SRV, Laos," *Le Matin* (in French), October 17, 1979, pp. 10, 11, FBIS, Asia and Pacific, IV, December 4, 1979, Vietnam, K8–K13, all from Reel 96, Series 92-300, POW/MIA.

**58.** P 030940Z DEC 79, POW/MIA and Inventory of the Records of the Senate Select Committee on POW/MIA Affairs. In an intelligence report that Hendon has seen and read in the declassified records held by the Library of Congress or the National Archives but cannot relocate, CIA officials in Bangkok reported in 1980 that Thai intelligence agents had interviewed a former Thai or Lao prisoner—Hendon cannot recall which—who reported that he had been transferred from Vieng Sai to Attopeu by plane in November 1979 and had been seated during the flight near some American prisoners previously held in Vieng Sai who were also being transferred to Attopeu. The former Thai or Lao prisoner reported that at a point during the flight when the plane was flying close to the Mekong River, one of the Americans (who was looking out the window at the time), began pointing out the window and excitedly exclaiming "Udorn!" "Udorn!" "Udorn!" while motioning for the other Americans to look out the window. This Thai or Lao prisoner said he took this to mean that the American who had spoken had been based at the Udorn air base during the war. Hendon found this report especially poignant due to the fact that while flying east of the Mekong in Lao airspace in December 1981 (while he and LeBoutillier were flying from Vientiane south to Savannakhet on a Lao military aircraft), he had seen the Udorn air base out of the right-hand side of the aircraft and had urged LeBoutillier to look out the window and see it in the distance. He had said to LeBoutillier, "That's the last thing a lot of our guys saw, John." This occurred many years before Hendon read the declassified report.

**59.** Hendon's interview with Tighe, La Jolla, CA, spring 1992.

**60.** December 12, 1979, NSA memorandum for [redacted], subject: Contact Report, in which a Col. Picinich of DIA is quoted, POW/MIA and Inventory of the Records of the Senate Select Committee on POW/MIA Affairs.

**61.** United States government six-page memorandum to DR [DIA Director Tighe] from: [redacted], December 18, 1979, subject: PW/MIA Report, DIA Case File 0412, Vol. III, POW/MIA.

## CHAPTER 19. 1980: RESCUE PLANS

**1.** Untitled DOD chart dated August 14, 1980, POW/MIA.

**2.** "Possible USG Statements on Americans Held in Indochina" and assorted papers, DIA Files, POW/MIA.

**3.** Defense Intelligence Agency, "Prisoners of War and Missing in Action in Southeast Asia, A Report, DIA Interim Report of Interview with [source name redacted]," DIA Source file 0846, POW/MIA.

**4.** Source's hand-drawn map titled "Camp K-55," ibid.

**5.** Copies of four annotated satellite images, DIA Source file 0846, POW/MIA.

**6.** Department of the Air Force, December 5, 1980, subject: [redacted], Male Born 18 Oct 36, RVN, Vietnamese Refugee, DIA Source file 0846, POW/MIA.

**7.** Defense Intelligence Agency, "Prisoners of War and Missing in Action in Southeast Asia."

**8.** Hendon's interview with Tighe, La Jolla, CA, spring 1992. Analysis shows that to get in and out of K-55, a U.S. rescue force would have had to traverse approximately 425 miles of hostile territory—whether the force launched and recovered from an aircraft carrier in the Gulf of Thailand, launched and recovered from the nearest staging area in Thai territory (the former U.S. air base at Ubon), or launched from one and recovered at the other. The former U.S. base at U-Tapao, Thailand, launch site for the marine force sent to rescue the crew of the *Mayagüez* in 1975, is even farther away. (Authors' annotated map.) By comparison, the U.S. force that had attempted to free the hostages in Iran earlier in 1980 had penetrated hostile airspace for a distance of some four hundred miles before disaster struck in the Great Salt Desert southeast of Tehran. ("Desert One," *Air Force* magazine, Vol. 82, no. 1, January 1999, and "The Plan: How It Failed," *Newsweek,* May 5, 1980.)

**9.** P R 022201Z DEC 80, with DIA map and heavily redacted United States Government memorandum, December 4, 1980, subject: American Prisoners in Laos, POW/MIA.

**10.** Authors' annotated color 1:250,000 map showing camp located at 17° 30' 46" N, 105° 25' 19" E, supporting DOD document containing handwritten map coordinates, Inventory of the Records of the Senate Select Committee on POW/MIA Affairs.

**11.** United States Government memorandum DATE: December 12, 1980, SUBJECT: PW Report TO: Director, DIA (ONLY), POW/MIA.

**12.** Heavily redacted annotated line drawing of prison camp as released by DOD in the general declassification of POW-related materials now on file at the Library of Congress and the National Archives; same line drawing with annotations added by Hendon from direct personal knowledge of the actual imagery; unannotated line drawing from satellite imagery taken from a different angle titled "Nhommarath Detention Camp, Ban Kouanpho, Laos, 10 December, 1980," Inventory of the Records of the Senate Select Committee on POW/MIA Affairs.

**13.** "Pocket Change Brief," a handwritten analyst's briefing, p. 9; CIA "Spot Report," January 6, 1981, both Inventory of the Records of the Senate Select Committee on POW/MIA Affairs.

**14.** Statement of Jerry O. Tuttle to Congressmen Hendon and LeBoutillier, Pentagon briefing, March 23, 1981, from "Briefings Presented" Inventory of the Records of the Senate Select Committee on POW/MIA Affairs.

**15.** NSA Hoen memorandum, December 30, 1980, subject: PW/MIA Meeting, DIA Source file 0846, POW/MIA.

**16.** December 31, 1980, hard copy of intercept, from National Security Agency, with handwritten notation, Microfilm Reel 1, POW/MIA.

**17.** Handwritten notes of Senate Select Committee intelligence investigator Bob Taylor, Inventory of the Records of the Senate Select Committee on POW/MIA Affairs.

**18.** Authors' two annotated color maps of the area; unclassified statement of Bob Taylor to Hendon, 1993. Taylor investigated the more sensitive and highly classified "special intelligence" for the Select Committee.

## CHAPTER 20. 1981: "GASOLINE"

**1.** Defense Intelligence Agency, S-9073/DI-7, memorandum for the Chairman, Joint Chiefs of Staff from Eugene F. Tighe, Jr., Lieutenant General, USAF, Director, January 28, 1981, subject: Current U.S. Prisoner of War Intelligence, "Miscellaneous PW File, Current POW Intelligence," POW/MIA.

**2.** Hendon's telephone interview with Lewis H. Burruss, December 4, 1996.

**3.** "Pocket Change Brief," p. 11.

**4.** Hendon's telephone interview with Herschel S. Morgan, January 3, 1997.

**5.** Intercept precisely as described to Hendon by a senior DOD official, spring 1981. Understandably, this highly classified intercept electrified U.S. officials at the time. The intercept has never been declassified, and it has never been determined why officials did not order a lightning raid on the camp immediately after it was received.

**6.** Hendon's personal recollections based upon his examination of satellite imagery of camp, hand-held photography of camp and occupants taken by the reconnaissance team, and statement of senior DOD official, all in spring 1981; DOD line drawings of satellite images of camp, Inventory of the Records of the Senate Select Committee on POW/MIA Affairs.

**7.** "Deposition questions/Mr. Bill Graver"; "Deposition questions/Mr. Tim Geraghty"; "Deposition Questions/Mr. John Stein"; memorandum for the record on Interview of Larry Waters, all Inventory of the Records of the Senate Select Committee on POW/MIA Affairs.

**8.** Interview notes, April 1, 1992, by Bob Taylor, William Gefferiss Graver, Inventory of the Records of the Senate Select Committee on POW/MIA Affairs.

**9.** Senate Select Committee investigator's handwritten notes of official record of May 21, 1981, meeting attended by Gens. Nelson and Gast and meeting the same day attended by Gens. Nelson and Tighe, Inventory of the Records of the Senate Select Committee on POW/MIA Affairs. Some familiar with the operation believed the trail to the leaker would lead west from the Pentagon up the George Washington Parkway to Langley. Others felt that, the generals' demands notwithstanding, it really didn't matter who had leaked he story because the damage had been done. Perhaps both were right. Graver, for his part, told Senate investigators in 1992 that CIA headquarters officials had had no intention of approving a second mission because they had received word that the press was onto the story. He also said that during the period of the mission he personally "didn't believe any POWs were being held against their will." (Interview notes, April 1, 1992, by Bob Taylor, William Gefferiss Graver, Inventory of the Records of the Senate Select Committee on POW/MIA Affairs.

**10.** "Parade," *Washington Post* edition, May 31, 1981, cover.

**11.** Hendon's personal knowledge.

**12.** *Prisoners of War/Missing in Action: Oversight, Hearings Before the Subcommittee on Asian and Pacific Affairs of the Committee on Foreign Affairs,* House of Representatives, 97th Cong., 1st sess., Part 1, June 25, 1981, p. 25.

**13.** Hendon and LeBoutillier's recollection of luncheon conversation.

**14.** Portions of declassified Briefing Book, Hendon files.

**15.** JCRC T81-024, May 1, 1981, subject: Refugee Report, Alleged Sighting of Captives in NVN, DIA Source file 0962, Inventory of the Records of the Senate Select Committee on POW/MIA Affairs.

**16.** The congressmen later learned that this ARVN officer, a major, had told U.S. officials that the group of American prisoners, which included one black, had arrived under guard at the prison's front gate at approximately 1:00 A.M. on January 10, 1981. When he heard talking, he got up to see what was going on, and it was then that he saw the Americans. He reported they were dressed in blue two-piece pajama-type outfits with vertical rust-colored stripes—which he said were of the same type given to foreign prisoners during the war—and were carrying small knapsacks on their backs. All of the American prisoners except the black had shoulder-length hair. The major said that the escorts who had brought the prisoners to the prison stood at the front gate talking to the prison guards for approximately five minutes. He said he then heard one of the Vietnamese say in the Vietnamese language, "This way, this way, quickly," followed by one or perhaps two of the Americans saying in English, "Let's go." The prisoners and their guards proceeded to the western section of the camp. The major said he never saw the Americans again. The prison where the Americans were seen is the Ha Nam Ninh "Me" camp, one of the several subcamps of the Ba Sao Prison complex located near Phu Ly, some thirty miles south of Hanoi. This prison complex is discussed in detail in subsequent chapters. (P 240301Z JUL 81, "Sighting of Americans in Phu Ly Prison Camp," DIA Source file 0997, POW/MIA.)

**17.** Memorandum for the record, July 20, 1981, subject: Lao Refugee [redacted], DIA Source file 0995, Inventory of the Records of the Senate Select Committee on POW/MIA Affairs. The congressmen later learned that this source passed a second polygraph and satellite imagery confirmed the existence of a camp at the exact location on Route 19 west of Muong Khoua he had described and drawn. This sighting is discussed in detail in Chapter 29.

**18.** R 210404Z AUG 81, "Alleged POW Sighting Vic Luang Prabang," DIA Source file 3018, Inventory of the Records of the Senate Select Committee on POW/MIA Affairs. Subsequent reporting from the U.S. embassy in Vientiane would show that news of this incident had caused grave concern among Australian diplomats stationed in Vientiane who feared that, coming on the heels of the publicity over Gnommorath, disclosure of the sighting might create a full-blown diplomatic incident. (R 260501Z SEP 81, subject: POW's in Laos, DIA Source file 3018.) Later, the UN official, fearing just such an incident himself and concerned for his career, rejected repeated pleas from U.S. officials in Vientiane and personal pleas from the two congressmen that he provide the United States with the exact location where the incident had occurred. (O 011005Z SEP 81, subject: Alleged POW Sighting in Laos, DIA Source file 3018; Hendon and Leboutillier personal knowledge.)

**19.** P 131015Z SEP 77, Subject: MIAS, "Fors" Casualty File, POW/MIA.

**20.** Upon returning to Bangkok following their meeting with Soubanh, the congressmen called on the Vietnamese at the SRV embassy. After a brief fifteen-minute discussion with the Vietnamese ambassador that was held in a decidedly hostile atmosphere, the congressmen were given a copy of an official demarche the SRV had presented to U.S. diplomats in Bangkok some weeks before. Included in the demarche was a revised formulation of the old Vietnamese litany concerning "unregistered POWs." The new version read, "All cases of Americans captured during the war and registered with the Centre responsible for P.O.W.s have already been brought to the attention of the U.S. side. . . . Cases of Americans reportedly captured but not registered with the Centre responsible for P.O.W.s require time for investigation and searching. Failure to register these cases was due to many reasons related to the war circumstances which led to their death or missing on the way from places of capture to the detention centers." (Copy of August 7, 1981, demarche given to congressmen by Vietnamese ambassador, Embassy of the Socialist Republic of Vietnam, Bangkok, evening of September 5, 1981, Hendon files.)

**21.** Memorandum from Congressmen Hendon and LeBoutillier to Bud McFarlane, May 12, 1982, Reference: POW/MIA Activities, Hendon files. Casey, a longtime friend of LeBoutillier's, had run unsuccessfully in 1966 for the congressional seat LeBoutillier now held. In September, LeBoutillier had arranged a meeting with Casey so that he and Hendon could brief the DCI on their efforts with the Lao and gain his support. The meeting, held in Casey's office at CIA headquarters at Langley, had been under way only a few minutes when Casey called one of his Asian experts and invited him to sit in. Casey introduced him to the two congressmen and said, "Have a seat. These boys have a plan to get some POWs out of Laos." When the man replied sarcastically, "Good luck," Casey exploded. "Don't give me that shit," he roared, "I am so *goddamned* tired of hearing that kind of talk around here. Now cut it out, goddamn it, and sit down and let's see what we can do to help!" The man sat down and the meeting continued. Hendon revered Casey from that moment on. (Hendon/LeBoutillier account of the meeting.)

**22.** O 040915Z JAN 82, FM AMEMBASSY VIENTIANE TO SECSTATE WASHDC IMMEDIATE 2318, subject: Lao Item Update: Visits.

## CHAPTER 21. 1982: "THE PRINCIPLE OF RECIPROCITY"

**1.** McFarlane memorandum, POW/MIA Activities.

**2.** McFarlane and Smardz, *Special Trust,* pp. 188, 172, 193.

**3.** McFarlane memorandum, POW/MIA Activities.

**4.** This new intelligence had come from a former ARVN captain who had been incarcerated in the Thanh Phong camp system in Thanh Hoa Province. The captain had told U.S. officials in February that when his wife had arrived at his reeducation camp to visit him during April or May of 1980, she had told him that she had just encountered two American prisoners on the road near the camp. She described the American prisoners as being very skinny. She told her husband that the Americans had implored her in the Vietnamese language to "go and tell any American whom she met that they were Americans and still being held prisoner." The captain told U.S. officials his wife had been very frightened by the encounter. (JCRC S82-001, March 27 1982, subject: Refugee Report, Hearsay of Americans Held in Thanh Hoa Province, DIA Source file 1298, POW/MIA.) In a subsequent interview, the captain told U.S. officials his wife had further described the two Americans as being tall and blond and wearing prison clothes. (JCRC S-82-001A, May 17, 1982, subject: Refugee Report, Hearsay of Two American POWs in Vietnam, DIA Source file 1298.)

**5.** R 100001Z MAY 82, subject: IR 2 722 0145 82 Laos/US POWs Reported in Laos, POW/MIA.

**6.** Memorandum, May 24, 1982, to Bud McFarlane from Congressman Bill Hendon and Congressman John LeBoutillier, reference: Follow up to meeting with the President; Memorandum, May 24, 1982, to Bud McFarlane, reference: Travel, both Hendon files. Just as the president had appeared deeply moved at the thought of recovering living POWs, so too had the congressmen been moved by Ronald Reagan's remarkable countenance, kindness, decency, and obvious compassion for the missing. In the months ahead they would learn that as a young man in Illinois in the late '20s and early '30s, lifeguard "Dutch" Reagan had made seventy-seven saves; that just after the Korean War, actor Ronald Reagan had volunteered for and then starred in the role of a Korean War POW in M-G-M's *Prisoner of War,* and the role had troubled him for years; and that during the Vietnam War, Governor Ronald Reagan had worn the POW bracelet of a Marine Corps helicopter pilot missing in Laos and had taken it off only when a survivor from the helicopter crew was released from captivity at Operation Homecoming and testified that the pilot had been killed in a firefight shortly after the crash.

**7.** Undated handwritten notes of telephone conversation between Hendon and Robert C. McFarlane, Hendon files. McFarlane would later tell staff attorneys for the Senate Select Committee on POW/MIA Affairs that "I thought it [shipping the medicine to the Lao] was a sensible idea. . . . I worked with Peter McPherson of AID to see if it was feasible. Peter found a way to do it." (Deposition of Robert C. McFarlane, pp. 49–50.)

**8.** Dr. Ponemek's list, in French, Hendon files.

**9.** "Fate of POWs, MIAs an Issue of the 'Highest' Priority, U.S. Says," AP in *Washington Post,* July 10, 1982, p. 2; "Weinberger: Some MIAs 'Assumed' Alive," *Army Times,* August 2, 1982; National League of Families of American Prisoners and Missing in Southeast Asia, *Newsletter,* August 2, 1982.

**10.** National League of Families of American Prisoners and Missing in Southeast Asia, *Newsletter,* August 2, 1982; Department of Defense, *POW-MIA Fact Book,* July 1983, p. 14.

**11.** National Security Council memorandum from LTC Richard Childress, USA, to Rep. Bill Hendon, August 3, 1982; National Security Council Memorandum from LTC Richard Childress, USA, to Rep. Bill Hendon, August 4, 1982, with attached price list, Hendon files.

**12.** Lao People's Democrate [*sic*] Republic . . . State Committee for Social Security and War Veterans, "Initial Project Regarding Rehabilitation of People's Livelihood in Provinces Heavily Affected by War in Laos During the Years 1964–72 (Provinces of Houaphan, Xiengkhouang, Khammouane, Savannakhet, Saravane, Attopeu and Paksong District)," Hendon files.

**13.** National League of Families of American Prisoners and Missing in Southeast Asia, memo to Board of Directors ONLY from Ann Griffiths, Executive Director, August 5, 1982, subject: League Trip to Southeast Asia, Hendon files.

**14.** Hendon's telephone interview with Earl Hopper, March 20, 1997.

**15.** Hendon's telephone conversations with Ron Miller, spring 1997. For an example of the new U.S. attitude Miller mentioned, see Department of State telegram 0 272325Z SEP 82, FM SECSTATE WASHDC TO [multiple addressees], Subject: Press Guidance: POW/MIA's, authors' files.

**16.** "Reception-Buffet," Tuesday, November 23, 1982, with guest list, Hendon files.

**17.** Statement of William Thomas to Hendon, Vientiane, Laos, November 23 1982.

## CHAPTER 22. 1983: A DRAMATIC CHANGE OF COURSE

**1.** "Address by the President to the National League of Families of American Prisoners and Missing in Southeast Asia," Hyatt Regency Hotel, Crystal City, Virginia, the White House, Office of the Press Secretary, January 28, 1983.

**2.** "Reagan Pledges Search for Men Missing in Vietnam," *Washington Post,* January 29, 1983, p. A4.

**3.** "Rebels Foil US Adventurers' Raid into Laos," *Bangkok Post,* January 31, 1983, p. 1.

**4.** PRIORITY 310611Z JAN 83, from FBIS Bangkok Th to [multiple addressees], "AFP: Thailand— Government Reacts to Reports on Commando Group," Hendon's Pentagon files.

**5.** "Thais Probe Adventurer's Search for POWs in Laos," *Washington Post,* February 22, 1983, p. 1.

**6.** "Bo Gritz: The Glory & the Search," *Washington Post,* March 3, 1983, p. D1.

**7.** Hendon's handwritten transcript of ABC's *Good Morning America* interview with Gritz, March 4, 1983, Hendon's Pentagon files.

**8.** "Gritz Insists POWs in Laos but Concedes He Has No Hard Proof," *Washington Times,* March 23, 1983, p. 1.

**9.** Mary McGrory, "Bo Gritz' Story Is Fascinating, but Does He Really Believe It?" *Washington Post,* March 24, 1983, p. A3.

**10.** For example, "Colonel Gritz's Dubious Mission," *Time,* April 4, 1983.

**11.** "Bo Gritz' Story Is Fascinating, but Does He Really Believe It?"

**12.** The CIA later reported the impact the Gritz mission reportedly had on LPDR officials and the ongoing "Lao Initiative." (Undated CIA memorandum, subject: Comments of Lao People's Democratic Republic (LPDR) Official on the Issue of Americans Missing in Action in the LPDR, CIA Files, Microfilm Reel 354, POW/MIA.)

**13.** Weinberger Links Salvadoran War to Global Competition," *Washington Post,* March 14, 1983, p. A15.

**14.** "Nicaraguan Warns Honduras on Raids," *New York Times,* April 10, 1983, p. 1.

**15.** *Proceedings and Debates,* 98th Cong., 1st sess., *Congressional Record,* Vol. 129, pt. 8, pp. 10134–137.

**16.** "President Appeals Before Congress for Aid to Latins," *New York Times,* April 28, 1983, p. 1; "President: Help Me Halt Latin Leftists," *USA Today,* April 28, 1983, p. 1; "Speech Seen as a Warning to Democrats," *Los Angeles Times,* April 28, 1983, p. 1.

**17.** Memorandum to Commodore Ring From Billy Hendon, February 22, 1983, Subject: Proposed Travel to Vientiane, Laos, Hendon Pentagon files.

**18.** This report was almost certainly declassified in the general declassification of POW-related documents that took place during and after 1992. However, it cannot be found in the current holdings of the Library of Congress and National Archives.

**19.** For example, letter from Mr. Glen Dale Shown, Jr. #93549, Fort Pillow State Farm, Fort Pillow, Tennessee to the Secretary of Defence [*sic*], May 5, 1983, Hendon's Pentagon files.

**20.** Hendon's precise recollection of Wolfowitz's statement.

**21.** Griffiths would later testify that "in the initial stages of the IAG it was more sessions to patronize the National League of Families and Ann Griffiths. . . . There was probably good intention there, but it was really mostly nonfunctional." *Oversight Hearings: Department of Defense, POW/MIA Family Issues, and Private Sector Issues, Hearings Before the Select Committee on POW/MIA Affairs,* United States Senate, December 1–4, 1992, p. 208.

**22.** For a list of IAG members and principal members later published by the League, see POW/MIA Interagency Group Members, 1/9/87, Elizabeth Stewart files.

**23.** Letter from Richard T. Childress, National Security Council, to Mr. George Brooks, Chairman of the Board, National League of Families of American Prisoners and Missing in Southeast Asia, May 17, 1983, Elizabeth Stewart files.

**24.** Statement of Carol Bates to Bill Hendon, 1985.

**25.** National League of Families of American Prisoners and Missing in Southeast Asia, *Newsletter,* May 31, 1983, AMG/32, Elizabeth Stewart files.

**26.** Ibid., November 27, 1979, AMG:9.

**27.** Ibid.

**28.** "Alternatives: Prepared by Ann Griffiths, 3/2/81," Elizabeth Stewart files.

**29.** POW/MIA Oversight, Subcommittee on Asian and Pacific Affairs, Committee on Foreign Relations, June 24, 1981.

**30.** Samples of league advertisements from National League of Families of American Prisoners and Missing in Southeast Asia, *Newsletter,* April 12, 1982, AMG/25, Elizabeth Stewart files.

**31.** "Shultz: Hanoi Holds Remains of U.S. MIAs" and "Shultz Accuses Vietnam of Withholding Remains of American Servicemen," *Washington Post,* June 29, 1983, pp. 1, A20.

**32.** Hendon's telephone interview with Earl Hopper, May 18, 2001.

**33.** "Remarks to the National League of Families Annual Meeting by Richard Childress, July 15, 1983," reprinted in *The Veterans Observer,* Dec.–Jan.–Feb. 1984.

**34.** National League of Families of American Prisoners and Missing in Southeast Asia, Ann Mills Griffiths, Executive Director to Family Members and Concerned Friends, August 12, 1983, Elizabeth Stewart files.

**35.** "Weinberger Visits Front Lines of Salvadoran War," *Washington Post,* September 8, 1983, p. A4; also photo in Oliver L. North with William Novak, *Under Fire* (Grand Rapids, MI: Zondervan, 1991).

**36.** "Central America Military Victory Called Necessity," *Washington Post,* September 13, 1983, p. A12.

**37.** "Prime Minister Of Grenada Dies in Military Coup," *Washington Post,* October 20, 1983, p. 1; "General Claims Power in Grenada," *Washington Post,* October 21, 1983, p. 1; "Caribbean Nations Discuss Response to Violence in Grenada" and "U.S. Says Situation Still Unclear as Naval Force Nears Grenada," *Washington Post,* October 23, 1983, p. A24; "U.S. Invades Grenada, Fights Cubans, Reagan Cites Protection of Americans," *Washington Post,* October 26, 1983, p. 1; "U.S. Troops in Grenada Invasion Exceed 6,000," *Washington Post,* October 29, 1983, p. 1; "Cuba Says Accord Reached for Return of Prisoners," *Washington Post,* October 30, 1983, p. A8.

**38.** "Student Evacuees Return, Praise U.S. Military," *Washington Post,* October 27, 1983, p. 1. That Grenada was on its way to becoming another Communist/Marxist-Leninist base in the Caribbean had been evident for many months. In late 1981, when the country had hosted its First International Conference in Solidarity With Grenada, prominent among those in attendance were ambassadors and/or high-ranking officials from the USSR, Cuba, Nicaragua, Bulgaria, Yugoslavia, East Germany, Libya, the PLO, South Yemen, Mongolia, North Korea, and Vietnam; Communist party representatives from Mexico, West Germany, the United States, and a number of small Caribbean nations; and officials representing such organizations as SWAPO (the South West Africa People's Organization), the Movement for the National Liberation of Barbados, the Chilean Resistance Movement, and the Patrice Lumumba Coalition of the U.S.A. (*Grenada Is Not Alone: Speeches by the People's Revolutionary Government at the First International Conference in Solidarity with Grenada, November 1981* (St. George's, Grenada: Fedon Publishers, 1982), pp. 144–47.)

**39.** "Undersecretary Urges More Salvadoran Aid," *Washington Post,* November 13, 1983, p. 1.

**40.** "Marines, Hondurans Storm Ashore in Mock Attack," *Washington Post,* November 19, 1983, p. 1.

**41.** "Pressure Builds for Concessions by Sandinista Regime," *Washington Post,* November 25, 1983, p. 1.

**42.** "U.S. Source Tells of Spy Flights Over Nicaragua," *Washington Post,* April 27, 1984, p. 1.

**43.** "President Defends Using Force," *Washington Post,* December 13, 1983, p. 1.

## CHAPTER 23. 1984: TRAGEDY AT ARLINGTON • A MISSED OPPORTUNITY IN THE OVAL OFFICE

**1.** Letter from Richard L. Armitage, Assistant Secretary of Defense, International Security Affairs to Ms. Ann Mills Griffiths, Executive Director, National League of Families of American Prisoners and Missing in Southeast Asia, January 21, 1984, Earl P. Hopper files.

**2.** National League of Families of American Prisoners and Missing in Southeast Asia, Memorandum to Board of Directors Only from Ann Mills Griffiths, February 17, 1984, subject: High Level Discussions, Earl P. Hopper files.

**3.** Letter from Col. Earl P. Hopper, Chairman of the Board, National League of Families of American Prisoners and Missing in Southeast Asia to Mrs. David Lewis, February 27, 1984, Earl P. Hopper files.

**4.** "Latin Panel Asks Aid of $8.4 Billion," *Washington Post,* January 12, 1984, p. 1.

**5.** "Nicaragua Says Copter Intruded," *Washington Post,* January 12, 1984, p. 1; "U.S. Pilot Killed in Honduras," *Washington Post,* January 12, 1984, p. 1; "In Managua, Nicaragua Denounces Incursion,"

*Washington Post,* January 13, 1984, p. 1; "Five Witnesses, Hondurans Say Border Crossed," *Washington Post,* January 13, 1984, p. 1; "A Condemnation, Helicopter Incident 'Unprovoked,'" *Washington Post,* January 13, 1984, p. 1; "Nicaragua Says It Shot Across Border at Chopper," *Washington Post,* January 18, 1984, p. A28.

6. "U.S. Buildup in Honduras Described," *Washington Post,* February 1, 1984, p. 1.

7. "Senate Votes, 84–12, to Condemn Mining of Nicaraguan Ports," *Washington Post,* April 11, 1984, p. 1.

8. "Mine Placed by U.S.-Backed Rebels Damages Soviet Tanker, Managua Says," *Washington Post,* March 21, 1984, p. A19.

9. "Nicaragua Asks World's Aid Against U.S. 'State Terrorism,'" *Washington Post,* March 14, 1984, p. A22.

10. William M. Hammond, *The Unknown Serviceman of the Vietnam Era* (Washington, DC: Center of Military History, United States Army, 1985), pp. 4–5.

11. Letter from Ann Mills Griffiths, Executive Director, National League of Families of American Prisoners and Missing in Southeast Asia to Honorable John O. Marsh, November 24, 1981, Ronald Reagan Presidential Library, Simi Valley, CA.

12. Secretary of the Army, memorandum for the Secretary of Defense, subject: Unknown Serviceman from the Vietnam Era, June 16, 1982; Secretary of Defense, memorandum for the Assistant to the President for National Security Affairs, subject: Selection of a Vietnam Unknown, August 23, 1982, both Ronald Reagan Library.

13. Memorandum for the Secretary of Defense, from Ann Mills Griffiths, Executive Director, National League of Families of American Prisoners and Missing in Southeast Asia SUBJECT: Proposed Interment of an unknown from the Vietnam Era, July 26, 1982, Ronald Reagan Library.

14. Memorandum for William P. Clark from Richard T. Childress, subject: Selection of a Vietnam Unknown, August 26, 1982, without Suggested Talking Points, POW/MIA.

15. Hammond, *Unknown Serviceman of the Vietnam Era,* p. 5.

16. Letter from Ann Mills Griffiths, Executive Director, National League of Families of American Prisoners and Missing in Southeast Asia to The Honorable John O. Marsh, March 15, 1984, Ronald Reagan Library.

17. Secretary of Defense, memorandum for the President, subject: Selection and Interment of an Unknown Serviceman from the Vietnam Era, March 16, 1984, Ronald Reagan Library.

18. Department of the Army, United States Army Central Identification Laboratory, Hawaii, Certification, Remains of TSN 0673-72 (X-26), March 21, 1984, signed by Johnie E. Webb, Jr., Maj, GS, Commanding, Ronald Reagan Library.

19. Memo for the record, April 4, 1984, subject: Documents to be Removed from X-26 File and Placed in the Blassie File, signed by Johnie E. Webb, Jr., Maj, GS, Commander, USA CILHI, with enclosure (statement of CPT. Richard S. Hess); Department of the Army, United States Army Central Identification Laboratory, Hawaii, Statement, April 4, 1984, signed by Johnie E. Webb, Jr., Maj, GS, Commanding, all Ronald Reagan Library.

20. "Unknown Soldier Is Selected," *New York Times,* April 15, 1984, p. 36, "Rites Slated For Vietnam 'Unknown,'" *Washington Post,* April 14, 1984, p. B1.

21. Letter to the President from Mrs. Anne M. Hart, Acting Chairman of the Board, National League of Families of American Prisoners and Missing in Southeast Asia, April 18, 1984, Ronald Reagan Library.

22. Hendon's telephone interview with Anne Hart, July 7, 2001.

23. Department of the Army, Office of the Assistant Secretary, memorandum for the Secretary of the Army, subject: Update on Vietnam Unknown, April 20, 1984, signed by William R. Gianelli, Assistant Secretary of the Army (Civil Works), Ronald Reagan Library.

24. Secretary of the Army, memorandum for the Secretary of Defense, subject: Update on Vietnam Unknown, April 23, 1984, Ronald Reagan Library.

25. The White House, memorandum for the President From Robert C. McFarlane, subject: Letter to the National League of Families in response to their letter at Tab B, May 4, 1984, Ronald Reagan Library.

26. The White House, letter from the President to Mrs. Anne Hart, Vice Chairman, National League of Families of American Prisoners and Missing in Southeast Asia, May 7, 1984, Ronald Reagan Library.

27. Hammond, *Unknown Serviceman of the Vietnam Era,* pp. 6–7.

28. "Duarte Meets Press" (photo), *Washington Post,* May 22, 1984, p. 1.

29. "Lowered Flags to Honor Unknown Soldier," *Washington Post,* May 22, 1984, p. A7.

30. "Demonstration" (photo), *Washington Post,* May 22, 1984, p. A11.

**31.** "A Rest in Honored Glory Awaits Unknown Soldier from Vietnam," *Washington Times,* May 25, 1984, p. 1.

**32.** "Vietnam Unknown Soldier Returned," *Washington Post,* May 25, 1984, p. 1.

**33.** Hammond, *Unknown Serviceman of the Vietnam Era,* pp. 20, 11.

**34.** "Reagan Honors Unknown American Killed in Vietnam War," *New York Times,* May 26, 1984, p. 9.

**35.** Ibid.

**36.** "Honored Symbol, Vietnam War's Unknown Buried In Arlington Tomb," *Washington Post,* May 29, 1984, p. 1.

**37.** "Respect, Sorrow, Pain, Anger, Pride," *Washington Times,* May 29, 1984, p. B1.

**38.** Hammond, *Unknown Serviceman of the Vietnam Era,* p. 7.

**39.** Statements of Earl Hopper, former chairman of the board, and Anne Hart, former vice chairman of the board, National League of Families of American Prisoners and Missing in Southeast Asia, June and July 2001.

**40.** "Reagan: 'A Grateful Nation Opens Her Heart in Gratitude,'" president's remarks at the funeral service and entombment of the Vietnam Unknown Serviceman, *Washington Post,* May 29, 1984, p. A8.

**41.** Hammond, *Unknown Serviceman of the Vietnam Era,* photo p. 27.

**42.** Ibid., pp. 13–14.

**43.** Just over a decade would pass before the truth about just what had actually occurred at Arlington began to filter out. The first hint came in July 1994, when activist Vietnam vet Ted Sampley of Kinston, North Carolina, publisher of a small veterans' newspaper highly critical of the government's efforts to recover live prisoners, reported that based on official documents he had uncovered, the Unknown could be identified and was in all probability Blassie. Sampley called on U.S. officials to open the tomb and perform DNA analysis—in widespread use by 1994—to determine if the remains were, in fact, those of Blassie. ("The Vietnam Unknown Soldier Can Be Identified," *U.S. Veteran Dispatch,* July 1994, p. 1, Hendon files.) When two years passed and no action had been taken, Sampley reprinted the article in the July 1996 edition of his newspaper, again calling on U.S. officials to open the tomb and perform DNA analysis on the remains. ("The Vietnam Unknown Soldier Can Be Identified," *U.S. Veteran Dispatch,* July 1996, p. 1, Hendon files.) When another year passed and there was *still* no response from the Pentagon, Sampley took his evidence to CBS News. In the fall of 1997, CBS investigators began filing Freedom of Information requests for documents pertaining to the naming and entombment of the Vietnam Unknown, and in early 1998 they began contacting U.S. officials for comment. At that point, in early January 1998, the house of cards constructed some fourteen years earlier began to collapse. "Ann Griffith [*sic*] believes if this story hits the airwaves it will cause a lot of problems . . . [and] will . . . put the government and past administration in a very bad light," one concerned Air Force official wrote in a January 12, 1998, e-mail to colleagues titled, "Possible Adverse Media on REFNO 1853-0-01, 1Lt Michael J. Blassie, Air Force." (From Perry, T Civ DPWCM(SMTP;PerryT@hq.afpc.af.mil), Monday, January 12, 1998 6:54 PM, to 'JOHNIE WEBB';'JOE HARTSELL', Cc: [multiple addressees], subject: Possible Adverse Media on REFNO 1853-0-01, 1Lt Michael J. Blassie, Air Force, from CBS News via National Alliance of Families.) "This will get very complicated and messy before it is resolved," CILHI's Webb was quoted as telling a government investigator by phone on January 14, after admitting that the remains in the tomb were, in fact, those of Blassie. (Blair, Mark, Memo for Record, subject: Lt Blassie—X-28 [*sic*]—Tomb of the Unknown for SEA, beginning "1545. 14 Jan 98. call Johnie Webb at CILHI. . . . I asked Mr. Webb if in fact . . . ," from CBS News via National Alliance of Families.)

On January 19, 1998, CBS reported that "a seven-month CBS News investigation has revealed that the identity of . . . [the] unknown serviceman is almost certainly known, and that some military officials, for whatever reason, knew it all along and tried to hide it." (CBS News "Up to the Minute" Web site, January 19, 1998, Hendon files.) The following evening, CBS reported that their investigation "has found evidence of a long-running cover-up. . . . A possible motive: One former high Pentagon official tells CBS News there was immense pressure from high up to find a Vietnam unknown and place his remains in the tomb by Memorial Day of the 1984 election year. . . . Pentagon officials tell CBS they have now interviewed specialists involved in selecting remains for the tomb who believed all along the remains were Blassie's." (Transcript of *CBS Evening News,* January 20, 1998, Hendon files.)

Blassie's mother responded to the CBS reports by asking that her son's remains be removed from the tomb and buried in his hometown of St. Louis, Missouri ("Report: U.S. Knew Unknown Soldier," AP, January 20, 1998, authors' files.) Mrs. Blassie's two U.S. senators, Republicans Christopher Bond and John Ashcroft, joined her in the request, telling Secretary of Defense William Cohen in a sharply worded letter that the Blassie family had an "absolute right to the return of the remains of their son and brother" and that the Department of Defense had a "sacred duty" to comply. In discussing the case, Bond told the *St. Louis Post-Dispatch* that it appeared the Pentagon had violated "the most basic requirements of human decency and dignity." ("Bond and Ashcroft Demand Answers About Pilot's Remains for His Family, Perform 'Sacred duty,' Senators Say in Letter to Defense Secretary," *St. Louis Post-Dispatch,* January 22, 1998.) Blassie's remains, along with some of his personal effects found with him at the time his partial remains were discovered in South Vietnam in 1972, were removed from the tomb shortly after midnight on May 14, 1998. ("Vietnam War Remains Removed From "Unknowns" Tomb," Reuters 14 REU 05-14-98 11:17 EST, authors' files; Blassie family photos.) The remains were later positively identified using DNA analysis. Lieutenant Blassie was buried with full military honors on July 11, 1998, at the Jefferson Barracks National Cemetery south of St. Louis. (" 'Unknown' Soldier Reburied with Full Honors in Missouri," AP in *Washington Times,* July 12, 1998.)

44. "U.S. Blames Hanoi for Icy Relations," *New York Times,* July 11, 1984.

45. "Remarks of the President at Ceremony for National POW/MIA Recognition Day," the White House, Office of the Press Secretary, July 20, 1984, authors' files.

46. "Reagan Says Laos Will Let U.S. Search Team Search Crash Site," *New York Times,* July 21, 1984, p. 1.

47. Deposition of Eugene F. Tighe, Jr., pp.191–95, 251–52.

48. For an interesting hearsay account describing Garwood's capture, see wartime intelligence report 6 029 0587 71, subject: Identification of a US Defector, June 2, 1971, POW/MIA.

49. Copy of note from Garwood Files, POW/MIA.

50. STOCKHOLM 0637 FM AMEMBASSY STOCKHOLM TO SECSTATE WASHDC IMMEDIATE 5885, Garwood Files, POW/MIA.

51. O P 140126Z FEB 79 ZFF6, FM SECSTATE WASHDC TO [multiple addressees], subject: Reported American in Vietnam, Hendon files; "Ex-Pow Wants to Leave VN," *Bangkok Post,* February 16, 1979.

52. Letter from Dermot G. Foley, Esq. to Col. Jerry Venanzi (USAF), May 15, 1985, Inventory of the Records of the Senate Select Committee on POW/MIA Affairs.

53. "Pfc. Garwood's Return Renews Families' Hopes," *New York Times* News Service in *Raleigh News,* May 25, 1979.

54. "Witness Says Garwood Told of POWs Who Stayed," AP in *Wilmington (NC) Morning Star,* January 23, 1981, p. 1B.

55. Hendon's contemporaneous phone notes, September 25, 1984, Hendon files.

56. Hendon recollection; also Dornan's account in "POWs Won't Be Found Without Cost," *Wall Street Journal,* April 24, 1985.

57. "U.S. Officials Skeptical but Seek More Information on Report of Vietnam POWs," *Los Angeles Times,* December 5, 1984, Garwood Files, POW/MIA.

58. Subsequent United States Government Memorandum from Julius Parker, Jr., Major General, USA, Deputy Director for Management and Operations to DR, December 17, 1984, subject: PW/MIA Weekly Report, Garwood Files, POW/MIA.

59. The corroborative nature of these reports is discussed at length at www. enormouscrime.com, Chapter 23.

60. Defense Intelligence Agency, memorandum for the Chief of Staff, United States Army, the Chief of Naval Operations, United States Navy, the Chief of Staff, United States Air Force, the Commandant, United States Marine Corps, U-20, 131/DC-2, from James A. Williams, Lieutenant General, U.S. Army, Director, February 1, 1985, subject: PW/MIA Briefing, 2 Enclosures, 1. DC-2 Memo dated 24 Dec 84, 2. DC-2 PW/MIA Affairs Division Briefing, Reel 58, Series 92-300, POW/MIA.

61. Rohrabacher's statement to Hendon in Udorn, Thailand, 1998, confirmed on the record during telephone interview May 4, 2004.

62. Department of the Navy, Headquarters United States Marine Corps, memorandum for the Commandant of the Marine Corps, 3461,INTC : MDJ :ljg, December 21, 1984, subject: Appraisal of Robert Garwood's Statements Concerning American POW's in Vietnam, Garwood Files, POW/MIA.

63. Letter from Ann Mills Griffiths, Executive Director, National League of Families of Prisoners and Missing in Southeast Asia to Mr. Norman Pearlstein, Managing Editor, *Wall Street Journal,* December 13, 1984, Garwood Files, POW/MIA.

## CHAPTER 24. 1985: "PROGRESS" IN THE SEARCH FOR REMAINS • FRESHMEN, STONEWALLED ON POWs, TURN TO PEROT • McFARLANE DROPS HIS GUARD

1. Hendon served on a congressional fact-finding mission that visited Honduras, El Salvador, and several other Central American countries in early 1985. The delegation, led by Rep. G. V. Mont-

gomery, left the region convinced that the situation there was extremely serious. And that, as Ronald Reagan had repeatedly said, the Sandinistas in Nicaragua and their allies, the Marxist-Leninist guerrillas operating inside El Salvador—and the Soviets and Cubans who were training, supporting, and supplying both—posed not only a potentially mortal threat to the pro-American governments of the region but also, given the specter of Soviet IRBMs being deployed inside Nicaragua, a very real and very serious threat to the national security of the United States. (Brief documentation of visit of "Codel Montgomery" to the region, Hendon files.)

2. Spectre photo and map of crash site location, *Americans Missing in Southeast Asia,* Part 5, p. 159.

3. Case #1962-1-01, Narrative, Department of the Air Force, December 21, 1973, subject: Continuance of Missing in Action Status Beyond Twelve Months—Case #478; Statement of Student Pilot and Instructor Pilot (Spectre 07) on Loss of Spectre 17, December 21, 1972, both Shields Files, POW/MIA; *Americans Missing in Southeast Asia,* Part 5, pp. 159–71.

4. *Americans Missing in Southeast Asia,* Part 5, p. 160.

5. "Bones of MiAs Found at Plane Crash Site in Laos," *Bangkok Post,* February 21, 1985, p. 6.

6. "Hope Rises for US MiA Search Teams," *Bangkok Post,* February 18, 1985, p. 5.

7. "Team Returns with Remains of MiAs," *Bangkok Post,* February 23, 1985, p. 1.

8. "Bones of MiAs Found at Plane Crash Site in Laos." DNA identification techniques were not in use at the time.

9. "Team Returns with Remains of MiAs." Webb, the reader will recall, had played a key roll in the entombment of Lt. Michael Blassie in the Tomb of the Unknown Soldier (see Chapter 23).

10. United States Department of State, Memorandum to the Secretary from EAP—Paul Wolfowitz, February 13, 1985, subject: "Proposed NSC Trip to Hanoi to Negotiate the Return of Remains," from portion of files of Senate Select Committee on POW/MIA Affairs declassified by the CIA in 2001, Inventory of the Records of the Senate Select Committee on POW/MIA Affairs.

11. United States Government memorandum 37,745/DB-3C, from Dennis M. Nagy, Assistant Deputy Director for Research to VO-D, March 15, 1985, subject: DB Examination of DC-2 PW/MIA Division of the Directorate for Collection Management, Inventory of the Records of the Senate Select Committee on POW/MIA Affairs.

12. Norman Polmar and Thomas B. Allen, *Spy Book: The Encyclopedia of Espionage* (New York: Random House, 1997), p. 160.

13. Defense Intelligence Agency, S-20,130/DC-2, from John R. Oberst, Colonel, USAF, Chief, Prisoner of War and Missing in Action Division to Honorable Billy Hendon, House of Representatives, January 30, 1985, Hendon files.

14. Memorandum for the record, January 22, 1985, signed by Robert J. Destatte, subject: Hendon's Request for Files, DIA Source file 1542, Inventory of the Records of the Senate Select Committee on POW/MIA Affairs.

15. Secretary of Defense, letter from William H. Taft, IV, Deputy Secretary of Defense, to Honorable William M. Hendon, U.S. House of Representatives, January 30, 1985, Hendon files.

16. Letters from Bill Hendon to Ms. Peggy Cifrino, Special Assistant for Foreign Affairs, Office of the Secretary of Defense, the Pentagon, February 1 and 5, 1985; letter from Bill Hendon to Caspar W. Weinberger, Secretary of Defense, the Pentagon, February 5, 1985, all from Hendon files.

17. Additional refusal by Solarz in *Americans Missing in Southeast Asia,* June 27, 1985, pp. 106–07.

18. Hand-drawn sketch on stationery of William Hendon titled "compound Ly Nam De," dated February 8, 1985, and signed by Robert Garwood, with contemporaneous annotations by Hendon; authors' black-and-white map titled "Area Along Ly Nam De Street Depicted in the Buffalo Hunter Photography"; DOD Buffalo Hunter photo of the compound (with DIA annotations) showing cistern at same location cited by the refugee and drawn by Garwood (point C2); same DOD Buffalo Hunter photo without DIA annotations but with annotations added by Hendon, all from Hendon files. Much of this information can also be found in the refugee's file (DIA Source file 1542, Inventory of the Records of the Senate Select Committee on POW/MIA Affairs) and in the numerous files relating to Garwood and his sightings (POW/MIA and Inventory of the Records of the Senate Select Committee on POW/MIA Affairs).

19. Letter from Bill Hendon to Robert C. McFarlane, May 2, 1985, point 3, Hendon files.

20. Handwritten memo for the record by senior analyst Robert J. Destatte, April 1, 1985, subject: [source name redacted], Ref meeting, 28 Mar 85, DC-2 staff members Trowbridge & [Destatte name redacted] with Congressional PW/MIA Task Force members Solomon, Longamarceno [sic], and Gilman, subject: SAB, DIA Source file 2225, POW/MIA; R 060402Z AUG 93, subject: IIR 6 024 0561 93/Hearsay Reports of U.S. PW's in Vietnam and Laos, DIA files, POW/MIA.

21. Robert J. Destatte memo for the record, April 1, 1985 POW/MIA.

**22.** Draft Complaint, United States District Court for the District of Columbia, Congressman Bill Hendon, 115 Cannon House Office Building, Washington, D.C. 20515, Plaintiff, v. Lt. General James A. Williams, USA, Director, Defense Intelligence Agency, Room 3E258, the Pentagon, Washington, D.C. 20301, Defendant, prepared by Martin Mendelsohn, Esq., attorney for plaintiff, Hendon files.

**23.** Letter from Bill Hendon to the President, April 16, 1985, Hendon files.

**24.** Letter from Robert C. McFarlane to Bill Hendon, April 30, 1985, Hendon files.

**25.** "POWs Won't Be Found Without Cost," *Wall Street Journal,* April 24, 1985, p. 30. Tighe favored a permanent presidential commission over a congressional commission. However, McFarlane had rejected the idea of such a commission in 1984.

**26.** (*Proceedings and Debates*, 99th Cong., 1st sess., *Congressional Record,* Vol. 131, no. 49, April 24, 1984, "Legislation to Establish the Perot Commision on Americans Missing in Southeast Asia."

**27.** The privilege of "revising and extending" one's remarks allows members to correct, edit, and/or amplify remarks made on the floor of the House prior to the publication of those remarks in the *Congressional Record*.

**28.** "Dear Colleague" letter from Bill Hendon, April 25, 1985, Hendon files.

**29.** United States Department of State, letter with date stamp JUN 25 1985 from William L. Ball, III, Assistant Secretary, Legislative and Intergovernmental Affairs, to the Honorable Dante B. Fascell, Chairman, Committee on Foreign Affairs, House of Representatives, Hendon files.

**30.** "Dear Colleague" letter to all members of Congress, May 2, 1985, from Gerald B. Solomon, Chairman, House Task Force on POWs and MIAs and Benjamin A. Gilman, Vice-Chairman, House Task Force on POWs and MIAs, Hendon files.

**31.** National League of Families of American Prisoners and Missing in Southeast Asia, letter from Ann Mills Griffiths, Executive Director, to the Honorable Bill Hendon, U.S. House of Representatives, May 1, 1985, Hendon files, National League of Families of American Prisoners and Missing in Southeast Asia, Memorandum to Regional and State Coordinators from Ann Mills Griffiths, Executive Director, April 26, 1985, subject: Update; National League of Families of American Prisoners and Missing in Southeast Asia, *Newsletter*, November 8, 1985, AMG/48, pp. 5–7, both Elizabeth Stewart files.

**32.** Office of the Clerk, U.S. House of Representatives, "99th Cong. Status Profile for H. Con. Res. 129."

**33.** Given future events, the actions of John McCain during this period should be noted: When Hendon and the others first introduced HCR 129, McCain began telling members that Perot had not agreed to serve as head of the commission and in fact, would refuse to serve if the resolution was passed—and for this reason anyone contemplating cosponsorship of the Perot Bill should reconsider his or her actions. Concurrently, McCain began disrupting briefings Hendon presented to members on the need for a commission by loudly objecting to items he did not agree with and/or storming out in protest when things did not go to his liking. Members would come to learn that four topics, especially, would set McCain off: suggesting in any way that Garwood was a credible witness, criticism of any kind leveled at Henry Kissinger, any inference that McCain and the other returnees released at Operation Homecoming had been ransomed out of Hanoi, and the fact that the intelligence indicated that the hundreds of servicemen who remained captive were still imprisoned because the promised ransom that had freed McCain and the others had never been paid. (Statements to Bill Hendon by numerous colleagues.) When it became clear in the last days of the congressional session that the Perot Bill had garnered broad bipartisan support and appeared headed for passage, McCain reversed course and signed on as a cosponsor.

**34.** Unknown to the tens of thousands of Americans who watched John Rambo's celluloid heroics that weekend, on May 28, the day after Memorial Day, the DIA received a report of American POWs performing forced labor in Laos, and the following day, a report of Americans POWs being detained in a jungle camp in southern Vietnam. Only two of the many reports of live POWs received during the year, the first involved ten Americans who had reportedly been seen performing forced labor on a construction detail in Sam Neua Province, Laos, in mid-1983, some two years earlier. The source who reportedly saw the POWs, a former Royal Lao officer who had worked with American pilots during the war, said that he had been imprisoned in the area and had seen the Americans—all of whom were Caucasian—when he was out of his camp gathering rocks to be used in the construction of a building. Guards told him the prisoners were former American pilots. He said that at the time he observed the Americans, they were carrying long pieces of metal of the type used in building construction. He described the men as being dressed only in undershorts and wearing sandbags tied to their feet for shoes. He also said that they had sandbags resting on their shoulders to cushion the weight of the heavy pieces of metal they were carrying. (P 280638Z MAY 85, subject: JCRC Report T85-186, Hearsay of 10 Americans Held in Vieng Xai Sam Neua, Laos, DIA Source file 3311, POW/MIA; authors' map.) The report from Vietnam quoted a former RVNAF NCO as telling U.S. officials in Bangkok that in early

1985, only months earlier, he and his brother, a former RVNAF second lieutenant, had personally observed U.S. POWs doing calisthenics just outside an underground detention facility located north-northwest of the coastal city of Nha Trang. According to the NCO, the Americans would come out of the underground facility in pairs or threes, exercise for a few minutes, and return underground; then two or three others would emerge and repeat the process. The NCO said the Americans were dressed in both striped and solid-color prison uniforms with collarless shirts, and that, compared to the armed Vietnamese guards who formed a semicircle around the entrance to the underground facility, they were very tall. The NCO provided U.S. officials with a map of the area and sketches of the facility and its surroundings. (R 291430Z MAY 85, subject: Retransmission of DIA/DC-2 MSG DTD [sic] 192021Z APR 85; P 071259Z JUN 85, subject: JCRC Report RP85-044R Americans Currently Detained in Vietnam, with source's drawings and maps, all DIA Source file 3114, POW/MIA; authors' map.)

**35.** *Americans Missing in Southeast Asia*, pp. 21, 25.

**36.** Ibid.

**37.** Hendon's telephone interview with Anne Hart, June 21, 1997.

**38.** "Questionable MIA Identifications Renew Families' Anguish," *Kansas City Times*, August 22, 1985, p. 1.

**39.** Hendon's telephone interview with Anne Hart.

**40.** National League of Families of American Prisoners and Missing in Southeast Asia, Chronology of US/Laos Relations, August 1981—October 21, 1985, Hendon files.

**41.** Hendon's telephone interview with Anne Hart; also "Convention on MIAs to Open Amid Dissension, High Hopes, Stronger Action Sought on Missing U.S. Servicemen," *Washington Post*, July 18, 1985, p. A6; The Vice President, Office of the Press Secretary, "Excerpts of Remarks by Vice President George Bush to the 16th Annual Meeting of the National League of Families, Washington, D.C., Friday, July 19, 1985"; "Laos Agrees To Search Crash Site, Bush Details Plan to Look for MIAs," *Washington Post*, July 20, 1985, p. A4.

**42.** 99th Cong., 1st sess., H. RES. 226, Directing the Secretary of Defense to furnish certain information to the House of Representatives relating to American prisoners of war in Southeast Asia, July 17, 1985.

**43.** "Two Soldiers Battle Pentagon to Prove POWs Still Alive," *Atlanta Journal Constitution*, September 29, 1985, p. 1. Reporting on the lawsuit in *The Washington Post* in mid-September, columnists Jack Anderson and Dale Van Atta declared themselves convinced that POWs remained alive and quoted one of their sources within the DIA as saying the number still alive could be as high as one hundred. Anderson and Van Atta quoted their source as saying his estimate was based on satellite photos, communications intercepts, and reports from human sources. "The evidence," the source was quoted as saying, "is overwhelming." (Jack Anderson and Dale Van Atta, "POWs Still Held in Southeast Asia," *Washington Post*, September 18, 1985.)

**44.** House of Representatives, 99th Cong., 1st sess., Report 99-260, Part I, *Resolution of Inquiry Concerning American Prisoners of War in Southeast Asia, Adverse Report*, September 10, 1985.

**45.** Jack Anderson and Dale Van Atta, "Access to MIA Files Being Blocked," *Washington Post*, September 27, 1985, p. F10.

**46.** Hendon's telephone interview with John LeBoutillier, June 29, 1997.

**47.** "POWs Probably Still Held in Vietnam, McFarlane Says," *Washington Times*, October 16, 1985, p. 1; "McFarlane Says POWs 'Have to Be' in Indochina," *USA Today*, October 16, 1985, p. 4A; "Some Vietnam MIAs Probably Live, McFarlane Says," *Washington Post*, October 17, 1985, p. A24.

**48.** "Fasting Amid Plenty," *Washington Post*, November 29, 1985, photo, p. A44.

**49.** "8 MIA Policy Protesters Arrested at White House," *Washington Post*, October 20, 1985, p. D4; "MIA Protest Completed with Arrests," New York *Daily News*, October 20, 1985, p. 4A.

**50.** Letter, from Bill Hendon to the Honorable Caspar W. Weinberger, Secretary of Defense, November 19, 1985, from Hendon files.

**51.** Letter from Richard L. Armitage, Assistant Secretary of Defense (International Security Affairs), to Honorable Bill Hendon, House of Representatives, November 27, 1985, Hendon files.

**52.** "Military's Identification Process Questioned, Exclusionary Method Doesn't Give Positive ID," *Daily Oklahoman*, November 22, 1985, p. 1.

**53.** "CILHI Identification Inspection Report of An OnSite Inspection of The Facilities and Procedures Of the U.S. Army Central Identification Laboratory in The Hawaiian Islands, December 9–12, 1985," Hendon files.

**54.** Ibid.

**55.** "Army Accused of Distorting Evidence in Its Identification of MIA Remains," *Philadelphia Inquirer*, March 2, 1986, p. 24-A.

**56.** "Army Lab Disputed on MIA Remains," *Washington Times,* March 31, 1986, p. 12C.

**57.** Letter from Samuel Strong Dunlap, Ph.D., to Honorable John O. Marsh, Secretary of the Army, July 10, 1986, Hendon files.

**58.** National League of Families of American Prisoners and Missing in Southeast Asia, "POW/MIA Briefing," October 21, 1985; Memorandum to the Congress from Ann Mills Griffiths, Executive Director, subject: POW/MIA Issue, October 21, 1985, from Hendon files.

**59.** James Litke, "Wrong Remains," AP, Hendon files. Perhaps the most mind-boggling aspect of the Spectre 17 "identifications" was the fact that, whereas the "experts" at CILHI had earlier taken the remains of Michael Blassie and, for reasons previously discussed, declared them unidentifiable and placed them in the Tomb of the Unknown Soldier, here these same "experts" had done the exact opposite—they had taken completely unidentifiable bone shards, chips, and fragments and used them to "positively identify" all thirteen members of the Spectre 17 crew.

**60.** "Reagan Phones Veteran," *Washington Post,* December 6, 1985, p. A16.

**61.** "Kissinger Doubtful Vietnam Has MIAs," *Bellevue (NE) Leader,* December 11, 1985, p. 1.

**62.** "National technical means" is "a U.S. term for the use of aircraft photography, satellite photography, the seafloor sound surveillance system, and other means of reconnaissance to provide arms control verification" (Polmar and Allen, *Spy Book,* p. 389.)

**63.** Transcript, "'60 Minutes' PW Segment," Reel 3, Series 92–300, POW/MIA.

**64.** As a general rule, supporters of a given piece of legislation can force hearings on that legislation once a majority of members (218 of 435) have signed on as cosponsors. On December 15, 1985, the number of members cosponsoring HCR 129 stood at 117. ("99th Cong. Status Profile for H. Con. Res. 129.")

## CHAPTER 25. 1986: TRENCH WARFARE

**1.** "Armitage Denies Cover-up of Prisoners in Indochina," AP in *Washington Times,* January 8, 1986, p. A7, with Hendon's handwritten margin note, Hendon files.

**2.** "100 Americans in Vietnam, White House," AP in Grays Harbor *Daily World,* Hendon files.

**3.** Ibid.

**4.** Hendon's warm relationship with the vice president was now permanently destroyed. More than six years would pass before two senior Reagan administration intelligence officials would independently declare that Hanoi's offer to trade living POWs for cash had, in fact, been received. According to one of those officials, the offer had been received by the administration on January 26, 1981, and was related not to remains but to living prisoners of war the Vietnamese were holding at the time. This official would recall among other things that the offer had been the topic of much discussion around the water coolers at Langley at the time. The other official reported that soon after taking office in 1981, "The Ronald Reagan administration received an offer from Vietnamese officials, transmitted through Canadian diplomats. They were reportedly willing to free an unspecified number of prisoners in return for reconstruction aid they believed that President Richard M. Nixon had promised when the Paris Peace Accords were signed in 1973." The specifics of what these two officials said and other information about the Vietnamese offer are discussed in detail in Chapter 31.

**5.** Defense Intelligence Agency, letter from Leonard H. Perroots, Lieutenant General, USAF, Director, to Lieutenant General Eugene F. Tighe, Jr., USAF (ret), January 16, 1986, Inventory of the Records of the Senate Select Committee on POW/MIA Affairs. Hendon considered Perroots, who had taken over as director in late 1985, to be another Jerry Tuttle, a first-class, no-nonsense military officer embarrassed by the mess he had found at the Special Office and committed to cleaning it up. Perroots, who upon first meeting Hendon over breakfast in the Chairman's Dining Room on E-Ring, had pledged "to hang up my jacket" rather than allow what was going on in the POW office to continue, had reached out to Hendon and his colleagues and, within the constraints imposed upon him by his civilian superiors, had attempted to provide the members with as much intelligence on live POWs as possible. The bulk of that intelligence was provided to the congressmen in classified briefings held in Hendon's office, at least one of which Perroots himself attended.

**6.** "Director's PW/MIA Task Force Report," with cover memorandum dated March 18, 1986, from Kimball M. Gaines, Colonel, USAF, Chief, Director's PW/MIA Task Force to DR [DIA Director Perroots], subject: Director's PW/MIA Task Force Review of the PW/MIA Division (VO-PW), Inventory of the Records of the Senate Select Committee on POW/MIA Affairs.

**7.** Statement of Kim Gaines to Hendon, spring 1986.

**8.** Gen. Tighe, Col. McGee, and Mr. McCreary were the members most actively involved in the investigation of the intelligence.

**9.** Defense Intelligence Agency, letter from Russell E. Dougherty, John Peter Flynn, Robert C. Kingston, Lyman Kirkpatrick, H. Ross Perot [unsigned], and Robinson Risner to Director, Defense Intelligence Agency, May 27, 1986, subject: Tighe Task Force Report, Inventory of the Records of the Senate Select Committee on POW/MIA Affairs.

**10.** Defense Intelligence Agency, letter from Eugene F. Tighe, Jr., John S. Murray, Lester E. McGee, Jr., Roberta Carper Maynard, John Francis McCreary, and Arthur G. Klos to Lieutenant General Leonard H. Perroots, USAF, Director, Defense Intelligence Agency, subject: Review of DIA'S PW/MIA Analysis Center, May 27, 1986, Inventory of the Records of the Senate Select Committee on POW/MIA Affairs.

**11.** "The Tighe Task Force Examination of DIA Intelligence Holdings Surrounding Unaccounted for United States Military Personnel in Southeast Asia," Inventory of the Records of the Senate Select Committee on POW/MIA Affairs.

**12.** The Iran-contra affair involved the sale of U.S.-made TOW antitank missiles, Hawk antiaircraft missiles, sophisticated radars, and other weaponry and military equipment to the government of Iran—which at the time was involved in a vicious war of attrition with its neighbor Iraq—and the diversion of a portion of the proceeds from those sales to Central America for use by the contra rebels in their war against the Sandinista government of Nicaragua. The entire operation was conducted in the strictest secrecy because both undertakings—the sale of arms to Iran and the funding of contra operations in Nicaragua—were prohibited at the time under U.S. law. For a thorough analysis of the Iran-contra affair, including an almost hour-by-hour account of McFarlane's and North's late-May 1986 visit to Tehran, see *Report of the Congressional Committees Investigating the Iran-Contra Affair, With Supplemental, Minority, and Additional Views,* 100th Cong., 1st sess., November 1987, H. Rep. 100-433, S. Rep. 100-216, pp. 237–42.

**13.** National Security Council, from Richard T. Childress, Director of Asian Affairs, memorandum for LTG Leonard H. Perroots, Director, Defense Intelligence Agency, June 18, 1986, subject: Tighe Report, with attachments, Reel 1, Series 92-300, POW/MIA.

**14.** Ibid.

**15.** Hendon's undated contemporaneous telephone notes of conversation with Perroots, and e-mail correspondence October 17, 2003, concerning the date of the Perroots telephone conversation, Hendon files. Associated relevant information is in Deposition of Leonard H. Perroots, Lt. Gen. (Ret.) USAF, Select Committee on POW/MIA Affairs, June 15, 1992, p. 148, Inventory of the Records of the Senate Select Committee on POW/MIA Affairs.

**16.** Letter from Robert K. Dornan, Bill Hendon, Christopher H. Smith, Frank McCloskey, David Dreier, Robert C. Smith, and John G. Rowland to the Honorable Ronald Reagan, the Honorable Thomas P. O'Neill, Jr., the Honorable Stephen J. Solarz, and the Honorable Gerald B. H. Solomon, July 31, 1986, Hendon files.

**17.** "U.S. POWs May Remain, House Task Force Report Sent to Reagan," *Washington Post,* August 2, 1986, p. A10. Not everyone had reacted as Perroots had to news of the congressmen's letter. On August 5, Bobby Wayne Esslinger, a representative of the Nebraska State Prison's Veterans Group, informed Hendon by letter from prison that he and members of his group had read of the congressmen's letter to the president in the *Omaha World Herald* and, citing reported instances during previous wars when prisoners had been "brought out for service . . . [on] so-called 'suicide' missions," volunteered (in return for their freedom if they were successful) to lead a group of his fellow prisoners back to Vietnam to attempt to rescue . . . our fellow comrades at arms and friends." (Letter from Bobby Wayne Esslinger to Bill Hendon, August 5, 1986, Hendon files.)

**18.** Brooks had served during 1985 as the DIA's assistant deputy director for collection management, essentially Tuttle's old position with direct line authority over the Special Office but with a slightly different title. While in that position, Brooks had personally conducted a detailed, in-depth, case-by-case analysis of the closely guarded analysts' working files. As a result, by the summer of 1986 he probably knew more about what was in those files than any other active-duty flag officer, with the possible exception of the DIA's Brig. Gen. James Shufelt, USA, who oversaw the day-to-day operations of the Special Office and, as head of the Interagency Committee on Indochina POWs (IAC), officially certified the analysts' "findings" that all the eyewitnesses were fabricators or had seen teenage Vietnamese "buffalo boys," Khmer half-breeds, ARVNs, Western tourists and missionaries, etc., and not American POWs.

**19.** United States Government memorandum, 084/JS, from Thomas A. Brooks, Rear Admiral, USN, Deputy Director for JCS Support, to DD, DR, July 7, 1986, subject: Review of Tighe Report, Reel 1, Series 92-300, POW/MIA.

**20.** See www.enormouscrime.com, Chapter 23, (3) "The American POWs Seen in the Ban Nok Jail Just East of the Plain of Jars in Northern Laos in 1978. Case #3037."

**21.** R 162330Z DEC 86, subject: Alleged Observation of Ten PWs in Laos in 1976, DIA Source file 3562, Inventory of the Records of the Senate Select Committee on POW/MIA Affairs.

**22.** See www.enormouscrime.com, Chapter 23, "The American POWs Reportedly Being Moved Around Nhge Tinh Province in Northern Vietnam During the Late 1970's and Early 1980's. Case #9689."

**23.** United States Government memorandum, C-1748/VO-PW, from Chief, Special Office for Prisoners of War and Missing in Action to ED, DD, DR thru VO, December 24, 1986, subject: VO-PW Analytical Efforts to Resolve Lao PW Sighting, Source file 3562, Inventory of the Records of the Senate Select Committee on POW/MIA Affairs.

**24.** The signature of the Special Office chief is redacted in the copy of the report available in the National Archives. Almost certainly the signer was Gaines, though there is the possibility Schlatter or Trowbridge could have signed in his absence, as they sometimes did.

**25.** Though at the time the activist congressmen were picking up only snippets of what Perroots and his men were doing, they all sensed that a dark cloud was again descending over the DIA. Soon it became painfully clear that Gaines and Schlatter, who only months before had been considered friends and comrades-in-arms in the effort to recover live prisoners, had followed Perroots's lead and, having joined hands with the very people they had so roundly condemned in the Gaines Report, were now hard at work assailing Tighe personally, his findings, and every piece of intelligence relating to living POWs that he and members of his task force had cited as credible.

**26.** Deposition of Eugene F. Tighe, Jr., pp. 216–20. Later, Perroots would contact at least one member of the Tighe task force and at least two members of the review panel, and seek to further change their minds about the task force's findings relative to live POWs. Although a copy of the letter Perroots sent to these members cannot be located in the declassified POW-related records housed at the National Archives and the Library of Congress, the responses that can be located indicate that Perroots was successful in the case of one task force member, Maj. Gen. John Murray, USA (Ret.), but failed miserably in his effort to sway two members of the review panel, Robert C. Kingston and Robinson Risner. (Undated letter from John S. Murray to LTG Leonard Perroots, USAF, Director, Defense Intelligence Agency, ref: Comment on Task Force Examination of DIA'S PW/MIA Analysis Center; letter from Robert G. Kingston, General, U.S. Army (Ret.) to Leonard H. Perroots, Lieutenant General, Director, Defense Intelligence Agency, December 12, 1986, Reference: My comments on your letter dated 29 October 1986; letter from Robinson Risner to Lt. General Leonard H. Perroots, Director, Defense Intelligence Agency, November 8, 1986, all Reel 1, Series 92-300, POW/MIA.) Risner, in fact, was now so convinced that his fellow countrymen remained captive that he later contacted the Lyndon Baines Johnson Library to amend statements about live POWs he had made in 1981 while being interviewed for the library's Vietnam War Oral History Project. In the 1981 interview, Risner, when asked if he believed all POWs had been returned at Operation Homecoming, had replied, "Well, I have always believed that all of the prisoners held in North Vietnam were repatriated. They were very desirous of establishing diplomatic relations with the United States. They also were very desirous of getting some [of] what they called reconstruction money from the U.S., about two and a half billion dollars. I believed that it would have been counterproductive to have retained any POWs. I'm sure that they were aware that if any additional live prisoners were discovered in North Vietnam they wouldn't have gotten any reconstruction money because the American people would have been really angry." His amended answer, dated December 1986, reads, "In the past year, during which time I have worked with DIA and others, I have become convinced, as has H. Ross Perot, that American POWs are being held in Laos and Vietnam against their will." ("Oral History Interview of Robinson Risner," Interview I, Date: November 4, 1981, Interviewee: Robinson Risner, Interviewer: Ted Gittinger, Place: General Risner's office, Austin, Texas, p. Risner—I—46, Lyndon Baines Johnson Library.)

**27.** *Hearings on Americans Missing or Prisoner in Southeast Asia, the Department of Defense Accounting Process,* Select Committee on POW/MIA Affairs, United States Senate, June 24 and 25, 1992, pp. 172–73.

**28.** District of Columbia, affidavit, sworn and signed by William Hendon, July 10, 1987, pp. 3–5, Hendon files.

**29.** Memorandum for the President from the Deputy Secretary of Defense, subject: H. Ross Perot's Efforts on Behalf of Prisoners of War and Missing in Action (PW/MIA), August 1, 1973, Shields Files, POW/MIA. Coauthor Stewart, fifteen at the time, and her mother and several of her brothers and sisters were among those who made the trip to Paris with Perot.

**30.** "Perot's Mission: To Return the Missing," *Detroit Free Press,* July 14, 1985, p. 1.

**31.** "The Viet Exodus Continues, Human Flow Has Not Changed Over the Years," *New Straits Times,* Kuala Lumpur, August 8, 1986, p. 2.

**32.** Authors' annotated 1:250,000 color map of area.

**33.** P 220939Z JAN 86, subject: JCRC Report T86-011, Hearsay Information of American Prisoners in Saravan Province, Laos in 1976 and 1983, DIA Source file 3906, POW/MIA.

**34.** P 221125Z JAN 86, subject: JCRC Report T86-010, Alleged Live Sightings of American Prisoners in Saravan Province, Laos in 1982, DIA Source file 3910, POW/MIA.

**35.** R 311013Z AUG 84, subject: Alleged Live U.S. PWs Held in Laos, DIA Source file 2626, POW/MIA.

**36.** P 240902Z JAN 86, subject: JCRC LNB Report T86-015, Sighting of Four Americans in Savannakhet Province, Laos in December 1985, DIA Source file 3885, POW/MIA.

**37.** Authors' annotated 1:250,000 color map of area.

**38.** 291046Z JAN 86, subject: JCRC Report M85-105, Rescue Attempt of 218 Live American Prisoners in Vietnam, Source Reports, Reel 48, Vol. XIV, pp. 106–15, POW/MIA.

**39.** Authors' annotated 1:250,000 color map of area.

**40.** P 030350Z FEB 86, subject: JCRC Report T86-031, Hearsay of American Prisoners Seen in Vietnam Near Khammouan Province, Laos in December 1985, JCRC Files, POW/MIA.

**41.** P 041733Z FEB 86, subject: JCRC Report T86-033, Report of 26 American Prisoners Seen in Khammouan Province, Laos in 1981, DIA Source file 3856, POW/MIA; authors' annotated 1:250,000 color map of area. Further corroboration of the sergeant's account was discovered in an intelligence report the DIA had received in 1980 that had reported the presence in March of that year of some fifty American POWs—a number of whom were reported to be in poor health—near the village of Ban Boneng, located some eight to ten kilometers up the road from the mine where the sergeant said he saw the twenty-six American POWs in 1981. (Authors' annotated color 1:250,000 map of area; handwritten letter to Mrs. Le Thi Anh dated Jully [*sic*] 2nd 1980, with date stamp SEP 9 1980, DIA Source file 0823, POW/MIA; R 122021Z SEP 80, subject: Request for Refugee Interview, and R 211200Z OCT 80, subject: Response to Request for Refugee Interview, both DIA Source file 3856, POW/MIA.

**42.** Central Intelligence Agency, memorandum for Assistant Vice Director for Collection Management, Department of Defense, Principal Advisor for Prisoner of War Missing in Action Affairs (International Security Affairs), Director, Vietnam, Laos and Cambodia, Bureau of East Asian and Pacific Affairs, Department of State, March 19, 1986, subject: Alleged Presence from 1982 to 1985 of U.S. Prisoners of War in a Ministry of Interior Detention Center South of Hanoi; R 121003Z SEP 86, subject: Collection Emphasis 86-0059—Request for Reinterview of VM Refugee [name redacted], both DIA Source file 5816, POW/MIA; R 070856Z NOV 88, subject: IIR 6 024 0010 89/Hearsay of Alleged Americans Held in SRV Prison, DIA Source file 6803, POW/MIA; authors' annotated 1:250,000 color map of area.

**43.** Multiple intelligence reports from former ARVN inmates of Binh Da reeducation camp and other intelligence, Camp Files, POW/MIA.

**44.** P 260532Z MAR 86, subject: JCRC Report T86-100, Hearsay of Two American Prisoners and the King of Laos Held in Houaphan Province, Laos, JCRC Files, POW/MIA; authors' annotated color 1:250,000 map of Sop Hao area.

**45.** P 070439Z MAY 86, subject: JCRC Report T86-180, Fifty American POW's Held North of Bien Hoa Town, with source's memory sketch of area, DIA Source file 5112, POW/MIA; authors' annotated 1:250,000 color map of area.

**46.** P 162245Z APR 85, subject: JCRC Refugee Report RP85-008 of 16APR85; American Prisoners in Vietnam," Camp Files, POW/MIA.

**47.** According to various intelligence sources, these facilities included a prison in downtown Bien Hoa known as "B-5," a sprawling reeducation camp located several kilometers east of Bien Hoa that had been used by the RVN government as a prison for Communist POWs during the war but that the victorious Communists had converted into a reeducation camp for captured Southerners, and a hard-labor camp located farther east along QL1 near the village of Trang Bom. (Authors' map.) The analysts had also learned from multiple intelligence sources that because the Suoi Mau complex was composed of several different facilities, over the years it had come to be known by several different names. Those names, all of which denoted the same reeducation camp complex, included "Bien Hoa detention centers," "B-5," "Suoi Mau," "Tan Hiep," "Suoi Mau-Tan Hiep," "Tan Hiep (Suoi Mau)," and "Trang Bom." (Multiple intelligence reports from former inmates of this reeducation camp system, and other intelligence, all from Camp Files, POW/MIA.)

**48.** Authors' annotated 1:250,000 color map of area.

**49.** United States Board on Geographic Names, *Official Standard Names Gazetteer, Laos,* 2d ed., p. 325; authors' annotated 1:250,000 map of Ban Daknong area.

**50.** R 290151Z MAY 86, fm [Redacted] to [redacted] [subject:] LPA Units Transfer of "Prisoners of War" in Central Laos in Mid-May, Reel 1, Series 92-300, POW/MIA.

**51.** During 1981: R 270825Z SEP 84, subject: Thai Citizen with Possible US POW/MIA Information; R 171816Z JUL 84, subject: Thai Citizen with Possible US PW/MIA Information, both DIA Source file 3057, POW/MIA; in mid-1981: JCRC T81-048, subject: Refugee Report, Hearsay of Americans in Laos, DIA Source file 1096, Inventory of the Records of the Senate Select Committee on POW/MIA Affairs; in June 1984: P 280811Z JAN 86, subject: JCRC Report T86-027, Alleged First Hand Observation of Two U.S. POWs in Laos During 1984, DIA Source file 3901, POW/MIA; in October 1984: R 130210Z FEB 85, subject: Report of Alleged Sightings of American POWs in Laos, DIA Source file 2676, Inventory of the Records of the Senate Select Committee on POW/MIA Affairs; in October 1985: Project Assignment Instructions, January 13, 1986, PWs allegedly Being Held in Vientiane Province, Laos, DIA Source file 3894, POW/MIA.

**52.** Authors' annotated 1:250,000 color map of area.

**53.** One page of the three-page CIA report, with Senate Select Committee stamp "005343" (denoting DIA Source 5343), Hendon files; one-page document, "Laos: VO-PW, AT-8, CIA Meeting, 29 July 1986," which identifies the CIA report as CIA FIR 317/09341-86; POW/MIA.

**54.** Source's hand-drawn map sketch (with authors' added color highlights), from P 081017Z SEP 86, subject: JCRC Report T86-384, Five Caucasians Reported in Laos, DIA Source file 5491, POW/MIA; authors' annotated 1:250,000 color map of area.

**55.** The militiaman had made his offer to return to the prison during interviews conducted by JCRC representatives in Thailand on September 5 and 6, 1986. The offer was never accepted. (P 191924Z AUG 87, subject: Source Directed Requirement, and all other documents contained in DIA Source file 5491, POW/MIA.)

**56.** Authors' annotated 1:250,000 color map of area.

**57.** R 201906Z SEP 86, from CIA to [multiple addressees], subject: POW/MIA: Alleged Relocation in June 1986 of 226 American Prisoners of War to Songhon District, Savannakhet Province, Laos From Vietnam, DIA Source file 5528, POW/MIA.

**58.** R 080722Z OCT 86 PSN 293124P21, subject: JCRC Report I86-37, Hearsay of Americans Sighted in the U Minh Forest, Near Binh Gia, Dong Nai, and Near Qui Nhon, JCRC Files, POW/MIA.

**59.** *The Tighe Report on American POW's and MIA's, Hearings and Markup Before the Subcommittee on Asian and Pacific Affairs of the Committee on Foreign Affairs,* House of Representatives, 99th Cong., 2d sess., October 15, 1986, ON H. Con Res 179 [*sic*], p. 8.

**60.** Ibid., p. 15.

**61.** Ibid., p. 25.

**62.** Ibid., p. 41.

**63.** Ibid.

**64.** Ibid., pp. 41–42, 45.

**65.** Ibid., pp. 43–44.

**66.** Ibid., pp. 48–49, 84–85.

**67.** E-mail "10/16/86, 14:10 *** To: NSRBM—CPUA JOHN M. POINDEXTER NSWRP.——CPUA JOHN M. POINDEXTER, NOTE FROM: RICHARD T. CHILDRESS, SUBJECT: POW/MIA Commission," in Tom Blanton, ed., *White House E-mail: The Top Secret Computer Messages the Reagan/Bush White House Tried to Destroy* (New York: New Press, 1995), p. 163.

**68.** *Report of the Congressional Committees Investigating the Iran-Contra Affair,* p. 261.

**69.** "How The West Was Won," "U.S. House," *Asheville Citizen,* November 6, 1986, p. 16.

**70.** "Clarke-Hendon III," *Asheville Citizen,* November 6, 1986, p. 13.

**71.** "Iran Says McFarlane, Others Came on Secret Mission to Tehran," *Washington Post,* November 5, 1986, p. A1.

**72.** "Secret Talks With Iran Described," *Washington Post,* November 6, 1986, p. A1.

**73.** "Hill Probes of NSC Planned," *Washington Post,* November 10, 1986, p. A1.

**74.** Mary McGrory, "Shaking Hands With the Devil," *Washington Post,* November 11, 1986, p. A3.

**75.** Haynes Johnson, "A Poisonous Post-Election Air," *Washington Post,* November 12, 1986, p. A3.

**76.** Daniel Schoor, "A Whiff of Watergate?"; Charles Krauthammer, "Somebody Should Resign"; Rowland Evans and Robert Novak, "Like 'a Shadow CIA,'" all *Washington Post,* November 12, 1986, p. A19.

**77.** "Reagan Denies 'Ransom' Was Paid for Hostages" and "President Was Told Arms Were Key to Iran's Help," *Washington Post,* November 14, 1986, p. A1.

**78.** "Cardinal John O'Connor Dies," www.cnn.com/2000/US/05/04/cardinal.oconnor.obit/.

**79.** "O'Connor Prods Prez on MIAs in Asia," *New York Post,* November 10, 1986, p. 20.

**80.** P 140224Z OCT 86, subject: JCRC Report T86-421, 20 Americans Being Held in a Bunker Near Vinh Quang Re-education Camp, C, 1980/81, DIA Source file 5753, POW/MIA. The Special Office analysts knew that the Vinh Quang Reeducation Camp complex was composed of two main prisons located along the western slope of Thud Ridge, northwest of Hanoi, and at least one nearby subcamp. (CIA Intelligence Information Report, April 15, 1981, subject: Prison Camps in North Vietnam: Nghe Tinh Province Prison No. 3 and Vinh Quang Prison (DOI: November 1980), DIA Source file 9687/2088, POW/MIA; R 090140Z AUG 86, subject: Absence of Americans at Reeducation Camp Two of Inter-Camp 4 in Ha Tuyen, and at the Vinh Quang Reeducation Camp in Vinh Phu, North Vietnam, Lien Trai IV Camp Files, Reel 278, Series 92-302, POW/MIA.) The northernmost of the two prisons was located near the village of Vinh Ninh at UTM grid coordinates WJ 550 803; the southernmost just outside the village of Dao Tru at WJ 547 783. (Authors' annotated color 1:250,000 map of area.)

The analysts also knew that a small number of American POWs had been detained at the northernmost of the two prisons near Vinh Ninh during the war, and that all held there had been released or accounted for at Operation Homecoming. U.S. intelligence officials had given this prison two different but similar wartime designations, "Vinh Ninh Prison no. 1, North Vietnam" and "Vinh Ninh PW Camp N-105," and had photographed it repeatedly throughout the latter part of the war. ("[Line Drawing] Derived From November 1970 Photography entitled 'Vinh Ninh Prison No.1, North Vietnam, WJ 550 803,'" Reel 363, Series 92-302, POW/MIA; annotated black-and-white reconnaissance photography, titled "Vinh Ninh Prison No 1, North Vietnam, WJ550803," Hendon files; annotated black-and-white reconnaissance photography titled "Vinh Ninh PW Camp N-105," Hendon files.) The returnees from "Vinh Ninh N-105" reported they had called the prison "Mountain Camp" or "Mountain Retreat." (Annotated black-and-white reconnaissance photograph titled "Mountain Retreat," Hendon files; P 210030Z MAR 73, 1. Returnee: Mr. Eugene A. Weaver; P 230056, 2 Mar 73. 1. Returnee: Mr. Eugene A. Weaver; O 042123Z APR 73, 1. Returnee: Purcell, Benjamin H. Rank: Col.; P 051540Z APR 73, 1. Returnee: Charles E. Willis, Civ; Commander, Naval Intelligence Command, Representative, Naval Hospital, Bethesda, Maryland 20014, Operation Homecoming/Navy, 3461—Ser S125, 20 April 1973, subject: Identification of Vinh Ninh PW Camp, N-105, all Vinh Quang Camp Files, Reel 286, Series 92-302, POW/MIA; P 300148Z MAR 73, subject: Unidentified Prisoner of War Camps in North Vietnam," Reel 389, Series 92-302, POW/MIA.)

The more southern of the two prisons near Dao Tru had also been identified and photographed during the war. This prison had been given the wartime designation "Vinh Ninh Prison No. 2, North Vietnam, WJ547783." ("[Line Drawing] Derived From November 1970 Photography titled 'Vinh Ninh Prison No. 2 (U/C), North Vietnam, WJ 547 783,'" Reel 363, Series 92-302, POW/MIA; annotated black-and-white reconnaissance photography titled "Vinh Ninh Prison No. 2, North Vietnam, WJ547783," Hendon files.) Though wartime officials had believed it possible that POWs had been held at the southernmost prison at Dao Tru during the war, no Americans who returned at Operation Homecoming reported being detrained there. (*Places and Dates of Confinement of Air Force, Navy and Marine Corps Prisoners of War Held in North Vietnam 1964—1973.*)

**81.** Senate intelligence investigators would later find that this refugee's prison chronology read like a case study of the North Vietnamese political prison system. He testified he had been held at Hoa Lo Prison in downtown Hanoi, Bang Liet/Thanh Liet Prison in the southwest Hanoi suburbs, Son Tay K-2 Prison on the western shore of Suoi Hai Lake in Son Tay Province, and Lam Son Prison, Cam Thuy Prison, and Thanh Lam Production Zone, all located in Thanh Hoa Province. DIA was in possession of large amounts of information about each of these six locations at the time the refugee's testimony was received.

**82.** Senate intelligence investigators would later determine that the Son Tay K-2 Prison (where the refugee said he was held from 1976 to 1986) was well-known to DIA analysts at the time the refugee's account was received. The investigators found that during the war, American intelligence officials had assigned the facility the official designation "Cam Dai Barracks and Possible PW Camp, N-36," after the nearby village of Cam Dai. (Defense Intelligence Agency, Basic Report, Military Logistics North Vietnam, Cam Dai Barracks and Possible PW Camp N-36, February 1973, Hendon files. Also North Vietnam, Photo Intelligence Briefing Notes on Briefing Board NO. DI-8-72-542 (U), August 1, 1972, installation: Cam Dai Barracks and Possible PW CAMP, N-36; annotated reconnaissance photo titled "North Vietnam, Cam Dai Barracks and Possible PW Camp N-36, 21 09 04N 105 22 18E, all from *Uncorrelated Information Relating to Missing Americans in Southeast Asia*, Vol. XV, Department of Defense, December 15, 1978, pp. 15, 207–15, 209.) None of the POWs released at Operation Homecoming reported they had been detained at Son Tay K-2/Cam Dai Barracks and Possible PW Camp, N-36. (*Places and Dates of Confinement of Air Force, Navy and Marine Corps Prisoners of War Held in North Vietnam 1964–1973.*)

**83.** The source's exact pronunciation was "EWE-ston," somewhat like the city Houston. DOD records show that one American serviceman with a similar-sounding name, Army Green Beret Sgt.

Charles G. Huston, went missing in Laos on March 28, 1968. (Department of Defense, *U.S. Personnel Missing, Southeast Asia (and Selected Foreign Nationals) (U),* Alpha, Chronological, and Refno Reports, June 1995, p. 23.) According to author John Prados, Huston and fellow Green Beret Sgt. George R. Brown were on the ground providing cover fire for members of their team during an emergency helicopter extraction when the chopper's ladder broke, sending a Rhade soldier and American Sgt. Alan L. Boyer, both of whom were halfway up the ladder at the time, plummeting back to earth. Prados, apparently quoting eyewitnesses aboard the helicopter or one of the backups operating nearby, writes that "Boyer did not move . . . [and] Brown and Huston were still shooting as the rescue chopper and its backups were forced to leave." (John Prados, *The Blood Road: The Ho Chi Minh Trail and the Vietnam War* [New York: John Wiley, 1999], p. 276.)

84. P 280752Z OCT 86, subject: JCRC Report M86-063A, 123 Caucasians Seen at Son Tay K3, 1976–1986; P1 30848Z NOV 86 PSN 515420P17 subject JCRC RPT M86-063B, Reinterview and Polygraph of Kuala Lumpur Walk-in [name redacted], both DIA Source file 5643, POW/MIA.

85. Source's hand-drawn map showing prison compound and surrounding area, from P 190838Z DEC 86, subject: JCRC Report T86-505, Observation of Two Caucasians Said to Be Americans Near Pleiku City and Hearsay of 20 Americans Held in Saigon, Reel 4, Group 66, Series 92-302, POW/MIA; authors' annotated DOD color 1:25,000 map of area showing double barbed-wire enclosed compound labeled "Tri Gia Binh" at exact location described by source.

86. P 190838Z DEC 86, subject: JCRC Report T86-505; Observation of Two Caucasians Said to Be Americans Near Pleiku City and Hearsay of 20 Americans Held in Saigon.

87. Map of Hanoi with DIA analyst's hand-drawn notation showing location of hospital, from R 191109 Z DEC 86, subject: JCRC Report HK86-091, Two Caucasians Observed in Moi Hospital, Hanoi City and Hearsay of Americans Held in the Ly Nam De Area, DIA Source file 5862, Inventory of the Records of the Senate Select Committee on POW/MIA Affairs.

88. R 191117Z DEC 86, subject: NCRC Report HK-86-V91 [cntd.].

89. Authors' annotated color 1:250,000 map of area south of the Mu Gia Pass; R 192238Z DEC 86, from CIA to [multiple addressees], subject: PW/MIA. Follow-up Information Concerning Alleged Live Missing in Action American in Khammouan Province, Laos, DIA Source file 5882, POW/MIA.

90. "GOP Leaders Warn Reagan, Fast Action Urged to Avert Long-term Damage," *Washington Post,* December 1, 1986, p. A1.

91. Colin Powell with Joseph E. Persico, *My American Journey* (New York: Ballantine Books, 1995), pp. 317–19.

92. "North's National Security Office To Be Abolished, Officials Say," AP in *The Asheville Citizen-Times,* December 25, 1986, p. 3.

93. Director Casey, prime target of the Democrats on the Hill, suffered a cerebral seizure at his office at Langley in mid-December and was diagnosed with brain cancer. Though unable to perform his duties as before, he would stay on as DCI until January 29, 1987, when he would resign. By early May, Casey would be dead. ("Regan to Testify to Senate Panel; Casey Hospitalized," *Washington Post,* December 16, 1986, p. A1; Joseph E. Persico, *Casey* [New York: Viking, 1990], pp. 557, 572.)

Donald Regan, the president's powerful chief of staff and another preferred target of Hill Democrats, would continue to serve under the most difficult of circumstances. On February 27, 1987, he, too, would resign. Regan would be replaced by a consummate Washington insider, the recently retired U.S. senator from Tennessee, Howard Baker. (Donald T. Regan, *For the Record* [New York: St. Martin's Press, 1988], pp. 414–15.)

Secretary of Defense Caspar Weinberger and Secretary of State George Shultz would both publicly and pointedly criticize not only the arms-for-hostages deal, but their boss, the president, as well, for having gone along with it. Weinberger would continue to serve until November 23, 1987, when he would resign. He would be replaced by National Security Advisor Carlucci, who in turn would be replaced by Powell. Shultz would serve out his term. ("SecDef Histories—Caspar Weinberger," www .defenselink.mil/specials/secdef_histories/bios/weinberger.htm; "SecDef Histories—Frank Carlucci," www.defenselink.mil/specials/secdef_histories/bios/carlucci.htm; Powell and Persico, *My American Journey,* p. 337; "George Shultz's Homepage," Hoover Institution, www-hoover.stanford.edu/bios/ shultz.html.)

All the while, Thomas Sutherland, dean of the American University's School of Agriculture in Beirut, and Terry Anderson, chief Middle East correspondent for the Associated Press, both of whom Reagan, Regan, Casey, Poindexter, McFarlane, North, and others had tried so desperately to free, remained in the hands of Hezbollah terrorists in Lebanon. Sutherland would not be released until mid-November 1991; Anderson, the longest held of all the hostages, not until early December of that year. (*Report of the Congressional Committees Investigating the Iran-Contra Affair,* p. 160; photos in Scott

Armstrong, *The Chronology: The Documented Day-by-Day Account of the Secret Military Assistance to Iran and the Contras* (New York: Warner Books, 1987); "Statement by Press Secretary Fitzwater on the Release of American Hostage Thomas Sutherland and British Hostage Terry Waite, November 18, 1991," http://bushlibrary.tamu.edu/papers/1911/91111802.html; "Bush Welcomes Anderson Release, Urges End to Terrorism," www.fas.org/news/iran/1991/911205-206498.htm.)

## CHAPTER 26. 1987: PEROT TO HANOI • A BOMBSHELL FROM GENERAL VESSEY • NO EVIDENCE?

1. 092058Z CIA, to [multiple addressees], subject: POW-MIA: Reported Recapture of Alleged Live Missing-in-Action American in Khammouan Province, Laos by the Lao People's Army, DIA Source file 5905, POW/MIA; authors' 1:250,000 color map of area showing the village of Boulapha (Ban Nalquang Nua), located some thirty kilometers southeast of Ban Napang at UTM grid coordinates XE 020 005. (*Official Standard Names Gazeteer, Laos*, p. 192.) DOD records show that Maj. Howard D. Stephenson, USAF, was a member of the flight crew of a Spectre gunship that was hit by antiaircraft fire on March 29, 1972, and crashed approximately ten kilometers southwest of the Tchepone (Sepone) airport at map coordinates 163900N 1060600E. Major Stephenson was officially listed as missing in action and still remains unaccounted for. (Department of Defense, *U.S. Personnel Missing, Southeast Asia (and Selected Foreign Nationals)*, p. 44; authors' 1:250,000 color map of area.)

2. "POW/MIA Issue Covered at Legion Conference, VA Budget, Combat Readiness, Home Loans Also Discussed," *Stars and Stripes*, February 23, 1987, p. 1.

3. "League Officials Order POW Sons and Daughters Jailed," *Bamboo Connection*, March 11, 1987, pp. 1–2.

4. National League of Families of American Prisoners and Missing in Southeast Asia, letter beginning "Dear Family Member," from Ann Mills Griffiths, Executive Director, March 16, 1987, files of Earl P. Hopper.

5. Deposition of H. Ross Perot, Select Committee on POW/MIA Affairs, July 1, 1992, pp. 45–46, Inventory of the Records of the Senate Select Committee on POW/MIA Affairs.

6. Letter from Bui Xuan Nhat, Ambassador, Acting Permanent Representative of the Socialist Republic of Vietnam to the United Nations, to His Excellency H. Ross Perot, March 19, 1987, ibid., Exhibit 8.

7. Deposition of General Colin L. Powell, Chairman, Joint Chiefs of Staff, Select Committee on POW/MIA Affairs, July 16, 1992, p. 55, Inventory of the Records of the Senate Select Committee on POW/MIA Affairs.

8. Document beginning, "3/21/87—3:40 P.M., Telecon With Colin Powell," with cover memorandum from Office of the Vice President, 3/21, to Jim from Craig L. Fuller, both from Deposition of James M. Cannon, Select Committee on POW/MIA Affairs, August 6, 1992, Inventory of the Records of the Senate Select Committee on POW/MIA Affairs.

9. Powell, despite his honorable service in Vietnam, was no friend to the unlisted, unreturned POWs. Steadfastly opposed to any attempt to rescue prisoners, hostages, or the like—in 1983 Powell had told the Joint Chiefs that "the Army could not stand another Desert One fiasco"—he was equally opposed to paying for prisoners, hostages, etc., believing that "ransom, however euphemized, is still ransom and should never be paid." (Powell and Persico, *My American Journey*, pp. 269, 297.) Later, in 1985, Powell had made it clear to the activist congressmen that he opposed making witnesses who had seen American POWs in captivity after the war available to them for independent interview. (See Chapter 24.) Then, when he became deputy national security advisor in late 1986, Powell had embraced Childress and kept him in his post. (See Chapter 25.) And still later, in 1992, Powell, then chairman of the Joint Chiefs of Staff, would tell Senate investigators that throughout the time he served as Secretary Weinberger's senior military assistant, President Reagan's deputy national security advisor and national security advisor, and now as chairman of the Joint Chiefs under President George H. W. Bush—a period of almost ten years during which the POW issue was very much a front-burner issue—rather than acquaint himself with the intelligence on live POWs, all of which he had ready access to, he had relied solely on his instincts when assessing the likelihood that American POWs remained alive in Indochina, and that his instincts had told him that none did. "I was aware that there were . . . reports of first-hand live sightings and that people were working on them," Powell would tell investigators, "but I never had occasion to see any of that material or examine any of it to make my own personal judgments about its veracity or accuracy, or reasonableness. . . . My best visceral instincts told me that it was unlikely that any remained alive." (Deposition of General Colin L. Powell, pp. 35–36.)

Searching for some explanation for Powell's actions, the authors came upon the following statements by Pulitzer Prize–winning author David Halberstam:

Vietnam never goes away. We've either had people criticizing it or whitewashing it and saying it was our finest hour. Everybody in this country is going to try and use it for partisan reasons and manage it. It's the second American civil war. It's really us against us.

When Clinton comes in as president, and Clinton meets Colin Powell, you have a president who not only didn't go to Vietnam but quite deftly danced around the ROTC in Arkansas. And you have Powell, who spent two tours in Vietnam and who believes the most important thing he ever did in his career was—not being a kid of Jamaican background, a City College of New York kid getting to be chairman of the Joint Chiefs or running the gulf war—but cleansing the Army of the viruses of Vietnam. So there you have the two sides of this divided America, and it's still unreconciled. (" 'Apocalypse' Then & Now," *Newsweek,* August 20, 2001, p. 48.)

"Cleansing the Army of the viruses of Vietnam." Could that have been it?

10. Deposition of H. Ross Perot, pp. 208–09.

11. Ibid., passim.

12. Letter to The Honorable Ronald Reagan, with attachment titled "Future Actions," from Ross Perot, April 8, 1987, Inventory of the Records of the Senate Select Committee on POW/MIA Affairs.

13. Robert Dornan, David Dreier, Duncan Hunter, James Hansen, Denny Smith, Don Sundquist, Robert Smith, and John Rowland. Soon, thirteen more GOP members would join in pledging $100,000 to the reward fund: Helen Bentley, Mike Bilirakis, Hank Brown, Dan Burton, Howard Coble, Larry Craig, James Inhofe, Arthur Ravenel, Toby Roth, Mac Sweeney, Pat Swindall, Curt Weldon, and Jack Davis. When private-sector pledges pushed the total to $2.4 million later in the summer, Hendon stopped soliciting additional contributors and, sometimes accompanied by POW/MIA relatives, began traveling to Southeast Asia to spread word of the reward. One additional unsolicited pledge pushed the total purse to $2.5 million, where it stands as of the date of publication of this book.

14. For example, "WANTED ALIVE: One U.S. Serviceman Missing in Vietnam, And These People Will Pay $1 Million Reward," *Fort Worth Star-Telegram,* April 28, 1987, p. 1; "POW Reward Offered," *Richmond News Leader,* April 28, 1987, p. 4; "$1 Million Offered for Live POW," *Washington Times,* April 28, 1987, p. 2A; "Group Offers $1 Million for Return of American POW," *Atlanta Journal,* April 29, 1987, p. 3A; "A Million Dollars for Freeing a US PoW, Congressmen Make Offer," *Bangkok World* (English), April 28, 1987, p. 1.

15. 100th Cong., 1st sess., H.R. 2260, "To direct the heads of Federal departments and agencies holding records concerning reported live sightings of American military personnel classified as prisoners of war or missing in action in Southeast Asia to make such records available to the public, April 30, 1987.

16. Deposition of Frank C. Carlucci, Select Committee on POW/MIA Affairs, June 26, 1992, p. 67, Inventory of the Records of the Senate Select Committee on POW/MIA Affairs.

17. "MIA Issue Shaped Perot's View of Bush," *Washington Post,* April 18, 1992, p. A1.

18. Deposition of Frank C. Carlucci, p. 70.

19. Letter from the Vice President, Washington, signed by George Bush, to Miss Tawny Wolfe, May 27, 1987, provided by the recipient in 1987, Hendon files.

20. "Laos," *National Geographic* 171, no. 6 (June 1987): 779.

21. *U.S. Childress Delegation Ends 3-Day Visit,* "Summary of Visit," OW280737 Hanoi VNA in English, May 28, 1987, and "AFP Says 'Some Success,' " BK280816 Hong Kong AFP in English, May 28, 1987, both FBIS, IV, May 29, 1987, VIETNAM, K1–K2; R 111506Z JUN 87, subject: [redacted] Reports on Meeting Between U.S. and Vietnamese Officials Regarding MIA Question, Hendon files.

22. Briefs, Vietnam-U.S.: Toughened Line on MIA Issue, FBIS Trends, July 1, 1987, p. 25, Hendon files.

23. "Viets Seek Financial Aid in MiA Search," *Bangkok Post,* July 11, 1987.

24. "Secretary Shultz, Resolving the POW/MIA Issue," United States Department of State, Bureau of Public Affairs, July 1987.

25. "U.S., Vietnam To Hold Talks On Fate of MIAs," *Washington Post,* July 25, 1987, p. A23. Traveling with Vessey would be Childress; Griffiths; the deputy chief of mission at the U.S. embassy in Seoul, South Korea (and former deputy assistant secretary of state and chairman of the POW/MIA Interagency Group), David Lambertson; former Tighe Task Force review panel member Robert Kingston; Vessey aide Brig. Gen. Steve Croaker; and a translator. (Handwritten undated phone notes, Hendon files.)

26. 031615Z AUG 87, from General Vessey to [multiple addressees], subject: POW/MIA Talks: Day One, Reel 57, Series 92-300, POW/MIA.

27. *The Vessey Mission to Hanoi: Hearing Before the Subcommittee on Asian and Pacific Affairs of the Committee on Foreign Affairs,* September 30, 1987, p. 6.

**28.** Ibid., pp. 12–13.

**29.** 031615Z AUG 87, POW/MIA Talks: Day One.

**30.** Barbara Crossette, "Vietnam-U.S. Meeting on Missing Ends With No Progress Reported," *New York Times,* August 4, 1987, p. A2.

**31.** "Vietnam Hints MIAs May Be in Bush Areas," *Washington Times,* August 11, 1987, p. A1.

**32.** Central Intelligence Agency, SNIE 14.3-87, "Hanoi and the POW/MIA Issue," Hendon files.

**33.** P 230812Z MAR 87, subject: JCRC Report M87-001, Escaped American POW Allegedly Seen Near Nam Can, 1984, DIA Source file 6182, POW/MIA (referenced sketch map not included in declassified DIA file, only a typewritten description of it titled "Key to sketch drawn by [source name redacted], Source of M87-001"); authors' annotated color 1:250,000 map of area showing reported location of sighting.

**34.** P 230812Z MAR 87, JCRC Report M87-001, DIA Source file 6182, POW/MIA.

**35.** United States Government, memorandum 10819/DI-7, November 6, 1981, subject: PW/MIA Daily Report; "Subject: Inputs to PMSEA3"; source's hand-drawn sketch, all DIA Source file 1074, POW/MIA.

**36.** R 271729Z MAR 87, FM CIA/DDO, TO DIA WASH DC//VO-PW, subject: Response to [redacted] Requirements, and Action Record, Source Name: [redacted], Case #6198, both Inventory of the Records of the Senate Select Committee on POW/MIA Affairs.

**37.** Letter from [name redacted] to Mr. Kimball Gaines, Col. USAF, Chief Sp. Ofc. POW/MIA, Defense Intel. Agency, April 20, 1987, DIA Source file 6744, POW/MIA.

**38.** Summary of Source Interview, DIA Source file 6744, POW/MIA; authors' annotated 1:250,000 color map of Kham Keut area.

**39.** R 051812Z JUN 87, subject: Evaluation of Rpt T87-221, DIA Source file 6744, POW/MIA.

**40.** P 290246Z APR 87, SUBJECT: JCRC RPT T87-163, Lao Resistance Report of 21 American Prisoners in Udomxai, Laos, DIA Source file 6356, POW/MIA.

**41.** P 300455Z APR 87, subject: JCRC Report T87-168, Limited Hearsay of American Prisoners in Northern Vietnam, JCRC files, POW/MIA. A number of ARVN soldiers who underwent reeducation in camps in Ha Nam Ninh Province would later tell U.S. officials that prior to periodic "inspections" of their camps by international organizations, inmates whom the Communists believed might make derogatory remarks about their treatment were moved out of the camps and detained elsewhere until the "inspectors" had completed their work and departed. The testimony of one such ARVN soldier received by the DIA in 1987 can be found in R 07 1005 DEC 87, subject: IIR 6 024 0141 88/Visits by International Organizations to Reeducation Camps in North Vietnam, DIA Source file 7173, Inventory of the Records of the Senate Select Committee on POW/MIA Affairs.

**42.** R 182113Z MAY 87, from CIA to [multiple addressees], subject: POW/MIA: Allegation of an Interrogation Center Still Holding U.S. Prisoners of War in an Unknown Location in Southwest Ha Nam Ninh Province in Early 1986, CIA files, POW/MIA.

**43.** P 2712332 MAY 87, subject: [redacted], DIA Source file 6462, Inventory of the Records of the Senate Select Committee on POW/MIA Affairs.

**44.** P 010927Z JUN 87, subject: JCRC Report T87-236, Hearsay of US POWs in Northern Vietnam, DIA Source file 6473, POW/MIA.

**45.** Handwritten memorandum for the record dated August 15, 1988, quoting CIA 021852Z May 1988, DIA Source file 6473, POW/MIA.

**46.** R 071708Z JUN 87, subject: JCRC Report T87-252, Observation of Caucasians Working on Road in the Lao Bao Area During April 1975, DIA Source file 6422, POW/MIA.

**47.** 01 251445Z JUN 87, from DIA Washington DC//VO-PW// to CIA Washington DC//DDO/PCS/INT-RR//, subject: Source Directed Requirement, REF: CIA 191518Z JUN 87, CITE 513862, TDFIRDB-315/22717-87, DIA Source file 6491, POW/MIA.

**48.** P 021012Z JUL 87, subject: IIR 6 024 0003 87/U.S. POWs Held in Ban Eun and Nong Hed, JCRC Files, POW/MIA.

**49.** R 300630Z JUL 87, subject: IIR 6 024 0040 87/Caucasians in Ha Nam Ninh Province, Source Reports, POW/MIA.

**50.** R 210715Z AUG 87, subject: IIR 6 024 0090/Indications of U.S. PWs [in] Vietnam, Service Intel Files, POW/MIA.

**51.** Authors' annotated 1:250,000 color map of Ban Kat area.

**52.** R 241024Z AUG 87, subject: IIR 6 024 U089 87/Sighting of Two US PWs in Northern Laos, DIA Source file 6933, POW/MIA.

**53.** R 080531Z SEP 87, subject: IIR 6 024 0735 87/Twelve American Pilots Held in Southern Sam Neua Province, DIA Source file 6955, POW/MIA.

**54.** JCRC T83-099, subject: Refugee Report, Hearsay of Sighting of Alleged Americans in Laos, Inventory of the Records of the Senate Select Committee on POW/MIA Affairs; authors' annotated 1:250,000 color map of Nong Co (Nong Kou) area.

**55.** 150159Z CIA to DIA WASH DC//VO-PW, subject: Alleged Location of Two POW Camps in Vietnam, CIA files, Inventory of the Records of the Senate Select Committee on POW/MIA Affairs.

**56.** R 110125Z SEP 87, subject: IIR 6 024 0146 87/US. POWs Detained in Caves Near Route 7, Source Reports, POW/MIA.

**57.** P 150933Z SEP 87, from DET 32 PSAA SEOUL KOR//CC//, subject: Possible Vietnamese Underground Prison Facility for US POW's, Source Reports, POW/MIA; authors' annotated 1:250,000 map of Hung Hoa area.

**58.** R 090802Z JUL 81, subject: IR 1 511 0234 81/Vietnam/Hearsay Report on American Prisoners Held in Hoang Lien Son Mountain Range. NVN/.

**59.** R 031051Z NOV 87, subject: IIR 6 024 0062 88/American PW in Ha Nam Ninh in March 1987, DIA Source file 7134, POW/MIA.

**60.** 42 American pilots being held in a Ha Nam Ninh prison camp in 1974: JCRC I79-040, January 4, 1980, subj: Refugee Report, Alleged Americans Held In North Vietnam, DIA Source file 4065, POW/MIA; a group of U.S. pilots being held at the Ba Sao/Rockpile prison camp complex through at least August, 1976: Central Intelligence Agency, memorandum for Assistant Vice Director For Collection Management, Department of Defense, Principal Advisor for Prisoners of War Missing in Action Affairs (International Security Affairs), Director, Vietnam, Laos And Kampuchea, Bureau of East Asian And Pacific Affairs, Department of State, subject: Alleged Imprisonment of a Group of U.S. Pilots in a House Near What Is Now the Nam Ha Reeducation Camp A in Ha Nam Ninh Province, Socialist Republic of Vietnam (SRV), Through at Least August 1976, DIA Source file 1695, Inventory of the Records of the Senate Select Committee on POW/MIA Affairs; about fifty U.S. pilots being held at the Ba Sao/Rockpile prison camp complex sometime between 1975 and April 1977: Defense Intelligence Agency, Resources and Installations Division [DB-4], undated Memo for Bill Hutchinson, DIA Source file 0130, Inventory of the Records of the Senate Select Committee on POW/MIA Affairs; American prisoners being held in Ha Nam Ninh Province as of May 1977: translation of letter beginning, "Dear Madame," DIA Source file 0125, Inventory of the Records of the Senate Select Committee on POW/MIA Affairs; two U.S. POWs with shaved heads being marched under guard toward the Ba Sao/Rockpile prison camp complex around Tet 1978: JCRC T80-057, Source file 0802, POW/MIA; white-skinned prisoners thought to be U.S. or French working in the fields around a reeducation camp in Ha Nam Ninh Province from 1975 to early 1979: R 300630Z JUL 87, subject: IIR 6 024 0040 87/Caucasians in Ha Nam Ninh Province, Source Reports, POW/MIA; many American prisoners being housed in a compound adjacent to a Ha Nam Ninh reeducation camp during 1979: P 010924Z JUN 87, subject: JCRC Report T87-236, Hearsay of US POWs in Northern Vietnam and handwritten memorandum for the record, dated August 15, 1988, quoting CIA 021852Z May 88, DIA Source file 6473, POW/MIA; a number of American POWs being detained in a separate compound inside the Ba Sao/Rockpile prison camp complex as late as mid-December 1979: P 200452Z FEB 80, subject: IR 6 013 6621 80, POW/MIA; three American prisoners being detained in a separate enclosure inside the Ba Sao/Rockpile prison camp complex as late as January 1980; DIA source file 0642; JCRC I80-014, August 1, 1980, subject: Refugee Report, Alleged Sighting of Caucasians near Ha Nam Ninh Camp, DIA Source file 0814, Inventory of the Records of the Senate Select Committee on POW/MIA Affairs; a group of American prisoners walking under guard along a road in Ha Nam Ninh/Ha Son Binh Province during the early 1980s; P 300445Z APR 87, subject: JCRC Report T87-168, Limited Hearsay of American Prisoners in Northern Vietnam, JCRC files, POW/MIA; a group of about ten American POWs entering a subcamp of the Ba Sao/Rockpile prison camp system located just east of Phu Ly City and known as "Camp My" early in the morning of January 10, 1981; P 240301Z JUL 81, Sighting of Americans in Phu Ly Prison Camp, DIA Source file 0997, POW/MIA; U.S. pilots begging for deliverance outside a jail in the vicinity of Phu Ly City in 1985: P 291904Z MAY 86, subject: JCRC Refugee Report RP86-048, 29 MAY 86, Alleged American Prisoners in Vietnam, JCRC Files, POW/MIA; U.S. POWs being detained in an interrogation center located southwest of Ninh Binh City in early 1986: R 182113Z MAY 87, subject: POW/MIA: Allegation of an Interrogation Center Still Holding U.S. Prisoners of War in an Unknown Location in Southwest Ha Nam Ninh Province in Early 1986, CIA files, POW/MIA.

**61.** "Veterans: MIAs Need More U.S. Attention," AP in unnamed veterans' newspaper, Hendon files.

**62.** "US Agencies to Step up Aid to Disabled in VN," *Bangkok Post,* December 23, 1987, p. 4.

## CHAPTER 27. 1988: "JUST TWO BAR OF SILVERS FOR EACH MAN"

**1.** "U.S. Is Asking Charitable Groups To Assist the Disabled in Vietnam," *New York Times,* January 3, 1988, p. 1.

**2.** "U.S. Encourages Private Charity for Vietnam," AP in *Washington Post,* January 3, 1988, p. A26.

**3.** In late December 1987, Robert Garwood had renewed an offer he had first made in December 1984 to accompany U.S. officials—this time activist Congressmen Frank McCloskey, Bob Smith, and John Rowland—to Vietnam and take them to the locations where he had seen American POWs in captivity long after Operation Homecoming. Administration officials at the White House, Defense Department, and State Department had joined forces to prohibit Garwood from boarding the U.S. government aircraft. (O 060108Z JAN 88, subject: Codel McCloskey—the Garwood Question; O 060314Z JAN 88, subject: Codel McCloskey; R 060935Z JAN 88, subject: Codel McCloskey: Korean Remains; P 081246Z JAN 88, subject: Codel McCloskey—en Route to Vietnam, all files of Frank McCloskey.) It would not be until the summer of 1993 that Garwood would finally make it to Vietnam with Smith and members of the senator's delegation and show them where he had seen the American POWs. Everyone on the delegation was tremendously impressed by Garwood's recall of past events and convinced beyond any doubt that he had been where he said he had been and had seen what he said he had seen. An ABC News *20/20* crew accompanying the delegation won an Emmy for its coverage of the trip, titled "Last Man Out."

**4.** "Hanoi Rejects U.S. Plan on Private Aid," *New York Times,* January 20, 1988, p. A3.

**5.** "U.S. Rejects Vietnam's Aid Demand," *Washington Post,* January 21, 1988, p. A18.

**6.** Testimony of Ann Mills Griffiths Before the Subcommittee on Asian and Pacific Affairs, Committee on Foreign Affairs, September 30, 1987, Elizabeth Stewart files.

**7.** "Families Beg Congressmen to Declassify POW Reports," *Washington Times.*

**8.** National League of Families of American Prisoners and Missing in Southeast Asia, "League Positions," April 27, 1988, Elizabeth Stewart files.

**9.** Powell and Persico, *My American Journey,* p. 336.

**10.** "Reagan Says Ties to Hanoi Hinge on Issue of the Missing," *New York Times,* July 30, 1988, p. A2.

**11.** The White House, Office of the Press Secretary, "Remarks by the President at Annual Meeting of the National League of POW/MIA Families," July 29, 1988.

**12.** "Reagan Applauds Vietnam's Agreement on Search for MIAs," *Washington Post,* July 30, 1988.

**13.** Hendon, Stewart, and Leo Hrdlicka, brother of Capt. David Hrdlicka, USAF, a confirmed yet unreturned POW captured in Laos in May 1965, were distributing reward flyers in northeast Thailand along the Mekong River boundary with Laos later in the summer when they were notified by members of the press that the first of the crash site excavations announced by President Reagan would begin in northern Vietnam within a matter of days. Asked by reporters in Thailand to comment on this development, Stewart said she was outraged that the United States would spend time excavating crash sites "while our prisoners starve in communist captivity nearby." Hrdlicka declared that for any U.S. official "to say this is progress is a slap in the face to my brother, Beth's dad and all the other prisoners of war." ("Relatives of MiAs Ridicule Joint Search," *Bangkok Post,* September 18, 1988, p. 2; "MiA Relatives: Free Live Prisoners Not Dead Bodies," *The Nation* (Bangkok), September 18, 1988, p. 2.) Hendon, speaking to a reporter in the United States several weeks later after the first series of excavations had been completed, said that "from press reports, it's clear that on the way to the crash sites the U.S. team almost stumbled over one of Vietnam's newest and most secure prison facilities, where the U.S. government has eyewitness accounts and volumes of intelligence showing American POWs being held there well into the 1980's. . . . For us to spend our time and resources digging around the wreckage of an airplane that crashed 20 years ago while American POWs starve nearby in communist prisons is unbelievable. . . . I've never seen anything that even comes close to this, as far as outrageous behavior on the part of the bureaucrats handling this issue. . . . For them to bypass the prisons they know without a doubt are there and dig around crash sites instead approaches criminal behavior against the men who still sit in communist prisons—some for as long as 20 years—waiting for Americans to bring them home." Asked by the reporter to comment on Hendon's statements, Schlatter, speaking on background, declared that the DOD possessed "probably 70 linear feet of files on the Vietnamese prison system that describes very accurately not only facilities, but inmate population, prisoners' daily routines and that kind of thing, [and that] "the only Americans that have been held in that system are those who returned in 1973, Americans arrested over the years for violating Vietnamese territorial waters, a few [of whom] were involved in some narcotics trafficking. . . . Every report I've been able to check out so far," Schlatter said, "has not been [an MIA] held captive." Schlatter went on to accuse Hendon and other POW activists of "blocking serious government efforts to determine whether Americans are alive in Vietnam. What troubles me," he declared, "is that the American public is going to begin looking on this issue as an issue of fruits and nuts, and its not. . . . It's a very real issue, and it's solvable, but they're holding the whole issue up to ridicule." ("Hendon: U.S. Hunts Bones While POWs Starve," *Asheville Citizen-Times,* October 16, 1988, p. A1.

**14.** Paragraph 6 of untitled, incomplete JCRC debrief of Lao refugee Major Sivilay, signed by Paul D. Mather, Lt Col, USAF, JCRC Liaison Officer, Hendon files.

**15.** P 040214Z FEB 86, subject: JCRC Report T86-032, Report of Four Caucasian Prisoners Seen in Saravan Province Laos in Nov 83, DIA Source file 3910, POW/MIA; authors' annotated map.

**16.** R 181131Z NOV 88, subject: JCRC RPT T88-605, Hearsay of American Prisoners in Southern Laos, DIA Source file 8607, POW/MIA; annotated color 1:250,000 map of area. Gadoury, when approached in the months ahead by other sources who said that they, too, were working to free American POWs in return for the $2.4 million reward, would repeat that there was no reward and that they should cease and desist in their efforts to free any American POW they might have seen, heard about, or have access to. (Gadoury's actions and those of other U.S. officials who told sources the same thing are discussed in detail in Chapter 29.)

**17.** R 050902Z JAN 88, subject: IIR 6 024 0157-88/Hearsay of Alleged American Prisoners Being Held in a Prison at Tay Hieu, 1978; R 280817Z MAR 88, subject: IIR 6 024 0285-88/Re-interview of Source SEA 1004-88 on Hearsay of Alleged American Prisoners Being Held in a Prison at Tay Hieu, both DIA Source file 9704, POW/MIA; authors' annotated 1:250,000 color map of area.

**18.** Two-page handwritten report in handwriting of DIA analyst Gen. Soutchay Vongsavanh dated January 15, 1988, DIA Source file 5491, pp. 41–42 POW/MIA.

**19.** Entire DIA Source file 5491, POW/MIA.

**20.** Authors' annotated 1:250,000 color map of area.

**21.** R 020504Z FEB 88, subject: IIR 6 024 0178 88/Reply to [redacted] VOP-05134: Three Alleged PW in Xepon, Laos, DIA Source file 7479, Inventory of the Records of the Senate Select Committee on POW/MIA Affairs.

**22.** R 140535Z OCT 86, subject: JCRC Report T86-422, Letter Reporting Three Americans in Laos, DIA Source file 5638, POW/MIA.

**23.** R 221220Z FEB 88, subject: JCRC Report T88-058, Hearsay of Activity in Northern Laos, DIA Source file 7565, POW/MIA.

**24.** P 270552Z FEB 88, subject: JCRC Refugee Report RP88-003, Hearsay Live Sighting of Americans Living in The U Minh Forest Area in 1987, DIA Source file 7605, POW/MIA.

**25.** [R] 050701Z APR 88, subject: JCRC Report T88-135, Hearsay Concerning 26 Americans Held in Minh Hai During 1985, DIA Source file 8006, POW/MIA.

**26.** [220229Z AP 88], from USDAO Bangkok TH//PW-MIA//, subject: IIR 6 024 0319-88/Alleged Sighting of U.S. PW Detained Near Nong Het, Source Files, Reel 5, Series 92-300, POW/MIA.

**27.** R 111800Z MAY 88, subject: JCRC Refugee Report RP88-015, Hearsay of 150 Alleged Americans Living in the U Minh Forest, Source Files, Reel 4, Series 92-300, POW/MIA.

**28.** R 180308Z MAY 88, subject: IIR 6 024 8320 88/Lao Government Policy for Retaining U.S. PW, USAF Intelligence Files, POW/MIA.

**29.** R 201106Z MAY 88, subject: IIR 6 024 0371-88/Hearsay of an Alleged Group of American PW in U-Minh Forest, SVN, DIA Source file 8076, POW/MIA.

**30.** R 220829Z JUN 88, subject: IIR 6 024 0 88/Hearsay of Alleged American P[risoners] Being Detained in Ha Tay Province, DIA Source file 8110, POW/MIA; authors' annotated 1:250,000 color map of area.

**31.** R 091029Z JUL 88, subject: JCRC Report M88-075, Hearsay of American Prisoners in Thanh Hoa Province, 1986, DIA Source file 8386, POW/MIA.

**32.** In addition to previous references to Americans being detained in Thanh Hoa Province, see report of more than twenty American pilots being held in Thanh Hoa: R 050955Z MAY 84, subject: American POWs remaining in Vietnam, DIA Source file 2220, Inventory of the Records of the Senate Select Committee on POW/MIA Affairs; Ten American POWs in Thanh Hoa: R 020330Z FEB 87, FM USDAO TOKYO JA, subject: IIR 6 852 0057 87/Collection Emphasis 86-0097-JCRC Report J-86-015, Alleged Knowledge of American Captives in Vietnam 301145Z JUL 86, DIA Source file 5360, Inventory of the Records of the Senate Select Committee on POW/MIA Affairs; Twenty-nine American POWs seen at a bath point in Thanh Hoa: JCRC M82-052, subject: Refugee Report, Hearsay of American Prisoners at Thanh Hoa Province, DIA Source file 1539, POW/MIA.

**33.** R 101711Z AUG 88, subject: [redacted] 6 024 0423-88/Hearsay of Alleged Americans Being Held South of the Nam Ngum Dam in 1983 [sic], DIA Source file 8326, Inventory of the Records of the Senate Select Committee on POW/MIA Affairs.

**34.** R 070924Z SEP 88, subject: [redacted] IIR 6 024 0454-88/Alleged American Prisoners in Vinh Phu Province Circa 1984, DIA Source file 8440, POW/MIA.

**35.** R 080820Z SEP 88, subject: [redacted] IIR 6 024 0456-88/Names of Alleged Live PW in Savannakhet Province; Enclosure 1 (sketch map of the camp off of Route 9 where the American POWs were reportedly held, and two-page letter of transmittal from the Royal Thai Navy captain, all DIA Source file 8417, POW/MIA.

**36.** DIA 1:50,000 black-and-white map; annotated black-and-white reconnaissance photo dated May 20, 1972, titled "Bang Liet PW Camp N-125; unannotated DIA black-and-white photo of same facility titled "Skidrow," all Hendon files.

**37.** R 161307Z NOV 88, subject: IIR 6 024 0018 89/Alleged Sighting of American Prisoners in Prison Near Hanoi in 1988; R 301021Z NOV 88, subject: IIR 6 024 0030 89/Reinterview of Source [name redacted] on Sighting of Alleged American Pilots in Hanoi Prison, with source's hand-drawn memory sketch, all DIA Source file 8223, POW/MIA.

**38.** P 081026Z DEC 88, subject: JCRC Report RP88-093, Alleged Movement of U.S. POWs, DIA Source file 8547, Inventory of the Records of the Senate Select Committee on POW/MIA Affairs.

**39.** Authors' annotated 1:250,000 color map.

**40.** R 221210Z DEC 88, subject: IIR 6 024 0032 89/Western Prisoners Allegedly Sighted in Nghe Tinh Province Early 1985, DIA Source file 9684, POW/MIA.

**41.** R 230634Z DEC 88, subject: IIR 6 024 0036 89/Alleged Detention of 12 PWs at Tham Kaeb, DIA Source file 8329, POW/MIA; authors' 1:250,000 annotated map of Ban Khalik area.

**42.** R 230510Z DEC 88, subject: IIR 6 024 0035 89/Four Alleged American Prisoners Sighted in Eastern Vientiane Province in August 1988, DIA Source file 8544, Inventory of the Records of the Senate Select Committee on POW/MIA Affairs; authors' annotated 1:250,000 map of Paksan, Laos, and environs.

**43.** Defense Intelligence Agency, Directorate for Imagery Exploitation, Imagery Analysis Memorandum, U-12-58559-88/DX5D, December 23, 1988, subject: Symbols near Sam Neua, Laos; "Markings in Rice Paddy Near Sam Neua, Laos," both Inventory of the Records of the Senate Select Committee on POW/MIA Affairs.

**44.** Department of the Air Force, Pacific Air Combat Operations Staff (PACAF), 7 SEP 1984, subject: PACAF E&E Code Letter Program [declassified], with declassified attachments, and United States Government memorandum, 1423/VO-PW, 20 DEC 88, subject: Request for Imagery Support [declassified], both Hendon files; declassified line drawing of satellite imagery and actual imagery, Inventory of the Records of the Senate Select Committee on POW/MIA Affairs. The reader will recall that in the case of the "Flying Tango Hotel" E&E code imaged just north of the Plain of Jars in 1973, the *T* (Tango), in accordance with instructions issued to some airmen, had been modified with "wings" rather than "feet," making it a "Flying T" or "Flying Tango." (See www.enormouscrime.com, Chapter 23, (3), Case #3037.)

**45.** Hendon and the activist families and vets, unaware during this period that Gadoury and other U.S. officials were telling would-be rescuers to cease and desist in their efforts to free American POWs for the reward, had continued distributing reward posters at border crossings all along the Mekong in eastern and northeastern Thailand. ("American Publicises Huge MIA Reward," *Bangkok Post*, December 21, 1988.)

## CHAPTER 28. 1989: ". . . THE STATUTE OF LIMITATIONS HAS BEEN REACHED"

**1.** Department of Defense, Department of State, *Final Interagency Report of the Reagan Administration on the POW/MIA Issue in Southeast Asia,* January 19, 1989.

**2.** John Scrivener, an American living with his family in Hong Kong, had purchased the trawler and renamed it the "Little John Thomas." See "Group Offers Reward in Bid to Find MIAs," *South China Sunday Morning Post,* February 5, 1989, p. 2; "Balloons Carry POW Reward Offer," *USA Today,* International Edition, p. 2; "Pair Set Off in Search of Missing Fathers," *South China Morning Post,* February 10, 1989, p. 3; "Hopes Offered on the Wind," *Hong Kong Standard,* February 13, 1989; "Exciting Times on the Boat Built for Adventure," *South China Morning Post,* June 2, 1990, p. 7.

**3.** P R 290503Z OCT 84, FM AMEMBASSY VIENTIANE, TO SECSTATE WASHDC . . . [and multiple addressees], subject: Alleged Presence of 30 US POWs Near Phou Bia in LAOS, DIA Source file 2551, POW/MIA.

**4.** O 210455Z MAR 89, FM AMEMBASSY VIENTIANE, TO SECSTATE WASH DC . . . , subject: Alleged "Colony" of U.S. Servicemen in Laos, DIA Source file 10011, POW/MIA.

**5.** 0231/PW-MIA, 21 MAR 1989, to DD, subject: Report of "Colony" of Americans Living in Laos, signed by Joseph A. Schlatter, Colonel, USA, Chief, Special Office for Prisoners of War and Missing in Action, with attached map, DIA Source file 10011, POW/MIA.

**6.** O R 230338Z MAR 89, FM SECSTATE WASHDC TO AMEMBASSY VIENTIANE . . . , subject: Reported "Colony" of U.S. Servicemen in Laos, DIA Source file 10011, POW/MIA.

**7.** 0 270106Z MAR 89, FM AMEMBASSY VIENTIANE, TO SECSTATE WASHDC, subject: Reported "Colony" of US Servicemen in Laos, DIA Source file 10011, POW/MIA.

**8.** Kyodo dispatch in O 071534Z JUN 89, subject: Japanese Says U.S. POW's Detained in SRV, DIA Source file 8799, POW/MIA.

**9.** O 080638Z JUN 89, retransmission of O 080624Z JUN 89, FM USDAO TOKYO JA, subject: IIR 6 852 0200 89/U.S. Military Personnel Imprisoned in Vietnam, DIA Source file 8799, POW/MIA.

**10.** United States Government memorandum, 0639/PW-MIA, Date: 08 JUN 1989, subject: Japanese Monk Reporting U.S. PWs in Vietnam, Thru: DD to DR, signed by Joseph A. Schlatter, Colonel, USA, Chief, Special Office for Prisoners of War and Missing in Action, DIA Source file 8799, POW/MIA.

**11.** "Freed Vietnam Captive Reports Seeing U.S. POWs," *Washington Post,* June 10, 1989, p. A10.

**12.** Defense Intelligence Agency, 12 JUN 1989, [Redacted]-0654/PW-MIA, to 1. Mr. Matt Reynolds, 2. Mr. Phil Robertson, 3. Mr. Steve Nelson, subject: U.S. Official Interview with Japanese Monk, signed by Joseph A. Schlatter, Colonel, USA, Chief, Special Office for Prisoners of War and Missing in Action; Office of the Assistant Secretary of Defense, International Security Affairs, letter to Honorable Dennis DeConcini, United States Senate from T. W. Wright, Rear Admiral, USN, Director, East Asia and Pacific Region, July 13, 1989, DIA Source file 8799, POW/MIA.

**13.** Memorandum for the record, subject: Congressional Request for Information Concerning Monk Ganshin Yoshida, July 10, 1989, DIA Source file 8799, POW/MIA.

**14.** DIA "Background Paper," June 12, 1989, subject: Japanese Buddhist Monk, Ganshin Yoshida, DIA Source file 8799, POW/MIA.

**15.** United States Government memorandum, 0651/PW-MIA, 12 JUN 1989, subject: Japanese Monk Update, signed by Joseph A. Schlatter, Colonel, USA, Chief, Special Office for Prisoners of War and Missing in Action, DIA Source file 8799, POW/MIA.

**16.** "700 Americans Are Still Rotting in Vietnam Prisons," *National Enquirer,* August 1, 1989, p. 1. Hendon interviewed Yoshida in Sapporo in 1990. He found him frail and still suffering the effects of his captivity, but his information—corroborated as it was by multiple, independent sources—was totally credible.

**17.** *American Legion Magazine,* November 1989, p. 51.

**18.** "Summary of Reporting on Japanese Monk," DIA Source file 8799, POW/MIA.

**19.** "To amend the Internal Revenue Code of 1986 to provide for the designation on income tax forms of overpayment of tax and contributions to reward the return of a Vietnam POW/MIA," 101st Cong., 1st sess., September 6, 1989, S 1587, http://Thomas.loc.gov/cgi-bin/query/z?c101:S.1587.

**20.** A little-known clause in the intelligence statutes required that intelligence reports containing the specific name of an American prisoner said to still be alive in captivity be made available to the named prisoner's next of kin immediately after the DIA received them. It was because of this requirement—and only because of this requirement—that over the years a number of the activist families had received reports indicating their fathers, husbands, sons, brothers, etc., were alive in captivity.

**21.** "At Game 3, Nature Took Awesome Swing," *Los Angeles Times,* October 18, 1989, p. A1.

**22.** " 'Scared to Death' at the 'Stick,' " *San Francisco Examiner,* October 18, 1989.

**23.** Ibid.

**24.** "Fear and Death in I-880 Collapse," *San Francisco Examiner,* October 18, 1989, p. A2.

**25.** "I-880 Excavation to Take a Week, Bodies Found in 31 Vehicles So Far," *San Francisco Examiner,* October 21, 1989.

**26.** "Bush Vows Aid During Quake Tour," *Washington Post,* October 21, 1989, p. A1.

**27.** "Survivor Pulled From Cypress Carnage, Miracle in the Ruins," "Buck Helm Is 'Tough as Nails,' " *San Francisco Examiner,* October 22, 1989, p. A1.

**28.** "Survivor of Quake Found in Oakland Freeway's Rubble," *Los Angeles Times,* October 22, 1989, p. A1.

**29.** "Buck Helm Is 'Tough as Nails.' "

**30.** " 'Miracle' Survivor,' Buck Helm Is Lowered From the Cypress Overpass," *Oakland Tribune,* photo via AP.

**31.** "Survivor of Quake Found in Oakland Freeway's Rubble."

**32.** Letter to the President from Elizabeth A. Stewart and twelve others, October 23, 1989, Elizabeth Stewart files.

**33.** National Security Council, letter to Ms. Elizabeth A. Stewart signed by Peter S. Watson, Director of Asian Affairs, December 4, 1989, Elizabeth Stewart files.

## CHAPTER 29. 1990: SABOTAGING THE HELMS/GRASSLEY INVESTIGATIONS • THE BUSH FINAL REPORT ON POWs • THACH'S HISTORIC VISIT TO WASHINGTON

**1.** Using methods outlined by the authors at www.enormouscrime.com, Chapter 23, DIA analysts had by 1990 debunked virtually all of the other eyewitness accounts of Americans held captive after Operation Homecoming.

**2.** Handwritten letter to Mrs. Dorothy M. Bodden, from [source name redacted], August 26, 1979; R 122135Z NOV 80, subject: Lao Refugee [name redacted], both DIA source file 0447, Inventory of the Records of the Senate Select Committee on POW/MIA Affairs.

**3.** "Affidavit of Bouakeau Phanavong," August 18, 1980, Hendon files.

**4.** Department of the Air Force, Headquarters Air Force Office of Special Investigations, Memorandum from Chief, USAF Polygraph Program to DIA/DI-7C, November 5, 1980, subject: (80HQD479-9) [source name redacted], DIA Source file 0447, POW/MIA.

**5.** Memorandum for the record, with handwritten date 27/3/81, subject: Re-evaluation of Polygraph Examination Results, signed by John E. Kennedy, Lieutenant Colonel, USAF, Chief, PW/MIA Branch, ibid.

**6.** "DIA Evaluation of Information Provided by Lao Refugee [source name redacted] (0447)," ibid.

**7.** This sighting is briefly mentioned in Chapter 20, note 16.

**8.** United States Government memorandum to DR, subject: PW/MIA Daily Report, July 30, 1981; Defense Intelligence Agency Staff Summary Sheet [redacted] 11901/DI-E2, subject: Request [redacted, replaced with handwritten word "Method"], with attached annotated map titled "Phonsaly Area Map" and hand-drawn map of camp titled "Thongnanoi Prison Camp at Muong Khoua," December 13, 1982; Memorandum, 11901/DI-E2 /Mr. Burns/50501/7 DEC 82/paf, "Memorandum for the [redacted] (BTB "THE DDO, CIA"), subject: Reported Presence of American Prisoners of War in the Lao People's Democratic Republic (U), signed by James A. Williams, Lieutenant General, U.S. Army, Director, December 27, 1982; also later written confirmation of imagery hit in Defense Intelligence Agency, Directorate for Research, [Imagery] Analysis Division, [Imagery] Analysis Memorandum SNF 06-55667-85, to DC-2B from [redacted], subject: U/I Facility vic Phongsaly Province, June 13, 1985, all from either DIA Source file 0995, POW/MIA or Inventory of the Records of the Senate Select Committee on POW/MIA Affairs. Hendon has personally seen and studied satellite imagery of the camp and states unequivocally that the camp was at the exact location cited by the source and conformed exactly to the source's description. (Defense Intelligence Agency, "DIA Evaluation of Information Provided by Lao Refugee [name redacted]," February 1990, DIA Source file 0995, POW/MIA; Defense Intelligence Agency, *SI Report*, April 30, 1992, edition, p. 7, Inventory of the Records of the Senate Select Committee on POW/MIA Affairs.)

**9.** Hendon's interview of source, Albuquerque, New Mexico, 1983; DIA Lao Desk analyst Gen. Southchay Vongsavanh's four-page handwritten meeting notes dated August 14, 1985, of reinterview of Source 0995, DIA Source file 0995, Inventory of the Records of the Senate Select Committee on POW/MIA Affairs.

**10.** Letter to the Honorable Louis Stokes, Chairman, Select Committee on Intelligence, from Gerry Sikorski, Member of Congress, November 17, 1988, DIA Source file 0995, POW/MIA.

**11.** Defense Intelligence Agency, U1402/VO-PW, letter to Mr. Tom Latimer, Permanent Select Committee on Intelligence, House of Representatives, from Joseph A. Schlatter, Colonel, USA, Chief, Special Office for Prisoners of War and Missing in Action, December 14, 1988, ibid.

**12.** Defense Intelligence Agency, [Redacted]1436/VO-PW, letter to Mr. Tom Latimer, Permanent Select Committee on Intelligence, House of Representatives, from Joseph A. Schlatter, Colonel, USA, Chief, Special Office for Prisoners of War and Missing in Action, December 27, 1988, ibid.

**13.** DIA Evaluation of PW/MIA Information Provided by Lao Immigrant [source name redacted], February 16, 1988, ibid.

**14.** Defense Intelligence Agency, "DIA Evaluation of Information Provided by Lao Refugee [name redacted]," February 1990, ibid.; Defense Intelligence Agency, *SI Report*, April 30, 1992, edition, p. 7, Inventory of the Records of the Senate Select Committee on POW/MIA Affairs.

**15.** *MIA/POW Reports, Congressional Record*, October 12, 1990, S 15034.

**16.** Months later, Grassley assailed Griffiths on the floor of the Senate, saying he had learned among other things that she "was the principal agent lobbying against access to POW files by Members of the U.S. Senate." (Ibid.)

**17.** Chapter 23 and www.enormouscrime.com, Chapter 23, (14) "The American POWs Seen by Robert Garwood at Five Separate Locations in Northern Vietnam From 1973–1979." Case 4983, 4982, 4979, 4980, and 4981.

**18.** All from "DIA Evaluation of PW/MIA Information Provided by American Stay Behind Robert R. Garwood (Protect), Sightings 04979, 04980, 04981, 04982, 04983," POW/MIA.

**19.** Authors' annotated 1:50,000 map of main Ba Sao/Rockpile compound.

**20.** R 100144Z JAN 89, subject: IIR 6 024 0046 89/Caucasian Prisoners Allegedly Incarcerated in Ba Sao Prison, Ha Nam Ninh Province 1983–87, with source's hand-drawn sketches, DIA Source file 8666, POW/MIA.

**21.** Authors' annotated 1:50,000 map of main Ba Sao/Rockpile compound.

**22.** R 150743Z AUG 89, subject: IIR 6 024 0352 89/Alleged Americans Sighted in Transit From Ba Sao Prison in 1984, DIA Source file 10721, POW/MIA.

**23.** "DIA Evaluation of PW/MIA Information From Vietnamese Refugee Source [name redacted] (08666)," DIA Source file 8666, POW/MIA.

**24.** "DIA Evaluation of PW/MIA Information From Vietnamese Refugee Source [name redacted] (10721)," DIA Source file 10721, POW/MIA. Hendon, accompanied by SRV/PAVN escorts, twice inspected the main Ba Sao/Rockpile Prison and its associated subcamps in mid-1993. Later, in 1994, using these two declassified intelligence reports as a guide, he, coauthor Stewart, and Lamont Gaston, head of VietNow, one of the nation's largest Vietnam veterans' organizations and among the most active on the live POW front, carefully inspected (under escort) the portions of the main Ba Sao/Rockpile Prison compound described in these two reports. They found that virtually every aspect of what both witnesses had said was supported by what they saw on the ground during their inspection—the quarry on the eastern slope of the mountain, the path up the mountain to the ridgetop, the small, now partially dismantled facility where the truck driver said he saw the American POWs forming up with their farm implements, the vast prison agricultural/security area nearby (still being farmed during 1994 by Vietnamese inmates housed in the still-active main prison, the guesthouse, the front gate, etc. As expected, no American prisoners were there. Had they been, Vietnamese officials of course would not have allowed Hendon and his associates to inspect the facility.

The Ba Sao/Rockpile inspection was only one of several prison inspections Hendon, Stewart, and Gaston were allowed to conduct during early March 1994. But just days after completing their inspection of Ba Sao/Rockpile, the three were denied entry into the large underground prison reported inside a mountain west of Son Tay and south of Hung Hoa (see Chapter 26 and this chapter). When they protested, Vietnamese authorities ordered them out of the country. An Associated Press account filed from Hanoi at the time quoted the head of the Vietnamese Office for Seeking Missing Persons as explaining that the location the three wanted to inspect was "a military security zone off-limits to foreigners; no exceptions." AP further quoted the official as saying, "[E]ven official members of the US MIA office in Hanoi have been refused entry to the site." ("MIA Team Forced out of Vietnam" and "Vietnam Refuses Americans Access to Alleged Prison," AP in *Hongkong Standard,* April 6, 1994; "U.S. Activists Barred From MIA Search, 3 Americans Told to Leave Vietnam," AP in *USA Today,* International Edition, April 5, 1994, p. A1.) In June 1995, when Hendon returned to Hanoi and again attempted to inspect the underground prison west of Son Tay and south of Hung Hoa, he was declared persona non grata and deported. (Letter to Bill Hendon, Kim Chi Hotel, 6 Doc Ngu Street, Hanoi, Vietnam, from Nguyen Xuan Phong, Director of Americas Department, Ministry of Foreign Affairs, June 8, 1995, Hendon files.) Immediately after Hendon's deportation, Lt. Col. Melvin Richmond, head of the U.S. POW/MIA office in Hanoi at the time, and other U.S. officials launched an official inspection. They first traveled to a group of rice fields located along the Red River just south of Hung Hoa, a point miles from the reported location of the prison inside the mountain. Then, after declaring the area to be the reported location of the underground prison (even though it obviously was not), the U.S. team inspected some rice fields, several small buildings, and a well; proclaimed to members of the press that no underground prison or POWs had been discovered either in the rice fields, in the buildings, or down in the well; and cited these findings as proof the reports about the prison inside the mountain were fabrications. (AP account of inspection filed from Hanoi, "Vietnam-US POWs, APn 6/19/95 2:15 AM," authors' files.) Richmond was later promoted to chief of the POW/MIA Special Office's successor office, the Defense Prisoner of War/Missing Personnel Office. As of January 2006, he remained in that position.

Between 1986, when Hendon first visited North Vietnam, until 1995, when he was declared persona non grata and deported, he personally inspected or attempted to inspect well over thirty prisons and other specific locations in North Vietnam where American POWs were reported detained after Operation Homecoming. The intelligence reports that gave rise to those inspections appear throughout this book and at www.enormouscrime.com, Chapter 23.

**25.** (P 211421Z JUN 90, . . . FM DET 32 PSAA SEOUL KOR//CC// . . . subject: IIR 1 512 0218 90/Underground Detention Facility for U.S. PW's in North Vietnam, DIA Source file 12845, POW/MIA.

**26.** Authors' two annotated color maps of Hung Hoa–Black River–Son Tay area.

**27.** Defense Intelligence Agency, "DIA Evaluation of PW/MIA Information Provided by Vietnamese Refugee Source [source name redacted]," DIA Source file 12845, POW/MIA.

**28.** See entire DIA Source file 12845, POW/MIA.

**29.** *Americans Missing in Indochina: An Assessment of Vietnamese Accountability,* pp. 5–6.

**30.** "Vietnam Refuses to Help, MIA Kin Told," *Washington Times,* July 16, 1990, p. A1. Schlatter would soon depart for a new DIA posting in Japan. He would return in July 1993 and serve as deputy director of the reconstituted Defense POW/MIA Office until his retirement on April 1, 1995. (Schlatter Web site, www.miafacts.org/.)

**31.** Handwritten letter from William M. Hendon, Chairman, the POW Publicity Fund with salutation "Dear Former Colleagues," with attachment, December 21, 1989, Hendon files.

**32.** R 160450Z OCT 89 PSN 547617P30, subject: JCRC Report T89-381, Hearsay of [Redacted] US POW in Laos, Milliner Casualty File, POW/MIA.

**33.** Hendon's, Stewart's, Mr. and Mrs. Milliner's, and others' personal recollections.

**34.** "Court Martial Urged on MiA US Officials," AP in *Bangkok Post,* August 29, 1990, p. 6; "MiA's Relatives Plan Courts-Martial Move," AP in *The Nation,* August 29, 1990, p. A4.

**35.** "Complaint," document filed with AFOSI by Hendon and the family members on September 19, 1990, Hendon files. Also "Hendon Demands Probe of JCRC Officers," *Stars and Stripes,* October 1, 1990, p. A1.

**36.** "Families Claim U.S. officials Thwarting Return of POWs," *Asheville Citizen,* October 22, 1990, p. A1. Though the Bush administration had only months before offered a $1 million cash reward for the capture of Panamanian dictator Manuel Noriega, the JCRC and other front-line U.S. personnel in Southeast Asia would continue until at least 1994 telling refugees and others with plans to free American POWs in return for the congressionally sponsored $2.4 million reward that there was no reward and that they should cease and desist with their plans to free American prisoners in order to claim the reward. Declassified intelligence reports and follow-up interviews show that between June 1991 and June 1993 alone, at least eight separate sources approached U.S. officials offering to help rescue living American POWs for the $2.4 million reward. Two of the offers related to POWs reportedly being held in northern Vietnam, two to POWs reportedly being held in Stung Treng Province in northeast Cambodia, and four to American prisoners reportedly being held in Laos. (R 081210Z APR 91, subject: JCRC Report T91-085, Hearsay of Three Live Americans in Nghe Tinh Province, Vietnam, DIA Source file 13749, POW/MIA; R 210944Z MAY 93, subject: Report of Walk-in Interview, DIA files, Case A-035, POW/MIA; R 200934Z SEP 91, subject: IIR 6 024 0736 91/Alleged First Hand Live Sighting of Five American Prisoners in Cambodia, Reel 6, Series 92-300, POW/MIA; R 070642Z JUN 91, subject: JCRC Report T91-184, Eyewitness Reports of Live Sighting of Four American Prisoners in Oudomxai Province, Laos; R 100554Z JUN 91, subject: JCRC Report T91-183, Eyewitness Reports Live Sighting of One American and Three Possible Filipinos in Lao Village; R 310439Z JUL 91, subject: JCRC Report T91-184A, Follow-on Communication From Source of Alleged First Hand Live Sighting of Americans in Laos; R 280926Z JAN 92, subject: IIR 6 024 0095 92/Follow-up Interview With Source of Information Described in SDR-VOP-05380, all DIA Source file 13867, Inventory of the Records of the Senate Select Committee on POW/MIA Affairs; Report of Interview, Name: Tanh Phommachack and Memorandum: Conversation With Bounpheng Vongsamphanh, 09/04/91, both DIA Source file 14102, Inventory of the Records of the Senate Select Committee on POW/MIA Affairs; Defense Intelligence Agency, U-0259/POW-MIA, 25 MAR 1991, to Headquarters, Air Force Military Personnel Center . . . , subject: Transmittal of Documents, Col Frank A Gould, USAF, with 2 enclosures; R 100537Z JUN 91, subject: JCRC Report T91-194, Hearsay of Four American [sic] Being Held in a Cave on the Phongsali Border, Laos; R 270831Z JAN 92, subject: IIR 6 024 0093 92/Stony Beach Follow-up Interview to JCRC Report T91-194, all DIA Source file 13875, Inventory of the Records of the Senate Select Committee on POW/MIA Affairs.) In every case, the declassified intelligence reports show that a U.S. government representative told the person or persons seeking the reward essentially, "Forget it, there is no reward, go back, don't do it." In one case, officials conveyed this message directly to one of Hendon's drivers who had helped Hendon and the activist families and vets distribute reward flyers in northeast Thailand. (R 201051Z FEB 92, subject: IIR 6 024 0124 92/Hearsay of Ten POW's on [sic] Laos, DIA Source files, POW/MIA.) The driver, known throughout the region for having assisted Hendon and the families and vets, had been approached by a third party in late 1991 who had said he had seen a group of ten American POWs under guard in Laos in November 1991 who were being forced to work on a coffee plantation in the mountainous area of Savannakhet Province in Laos. He said that he would help arrange their escape in return for the reward Hendon and the others were offering. JCRC representatives told both the driver and the man who had volunteered to help free the American prisoners to cease and desist in their efforts. In another case reported in June 1991, a source reported to the JCRC that he had personally observed two American POWs being guarded by approximately thirty Cambodians in northeastern Stung Treng Province earlier in the month, and that the commander of the guards asked his help in returning the two prisoners to U.S. custody in return for a reward. (R 011049Z JUL 91, subject: IIR 6 024 0436 91/Report of Two Americans in Stung Treng Province CB, DIA Source file 13933, POW/MIA.) The official JCRC report of this sighting read in part: "Source was told that it is very important to help any Americans to get out of CB and return to his [sic] family in the U.S. However, there was no reward for the return of live Americans nor for the return of U.S. remains. He was asked to make sure that . . . the guard commander understood that this was U.S. policy."

37. R,W,4—AM-US-VIETNAM, . . . 10-17 0637—AM-US-VIETNAM, 590, "US, Hanoi Agree on New Levels of Cooperation," authors' files.

38. "Vietnam's MIA Vows," *Washington Post,* October 19, 1990, p. A22.

39. *Interim Report on the Southeast Asian POW/MIA Issue,* by the U.S. Senate Committee on Foreign Relations Republican Staff, October 29, 1990.

40. "POWs Still in Vietnam, '74 Report Says," *Washington Times,* October 29, 1990, p. A7.

41. R,W,4—AM-POW-MIAREPORT [*sic*], . . . 10-29 O533—AM-POW-MIA REPORT, 480, "Report Doubts Contentions No US POWs Still in Asia," authors' files.

42. Copy of official citation, authors' files.

43. National League of Families of American Prisoners and Missing in Southeast Asia, *Newsletter,* December 6, 1990, AMG:83, Elizabeth Stewart files.

## CHAPTER 30. 1991: ONE LAST CHANCE TO SAVE THE UNLISTED, UNRETURNED POWs

1. All information about Colonel Peck presented in this chapter was taken from the following two documents: Office of the Assistant Secretary of Defense, Command, Control, Communications and Intelligence, January 28, 1992, subject: Memorandum for the Record—POW/MIA Management Inquiry, signed by Ronald J. Knecht, Special Assistant to the ASD(C3I), and United States Government memorandum, U-0173/POW-MIA, TO: DR [Lt. Gen. Soyster], signed by Millard A. Peck, Colonel, Infantry, USA, February 12, 1991, subject: Request for Relief, POW/MIA and Inventory of the Records of the Senate Select Committee on POW/MIA Affairs.

2. Sheafer lobbied hard for Peck's appointment with DIA director Lt. Gen. Ed Soyster, USA. Soyster would later say he chose Peck "on the basis of his outstanding service record and his evident familiarity with the region, developed during three distinguished wartime tours of duty in Vietnam and on the recommendation of Rear Admiral Sheafer."

3. *Congressional Record,* Senate, March 14, 1991, pp. S3436–45.

4. *Congressional Record,* Senate, May 9, 1991, S Res. 118, p. S5606. A temporary office was quickly opened as Vessey had promised, but then, in one of the great rub-your-face-in-it moves of the postwar period, the Vietnamese insisted over strong U.S. objections that the permanent POW/MIA Office be housed in a compound virtually adjacent to the Ngoc Ha Water Works in the western part of the city. (Tran Viet Anh, *Hanoi Atlas, Tourist Maps* [Hanoi: The Gioi Publishers, 1997], p. 20; also Garnett "Bill" Bell with George J. Veith, *Leave No Man Behind,* [Madison, WI: Goblin Fern Press, 2004], pp. 344, 390.) Why the U.S. objections? Perhaps the most glaring was the fact that wartime intelligence had shown U.S. POWs were confined as human shields at the Ngoc Ha Water Works during the war, but none of the returnees reported they had been held at the facility. (See Chapter 4.)

5. "Quitting Time," *U.S. News & World Report,* May 13, 1991, p. 26; "Colonel's Letter on MIAs Sparks Inquiry," *Washington Times,* May 16, 1991, p. A6; "Ex-Official's Memo Calls US MIA Effort a Charade, Travesty," AP in *Orange County Register,* May 22, 1991, p. B10; "Pentagon Official Resigns, Alleges Cover-Up On MIAs," *Los Angeles Times,* May 21, 1991, p. A1; "Ex-Official Alleges Administration Coverup On POW/MIA Issue," *Washington Post,* May 22, 1991, p. A13; "Bush Is Said To Ignore the Vietnam War's Missing," *New York Times,* May 22, 1991; "Colonel Says Support-Group Leader Hinders Search for Vietnam POWs," *Washington Times,* May 21, 1991, p. A4.

6. United States Senate, Committee on Foreign Relations Republican Staff, *An Examination of U.S. Policy Toward POW/MIAs,* May 23, 1991.

7. "Report: Government Leaves MIAs to Rot in Prison," *Sacramento Union,* May 24, 1991, p. A1.

8. "Panel Sharply Critical of U.S. Efforts on MIAs," *USA Today,* May 24, 1991.

9. "Veterans Call for Probe of PoW, MIA 'Coverup,'" *Bangkok Post,* May 26, 1991.

10. "DOD Finds No Evidence of Peck Allegations," DOD press release, June 13, 1991, Inventory of the Records of the Senate Select Committee on POW/MIA Affairs.

11. "Cheney: POW Charges Unfounded," *Washington Times,* June 20, 1991, p. A4.

12. In later testimony, Assistant Secretary of Defense Carl Ford called the source a "confidential informer." ("Does Photo Show 3 Vietnam M.I.A.'s?" *New York Times,* July 18, 1991.) According to a now-declassified DOD memorandum, the State Department identified the source as "Former Cambodian President In Tam." (Declassified DOD memorandum, subject: Chronology of 1990–91 Reporting on Major John L. Robertson, Lieutenant (JG) Larry L. Stevens, and Major Lynn A. Lundy, Reel 300, POW/MIA.

13. "'Photo' Puts POW/MIA Issue Back in Focus," *Chicago Tribune,* July 21, 1991, p. A1.

14. "Scowcroft: No Evidence MIAs Alive," *Washington Post,* July 27, 1991, p. A1; "Scowcroft: No MIAs Still Alive," *Atlanta Journal and Constitution,* July 27, 1991, p. A1.

15. "Dole: Special Panel Should Look for MIAs," *Atlanta Journal and Constitution,* July 29, 1991, p. A16.

16. "Pentagon Assigns More MIA Investigators," *Washington Post,* July 31, 1991, p. A5; Dick Cheney, "The POW-MIA Effort: Our Fullest Support," *Defense* 92 (January/February 1991): 13.

17. OSD/ISA, "A POW/MIA Status Report," DOD briefing presented by Cheney and officials accompanying him to ten senators at Senator Dole's office, July 29, 1991, POW/MIA.

18. "Washington Wire," *Wall Street Journal,* August 2, 1991, p. A1.

19. "Press Conference by the President," the White House, Office of the Press Secretary, August 2, 1991, p. 2.

20. "Senate Approves Special Panel To Probe Vietnam MIAs' Fate," *Washington Post,* August 3, 1991, p. A18.

21. O 300014Z Aug 91, FM SECSTATE WASHDC TO AMEMBASSY BANGKOK IMMEDIATE, Inventory of the Records of the Senate Select Committee on POW/MIA Affairs.

22. "Senator Pursues 'Hot' MIA Leads," *USA Today,* August 13, 1991, p. 3A.

23. "Sen. Kerry Doubts MIA Claims," *Washington Times,* September 8, 1991, p. A2.

24. Hendon's precise recollection of Zwenig's statement to him.

25. Sedgwick D. Tourison Jr., *Talking With Victor Charlie* (New York: Ivy Books, 1991), pp. 265–66.

26. Memorandum to Bill/Al, from Bob T., November 18, 1991, Subject: Several Specific Types of Documents the Committee Should Request; draft memorandum to Bill Codinha, from Dino Carluccio, subject: Investigative Plan for Vietnam, December, both Hendon files.

## CHAPTER 31. 1992: THE FRAGGING

1. "It Has To Come Out," *Daily Oklahoman,* January 1, 1992, p. 12.

2. "Viets Held POWs After '73: Ex-Spy"; "Ex Sov General: Yanks Still in Viet in '78," New York *Daily News,* January 2, 1992, pp. 1, 2.

3. For examples, "Soviets Questioned 3 U.S. POWs in Vietnam in '78, KGB Ex-Officer Says," AP in *Washington Post,* January 3, 1992, p. A16; "KGB Ex-General: Soviets Interrogated POWs in Vietnam After War Was Over," *Atlanta Journal and Constitution,* January 3, 1992; "New Interest In Missing Servicemen May Imperil Move Toward Hanoi Ties," *New York Times,* January 6, 1992, p. A3. Several weeks later Hendon, representing Smith, sat in as William Codinha, the committee's chief counsel, and intelligence investigator Bob Taylor interviewed Kalugin in Los Angeles about the reported incident involving the three American POWs. Hendon states unequivocally that he has never, ever—before or since—encountered a more credible witness than Oleg Kalugin.

4. Center for Security Policy, " 'POW-Gate'? Boren Signals Lid to Blow on Scandalous 25-Year, Bi-partisan Cover-up," January 21, 1992, authors' files.

5. The select committee had, on paper at least, two separate staffs. One was made up of staffers employed by the committee itself (approximately twenty people), the other of staffers employed by the individual senators or at their discretion and assigned to the committee as the senator's "designee" (just over a dozen). In reality, the two staffs functioned as one. ("Senate Select Committee on POW/MIA Affairs, Staff Phone List—Office Use Only, 02-02-92," Hendon files.)

6. "Inside the Beltway," *Washington Times,* January 10, 1992, p. A6.

7. "Alan C. Ptak, Deputy Assistant Secretary of Defense (Prisoner of War/Missing in Action Affairs)," from *Oversight Hearings: Department of Defense, POW/MIA Family Issues, and Private Sector Issues,* Hearings Before the Senate Select Committee on POW/MIA Affairs, December 1–4, 1992, p. 1280.

8. Unsigned handwritten meeting notes titled "Staff Meeting, 1-24-92," Inventory of the Records of the Senate Select Committee on POW/MIA Affairs.

9. Defense Intelligence Agency, Deserters in South Vietnam, enclosure to letter I-6798/76 from Roger E. Shields, Deputy Assistant Secretary, Office of Assistant Secretary of Defense, International Security Affairs, Department of Defense to Mr. J. Angus MacDonald, Staff Director, U.S. House Select Committee on Missing Persons in Southeast Asia, June 30, 1976, Hendon files.

10. John Aloysius Farrell, "The Avenger," *Boston Globe Magazine,* February 9, 1992, p. 28.

11. Office of the Assistant Secretary of Defense, letter U-219/DOD POW/MIA CDO from Margaret R. Munson, Director, DOD POW/MIA Central Documentation Office, to Mr. J. William Codinha, Chief Counsel, Senate Select Committee on POW/MIA Affairs, 1 encl "SI Report," March 10, 1992, 231 pages, Hendon files.

12. Defense Intelligence Agency, SI Report, 59 pages, Inventory of the Records of the Senate Select Committee on POW/MIA Affairs.

13. SI Report, refugee sources 2027, 2041, 3811, and 12773.

14. SI Report, refugee sources 0468, 1564, 2299, 3591, 6902, 10725, 11247, 12522, 12686, 13045, and 14079.

15. SI Report, refugee sources 3814, 5454, 7984, 8147, and 11352.

16. Headquarters 6499th SP Acty GP, report 1516 0788 70, p. 9, POW/MIA.

17. Defense Intelligence Agency, Directorate for Defense Intelligence, Plans and Policy Division, PW/MIA Branch, "Report of Sightings at Yen Bai," February 15, 1980, Inventory of the Records of the Senate Select Committee on POW/MIA Affairs.

18. Even worse, McCreary and Hendon had discovered while reading the SI Report that the outcome section of every live sighting "investigation" did not even allow for the possibility of a live POW ever being discovered. As listed in the SI Report, the *only* allowable findings, conclusions, or outcomes of the investigations were, by category: the sighting is unresolved and no further action is possible; the sighting is of a known, identified individual or incident [i.e., returnees, Garwood, etc.]; the sighting is of unidentified individuals who are not POWs; the sighting is a fabrication; or the sighting is a possible fabrication. There was no category for the finding "the sighting is of a POW." There was no category, "the sighting is true."

19. Investigators' time cards, various notes, etc., Hendon files.

20. Photos taken in 1992 of the map, which is now housed at the National Archives. Later, using color-coded pins rather than flags, Hendon plotted the exact same reports on an exact copy of the map used by the investigators. He then added yellow squares signifying SIGINT and IMINT hits (see additional photos).

21. *Briefing for the Senate Select Committee on Prisoners of War and the Missing in Action,* April 8, 1992, pp. 10–17, Inventory of the Records of the Senate Select Committee on POW/MIA Affairs.

22. Memorandum for the record, April 13, 1992, subject: 9 April Senate Select Committee on POW/MIA Affairs Briefing, signed by DOD officials Charles Wells and Mark Bitterman, and memorandum to Senator Bob Smith from Billy Hendon, subject: Senators Briefing Thursday 9 April 92, date: 15 April 92, both Hendon files.

23. Hendon's recollection of McCain's statement; also McCain and Salter, *Worth the Fighting For,* p. 250.

24. United States Senate, Office of Senate Security, receipt form, April 10, 1992, Hendon files.

25. Hendon's handwritten notes made at conclusion of meeting, Hendon files.

26. Memorandum to Investigators from The Honorable John F. Kerry, USS, Chairman, through Frances Zwenig, Staff Director, April 15, 1992, Hendon files.

27. Memorandum to J. William Codinha from Vietnam/Laos Investigators, subject: Document destruction, April 16, 1992, Hendon files.

28. Memorandum to The Honorable John F. Kerry, USS, Chairman from Dino L. Carluccio, Deputy Staff Director, April 16, 1992, cc: Frances Zwenig, J. William Codinha, Hendon files.

29. Hendon's recollections of what occurred.

30. Two pages of Senate Select Committee press clips; also United States Senate, Select Committee on POW/MIA Affairs, "Comments Made During Trip to Southeast Asia by the Senate Select Committee on POW/MIA Affairs," April 16–27, 1992, 1. Bangkok, Thailand Press Conference—April 19, 1992, all from Hendon files.

31. Hendon's recollection of the telephone conversation.

32. C-SPAN tape.

33. Kerry would later explain he had selected this prison after consulting with General Needham and his staff.

34. C-SPAN tape.

35. Brinkley, *Tour of Duty,* p. 449.

36. "Senators' Prison Visit Tests New Vietnamese Openness," *Boston Herald,* April 23, 1992, p. 8.

37. "Vietnam Allows 4 U.S. Senators to Search Prison," *Los Angeles Times,* April 23, 1992, p. A13.

38. "Senators Visit Prison In Vietnam," *Washington Post,* April 23, 1992, p. A32.

39. "U.S. Easing Vietnam Trade Embargo," *Washington Post,* April 28, 1992.

40. "Open Doors but Little Evidence Greet Senators in Vietnam," *Congressional Quarterly,* May 2, 1992, p. 1174; "Senators Tour Vietnamese Jail, Find 'No Smoking Gun,'" *Stars and Stripes,* May 4–10, 1992, p. 1.

41. See www.enormouscrime.com, Chapter 23, (8) "The American POWs Seen Getting off of a Prisons Management Department Bus Inside the K-4 Prison at Xuan Loc in Long Khanh Province in Southern Vietnam in 1979." Case 2395.

42. One of the many criticisms set forth in the 1985 Brooks Report was that the analysts at the Special Office "had never employed some of the most basic analytic tools such as plotting all sightings on a map to look for patterns, concentrations, etc.," and one of the report's many recommen-

dations was that the analysts begin using this technique at once. As previously noted, the analysts and their civilian and military managers never instituted this recommendation, and it was not until the Senate Select Committee's intelligence investigators began their own study of the postwar intelligence six years later that this "most basic analytic [tool]" was employed. (Three-page Brooks Report, officially cited as Defense Intelligence Agency, C-109/DC, 25 SEP 1985, Memorandum for BGEN Shufelt (VO) from Thomas A. Brooks, Commodore, USN, Assistant Deputy Director for Collection Management, subject: The POW/MIA Issue (U), Inventory of the Records of the Senate Select Committee on POW/MIA Affairs.

**43.** Stenographic transcript of *Hearings Before the Select Committee on POW/MIA Affairs,* United States Senate, Executive Session (Staff Briefing), May 12, 1992 (117 pages), Hendon files.

**44.** C-SPAN tape.

**45.** Ibid.

**46.** When Brig. Gen. Tom Needham of the JTF/FA, who had "assisted" Kerry with the "short notice" inspection of Thanh Liet, had first learned of the investigators' plan after the Hendon-Carluccio in-flight conversation back in April, he had warned the DIA in Washington that every effort should be made to head off the plan and that if Smith's men were allowed to conduct their own investigations, "the end result will be bad for everyone concerned." (R271122Z AP 92, FM USDAO BANGKOK TH//PW-MIA//, TO DIA WASHINGTON DC//DO/DOF/DOF-3/PW-MIA//, subject: CMDR JTF-FA'S Perceptions of Codel Kerry Visit to Southeast Asia (U), paragraph 3, Inventory of the Records of the Senate Select Committee on POW/MIA Affairs.

**47.** Department of Defense cable, no day/time group number but identified as PAGE:0016 and beginning "DOI: 68000000," with authors' handwritten notation "Source 11352" and typewritten notation "the High School Student," DIA Source file 11352, POW/MIA.

**48.** P 200416Z DEC 85, subject: JCRC Report HK85-104, Capture of One U.S. Pilot in Hanoi City, with authors' typewritten notation "the Electrician," DIA Source file 3814, POW/MIA.

**49.** R 200957Z JUN 88, subject: JCRC Report HK88-029, Crash of U.S. Aircraft in Hanoi/Hearsay Capture of Pilot, with authors' typewritten notation "the Tailor," DIA Source file 8147, POW/MIA.

**50.** R 280740Z APR 88, subject: JCRC Report T88-180, Capture of Two American Pilots in Hanoi During 1971–72, with source's hand-drawn sketch of Truc Bach Lake area, all pages with authors' typewritten notation "the Table Tennis Instructor," DIA Source file 7984, POW/MIA.

**51.** P 250447Z AUG 86, subject: JCRC Report M86-038, American Pilot Who Parachuted Into Hanoi, with authors' typewritten notation "the Architect," DIA Source file 5454.

**52.** The five-man HUMINT team was McCreary, Hendon, LeGro, Holstein, and Nicklas; Taylor, the sixth intelligence investigator, worked mostly the "special intelligence," IMINT and SIGINT, and thus was not polled.

**53.** United States Senate, memorandum, with handwritten date 3 June 1992, containing handwritten tally of individual intelligence investigators' estimates of number of U.S. POWs being detained by the governments of Vietnam and Laos, Hendon files. Hendon's and Holstein's estimates of the total number of POWs being held as of early June (650) represented approximately 30 percent of those Americans still unaccounted for in Southeast Asia at the time; McCreary's estimate (850), approximately 38 percent. (As of March 12, 1992, the latest figures available to the committee at the time, DOD carried 2,235 persons on its official roll of Americans still unaccounted for in the region.) (Unaccounted for Americans, Hendon files.)

**54.** "POW-MIA Panel Aide Loses Security Clearance," *Washington Post,* June 24, 1992, p. A12. The alleged offense involved the distribution to members of the committee by Hendon and Carluccio of a 1985 internal DIA review of the Special Office conducted by Commodore Thomas Brooks, the DIA's assistant deputy director for collection management at the time, which, among other things, recommended that the analysts begin using cluster analysis when analyzing intelligence reports about live POWs. (Defense Intelligence Agency, C109/DC, 25 SEP 1985, memorandum for BGEN Shufelt (VO) from Thomas A. Brooks, subject: The POW/MIA Issue, Inventory of the Records of the Senate Select Committee on POW/MIA Affairs.)

**55.** Hendon resignation letter, Hendon files.

**56.** Statement of Carluccio to Hendon, February 17, 1998, and Hendon handwritten meeting notes, Hendon files.

**57.** "Under the Volcano," *U.S. News & World Report,* July 20, 1992, p. 20.

**58.** "POW-MIA Panel Aide Loses Security Clearance"; Hendon's conversations with Carluccio.

**59.** "Senator Sure MIAs Were Still Alive in '89," *USA Today,* June 24, 1992, p. A1.

**60.** "Senate Panel Asks Bush to Release all POW-MIA Files," *Washington Times,* July 3, 1992, p. A3.

**61.** *Hearings on Americans Missing or Prisoner in Southeast Asia,* the Department of Defense Accounting Process, U.S. Senate, Select Committee on POW/MIA Affairs, June 24, 1992, pp. 3–4.

**62.** Hendon's telephone interview with Sampley, 1999.

**63.** "Senate Urges White House To Release Secret POW Papers," *Washington Post,* July 3, 1992, p. A5; The White House, Office of the Press Secretary, July 22, 1992, executive order, "Declassification and Release of Materials Pertaining to Prisoners of War and Missing in Action."

**64.** *Analysis of Live Sightings. Hearings Before the Senate Select Committee on POW/MIA Affairs,* August 4 and 5, 1992, pp. 1–3.

**65.** Ibid., pp. 13–14.

**66.** Ibid., pp. 15–16.

**67.** Ibid., p. 17.

**68.** The fact that Ho died on the 2nd was kept secret for fear it would dampen future National Day celebrations, and so the Vietnamese announced at the time of his death that Ho had died on the 3rd. Only long after the war did Vietnamese authorities rectify their "mistake" and move Ho's date of death back to the 2nd.

**69.** "Ho Chi Minh Mausoleum Inaugurated," "Politburo Decision," FBIS, Asia and Pacific, IV, August 29, 1975, North Vietnam, K6.

**70.** Ilya Zbarsky and Samuel Hutchinson, *Lenin's Embalmers* (London: Harvill Press, 1998), pp. 181–85.

**71.** "Inauguration Ceremony," FBIS, Asia and Pacific, IV, August 29, 1975, North Vietnam, K7; "Mausoleum for Ho Opens," AP in *Bangkok Post,* August 30, 1975, p. 2; "Ho Chi Minh Mausoleum Inaugurated," FBIS, Asia and Pacific, IV, September 2, 1975, North Vietnam, K1–K2.

**72.** "30th National Day Celebrated," "Grand Meeting," FBIS, Asia and Pacific, IV, September 2, 1975, North Vietnam, K2–K3; "S.E. Asia Delegations Attend Ceremonies," "PRC Visitors," FBIS, Asia and Pacific, IV, September 2, 1975, North Vietnam, K5; "Souphanouvong Delegation," FBIS, Asia and Pacific, IV, September 2, 1975, North Vietnam, K7; "President Ho Chi Minh's Mausoleum," *Viet Nam Courier,* September 1975.

**73.** P 111238Z FEB 86, subject: JCRC Report T86-039, Alleged Firsthand Observation of Live American POWs in Vietnam and Laos, DIA Source file 8682, POW/MIA.

**74.** P 300843Z SEP 86, subject: JCRC Report HK86-67, Hearsay of U.S. Pilots Held in Hanoi (U); R 100924Z DEC 86, subject: IIR 6 842 0127 87/Lynam [*sic*] De Jail Possible POW Camp in Vietnam (U), both DIA Source file 5633, Inventory of the Records of the Senate Select Committee on POW/MIA Affairs.

**75.** P 181132Z SEP 87, subject: American Prisoners of War Detained as Late as 1985, DIA Source file 7591, POW/MIA.

**76.** R 151012Z OCT 88, FM CIA, TO DIA, subject: Information on POW's in Hanoi Area, DIA Source file 8113, POW/MIA.

**77.** R 060639Z MAR 89, subject: IIR 6 024 0097 89/Reinterview of [redacted] on Alleged Sighting of Americans in Hanoi in 1986, DIA Source file 8621, POW/MIA.

**78.** R 130142Z MAR 90, subject: IIR 6 024 0376 90/Operations to Recapture Alleged Escaped American PWs in 1977 and 1984 and Hearsay of Detention of Alleged American PWs in Hanoi in 1986, DIA Source file 10675, POW/MIA.

**79.** Hendon debrief of defector Le Quang Khai; also Deposition of Le Quang Khai (transcribed from an audio recording), June 26, 1992, Inventory of the Records of the Senate Select Committee on POW/MIA Affairs.

**80.** Ted Gup, "The Ultimate Congressional Hideaway," *Washington Post Magazine*, May 31, 1992, pp. 11ff.

**81.** ("Bunker Comes Out of Hiding," "Under the Greenbrier, A Relic of the Cold War Opens Its Doors to Public," *Washington Post,* July 26, 1997, p. B1.) In 1995, the Greenbrier began offering tours of the underground facility to guests staying at the hotel, and in the summer of 1997 the facility was opened to public tour. As part of their research for this book, the authors inspected the underground facility in detail in February 1998. They found it to be almost exactly as Gup's sources had described.

**82.** See www.enormouscrime.com, Chapter 23, (14), Case 4983, 4982, 4979, 4980, and 4981, Ly Nam De Sighting #5; also R 281115Z NOV 88, subject: IIR 6 024 0026 89/Alleged Americans Sighted in Hanoi in 1986, DIA Source file 8621, POW/MIA; R 082202Z SEP 89, subject: DRAFT IR HK-051-89/Two Alleged American Pilots Sighted in Detention in Ba Dinh Ward, Hanoi, in 1988, DIA Source file 10919, POW/MIA.

**83.** *ANALYSIS OF LIVE SIGHTINGS,* August 4 and 5, 1992, pp. 76ff; also condensed version of Sydow's and Destatte's sworn statements in *Oversight Hearings: Department of Defense, POW/MIA Family Issues, and Private Sector Issues,* pp. 14–15.

**84.** "Pentagon doubts reports of Hanoi holding POWs in underground jail," *Washington Times,* August 5, 1992, p. A5.

85. "Panel Grills Pentagon Over POWs," *Los Angeles Times*, August 5, 1992, p. A10.

86. Kathleen Callo, "Vietnam Dismisses Claims of Underground POW Camp," Reuters, August 6, 1992, Hendon files.

87. "U.S. Movie Industry Blamed for POW-MIA 'Myth,'" FBIS-EAS-92-159, August 17, 1992, Southeast Asia, p. 51.

88. "Partial Transcript of Briefing by Russian Ambassador Rashid Khamidouline in Hanoi to Reuters and BBC—on 15 August 1992," Hendon files.

89. Ibid.

90. "Quick Look, Hanoi Underground Facilities," August 21, 1992, Springfield Research Facility, Springfield, Virginia; in 2006, the authors discovered two additional SR-71 images of the mausoleum taken during its construction. These were enclosures to a September 25, 1992, memorandum from Michael J. Shore, Chief, Strategic Command and Control Division, Defense Nuclear Agency, Memorandum for DIA/POW, subject: Underground Facilities—Hanoi Area, with declassified SR-71 photos, Inventory of the Records of the Senate Select Committee on POW/MIA Affairs. See the images and authors' analysis at www.enormouscrime.com, Chapter 31.

91. P 271121Z AUG 92, subject: IIR 6 024 0534 92/Alleged Captive Americans in Ho Chi Minh Mausoleum, Hanoi, Vietnam, DIA Source file 15589, POW/MIA.

92. "Do Muoi Interviewed on Capital Construction," FBIS, Asia and Pacific, IV, April 6, 1972, North Vietnam, K12; "Communiqué Issued," FBIS, Asia and Pacific, IV, June 9, 1975, North Vietnam, K7–K9; portion of Central Intelligence Agency, Directorate of Intelligence, "Government Structure of the Socialist Republic of Vietnam: The Machinery of State," April 1990.

93. Senate Select Committee intelligence investigators later discovered that Air Force Lt. Col. Henry M. "Mick" Serex, an electronic warfare officer, had been missing since April 2, 1972, when his EB-66, code-named "Bat 21," was shot down over the Demilitarized Zone while accompanying a B-52 strike during the Easter invasion. (Defense Prisoner of War/Missing in Action Office, "U.S. Personnel Missing, Southeast Asia (and Selected Foreign Nationals) (U)," June 1995, p. 42.) Air Force records indicate Bat 21 was hit by a surface-to-air missile while flying at an altitude of approximately twenty-six thousand feet. An intercepted PAVN radio communication reported the shootdown and stated that PAVN personnel had "sighted orange parachutes in the area." (O 032052Z, APR 72 FM DIRNSA [Director, National Security Agency], Summary . . . Shootdown of AN-3B-66 [sic] by Battalion 86, 274TH SAM Regiment, released by NSA on January 29, 2001, pursuant to the Freedom of Information Act, Case #J9137-98, files of Mr. Rich Daly.) One of those parachuting from the plane, navigator Lt. Col. Iceal Hambleton, USAF, reached the ground alive and evaded capture until rescued eleven days later. Though Hambleton reported no knowledge that any of his fellow crewmen might also have survived, an Air Force report filed shortly after his rescue states that "although no contact was established with the [other] crewmembers of Bat 21, the possibility of survival is good, since one member of the crew ejected unobserved and evaded capture until his rescue. Since there were hostile forces in the immediate area, it is possible that the other crewmembers ejected unobserved, are evading capture, or have been captured by the hostile forces." ("SUMMARY OF FACTS AND CIRCUMSTANCES"; untitled typewritten USAF after-action report with handwritten note "why is this here," both Casualty Files, POW/MIA.)

The events surrounding the shootdown of Bat 21 and the subsequent rescue of Lieutenant Colonel Hambleton were the basis for the 1988 action-adventure film *Bat 21*, starring Gene Hackman and Danny Glover. Lieutenant Colonel Serex's name was not mentioned in the film. According to available declassified U.S. government records, no information pertaining to Serex was received by the government from any official or unofficial source from his date of shootdown (April 2, 1972) until his name was imaged in the field outside the Dong Vai Prison in northern Vietnam on June 5, 1992.

94. Deposition of Robert George Dussault, pp. 75–81, with Hendon's handwritten explanatory notes.

95. "Panel on POWs Deeply Divided Over Direction," *Los Angeles Times*, November 19, 1992, p. A2; handwritten memorandum of October 6 from Frances A. Zwenig, Staff Director, Senate Select Committee on POW/MIA Affairs to JK [John Kerry], declaring she is working with DIA to prepare a script for DIA officials to use at the upcoming imagery hearings. Hendon files.

96. R 040642Z MAR 88, subject: JCRC Report T88-076, Hearsay of American POWs Previously Held in Dong Vai Prison; Speculation Concerning American POWs Held Subsequent to 1973, DIA Source file 0080, POW/MIA; JCRC M80-015, 31 JANUARY 1980, subject: Refugee Report, Alleged Sighting of Caucasians in Captivity, NVN, DIA Source file 0558, POW/MIA; R 201107Z DEC 90, subject: IIR 6 024 0202 91/Hearsay of American PWs Held at Dong Vai Reeducation Camp, Quang Ninh Province, DIA Source file 13549, POW/MIA; R 031022Z OCT 89, subject: IIR 6 024 0006 90/Absence

of Americans at the Quang Ninh Reeducation Camp, AUG 77, Inventory of the Records of the Senate Select Committee on POW/MIA Affairs; TOT: 170428Z FEB 88 CIA, subject: Alleged Hearsay Live Sighting Reporting From [source redacted], Inventory of the Records of the Senate Select Committee on POW/MIA Affairs; JCRC HK81-007, subject: Refugee Report, Alleged American Prisoners in Quang Ninh and Memorandum for Record, 21 October 1983, subject: Telecon between Vietnamese Refugee [name redacted] and DC-2 analyst [name redacted], both DIA Source file 1228, Inventory of the Records of the Senate Select Committee on POW/MIA Affairs; www.enormouscrime.com, Chapter 23, (4) "The American POWs Reportedly Transferred From the Cam Thuy Maximum Security Prison in Thanh Hoa Province to the Dong Vai Maximum Security Prison North of Hong Gai in 1982." Case 1733.) None of the American POWs released at Operation Homecoming in 1973 reported that they had been held at Dong Vai. (*Places and Dates of Confinement of Air Force, Navy and Marine Corps Prisoners of War Held in North Vietnam 1964–1973.*)

97. "DASD PTAK Addresses AMC," *Department of Defense POW/MIA Newsletter,* October 1992, p. 2, files of William Stewart.

98. Deposition of Robert George Dussault.

99. Handwritten investigator's notes titled "Questions For JSSA" and "Questions For DIA/CIA Photo Interpretors [*sic*]," both from Working Files of Committee Investigator Bob Taylor, 1991–1992, Inventory of the Records of the Senate Select Committee on POW/MIA Affairs; "Joint Document by LWB & CLL Concerning Unresolved Differences in Their Analyses of Imagery Over Sam Neua, Laos and Adjacent to the Dong Vai Prison in Viet Nam," p. 2; Hendon's handwritten notes dated October 2, 1992, of telephone conversation with someone who had attended the August 2 briefing, both Hendon files; authors' color map. The name of the missing pilot was Wrye, along with the four-digit number 1104. RF101 pilot Maj. Blair C. Wrye, USAF, was shot down over North Vietnam on August 12, 1966. (Defense Prisoner of War/Missing in Action Office, "U.S. Personnel Missing in Southeast Asia (and Selected Foreign Nationals) (U)," p. 51.)

100. "Pentagon's Cooperativeness on POW Probe Questioned, Grassley Criticizes DIA's 'Mind-Set to Debunk,'" *Washington Post,* October 9, 1992, p. A3; *Hearings on Symbols,* Hearings Before the Senate Select Committee on POW/MIA Affairs, "Second Session on Symbols," October 15, 1992, p. 8.

101. *Dateline NBC,* October 6, 1992, transcript prepared by Burrelle's Information Services, p. 5, authors' files.

102. Office of the Assistant Secretary of Defense, Command, Control, Communications and Intelligence, memorandum for the record, October 7, 1992, subject: Telephone Call from Senator Kerry, signed by Ronald J. Knecht, authors' files; also "Panel on POWs Deeply Divided Over Direction," *Los Angeles Times.*

103. *Hearings on Symbols,* pp. 17ff.

104. Ibid., pp. 11ff.

105. Department of the Air Force, Joint Services SERE Agency, memorandum from Robert G. Dussault, GS-15, DAF, Deputy Director, to DD, subject: Analysis of 22 Jan 88 "USA" Photo (CDO Ltr, 23 Jun 92), June 29, 1992, Hendon files; *Hearings on Symbols,* p. 72. Another DOD witness, Thai-based JCRC interviewer Gadoury, would testify later in the day that he believed the "USA/Walking K" was a hoax perpetrated by a member of a POW activist group. (*Hearings on Symbols,* pp. 68ff.)

106. *Hearings on Symbols,* p. 16.

107. "Perot Has Narrow Lead in Post–ABC News Poll," *Washington Post,* June 2, 1992, p. A1.

108. For a fascinating account of how voters abandoned Bush in the last days of the campaign and threw their support to Perot (for reasons unrelated to the POWs), see Bob Woodward, *Shadow: Five Presidents and the Legacy of Watergate* (New York: Simon & Schuster, 1999), pp. 202–05.

109. Hendon's conversations with Senators Brown and Smith, 1992.

110. Kerry would enter the following statement into the official committee record: "Let me just say for the record that when we were [on] our trip . . . last week, we were given access to classified information. Through both technical sources and classified sources, we have learned, at least to the satisfaction of those on the trip, that in fact there is no underground, quote, prison or facility in that particular location." (*Oversight Hearings,* p. 1234.)

111. [Select Committee on] POW/MIA Affairs, fax cover sheet, to Pat Petty from Bob Taylor, 22 July 2:10; also Select Committee on POW/MIA Affairs, letter from J. William Codinha from Robert M. McNamara, Jr., Assistant General Counsel, Department of the Treasury, July 22, 1992; both Inventory of the Records of the Senate Select Committee on POW/MIA Affairs.

112. The White House, letter from Brent Scowcroft to Honorable Robert C. Smith, August 28, 1992, Hendon files.

**113.** Letter from Nicholas F. Brady to the Honorable John Kerry, Chairman, Select Committee on POW/MIA Affairs, July 24, 1992, Inventory of the Records of the Senate Select Committee on POW/MIA Affairs.

**114.** Department of the Treasury, United States Secret Service, letter from John W. Magaw, Director, to the Honorable John F. Kerry, Chairman, Select Committee on POW/MIA Affairs, July 24, 1992, Inventory of the Records of the Senate Select Committee on POW/MIA Affairs.

**115.** Memorandum with stamp "COMMITTEE CONFIDENTIAL," to Members, Senate Select Committee from J. William Codinha, Chief Counsel, July 29, 1992, re: Deposition of Secret Service Agent, Hendon files.

**116.** "White House, Senate at Odds on POW Issue," *Los Angeles Times*, Washington edition, August 7, 1992, p. A2.

**117.** "Panel Awaits Agent's Story on POW Swap," *Washington Times*, August 11, 1992, p. A4.

**118.** (*POW/MIA'S*, p. 284.)

**119.** United States Senate, Select Committee on POW/MIA Affairs, draft letter from all members to Mr. John F. Syphrit, November 4, 1992, Inventory of the Records of the Senate Select Committee on POW/MIA Affairs; Memorandum to Sen. Smith from JWC, November 17, 1992, re: Syphrit Letter; Department of the Treasury, letter from Peter K. Nunez, Assistant Secretary (Enforcement), to the Honorable John F. Kerry, Chairman, Select Committee on POW/MIA Affairs, November 18, 1992, Hendon files.

**120.** Memorandum to Members, Senate Select Committee on POW/MIA Affairs from J. William Codinha, Chief Counsel, November 18, 1992, re: John Syphrit, Former Secret Service Agent, with exhibits, Hendon files.

**121.** Hendon's phone notes, Hendon files.

**122.** "MIA Panel Won't Call Secret Service Agent," *Washington Times*, November 25, 1992, p. A4.

**123.** Sydney Schanberg, "It's Operation Censor in Draft POW Report," *New York Newsday*, January 7, 1993.

**124.** *OVERSIGHT HEARINGS*, pp. 1–245.

**125.** Ibid., pp. 247–696; "Cash Is Object of POW Search, Senators Charge," AP in *Washington Times*, December 4, 1992, p. A4. Hendon, like most of the other activists, had himself been accused during the late 1980s of committing similar "fraud." This charge had first been leveled by IAG Principal Member Griffiths and IAC Chairman James Shufelt after Hendon, McDaniel, and the congressmen announced the creation of the $2.4 million reward. According to Shufelt, the charge of fraud was based, among other things, on the following statement Hendon and McDaniel had included in one of their fund-raising appeals. The statement, which Hendon and McDaniel had reprinted with permission from a syndicated 1985 Jack Anderson column, read as follows: "According to a key source in the Defense Intelligence Agency, approximately one hundred POWs still remain. He based this estimate on satellite photos, communications intercepts [and reports from human sources]. The evidence, he said, 'is overwhelming.'" (Defense Intelligence Agency, letter U-1520/VO-PW, with date stamp 22 NOV 1987, from James W. Shufelt, Brigadier General, USA, Deputy Director for Operations, Plans and Training, to Honorable Stephen J. Solarz, Chairman, Subcommittee on Asian and Pacific Affairs, Committee on Foreign Affairs, House of Representatives, Hendon files.) At the request of Solarz, the U.S. postal inspector investigated the alleged "fraud." No charges of any kind resulted from the investigation. In early 1992, an investigation conducted by a Senate Select Committee fraud investigator—a former assistant U.S. attorney hired by Kerry—had again cleared Hendon of all charges of fraud. In reporting the results of his investigation to Codinha on April 1, 1992, the investigator had stated the following: "I have carefully re-studied the Hendon file. There are no allegations with substance of fraud or proof of fraud in the file. This includes the legal definition and the everyday meaning of the word. The Hendon review has no significance on the issue of whether the Committee should continue the fraud investigation. The effect of League and DIA statements has been to paint Hendon as making false statements. He has not. League and DIA object to his activity of offering rewards for POWs and his criticism of DIA practices. At this point, Hendon can be cleared by the Committee of charges of fraud. This would clear the air of baseless charges and be an act of fairness to Hendon." (United States Senate, Select Committee on POW/MIA Affairs, Memorandum to J. William Codinha, Counsel, from Senator Bob Smith, Vice Chairman, August 25, 1992, re: Fraud, in *Oversight Hearings*, pp. 247–57.

**126.** "*Oversight Hearings*, pp. 697–1033.

**127.** Ibid., pp. 1035–1674. The more vocal of the activist vets, long aware of what they perceived as the orchestrated Kerry/McCain/Bush administration sellout on the live prisoner issue, had attended the hearings in force and, to Kerry's and McCain's displeasure, had periodically made their feelings known from the spectator area. Kerry had ejected one of the vets, Sampley, after Sampley groaned loudly in disgust when Sybil Stockdale testified she was certain no POWs remained alive and that, in fact, none had been left behind in the first place. (Ibid., p. 717.)

**128.** "All P.O.W.'S Freed, Ex-Admiral Says," *New York Times,* December 4, 1992.

**129.** Panel Finds No Data on Live U.S. POWs," AP in *Washington Times,* December 5, 1992, p. A3.

**130.** McCain, who had earlier ridiculed the "USA/Walking K" imagery by explaining to *Dateline NBC* that "guards do not generally allow prisoners to go out and stamp out U-S-A in large letters so that it can be photographed [by] satellite or by airplane. That's not their habit," would seize on the DIA's young-boy-copied-the-USA-off-an-envelope explanation and cite it in the future as the reason the message in the rice paddy should be ignored. (McCain and Salter, *Worth the Fighting For,* p. 257.) When doing so, however, he would offer no explanation for the "walking K" portion of the message, which he had earlier told *Dateline* had "caught in [his] throat enormously" when he had first seen it, nor would he address exactly why a Laotian child had taken time to dig out of the ground three twelve-foot-tall letters that together stretched a distance of some thirty-seven feet.

**131.** "Aides at Odds On Response To Vietnam," *Washington Post,* December 5, 1992, p. A3.

**132.** Brinkley *Tour of Duty,* p. 448.

**133.** "New Gestures Cited on MIAs, Kerry Says Hanoi Offering More Access," with accompanying Agence France-Presse photo "Sen. John Kerry (right) and a U.S. delegation face Vietnamese officials yesterday in Hanoi, where they met for a final round of talks on American POWs and MIAs before Kerry's Senate panel issues a report," *Boston Globe,* December 18, 1992, p. 3.

**134.** "Vietnam Hands Over More MIA Information," *Washington Times,* December 18, 1992, p. 2.

**135.** Brinkley, *Tour of Duty,* p. 450.

**136.** Hendon's notes of telephone conversation with Bob Smith, May 22, 2004.

**137.** Ibid.

**138.** "Colliers International Opens Office in Vietnam," *Business Wire,* December 21, 1992, authors' files.

**139.** Statement of Senator Kerry confirming Forbes "is a cousin," letter from Sen. John Kerry to Mr. Jeff Brailey, late March 1993, authors' files.

**140.** "NTM Imagery Analysis Report of POW/MIA Related Photography," December 7, 1992, Prepared by Colonel (Ret.) Lorenzo W. Burroughs, copy faxed by OASD (C3I) 12/14/92; "Joint Document by: LWB & CLL Concerning Unresolved Differences in their Analyses of Imagery Over Sam Neua, Laos and Adjacent to the Dong Vai Prison in Viet Nam," December 17, 1992, p. 2, both authors' files.

**141.** "Joint Document by: LWB & CLL." Burroughs later explained to *Dateline NBC* that the "X" in the "GX 2527" E&E code at Dong Vai was "a walking X." When the *Dateline* correspondent asked, "And the walking X means that it has been modified in a way that only air crews are supposed to know?" Burroughs replied, "That's how they are trained, and all of them are trained to do that." (*Dateline NBC* transcript, p. 3, authors' files.) Burroughs also later drew a memory sketch of the June 5, 1992, imagery showing the Dong Vai Prison, the nearby field, and the "G/Walking X 2527" in a remote part of the field. (Hand-drawn sketch of Dong Vai Prison and adjacent area titled "Dong Mang (Dong Vai [sic] Prison Area, June 1992" with notation "LWB/6-31-'93" in lower left-hand corner, authors' files.) Declassified information shows that the four-digit authenticator 2527 belongs to 1st Lt. Peter J. Matthes, USAF, who went missing on November 24, 1969, when the C-130 A aircraft he was aboard—call sign "Blind Bat 12"—was shot down while on a nighttime FAC mission over the Ho Chi Minh Trail in Laos. (Defense Prisoner of War/Missing in Action Office, "U.S. Personnel Missing in Southeast Asia (and Selected Foreign Nationals) (U)," p. 30. One beeper was heard following the loss of Matthes's aircraft, but nothing was heard from Matthes or any other member of the crew of Blind Bat 12 until the "G/Walking X" followed by Matthes's four-digit authenticator had shown up in the June 5 1992, imagery of Dong Vai Prison. (X 241515Z NOV 69, (Specific Subject) Initial Combat Loss, Casualty Files, "REFNO 1530-0-04, MATTHES, P.R.," POW/MIA. Also *POW/MIA'S,* p. 215.)

## CHAPTER 32. 1993–1995: "THE VIETNAMESE KNOW HOW TO COUNT"

**1.** "In November 1991, Tourison joined the staff of the Senate Select Committee on POW/MIA affairs [sic] and was a major author of its final 1993 report." (Sedgwick Tourison, *Secret Army, Secret War* [Annapolis, MD: Naval Institute Press, 1995], dust jacket.)

**2.** Schanberg, "It's Operation Censor in Draft POW Report."

**3.** Farrell, "The Avenger."

**4.** *POW/MIA'S,* p. 10.

**5.** Ibid.

**6.** Ibid., p. 9.

**7.** It should be noted that the members admitted later in the report what had actually occurred: that Kerry had informed the Vietnamese of his desire to visit Thanh Liet on the day prior to the actual inspection. The members made no mention, however, of the fact that Kerry and Zwenig had deceived the POW/MIA families and hundreds of thousands of Vietnam vets and other concerned Americans and severely damaged the cause of the unlisted, unreturned POWs by declaring ad nauseam after the "raid" and especially during the C-SPAN Memorial Day special *Vietnam Revisited* that the "raid" on Thanh Liet had been conducted with just ninety minutes' notice. (Ibid., p. 384.)

**8.** Ibid., p. 81.

**9.** Ibid., pp. 450–54.

**10.** The Gulf of Tonkin resolution.

**11.** Untitled memorandum to Nancy Soderberg from Richard Bush, February 2, 1993, re "Urgent Matter Regarding POW/MIAs in Vietnam," with National Security Council declassification authorization contained in letter from William H. Leary, Senior Director, Records and Access Management, to Ms. Carla J. Martin, Office of Senate Security, February 11, 1997, authors' files.

**12.** "Richard C. Bush III," www.brook.edu/scholars/rbush.htm; www.scienceblog.com/community/older/archives/K/2/pub2737.html.

**13.** Morris's statement to Hendon, Mayflower Hotel, Washington, DC, April 1993.

**14.** English copy with fax ID "MAR-22-1993 09:55 From Task Force Russia to Pentagon P. 02," beginning "*Top Secret*, Central Committee of the Communist Party of the Soviet Union," with attached copy in Russian, authors' files.

**15.** "Nominee Favors Ties to Vietnam," *Washington Times,* April 1, 1993.

**16.** Defense Intelligence Agency, U-0480/PW with date stamp 12 APR 1993, Memorandum for the Acting Deputy Assistant Secretary of Defense for POW/MIA Affairs from Robert R. Sheetz, Director, Special Office for Prisoners of War and Missing in Action, subject: Vietnamese POW/MIA Document from Russian Archives, authors' files.

**17.** U.S. to Press Hanoi to Explain '72 P.O.W. Report," *New York Times,* April 13, 1993, p. A1.

**18.** "Soviet Document Indicates POW Deception by Hanoi, U.S. Officials Cautious About 1972 Account," *Washington Post,* April 13, 1993, p. A20.

**19.** "Vietnam's 1972 Statement on P.O.W.'s: Triple the Total Hanoi Acknowledged," *New York Times,* April 13, 1993, p. A6.

**20.** "A '72 Report on P.O.W.'s Is a Fake, Vietnam Asserts," *New York Times,* April 14, 1993, p. A6.

**21.** "Asians Classified as American, POW Expert Says," *Washington Post,* April 15, 1993, p. A21.

**22.** R 111350Z JUN 85, subject: Identification of SVN Commando Groups, . . . POC IN DIA/DC-2 Is Sedgwick Tourison, DIA Source file 2460, POW/MIA.

**23.** Department of Defense and Central Intelligence Agency, *A Joint Report: A Review of the 1998 National Intelligence Estimate on POW/MIA Issues and the Charges Levied by A Critical Assessment of the Estimate* (1999-5974-IG), (00-OIR-04), February 29, 2000, p. 107, authors files. Shortly after the White House meeting, the senior official would tell a U.S. senator what he had personally heard the president tell Vessey, and the senator would later relate that information to Hendon. (The official's name is known to the authors but will not be revealed.) The official's account of what the president told Vessey appears in redacted form on page 107 of the now-declassified joint DOD/CIA *Joint Report.*

**24.** "Clinton Bars Thaw With Hanoi Until Fate of POWs Resolved," REU 04-15-93 15:43 EST 49 Line, BC-VIETNAM-USA-CLINTON, authors' files.

**25.** "The Vietnamese Know How to Count," *Washington Post,* April 18, 1993, p. C7.

**26.** "Doubts on MIA's," *Washington Post,* April 20, 1993, p. A1; "U.S. General Questions Alleged Pow Document," ibid., p. A15; "U.S. General Expresses Doubts About Alleged Pow Document," ibid., p. A17.

**27.** "Vessey Faults Russian Paper On U.S. POWs, *Emissary Calls Document Inaccurate, Highly Inflated,*" *Washington Post,* April 22, 1993, p. A25.

**28.** "U.S. Team Gives Hanoi MIA Archive, Documents Captured From Wartime Foes," *Washington Post,* July 17, 1993, p. A12.

**29.** "No U.S. POWs in Vietnam, Senior U.S. Official Says," 74 Reuters 12-14-93 07:42 AET, BC-VIETNAM-USA-POWS, authors' files.

**30.** "Clinton Aides Ready to Urge Lifting of Vietnam Embargo," *Washington Post,* December 31, 1993, p. A26.

**31.** "Clinton Drops 19-Year Ban on U.S. Trade With Vietnam; Cites Hanoi's Help on M.I.A.'s," *New York Times,* February 4, 1994, p. A1.

**32.** "Top-Level U.S. Delegation Lauds Search for MIAs," AP in *Washington Times,* July 4, 1994, p. A16.

**33.** For example, "Mission in Vietnam," *USA Today,* International Edition, March 15, 1995, p. 4A.

**34.** "Giap: U.S. Morally, Legally Liable for War," Kyodo in FBIS, Southeast Asia, FBIS-EAS-95-083, May 1, 1995, p. 85.

**35.** For example, "Senior Clinton Aides Urging Full Relations With Vietnam," *New York Times,* May 20, 1995, p. A1.

**36.** "U.S. Grants Full Ties to Hanoi; Time for Healing, Clinton Says," *New York Times,* July 12, 1995, p. A1.

## CHAPTER 33. 1995–2005: "WAR LEGACIES"

**1.** "Meets With Cam," FBIS, Southeast Asia, FBIS-EAS-95-151, August 7, 1995, p. 66.

**2.** "Vietnam Says It Needs More U.S. Aid," 4 AP 07-11-96 13:29 EST . . . AM-VIETNAM, 0398; "Vietnam Says MIAs Not the Only Post-War Issue," 49 REU 07-11-96 09:55 EST . . . BC-VIETNAM-USA-MIA.

**3.** "As MIAs Go Home, Vietnam Says U.S. Could Do More," 2 REU 05-20-97 05:32 . . . BC-VIETNAM-USA.

**4.** "War's Cost to Vietnam," Reuters in *New York Times,* June 16, 1997.

**5.** Untitled Kyodo dispatch datelined "Hanoi, July 26 (Kyodo)," via AP-NY-07- 26-97 0958EDT, authors' files.

**6.** "Vietnamese General: US Should Help," AP-NY-04-08-00 0451EDT; "Gen.: US Should Help Vietnam," AP-NY-04-08-00 1211EDT; "General Invites Americans to Vietnam," AP in *Charlotte Observer,* April 9, 2000, p. 28A.

**7.** "FM Spokeswomen [*sic*] on Significance of Visit of President Clinton," "News," Embassy of the Socialist Republic of Vietnam in the United States of America, VN/US relations 10/24/2000, with attachment "News from Viet Nam Ministry of Foreign Affairs, Answers by MOFA's spokeswoman Phan Thuy Thanh to foreign correspondents on 24 October 2000," www.vietnamembassy-usa.org.

**8.** "Vietnam Demands War Reparations," AFP 250840 GMT 00.

**9.** (See "McCain Trounces Bush by 18 Points; Gore Deals Bradley His Second Defeat," *Washington Post,* February 2, 2000, p. A1; "Arizonian Gains Stature; S.C. Awaits," ibid.; "Arizona Insurgent Issues a Wake-Up Call," *Washington Post,* p. A6; "Polls Show McCain Is Surging in S. Carolina," *Washington Post,* February 4, 2000, p. A1; "A battle for veterans joined in S. Carolina," *Washington Times,* February 4, 2000, p. A1; "Five Senators Rebuke Bush For Criticism of McCain," *Washington Post,* February 5, 2000, p. A10; "Bush and McCain Clash, *GOP Rivals Debate Blame for Negative Campaigning," Washington Post,* February 16, 2000, p. A1; Mary McGrory, *"McCain's Uncivil War Bind," Washington Post,* February 17, 2000, p. A3; "Bush Wins in Huge Turnout," *Washington Post,* February 20, 2000, p. A1; *"Texas Governor Regains the Momentum,"* ibid., and "Negative Tone Took A Toll on Image of McCain as Reformer," *Washington Post,* p. A10.)

**10.** (See "Kerry Stresses Military Past, *He Invokes Vietnam Service to Reach Voters, Push Agenda," Washington Post,* February 1, 2004, p. A4; www.swiftvets.com; "FACT CHECK: Swift Boat Veterans for Bush," @ www.johnkerry.com/rapidresponse/080504_truth.html; "Vietnam vets feel validated by John Kerry's ascent," *Washington Post,* July 29, 2004, p. A1; "The Vietnam Vet, Leaving No One Behind," *Washington Post,* p. C1; "Kerry files FEC complaint against swift boat group," CNN "INSIDE POLITICS," August 21, 2004 @ www.cnn.com/2004/ALLPOLITICS/08/20/kerry.swiftboat/; "Kerry invokes ghost of bitter Bush-McCain race," *The State* (Columbia, S.C.), August 24, 2004 @ www.thestate.com/mld/thestate/9478474.htm?template=contentModules/printstory.jsp; Dispute Over Kerry's Vietnam Service Cuts Both Ways, *Washington Post,* August 25, 2004, p. A4; "Swift boat ads appear to have effect in polls," *Philadelphia Inquirer,* August 27, 2004 @ www.philly.com/mld/philly/news/special_packages/election2004/9507779.htm; "The Vets Attack," *Newsweek,* November 15, 2004 @ www.msnbc.msn.com/id/6420967/site/newsweek/print/1/displaymode/1098/, and "Kerry campaign manager admits underestimating Swift boat ads," AP in *Boston Globe,* December 15, 2004 @ www.boston.com/news/polituics/president/bush/articles/2004/12/15/kerry_campaign_ma . . . ).

## EPILOGUE. A PROPOSAL FOR PRESIDENT BUSH

**1.** Robert Dallek, *Flawed Giant: Lyndon Johnson and His Times, 1961–1973* (New York: Oxford University Press, 1998).

**2.** Peterson, a former Vietnam War POW, former U.S. congressman, and Clinton's ambassador to the SRV, told *People* magazine in Hanoi in the spring of 2000 that there was "not a shred of evidence" that any American POWs survived after Operation Homecoming.

**3.** Paul, "POWs Won't Be Found Without Cost."

**4.** General Khamtay has been at the epicenter of the live POW issue in Laos ever since his wartime service as, first, commander in chief of all Pathet Lao forces, and from 1972 until today as, variously, supreme commander of the People's Liberation Army, minister of national defense, deputy prime minister, fourth-ranking member of the Political Bureau of the Lao People's Revolutionary Party (the Pathet Lao), and finally as president of the LPDR. (IIR 1 515 0049 70, subject: (U) NVA/PL Policy Towards Allied POWs, June 16, 1970, POW/MIA; "National Government, Peoples Democratic Republic of Laos," Gareth Porter files; Central Intelligence Agency, National Foreign Assessment Center, CR 79-10822, "Lao People's Democratic Republic Party and Government Structure," May 1979 [unclassified], Hendon files; Lao Embassy home page, http://laoembassy.com/lao_pdr.htm.) For explosive examples of Khamtay's postwar role in the POW issue, outlining how Khamtay personally maintained "a central and highly classified record" of American pilots captured in Laos and how those pilots would not be returned until the LPDR received postwar reconstruction aid (and recall that it was Khamtay who personally signed the intercepted late-1980 directive ordering PL officials in Attopeu Province to deliver a group of American POWs to the Attopeu airfield at 12:30 P.M. on December 28, 1980, so the prisoners could be flown to a more secret location), see CIA Intelligence Information Cable, June 27, 1977, subject: Records Maintained by a Senior Lao Government and Communist Party Official [Khamtay] Listing American MIA From the War in Laos, CIA files, Microfilm Reel 411, POW/MIA.

5. "Souboun, Ponemek: Organization of the Government State and Government Leaders," www.laoembassy.com/officials/government.htm.

## · ACKNOWLEDGMENTS ·

We jointly dedicate *An Enormous Crime* and the good that can come from its publication:

To every American fighting man who set foot in the jungles of Southeast Asia during the Vietnam War. And every airman—Air Force, Navy, Army, Marine, Raven, and the others—who flew in those skies. And every sailor who navigated or sailed those waters. To every chaplain who comforted these brave men; every medic, doctor, and nurse who cared for their wounds; every supply clerk and truck driver and cook and file clerk and all the others who supported them; and every CIA employee, every State Department employee, every USAID employee, and every other American civilian who provided similar support or contributed in other ways to the war effort. To every American who served in the Vietnam War in any capacity—and especially to those servicemen we are convinced are still serving our country today in the underground prisons and prison caves of Indochina—we dedicate this book to you.

To the memory of the POW/MIA family members we worked closely with over the years who died before receiving the answers they fought so hard for and so justly deserved: Col. Budd Donahue, USAF, and Shirley, parents of Morgan; Bob and Evelyn and Pat Cressman, parents and brother of Pete; Vera Hart, mother of Tommy; Marian Shelton, wife of Charles; Dr. Robin Gatwood Sr., father of Robin Jr.; Jean MacDonald, mother of George; Deborah Robertson Bardsley, daughter of John Robertson; Dovie Widner Huffman, mother of Danny Widner; Errol Q. Bond, father of Ronnie; Reg Lester, father of Rog; and Jane Duke Gaylor, mother of Charles Duke Jr.

To our close friends among the POW/MIA families who continue their courageous fight for answers, and all Americans who support them.

*Especially* to the activist Vietnam vets—the bikers, the hunger strikers, you who have marched and stood vigil and organized events and attended rallies and protested and conducted fund-raisers and done research and published newsletters and press releases and newspapers and manned booths and given speeches and built memorials and flown flags and lobbied your elected representatives relentlessly in support of your abandoned brothers. Your individual actions are inspiring; their collective impact enormous. And maybe historic, for if any of the prisoners whose stories appear in these pages ever get home alive, it will be because of your actions, and yours alone.

And finally, to our remarkable publisher, Tom Dunne. We promised you a completed manuscript in eighteen months—it took us ten years! Talk about dedication, perseverance, and commitment (yours, not ours). We could never have done it without you, Tom, or without the fine help and guidance we received from John Parsley and Peter Meyer, the crackerjack editors you assigned to us, and the many other outstanding folks at Thomas Dunne Books/ St. Martin's Press. Thank you for giving us the opportunity to tell these brave men's stories.

—BILL HENDON
Washington, DC

—ELIZABETH STEWART
Winter Haven, Florida

# · INDEX ·

*Note:* Following Vietnamese practice, a name like "Le Duc Tho" appears in the index under the family name, "Le," but is referred to in the text by the given name, "Tho". Cambodian and Laotian names appear under the family name, which comes first, for example "Lon Nol" and "Soutchay Vongsavanh."

A Shau Valley, 121, 518–20n.32
Abrams, Gen. Creighton, 56
AC-130 Spectres, 247, 266–69
Ackerman, Gary, 275
Agence France-Press (AFP), 38, 233, 481
Albright, Madeleine, 480, 484
"Alcatraz". *See* Ministry of Defense Citadel, Hanoi, POW camp (N-67)
Aldrich, George, 47, 64
Allard, Mrs. Phyllis, 104–5
Allard, Spec. 4 Richard M., 104–5
Allen, Richard, 225, 288, 289, 458–59
Alvarez, Lt. (j.g) Everett, Jr., 77, 80, 81, 413
American Defense Institute, 328
American Ex-Prisoners of War, 254
American Friends Service Committee, 346
American Gold Star Mothers, 254
American Legion, 254, 318, 324
Americans remaining in Vietnam after the war
  categorized as
    deserters, 263–64, 296–97, 412, 422–23
    progressives, 203
    remaining voluntarily, 150–51, 257, 263–64, 369
    unaccounted for by DOD, 555n.53
    "unregistered," so-called by Vietnamese, 163, 524n.20
    in wild parts of Vietnam, as suggested by Vietnamese, 334–35, 394
    yachtsmen, drug runners, and criminals, 372
  deceased, remains of turned over to Americans, 164
  in hiding, 157, 172, 323
  *See also* prisoners of war, American
AMVETS, 254
Anderson, Jack, 559n.125
Anderson, Terry, 540n.93
Andrews, Duane, 454–55
Applegate, Douglas, 256, 275
Armey, Dick, 275
Armitage, Richard, 231, 238, 239–40, 246, 248, 269, 282, 286, 287, 289, 324, 484

Army of the Republic of Vietnam (South) (ARVN)
  American POWs sighted by extroopers of, 103–4, 200–202, 207–10
Ash, Roy L., 84
Ashcroft, John, 529n.43
Aspin, Les, 275
Association of the Southeast Asian Nations (ASEAN), 244
Attopeu, 522n.58
  American POWs reported, 204, 416, 562n.4
Attopeu Province, Laos
  American POWs reported, 204, 212
Australians, 524n.18

Ba Dinh Square, 436–37
  American POWs reported, 438
Ba Ra Mountain
  American POWs reported, 159
Ba Sao/Rockpile Prison Camp, 176, 386–88, 512n.2
  American POWs reported, 524n.16
  prison inspection by Hendon and colleagues, 550n.24
Ba Vi
  American POWs reported, 151
Ba Vi Mountain
  American POWs reported, 359–60
Bac Giang City, 43
  POW camp, 29
  prison, 96
Bac Ninh City
  American POWs reported, 194–95
Bach Mai, 47
  hospital bombing, 63
Bach Mai Airfield, Hanoi, 43, 96
Bai Bang
  American POWs reported, 176, 196, 512n.4
Baker, Howard, 325, 329, 540n.93
Baker, James, III, 226, 263, 369–70, 484
Ban Boneng
  American POWs reported, 537n.41
Ban Daknong. *See* Nong Tha
Ban Don
  American POWs reported, 306

Ban Eun (aka Ban Na Eune)
  cave prison, 342
Ban Hang Long
  American POWs reported, 27
Ban Hoei. *See* Binh Hoei
Ban Kat. *See* Ban Long Kat
Ban Khilek
  American POWs reported, 363
Ban Long Kat (aka Ban Kat)
  American POWs reported, 343
Ban Me Thuot, 121
Ban Na Eune. *See* Ban Eun
Ban Na Keo. *See* Ban Nameo
Ban Nakay Teu
  information on, withheld by CIA, 154
  POW camp, 28
Ban Napang
  American POWs reported, 335
Ban Phontiou
  American POWs reported, 308
Bang Liet/Thanh Liet Prison (N-125; "Skidrow";
    6 miles SW of Hanoi), 95, 361–62, 370,
    373, 505n.10, 539n.81
  Kerry's surprise inspection of, 424–26, 428,
    561n.7
*Bangkok Post,* 233
Barker, Bernard, 119
Barton, Joe, 275
Bat Bat
  American POWs reported, 385
  prison, 318, 320 (map)
  *See also* "Briarpatch" POW camp
Bates, Carol, 242–45
Bay of Pigs invasion (Cuba), 3–9
  prisoners' trial for treason, 6
  release of freedom fighters, 7–8, 65
Baytong Mountain
  American POWs reported, 339
Bell, Garnett E. "Bill," 428
Ben Cat, 123
Bennett, Charles, 275
Benson, Steve
  cartoon by, 479
Bentley, Helen, 275, 542n.13
Berger, Samuel R. "Sandy," 471, 472, 484
B-52 bombings of North Vietnam, 59–60
B-5 reeducation camp, 537n.47
Bien Hoa
  American POWs reported, 144, 309–10
  camp complex near, 537n.47
  reeducation camp, 130
biker vets, 350
Bilirakis, Mike, 275, 542n.13
Binh Da Village "Camp 52," 309
Binh, Madame (VC), 57
Binh Dinh Province
  American POWs reported, 20, 22,
    23–24
Binh Hoei (aka Ban Hoei)
  cave prison, 343

Binh Thuy Air Base
  American POWs reported, 171
*binh tram* (base camps on the Ho Chi Minh
    Trail), 20
Black, Capt Jon D., 38
"Black Ferry" camp (N-89), Hanoi, 37
Blassie, Lt. Michael, J., 251–52, 529n.43
Blinded Veterans Association, 254
Bo Djuong
  American POWs reported, 152, 188–91,
    506n.38
  prison, 152
  *See also* "Dogpatch" Camp
Bo Ha Village, 44
boat people, 184–85
Boehlert, Sherwood, 275
Boland, Edward, 275
bombing
  and collateral damage, 46, 63
  POW appeals to stop, 47
  tally of damage, kept by North Vietnamese,
    13, 46, 65, 68, 87
Bond, Christopher, 529n.43
bones
  fragments identified as KIA victims,
    277–78
  purchased from North Vietnamese, 269
Bong Son (aka Hoai Nhon)
  American POWs reported, 192
Boren, David, 409
*Boston Globe Magazine,* 412
*Boston Herald,* 425
Boulapha District
  American POWs reported, 323, 335, 541n.1
Bounkeut Sangsomsack, 369–70
bourgeoisie tradesman
  crackdown on, 183
Boxer, Barbara, 275
Boyd, Capt. Charles G., 81
Boyer, Sgt. Alan L., 540n.83
Brace, Ernest C., 143
Bradley, Ed, 286
Brady, Nicholas, 458
"Briarpatch" POW camp (33 miles WNW of
    Hanoi), 95
  *See also* Bat Bat.
bridges
  bombing of, 34–35
Brigade 2506 (in Bay of Pigs invasion), 3, 8
Brinkley, Douglas
  quoted, 408
Brooks, George, 242, 351
Brooks, Jack, 275
Brooks, Rear Adm. Thomas, 279, 296–97, 460,
    535n.18
Brown, Sgt. George R., 540n.83
Brown, Hank, 275, 405, 422, 457, 460,
    542n.13
Brown, Harold, 171, 484
Broyhill, Jim, 275

Brzezinski, Zbigniew, 160, 171, 473, 484
quoted, xiii
Bu Dop
American POWs reported, 175, 180
Bu Gia Map
American POWs reported, 159, 174–75
Buchanan, Patrick J.
quoted, 120
Buffalo Mountain. *See* Phou Ngoua
Bunker, Ellsworth, 51, 53
Burch, J. Thomas, Jr., 482
Burroughs, Col. Lorenzo "Larry," 464
Burruss, Lt. Col Lewis H. "Bucky," 215–18
Burton, Dan, 275, 542*n*.13
Bush, George H. W.
(1989) Inaugural Address, 367–68
(1989) at Loma Prieta earthquake site, 375–77
(1992) loses presidential reelection, 457
author's proposal to, 484
CIA chief, 152–53, 154
POW/MIA policy, 367–77, 403, 411–12
quoted, 367
"the statute of limitations has been reached,"
367–68
as VP, 278, 288, 289, 304, 329–31
mentioned, 313, 327
Bush, George W.
(2000) presidential election, 482
authors' proposal to, 483–85
POW/MIA policy, xiii
Bush, Richard, 469–71
Bush report (1990), 391
Byrd, Robert C., 83
Byron, Beverly, 275

Ca Mau Peninsula
American POWs reported, 335, 357, 416
Ca Tot prison, 179
Cam Chu. *See* Cam Thuy
Cam Lo district (in Quang Tri Province), 113
American POWs reported, 22
Cam Thuy (aka Cam Chu)
POW camp, 29
prison, 539*n*.81
Cambodia, 69, 184
American POWs transported through, 20, 22,
23
Americans captured in, 19
cease-fire in, 500*n*.8
Khmer Rouge, 109
photo said to be of three American POWs in,
403–4
POW camp in, 25
Vietnamese invasion of, 187–88
"Camp Faith" prison (9 miles W of Hanoi), 95
Camp Holloway, 321
"Camp Hope" prison (22 miles WNW of
Hanoi), 95
Camp K-55, 207, 209 (map), 522*n*.8
Campbell, Carroll, 275

Cao Bang Province
American POWs reported, 104, 152, 188,
415, 416, 506*n*.38
Cao Van Vien, Gen., 122
capture cards (used when capturing American
prisoners of war), 14–15
Carlucci, Frank, 322–23, 329, 484, 540*n*.93
Carluccio, Dino, 407, 422, 423, 432, 555*n*.54
Carper, Tom, 275
Carroll, James
quoted, 408
Carter, Jimmy, 140, 159, 484
(1977) praises Woodcock Commission, 165–66
and POW/MIA issue, 170–71, 206
Casey, William J., 223, 288, 301–3, 458–59,
524*n*.21, 540*n*.93
cash-for-bones offer, 269
Cassanova, Gino, 285
Castro, Fidel, 3–9
(1961) U.S. attempt to overthrow, 3–4
(1962) Havana ceremonies honoring rise to
power, 8–9
(1973) visit to Vietnam, 112–14
Cat Lai
reeducation camp, 130
CBS News, 529*n*.43
Central America
Marxist-Leninist problem in, threatening
American security, 236–38, 244, 247–48,
530–31*n*.1
U.S. actions in, 246–49
Central Highlands, 15
(1975) PAVN campaign, 121–23
American POWs reported, 416
Central Identification Laboratory (CIL), 250–51
*See also* "Central Identification Laboratory,
Hawaii (CILHI)
Central Identification Laboratory, Hawaii
(CILHI), 269, 277–78, 282–85
Central Intelligence Agency. *See* CIA
Chandler, Londa, 350–51
Chapa (aka Sa Pa)
American POWs reported, 173
Charlotte Motor Speedway, 328–29
Charney, Dr. Michael, 284
Chau. *See* Dang Viet Chau
Cheney, Dick, 275, 403, 404, 411, 442, 484
Cheo Reo. *See* Phu Bon
*Chicago Tribune*, 404
Chieu Hoi (open arms) program, 18
Childress, Lt. Col. Richard T., 229, 240–41,
244–45, 248, 250–51, 256–57, 263, 269,
287, 295–96, 299, 314, 315, 323, 324,
329, 331, 350, 354, 460, 541*n*.9, 542*n*.25
China, Communist
(1979) invasion of North Vietnam, 188,
191–92
enraged by persecution of ethnic Chinese, 184
Chinese, ethnic (Hoa), in Vietnam, 182–83
Communist persecution of, 183–84, 514*n*.30

"the Chinese mortician"
  American POWs reported by, 199–200
Cholon, 343
Chou En-lai, 500n.8
Christopher, Warren, 480
Chwan, Dana, 351
CIA
  all-Asian reconnaissance team of, in Laos,
    215–17
  information sources, 18
  information supplied by, 161, 163–64
  information withheld by, 152–54, 167
  on number of POWs, 75
  rejects proposition of live MIAs in Indochina,
    212, 335
  in Vientiane, 26
CINCPAC
  POW/MIA task force, 71–72, 94
Clancey, Pete, 353
Clapper, Lt. Gen James R., 435, 442, 445, 460
Clark, William, 116, 223, 225, 250–51
Clements, William P., 87
Clinton, Bill, 484, 542n.9
  (1992) elected president, 457
  (2000) visit to Hanoi, 481
  POW/MIA policy, 471–77
cluster analysis, 415, 467
Co Xa Island (in Red River)
  prison on, 34–35
Coats, Dan, 275
Coble, Howard, 542n.13
Coc Mi. See Phong Quang
Codinha, William, 411, 420–22, 458, 553n.3,
    559n.125
Coehlo, Tony, 275
Cohen, William, 484, 529n.43
Coker, Lt. Cmdr. George, 141–42
collateral damage, 46, 63
collective farms, 182–83
Colliers International, 464
Colson, Charles, 63, 98, 118, 119
Combined U.S./South Vietnamese Military
    Interrogation Center (CMIC), 17
Command History (MACV publication), 18–19
commando teams
  of former Green Berets, 233–36
  South Vietnamese working for Americans
    during the war, 473–74
Committee of Inquiry (later Commission of
    Inquiry) (North Vietnam), 13, 68
Committee to Re-elect the President (CRP),
    98
commo-liaison stations (on Ho Chi Minh
    Trail), 20
Communism
  in Central America, 3
Congress, U.S.
  opposition to war reparations, 83–84, 86–87
Congressional Medal of Honor Society, 254
"Convoy of Tears," 123

Costa Rica, 238, 247
Council of National Reconciliation and
    Concord (proposed "Coalition
    Government"), 48–49, 54, 57
court-martial complaint against JCRC officers
    (1990), 393
cover-up issue (regarding U.S. abandonment of
    POWs in Vietnam), 105–7, 240, 409
  charge of, 263, 395, 402
  denied, 292, 467
  reasons for, 409
Cox, Christopher, 425
Craig, Larry, 275, 542n.13
Crane, Phil, 275
crash site excavations, 476, 545n.13
Croaker, Brig. Gen. Steve, 542n.25
Cronkite, Walter, 93
Cu Loc, 43
  POW camp N-53, 47, 517n.25
Cuba
  (1961) Bay of Pigs invasion, 3–9
  and Grenada, 246
  and Vietnam, 31, 113
Cuban missile crisis (1962), 7
"Cubans," in Watergate affair, 100–101, 119
Cuomo, Mario, 280
Cushman, Gen. Robert, Jr., 56

Da Nang, 123
  American POWs reported, 192–93
Daily Oklahoman, 282, 408–9
Dak Chung
  American POWs reported, 352, 365
Dang Viet Chau, 87–92, 109–11
Dao Tru
  prison, 539n.80
  See also Vinh Quang
Dar Lac Province
  American POWs transported through, 24
Daschle, Tom, 275, 405, 457, 460
Dash, Samuel, 101
Dateline NBC, 452–54
Dau Tieng (aka Tri Tam)
  American POWs reported, 207–10
  See also Camp K-55
Daub, Hal, 275
Davis, Jack, 542n.13
DC-2. See Special Office for POWs/MIAs (of
    DIA)
Dean, Charles, 520–21n.34
Dean, Howard, 520n.34
Dean, John, 98–100, 101–2, 120
DeConcini, Dennis, 405
Defense Intelligence Agency (DIA), 185,
    197–99, 271, 289–91, 559n.125
  (1991) investigates itself on POW/MIA policy,
    403
  information withheld by, 154, 278–79, 282
  See also Special Office for POWs/MIAs
Defense Nuclear Agency, 446

Defense Prisoner of War/Missing Personnel
    Office (DPMO), 483, 550n.24, 552n.2
Delay, Tom, 275
Delta Force team, JSOC, 215–18
demilitarized zone (DMZ)
    American POWs moved across, 24
Democratic National Committee (DNC), 98
Democratic Republic of Vietnam (DRV, "North
    Vietnam")
    (1964) sending supplies and troops to South
        Vietnam, 11
    (1972) Paris peace talks, 47–49, 73
    (1973) ratifies Paris accords, 84–86
    (1973) resumes war in South Vietnam, 114
    five-year plan and shopping list, 88–92, 138
    normalization of relations, linked with repa-
        rations, 167–68
    propaganda of, 257
    See also North Vietnam (area); Socialist
        Republic of Vietnam after 1975
Democrats
    in Congress, 315
Denton, Capt. Jeremiah, 80, 81
    quoted, 108
Department of State
    hard-liners in, 224–25, 347–48
"Desert 1" rescue attempt in Iran, 215, 221,
    522n.8, 541n.9
deserters, American, 263–64, 296–97, 412,
    422–23
Destatte, Robert, 273, 442, 461
Dien Bien Phu
    battle of, 37, 114
"Dirty Bird" prison, Hanoi, 95, 96, 141
"Dirty Dozen" missions, 240
Disabled American Veterans, 254
distress signals, 452–56
    four-digit authenticator numbers, 452, 464,
        560n.141
    "GX," 464, 560n.141
    "K" dug out in a field, 452–55, 560n.130
    "K" letter in Morse Code, 154, 155, 211
    in laundry on roof, 512n.1
    many called hoaxes, 558n.105
    satellite imagery of, 449–50
    "T" letter with wings ("Flying Tango"),
        547n.44
    "X," walking, 560n.141
DNA analysis, 529n.43
Do Muoi, 424–25, 428, 448, 485
Dobrynin, Anatoly, 53, 153
Dodd, Thomas, 5
"Dogpatch" Camp (Luong Lang PW Camp
    N-124; 105 miles NNE of Hanoi), 95,
    188–91, 507n.38, 514n.2
Dole, Robert, 280, 404, 405, 432
dollar
    devaluation of (1973), 86
Donahue, Lt. Morgan Jefferson, 338–39
Dong. See Pham Van Dong

Dong Ha, 113
    bridge at, blown up, 501n.27
Dong Hoi, 112, 121
Dong Khe City
    American POWs reported, 152
Dong Khe County
    American POWs reported, 152
Dong Mang. See Dong Vai
Dong Nai. See Long Khanh
Dong Vai (aka Dong Mang)
    imagery of, 451, 464, 512n.1
    prison, 154, 365, 449–50, 464
Donovan, James, 7
Dorgan, Bryon, 275
Dornan, Robert K., 260–61, 271, 275,
    542n.13
Dougherty, Gen. Russell, 292
Dreier, David, 275, 542n.13
Duarte, José Napoleón, 252
Dung. See Van Tien Dung
Dussault, Robert G., 449, 451–52

Eastwood, Clint, 233, 235
Edelman, Marian Wright, 160, 163
Edgar, Bob, 275
Edwards, Mickey, 275
Ehrlichman, John, 63, 99, 102, 108, 118, 119
Eichmann, Adolf, 6
Eisenhower, Milton S., 4
El Salvador, 236–37, 252, 530–31n.1
Elder, David, 346–47
elections, U.S.
    (1972) presidential, 48
    (1982) midterm, 203
    (1986) midterm, 315
    (1992) presidential, 456–57, 558n.108
    (2000) presidential, 482
    (2004) presidential, 482
Ellsberg, Daniel, 99
Elvin, John, 410
"an enormous crime has been committed"
    (Kissinger), xiii
Ervin, Sam J., 99
Ervin Committee, 99
escape and evasion codes, 155
Esslinger, Bobby Wayne, 535n.17
Evans, Lane, 275
Evans, Rowland, 280, 316
An Examination of U.S. Policy Toward POW/MIAs
    (Helms Report), 403
eyewitness accounts
    debunking of, 378–91, 444

farming
    forced, in reeducation campaign, 182–83
"Farnsworth" prison (18 miles SW of Hanoi),
    95
Farrell, Jack, 412
Fazio, Vic, 275
films about the Vietnam War, 276, 557n.93

*Final Interagency Report of the Reagan Administration on the POW/MIA Issue in Southeast Asia,* 354, 367–68
Flynn, Lt. Gen. John Peter, 292
Foley, Maj. Brendan, 258
Foley, Dermot, 258
Fonda, Jane, 47
food shortages in Vietnam after the war, 183
Forbes, Stewart, 464
Ford, Carl, 460, 461
Ford, Gerald, 116, 119, 136–37
Foreign Broadcast Information Service (FBIS), 47, 504*n*.29
Forest (aka U-Minh Forest), 390
   American POWs reported, 357
Forget-Me-Not Association, 350–51
"Fort Apache". *See* Gnommorath
Franklin, H. Bruce
   quoted, 399
French
   in North Vietnam, 30, 37
   troops remaining after the Indo-China War, as "ralliers," 296
Frost, Martin, 275
Fulbright, J. William, 71, 86
Fuller, M. Sgt. James R., 278, 284

Gadoury, SM Sgt. William, 351–53, 392–93, 461, 546*n*.16, 558*n*.105
Gaffney, Frank, 409
Gaines, Col. Kim, 290–91, 460, 536*n*.25
Garwood, Pvt. Robert Russell, 151, 257–65, 272, 286, 413, 416, 532*n*.33
   (1979) return to U.S., 257–58
   (1981) trial for treason, and testimony, 258–59
   (1993) revisits Vietnam with House delegation, 545*n*.3
   activities in North Vietnam as a POW choosing not to return, 257
   knowledge of POW camps, 385
   meetings with Hendon, 259–60
   officialdom's minimizing of damage from revelations, 266
   request to revisit Vietnam, refused by State Department, 347–48
   sightings of, by many informants, 413, 416, 520*n*.34
   *Wall Street Journal* story, 260–61
"gasoline" not wanted on the issue, 218
Gaston, Lamont, 550*n*.24
Gates, Robert, 301
Gay, Arlo, 416
Gayler, Adm. Noel, 75
Geller, Jeff, 246
Gia Lai (aka Pleiku) Province
   American POWs reported, 22
Gia Lam, 34
   American POWs reported, 385
Gia Lam Field, 79–81, 497*n*.20

Giap. *See* Vo Nguyen Giap
Gilman, Benjamin A., 136, 137, 271–72, 275, 279, 314
Gingrich, Newt, 275
Glickman, Dan, 275
Gnommorath
   American POWs reported, 210–12, 215–18, 365, 416, 455
   dubbed "Fort Apache," 218
   mission to, compromised, 218, 220–21
Gober, Herschel, 475, 476, 484
Godley, G. McMurtrie "Mac," 93
Gold Star Wives of America, 254
Gonzales, Virgilio, 119
Gonzalez, Henry, 136
Gougelman, Tucker, 416
Grassley, Charles, 373–74, 384–85, 402, 405, 419, 422, 432, 452, 454, 456, 457, 460
   investigation of MIA reports, 378–79, 395–96
Graver, William G., 218, 523*n*.9
Gray, Warren, 461
Green Berets
   commando team of former, 233–36
   who sued the administration, 286
Greenbrier Hotel, West Virginia
   United States Government Relocation Facility at, 440–41, 556*n*.81
Gregg, Judd, 275
Grenada
   as a Marxist-Leninist base, 527*n*.38
   U.S. invasion of, 246–47
Griffin, Robert, 166
Griffiths, Ann Mills, 248, 251–52, 254, 256, 264–65, 269, 270, 275, 278, 285, 287, 314–15, 323, 324, 329, 331, 346, 349, 350, 354, 394, 396, 401, 403, 460, 461, 542*n*.25, 559*n*.125
   POW/MIA advocacy, 242–46
Gritz, Lt. Col. James "Bo," 233–36, 240
Gross, H. R., 83
Guatemala, 238
Gulf of Tonkin, 11–12, 77
Gulf of Tonkin Resolution (1964), 12
Gup, Ted, 440–41
"GX" distress signal, 464, 560*n*.141

Ha Dong (suburb of Hanoi), 96
Ha Nam Ninh Province
   American POWs reported, 524*n*.16
   *See also* "Rockpile" prison
Ha Nam Ninh Province
   American POWs reported, 339, 340, 341, 345–46, 386–88
   reeducation camp, 342, 543*n*.41
Ha Son Binh. *See* Hoa Binh
Ha Van Lau, Col., 68
Habib, Philip, 65, 71
Hai Duong
   American POWs reported, 151

Haig, Gen. Alexander, 47, 48, 52–53, 56, 69, 108, 484
Haiphong, 148
  (1972) bombing of, 495n.84
  (1972) mining of harbor, 46
  American POWs reported, 175
  prison, 29
Haldeman, H. R., 55, 63, 83, 99, 101–2, 108, 118, 119
Hall, Stephen, 246
Ham Tan
  American POWs reported, 145–146, 193
Ham Yen
  American POWs reported, 175, 176, 197, 512n.4
Hambleton, Lt. Col. Iceal, 557n.93
Hamilton, Lee, 279
Hammond, William M., 249–50
Hanoi
  American POWs reported, 32–43, 195–96, 203, 239, 340, 416, 438
  beltway, 195
  main waterworks (Vic. Truc Bach Lake), 42, 96
  Ministry of Defense Citadel. See Ministry of Defense Citadel
  Ministry of Interior hospital, 321–22
  Nga Tu So intersection, 195–96
  Ngoc Ha waterworks (N-63), 42, 96, 552n.2
  POW camps in, 29, 31 (map)
  POW/MIA office planned for, 395, 402
  Presidential Palace, 96
  Trung Qui Mo munitions factory, 43
  Zoological Garden, POW camp at, 42
Hanoi Thermal Power Plant
  American POWs as human shields at, 32–34, 96, 141
Hansen, James, 275, 542n.13
hard-liners, in U.S. administrations, 224–25, 304, 347–48
Hardi, Ambassador from Indonesia, 163–64
Harriman, Averell, 65, 71
Hart, Anne, 252, 277–78, 285
Hart, Capt. Thomas T., III, 252, 277, 282–83
Hartnett, Tom, 275
Harvey, Lt. Col. Joe, 392–93
Harville, Vic
  cartoon by, 456
Hayes, Wayne L., 86
Helm, Buck, 376
Helms, Jesse, 373–74, 402, 403, 405, 410–11, 460
  final report, 403
  investigation of MIA reports, 378–79, 395
Helms, Richard, 34
Hendon, Bill (author), 115, 220–31, 238–41, 259–63, 271–75, 282, 286, 288–90, 296, 301–3, 315, 328, 368, 380, 382–83, 392–93, 405–7, 412, 414–23, 427–32, 452–53, 459, 468, 530–31n.1, 545n.13, 550n.24, 555n.54, 559n.125

(1981–82) trips to Laos, 223–25, 228–29, 230–31
(1982) loses reelection bid, 230
(1983) desk job at the Pentagon, 238–41
(1984) returns to Congress, 260
(1986–95) visits to Vietnam to look for POW prisons, 550n.24
(1986) loses reelection bid, 315
(1989) visit to South China Sea, 368
(1992) security clearance revoked, and leaves committee, 432, 555n.54
(1995) deported from Vietnam, 550n.24
accused of fraud re POW/MIA issues, and exonerated, 559n.125
accused of impeding release of POWs, 545n.13
and Garwood, 259–60
introduces HCR 129 ("Perot resolution"), 274–75
offers reward for rescuing a POW, 328
Heng Samrin, 437
Hezbollah, 295, 540n.93
Hien. See Phan Hien
Hitler, Adolf, 3
Ho Chi Minh, 31, 42, 78, 85, 113, 124
  death and preservation of body, 436, 556n.68
  quoted, 11
Ho Chi Minh City (former Saigon)
  American POWs reported, 139, 416
  Cholon district, 183
Ho Chi Minh Mausoleum, 457, 463
  American POWs reported, 438, 441
  building of, 436–37, 445–46, 448
  underground tunnels, 426, 434–48, 457, 462–64
Ho Chi Minh Trail, 16, 19–20, 21 (map), 75, 121
  American POWs reported, 20–23
  used to move POWs from South Vietnam to North Vietnam, 97
Hoa Binh (aka Ha Son Binh) Province
  American POWs reported, 188–91, 339–40
Hoa Lo Detention/Interrogation Center, Hanoi (no "N" number, not the same as Hoa Lo prison), 30–31, 97
  American POWs reported, 30
Hoa Lo prison, Hanoi (N-43) ("Hanoi Hilton"), 29–30, 38, 80, 95, 97, 143, 191, 505n.10, 539n.81
  American POWs reported, 30, 60
Hoa Lo Street, Hanoi, 29
Hoai Nhon. See Bong Son
Hoang Duc Nha, 50–51
Hoang Lien Son mountain range
  prison, 345
Hoc Mon
  reeducation camp, 130
Hoi Chanhs (VC who turned themselves in), 18
Holbrooke, Richard, 160, 161, 166, 168, 171, 484

Holler, Richard
  quoted, 156
Holstein, Dr. John, 407, 415, 419, 431–32
Hon Gai, 148
  American POWs reported, 151, 154, 413, 449
Honduras, 238, 247
Hopper, Col. Earl, 229, 244, 248, 253, 278
hostage crisis
  to be avoided, per Casey, 303
hostages
  American, in Lebanon, 295, 315–16, 332,
    540n.93
  traded for arms, in Iran-contra affair, 316
Houaphan Province. See Sam Neua Province
Houay Khong
  American POWs reported, 360
House Committee on Foreign Affairs, 274
  Asian and Pacific Affairs Subcommittee, 272,
    313–15
House Concurrent Resolution 114 (HCR 114),
    329
House Concurrent Resolution 129 (HCR 129;
    "Perot Bill"), 274–76, 313–15, 532n.33
House Permanent Select Committee on
    Intelligence (HPSCI), 278–79
House Resolution 2260 (HR 2260), 329, 349
House Select Committee on Missing Persons in
    Southeast Area (Montgomery
    Committee), 135–44, 152–55
  final report, 155
  testimony to, 141–44
House Committee on Veterans Affairs, 256
Hrdlicka, Capt. David L., 27, 545n.13
Hrdlicka, Leo, 545n.13
Hue, 123
Hugel, Max, 459
human intelligence (HUMINT), 434–35
  corroboration of, 414–19
humanitarian issue, 332–34
Humphrey, Hubert H., 83
Hung Hoa
  American POWs reported, 389
  underground prison, 344
Hunt, Howard, 63, 99, 100–101, 119
Hunter, Duncan, 275, 282, 542n.13
Huston, Sgt. Charles G., 539–40n.83
Hyde, Henry, 275

Ia Drang Valley, 15
Ikle, Fred. C, 246
imagery intelligence (IMINT), 450–56
  disappearing, 451, 511n.1
In Tam, 552n.12
income tax forms checkoff box pertaining to
    MIAs, proposed, 373–74
"indemnification," 4, 9
Indochina
  Nixon's rebuilding offer, 67–68, 83, 88
Indonesia, 163
Inhofe, James, 542n.13

intelligence
  sources of information, 29
  use of pattern analysis and cluster analysis
    in, 414–19
Interim Report on the Southeast Asia POW/MIA
    Issue (Senate), 395
International Control Commission (ICC), 59
International Monetary Fund, 475
Iran
  hostage crisis (Carter's), 247. See also "Desert
    One"
  sale of arms to, 295
Iran-contra affair, 295, 315–17, 332, 535n.12
Isom, Harriet
  shares information on MIAs with Lao official,
    368–70
issues. See cover-up issue; humanitarian issue;
    live POW issue; normalization of rela-
    tions issue; POW/MIA issue; war repara-
    tions issue

Jacobs, Andy, 275
Jacobson, David, 315
Japanese
  in Laos, post-Vietnam War, 226
  in North Vietnam, post-Vietnam War, 37
Jaworski, Leon, 118
Jeffords, Jim, 275
Johnson, Haynes, 316
Johnson, Lyndon B., 66
  (1964) continues JFK's policies in Vietnam,
    11
  and Vietnam War, 28, 65
Johnson, Maj. Samuel R., 81
Joint Casualty Resolution Center (JCRC),
    185–87, 351, 392, 551n.36
  court-martial complaint against officers of
    (1990), 393
Joint Chiefs of Staff (JCS), 56–57, 65, 75, 83
Joint Communiqué, U.S.-DRV (1973), 82
Joint Economic Commission, U.S.-DRV, 82–83,
    85–92, 109–11, 138
Joint POW/MIA Accounting Command, xiii
Joint Prisoner Recovery Center (JPRC), 35
Joint Services SERE Agency (JSSA), 448–49, 453,
    464
Joint Special Operations Command (JSOC),
    215–18
Jones, Jim, 275

"K," letter
  dug out in a field, 362, 452–55, 560n.130
  in Morse Code, 154, 155, 211
  "walking," 452–53, 560n.130
Kaiser, Robert, 316
Kalugin, Mag. Gen. Oleg, 407, 409, 553n.3
Kaptur, Marcy, 275
Karnow, Stanley
  quoted, 399
Kasich, John, 275

Kassebaum, Nancy Landon, 405, 460
Katon Mountain
    cave prison, 355
Katum
    American POWs reported, 157, 175, 207–8
    reeducation camps, 172, 180
Kay, Emmet, 416
Kelley, Steve
    cartoon by, 479
Kemp, Jack, 275
Kennedy, Edward M., 71, 86
Kennedy, Jacqueline, 8
Kennedy, John F.
    (1961–62) and Bay of Pigs invasion, 3–9
    (1963) assassination, 11
Kennedy, Robert F., 7
Kerrey, Bob, 405, 460, 465
    quoted, 408
Kerry, John
    (1991) after quick visit to Hanoi doubts any
        living POWs, 405
    (1991) chairs Senate POW/MIA committee,
        405–7, 412
    (1991) goes to Hanoi for fact-finding, 420–26
    (1991) surprise inspection of a prison,
        424–26, 428, 561n.7
    (1992) first trip that year to Hanoi, 457
    (1992) second trip to Hanoi, and tour of Ho
        Chi Minh Mausoleum, 462–64
    (2004) in presidential campaign, attacked for
        Vietnam service, 482
    author's invitation to, 484
    hearings by, 418–19, 426–27, 434–52,
        454–56, 457–62
    and POW numbers, 432–34, 473
    "you don't leave anyone behind," 408
K-55. See Camp K-55
Kham Keut, Laos
    American POWs reported, 306–8, 416
Khamidouline, Rashid, 445–46
Khammouan. See Thakhek
Khammouane Province
    American POWs reported, 322, 363, 537n.41
Khamtay Siphandone, 485, 562–63n.4
Khe Sanh
    POWs captured at, 44
Khmer Rouge, 109, 184, 187, 500n.8
Kim Boi District, 514n.3
    American POWs reported, 188, 189
Kingston, Gen. Robert, 292, 536n.26, 542n.25
Kipling, Rudyard
    on dealing with the Orient, 50
Kirkpatrick, Lyman, 292
Kissinger, Henry, 500n.8, 532n.33
    (1972–73) Paris peace talks, 47–60, 63–70,
        72–76
    asks why Vietnamese would hold POWs,
        285–86, 504n.18
    author's proposal to, 484
    and Central America, 248

    declares the Paris Peace Accords dead, 140
    eager for a deal at Paris peace talks, 48
    "an enormous crime," xiii
    foreign affairs power in Nixon's last term,
        108–9
    goal of getting out of Vietnam, 116–18
    Hanoi visit, 78–83
    knowledge of number of POWs held, 93, 103
    "my most thrilling moment," 49
    negotiating prowess, 53, 55
    and Nobel Prize, 51, 115
    and Paris Peace Accords compliance, 111
    "peace is at hand," 52
    on POW numbers, 473
    on reparations, 67
    speech about negotiating with DRV, 135–36
    supports aid to North Vietnam, 63, 87
Klein, Joe
    quoted, 408
Kleisner, Ted, 441
Klos, Arthur G., 291
Knecht, Ron, 460
Kohl, Herb, 405, 460
Kontum City, 121
Kontum Province, 15
    American POWs reported, 22, 23, 192
Korean prisoners of war in Vietnam, 22
Korean War, 255–56
Krauthammer, Charles, 316

Lai Chau
    prison N-101, 508n.1
Lai Chau Province
    American POWs reported, 156
Laird, Melvin, 56, 71
Lake, Anthony, 471, 480, 484
Lam Son
    prison, 539n.81
Lambertson, David, 542n.25
Lang Son
    prison camp N-104, 517n.25
Lang Son Province
    American POWs reported, 104, 415
Lao Bao
    American POWs reported, 341
Lao Cai
    American POWs reported, 173, 191
    prison N-80, 514n.6
Lao Cai Province
    American POWs reported, 415
"Lao Initiative," 224–31, 236–41
Lao National Route 12
    American POWs reported, 308
Lao Peace Accords (1973), 139
Lao People's Democratic Republic (LPDR),
    138–39
Lao People's Liberation Army (LPLA), 323
Laos
    American POWs held back in, 93, 143–44
    American POWs reported, 222, 226

Laos (*continued*)
  American POWs transferred to North
      Vietnam, 27–28, 143
  Americans captured in, 19, 74, 75, 139
  called "soft underbelly" of Communist
      Indochina, 221
  medical supplies sent to, as aid, 223–27
  negotiations with, 233
  Pathet Lao victory, 503n.6
  royal family imprisoned, 309, 516n.23
  shopping list of reconstruction aid in
      exchange for POWs, 229–30
  wartime intelligence on, 26–28
Latin America
  communism and anticommunism in, 3
Lawrence, Rear Adm. William P., 142–43
Le Dinh, 202–4
Le Duan, 121, 123
Le Duc Tho, 500n.8
  (1972) Paris peace talks, 48–49, 50, 53–55,
      57–58, 64, 67, 68–69
  and fall of RVN, 123, 128
  greets Kissinger in Hanoi, 81
  Hanoi celebrations, 77–78
  in Hanoi during bombings, 59
  last meeting with Kissinger, 116
  and Paris Peace Accords compliance, 109
  refuses Nobel Prize, 115
Le Phuong, Col., 127
Le Van Bang, 423, 428
League, the. *See* National League of Families of
      American Prisoners and Missing in
      Southeast Asia
leaks, 218, 523n.9
Leath, Marvin, 275
Lebanon
  American hostages in, 295, 315–16, 332,
      540n.93
LeBoutillier, John, 116, 220–28, 230, 234,
      280–81, 380, 524n.21
Legion of Valor, 254
LeGro, William "Bill," 407, 413, 415, 419, 431
Leland, Mickey, 275
Leoffler, Tom, 275
Lerner, Max
  quoted, 82
Lewis, Jerry, 275
Liddy, G. Gordon, 100–101, 119
*Life* magazine, 38
live POW issue, 71, 141, 161, 212, 330–31, 335.
      *See also* prisoners of war, American:
      numbers
Loc Ninh, 123
  American POWs reported, 175, 179–80,
      200–202
Loc Ninh Province
  POW camp in, 25
Logan Act, 5
Loma Prieta earthquake, in California (1989),
      374–77

Lon Nol, 51, 69
Long Bien, 34
Long Bien Bridge, Hanoi, 480
  American POWs as human shields at, 34–37,
      96, 153
Long Binh
  American POWs reported, 144
Long Khanh
  reeducation camp, 130
Long Khanh (aka Dong Nai) Province
  American POWs reported, 194, 517n.25
Lord, Winston, 47, 72–73, 78, 109, 472,
      475–76, 480, 484
*Los Angeles Times,* 234, 426
Lott, Trent, 275
Lowe, John, 258–59
Lowery, Bill, 275
Lu Van Loi, 48
Luang Prabang Province
  American POWs reported, 343
"Luong Lang" PW Camp N-124, 506n.38
  *See also* "Dogpatch" Camp
Luu Xa, 44, 96
Ly Nam De Street, Hanoi, 38, 41, 96
  American POWs reported, 271–73, 282, 286,
      309, 385
  POW camp (N-62) ("Plantation"), 38, 95,
      143, 505n.10

M-16s from Vietnam turning up in Central
      America, 241
Ma Da woods
  American POWs reported, 309–10
Macdonald, 2nd Lt. George D., 278, 282–83
Mack, Connie, 275
MacKay, Buddy, 275
Madigan, Ed, 275
Magaw, John, 458
Magruder, Jeb Stuart, 101, 120
Mai Son
  American POWs reported, 191, 515n.20
*Manchester Union Leader,* 395
Maneta, Norman, 275
Mansfield, Mike, 159, 165
Marine Corps League, 254
Marsh, John O. "Jack," 107, 250, 285
Martin, Lynn, 275
Martinez, Eugenio, 119
Marxism-Leninism
  in Central America, 236–38, 244, 247–48,
      530–31n.1
  in Grenada, 527n.38
Matthes, 1st Lt. Peter J., 560n.141
May Tao mountain
  American POWs reported, 145–46
Maynard, Roberta Carper, 291
McCain, Adm. John S., Jr., 142
McCain, Cdr. John S., III, 275, 484
  at hearings, 418–19, 426–27, 432, 435, 442,
      460, 532n.33

on a news show, 452
opinions on POW/MIA issues, 142, 399, 408,
    461, 532n.33, 560n.130
as POW, 143
POW camps where he was held, 505n.10
on Senate Select Committee, 405
shootdown over Hanoi, 413, 429–31, 505n.10
McChristian, Maj. Gen. Joseph A., 18
McCloskey, Frank, 275, 329, 347, 545n.3
McCloskey, Paul N. "Pete," Jr., 136, 137
McCollum, Bill, 275
McCord, James, 99, 100–101, 119
McCreary, John Francis, 291, 407, 412, 414–20,
    427, 431–32, 434–35
McCurdy, Dave, 275
McDaniel, Capt. Eugene "Red," 328, 559n.125
McFarlane, Robert "Bud," 115–16, 225–28, 231,
    241, 252, 261, 263, 269, 274, 280–81,
    295, 484
  in Iran-contra affair, 315–16
McGee, Col. Lester, 291
McGonigle, Kevin, 353
McGrory, Mary, 316
McIntyre, Sgt. 1st Class Melvin, 286
McKernan, John, 275
McNamara, Robert, 34
McPherson, Peter, 223
medical assistance to Indochina
  to Laos, 223–27
  NGOs proposed to supply, 333–34, 346–47
  to Vietnam, 116
Meese, Edwin, III, 223, 317
Mekong Delta, 122
Melton, Staff Sgt. Todd, 197, 520n.32
Memorial Day ceremonies
  (1981), 219
Mengele, Josef, 273
Michel, Bob, 275
Mikulski, Barbara, 275
Military Assistance Command Vietnam
    (MACV), 18
military interrogators, 17–18
  rating system for interrogations, 17
Military Order of the Purple Heart,
    254
Miller, Ron, 229
Milliner, William P., 392–93
Mills, Wilbur D., 83
Milne, Mike, 346
Minh Hai Province
  American POWs reported, 357
Ministry of Defense (DRV), 37
Ministry of Defense Citadel, Hanoi, 39 (map)
  American POWs as human shields at, 37–42,
    96
  American POWs reported, 441–42
  POW camp (N-67) ("Alcatraz"), 38–39, 95,
    96, 141
  underground bunkers, 480
  underground prison, 426, 434–48

missing in action (MIA)
  DIA's SI Report of, 413
  officially declaring them dead, 171
  question as to whether they are dead, KIAs,
    or POWs, 71, 141, 161, 212, 335
  search for remains, 133, 134–35
Mitchell, George, 405
Mitchell, John, 100, 118, 119
Moi Pass
  sighting of American POWs, 20
Molinari, Guy, 275
Mondale, Walter, 260
Montgomery, G. V. "Sonny," 135–44, 152–55,
    159, 236, 530–31n.1
Moorer, Adm. Thomas, 56, 57, 72, 83
Morgan, Lt. Col. Herschel "Scotty," 81, 216
Morris, Capt. Robert, 104
Morris, Steven, 469–75
Morse code
  distress signals in, 154, 155, 211
"mortician, the Chinese"
  American POWs reported by, 199–200
Mount Bia. See Phou Bia
"Mountain Camp" prison (40 miles NW of
    Hanoi), 95
  See also Vin Quang
Mu Gia Pass
  American POWs reported, 308, 323
Muang Ngoy
  American POWs reported, 311
Muang Udomxai
  American POWs reported, 339
Mulligan, Capt. James, 81
Muong Fuong
  American POWs reported, 310–11
Muong Khoua
  American POWs reported, 381–84
Murray, Maj. Gen. John S., 291, 493n.10,
    536n.26
Muslims, Vietnamese (Cham), 180

Na Sam
  American POWs reported, 152
Nagy, Dennis M., 271, 460
Nakhon Phanom, Thailand, 216
  Air Force Base, 268
Nam Can
  American POWs reported, 335–38
  prison camps, 338
Nam Dinh
  thermal power plant, 43, 96
Nam Ngum dam
  American POWs reported, 360
Nam Ngum Reservoir
  American POWs reported, 310
Nance, Rear Adm. James "Bud," 410–11, 412
Napang
  American POWs reported, 322
National Enquirer, 373
National Forget-Me-Nots, 187

*National Geographic,* 331
National Interrogation Center (NIC), 17
National League of Families of American
    Prisoners and Missing in Southeast Asia,
    70, 117–18, 187, 229, 235, 248, 254, 258,
    264, 270, 324, 332, 391–93, 401, 559*n*.125
  (1984) declines to participate in Unknown
    Soldier ceremonies, 254
  (1987) activists attempt takeover of office, 324
  (1988) Reagan's speech to, 350–51
  co-opting of, by Reagan administration,
    242–46
  newsletter known as the "POW Death
    Warrant," 245
  officials' speeches to, 244–45
National Photographic Interpretation Center
    (NPIC), 451
National POW/MIA Recognition Day, 255
National Security Advisor, 404
National Security Agency (NSA), 204, 269, 310
National Security Council (NSC), 229, 377
  Office of Politico-Military Affairs, 323
National Vietnam and Gulf War Veterans Coali-
    tion, 482
Needham, Brig. Gen. Thomas, 423, 424–25,
    428, 461, 555*n*.46
Negroponte, John, 47, 48, 49, 58, 69, 206, 484,
    493*n*.10
Nelson, Bill, 275
Nessen, Ron, 134
new economic zones (SRV), 182
*New York Post,* 317
*New York Times,* 106–7, 299–301, 347, 350–51,
    472
Newberry, Robert J., 483
news broadcasters
  downplaying coverage of witness stories,
    106–7
Nghe Tinh Province
  American POWs reported, 343, 354, 363
Nghia Lo
  American POWs reported, 175, 178, 181
Nghia Lo Province
  American POWs reported, 150
Ngoc Ha waterworks, Hanoi, 42, 96, 552*n*.2
Nguyen Co Thach, 48, 78, 326, 327, 332–34,
    346–47, 348
  (1990) visits Washington, 394
Nguyen Cong Nhuan, Col., 424–25, 428
Nguyen Duy Trinh, 69, 77–78, 132, 162
Nguyen Manh Cam, 424–25, 462
Nguyen Phu Duc, 56
Nguyen Thanh Son, 106–7
Nguyen Van Linh, 331
Nguyen Van Thieu
  (1973) learns of and rejects Paris peace plan,
    49–53
  (1975) and fall of South Vietnam, 121–22
  estimate of number of PAVN troops left in
    South, 493*n*.10

Nguyen Xuan Phong, 423, 424–25, 428
Nha Trang
  American POWs reported, 533*n*.34
*Nhan Dan* Communist newspaper, 76
Nicaragua, 237–38, 247–49, 530–31*n*.1
Nicklas, Col. Harold "Nick," 407, 415, 419, 431
Nixon, Richard
  (1972) first bombing, 46
  (1972) reelection, 52
  (1972) second "Christmas" bombing, 63
  (1972–73) and Paris Peace Accords, 51–53,
    55–57
  (1973) fights for aid to North Vietnam, 83–87
  (1973) getting Vietnam "out of the way,"
    102–3, 105–6
  (1973–74) Watergate problem, 98–103, 108,
    118–20
  (1974) impeachment charges and resigna-
    tion, 118–19
  on negotiating, 63
  offer to rebuild Indochina, 67–68, 83, 88
  and Paris peace talks, 49, 81
  and POW/MIA issue, 303
  on ransom, 6
  and Thieu, 51
  and Vietnam War, 28
Nixon secret letter promising postwar aid to
    North Vietnam (1973)
  (1972) promised by Kissinger, 68–69
  cited by DRV, 137–38, 140–41, 162, 167
  cited by SRV, 458, 476
  confirmed by Dong, 79, 85–86
  delivered, 74
  existence of, 136
  Vietnamese reliance on, 347
Nobel Peace Prize
  to Kissinger and Le Duc Tho, 51, 115
Noi Bai International Airport (postwar name of
    Phuc Yen airbase), 46, 497*n*.20
"Noi Coc PW Camp N-129," 512*n*.2
  *See also* "Rockpile" prison
Nong Co (aka Nong Kou)
  American POWs reported, 343
Nong Hed (aka Nong Het), Laos
  American POWs reported, 311–12, 358, 359
  cave prison, 342
Nong Het. *See* Nong Hed
Nong Kou. *See* Nong; Nong Co
Nong Tha (aka Ban Daknong)
  American POWs reported, 310–11
nongovernmental organizations (NGOs)
  and medical assistance to Vietnam, 333–34,
    346–47
Noonan, Peggy
  quoted, 120
Noriega, Manuel, 551*n*.36
normalization of relations (issue)
  linkage with reparations, 167–68
  *See also* Socialist Republic of Vietnam
North, Oliver, 116, 246, 295, 323

North Korea, 256
North Vietnam (area, NVN)
    air wars over, 28–29, 46–47, 59–60, 67
    American POWs in, 28–46
    prisons in, 95–96, 372
    rebuilding of, 112
    South Vietnamese "spies" in, 149–50
    *See also* Democratic Republic of Vietnam
North Vietnam Communist Party Central
        Committee, 12–11
Novak, Robert, 280, 316
Nui Ba Den (Black Virgin Mountain)
    American POWs reported, 157, 207

Oberst, Col. John, 262–63, 279, 291
Oberstar, Jim, 275
O'Connor, Cardinal John Joseph, 317–18
Ogburn, Capt. Benjamin R., 258
Oglesby, M. B., 262–63, 288
O'Neill, Thomas P. "Tip," Jr., 296
Op Plan 34-A, 11
Operation Homecoming, 303, 532*n*.33
    debriefing of returned POWs, 28, 92–95
    full list of POWs not supplied by DRV, 71,
        73–75
    POWs not returned at, 98, 257, 507*n*.38
Operation Linebacker, 28, 46–47, 59, 67
Operation Linebacker II ("Christmas bomb-
        ing"), 28, 57, 59–60, 63–64, 68
    condemnations of, 47
Operation Pocket Change, 215–18
Operation Rolling Thunder (1965–68), 28
Oriental culture
    environment of, effect of reinterviewing on
        credibility of sources, 293
    face consciousness, 425
    Kipling's advice to Westerners, 50
Ortega, Daniel, 237, 247, 249
Ortega, Humberto, 237
Ottinger, Richard, 137
Oudom Sai City, Laos
    American POWs reported, 339
Oudom Sai Province
    American POWs reported, 343

Paksan, Laos
    American POWs reported, 364–65
    in cave, 354
Pakse, 139
    remains from, 283
Panama, 238
Panetta, Leon, 275
*Parade* magazine (Sunday supplement),
        218–19
Paralyzed Veterans of America, 254
Paris Peace Accords (1973 treaty), 48–60
    (1973) celebrations in Hanoi over, 76–78
    (1973) ratified by North Vietnam, 84–86
    (1975) North Vietnam demands that it be
        respected, 132–33

(1975–76) declared meaningless by U.S., 134,
        140
    Articles 1 and 4 (Vietnam's national rights),
        132
    Article 8(b) (MIAs), 137
    Article 21 (reparations), 132, 134, 303, 476
    Article 22 (normalization), 132
    failure to comply with war reparations ar-
        ticle, 109, 111
    linkage of Articles 21 and 8(b), 65–70,
        132–35, 155, 162–63, 169, 331–33,
        394–95, 458, 504*n*.18
    linkage of Articles 21 and 22, 167–68
    list of POWs supplied by DRV believed to be
        incomplete, 73–74
    signing, 69
Paris peace talks (1968), 65–66, 68
    Communist ransom demands, 65
Paris peace talks (1972–73), 28, 47–49, 53–55,
        57–58, 64–74
    North Vietnamese peace plan, 48
    *See also* Paris Peace Accords
Parker, Dr. Donald, 284, 285
Passman, Otto, 86
Pathet Lao (PL), 138–39, 193, 503*n*.6, 504*n*.31
    (1977) Woodcock Commission visits, 164–65
    (1979) radio transmission about POWs, 204
    American POWs captured by, 26–28
    pattern analysis, 414–19
Paul, Bill, 260, 484
Paulson, Rear Adm. Jerry, 242
Pearl Harbor attack (1941), xv
Pearlstein, Norman, 264–65
Peck, Col. Millard "Mike," 396, 399–403, 404,
        552*n*.2
People's Army of Vietnam (North) (PAVN)
    captured soldiers, interrogation of, 14, 16–19
    defectors from, reports of American POWs
        from, 106–7, 202–4
    instructed to capture Americans alive, 13–15
    remain in South in 1972 peace plan, 48–49,
        54, 57, 112–13, 493*n*.10
People's Liberation Army (Chinese Army)
        (PLA), 191–92
Perot, H. Ross, 484
    (1987) Hanoi trip, 325–27
    (1987) report on Hanoi trip, 327–30
    (1992) runs for president, 457, 558*n*.108
    advice to negotiate for release of POWs ("cut
        a deal and pay"), 304, 313–14, 487
    asked to head a commission, 272–75, 313–14
    forming the "Perot Commission," 273–75, 296
    longtime friend of the POWs, 303
    and POW/MIA issue, 292, 303–4
    studies the POW/MIA issue, 318, 322–23,
        324–30
    "we set the screen so tight that nothing can
        get through," 313
Perot Bill. *See* House Concurrent Resolution
        129

Perrin, Dan, 403
Perroots, Lt. Gen. Leonard H., 289–91,
        295–301, 460, 534n.5, 536n.25, 536n.26
Peterson, Capt. Douglas B."Pete," 94, 480, 484,
        507n.38, 514n.2, 562n.2
Pham Hong Thai Street, Hanoi, 32
Pham Hung, 123
Pham Van Dong, 42, 54, 69, 78–79, 81, 82–83,
        84–86, 111–12, 132, 135, 138
Phan Hien, 48, 137–38, 162–63, 166–68
Phan Thiet
    American POWs reported, 175, 178
Phnom Penh, 51, 187
Pho Lu
    American POWs reported, 157
Phong Quang (aka Coc Mi) prison complex,
        173–74, 188, 189, 506n.33
    American POWs reported, 151, 157
Phong Saly Province
    American POWs reported, 381–84
Phou Bia (Mount Bia)
    American POWs reported, 368–69, 373
Phou Ngoua (Buffalo Mountain), 304–5
    American POWs reported, 305–6
Phu Bon (aka Cheo Reo), 121, 123
Phu Khanh Province
    camp, 306
Phu Khoung District, Tay Ninh Province
    American POWs reported, 180–81
Phu Loi
    American POWs reported, 144
Phu Ly
    American POWs reported, 175, 176
    prison camp, 512n.2
    See also "Rockpile" prison
Phu Tho
    American POWs reported, 175, 318
Phuc Yen MiG base, 497n.20
    American POWs reported, 44–46, 96
Pickle, Jake, 275
pilots and aircrewman, American
    shot down and taken prisoner, 29, 30
Pilots in Pajamas (East German documentary),
        38
Plain of Jars (Plaine des Jarres, PDJ), 231
Plateau Gi
    American POWs seen north of, 192
Pleibong, Central Highlands, Reeducation Camp
    American POWs seen north of, 192
Pleiku, 121
    American POWs seen north of, 20, 321
Pleiku Province
    American POWs reported, 20
Poindexter, John, 288, 315, 317, 322
Polgar, Thomas, 117 quoted
"Policy on Treatment of American Prisoners"
        (North Vietnamese pamphlet), 11
polygraphs, 294
Ponemek Daraloy, Dr., 228–29, 231, 239, 241,
        485

Porter, D. Gareth, 111–12, 137
POW camps
    cave prisons, 26–28
    located at a safe distance from the Chinese
        border after 1978–79, 192
Powell, Maj. Gen. Colin, 282, 322–23, 325,
        329, 349, 354, 475, 484, 540n.93
    attitude on POW/MIA issue, 541–42n.9
Powers, Francis Gary, 7
POW/MIA activists
    congressmen
        (1988) trip to Vietnam, 347
    organizations, 240
        accused of fraud, 461
    rescuers
        accused of exploiting, 236
POW/MIA families
    officials' speeches and promises to, 229,
        232–33, 353
    unhappy with Montgomery Committee's
        findings, 159
POW/MIA Interagency Committee (IAC), 314
POW/MIA Interagency Group (IAG), 242–45,
        314, 324, 329
POW/MIA issue
    (1988) final interagency report, 354
    considered a hoax by some, 399
    intelligence reports on, obtained by Senate
        Select Committee on POW/MIA Affairs,
        407, 412–18
    linkage with war reparations issue, 65–70,
        132–35, 155, 394–95
    political cartoons about, 275, 348, 456, 479
    private sector attempts to deal with, 235–36
    public opinion polls about, 404
Presidential Commission on Americans Missing
        and Unaccounted for in Southeast Asia
        (Woodcock Commission), 159–66
Principi, Anthony, 411
prison system (DRV, SRV)
    DIA knowledge of, 372
    in North Vietnam, 95–96
    supersecret second tier of, 389
prisoners of war, allied, 44
prisoners of war, American
    captured during the war
        (1970) wartime intelligence reports, 24–25
        appeals from, to stop bombing, 47
        captured alive, Communist policy, 12–15, 26
        killed by American weaponry while being
            withdrawn from the battlefield, 15
        in North Vietnam, 28–46
        revenge killings of, upon capture, 15–16
        sent to North Vietnam for long-term
            imprisonment, 19–25
        treatment of, after capture, 15, 18–19, 26
        wounded, treatment of, 15, 18
    contacting next of kin about, 548n.20
    escapes
        attempts, 23, 196

hiding in a bunker, 144
seeking asylum with Swedes, 196–97
information on, sources, 185–87
in Laos, 93, 143–44
life and activities in captivity
appearing "skin and very old," 338
diet fed to, 362
exercising, 33, 533n.34
in good spirits, 36
personal appearance, 40
numbers
belief by veterans that hundreds are alive, 346
number held by VC, 25
number privately stated to the North Vietnam Politburo, 469–75
number reported sighted in North Vietnam, 44–46
number sent from south to North Vietnam, 24–25, 97
number that Kerry reckoned, 433–34, 435
number that North Vietnam claimed to hold after signing Paris Peace Accords, 69–75
number that Senate Select Committee investigators reckoned, 431–32, 555n.53
number that U.S. government reckons, 71–75
official doubts that any POWs are alive, 330–31
Soviet knowledge of, 409
returned at Operation Homecoming
(1973) released by North Vietnam, 79–81
debriefing reveals POWs held back, 92–95
North Vietnam's lists of, presented at Paris peace talks, 73–75, 79
North Vietnam's refusal to provide a full list, 71
returnees' opposition to war reparations, 83
secretly held back. See also sightings of American prisoners of war
(1979) moved within Vietnam, 205 (map)
(1980–81) rescue plans, 206–12, 215–21
(1981) Hanoi's offer to ransom, reportedly, 288, 534n.4
advertisements asking for information about, 187
American public's belief that there are some, but no public support for rescuing them, 197–99, 302–3
ask to send and receive mail, 196
attempts by commandos to liberate, 233–36
called deserters, 263–64
called stay-behinds, trying to live out their years in privacy, 264
captured after 1972, 75
cover-up of knowledge of, 105–7, 240
debate about whether any are alive, 285–87, 291–312

government abandonment of, denied, 450–51
in Laos, 93, 143–44
not returned at Operation Homecoming, 98, 257, 507n.38
number of, 92–98
official claim that there is no proof, 287
official stated belief that there are none, 117–18, 142, 255
official stated belief that there are some, 229, 280–81, 289
official Washington uninterested in recovering, 160
officially declaring them dead, 171
Perot's advice to negotiate for release of ("cut a deal and pay"), 304, 313–14, 487
question why Vietnamese would hold them, 285–86, 504n.18
Tighe's report on, 291–312
Watergate held responsible for their fate, 120
whether they have been executed, 487
usefulness of, to Vietnamese
Communist policy to hold as hostages in return for war reparations, 11–13, 18, 65–66
filming of, for propaganda, 194–96, 518n.28
as human shields, 31–46, 45 (map), 59, 96, 141, 153
for prisoner exchanges, 515n.20
See also sightings of American prisoners of war
"Prisoners of War in Indochina" (RAND report), 66–67
prosthetics-to-Vietnamese initiative, 346–47
Provisional Revolutionary Government (the Vietcong) (PRG), 113–14
Ptak, Alan C., 411, 442, 450–51, 461

Quang Binh Province, 112
American POWs reported, 23
American POWs transported through, 22
Quang Ngai Province
POW camp in, 25
Quang Nihn Province, 77
Quang Tin Province, 15, 49
Quang Tri Province, 15
American POWs reported, 22
Qui Nhon
American POWs reported, 363
Quinn, Ken, 460, 461
Quyet Tien
American POWs reported, 172–73
prison complex, 510n.49

ralliers, French, 297
"Rambo" (Stallone character), 276, 295, 445
Rambo: First Blood Part II, 275–76
RAND Corporation, 66

ransom demands
  belief that giving in would set a precedent,
    5–6
  "Cuban" style, 140
  Cuba's, after Bay of Pigs invasion, 4–9
  North Vietnamese, for unlisted POWs,
    132–35, 287–88, 458–60, 532*n*.33, 534*n*.4
  a secret service agent's report of offer made
    in 1981, 287–88, 458–60
  rejection of, as a matter of principle, 155,
    541*n*.9
Ravenel, Arthur, 542*n*.13
Reagan, Ronald
  (1981) author meets with, 225–27
  (1981) pledges release of POWs, 219–20
  (1983) and Unknown Soldier from the
    Vietnam War controversy, 252–55
  (1984) reelection, 260
  (1986) Iran-contra affair, 316–17
  (1986) Vietnamese ransom offer, 287–88,
    458–60
  (1987) Perot's report to, 327–30
  aides' desire to save him from himself, 236,
    241, 256
  criticized for Iran-contra affair, 316–17
  "gave the poisoned pot another stir," 236
  hard-liners in administration of, 304
  military's high regard for, 215
  personal decency and concern for POWs,
    525*n*.6
  POW/MIA policy, 244–45, 255–56, 260–64,
    317–18, 329–32, 346–47, 350–51,
    353–54, 367
  requests a vet to end hunger strike, 285
  speeches on Central America, 237–38, 247
  speeches on POW/MIAs, 232–33
  "your long vigil is over," 232, 245
  mentioned, 296, 313, 322
Reagan report (1989). *See Final Interagency
    Report of the Reagan Administration on the
    POW/MIA Issue in Southeast Asia*
Reaid, M. Sgt. Rollie K., 282–83
Red River, 34–37
Redman, Chuck, 348
reeducation campaign (SRV)
  (1975) moderate beginning of, 128–32
  (1976) transfer of long-term prisoners to
    North Vietnam, 147–50, 149 (map)
  camps, 537*n*.47
  and creation of witnesses for American intel-
    ligence, 149–51
  international inspectors of, 543*n*.41
refugees, Vietnamese, 127, 175
  discrediting of testimony of, 296–99, 352–53
  Hendon's requests for files on, 271
  information from, 185–87, 292, 514*n*.35
  movement of, 182–85, 186 (map)
  and relief workers at refugee camps, 185
Regan, Donald, 280, 540*n*.93
Rehnquist, William H., 118

Reid, Harry, 275, 405, 460, 484
remains recovery effort, 242, 244, 255–56,
    266–69, 283, 351
  bones purchased from North Vietnamese,
    269
  Vietnamese accused of withholding remains,
    244
"reparations," 5
  Kissinger's rejection of word, 67
Republic of Vietnam (RVN)
  (1973) reaction to Paris Peace Accords, 49–53
  (1975) fall of, 120–24, 122 (map)
  (1975) roundup of officials and military by
    victorious Communists, 124, 127–32
  Air Force (RVNAF), 127
  *See also* South Vietnam (area)
Republicans
  in Congress, 315
Resolution of Inquiry filed by Hendon (1985),
    278–79
Reuther, Walter P., 4, 5
reward for rescuing a Vietnam War POW
  advertising of, in Southeast Asia, 368,
    545*n*.13
  denial of existence of, official U.S. policy of,
    352–53, 392, 551*n*.36
  fraud accusation, 559*n*.125
  posted by Hendon and McDaniel, 328–29
  present size of (2006), 542*n*.13
  U.S. government policy against private
    rewards, 393, 551*n*.36
Richardson, Bill, 275
Richardson, Elliot, 83, 87
Richmond, Lt. Col. Melvin E., 483, 550*n*.24
Ridge, Tom, 275
Ring, Commodore Stu, 238
Riordan, Lt. Col. Jim, 238
Risner, Lt. Col. Robinson, 81, 292, 536*n*.26
Robb, Charles, 405, 422, 460
Roberts, Pat, 275
"Rockpile" prison (32 miles S of Hanoi), 95
Rodino, Peter, 118
Rodman, Peter, 47, 74, 78, 484
Roemer, Buddy, 275
Rogers, William P., 69, 73, 84, 86, 109
Rohrbacher, Dana, 264
Rolling Thunder protest movement, 349–50
Roosevelt, Eleanor, 4
Rosenthal, James, 160, 161, 163–64, 166, 171,
    484
Roth, Toby, 542*n*.13
Rowe, Lt. Col. Nick, 218–19
Rowland, John, 265, 271, 275, 347, 542*n*.13,
    545*n*.3
Rush, Kenneth, 56
Russian document on American POWs (the
    "1205 document"), 469–75
Russo, Marty, 275
Rutledge, Capt. Howard, 80, 81
Ryan, Lt. Gen. Michael, 475

Sa Dec
  American POW reported, 172
Sa Pa. *See* Chapa
Sadoi
  cave prison, 343–44
Saigon, 122
  (1975) fall of, 123–24
  (1975) renamed Ho Chi Minh City, 123
Salter, Mark, 412, 418, 434
SAM-2s, 63–64
Sam Neua Province (aka Houaphan Province),
      Laos, 59
  American POWs reported, 93, 97, 139, 154,
      193–94, 204, 309, 342, 343, 357, 379,
      381, 416, 532n.34
  POW camps in, 26–28
  seminar camp system, 515n.23
Sampley, Ted, 433–34, 468, 529n.43,
      559–60n.127
San Francisco earthquake (1989), 374–77
Sandinistas, 247–48, 530–31n.1
Saravan Province, 304
satellite photography, 154, 449–50
Savang Vatthana, King, 138, 139
Savannakhet
  hospital at, 223–24
Savannakhet Province, Laos
  American POWs reported, 312, 361, 416
Saxton, Jim, 265, 271, 275
Schanberg, Sydney, 460
Schlatter, Lt. Col. Joe, 290–91, 349, 369–70,
      371–72, 382–84, 385, 391–92, 460,
      536n.25, 545n.13
  honored, 395
Schlesinger, James, 93
Schmidt, 1st Lt. Walter R., Jr., 197,
      518–20n.32
Schneider, Lt. Col. Keith, 284
Schoor, Daniel, 316
Scott, Hugh, 86
Scowcroft, Brig. Gen. Brent, 75, 83, 105, 116,
      140, 404, 410, 458, 484
Scrivener, John, 547n.2
Searle, James A., Jr., 441
Secord, Richard, 236
Senate Committee on Foreign Relations, 166,
      374, 394
  report on POW/MIAs, 403
Senate Select Committee on POW/MIA Affairs,
      72, 405–65
  created, 404–5
  destruction of investigators' documents,
      419–22
  final hearings, 460–62
  final report, signed by all twelve members,
      465
  personnel changes prompted by Kerry,
      410–11
  principal findings, 465–68
  the "Numbers Hearing," 433–34

Sepone (Tchepone)
  American POWs reported, 355
Serex, Lt. Col. Henry M. "Mick," 557n.93
"SEREX" dug in field, 449–50
Shatner, William, 235
Shaw, Clay, 275
Sheafer, Rear Adm. Edward D., 400
Sheehan, Neil
  quoted, 399
Sheetz, Robert, 460, 461, 473
Shelby, Richard, 275
Shelton, Charles, 27
Shelton, Mike
  cartoons by, 275, 348
Shields, Maj. Robert, 253
Shields, Dr. Roger, 105–6, 161
Shrok Xa Neo POW Camp
  American POWs reported, 202
Shufelt, Brig. Gen. James, 314, 535n.18,
      559n.125
Shultz, George, 244, 255, 269, 332, 348, 484,
      540n.93
Shumaker, Lt. Cmdr. Robert Harper, 80, 81
SI Reports, 413, 554n.18
sightings of American prisoners of war (topic
      includes first-hand sightings, second-
      hand reports, SIGINT, HUMINT, IMINT,
      and other forms of intelligence gather-
      ing)
  (1966) on Ho Chi Minh Trail, 20–23
  (1969), 27
  (1970s), 338
  (1972), 388–91
  (1973–78), 342
  (1973–79), 385, 441
  (1973–89), 416
  (1974), 203
  (1975), 139, 341, 349
  (1975–76), 379–81
  (1975–79), 342, 413–14
  (1976), 144–46, 145 (map), 151–52, 305–6
  (1976–1986), 318–22
  (1977), 156–59, 158 (map), 171–75, 338, 385,
      439, 441, 442
  (1978), 175–82, 177 (map), 200–202, 271–73,
      286, 363, 385, 441, 442
  (1978–79), 354
  (1979), 188–97, 190 (map), 341, 363, 438,
      441, 442
  (1980), 207–10, 212, 441, 442
  (1980–1981), 318
  (1980–1986), 306–12
  (1980–81), 222
  (1980s), 339
  (1981), 217–18, 358, 441, 442
  (1981–82), 340
  (1982), 305–6, 341, 441, 442
  (1983), 239, 386–87, 441, 442
  (1984), 335, 344, 358, 360, 369, 437, 439,
      441, 442

sightings of American prisoners of war
  (*continued*)
  (1985), 306–12, 343, 357, 360, 363, 438, 439,
    441, 442
  (1986), 305–6, 307 (map), 318–22, 335, 339,
    340, 341, 343, 359, 360, 439, 441, 442
  (1987), 337 (map), 338, 343, 345, 354, 355,
    362, 365
  (1988), 331, 352, 356 (map), 357, 359, 361,
    363, 364, 365, 439, 441, 442
  (1989), 369, 370, 387
  (1992), 464
  (2005 and 2006 receipt of reports), 483
  by ARVN releasees, 103–4, 200–202, 207–10
  confirmation of, 232
  declassification urged (HR 2260), 329, 349,
    434–35
  standard of evidence of, eyewitness testi-
    mony discounted, 377–78
Sihanouk, Prince Norodom, 500*n*.8
Sikorski, Gerry, 382–83
Siphandone, Gen. Khamtay. *See* Khamtay
  Siphandone
Sirica, John J., 100–101, 118
*60 Minutes*, 286–87
Skelton, Ike, 275
"Skidrow". *See* Bang Liet/Thanh Liet Prison
Smith, Bob, 275, 288, 301, 329, 347, 349, 384,
    385, 402, 404, 409–12, 419, 422, 423,
    432, 434–35, 451–52, 454–56, 457–60,
    542*n*.13, 545*n*.3
  concern with POW/MIA issue, 265, 271
  vice chairman of Senate Select Committee,
    405–7
  winds up Senate Select Committee report,
    462–65
Smith, Chris, 275
Smith, Denny, 275, 542*n*.13
Smith, Maj. Mark, 286
Snowe, Olympia, 275
Socialist Republic of Vietnam (SRV, after 1975)
  (1977) Woodcock Commission visits, 164
  American negotiating style with, rude and
    arrogant, 326
  feels entitled to respect, as victor in Vietnam
    War, 326
  National Day, 556*n*.68
  normalization of relations with, 159–70, 313,
    327–28, 472, 474–77, 480–82
  offers to ransom unlisted POWs, 132–35,
    287–88, 458–60, 532*n*.33, 534*n*.4
  prison system, 372, 389
  radio and newspaper pronouncements,
    168–70, 445
  "shopping list" of desired aid, 164
  trade embargo, 464, 476
Soderberg, Nancy, 469–71
Solarz, Steven, 272, 275, 276, 279, 296, 313–15,
    349, 559*n*.125

Solomon, Gerald, 271–72, 275, 279, 296, 314
Son La Province, west of Hanoi
  American POWs reported, 150, 174, 191
  possible prison N-29, 511*n*.58
Son La, village north of Hanoi (aka Son Lau)
  American POWs reported, 181
Son Tay
  American POWs reported, 385, 388–91
  "Camp Hope" prison, 95, 318–21, 320
    (map)
  K-2 prison, 539*n*.81, 539*n*.82
  underground prison, 550*n*.24
Song Be. *See* Phuoc Binh
Song Thuong Bridge, 43, 96
Songhon district, Savannakhet Province
  American POWs reported, 312
Sop Hao, 516*n*.23
  American POWs reported, 192, 193–94,
    309
  cave, 357
Soubanh Srithirath, 139, 223–25, 228–29, 231,
    485
Soulivong Phasitthideth, 231
Souphanouvong, Prince, 26
Soutchay Vongsavanh, Gen., 297
South Vietnam (area, SVN)
  (1964) buildup of U.S. forces, 11
  (1972) North Vietnamese invasion of, 46
  *See also* Republic of Vietnam *until 1975*
South Vietnamese
  commandos working for American military,
    473–74
  refugees from defeated South Vietnam, 127
  resistance units, after the war, 308
Southeast Asia, culture of. *See* Oriental culture
Souvanna Phouma, 69
Soviet Union
  arms and missiles in Central America,
    237–38, 530–31*n*.1
  information about American POWs in
    archives, 469–75
Soyster, Lt. Gen. Ed, 401, 402, 552*n*.2
Special National Intelligence Estimate (SNIE)
  "Hanoi and the POW/MIA Issue," 335
Special Office for POWs/MIAs (of DIA), 185,
    197–99, 242–45, 261–63, 369, 399–403,
    520*n*.34
  (1985) Brooks Report, critical, 427,
    554–55*n*.42, 555*n*.54
  (1985) congressional praise for, 279
  (1985) internal review of, 269–71
  (1986) internal review of ("Gaines Report"),
    critical of the unit, 289–91, 400, 418
  (1990) praise and honors to, 395–96
  (1991) Peck's memo critical of, 401–3
  called a "black hole," 400
  criticized by Senate Select Committee, 427
  mind-set to debunk reports of live POWs,
    197–98, 240, 274, 290, 401

Spectre 17 crash investigation, 266–69, 277–78, 282–85
Spence, Floyd, 275
Sprat, John, 275
Spurgeon, Lt. Col. James D., 254, 393
Standerwick, Lynn, 254
Standerwick, Col. Robert, 254
Standerwick, Robert (son of the colonel), 254
Stark, Pete, 275
*Stars and Stripes*, 103–4
stay-behinds, 263–64
Stenholm, Charles, 275
Stephanopoulos, George, 474
Stephenson, Maj. Howard D. (gunship pilot), 323, 335, 541*n*.1
Stetson, Nancy, 406
Stevens, Ted, 86
Stewart, Elizabeth A. (coauthor), 376–77, 393, 545*n*.13
    visits Vietnam to inspect prisons, 550*n*.24
Stewart, Jim, 393
Stockdale, Cmdr. James B., 81, 154, 461
Stockdale, Sybil, 461, 559–60*n*.127
Stokes, Louis, 275, 382
Stung Treng Province, Cambodia
    American POWs reported, 551*n*.36
Sturgis, Frank, 119
Sullivan, William, 47, 64, 78, 79
Sundquist, Don, 275, 542*n*.13
Suoi Cut
    American POWs reported, 157
Suoi Mau prison camp complex, 310, 537*n*.47
survival, evasion, resistance and escape (SERE), 448–49
Sutherland, Thomas, 540*n*.93
Swedish ambassador to Vietnam, 258
Swedish engineers
    encounter American POWs, post–Vietnam War, and refuse asylum, 176, 196–97, 512*n*.4
Sweeney, Mac, 542*n*.13
Swift Vets and POWs for Truth, 482
Swindall, Pat, 542*n*.13
Switzer, Col. R. E., 258
Sydow, Gary, 442, 461
Syphrit, John, 457–60

"T," letter, distress signal, 547*n*.44
Taft, Will, 271
Tam Hung Village
    American POWs reported, 179
Tan Hiep prison camp, 537*n*.47
Tan Lap-Phu Tho prison complex, 174, 176–78, 181–82, 511*n*.57
    Xom Giong possible prison N-54, 511*n*.57
Tan Son Nhut, 123
Tauzin, Billy, 275
Tay Hieu Prison/State Farm, 354
Tay Nguyen (Central Highlands), 121–23

Tay Ninh Province
    American POWs reported, 23, 157, 178–79, 180–81, 193, 207
    POW camp in, 25
    reeducation camp in, 129, 130
Taylor, Robert "Bob," 407, 419, 553*n*.3
Tchepone. *See* Sepone
Tet Offensive, 65
T-15 POW camp, 25
Thac Ba Lake
    American POWs reported, 151, 272–73, 385, 428
Thach. *See* Nguyen Co Thach
Thai Nguyen City (north of Hanoi)
    POW camp, 44, 96
Thai Nguyen Province
    American POWs reported, 104
Thai Phi Long, Maj., 129–32, 147–48, 150, 515*n*.10
Thailand, 234, 351, 504*n*.31
Thakhek (aka Khammouan)
    American POWs reported, 308
Tham Kaeb
    American POWs reported, 363
Tham Seua (Tiger Cave)
    American POWs reported, 308
Thang. *See* Ton Duc Thang
Thanh Hoa Province
    American POWs reported, 226, 525*n*.4
    prison camps in, 29, 360, 525*n*.4, 539*n*.81
Thanh Lam Production Zone, 539*n*.81
Thanh Liet Prison. *See* Bang Liet/Thanh Liet
Thanh Phong
    prison camp system, 525*n*.4
Thien Ngon
    American POWs reported, 175, 179
Thieu. *See* Nguyen Van Thieu
Tho. *See* Le Duc Tho
Thomas, Bill (Congressman), 275
Thomas, William W., Jr., 224, 230–31
Thurmond, Strom, 411
Tighe, Brig. Gen. Eugene F., Jr., 72, 74–75, 197–212, 215–22, 256–57, 260, 274, 276, 286, 288–89, 291–95, 299–301, 313, 385, 407
    testimony that POWs are being held, 220–21
Tighe Report (on unaccounted for U.S. military in Southeast Asia), 292–301
    attempt to discredit and rewrite, 296–99, 304
Tighe Task Force, 291–92, 299
Ton Duc Thang, 78, 85, 124
Torricelli, Bob, 275
Tourison, Sedgwick D. "Wick," Jr., 18, 406–7, 412, 465–66, 473–74
Tractors for Freedom Committee (re Cuba), 4–6
Trai Ba Sao (Camp Ba Sao)
    American POWs reported, 176
    *See also* "Rockpile" prison

Tran Hoang Quan School, 343
Tran Phu Military Compound, Hanoi, 40
Tran Phu prison (Haiphong), 29, 175–76,
    511n.1
Tran Van Quang, Gen., 472, 473, 485
Trang Bom
    prison camp, 537n.47
Trang Lon
    reeducation camp in, 129
tri-border area
    American POWs reported, 352
Tri Tam
    American POWs reported, 207
    See Dau Tieng
Trinh. See Nguyen Duy Trinh
Trowbridge, Charles, 262
Truc Bach Lake, 32, 429–31
    American POWs reported, 413, 429–31
Trung Qui Mo munitions factory, 96
Truong Chinh, 85
Tucker, Lt. Cmdr. Edwin, 413
Tuttle, Rear Adm. Jerry O., 198–212, 215, 260,
    520n.40
Tuy Hoa City
    American POWs reported, 22, 24
Tuyen Quang City
    POW camp near, 44
Tuyen Quang Province
    American POWs reported, 415

U-Minh Forest
    American POWs reported, 312, 357, 359, 416
    POW camp in, 25
U-Tapao air base, 59
Ubon, Thailand, 267, 522n.8
Udorn air base, 522n.58
United Nations
    refugee official from, 524n.18
United States Air Force (USAF)
    6499th Special Activities Group, 24–25
    escape and evasion codes, 155
    Joint Services SERE Agency (JSSA), 448–49
    Office of Special Investigations (AFOSI), 393
United States Army (USA)
    1st Airborne, American POW from, 20
United States government (USG)
    becomes convinced that American POWs are
        alive, 197–99
    joint communiqué, U.S.-DRV (1973), 82
    knowledge of POWs held back at Operation
        Homecoming, 98
United States Government Relocation Facility,
    440–41
United Vietnam Veterans Organization, 254
Unknown Soldier from the Vietnam War con-
    troversy, 249–55, 529n.43
U.S. News & World Report, 402
"USA" dug out in a field, 362–63, 452–55,
    560n.130

USA Today, 347
USS Maddox, 11–12
USS Turner Joy, 12
"UY-STON," 319–21, 487, 539n.83

Van Ban
    American POWs reported, 173
Van Tien Dung, Gen., 114–15, 120–24, 127
Vance, Cyrus, 71, 160, 168, 171
Vander Jagt, Guy, 275
Venanzi, Col. Jerry, 238
Vento, Bruce, 275
Vessey, Gen. John W. "Jack," Jr., 253, 326–27,
        329, 331–34, 346, 394, 402, 461, 472–75,
        484, 561n.23
    (1987) trip to Hanoi, 332–34
Veterans of Foreign Wars (VFW), 254, 403
Veterans of the Vietnam War (VVnW), 346
Veterans of World War I of the USA, 254
Vieng Sai, 515n.23
    American POWs reported, 204, 379–81
Vientiane, 26, 69, 143
    hospital at, 228
    U.S. embassy in, 368–70
Vientiane Province
    American POWs reported, 360
Vietcong (VC), 75, 112–14
    instructed to capture Americans alive, 18–19
    number of American POWs held by, 25, 73
Vietminh, 20, 66, 114–15
Vietnam. See Democratic Republic of Vietnam;
        North Vietnam; Republic of Vietnam;
        Socialist Republic of Vietnam; South
        Vietnam
"Vietnam—It ain't over till it's over," 275
Vietnam Revisited video, 427–28, 561n.7
Vietnam veterans
    films about, 276
    protests by, 281, 285, 346, 349–50, 353,
        559–60n.127
    at Unknown Soldier ceremonies, 254
    willingness to engage in rescue missions,
        219, 240, 535n.17
Vietnam Veterans Memorial, 353, 481
Vietnam Veterans of America, 254
Vietnam War
    (1972) close of, 46–60
    (1972) Nixon's decision to end, 55–57
    (1973) resumes between North Vietnam and
        South Vietnam, 115–17
    (1975) fall of South Vietnam, 120–24
    continuing role in American politics, 481–82,
        483–85
    effect on Army, 542n.9
    escalation of, 28, 65
    films about, 276, 557n.93
    Oral History Project, 536n.26
    "we didn't win this war" (Perot), 314
    wounds of war heal slowly, 481

Vietnamese language, phonetic rendering of English phrases into, 14, 18–19, 46
Vietnamese refugees. *See* refugees, Vietnamese
VietNow, 550*n*.24
Vinh, 116, 148
Vinh Linh (village), 112
Vinh Linh Special Zone (DMZ)
  American POWs reported, 23
Vinh Ninh
  POWs at, 539*n*.80
Vinh Phu Province
  U.S. POW report, 140
Vinh Quang
  reeducation camp, 318, 340, 360–61, 539*n*.80
Vo Nguyen Giap, Gen., 114–15, 121, 122, 123, 327, 476, 481, 485
Vo Van Sung, 136
Voice of America, 368

Wade, Gen. Horace M., 56
*Wall Street Journal*, 260–61, 264–65, 274, 404
Walters, Barbara, 87
Walters, Lt. Gen. Vernon A. "Dick," 152–53, 324
war reparations (issue), 64–69, 79, 109–11, 116, 132–35
  congressional opposition to, 83–84, 86–87
  continues to be raised by Vietnamese, 480–81
  medicines offered as first "tranche" (install-ment), 116
  U.S. administration opposition to discussing, 331–32
  U.S. domestic opposition to, 82–84
Washington, D.C.
  damage control and spin doctors in, 281
  outsiders and insiders in, 280
*Washington Post*, 108, 118, 218, 234, 315–16, 353, 367, 394–95, 426, 440, 461–62, 475
*Washington Times*, 349, 402, 410
Watergate affair, 55, 63, 98–103, 118–20
  contribution of, to the fall of Southeast Asia, 120
Watson, Peter, 377
Webb, Maj. Johnie, 251–52, 269
Weber, Vin, 275
Weinberger, Caspar, 229, 237, 246–47, 250–52, 254, 271, 272, 282, 540*n*.93
Weiss, Cora, 71
Weldon, Curt, 542*n*.13
Wells, William W., 161
West German engineer
  encounters American prisoners of war, 196–97, 512*n*.4

*West Virginia*
  trapped sailors in, xv
Westmoreland, Gen. William C., 234
White Sulfur Springs, West Virginia
  United States Government Relocation Facility at, 440–41, 556*n*.81
Williams, Lt. Gen. James A., 262–63, 279, 460
Williams, Maurice J., 88–92, 109–10
Wilson, Charlie, 275
Wirth, Timothy, 275
Wolf, Frank, 275
Wolfowitz, Paul, 231, 240–41, 269, 276, 287, 289, 324, 411, 442, 484
Woodcock, Leonard, 159–66, 484
Woods, Rose, 100
World Bank
  employees in Vietnam, 258
Wrye, Maj. Blair C., 558*n*.99
Wyden, Ron, 275

"X," letter, distress signal, 560*n*.141
"X-26" unidentifiable remains, 251–52
Xieng Khoang Province, Laos, 231
  American POWs reported, 416
Xom Giong. *See* Tan Lap-Phu Tho prison complex
Xuan Loc
  American POWs reported, 194, 427, 517*n*.25
Xuan Thuy, 48, 53

yachtsman claim, 372
Yarborough, Brig. Gen. William, 234
Yen Bai, 148
  American POWs reported, 150, 151, 191, 257, 272, 345, 385
Yen Phu Thermal Power Plant, Hanoi, 32
York, Michael, 353
Yoshida, Iwanobu, 370–73
Yost, Charles W., 160
Young, C. W., 275
Young, Don, 275

Zagladin, Vadim V., 237
Ziegler, Ronald, 102
"Zoo" prison (in village of Cu Loc, a suburb of Hanoi), 95, 517*n*.25
Zumwalt, Adm. Elmo, 56
Zwenig, Frances, 406, 411, 418, 419, 423, 425, 428
  quoted, 408